AFFORDABLE HOUSING IN THE URBAN GLOBAL SOUTH

The global increase in the number of slums calls for policies which improve the conditions of the urban poor, sustainably. This volume provides an extensive overview of current housing policies in Asia, Africa and Latin America and presents the facts and trends of recent housing policies. The chapters provide ideas and tools for pro-poor interventions with respect to the provision of land for housing, building materials, labour, participation and finance. The book looks at the role of the various stakeholders involved in such interventions, including national and local governments, private sector organisations, NGOs and community-based organisations.

Jan Bredenoord is an urban planner and housing researcher. His PhD was on management instruments for cities (1996). Strategic urban and regional planning is his specialism. Since 1990 he has been working frequently in developing countries as a consultant on housing and planning. Since 2000 his research at Utrecht University has focused on affordable housing, self-help housing, land-for-housing programmes, housing cooperatives, and sustainable development. He has published in edited volumes and in scientific journals.

Paul van Lindert is Associate Professor in International Development Studies at Utrecht University. His PhD was on migration, urbanisation and housing strategies in Bolivia (1991) and he has published extensively on these and other topics in edited volumes and international journals. As a human geographer, his other research and teaching interests include: multi-local livelihoods, rural–urban relations; regional and local development; development planning; local governance; and (municipal) international cooperation.

Peer Smets is Assistant Professor at the Department of Sociology, VU University, Amsterdam, the Netherlands. His PhD was on housing finance and the urban poor in India (2002). His research focuses mainly on urban habitat conditions (housing and its living environment) in low-income neighbourhoods in southern and western countries, and perceptions which determine their liveability. He has published on urban segregation, housing, housing finance, government bureaucracy, and social life in neighbourhoods.

AFFORDABLE HOUSING IN THE URBAN GLOBAL SOUTH

Seeking sustainable solutions

Edited by Jan Bredenoord, Paul van Lindert and Peer Smets

First published 2014
by Routledge
2 Park Square, Milton Park, Abingdon, Oxon, OX14 4RN

and by Routledge
711 Third Avenue, New York, NY 10017

Routledge is an imprint of the Taylor & Francis Group, an informa business

© 2014 selection and editorial material, Jan Bredenoord, Paul van Lindert and Peer Smets; individual chapters, the contributors

The right of Jan Bredenoord, Paul van Lindert and Peer Smets to be identified as author of the editorial material, and of the individual authors as authors of their contributions, has been asserted in accordance with sections 77 and 78 of the Copyright, Designs and Patents Act 1988.

All rights reserved. No part of this book may be reprinted or reproduced or utilised in any form or by any electronic, mechanical, or other means, now known or hereafter invented, including photocopying and recording, or in any information storage or retrieval system, without permission in writing from the publishers.

Trademark notice: Product or corporate names may be trademarks or registered trademarks, and are used only for identification and explanation without intent to infringe.

British Library Cataloguing in Publication Data
A catalogue record for this book is available from the British Library

Library of Congress Cataloguing in Publication data
   Affordable housing in the urban global south : seeking sustainable solutions / edited by Jan Bredenoord, Paul van Lindert and Peer Smets.
     pages   cm
   Includes bibliographical references and index.
   1. Housing–Developing countries. 2. Housing policy–Developing countries.
   3. Urban poor–Developing countries. I. Bredenoord, Jan. II. Lindert,
P. van. III. Smets, Peer.
   HD7391.A44 2014
   363.5'561091724–dc23
   2013043282

ISBN: 978-0-415-62242-4 (hbk)
ISBN: 978-0-415-72893-5 (pbk)
ISBN: 978-1-315-84953-9 (ebk)

Typeset in Bembo
by Out of House Publishing

Printed and bound in Great Britain by
TJ International Ltd, Padstow, Cornwall

In memory of a great teacher, researcher, colleague and friend
Jan van der Linden

CONTENTS

List of figures   *xi*
List of tables   *xiii*
List of boxes   *xv*
Notes on contributors   *xvi*
*Foreword: Housing in an urban planet. Seeking the
nexus housing–sustainable urbanization by Claudio Acioly Jr.*   *xxi*
Acknowledgements   *xxv*

1   Introduction: governance, sustainability and affordability of low-income housing   1
     Peer Smets, Jan Bredenoord and Paul van Lindert

PART I
Thematic perspectives   15

     Introduction to Part I   15
     Peer Smets, Paul van Lindert and Jan Bredenoord

2   Policy and politics in urban land market management: lessons from experience   19
     Geoffrey Payne

3   The new political economy of affordable housing finance and urban development   40
     Bruce Ferguson, Peer Smets and David Mason

4 Backing the self-builders: assisted self-help housing as a sustainable housing provision strategy 55
Jan Bredenoord and Paul van Lindert

5 The resilience of self-built housing to natural hazards 73
Earl Kessler

6 Renting a home: the need for a policy response 87
Alan Gilbert

7 Housing cooperatives in the developing world 102
Sukumar Ganapati

8 The transnational experience of community-led development: the affordable shelter challenge 117
Beth Chitekwe-Biti, Sheela Patel and Diana Mitlin

PART II
Asia 133

Introduction to Part II 133
Peer Smets, Jan Bredenoord and Paul van Lindert

9 New frontiers and challenges for affordable housing provision in India 137
Urmi Sengupta

10 How the poor house themselves in Pakistan today 154
Arif Hasan

11 Self-help housing in Indonesia 166
Devisari Tunas and Laksmi T. Darmoyono

12 Community contracting in neighbourhood improvement and housing: Indonesia and Pakistan 181
Florian Steinberg

13 Housing futures: housing for the poor in Sri Lanka 192
Sharadbala Joshi and M. Sohail Khan

14 Affordable housing policies in urban China 204
Mingye Li and Jean-Claude Driant

PART III
Latin America   **219**

    Introduction to Part III   219
    Jan Bredenoord, Paul van Lindert and Peer Smets

15 Affordable housing for low-income groups in Mexico
     and urban housing challenges of today   223
     Jan Bredenoord and Lorena Cabrera Montiel

16 Half a century of self-help in Brazil   241
     Suzana Pasternak and Camila D'Ottaviano

17 Housing policy in Colombia   256
     Alan Gilbert

18 Incremental housing in Peru and the role of the social housing sector   271
     Ana María Fernández-Maldonado

19 From shortage reduction to a wellbeing approach: changing paradigms
     in Ecuadorian housing policies   286
     Christien Klaufus and Laura Cedrés Pérez

20 Self-help housing and upcoming policies for affordable housing
     in Nicaragua   300
     Jan Bredenoord and Bart van der Meulen

PART IV
Africa   **317**

    Introduction to Part IV   317
    Paul van Lindert, Jan Bredenoord and Peer Smets

21 Pathways towards self-help housing innovations in Egypt   321
     Ahmed M. Soliman

22 Changing housing policy in South Africa   336
     Marie Huchzermeyer

23 Dashed hopes? Public–private partnership and sustainable urban
     low-income housing delivery in Nigeria   349
     Uche Cosmas Ikejiofor

24 Housing and the urban poor in Kenya: opportunities for increased partnerships and innovative practices 363
Bob Hendriks

25 Urban low-income housing in Ghana 381
Paul W. K. Yankson and Katherine V. Gough

Conclusion 395

26 Pro-poor housing policies revisited: where do we go from here? 397
Paul van Lindert, Peer Smets and Jan Bredenoord

Index 404

LIST OF FIGURES

1.1	Sustainability and complex flow networks as function of the trade-offs between efficiency and resilience	8
1.2	Housing affordability: basic components	10
2.1	Riverbank settlement in Phnom Penh, Cambodia	21
2.2	*Kampung* settlement in Surabaya, Indonesia	21
2.3	Congenial high-density neighbourhoods in Shanghai, China, contrasted with more recent high-rise developments	29
3.1	The affordable housing finance continuum	48
4.1a	The development of neighbourhood Santa Rosa Cinco Dedos in La Paz, Bolivia (1984)	60
4.1b	The development of neighbourhood Santa Rosa Cinco Dedos in La Paz, Bolivia (1995)	60
4.1c	The development of neighbourhood Santa Rosa Cinco Dedos in La Paz, Bolivia (2006)	61
4.2	Sites-and-services project Nuevo Pachacutec, Ventanilla, Peru	61
4.3	Neighbourhood improvement with playground, San Borja, Lima	67
6.1	Mexico City: in the early twentieth century even the well-off lived in rental housing	90
6.2	Middle-income rental housing in Bogotá, Colombia	92
8.1	Incremental housing construction in Pune, India	119
8.2	Milan Nagar cooperative housing construction in Mankhurd, Mumbai	122
9.1	Urban income pyramid in India	144
9.2	Sukhobristi Master Plan and building features	146
14.1	ECH floor space and total residential building proportion in China (1997–2008)	208
14.2	ECH housing units in Nanjing (top) and Low Rental Housing units in Chongqing (bottom)	209

15.1	Self-built housing in Nezahualcóyotl	226
15.2	Housing complex El Cortijo in Tlalnepantla	230
15.3a	Uninhabited row-houses in Galaxia La Calera, Puebla	236
15.3b	Uninhabited apartments in Villa San Carlos, Puebla	236
17.1	Bogotá: now consolidated shelter but building self-help housing on a hillside is not easy	258
17.2	ABC housing for sale in Bogotá	261
17.3	Not much space in ABC housing for sale in Bogotá	267
18.1	Conventional and informal ways of urban development	273
18.2	Relative construction costs of a project dwelling and a *barriada* dwelling	274
18.3	Main phases of the social housing projects and the sector responsible for their implementation	276
18.4	Current types of state involvement in housing in Peru	277
18.5	Housing finance system according to socio-economic sector (NSE)	279
18.6	Number of Mivivienda Credits granted, 2001–2011	280
18.7	Dwelling built through Techo Propio 'building in own property' in Collique, Comas	281
18.8	Techo Propio subsidies granted in its three modalities, 2003–2012	281
18.9	Number of loans and subsidies (left) and amount of money they represent (right) in the three social housing programmes, 2006–2011	282
19.1	National Development Plan: administrative reforms	290
20.1	Street view in Colonia Maestro Gabriel, Managua	304
20.2	Cooperative housing in León South East	305
20.3	Modest housing in Barrio Granada, Managua	306
21.1	New towns in Upper Egypt	327
21.2	*Ibni Beitak* scheme in Sadat City	329
21.3	Incremental house construction in Sadat City	332
22.1	The Isiqalo informal settlement in Philippi – Cape Town, 2012.	341
22.2	Backyard rental shacks in Tembisa, Johannesburg/Ekurhuleni, 2012	341
22.3	Neglected inner city buildings in Johannesburg provide opportunities for informal occupation	342
24.1	Existing and emerging housing provision in Kenya	366

LIST OF TABLES

3.1	Mortgage finance as a share of GDP	43
3.2	Methods of production and financing of new Brazilian housing per annum	46
4.1	Formal versus informal housing provision	57
4.2	Modalities of housing provision for urban poor and the role of self-help construction	62
4.3	Assisted self-help housing options: different components and actors	64
4.4	Assisted self-help housing components: variation in policy packages	65
5.1	Climate change participation	82
6.1	How to improve the environment for rental housing	98
9.1	Urban housing shortage in India	139
9.2	Low-cost and affordable housing in India	142
9.3	Affordability ratio of different income groups	143
9.4	Housing categories scenario in India	143
10.1	Population of *katchi abadis*	157
11.1	PERUMNAS housing production from 2000 to 2010	172
11.2	Comparison of flat price, income and housing credits	173
11.3	Different forms of low-income self-help housing in Indonesia	174
14.1	Principal characteristics of Chongqing and Nanjing	212
15.1	Housing policies and financial stages	227
15.2	Housing types in the Mexican subsidized housing market	230
15.3	Overview of housing finance operations in Mexico, 2006–2011	233
16.1	Housing loans granted by BNH (1964–1985)	244
16.2	Subsidies per income band for the acquisition or construction of new properties in MCMV (2009–2010)	251

16.3	Housing units contracted according to income band (2009–2010)	251
16.4	Housing units contracted, 0 to 3 minimum wages (2009–2010)	252
16.5	MCMV-E programme by September 2012	253
18.1	Peruvian housing deficit according to the national census of 1993 and 2007	272
18.2	Supply and demand of housing units in Metropolitan Lima in 2011	279
19.1	Housing shortages in Ecuador, 2010	287
19.2	Housing types in existing housing stock in Ecuador, 2010	288
19.3	Paid grants for new housing and home improvement during former and current government terms, 2011	296
20.1	Housing classification per income category in Nicaragua	303
20.2	Typology of social housing solutions in Managua and León (November 2012)	313
21.1	The National Housing Project (NHP) under the Mubarak Election Program (2005–2011)	330
23.1	Summary of case studies of selected PPP projects showing on-site facilities and selling prices of house types	356
24.1	Kenya country statistics	365
24.2	KENSUP	369
24.3	Registered self-help housing initiatives in Kenya, 1990–2011	373
25.1	Changes in price of housing land for indigenes in urban/peri-urban areas in Ghana, 1995–2005	385
25.2	Changes in price of housing land for migrants in urban/peri-urban areas in Ghana, 1995–2005	385
25.3	Trends in price of indigene and migrant housing land per acre in selected areas of Accra and Kumasi, 1995–2005	386
25.4	Sources of housing finance in some selected low-income urban communities in Ghana	387

LIST OF BOXES

2.1	Examples of innovative approaches to urban land development	22
2.2	Impacts of inequality on access to land	32
5.1	The Solanda Project in Quito, Ecuador	75
5.2	The Haiti Experience	76
5.3	Emergency shelter kits	78
5.4	Timor L'Este Case Study	79
11.1	Government initiated self-help programme: Swadaya	174
11.2	Self-help *Kampong* Improvement in Jetisharjo, Yogyakarta	175
14.1	Chongqing	212
14.2	Nanjing	214
15.1	Social housing finance in Mexico	231
15.2	Examples of assisted self-help housing in Mexico	234
19.1	Ciudad Victoria, Guayaquil	292
19.2	The 'dream-house competition' in self-help housing	294
20.1	León South East	301
20.2	Anexo Barrio Grenada, Sector 17: a neighbourhood in the outskirts of Managua	309

NOTES ON CONTRIBUTORS

Claudio Acioly Jr. is an architect and urban planner with over 30 years of experience as practitioner, technical and policy advisor, consultant, and training and capacity development expert in over 30 countries across Asia, Africa, Europe, Latin America and the Caribbean. He is currently chief of Training and Capacity Development at UN-Habitat. During the period 2008-2012 he was chief of Housing Policy at UN-Habitat, coordinator of the United Nations Housing Rights Programme, and coordinator of the Advisory Group on Forced Evictions for the Executive Director of UN-Habitat. He has published widely and lectured on housing, slum upgrading, land policies and community-based action planning.

Jan Bredenoord is an urban planner and housing researcher and was educated at Delft University of Technology. His PhD was on strategic urban planning and management for cities (1996). For the past 20 years he has worked as an international consultant on housing and planning, and was a part-time research fellow at Utrecht University. His current work is focused on affordable housing for low-income households and sustainable urban housing. E-mail: janbredenoord@planet.nl

Lorena Cabrera Montiel is an architect and urban planner. She has worked in the public and private sectors, and at the University of Puebla, Mexico. Currently she is pursuing a PhD on housing and urban growth at the Institute of Geography, UNAM. Her fields of expertise include urban planning, housing finance and real estate. E-mail: lorecamo@gmail.com

Laura Cedrés Pérez works as a technical expert at the UN-Habitat Program in Ecuador and as Visiting Professor at FLACSO, Ecuador. She holds a Bachelor's degree in political sciences, a Master's degree in international cooperation and development, and another in urban management. She has been involved in the development of new urban and housing policies in Ecuador. E-mail: lauracedres@hotmail.com

Beth Chitekwe-Biti is the Executive Director of Dialogue on Shelter, a Zimbabwean NGO that works in partnership with the Zimbabwe Homeless People's Federation. The two organisations, which are affiliates of the international network SDI, work to secure tenure and services for the urban poor in Zimbabwean towns and cities. Beth holds a PhD from the University of Manchester. E-mail: btchitekwebiti@gmail.com

Uche Cosmas Ikejiofor is a registered architect-planner with 25 years' experience working for the federal government of Nigeria. He currently holds the position of Deputy Director and Federal Controller in the Federal Ministry of Lands, Housing and Urban Development. An Adjunct Professor in the Department of Urban and Regional Planning of Caritas University, Enugu, Nigeria, Dr Ikejiofor's interests and expertise are in the areas of land delivery processes and housing strategies. E-mail: ikejioforcu@gmail.com

Laksmi T. Darmoyono is a PhD student in the Planning Department, Faculty of Spatial Sciences, University of Groningen. Her research focuses on a feasibility study for property investment, low-income urban neighbourhoods, value-capture for infrastructure provision, and institutional design. She has worked as a professional urban designer at several urban design companies in Asia and the Middle East. E-mail: laksmi.darmoyono@gmail.com

Camila D'Ottaviano is an architect and urban planner, with Master's and PhD degrees in architecture and urbanism. She is PhD Professor at the School of Architecture and Urbanism at the University of São Paulo. Her main areas of experience are in architecture and urban planning, with an emphasis on the areas of housing, urban design, city history, habitat and demographics. E-mail: camila.dottaviano@gmail.com

Jean-Claude Driant is Professor at the Paris School of Urban Planning, University Paris-Est. He is the director of Lab'Urba, an urban research team in the University of Paris-Est. He works mainly on the interactions between real estate markets and housing policies at both central and local levels in France and Europe. E-mail: driant@u-pec.fr

Bruce Ferguson consults in international affordable housing finance, value chains for housing products, urban infrastructure and the environment from Venice, California. His background includes: staff positions at the World Bank, IADB, Abt Associates, Urban Institute, MIT, mortgage banks and community development corporations; 45+ papers and chapters, and 4 books; and numerous donor project documents and client reports. E-mail: brucewferguson@hotmail.com.

Ana María Fernández-Maldonado is Senior Researcher in the Department of Urbanism at the Faculty of Architecture, Delft University of Technology. She has worked as an urban planner and researcher in topics related to rapid urbanisation and informal housing processes, including planning, housing policies, polycentric developments, comparative planning and knowledge-based urban development. E-mail: A.M.FernandezMaldonado@tudelft.nl

Sukumar Ganapati is Associate Professor in the Department of Public Administration and the director of the PhD programme in Public Affairs at the Florida International University. His main research interests are in housing, community development, and e-government solutions. His publications have appeared in planning and public administration journals. E-mail: ganapati@fiu.edu

Notes on contributors

Alan Gilbert is Professor Emeritus at University College London. He has published extensively on housing, poverty, employment and urban governance in developing countries, particularly those in Latin America. He acts as an advisor to several international institutions including the Inter-American Development Bank and UN-Habitat. E-mail: a.gilbert@ucl.ac.uk

Katherine V. Gough is Professor in the Department of Geography, Loughborough University. Her research on urban issues in the Global South focuses in particular on: housing and home; youth mobility and entrepreneurship; rural–urban dynamics; governance and planning; and comparative urbanism. She has a special interest in conducting comparative research and longitudinal studies. E-mail: k.v.gough@lboro.ac.uk

Arif Hasan is a Karachi-based architect planner, research and activist. He is a Visiting Professor at the Department of Architecture & Planning, NED University, Karachi; Chairperson of the Orangi Pilot Project-Research & Training Institute and of the Karachi Urban Resource Centre; and a founding member of the Asian Coalition for Housing Rights, Bangkok. E-mail: arifhasan@cyber.net.pk

Bob Hendriks is an independent international consultant with 19 years of experience in the areas of affordable housing, slum upgrading, land and tenure, inclusive governance, institution/capacity building and inclusive growth. He has a PhD in international development studies, human geography and planning. Clients include IHS, UN-Habitat, EU, World Bank and SNV. E-mail: bobhendriks@yahoo.com

Marie Huchzermeyer is a Professor in the School of Architecture and Planning, University of the Witwatersrand. Her research is on housing policy, informal settlements and private rental housing. Much of her research takes a rights-based and comparative approach, spanning South Africa, Brazil and more recently Kenya. E-mail: marie.huchzermeyer@wits.ac.za

Sharadbala Joshi is a consultant with broad experience in community-responsive housing and settlement development, project strategising, scoping, monitoring and documentation for integrated settlement development and affordable housing for bilateral/multilateral agencies, (I)NGOs, local governments and private sector. Her research and papers focus on affordable and assisted self-help housing, settlements upgrading, redevelopment and resettlement. E-mail: Sharadbala.Joshi@gmail.com

Earl Kessler earned his Master's of architecture from MIT in Planning for Developing Countries. He was director of the USAID Regional Urban Development Offices (RUDO) in Bangkok, Thailand and Delhi, India. He was deputy executive director of the Asian Disaster Preparedness Center/Bangkok. He is now an independent consultant. E-mail: kesslerearl@gmail.com

Christien Klaufus works at the Centre of Latin American Research and Documentation (CEDLA) as Assistant Professor of Human Geography. She specialises in urban studies and the Andean region. Christien holds a Master's degree in architecture and a PhD in cultural anthropology. Before working at CEDLA she was employed at Delft University of Technology. E-mail: c.j.klaufus@cedla.nl

Mingye Li is a PhD candidate at the Paris School of Urban Planning, University Paris-Est. She is working on Chinese urban development, urban governance and social housing policies. E-mail: limingyenju@gmail.com

David Mason is a consultant with the World Bank. He specialises in urban planning, affordable housing and microfinance, with research and practice experience in Mongolia, Nicaragua and Mexico. He holds a PhD in urban planning from UCLA. E-mail: dmason@worldbank.org

Diana Mitlin directs the Global Urban Research Centre at the University of Manchester and also holds an appointment at the International Institute for Environment and Development (www.iied.org). Her work focuses on urban poverty and inequality including urban poverty reduction programmes and the contribution of collective action by low-income and otherwise disadvantaged groups. E-mail: diana.mitlin@manchester.ac.uk

Suzana Pasternak is an architect and urban planner with Master's and PhD degrees in public health. She is full Professor at the School of Architecture and Urbanism, University of São Paulo. Her experience is in the area of urban and regional planning, with an emphasis on the fundamentals of urban and regional planning. E-mail: suzanapasternak@gmail.com

Sheela Patel is the Founder-Director of the Society for Promotion of Area Resource Centres (SPARC), an NGO that has been working since 1984 to support community organisations of the urban poor in their efforts to access secure housing and basic amenities, and seek their right to the city. She is also a founder and current chairperson of Slum/Shack Dwellers International (SDI). E-mail: sparcssns@gmail.com

Geoffrey Payne is a housing and urban development consultant. He established Geoffrey Payne and Associates in 1995 (www.gpa.org.uk) and has since undertaken research, consultancy and teaching assignments throughout the world for international donor agencies and NGOs. He has published widely on land tenure and property rights, housing policy and related issues. E-mail: gkpayne@gpa.org.uk

Urmi Sengupta is a lecturer in spatial planning in the School of Planning, Architecture and Civil Engineering at Queen's University Belfast. She received her PhD from Newcastle University. Her fields of expertise include land and housing issues in the Global South, housing design, informalities in cities, inclusion and governance, urban evaluation and indicators. She has published widely in leading journals and advises various NGOs/grassroots organisations in India and Nepal. E-mail: u.sengupta@qub.ac.uk

Peer Smets is Assistant Professor in the Department of Sociology, VU University, Amsterdam. His research focuses on housing and social life in the low-income neighbourhoods of the cities of southern and western countries. He has published on urban segregation, housing, housing finance, government bureaucracy, communities and social life in neighbourhoods. E-mail: p.g.s.m.smets@vu.nl

M. Sohail Khan is Professor of Sustainable Infrastructure at Loughborough University. He has led several international research projects and has published more than 200 journal papers, book chapters and conference papers. He has served on several international scientific committees/panels. E-mail: M.Sohail@lboro.ac.uk

Ahmed M. Soliman is currently working as an Emeritus Professor of Urban Planning and Housing and was former Chairman of the Architecture Department in the Faculty of Engineering at Alexandria University. He has published widely on issues of housing informality in several international journals and contributed chapters in various books. E-mail: ahmsoliman@yahoo.com

Florian Steinberg is a senior urban development specialist who has worked on long-term assignments for the Institute for Housing and Urban Development Studies (IHS) and with the Asian Development Bank (ADB), Manila, covering urban projects in Southeast Asia. He is a specialist in urban management, urban planning and renewal–rehabilitation, settlement upgrading, urban infrastructure planning, climate change adaptation and institutional development. E-mail: florian_steinberg@yahoo.de

Devisari Tunas is currently working as a research fellow at the National University of Singapore. Her research topics include sustainable urban development and empowerment of social capital. She obtained her PhD degree in urbanism from Delft University of Technology on the spatial economy of urban informal settlements. E-mail: tunastunas@gmail.com

Bart van der Meulen is a Dutch-born political scientist who has lived in Nicaragua since 1994. He worked at the Embassy of the Netherlands in Managua and did many assignments on urban planning, governance and city linkages. Since his retirement he has worked as a volunteer at the Instituto de Historia de Nicaragua and Centroamérica. E-mail: meulenbart@gmail.com

Paul van Lindert is Associate Professor in Human Geography, Planning and International Development at Utrecht University. He has taught as Visiting Professor at various universities in Latin America and Africa. His research includes urban development and planning, city networks and city-to-city cooperation, rural–urban relations, regional and local development, local governance and multi-local livelihoods. E-mail: p.h.c.m.vanlindert@uu.nl

Paul W. K. Yankson is Professor in the Department of Geography and Resource Development, University of Ghana. He is an urban/regional planner with research interest in a number of urban and regional development issues in Ghana including land and housing, urban and regional economic development issues, governance and decentralisation. He has published articles in both local and international journals as well as contributed chapters in books as single or joint authorship papers. E-mail: pyankson@ug.edu.gh

FOREWORD: HOUSING IN AN URBAN PLANET

Seeking the nexus housing–sustainable urbanization

Claudio Acioly Jr. (UN-Habitat)

The housing sector has interfaces with practically every single part of a country's economy. Never was this made so clear until the world faced the global financial meltdown that revealed its deep roots in the housing market and particularly in the housing finance industry. Housing is more than simply bricks and mortar, a roof over walls and foundations. It is far more complex than houses and buildings on a parcel of land. Housing is a human right as defined by the Covenant of Economic, Social and Cultural Rights, the Habitat Agenda and international instruments. This has been recognized by more than a hundred national constitutions and policies that attempt to create the necessary conditions through which individuals and households progressively achieve access to adequate housing where they can lead a life with dignity and safety. Housing is a powerhouse for economic development, prosperity and wealth creation involving a multitude of institutions, regulations, policies, different stakeholders and significant government participation in the supply of land, infrastructure and finance.

The importance of housing cannot be better emphasized than by the propositions and experiences depicted in this book. Housing also encompasses a chain of economic and productive relations in the building construction sector and labour markets that altogether have a significant impact on cities and human settlements. The typology of housing, its design, densities, standards and regulations set by bylaws, planning and building codes have an enormous influence on urban planning and urban design and the way land is assembled, sub-divided and used for residential purposes. Housing is inexorably linked to urban extension and by default to sustainable urbanization defining land uses and the urban form of cities. The increasing demand for housing and the markets that evolve from this demand, including the demand for land, is defining the urban form of cities, the modes of urban growth and the location of neighbourhoods, particularly those where low-income households find housing accommodation. Thus housing is multi-dimensional, multi-disciplinary and multi-institutional, and has a range of economic, political, social, legal and technological attributes that influence policy options and the behaviour of providers and consumers in the market. This book reveals the various dimensions of housing and the variety of approaches to address housing needs in cities.

All these elements mentioned above make housing a special commodity, a private good that is produced by significant public sector participation. Whenever the public sector fails to intervene and facilitate accessibility and affordability, people, and particularly those with low incomes, resort to informal land developments, informal housing and all sorts of informality. This is more critical in the absence of affordable housing finance leading to more scarcity of affordable housing and pumping prices to scandalous levels when compared with average household incomes. This leads to pervasive social exclusion and spatial segregation. The unavailability of affordable housing options at scale and diversity in type, location, price and standard is one of the deep-rooted causes of slum formation and excludes more people from the benefits of urbanization and agglomeration. Today, nearly one third of the global urban population lives in slum conditions and this reminds us about the need to increase our understanding of housing as an important step to formulate alternative and innovative policies so that those who are not capable to pay for it through the market may receive some degree of government assistance. This book is a welcome and valuable contribution to this search for solutions and approaches.

The studies and articles that comprise this volume coordinated by Jan Bredenoord, Paul van Lindert and Peer Smets reveal unequivocally this multi-dimensional and multi-disciplinary dimension of housing and make an indispensable contribution to the bulk of knowledge that is needed to advance our understanding of housing in its broadest sense. They also help us to critically analyze the formulation of policies aiming at greater accessibility to adequate housing, particularly for those with low incomes. Not only have the editors gathered solid international scholars, researchers and practitioners around this volume but they have also managed to cover regional aspects, providing the reader with global references and lessons from countries of Asia, Latin America and Africa. The authors of the various chapters also provide us with a range of policy options such as rental housing, housing cooperatives, self-help housing and land policies that altogether form a robust reference for the discussion on policy and institutional reforms. UN-Habitat welcomes this kind of global perspective and critical analysis of policies and practices.

In my work for UN-Habitat, the United Nations Human Settlements Programme, where I led the work on housing policies and housing rights, I frequently had close exchange with local practitioners and policy makers in various countries. My involvement in policy dialogues and development of national housing strategies and policies in countries of Africa, Asia, Latin America and Eastern Europe during my tenure at UN-Habitat revealed to me that knowledge and references about different housing experiences are in great demand. This book helps to fill this gap. The volume actually addresses the needs of different groups. Those who work in the field of housing and are concerned with the living conditions in cities will find this volume extremely useful and resourceful, and those seeking for references and lessons learned to sustain the formulation of policies in their own contexts will find a wealth of experience and knowledge in the various chapters of the volume. Scholars and researchers will certainly find inspiration from the various sections of the publication and identify areas where we need further investigation and robust research that can contribute to the global debate about such an important dimension of urban development in the twenty-first century.

This timely book comes exactly at a moment when the international community is reflecting on the post-2015 development agenda, taking stock of the Millennium Development Goals (MDGs) and formulating a new international agenda reflected into the recently drafted

Sustainable Development Goals that must follow the agreements made during the Rio+20 Conference, the Third United Nations Conference on the Environment and Development that was held in Rio de Janeiro in 2012. In the final document emanating from the conference, entitled 'The Future We Want', housing, and particularly urbanization and the role of cities, has not been articulated as one would have expected given that today the majority of the world's population is already living in cities, and the numbers are going to increase in the following decades. This book serves a purpose. It helps to remind those involved in this crucial international discussion that the MDG focusing on the improvement of the living conditions of slum dwellers is an unfinished business and that affordable housing and wider accessibility to adequate housing are part and parcel of the equation of building a better and more equitable urban world. Understanding the sorts of institutional and policy bottleneck preventing scaled-up supply of serviced land, as depicted by the book, and addressing other constraints in the infrastructure, building and finance sectors will help in identifying ways and policy options that need to be included in the new development agenda.

Finally, the richness contained in the various chapters of the book is an invaluable contribution to the international debate about the new urban agenda that is in the making. The General Assembly of the United Nations has already decided on the third United Nations Conference on Human Settlements, Habitat III, which has as its theme 'Housing and Sustainable Urbanization'. The conference, scheduled for 2016, is expected to take stock of the implementation of the Habitat Agenda. Governments are expected to review their experiences and involve their civil society in this exercise, assess the extent to which the ingredients of the Istanbul Plan of Action (Istanbul, 1996) have been implemented and, based on that, make suggestions for the formulation of an urban development agenda for the next 20 years. This volume makes a substantive contribution to this process. It brings to a wider audience the challenges of making affordable housing options available in different parts of the world. It also helps us to highlight the role of housing in the configuration of the new agenda.

The Habitat Agenda (1996) was undersigned by more than 190 heads of States who agreed to promote the full and progressive realization of the right to adequate housing as defined in international instruments, and to promote policies and approaches to attain sustainable urban development. The chapters of this book very much reflect the concerns outlined under the two pillars of the Habitat Agenda (1) Adequate Shelter for All and (2) Sustainable Urbanization. The implementation of the Agenda and the work carried out thereafter by a multitude of public, private, academic and community-based actors since its adoption in 1996 have helped to promote ways to monitor and understand housing markets and develop sound indicators to sustain policy decisions; there has been increasing stakeholders' participation and involvement of communities in decision making and in mobilizing finance and credit as advocated by the Agenda; we have also seen an increase in the deployment of land management tools to unlock land for housing and bring it to scale. The Agenda also promoted the need to establish an enabling policy environment by recommending governments to review their policy, regulatory and administrative constrains hindering land delivery systems, and accessibility to adequate housing so that other actors could get actively involved in housing production. The cases and experiences depicted in this book reflect this search for mechanisms in various parts of the world and provide us with the lessons learned from their implementation. There is a wealth of knowledge revealed by their authors, which makes the book a must for housing researchers and practitioners alike.

The Habitat Agenda defined a broad meaning of shelter. Its implementation helped further define the seven elements of housing adequacy as depicted in the Covenant of Social Economic and Cultural Rights and the Fact Sheet on the Right to Adequate Housing e.g (1) Security of tenure *(and protection from forced eviction)*, (2) Availability of services, materials, facilities and infrastructure, (3) Location, (4) Habitability, (5) Affordability, (6) Accessibility and (7) Cultural adequacy (UN-Habitat and Office of United Nations High Commissioner of Human Rights 2010), which are reflected into the various chapters comprising this volume. In that respect, the book makes a creditable contribution to our understanding of these adequacy dimensions and how policies address them locally. Seen by the United Nations Committee on Economic, Social and Cultural Rights as the right to live somewhere in security, peace and dignity, the recognition of housing rights as a component of the right to an adequate standard of living (see the Universal Declaration of Human Rights) has triggered a large amount of policy, institutional and legal work to create the conditions for countries to fulfil and protect this right of their populations. Rather than having houses built by the State for its entire population, this legal and conceptual framework actually advocates for measures and the adoption by governments of institutional, policy and financial mechanisms to enable greater accessibility to adequate housing, prevent homelessness, curb discrimination and prohibit unlawful forced evictions. This book covers governance, affordability, and sustainability of policies, institutions, and housing production, which represent a contribution about our understanding and implications of the efforts undertaken in various parts of the world for the realization of the right to adequate housing. Only this makes the book an indispensable companion for housing practitioners.

References

UN-Habitat and Office of United Nations High Commissioner of Human Rights (2010) *The Right to Adequate Housing*, Fact Sheet 21. Geneva: OHCHR.

ACKNOWLEDGEMENTS

The edited volume that we present here is about the dimensions of affordability and sustainability of current housing policies and practices in the urban Global South. Over 30 colleagues – all of them experts in the field of affordable housing – collaborated with us by sharing their expert knowledge. and thus co-creating a state-of-art book which combines thematic reviews with local empirical evidence from a wide variety of regional contexts.

Usually, the production of a volume like this is the result of a conference or seminar, where experts present their respective papers and discuss their ideas and findings with other participants. At some later stage they then may be invited to submit an adapted version of their work for publication in a book. The journey of the making of this volume has been a different one.

It started off with the publication of a special issue of *Habitat International* in 2010. Being invited as guest editors by *Habitat International* for such a special issue, we delivered a timely collection of specialized papers which picked up the dialogue theme 'Equal Access to Shelter' at the Fifth World Urban Forum (WUF) that was held in Rio de Janeiro in March 2010. It specifically highlighted the role of (assisted) self-help in facilitating shelter development for the urban poor of the Global South. At the WUF in Rio, we received suggestions from many colleagues to further develop our ideas and to expand the thematic notions on affordable and sustainable housing provision. Charles Choguill, the editor of *Habitat International*, was among the first people who inspired us to follow up on our joint special issue venture, for which we are greatly indebted to him.

On the basis of these experiences, we aimed at opening up a discussion about housing policies and practices, which form the basis for this volume. We are of course extremely grateful to all authors of the chapters in this book, each of whom responded unreservedly to our invitation to collaborate with our project. The authors have different disciplinary backgrounds, including architecture, urban planning, geography, sociology, public administration, economics and political science, which is also expressed in their analytical approaches of the housing question. All chapters are original contributions which have been written specifically for this book. Claudio Acioly Jr at UN-Habitat kindly accepted our invitation to write a foreword and we greatly appreciate the pointed way in which he did so by sharing his expert view on the post-2015 habitat agenda and its dimensions of housing adequacy. We indeed hope and expect that our collective effort of composing this book will substantially contribute to the development of the new international agendas on housing and sustainable urbanization.

We are also very grateful to Nicki Dennis and Alice Aldous at Earthscan, who from the moment of our first book proposal to the final stage of publication were extremely encouraging and responsive to our queries. Moreover, thanks are due to Laila Grieg-Gran, Hannah Champney and Jamie Hood for their involvement in the final production stage. Three anonymous referees provided constructive comments, which we highly appreciated. We also thank Michelle Nuijen for the language amendments of many chapters of this book; and Margot Stoete and Ton Markus for the graphic illustrations and cartography. We consider ourselves very lucky to have such capable colleagues at Utrecht University.

Jan Bredenoord, Paul van Lindert and Peer Smets

1
INTRODUCTION

Governance, sustainability and affordability of low-income housing

Peer Smets, Jan Bredenoord and Paul van Lindert

Today the urban Global South is the part of the world that faces the most rapid urbanization processes. Here, cities grow in size and number, which makes it rather difficult for the poorer sections of society to find adequate shelter and security of tenure. This has led to an increasing number of dwellers living in poor housing conditions: an estimated 2 billion by 2030. One of the big challenges is aiming at 'inclusive cities for all', including the urban poor, which could be achieved via better housing policies designed for the total urban low-income population (UN-Habitat 2003). Therefore, given the characteristics outlined above, affordable and sustainable housing solutions for the poor are needed in the Global South. As a consequence of limited incomes and weak national and local housing policies in a number of countries, affordable housing is out of reach for millions of low-income families. While the upgrading of poor housing conditions is indispensable, a range of affordable housing alternatives ought to be promoted in order to bring sufficient 'decent' housing solutions to the low-income brackets in particular. Other contemporary challenges are concerned with a turning away from settlement deterioration, new informal settlement formation and a severe lack of sufficient housing production mechanisms.

Seen against the background of significant political, economic, social and environmental changes throughout the world, difficulties, challenges and opportunities are different from the past. New shelter strategies for the millions of people without decent homes are urgently needed in this twenty-first century.

A large part of the world's affordable housing delivery is self-managed housing, or (assisted) self-help housing and the 'build as you go' approach. As these housing delivery practices have received less attention (at least in a number of countries), this book gives much consideration to self-managed housing with grassroots incentives. Incorporating this in public and formal social housing delivery systems is invaluable; ignoring or combating it is unwise. Self-managed housing limitations in particular deserve attention, especially in irregular land developments. As not all houses are being built durably and through sustainable construction, this includes the low quality of housing.

This book has three objectives. First, this volume intends to contribute to the debate about the international habitat and housing agenda. Second, and based on the experiences gained from a variety of locations, its aim is to seek innovative and sustainable solutions that can bring affordable low-income housing production to scale. In this respect, the diversity of urban and regional contexts, but also the range of relevant stakeholders involved, is taken into account. In addition, attention is paid to both the potential and limitations of aided and non-aided self-help housing. Third, this book aims at placing the search for sustainable solutions for affordable low-income housing under the umbrella of governance. Therefore stakeholders have to work together without knowing the exact results, which requires some sense of resilience. Towards this end, the next section briefly focuses on the history of low-income housing and its policies in the city. This is followed by a discussion of the relevant concepts of governance, sustainability and affordability.

A brief history of low-income housing

The development of effective housing policy and planning should be seen not only in relation to the nature of housing, but also in relation to the tensions between housing as a consumption good and housing as an economic good with a market value. As a consumption good, housing serves as the basis for households and individuals to avoid impoverishment and increase their wealth and well-being. For some, housing is just a roof, while others regard it as their most valuable possession (Beall and Fox 2009: 125–127).

The provision of housing by governments is a relatively recent phenomenon. Newly independent states in Asia and Africa set up many large-scale housing projects, which partly mirrored post-war European welfare states and the injustices of the colonial period. Moreover, while such developments nourished the pride of the newly formed countries, these housing projects were not affordable for the urban poor (Beall and Fox 2009: 127). UNCHS (1996) estimated that less than 10 per cent of the housing stock in low- and middle-income countries was public housing. Consequently, the urban poor have had to employ self-help in constructing shelter in an incremental manner (e.g. Mangin 1967; Turner 1976). This was followed by sites-and-services schemes and settlement upgrading plans. These approaches, which have become part of the urban fabric, tend to be 'uniform solutions' implemented as pilot projects in many cities in the urban Global South. However, recent sites-and-services projects are often less popular; many are typically located far from income-generating activities and lack sufficient access to public transport and the city (see e.g. Bredenoord and Verkoren 2010: 360–361; Fernández-Maldonado and Bredenoord 2010; Klaver 2011).

The government's role as a housing provider changed into a role as an enabler of housing markets. In this respect, the government takes care of the legislative, institutional and financial framework (Pugh 1997). As a result, a stakeholder approach gained ground under the umbrella of urban governance. Although the western-based approach of neoliberalism focuses on the formal sector and neglects the informal sector (Brenner and Theodore 2002; Peck *et al.* 2013; Rolnik 2013), studies surrounding the urban Global South include the formal as well as the informal sector; each plays a vital role in the production of housing (e.g. Smets 2004; Simone 2010).

Whether it concerns owner-occupied or rental housing, dwellings should be built and basic facilities provided. Therefore, land, construction materials, building skills and knowledge, and finance are required. Each is outlined in the following paragraphs.

Although housing occasionally may be constructed above water, land is generally a necessary component of housing construction. The discussion on land and land titling – as a means to ensure security of tenure – has received a boost since the publication of De Soto (2001). The assumption is that land titling will help households and individuals realize asset value that encourages self-help construction and improvement. Although these assumptions have been criticized (Gilbert 2002; Smets 2003), titling processes nonetheless are widespread. Payne (Chapter 2) elaborates on such land issues.

Moreover, construction materials have received attention since cheaper materials could lead to lower production costs. The literature generally calls this low-cost housing rather than low-income housing (Smets 2004). More recently attention has also been given to the sustainability of building materials (see Kessler, Chapter 5).

As building skills and knowledge are necessary for shelter construction, building skills development and the transfer of this knowledge to self-builders is required. Some initiatives involved in building skills and knowledge aim at sustainable house construction, for example those provided by the Technical Training Resource Centre in Karachi. Other examples encompass private sector organizations such as the CEMEX cement company in Mexico (see Box 15.2) and many housing non-governmental organizations (NGOs) (see also Bredenoord and Van Lindert, Chapter 4).

Finally, unless compensated by self-help, finance is needed for all parts of the construction process. Although finance can be derived from the formal financial sector, it is not easily accessible for the poorer segments of society (Ferguson and Smets 2010; Smets 1997). Therefore, dwellers also use informal forms of finance such as small loans from family members, colleagues, neighbours, friends, moneylenders, and pawnbrokers, as well as funds from financial self-help groups (Smets 2004).

Governance and the stakeholders

Over the past few decades, the 'enabling approach' has gained a permanent place in the international habitat discourse (UNCHS 1990). It became generally accepted that the principal role of governments should not be the provision of housing to all citizens but rather the enabling of 'housing markets to work' (Mayo and Angel 1993). It was not coincidental that this shift took place in an international ideological environment of neoliberal supremacy. In the context of renewed market thinking and a gradual retraction of the state, the role of central governments and multilateral development institutions is also restrained within the public sector in habitat sector policies. Priority was given to the development of more efficient finance systems for housing construction by the formal sector, for example the national housing banks. Thus, there was an increasing awareness that the state could not – and should not – act as the provider of housing. The initiatives from civil society and the private sector are influenced by the 'new' role of the state concerning the responsibility to establish the appropriate financial, legal and regulatory frameworks.

In the 1990s, much work was done on the development of the roles, values and responsibilities of governments with respect to the urban habitat. A leading motive was that self-help initiatives by households and communities, which account for the lion's share of total urban housing supply and neighbourhood upgrading, should be stimulated as much as possible by means of a proactive attitude on the part of the government. As such, the role of the government was to shift towards other activities such as the guaranteeing of housing security, the supply of land for housing, the facilitation of credit facilities, the development of an appropriate public transport system, adequate solid waste management and basic service provision in general. In addition, local government should be better equipped to complement the many neighbourhood level initiatives and interventions in a strategy of citywide inclusive development. The worldwide trend towards public sector reforms and the decentralization of political power and public responsibilities to municipalities also supports this new role of local government with respect to housing and the provision of collective services (van Lindert and Verkoren 2010).

In the 1990s and 2000s the acknowledgement of the important role that local governance has to play became firmly rooted in general thinking about sustainable urban development. Testimonies to this paradigm shift were the Local Agenda 21, launched at the important Earth Summit in Rio de Janeiro in 1992, and the Habitat Agenda, proclaimed at the City Summit in Istanbul in 1996. Both agendas aim at an enhanced involvement of civil society and the private sector, in order to arrive at truly participatory planning processes at the municipal level (Metropolis 1994). Starting from the principles of partnership, capacity strengthening, and the exchange of knowledge, the Habitat Agenda expressly claims that cooperation between all actors, from public to private, including community-based organizations, non-governmental organizations and individuals, is necessary in order to arrive at sustainable urban development. The Habitat Agenda attaches major significance to the strengthening of civil society at all levels and to the participation of all actors in the decision-making process (UNCHS 1996).

Today, after over two decades of systematizing available knowledge on urban development interventions, it has become generally accepted that the design of sustainable urban and housing development strategies should be based on the following three basic principles.

First, it is recognized that sustainable urban development will only be possible if policies and strategies are embedded in a multi-disciplinary, holistic, and pluralist approach, and that long-term programme support is needed for institutional capacity building. As such, good local governance and urban management, appropriate regulatory frameworks, sustainable environmental management, and the development of local – often neighbourhood-based – economic activities, are essential preconditions to reduce urban poverty and to redistribute resources in such a way as to include the urban poor in the formal city (Gilbert *et al.* 1996; Shah and Shah 2006).

A second key principle – partnership – focuses on cooperation between the public, civic, and private sectors. Local multi-sector partnerships may create the synergies that are absolutely necessary for a successful approach to urban development (Batley 1996; Payne 1999; Corrêa de Oliveira 2004). External partnerships are just as important, as strategic alliances with donor organizations may provide complementary human and material resources that are indispensable for urban development programmes (Brinkerhoff and Brinkerhoff 2004; Smets and Salman 2008).

The third essential ingredient for successful development programmes is the active involvement and participation of the inhabitants. Ownership and empowerment, both important catchwords in the general development discourse, have also secured first rank positions on the agendas of urban planning and housing. Without an outspoken population that has access to decision-making in all stages of project and policy formulation, from the very first stages of needs assessments until the final implementation phase, the chances of attaining sustainable solutions are slim (Abbott 1996; Moctezuma 2001; Van Lindert and Nijenhuis 2003).

In the thematic and country policy chapters that follow in this book, many examples will expose the relevance of these principles. Indeed, none of the various national housing policies in the Global South escapes from the rule that proper institutions are vital to an effective functioning of land and housing markets. Collaboration between the public and the private sectors with respect to the provision of land, housing, and collective services is also an issue that is highlighted in various chapters of this volume – in particular by Ikejiofor in Chapter 23 on public–private partnerships in Nigeria (cf. Ibem 2011). In India, the so-called Transferable Development Rights (TDRs) instrument has motivated private land developers also to include elements of affordable (low- and middle-income) housing provision in their essentially profit-driven ventures (see e.g. Chitekwe-Biti *et al.*, Chapter 8; Sengupta, Chapter 9; and Box 2.1). Close and interdependent relations also exist between public institutions and the financial sector. Exemplary in this respect is the so-called *Ahorro-Bono-Crédito* or ABC model, as developed in Chile and replicated in many Latin American countries (see the chapters on housing policies in Colombia, Peru and Ecuador). In the ABC model, the central state supplies subsidies while the mortgage loans are provided by the private financial system. Housing construction is entirely realized by private companies. Outstanding mortgage loans are guaranteed by a public (housing) bank.

In the low-income housing sector a myriad of actors engage in the everyday art of housing production. The producers of housing include, for example, formal construction companies, private land and housing developers, informal contractors, local craftsmen, NGOs, housing cooperatives, housing associations, and last but not least the residents themselves. Once the residents of informal settlements perceive their tenure condition as being sufficiently secure, they will often engage over the course of many years in self-help and self-managed incremental construction activities.

At the same time, however, the ambition of many of the urban poor to realize 'a home of one's own' (Moser 1982) is still far from reality. Therefore, the rental housing segment is also of great importance for the functioning of urban housing markets. In Chapter 6, Gilbert focuses on that important modality of housing tenure. Rented housing meets in particular the needs of youngsters, students, retired people and low-income families without purchasing power for decent housing, as well as temporary workers and first stage migrants who do not have the possibility of self-managed housing. However, the production of public and private rental housing lags behind the demand, as a consequence of inadequate political attention to (financing of) social rental housing units by governments, the presence of defective housing associations and the one-sided attention on the stimulation of private house property.

Many of the chapters in this volume also demonstrate that the traditional forms of vertical hierarchies of power and centralized decision-making have been slowly eroding. Although powerful patterns of patronage and clientelism still exist, solutions are sought to deal with them. Van der Linden (1997: 89) remarks that in a patronage-dominated environment:

> the rights and interest of the poor are probably best safeguarded by a rather centralized top-down approach with no tolerance for exceptions. … Having access is the best guarantee for participation and seemingly democratic procedures stand in the way of participation. … [This is because] poor people are very dependent on their leaders and will not easily antagonize them. Therefore, in a culture of patronage, having a say or a vote is not as meaningful as it might seem. At the same time, when government officers try to communicate with the people through their leaders, they confirm and even reinforce the leaders' claims that nothing can be done except through them, thus increasing people's dependence instead of empowering them at the grassroots level.

Once people at the grassroots come up with their own organizations, Van der Linden (1997: 89–90) identifies three points of attention. First, organizations representing the grassroots are more effective in doing so when they are not set up by a public sector organization. Second, representative leadership is best enabled when people have access to goods, services and information, even without those leaders. Third, public officers and leaders should discuss matters in open meetings and decisions taken should be made accessible to the public. In this way, scarcity as well as the distance between public sector institutions and citizens declines.

In the relationships between civic society and the state, newer forms of engagement and popular participation have emerged. Local governance is increasingly characterized by 'institutionalized' interactions between public, private, and civil society sectors (communities and citizens). The resulting 'governance networks' may then 'contribute to agenda setting, decision-making, or policy implementation' (Van Bortel 2012: 93; cf. Baud *et al.* 2011). The thematic chapters on the potential of assisted self-help housing (Bredenoord and Van Lindert, Chapter 4), on housing cooperatives (Ganapati, Chapter 7) and on the vitality of community-led development (Chitekwe-Biti *et al.*, Chapter 8) explicitly focus on the functioning of such governance networks; many country policy chapters also underline the relevance of co-production (Mitlin 2008), as the examples of housing cooperatives, community contracting and community-led development in particular demonstrate.

Sustainability

Popularized by the Brundtland report (WCED 1987), sustainable development is commonly defined as the long-term balance between society, the environment and economic growth – a world where human and natural systems can continue to exist and even thrive in tandem over a long period of time. However, due to global warming and its effects, the long-term prospects for the healthy urban habitat are under threat of climate change. Climate change increasingly affects several countries, and many urban neighbourhoods and even whole cities are threatened by rising sea levels, flooding rivers, tsunamis, hurricanes, heavy rains and severe drought. These conditions make urban planning more important than in the past, as adequate planning, such as risk- and water management can prevent houses from being built in danger zones. The construction of houses in risk zones – for example areas prone to earthquakes and volcanic eruptions, but also where heavy industry is located or hazardous materials are stored – must be prevented or restricted. Yet making reliable weather and climate predictions in order to determine the best planning path is difficult in areas with changeable weather patterns. However, while minimizing risk is possible through climate change adaptation or mitigation, depending on the available options, as well as available climate change finance and calculations of risks, making decisions on disaster reduction strategies is a political task. Yet as a public and communal responsibility, governments as well as households must be aware of the consequences and possibilities for prevention, protection and mitigation (e.g. Urry 2011).

Sustainability also has become an important concept in relation to environmental integrity. Human intervention results in the pollution of land, air and water, but also the disturbance of nature's equilibrium, including the loss of biodiversity. Therefore one should look into 'alternatives to traditional patterns of physical, social and economic development that can avoid problems such as exhaustion of natural resources, ecosystem destruction, pollution, overpopulation, growing inequality, and the degradation of human living conditions' (Wheeler 2003: 487).

Insights concerning environmental sustainability can also be applied to low-income housing in the urban Global South. Specifically, more attention should be paid to the interplay between technical and social solutions for sustainable change with respect to behaviour, economic or governance shifts (Williams 2009), which are mediated through physical spaces and the built environment (Keivani 2009).

In order to unpack the complex relationships between sustainability and low-income housing in cities, it is useful to distinguish the following five relevant fields: ecology and energy; technology and production; economy; social considerations; and targeted policies (based on Dietz and O'Neill 2013; Keivani 2009; McGranahan and Satterthwaite 2003; Thiele 2013; Williams 2009).

First, low-income urban housing cannot be made sustainable unless the themes of ecology and energy are taken into consideration. Sustainability may be improved, for example, through interventions that lower the carbon footprint and hazard-resilient measures as well as by urban planning that leads to a densification of the built-up area. Moreover, there are many other planning measures that prevent or counteract housing situations that are far from sustainable.

Second, technology and production can play an important role in the development of sustainable disaster-proof building materials. For example, prefab building components can be recycled and locally produced building materials minimize transport costs; each improves the sustainability of low-income housing.

Third, the economy is another important determinant of sustainability. As such, one should also take into account the limits of the neoliberal models exemplified by the recent global financial crisis. Moreover, dwellings should offer the possibility of home-based economic activities which in turn can stimulate the development of local economies. This could occur through community contracting for dwelling and neighbourhood improvement (for more on community contracting, see Steinberg, Chapter 12).

Fourth, the social component of sustainability should not be forgotten. Here one could think of community development and involvement, local culture, identity formation, social cohesion, as well as feelings of social investment in the form of responsibility and ownership.

Fifth, targeted policies are needed to reduce carbon emissions and prevent man-made hazards as well as to guide sound and informed city planning that includes pro-poor measures. Targeted policies are also needed for increased collaboration between national and local state levels as well as urban management to urban governance.

Figure 1.1 illustrates a model based on natural ecosystems whose existence over time is determined by 'sufficient self-directed identity as well as flexibility to change' (Lietaer *et al.* 2010: 5). Here, the flexibility to change – also called resilience – refers to 'the capacity of a system to absorb disturbance and reorganize while undergoing change so as to retain essentially the same function, structure, identity, and feedbacks' (Walker *et al.* 2004). This model also can be applied to housing provision and the complex relationships between sustainability and low-income housing in cities particularly regarding the five fields outlined above.

Ecosystems survived over time by adjusting to changing circumstances resulting in a search for equilibrium between the two opposing poles of efficiency and resilience. The healthiest systems have an optimum balance between the two extremes, which may be described by the term sustainability (see the window of viability in Figure 1.1). Once the balance between resilience and efficiency is disturbed the system becomes unstable. Too much efficiency leads to fragility, which goes together with too little diversity and connectivity. Moreover, too much resilience causes stagnation accompanied by too much diversity and connectivity (Lietaer *et al.* 2010: 6).

8 Peer Smets, Jan Bredenoord and Paul van Lindert

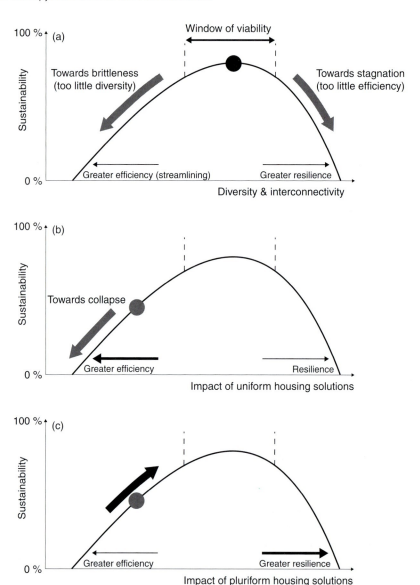

FIGURE 1.1 Sustainability and complex flow networks as function of the trade-offs between efficiency and resilience (Lietaer et al. 2009).

As with natural ecosystems, the modern urban world is characterized by constant improvements in system efficiency. However, too much efficiency will lead to brittleness and little diversity resulting in crashes and destruction, whereas too much resilience is characterized by too much diversity and a lack of coherence and purpose to growth, eventually leading to little efficiency and stagnation (see second graph in Figure 1.1).

Based on economic logic, similar analogies can be applied to our global financial system, which attempts to improve economic efficiency. However, the World Bank could trace more than 96 banking crises and 176 monetary crises since the early 1970s, when President

Nixon introduced the floating exchange regime. These crashes can also be found back in Schumpeter's notion of 'the creative destruction of capitalism' referring to the rise and fall of enterprises (Caprio and Klingebile, in Lietaer *et al.* 2010: 3). The financial crisis, which started in the United States and has spread over many parts across the globe, is already having a detrimental impact in cities in the Global South (see Ferguson *et al.*, Chapter 3 in this volume).

The tendency when coping with a crisis, whether it is from an economic or housing perspective, is to increase efficiency and to start again from the bottom line up. By so doing, the window of viability will not be reached at all. Once the focus is on creating diversity, a balance between efficiency and resilience can be more easily reached. This is especially true of housing solutions (see graph at bottom of Figure 1.1).

The sustainability model discussed above is also useful to understand the relationship between sustainability and the provision of low-income housing. A simple example will do. In the past, sites-and-services schemes were seen as a universal solution for dealing with the housing deficit, but in reality many sites-and-services were rather desolated areas that did not serve their target group. A better approach is to create a diversity of housing options for the urban poor, as illustrated for example by Hasan (Chapter 10). Once there is a housing diversity, chances that sufficient housing solutions will survive – and thus will reach the window of viability – are big. This is where sustainable shelter solutions can be found.

Finally, Thiele (2013: 198) warns us that '[s]ustainability is Janus-faced and two handed. It is future-focused but with an eye to its inheritance. And while it deftly manages the rate and scale of change with one hand, it also firmly grasps the need to conserve core values and relationships.'

Affordability

To discuss the concept of affordability, three different approaches will be used in the following order: (1) housing expenditure-to-income ratio; (2) the residual income approach; and (3) the incremental affordability approach.

Both in practice and in literature, affordability is a fuzzy concept with different meanings. Nonetheless, affordability has to do with a combination of the household's earning capability, as well as the availability of savings and credit. Housing loans will normally be provided if the lender is to a large extent sure that the loan will be repaid. In general, the affordable amount of a housing loan is determined by taking into account the capital costs required, the financing terms, the size and regularity of the household income and physical possessions, and the propensity to 'consume' housing. The most widespread idea is that once capital cost, terms, and household income are known, the ability to buy housing and the readiness to invest will automatically follow (Lee 1990: 64). Such discussions about affordable housing started at the end of the nineteenth century/beginning of the twentieth century in the western world. Initially, affordability was seen as 'one week's pay for one month's rent'. Mortgage providers started to use a *housing expenditure-to-income ratio*; this was a maximum of 25–30 per cent of the average household income that could be spent on housing. Here, housing expenditures could entail construction costs or rent paid for a dwelling. In addition to the housing expenditure-to-income ratio, attention also will be paid to the residual approach and the incremental affordability approach. The housing expenditure-to-income ratio is a rule of thumb measure which is often used for public policy purposes, for describing typical household expenditures for

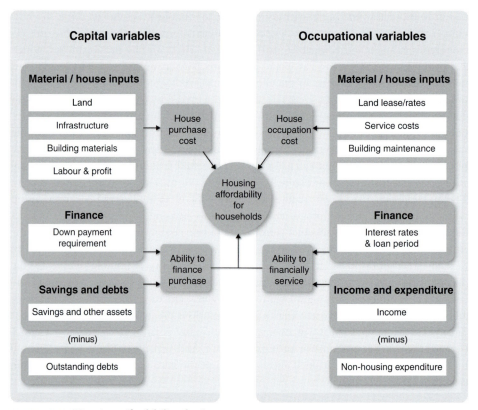

FIGURE 1.2 Housing affordability: basic components.
Source: Majale *et al*. (2011: 11).

housing, predicting the household's ability to pay a rent or housing loan instalment, or selecting households for a rental unit or housing loan. Although this measure is criticized because of the imprecise determination of a household income and the assumption that people are willing to spend this proportion of their income on housing, it is still widely used (Hulchanski 1995: 471–484).

Apart from looking at the size of the household income, housing can also be made affordable by reducing the housing costs by means of economizing on the construction costs, or by providing subsidies. Here the focus is low-cost housing, implying that low costs make the house affordable (see e.g. Baker, as discussed by Sengupta, Chapter 9).

Although a ratio provides insight into the affordability of housing costs – rent or repayment of a housing credit – it does not take into account that sufficient means remain for other necessities of life to avoid falling below the poverty line. Stone (2006) argues that the ratio approach provides misleading figures. A more realistic picture can be given by looking into the interaction between income, housing cost and the costs of non-housing needs which are also determined by the size of the household. Therefore, a second measure – called the *residual income approach* – offers measures which better reflect reality.

Above, affordability is seen as an income problem, but it can also be treated as a housing market problem. This implies that once it is considered a market problem, public intervention is needed to provide physical housing. For this purpose the government takes into account the adjustment of the denominator of the rent-to-income ratio (Linneman and Megolugbe 1992: 387).

Affordability has many components and measures, which are presented in Figure 1.2.

Here a distinction is made between capital variables (house purchase costs) and occupational variables (costs associated with keeping the house). A household's ability to buy a house depends on the purchase costs (including land, infrastructure, building materials, labour, and profit) and the ability to obtain financing; these in turn are mainly determined by the amount of down payment required, household savings, and the size and length of the instalments to repay the housing loan. After purchase, occupation costs encompass immaterial costs such as land lease, service costs, and building maintenance, but also financial costs dependent on the loan term, interest rate and the available household budget once the non-housing costs are deducted. This model goes beyond the simplified house-purchase-price to household-income model (Majale *et al.* 2011: 10–11). '[T]he lack of housing finance or unsupportive finance terms (for instance, high down payment requirements, high interest rates, and short loan periods) also directly limit housing affordability especially for lower- and middle-income groups' (Majale *et al.* 2011: 11).

Finally, the *incremental affordability approach*, which entails the incremental financing of smaller, short-term loans, should be applied alongside incremental building practices. With small and irregular incomes, such loans fit the livelihood strategies of the poorer sections of society. People with small budgets require flexibility in expenditure patterns that allow for possibilities of changing priorities. Consequently, expenditures on housing can only last for a relative period of time (e.g. Smets 1999, 2004, 2006; Ferguson and Smets 2010; Ferguson and Navarette 2003). In the Indian city of Hyderabad, Smets (2006) initially found that housing loans among the urban poor can last up to five years. However, a more in-depth analysis conducted by Smets – although not yet published – shows that the poorest sections take out credit for a maximum of three years, but preferably less than this.

The incremental affordability approach has been criticized by, for example, Pugh (1994) and Malpezzi (1994), who claim that Turner's self-help approach misconceived the economics and finance of self-help housing. However, their line of affordability thinking neglects the livelihood strategies of the urban poor; they state that decisions concerning the construction of a dwelling would be more efficient if financial decisions could be separated from individual building decisions. This would permit building a house now and paying for it later, which means repaying the housing loan in instalments. It is suggested that it is better to enjoy the benefits of a complete housing unit now, instead of consuming it incrementally. To take the argument one step further, one could say, by referring to Renaud (1987: 30), that the methods of financing dictate the mode of construction. Larger loans would lead to building in one go, which avoids the waste of resources. As incremental building often takes place with inferior materials, the improvement or extension of the existing structure requires that parts of the shelter frequently have to be demolished. Sometimes, only a fraction of the material can be reused. Despite these critiques on the incremental affordability approach, the urban poor will be better helped with affordability measures that fit their livelihood strategies.

Even though the concept of affordability can be used for all income groups, in this book the focus is entirely on affordability for low-income households. However, one should take into account that the use of affordability criteria should be adjusted to the specific contexts.

Moreover, housing can be made affordable by cross subsidies, which Payne, for example, illustrates in Chapter 2. Moreover, this volume also illustrates special arrangements such as in India, where developers are allowed to avoid building norms if they allocate a certain percentage of the buildings to low-income families.

Contents of the book

The book consists of four parts. The first part deals with low-income housing and the components needed for its production. The following sections cover a series of selected countries in Asia, Latin America and Africa. The book ends with drawing conclusions as well as a look ahead.

References

Abbott, J. (1996) *Sharing the City: Community Participation in Urban Management*. London: Earthscan.
Batley, R. (1996) 'Public-Private relationships and performance in service provision', *Urban Studies*, 33(4–5): 723–751.
Baud, I., Pfeffer, K., Sydenstricker, J. and Scott, D. (2011) *Developing Participatory 'Spatial' Knowledge Models in Metropolitan Governance Networks for Sustainable Development. Literature Review*. Bonn: EADI. Online. Available at www.chance2sustain.eu/fileadmin/Website/Dokumente/Dokumente/Publications/Developing_Participatory_Knowledge_Models.pdf (accessed 16 September 2013).
Beall, J. and Fox, S. (2009) *Cities and Development*. London, New York: Routledge.
Bredenoord, J. and Verkoren, O. (2010) 'Between self-help – and institutional housing: a bird's eye view of Mexico's housing production for low and (lower) middle-income groups', *Habitat International*, 34(3): 359–365.
Brenner, N. and Theodore, N. (2002) 'Cities and geographies of "actually existing neoliberalism"', *Antipode*, 34(3): 349–379.
Brinkerhoff, D.W. and Brinkerhoff, J.M. (2004) 'Partnerships between international donors and non-governmental development organizations: opportunities and constraints', *International Review of Administrative Sciences*, 70: 101–124.
Corrêa de Oliveira, M.T. (2004) 'Multi-sectoral partnerships in Brazil: a new scenario of its limits and possibilities', in D. Kruijt, P. van Lindert and O. Verkoren (eds) *State and Development: Essays in Honour of Menno Vellinga*. Amsterdam: Rozenberg.
De Soto, H. (2001) *The Mystery of Capital: Why Capitalism Triumphs in the West and Fails Everywhere Else*. London: Black Swan.
Dietz, R. and O'Neill, D. (2013) *Enough is Enough: Building a Sustainable Economy in a World of Finite Resources*. San Francisco: Berrett-Koehler Publishers.
Ferguson, B. and Navarette, J. (2003) 'A financial framework for reducing slums: lessons from experience in Latin America', *Environment and Urbanization*, 15(2): 201–216.
Ferguson, B. and Smets, P. (2010) 'Finance for incremental housing; current status and prospects for expansion', *Habitat International*, 34(3): 288–298.
Fernández-Maldonado, A.M. and Bredenoord, J. (2010) 'Progressive housing approaches in the current Peruvian policies', *Habitat International*, 34(3): 342–350.
Gilbert, A. (2002) 'On the mystery of capital and the myths of Hernando de Soto: what difference does legal title make?', *International Development Planning Review*, 24(1): 1–19.
Gilbert, R., Stevenson, D., Girardet, H. and Stren, R. (1996) *Making Cities Work: The Role of Local Authorities in the Urban Environment*. London: Earthscan.
Hulchanski, J.D. (1995) 'The concept of housing affordability: six contemporary uses of the housing expenditure-to-income ratio', *Housing Studies*, 10(4): 471–491.

Ibem, E.O. (2011) 'The contribution of Public-Private Partnerships (PPPs) to improving accessibility of low-income earners to housing in southern Nigeria', *Journal of Housing and the Built Environment*, 26: 201–217.

Keivani, R. (2009) 'Introduction: a review of the main challenges to urban sustainability', *International Journal of Urban Sustainable Development*, 1(1–2): 5–16.

Klaver, W. (2011) 'The key drivers behind the process of neighbourhood improvement: a study of the process of neighbourhood improvement in Nuevo Pachacútec, Municipality of Ventanilla, province of Callao, metropolis of Lima, Peru', Master's thesis, Utrecht University.

Lee, M. (1990) 'The affordability criterion: inefficient, inequitable and immoral?', in M. Raj and P. Nientied (eds) *Housing and Income in Third World Urban Development*. Bombay, Calcutta, New Delhi: Oxford University Press and IBH.

Lietaer, B., Ulanowicz, R. and Goerner, S. (2009) 'Options for managing a systemic bank crisis', *Surveys and Perspectives Integrating Environment and Society*, 2(1): 1–28.

Lietaer, B., Ulanowicz, R.E., Goerner, S.J. and McLaren, N. (2010) 'Is our monetary structure cause for financial instability? Evidence and remedies from nature', *Journal of Future Studies*, 14(3): 89–108.

Linneman, P.D. and Megbogbe, I.F. (1992) 'Housing affordability: myth or reality?', *Urban Studies*, 29(3/4): 369–392.

McGranahan, G. and Satterthwaite, D. (2003) 'Urban centers: an assessment of sustainability', *Annual Review of Environment and Resources*, 28: 243–274.

Majale, M., Tipple, G. and French, M. (2011) *Affordable Land and Housing in Asia*. Nairobi: UN-Habitat.

Malpezzi, S. (1994) '"Getting the incentives right": a reply to Robert-Jan Baken and Jan van der Linden', *Third World Planning Review*, 16(4): 451–466.

Mangin, W. (1967) 'Latin American squatter settlement: a problem and a solution', *Latin American Research Review*, 2: 65–98.

Mayo, S.K. and Angel, S. (1993) *Housing: Enabling Housing Markets to Work*. Washington, DC: World Bank.

Metropolis (1994) *Towards a Local 'Agenda 21'. An urban synthesis of Agenda 21; a guide for local authorities*. Paris: METROPOLIS/UTO/IULA/SUMMIT.

Mitlin, D. (2008) 'With and beyond the state – co-production as a route to political influence, power and transformation for grassroots organizations', *Environment and Urbanization*, 20(2): 339–360.

Moctezuma, P. (2001) 'Community-based organization and participation in south-east Mexico City', *Environment and Urbanization*, 13(2): 117–133.

Moser, C. (1982) 'A home of one's own: squatter housing strategies in Guayaquil, Ecuador', in A. Gilbert, J. Hardoy and R. Ramírez (eds) *Urbanization in Contemporary Latin America*. Chichester: John Wiley.

Payne, G. (ed.) (1999) *Making Common Ground: Public-Private Partnerships in Land for Housing*. London: Intermediate Technology Publications.

Peck, J., Theodore, N. and Brenner, N. (2013) 'Neoliberal urbanism Redux?', *International Journal of Urban and Regional Research*, 37(3): 1091–1099.

Pugh, C. (1994) 'Development of housing finance and the global strategy for shelter', *Cities*, 11(6): 384–392.

Pugh, C. (1997) 'Viewpoint. The World Bank's millennial theory of the state: further attempts to reconcile the political and the economic', *Third World Planning Review*, 19(3): iii–xiv.

Renaud, B. (1987) 'Another look at housing finance in developing countries', *Cities*, February: 28–34.

Rolnik, R. (2013) 'Late neoliberalism: the financialization of homeownership and housing rights', *International Journal of Urban and Regional Research*, 37(3): 1058–1066.

Shah, A. and Shah, S. (2006) 'The new vision of local governance and the evolving roles of local governments', in A. Shah (ed.) *Local Governance in Developing Countries*. Washington, DC: World Bank.

Simone, A. (2010) *City Life from Jakarta to Dakar: Movements at the Crossroads*. New York, London: Routledge.

Smets, P. (1997) 'Private housing finance in India: reaching down-market?', *Habitat International*, 21(1): 1–15.

Smets, P. (1999) 'Housing finance trapped in dilemma of perceptions: affordability criteria for the urban poor questioned', *Housing Studies*, 14(6): 821–838.
Smets, P. (2003) 'The market does not work for all; and not just because of lacking property titles', *Focaal – European Journal of Anthropology*, 41: 193–196.
Smets, P. (2004) *Housing Finance and the Urban Poor*. New Delhi, Jaipur: Rawat.
Smets, P. (2006) 'Small is beautiful but big is often the norm: housing microfinance in discussion', *Habitat International*, 30: 595–613.
Smets. P. and Salman, T. (2008) 'Countering urban segregation: theoretical and policy innovations from around the globe', *Urban Studies*, 45(7): 1307–1332.
Stone, E. (2006) 'What is housing affordability? The case for the residual income approach', *Housing Policy Debate*, 17(1): 151–184.
Thiele, L.P. (2013) *Sustainability*. Cambridge, Malden: Polity.
Turner, J. (1976) *Housing by People: Towards Autonomy in Building Environment*. London: Marion.
UNCHS (1990) *The Global Strategy for Shelter to the Year 2000*. Nairobi: United Nations Centre for Human Settlements.
UNCHS (1996) *The Habitat Agenda: Goals and Principles, Commitments and Global Plan of Action*. Istanbul: United Nations Centre for Human Settlements.
UN-Habitat (2003) *The Challenge of Slums*. London: Earthscan.
Urry, J. (2011) *Climate Change and Society*. Cambridge: Polity.
Van Bortel, G. (2012) 'Institutions and governance networks in housing and urban regeneration', in S.J. Smith, M. Elsinga, L.F. O'Mahony, O.S. Eng, S. Wachter and R. Ronalds (eds) *International Encyclopedia of Housing and Home*. Oxford: Elsevier.
Van der Linden, J. (1997) 'On popular participation in a culture of patronage: patrons and grassroots organizations in a sites and services project in Hyderabad, Pakistan', *Environment and Urbanization*, 9(1): 81–90.
Van Lindert, P. and Nijenhuis, G. (2003) 'Popular participation and the participatory planning practice in Latin America: some evidence from Bolivia and Brazil', in I.S.A. Baud and J. Post (eds) *Realigning Actors in an Urbanizing World: Governance and Institutions from a Development Perspective*. London: Ashgate.
Van Lindert, P. and Verkoren, O. (eds) (2010) *Decentralized Development in Latin America: Experiences in Local Governance and Local Development*. Dordrecht: Springer.
Walker, B.H., Holling, C.S., Carpenter, S.R. and Kinzig, A.S. (2004) 'Resilience, adaptability and transformability in social-ecological systems', *Ecology and Society*, 9(2): art 5.
WCED (1987) *Our Common Future*. Oxford: Oxford University Press.
Wheeler, S. (2003) 'Planning sustainable and livable cities', in T.T. LeGates and F. Stout (eds) *The City Reader*. London, New York: Routledge.
Williams, K. (2009) 'Sustainable cities: research and practice challenges', *International Journal of Urban Sustainable Development*, 1(1–2): 128–132.

PART I
Thematic perspectives
Introduction

Peer Smets, Paul van Lindert and Jan Bredenoord

The production and consumption of owner-occupied and rental housing cannot be seen as separate from the fundamental elements needed for the construction process: land, finance, construction skills and building materials. Such elements of the building process are needed locally but should be seen from a political economy perspective. The political economy perspective offers insight into the impact of neoliberalism, different crises concerning finance, climate, energy and resources, but also into the policies and practices of global institutions such as the World Bank and UN institutions. Moreover, the fulfilment of public tasks concerning urban planning and development – in other words creating good conditions for housing – is difficult enough for national and local governments, which have certain limitations regarding the investment in housing. This is why poor residents cannot count on their governments alone for housing. The involvement of the private sector – e.g. building companies, financial institutions and banks – and resident participation is essential for large-scale house production in developing countries. This thematic part will discuss insights in construction elements, low-income housing types and its embeddedness in the local context. Below, the different contributions will be presented.

In Chapter 2, *Geoffrey Payne* addresses ways in which urban land markets are managed and assesses a whole range of constraints that restrict access to land, housing and services to large sections of urban populations. Such constraints are of a political, legal, technical, regulatory, financial or attitudinal nature that may operate independently, but often reinforce one another. Using a political economy perspective, Payne argues that it is extremely challenging to remove market constraints on affordable and sustainable land because it is the leading stakeholder groups that actually benefit from the status quo. In fact, Payne continues, in order to meet these challenges, 'elite' groups must be convinced that changes in the functioning of the land markets can be in their interest, as much as it will be in the interest of those without access to land, failing which alternative 'champions of change' will need to be identified and supported. A precondition is to assert the right of the poor to the city. That should be a first priority to all those with professional responsibilities in urban planning and land use management. The contribution of the poor majority to solving urban housing deficits should also be promoted in ways which can be integrated into existing plans.

In Chapter 3, *Bruce Ferguson, Peer Smets and David Mason* also use a political economy approach to look into the issue of housing finance. They show that governments, land and housing developers, public mortgage finance systems as well as housing and land subsidy mechanisms are creating a habitat disaster for most of the population in many countries in the urban Global South. Moreover, in the aftermath of the implosion of the great property/housing debt bubble in Western Europe and the United States, real property lending and the real estate and financial sectors still operate in a dysfunctional manner at all levels. The next huge global debt bubble is highly likely to be followed by a bust in the new engines of global economic growth and real home lending, much of it at very high rates to low- and moderate-income households in cities of developing and emerging countries. These developments ask for a thorough reconsideration of current 'enabling housing markets' approaches which dramatically worsen housing gaps for low-income groups. This chapter also shows that alternatives can be found in a diversity of new market-based products from the private sector in Latin American, Asian and African cities.

In Chapter 4, *Jan Bredenoord and Paul van Lindert* elaborate on the occurrence and the importance of (assisted) self-help housing as a sustainable housing provision strategy for low-income households. The chapter elaborates on the variety of housing supply modalities for the urban poor and the vital role of self-help construction within such modalities. While emphasizing that various arrangements of outside support may be pertinent to the needs of different categories of households, the authors propose a differentiated approach of assisted self-help housing policies. Such policy packages may range from, for example, the provision of land with basic services; core houses on plots within a sites-and-services scheme; technical assistance with self-help and housing microfinance schemes; and mutual self-help housing realized in the framework of housing cooperatives. Attention is also given to some of the main limitations of self-help housing such as low housing densities, slow construction pace and sometimes low technical quality of the housing. The authors call for a reintroduction of assisted self-help housing into national and local housing policies, including a range of separate instruments that support self-help housing of target groups that operate under different conditions.

In Chapter 5, *Earl Kessler* links up with this discussion by presenting ways of support that are both suitable for self-help housing and include solutions that are more sustainable and resilient to natural hazards and climate change. Kessler argues that natural disasters and climate change will change the shape of cities and influence the choice of building technologies and materials, including those concerning self-build housing. Therefore, new self-help shelter programmes should be designed for resilience against climate change in order to diminish disaster risks. The constructive role of self-help shelter kits and core housing schemes in reconstruction programmes exposes the connection between disaster reconstruction and longer-term urban and shelter development. In addition, the housing strategies including urban design should increasingly utilize recycled building materials and develop renewable resources. In this context, bamboo is presented as a most promising construction material in terms of its climate-friendly technology and its suitability for self-help housing.

In Chapter 6, *Alan Gilbert* focuses on the vital role of rental housing for the poor in many cities of the Global South. One of the major explanations is that many households need rental housing because they cannot afford to be homeowners or because they do not yet want to assume the responsibilities that home ownership involves. It is remarkable that most rental accommodation for the poor is offered by small-scale landlords and most of it becomes available in the informal segments of the housing market. The expansion of the rental housing market for lower income groups across the cities of Latin America, Asia and Africa is largely an effect of incremental construction by owner-occupiers in the consolidated peripheries of cities. In view of the importance of rental housing, it is surprising that only a few governments have addressed this issue beyond policies of rent control. Gilbert argues that governments and international institutions such as multilateral development banks and UN agencies should put the issue of how to increase the supply of affordable rental housing much higher on their political agendas.

Sukumar Ganapati explains in Chapter 7 how housing cooperatives since the 1990s have grown across Asia, Latin America and Africa. For each of these regions, he distinguishes a different steering mechanism behind the formation of housing cooperatives, implying distinct institutional structures with varying influence of state institutions (mainly in Asia) and of (international) non-governmental organizations (mainly in Africa). In contrast, the Latin American housing cooperative is based on the tradition of urban social movements in that region. In each of the three regions, however, housing cooperatives have increasingly been recognized as effective vehicles able to secure affordable housing for their members. In addition to providing tenure security, housing cooperatives also are very effective in fostering community action. Ganapati argues that, across the Global South, housing cooperatives have increased in importance as collective institutions which fill the gap between the public and the private sectors. These cooperatives enable both collective and individual ownership of land and housing, while at the same time facilitating access to finance and promoting or assisting (mutual, self-help) construction. In order to enhance these roles of housing cooperatives, it is of vital importance that appropriate institutional frameworks are put in place.

In Chapter 8, *Beth Chitekwe-Biti, Sheela Patel and Diana Mitlin* pay attention to self-organized communities who have sought to improve their own habitat situation. Many of these groups recognize that problems cannot be addressed by either households or individual communities alone, and so have aligned with each other to form networks and have a political impact. This chapter explores the experiences of Shack/Slum Dwellers International (SDI), one such network. Through an exploration of SDI affiliate work in India and Zimbabwe, the authors debate how to address the shelter needs of the 1 billion people who currently lack safe and secure homes in the cities of the Global South. The discussion highlights the lack of investment finance, and the difficulties of effectively addressing housing needs by means of subsidy programmes which are currently unavailable. The case studies of Mumbai and Harare respectively demonstrate the capacity of grassroots organizations to secure political commitment towards implementing pro-poor measures, including affordable housing and improving liveability in informal settlements. The chapter presents suggestions for, among other things, increased affordability and the creation of a more inclusive social process through the use of tools such as mapping and enumeration, house modelling and savings schemes. Key to such solutions, however, is collective action through which the communities can engage the state and effectively influence housing and urban planning interventions.

2

POLICY AND POLITICS IN URBAN LAND MARKET MANAGEMENT

Lessons from experience

Geoffrey Payne[1]

Introduction

This chapter poses a challenge to all those with professional responsibilities in land administration. How can policies and programmes be formulated *and* implemented at the scale and speed necessary to improve access to land on affordable and appropriate terms to all those in need, particularly the vulnerable and poor unable to conform to current financial and regulatory requirements? The constraints imposed by local and global market forces and current levels of inequality in all countries (developed as well as developing) have unleashed economic forces which have destabilised the markets themselves.[2] The formulation and implementation of smarter, more innovative forms of market regulation to reduce urban inequality has therefore become essential to the wider public interest and to market stability.

So what constraints exist, what options are available and what action will be needed to ensure their adoption? Sadly, examples of significant progress are all too rare. The fact that dramatic progress has not yet been achieved demonstrates the complexity of the challenge, but also demonstrates that no silver bullets exist to effect structural change overnight. It does, however, show that unless major changes are made soon, the problems will continue to increase more rapidly than the solutions.

This chapter is based on practical and academic experience of the forces and interests driving urban development and options for the urban poor to benefit from the economic development which they help to generate. Whilst this experience has revealed many inspiring examples of political leadership and imaginative administration, it has also revealed the prevalence, in countries at all levels of economic development, of powerful forces which reflect the vested interests of a small elite. As such, it is clear that urban planning and land use management need to be regarded ultimately as politically driven. The chapter therefore addresses the issues from a political economy perspective.

Following an outline of the challenge facing professionals active in the sector, the political, institutional, legal, technical, regulatory, financial and attitudinal constraints to progress are summarised. A political economy perspective is then used to assess the impact of political, administrative and commercial elites on options for the urban poor to meet their basic needs for land, housing and services. The chapter concludes with a range of options for meeting the challenges ahead.

The scale and nature of the challenge

The scale of urbanisation and urban growth today are without historical precedent. A large proportion of this urban population growth will take place in sub-Saharan Africa and growth rates are similarly high in Asian countries, where the proportion may be lower but the total numbers even higher.

It is hardly surprising that urban land and housing markets are not operating efficiently or equitably. Faced with the inexorable increase in urban populations, and with restricted resources, governments deserve a great deal of sympathy. After all, it took the United Kingdom the best part of a century to develop an effective institutional response to urban growth when it had a small population and enjoyed relative affluence. Countries experiencing urbanisation today have far fewer resources per capita and, in most cases, far larger populations. It is also understandable that urban managers and policymakers throughout urbanising countries feel overwhelmed and under-resourced in dealing with such unprecedented numbers, especially given the increasing extent of urban poverty. The rate of growth in secondary cities in Africa and elsewhere also puts acute pressure on local governments to take action at a time when many lack adequate powers or institutional capability.

Despite the enormous challenges they pose, urban areas are, and always have been, more efficient at creating large-scale, high value employment than rural areas, though much of the growth in employment has been within the informal, rather than the formal, economy. Urbanisation has been taking place for several decades in Latin America and Asia, and no amount of wishful thinking, wilful neglect, hostility or indifference on the part of unsympathetic officials, politicians or professionals is going to stop it (Figure 2.1). Furthermore, a failure to provide adequate land, housing and services has not reduced urban growth – it simply consigns larger numbers of people to substandard living conditions (UNFPA 2007: 67).

It is important to recognise that some countries have made a major commitment to improving the living conditions of the increasing numbers of urban poor households (see Figure 2.2) and the fact that

> more than 200 million slum-dwellers have gained access to either improved water, sanitation or durable and less crowded housing shows that countries and municipal governments have made serious attempts to improve slum conditions, thereby enhancing the prospects of millions of people to escape poverty, disease and illiteracy. However, in absolute terms, the number of slum-dwellers in the developing world is actually growing, and will continue to rise in the near future.
>
> *(MDG 2010, cited in UNFPA 2011: 86)*

How long the poor will tolerate being unable to access basic housing and services, especially when they see the comforts enjoyed by a more fortunate minority, should raise concerns among donors and enlightened city managers on all continents.

FIGURE 2.1 Riverbank settlement in Phnom Penh, Cambodia. Photo by Geoffrey Payne.

FIGURE 2.2 *Kampung* settlement in Surabaya, Indonesia. Photo by Geoffrey Payne.

Constraints to progress

A wide range of innovative approaches to land development have been introduced and flourished under a range of political regimes and conditions (see Lipman and Rajack 2011 for examples and also the summary in Box 2.1). Identifying the conditions under which specific policy instruments are likely to be accepted and implemented is, however, fraught with difficulties and dissent.

BOX 2.1 EXAMPLES OF INNOVATIVE APPROACHES TO URBAN LAND DEVELOPMENT

Land pooling/land readjustment (LP/LR), a technique for managing and financing urban land development, in which land parcels in selected urban fringe areas are assembled into planned layouts of roads, public utility lines, public open spaces and serviced building plots. Some plots are sold for cost recovery and the others are distributed to the landowners in exchange for their land parcels. LP/LR projects exist in many Asian countries.

Transferable Development Rights (TDR) separate the right to develop land from the land itself. It involves purchasing development rights – usually from areas where development is to be discouraged – and using them to develop land in another location – in areas where more development or density is desired. While TDR does not always increase the supply of land, it can increase the supply of land for a particular use, for example affordable housing. It is widely applied in Mumbai, India.

Land sharing is a means of putting land to the most efficient financial and social use by accommodating existing occupants in ways which enable the landowners to generate a financial benefit. It is widely applied in Thailand, India and other countries.

Community land trusts (CLTs) are similar to cooperatives in that they are private non-profit corporations created to acquire and hold land for the benefit of a community.

Guided land development (GLD) is a land management tool for guiding the conversion of privately owned land in the urban periphery from rural to urban uses. It uses the provision of infrastructure as a mechanism to guide urban development and has been implemented widely in Pakistan, and also used in Egypt, Thailand and elsewhere.

Site development briefs – public sector agencies prepare site development and design briefs and invite a range of groups to respond with proposals. This should encourage more market-sensitive and demand-led approaches, whilst reducing the burden on scarce public sector resources.

Requests for proposals (RFPs) involve an invitation to suitably qualified developers to submit proposals for a specific site. RFPs specify a number of mandatory requirements, plus a number of additional optional elements. Developers are invited to submit proposals that meet all the mandatory requirements and include additional elements. They are a means for realising a public benefit from a private development. From the developers' perspective, the RFP approach increases access to highly desirable sites for

> development and offers an attractive alternative. RFPs have been widely implemented in Eastern Europe and Russia.
>
> **Concession of Real Right to Use (CRRU) and ZEIS (Special Zone of Social Interest).** CRRU is a legal instrument to secure land tenure rights to occupants in Brazil's *favelas* (informal settlements) without transferring property from the owner to the possessor. It can also be registered in the name of an individual or a group, giving maximum flexibility at minimum cost. It can also be inherited and used as collateral for a loan. In Brazil, by designating a *favela* as a special residential zone ('*ZEIS*'), settlements can be regularised and upgraded with the active participation of local communities.
>
> *Source*: Lipman and Rajack (2011).

Clearly, authoritarian regimes and conservative administrations are unlikely to embrace approaches which may undermine their power, such as community participation in decision-making. However, they are also free from the constraints imposed by a multiplicity of conflicting stakeholder interests and can therefore push through innovative approaches that they consider beneficial. China, Rwanda, Singapore, Tunisia and some Gulf states are examples where innovative approaches have been introduced by relatively authoritarian governments.

Sadly, these innovative approaches have not been as widely implemented as their merits justify, forcing large and increasing numbers of people into a range of unauthorised methods for accessing land (*The Economist* 2012). As a result, some citizens' organisations have undertaken autonomous actions in order to meet their basic needs (IIED 2008: 2). The irony is that land policies and programmes designed to ensure planned development have led to the very opposite.

This raises two critical questions. First, have the positive attributes of urban growth and the contribution of the poor majority been effectively communicated to politicians and urban managers in urbanising countries in ways which they can accept as a basis for policy and practice? If not, then a major effort is required by professional researchers and practitioners to address this failure. Second, if urban managers *have* been made aware of the inevitability of urban growth and its positive attributes, as well as the contribution of the poor to economic development, then why has so little changed?

In addressing these two questions, it is necessary to explore the full range of political, institutional, legal, technical, regulatory, financial and attitudinal constraints. These operate independently and in concert to restrict access to land, housing and services on terms that are affordable and appropriate for large sections of the urban population. The following sections discuss these constraints in turn.

Political constraints

National, provincial and municipal governments, especially those in democracies concerned about winning the next election, tend to have short-term priorities that over-ride long-term strategic planning or expenditure, and relationships between political cycles and forced evictions and relocations are apparent.[3]

Similarly, urban constituencies are often more progressive and less conservative than the more numerous rural constituencies, producing national and regional governments that may be different from municipal ones. This is especially so in the case of large cities, where local government can provide a powerful platform for local politicians seeking power at the national level.[4] Even when the party in power nationally and locally is the same, tensions may exist if ambitious politicians at the local level are seen as threatening the authority of the national leadership.[5] This situation is made worse if national government fiscal policies capture an excessive proportion of the revenues generated at the urban level, frustrating the ability of local government to undertake long-term land use planning.[6]

Institutional constraints

Given the competition between central, regional and local government agencies for scarce resources and influence in order to protect their positions, there is a common tendency for agencies not to collaborate, a tendency which sometimes also applies to the donor community itself. Given that information is a form of power, especially in the context of lucrative urban land markets, many government agencies seek to concentrate power and resources within themselves. Decentralisation, while frequently promoted, often takes the form in practice of devolving responsibilities, but not authority or control over resources.

Bureaucratic inertia, personal vested interests and fear of failure on the part of officials at all levels are a further consideration and often inhibit the development of a flexible, pragmatic approach to new challenges, unless it is seen as providing, or increasing, opportunities for greater control or abuse. In the capital of the Solomon Islands, Honiara, all land within the municipal boundary is government owned. Yet the Commissioner of Lands retains the same untrammelled discretionary powers to allocate land as existed when the country was under colonial administration and the population was less than 5,000. Such arrangements are an open invitation to abuse and poor governance.

Apart from the prestige and social status afforded to the administrative elite, such as the Indian Administrative Service (IAS) national and state cadres, for which competition to enter is intense, the lower pay levels and social status available in the middle and lower ranks of the public sector tend to result in less talented graduates being recruited. At the same time, the frequent moving of senior staff between government departments severely reduces administrative continuity. This reduces the ability of the public sector to operate with the same level of competence as the private sector entities which they are required to regulate in the public interest. This is particularly the case in land administration agencies where the sums involved in land management provide enormous temptation to even the most honest of staff (Van der Molen and Tuladhar 2007: 4–5).

A further consideration is that public sector officials are insulated from economic realities by the fact that they are spending taxpayers' money and not their own, so are not affected personally by the costs of their proposals. In some respects, pressure to spend an annual budgetary allocation may actually encourage a wasteful approach, since any savings may result in a reduced budget in future years, thereby reducing the resources and influence enjoyed by those leading such agencies. The gap between pay and conditions in public and private sectors is now far narrower in many developed countries and this, together with the frequent movement of professional staff between public and private sectors, makes it easier to create innovative public–private sector partnerships in land (PPIAF 2011). In urbanising countries, the higher salaries offered by the private sector make it less attractive for talented and committed students to work in the public sector, weakening the ability of the land administrations to extract a good deal in negotiations with private land developers.

A concentration of powers enjoyed by some public sector agencies may help to maximise influence over private investment in the public interest. However, any monopolistic powers also increase the powers of patronage and potential for rent-seeking which can militate against innovation and good practice.[7] Similar concerns regarding the limitations of concentrating powers in a single agency have been expressed in the case of the Delhi Development Authority in India, which has become the largest landowner in the city, but which has been accused of disproportionately benefiting high-income groups, rather than those in greatest need (see UNESCAP 1995: 37; *The Hindu* 2014). These cases are far from unique.

In Chinese cities, regulatory issues and conflicts over land have proliferated following the introduction of private land leases. In a system where private ownership of land is still not recognised, government retains a paramount role in urban land allocation and development.[8] The 1998 Land Administration Law (LAL) empowers local governments to acquire land from rural collectives on the basis of 'public interest', which has created many problems, especially for the urban poor and those on the periphery. In 1995, when official statistics on land leases became available, about 43,000 hectares of land were leased by various governments in the country and by 2006, as a result of the powers granted to local government by the LAL, this figure had increased by over five times to 232,500 hectares (Su 2008: 5). The monopoly power over land access granted to local governments, and their dependence upon land sales to developers as a major source of revenues, has led to acute distortions in land delivery across the country (UBS Investment Research 2011: 1).

Legal constraints

The legal framework in many currently urbanising countries is often far more complex than in more affluent countries which are already heavily urbanised and which have greater resources to address their problems. This is not just because countries that underwent the transformation earlier have had more time to evolve a coherent legal framework for managing land which enjoys social legitimacy, but because countries urbanising today often have to cope with a range of historical influences and pressures which were once imposed on their indigenous legal systems through colonialism or other external pressures.[9] This is particularly applicable in the case of land, where customary practices are overlaid by concepts and practices imposed under colonialism.

Another source of legal constraint in land administration is when countries undergo major transformations in their political, institutional and legal structures. For example, when communism collapsed throughout Eastern Europe and Cambodia recovered from the Khmer Rouge regime, previous legal frameworks in land management cast a long shadow.

A final legal constraint that impedes access to serviced land is if there are legal constraints on installing water supply or sewer networks in unregistered settlements. This does not apply, however, in Colombia, as the constitution permits all residents to obtain access to water, electricity and sewer networks on the simple condition that they can afford to pay for them.[10] This has significantly accelerated the improvement of informal settlements throughout the capital city of Bogotá.

Technical and regulatory constraints

One regulatory constraint relates to the widespread tendency to regard the formulation of spatially based 'master plans' specifying approved land uses and relevant regulatory requirements as an acceptable basis for urban management despite the rapidly changing opportunities and constraints applicable in a globalising world. Such plans often take long to prepare and cannot keep pace with rapidly changing needs and resources. For example, the current master plan for Lahore, the 'Integrated Master Plan for Lahore-2021', was approved in 2005 and is simply a refined version of a draft submitted in 1998, when the population was significantly smaller and the economic parameters noticeably different.[11]

Another regulatory constraint in land is that of the floor space index[12] (FSI). This methodological approach is widely criticised (e.g. Bertaud and Brueckner 2004; Bertaud and Buckley 2005; Brueckner 2007) as impeding the efficient development of urban land compared to what would have been the case had market forces determined the density and height of urban development. Seen in long-term strategic terms, it might be argued that while a 'common-sense FSI' as advocated by Bertaud and Buckley (2005) is advisable, a degree of restriction can help in guiding development to what may be considered more appropriate locations and helping to create a multi-nucleated urban spatial structure, rather than the conventional central business district (CBD) of a mono-centric spatial urban structure.[13]

Administrative procedures[14] in processing applications for land development are often cumbersome, time-consuming and expensive, without even the certainty of a positive outcome for applicants. For example, Payne and Majale (2004) found that in Tanzania, it could take seven years or more to complete a formal transfer of land titles, and in Kenya, a potential developer had to contend with over 22 Acts of Parliament that relate to urban development. These cumbersome procedures conspire to force large sections of the population, including even some middle- and high-income groups, to develop land and modify property without official approval.

Williams (2008: 25–27) cites several studies to demonstrate that communication and consultation strategies are critical to the introduction of innovative land policy instruments. They are tools for reaching out to people, for promotion and advocacy, as well as for social mobilisation through information sharing. Adequate time for negotiations and discussions should be taken into consideration since constructive negotiations can take from six months to two years, depending on the scale and complexity of the project. Communication and consultation strategies have been active for many years in Mumbai, where Bombay First has been an active forum for multi-stakeholder debate for some years and where civil society groups have launched offers of partnership with state and municipal government agencies (Patel and Arputham 2007). Projects such as the redevelopment of the Dharavi settlement in Mumbai raise major opportunities for innovative collaboration between government and civil society groups, yet such partnerships are not without their own dangers, since they may compromise the independence and integrity of civil society groups and limit their ability, in practice if not in theory, to later criticise the hand that feeds them.

Financial constraints

As emphasised above, urban growth is an asset-generating process. However, it is often not a lack of finance that impedes the development of economically efficient and socially inclusive urban land and housing markets, but reluctance on the part of those who formulate or approve policy to pay their fair share of the costs of urban development in the form of property taxes and other charges (Bredenoord and Van Lindert 2010). Increasingly, private sector urban developments consisting of whole townships, or even mini-cities, such as Rajarhat and Lavasa in India, are being developed on the urban periphery, or well outside the administrative boundaries of existing cities, so that the affluent minority can enjoy the amenities to which they feel entitled, while retaining the opportunity to maximise their economic opportunities in the established cities without paying the relevant taxes which enable the cities to develop and flourish.

A further constraint is the claim by central governments on land and property revenues generated within urban areas. Given the concentration of economic activity within urban areas, it is inevitable that a proportion of such revenues will be claimed by central government to meet a range of national needs. However, where this denies cities the ability to maintain their development, there is a real risk that it will impede the ability of urban areas to generate such revenues. A balance therefore needs to be struck in order to ensure that the long-term needs of both local and national governments are met. This balance was sought in Bolivia's 1994 Popular Participation Law 1551, which provides that all revenues received by the Ministry of Finance are subject to a 20 per cent transfer to a distinct fund which is then reallocated to local governments according to their population size. This works to strengthen the resource base of local authorities and improve democratic accountability.[15]

Attitudinal constraints

Of all the constraints listed above, the attitudes of policymakers may be one of the greatest factors influencing the ability of the urban poor to access land on affordable terms. Despite entrenched economic inequality, few countries can match Brazil's recent record in addressing the needs of the urban poor through participatory budgeting, the introduction of the City Statute in 2001 and the creation of a Ministry of Cities in 2003. The City Statute is a federal law which regulates and expands the constitutional measures on urban policy and acknowledges a legal right to the city of urban residents in Brazil (Cities Alliance 2010: 61).

Despite the examples of innovative and cost-effective programmes and projects for land development and administration around the world published in the academic literature and presented at numerous international conferences such as the World Urban Forums, the World Bank annual land policy conferences, plus those recognised by the Dubai Best Practice Awards, and the annual Habitat Awards, some political, social and economic elites appear as ambivalent towards urban growth, and particularly the presence of the urban poor, as they were before all these initiatives were launched.[16] The professional community has so far failed to change this inbuilt, and factually unjustified, constraint; possibly because many senior professionals are part of the problem, rather than the solution. This may be because they are the product of an educational system that was essentially technically focused and lacked a political economy dimension or because they are drawn from the upper echelons of society whose interests they share.

Urban inequality and insights of a political economy approach

A key constraint to the adoption of innovative policy instruments may be that leading stakeholder groups actually benefit from the status quo to the extent that they do not see it as in their interests to change. After all, for politicians, keeping the poor majority under conditions of insecurity and substandard living conditions enables them to maintain power through vote banks created by promising to relieve poor conditions, even if the promises are never fulfilled. For public sector officials, it enables them to maintain a degree of control over private sector groups, whether this is seen as in the interests of the public, or their own private interests. For private developers, it enables them to maintain high profit margins due to the shortage of supply relative to demand, while even non-governmental organisations (NGOs) benefit from the continued flow of funds from developed countries through both donor-funded programmes and charities in the West.

The rising power of elites

The situation in many urbanising countries is also influenced by the fact that the political, administrative and economic elites are drawn from a narrow section of society, educated in prestigious schools and colleges, and enjoy membership of exclusive clubs. This is consistent with the writings of Pareto (1927), Burnham (1941), Wright Mills (1956) and Gonzalez (2006, 2009), who promulgate what is known as 'elitist theory', by which many social scientists claim that American and other national politics are best understood through the generalisation that nearly all political power is held by a relatively small and wealthy group of people sharing similar values and interests, and mostly coming from relatively similar privileged backgrounds. Most of the leaders in all, or nearly all, key sectors of society are recruited from this same social group, and elite theorists emphasise the degree to which interlocking corporate and foundation directorates, old school ties and frequent social interaction tend to link together and facilitate coordination between the other leaders in business, government, civic organisations, educational and cultural establishments, and the mass media.

Analysts of elitist theory differ somewhat among themselves on such questions as how open the power elite is to change or 'new blood', the exact degree of agreement or disagreement that usually prevails within its ranks and the degree of genuine concern (or lack thereof) for the broader public welfare that enters into their choices of public policy goals, but all such theorists broadly share the notion that it is these few thousand 'movers and shakers' who really run their country and determine the basic directions of public policy, certainly not the manipulated and powerless masses of ordinary voters choosing among candidates at election time.[17]

A parallel theoretical perspective known as 'regime theory' seeks to explain the ways in which a small group dominates decisions on urban management. Based again on American experience, Stone (1989: 4) notes that the result of applied regime theory is 'an informal, yet relatively stable group with access to institutional resources that enable it to have a sustained role in making governing decisions'. Evidence in support of this theory in the Bangladeshi urban context is described by the eminent researcher Nazrul Islam (*Daily Star* 2007), who claims that 'the corruption of the politicians, which has been widely recognized by one and all, is only possible because of the connivance of the corrupt bureaucrats'. Furthermore, 'bureaucrat capital controls more than 90 per cent of all capital assets in Bangladesh, which includes the infrastructure, public corporations, large tracts of valuable land, the nationalized banks, and so on'. As the power and confidence of the urban elite have increased, so they are reflected in policies on land management: official standards and norms reflect their interests. Thus, gated communities, or even new towns, are developed for affluent groups; and property taxes based

FIGURE 2.3 Congenial high-density neighbourhoods in Shanghai, China, contrasted with more recent high-rise developments. Photo by Geoffrey Payne.

on market values are minimal, or not collected. At the same time, slum clearance programmes evict the poor from their homes to peripheral and badly serviced locations, resulting in the spatial, as well as social, segregation of urban areas. Elitist concepts of progress are based on images of city states such as Singapore or Dubai and are imposed locally no matter how inappropriate to local needs, resources or conditions (see Figure 2.3).

Inequality and its impacts

Of course, it can be argued that all societies are ruled to some extent by elites. The issue is therefore the extent to which such elites control the wealth and allocation of resources in their respective countries. A key proxy for assessing the concentration of power within a country is to assess the distribution of wealth, or the degree of inequality. In this respect, the UNDP (United Nations Development Programme) human development indicators provide revealing information. The 2011 report cites a number of sources to report that 'the gap between the rich and the poor widened over the last two decades in more than three-quarters of Organisation for Economic Co-operation and Development [OECD] countries and in many emerging market economies' (UNDP 2011: 29). Income has also become more concentrated among top earners in China, India and South Africa. In China, for example, the top 20 per cent of income earners had 41 per cent of total income in 2008, and the Gini coefficient[18] for income inequality rose from 0.31 in 1981 to 0.42 in 2005 (UNDP 2011: 135–138). Whilst it could be expected that higher levels of inequality may be inevitable in countries at early stages of economic development, the majority of countries with both significant concentrations of wealth and high levels of inequality are at relatively high, or very high levels of economic development. This suggests that inequality does not necessarily reduce with levels of economic development and in many countries increases or remains high, thereby providing evidence in support of elitist theories.

Income inequality is not just a major problem nationally. Evidence (e.g. Wilkinson and Pickett 2010; Chomsky 2013; Monbiot 2013: 30; Oxfam 2014) shows that it is increasing internationally to the point where multinational corporations and a few individuals are now wealthier than many countries.[19] In a pioneering political economy study of urban planning and housing in urbanising countries, Jenkins *et al.* (2007: 49) note that

> a new trans-national community is emerging, made up of people from different nations, but with similar ideas and values as well as patterns of behaviour. On the other hand, national societies are undergoing a process of disintegration, including the destruction of indigenous economies and concentrations of property and income. The resulting process of marginalisation leads to increasing repression and authoritarianism in both under-developed and developed countries.

Much of this trans-national community building and associated repression occurs in developing country cities which are depicted as hubs of global growth and wealth creation.[20]

Such inequality is reflected in patterns of land and property ownership which conspire to force up prices and rents and push those unable to pay into peripheral areas or substandard living conditions. Even 'developed' countries suffer from the concentration of land in few hands and Cahill (2001: 209) reports that 40 million of the 60 million acres of land in the United Kingdom are owned by just 157,000 owners/families. Such concentration of wealth and property forces up prices and rents, inhibiting efforts to improve access to land, services and livelihoods for the majority of the population, especially the urban poor. To make matters even more regressive, such properties are not necessarily taxed at anything like their market values,[21] if at all. Progress will not be made without addressing this issue both nationally and internationally.

It would be incorrect to conclude from the foregoing assessment that the dominance of entrenched elites has turned the remainder of the urban population in emerging countries into passive victims. Countless examples exist of the determination with which the poor resist attempts to exclude them from prime locations for accessing livelihood opportunities and rebuild their modest dwellings despite repeated evictions. These are all testament to the resilience of the poor in challenging elitist attempts to impose urban plans and policies which seek to deny their right to the city. In this respect, urban areas are an arena in which the outcomes of competing interests are expressed in physical form. The key players in this contest are not only the elite as represented by government agencies and their policies and official norms, but a range of civil society groups, academic and professional associations, international donors and the media. Of course, the scope for influencing official policies and improving access to land and housing for the poor will be different from one context to another. Thus, in democracies, evictions are more likely to decrease dramatically before elections, even in countries with powerful elites, such as Cambodia (STT 2011: 3), whereas in China, the government has stamped down ruthlessly on protests by farmers on the urban periphery over unfair compensation when their land is commandeered for sale to private developers,[22] though there are also cases where protests have produced positive results for both sides.[23]

Attempts to improve access to land by low-income groups clearly need to address the vested interests which seek to reinforce the status quo, and to confront existing legal and regulatory regimes that may work against their goals. When the combined interests of the political, commercial and administrative elite coalesce around a shared vision of how society should be structured, they will inevitably seek to promote forms of urban development which reflect that vision. The more power is concentrated in an elite, the greater its ability will be to inhibit change, or channel it in directions which do not threaten its interests. This was noted in a literature review of access to land markets by Williams (2008: 14), who found that

> there seems to be resistance to change and innovation among technicians and administrators. This resistance is fuelled by government, ministry and state officials' perceptions that changes in the legislations and programs will have a negative impact on their roles, their power and their jobs.

Williams (2008: 18–19) also found extensive evidence that government officials and politicians are sometimes more the problem than the solution due to conflicts of interest and legislation blocking or restricting the scope of transformative land management initiatives in order to protect the status quo.

The political realities of land administration and urban planning are noted by Jenkins *et al.* (2007: 201), who observed that

> a new form of planning – which has existed in subordinate ways since the 1960s – is emerging, where the planner is seen not as a neutral agent but as a proponent, whether on behalf of government, the private and non-governmental sectors, or civil society.

Williams (2008: 18) also argues that 'although partnerships require stakeholder participation to be politically neutral, individual and political interests can supersede planning considerations, fiscal liabilities and even legal limitations in determining land supply'. She cites Jenkins (2001) as demonstrating that

> this is one of the main challenges in partnerships between government officials and informal developers, who in many cases are the same people. Some politicians have become the informal sources of land and act through brokers and staff in government agencies responsible for land control.

The institutional structure of land administration seems to make little difference in overcoming the resistance of an entrenched elite. For example, the multiplicity of state and local agencies responsible for land in Mumbai and the single agency in the capital New Delhi (the Delhi Development Authority) both reflect situations in which the ability of the poor to access land on affordable terms is highly constrained and where official policies are not necessarily fully implemented. This has caused considerable concern within India and has prompted a major international conference on the subject.[24] As a UN-Habitat report (2008: 60) notes, 'unequal access to land is closely linked to income inequality in both China and India'. They are not the only countries to which this applies (see Box 2.2).

> **BOX 2.2 IMPACTS OF INEQUALITY ON ACCESS TO LAND**
>
> **In India, Trinidad and Tobago, and Uganda**, Bahl and Martinez-Vazquez (2007) cite the examples of central government officials not only resisting transferring their powers to local officials, but also resisting conferring the rights of ownership to their citizens.
>
> **In Kenya**, the spokeswoman for a local NGO working on land issues for the urban poor recently stated, 'the people who are appointed to solve the problems of the poor are the very people who are keeping them in poverty'.
>
> **In India**, Shirish Patel (one of the original proponents of Navi Mumbai) believes that 'government and developers have a strong interest in keeping property prices high' (*The Economist* 2007: 8). Vijay Mahajan, of Bombay First, agrees that 'the higher the prices, the more builders can charge. As for the politicians, they profit from an invisible line that runs directly from slumlord to local politician to state minister to his boss. Money runs up along this line, and so do votes. In return, the government lets the slums remain undemolished. It is a pay-and-stay arrangement' (*The Economist* 2007: 8).
>
> **In Brazil**, Henderson (2007: 24) concludes that 'based on modelling from Brazil, it appears that forcing lower income migrants into the informal [housing] sector is, in part, *a strategic device used by existing residents* [emphasis added] to limit population growth, to fiscally exploit migrants by taxing them with few public services in return, and to avoid the fiscal externalities imposed by migrants who pay less than the full cost of public services if they were admitted to the formal sector'. This overlooks the fact that many low-income groups pay far higher unit costs for inferior services such as water, but implies that as the poor cannot pay the full costs of formal sector provision, the higher income groups are justified in discouraging them from living in the cities.
>
> **In the Philippines**, Strassmann (1996) and Dekker (1992) observe that among Manila politicians and officials, their 'personalism resulted in the concentration of land in the hands of those who use land mainly for investment purposes enhancing the vacancy of relatively scarce land'. At Malacañang Palace, the President's official residence in Manila, high officials are purported to believe that raising idle land taxes and making related land reforms was impossible because of the strong opposition from some Congressional leaders who owned vast urban properties and because of influential private sector individuals (Shatkin 2007: 12–14).

In summary, it can be argued that an ambivalent and occasionally hostile attitude towards the urban poor by the social and economic urban elite, reinforced by corruption and collusion within government agencies, have all reinforced constraints to the large-scale adoption of innovative and progressive land policy instruments.[25]

Given this situation, the assertion made at the start of this section that leading stakeholder groups benefit sufficiently from the status quo that they do not see it as in their interests to change, appears well founded and largely explains the frequent failure to implement progressive approaches at the scale and speed required. Prospects for change will therefore depend upon convincing such political, commercial and administrative elites that they have more to gain by embracing change or, at least, little to lose. A failure to address inequality has been identified as a key factor in recent upheavals in north and southern Africa, the Middle East and East Asia and is also threatening global economic stability (see e.g. Hutton 2013). As catalysts of change and development, it is vital that cities do not exacerbate such levels of inequality that large sections are unable to meet their basic needs for access to land, shelter and services. As Wilkinson and Pickett (2010) and Oxfam (2013) demonstrate, if governments do not invest in efforts to reduce inequality in order to avoid a range of negative social consequences such as high levels of crime, drug dependency, depression, divorce, obesity and other social ills, they are forced to spend even more on coping with the consequence of such negative social outcomes of inequality.

Meeting the challenge

The political economy approach adopted in this chapter began by speculating that as long as existing elites benefit sufficiently from the status quo, they will not see it as in their interests to change. On this assumption, change is likely to come from only two approaches: (1) the elites must be persuaded that they will benefit as much, or even more, from change than they do from the status quo and at minimum risk; or (2) 'champions of change' will need to be identified and supported. Elites also need to be made aware of the risks to their interests of inaction.

The scale of the problems being faced and the two overlapping approaches place professionals, whether academic or practising, in a vital position of responsibility for educating policymakers, administrators *and* the wider public of the implications of existing policies and programmes and the potential benefits to all of alternatives. It also means accepting that land administration and urban planning are ultimately political activities in which professionals have a duty to inform and educate through whatever means are available. It is therefore incumbent upon the professional community to present the most effective arguments in favour of socially and economically sustainable policies and to demonstrate the negative consequences of alternatives. To date, the professional community involved in urban development and land management has failed to convince policymakers of the need to enable the large proportion of the urban poor to share in the benefits of development that they help to create. This may be because many senior professionals were recruited from the social elite and were not educated with a sufficient awareness of the social, economic and political implications of planning concepts and norms. Greater efforts are therefore needed to ensure that academic and vocational courses include the political economy aspects of planning and land administration so that future generations are more effective in promoting more sustainable approaches.

In the short term, leverage can also be improved by identifying and taking full advantage of 'windows of opportunity', for example just before and after elections, when a new government comes to power, or when the spotlight is on the elites for other reasons, such as during the 'Arab Spring', or the response of the authorities in India to the rape and murder of a student in December 2012 which galvanised public opinion on the need to address women's rights at the national and international level.

Naming and shaming those acting as obstacles to helping the poor can also help as no government enjoys criticism, though some react by seeking to silence or constrain local public and social media and co-opt professionals. Even when the scope for change is limited, it is essential that professionals in land administration retain their intellectual independence and identify any options available at a given time and place. A precondition for progress is to assert the right of the poor to the city and access to land in locations where they can benefit as much as they contribute collectively. This can be promoted by:

- reviewing institutional, regulatory and other constraints to increasing the supply of urban land, services and credit in line with existing and projected levels of need;
- building on existing supply options and forms of land tenure and property rights which enjoy social legitimacy, or introducing others based on international experience to create a diverse range of supply options reflecting evolving patterns of demand;
- formulating and enforcing equitable tax and other revenue-generating measures (e.g. capturing part of the increased values generated by granting planning permission) to finance such increased supply;
- devolving powers *and* resources to local levels;
- creating a sense of civic responsibility in which all sectors, public, private and civil society groups develop a shared vision and strategy;
- regularising and upgrading existing slums and informal settlements where possible, but not necessarily with full property titles;
- concentrating resources on those elements, such as the planning of public transportation, utility networks and facilities, which communities cannot resolve by themselves;
- assessing the impact of subsidies on the intended beneficiaries and the land market to ensure the subsidies are achieving their intentions and modifying if necessary;
- improving public access to information, land and housing markets, and land administration to improve urban governance;
- accepting the principle of incremental development as practised by the poor; and
- providing the professional capability and administrative continuity at senior levels to ensure that policies are implemented.

International agencies have invested many millions of dollars in improving land administration throughout the world, though the amounts are small compared to the resources required and the resources generated by urban land markets. In this sense, the influence that donor agencies exert through the legitimacy they give to forms of land administration may be as important as the funding itself. Thus, the World Bank family and the Global Land Tool Network in UN-Habitat are in a powerful position to promote approaches that make urban land markets more equitable as well as efficient. The development banks have in the past supported market-based policies that have exacerbated rather than resolved the problems facing the urban poor. However, this has changed in some key respects on the basis of previous experience and recent approaches are more soundly based on improving equity as well as efficiency in land administration. Their ability to realise this potential depends, of course, on having partners in client governments willing to endorse voluntary codes of conduct and related policy recommendations for improving interaction with and opportunities in pro-poor urban land management.

Civil society groups at both national and international levels have expanded their roles in land issues dramatically over recent decades and are now represented on the governing councils of major bodies such as UN-Habitat (2011: 30). Some, such as Shack/Slum Dwellers International (SDI), have attracted substantial international funding for their own programmes. This opens doors to government ministers keen for the endorsement and projects such organisations bring with them. However, there is also a need to support a wide range of local civil society groups in addition to well-established and well-known NGOs to ensure that the sector as a whole can flourish. Only through the adoption of more inclusive approaches to urban land management will the rapidly urbanising developing world enjoy the full benefits of the economic powers released in cities. As global policymakers and municipal governments seek to build economic and social resilience into the cities that will drive global prosperity in the twenty-first century, they must face the needs of burgeoning urban poor populations. Transparent and effective implementation of tools for land access and administration will be a key determinant of their success in this process.

Notes

1. This chapter builds on work undertaken for the World Bank on addressing land market and economy-wide constraints and later incorporated into Lipman and Rajack (2011). The author would like to express warmest thanks to Robin Rajack of the World Bank for permission to draw on this work, to Hamish Stewart and Tony Lloyd-Jones for help in editing and to Isabel Wetzel and Emma Johnson for help in sub-editing. As always, the author assumes full responsibility for any errors. The author dedicates this chapter to his parents.
2. The World Economic Forum's Global Risks Report (2013: 10) analyses 50 global risks in terms of impact, likelihood and interconnections, with severe income disparity ranking as the most likely global risk projected to manifest over the next decade.
3. Countries where the absence of a national housing strategy augments social and economic constraints on growth range from Canada to Cameroon. On the situation in Canada see Shapcott (2012).
4. The growth of Bal Thackeray's Shiv Sena political organisation beyond Mumbai is illustrative of this problem. For a detailed discussion of the phenomenon, see Fernandes (2004).
5. This is very much the case at present in the UK where the elected mayor of London, Boris Johnson, is widely seen as using his position to challenge the Prime Minister, David Cameron, for leadership of the Conservative Party. The situation in the UK is not unique.
6. For example, whilst the population of Mumbai accounts for only about 1.5 per cent of India's total population, the city accounts for approximately 30 per cent of all central government revenues, making it extremely difficult for the city to finance the urban environment and living conditions for the poor. In response to such financing pressures, municipal governments must seek to raise funds in controversial ways which impact on access to land for the poor majority. In Mumbai, the local government plans to spend R1 trillion (US$22 billion) on infrastructure from 2010 to 2015, with funds raised through land sales in the Bandra Kurla area and through auctioning rights to public–private partnerships on profitable public services (McKinsey 2010: 23).
7. For example, 30 per cent of all land in Lahore, Pakistan, is held by government and the Lahore Development Authority (LDA) owns and controls 80 per cent of this, giving it exceptional powers to regulate land prices. By restricting supply, it is able to maximise unit profits, which acts as a powerful disincentive to change. Of the 30,000 new housing units needed annually in Lahore, the LDA only contributes about 2,000, with the formal private sector adding a further 5,000. The shortfall is met through various informal processes. Private communication to the author.
8. According to national law, land transfer in China is not facilitated through ownership certificates, but rather through land use rights (LUR) transfer. The law allows for land to be transferred, mortgaged or leased to individuals or organisations. The Land Administration Law sets the duration of the lease depending on land use category to 70, 50 or 40 years for residential, industrial or commercial use, respectively.
9. For example, the historical fluidity of rising and declining Vietnamese, Siamese, French, and later Soviet and American influence over what is today Cambodia, mean that various competing approaches to land management are all grounded in distinct socio-legal traditions, which further complicate the implementation of international, and mainly Western European, legal norms in land administration.

10 Gilbert (2011: 8) suggested that by 2010 'virtually every household in Bogotá was connected to the electricity, water and sewerage networks'.
11 For details on the Lahore plan see Hadeem and Nadeem (2006). Other problematic master plans include one for Kigali that will take decades to realise and does not deal effectively with the majority urban residents who are currently housed informally; the latest Master Plan for Kaduna city in Nigeria makes reference to a 1965 Master Plan, in spite of the vastly different conditions today; with population growth rates of 8 per cent, the city of Abuja's latest Master Plan is unlikely to be able to cope with the pace of growth.
12 Also known as the floor area ratio, or FAR.
13 Such a creative use of FSI can be seen in the case of Mumbai in India, where it has been combined with Transferable Development Rights (TDR) to encourage new investment and development away from the congested areas of south Mumbai to other areas to the north and east, including the largely self-financed strategic development of Navi Mumbai. A further consideration is that the physical constraints applicable to Mumbai, and many other cities, make increasing densities and FSI in the existing CBD impractical in terms of public transportation capacity, apart from the even greater concerns about environmental vulnerability due to climate change and possible increases in sea level.
14 Research in Bolivia, India, Lesotho, South Africa, Tanzania and Turkey undertaken by Geoffrey Payne and Associates for the UK Department for International Development (DFID) found that in each country, administrative procedures represented the greatest single regulatory constraint to enabling the urban poor to obtain legal and affordable shelter (see Payne and Majale 2004). Similar research by de Soto (1989: 142) found, for example, that in Peru, it may take 83 months to obtain all the official permits required to access and develop a plot of land legally.
15 The Popular Participation Law, 'Ley de Participación Popular' (LPP), subdivided Bolivian territory into 314 municipalities, which were each given a per capita share of national resources, under the principle of *coparticipación*. See Altman and Lalander (2003: 63).
16 See Jones and Corbridge (2010) for a general overview. As the proportion of poor people in the urban population increases, these disputes are likely to become acute. Satterthwaite (2004) estimates that in some of the world's poorest countries – Angola, Bangladesh, Chad, Guatemala, Haiti and Niger – over half the urban population is poor, and for a small number of countries, such as Honduras and Mongolia, the proportion of poor people in urban areas is greater than in rural areas.
17 Johnson (1994–99). In a recent interview with the Al Jazeera television network, the political commentator and academic Noam Chomsky (2013) claims that a small business elite now exists which can no longer control people by force, so uses vast resources to control attitudes and information and keep the mass of the population uninformed and marginalised so they can retain control.
18 The income Gini coefficient is the measure of the deviation of the distribution of income (or consumption) among individuals or households within a country from a perfectly equal distribution. A value of 0 represents absolute equality, a value of 100 absolute inequality. According to UN-Habitat (2008: 51), a Gini coefficient of 40 or more represents an international alert line, while a level above 45 suggests that inequality is approaching 'dangerously high levels. If no remedial actions are taken, [this] could discourage investment and lead to sporadic protests and riots'. In some cases, data are presented as between 0 and 1.0.
19 Monbiot (2013: 30) also reports that 'in 2012, the world's richest 100 people became US$241 billion richer. They are now worth US$1.9 trillion, just a little less than the entire output of the United Kingdom. This is not by chance. The rise in the fortunes of the super-rich is the direct result of policies.'
20 The global business services consultancy McKinsey Global Institute (2011: 4) refers to 423 emerging market 'mega- and middleweight cities' contributing more than 45 per cent of global growth from 2007 to 2025, and note that 407 emerging market middleweight cities will contribute nearly 40 per cent of exchange-rate adjusted global GDP growth, more than the developed world and developing region megacities put together.

21 For example, council taxes in the United Kingdom are based on 1991 property values, despite the fact that average prices in London increased 3.5 times in just 16 years between 1995 and 2011 and in Westminster, central London by 45 per cent in just five years to 2012, providing existing property owners with a large subsidy they are unlikely to forgo without a fight (www.landregistry.gov.uk/public/house-prices-and-sales/search-the-index).
22 See, for example, www.guardian.co.uk/world/2012/apr/03/chinese-police-land-grab-protests.
23 See, for example, www.bbc.co.uk/news/world-asia-china-16571568.
24 'Inclusive urban planning' conference, organised by the Ministry of Housing and Urban Poverty Alleviation, Government of India, New Delhi, 18–19 February, 2013. Online. Available at http://pib.nic.in/newsite/erelease.aspx?relid=92220 (accessed 14 January 2014).
25 International development agencies cannot escape a share of responsibility for the present impasse. Most allocate inadequate proportions of staff and financial resources to addressing urban issues and reducing urban poverty, despite the fact that in 2010–2011, the world has become more urban than rural and the population living in slums is projected to more than double by 2030 unless firm and concrete action is taken. They are also often as guilty of limited inter- and intra-agency coordination as the governments they seek to advise.

References

Altman, D. and Lalander, R. (2003) 'Bolivia's Popular Participation Law: an undemocratic democratisation process?', in A. Hadenius (ed.) *Decentralisation and Local Governance*. Stockholm: Almqvist & Wiksell International.

Bahl, R. and Martinez-Vazquez, J. (2007) *The Property Tax in Developing Countries: Current Practice and Prospects*, Lincoln Institute of Land Policy Working Paper. Online. Available at www.lincolninst.edu/pubs/dl/1256_Bahl%20Final.pdf (accessed 2 February 2012).

Bertaud, A. and Brueckner, J.K. (2004) *Analyzing Building-Height Restrictions: Predicted Impacts, Welfare Costs, and a Case Study of Bangalore, India*. World Bank Working Paper WPS3 290. Washington, DC: World Bank.

Bertaud, A. and Buckley, R. (2005) *Reforming Mumbai's Real Estate Raj: A Prelude to a Business Plan*. Washington, DC: World Bank.

Bredenoord, J. and Van Lindert, P. (2010) 'Pro-poor housing policies: rethinking the potential of assisted self-help housing', *Habitat International*, 34(9): 278–287.

Brueckner, J.K. (2007) 'Government's land-use interventions: an economic analysis', paper presented at the World Bank Urban Research Symposium, 14–16 May, Washington, DC.

Burnham, J. (1941) *The Managerial Revolution: What is Happening in the World*. New York: John Day.

Cahill, K. (2001) *Who Owns Britain? The Hidden Facts Behind Landownership in the UK and Ireland*. Edinburgh: Canongate.

Chomsky, N. (2013) 'The responsibility of privilege'. Online. Available at www.aljazeera.com/programmes/talktojazeera/2013/01/201311294541129427.html (accessed 8 February 2013).

Cities Alliance (2010) *The City Statute of Brazil: A Commentary*. São Paulo: Cities Alliance and Ministry of Cities.

Daily Star (2007) March: 5–11.

De Soto, H. (1989) *The Other Path: The Invisible Revolution in the Third World*. London: I.B. Taurus and Co.

Dekker, E. (1992) *Conventional Housing in Manila: The Development of a Residential Subdivision and Government Involvement*. Urban Research Working Paper 28. Amsterdam: Vrije Universiteit.

Fernandes, L. (2004) 'The politics of forgetting: class politics, state power and the restructuring of urban space in India', *Urban Studies*, 41(12): 2415–2430.

Gilbert, A. (2011) 'Public service delivery in Bogotá: a success story?', *International Journal of Urban Sustainable Development*, 3(1): 8–25.

Gonzalez, G.A. (2006) *The Politics of Air Pollution: Urban Growth, Ecological Modernization, and Symbolic Inclusion*. Albany: State University of New York Press.

Gonzalez, G.A. (2009) *Urban Sprawl, Global Warming, and the Empire of Capital* Albany: State University of New York Press.

Hadeem, R. and Nadeem, O. (2006) 'Challenges of implementing urban master plans: the Lahore experience', *International Journal of Human and Social Sciences*, 1(1): 46–53.

Henderson, J.V. (2007) 'The effect of residential land market regulations on urban welfare', paper presented at the World Bank Urban Research Symposium 2007 on Urban Land Use and Land Markets, 14–16 May, Washington, DC.

Hutton, W. (2013) 'Davos man thrives while the rest of us pay for his excesses', *Observer* 20 January. Online. Available at www.guardian.co.uk/commentisfree/2013/jan/20/davos-world-economic-forum-bad-capitalism (accessed 1 March 2013).

IIED (2008) 'Citizen driven action on urban poverty reduction', *Environment and Urbanization*, Brief No. 17. Online. Available at http://pubs.iied.org/pdfs/10578IIED.pdf (accessed 15 January 2012).

Jenkins, P. (2001) 'Strengthening access to land for housing for the poor in Maputo, Mozambique', *International Journal of Urban & Regional Research*, 25(3): 629–648.

Jenkins, P., Smith, H. and Wang, Y.P. (2007) *Planning and Housing in the Rapidly Urbanising World*. London: Routledge.

Johnson, P.M. (1994–99) 'A glossary of political economy terms', Department of Political Science, Alburn, AL36849.

Jones, G. and Corbridge, S. (2010) 'The continuing debate about urban bias: the thesis, its critics, its influence, and its implications for poverty reduction strategies', *Progress in Development Studies*, 10(1): 1–18.

Lipman, B. and Rajack, R. (2011) *Memo to the Mayor: Improving Access to Urban Land for All Residents: Fulfilling the Promise*, Urban Development Series Knowledge Papers, No. 11. Washington, DC: World Bank.

McKinsey (2010) 'India's urban awakening: building inclusive cities, sustaining economic growth'. Online. Available at www.mckinsey.com/insights/mgi/research/urbanization/urban_awakening_in_india (accessed 2 February 2012).

McKinsey Global Institute (2011) *Urban World: Mapping the Economic Power of Cities*. McKinsey and Company.

Monbiot, G. (2013) 'If you think we're done with neoliberalism, think again', *The Guardian*, 15 January: 30.

Oxfam (2013) 'The cost of inequality: how wealth and income extremes hurt us all'. Online. Available at www.oxfam.org/sites/www.oxfam.org/files/cost-of-inequality-oxfam-mb180113.pdf (accessed 2 February 2012).

Oxfam (2014) 'Working for the few: political capture and economic inequality', Oxfam briefing paper, 20 January. Available at http://policy-practice.oxfam.org.uk/blog/2014/01/working-for-the-few.

Pareto (1927) *Manual of Political Economy*. New York: Augustus M. Kelley, 1971 (translation of French edition from 1927).

Patel, S. and Arputham, J (2007) 'An offer of partnership or a promise of conflict in Dharavi, Mumbai?', *Environment and Urbanization*, 19(2): 501–508.

Payne, G. and Majale, M. (2004) *Urban Housing Manual: Making Regulatory Frameworks Work for the Poor*. London: Earthscan.

Public-Private Infrastructure Advisory Facility (PPIAF) (2011) 'Work Program 2011–2013'. Online. Available at www.ppiaf.org/ppiaf/sites/ppiaf.org/files/documents/PPIAF_Supports_Cities.pdf (accessed 20 January 2013).

Satterthwaite, D. (2004) *The Under-Estimation of Urban Poverty in Low and Middle-Income Nations*, IIED Poverty Reduction in Urban Areas Series, Working Paper No. 14.

Shapcott, M. (2012) 'Universal Periodic Review Canada 2013: Submission on behalf of The Wellesley Institute'. Online. Available at www.wellesleyinstitute.com/wp-content/uploads/2012/10/wellesleyinstituteUPRCanada2013.pdf (accessed 2 February 2012).

Shatkin, G. (2007) *Collective Action and Urban Poverty Alleviation: Community Organizations and the Struggle for Shelter in Manila*. London: Ashgate Publishing.

Stone, C.N. (1989) *Regime Politics*. Lawrence, KS: University Press of Kansas.

Strassmann, W.P. (1996) 'Limits to market empowerment for housing in developing countries: the case of land', *Journal of Economics*, 30(2):11–22.

STT (Sahmakum Teang Tnaut) (2011) 'Displaced families: Phnom Penh 1990–2011' facts and figures, May. Online. Available at www.teangtnaut.org and http://teangtnaut.org/PDF/F%26F%20displaced%20PP%20families%202011%20update.pdf (accessed 2 January 2012).

Su, F. (2008) *Land Markets in China's Modernization: Regulations, Challenges, and Reforms*. National University of Singapore East Asia Institute Background Brief No. 418.

The Economist (2007) 'The strange allure of the slums: people prefer urban squalor to rural hopelessness', 3 May. Online. Available at www.economist.com/node/9070714 (accessed 1 March 2013).

The Economist (2012) 'Tangles over tenure: deciding who owns shantytowns would help their residents', 22 September. Online. Available at www.economist.com/node/21563338?fsrc=scn/tw_ec/tangles_over_ten (accessed 20 January 2013).

The Hindu (2014) 'DDA shelves new housing scheme', New Delhi, 1 February.

UBS Investment Research (2011) 'Local government debt – how bad and how will it end?' Online. Available at www.easyforexnews.net/wp-content/uploads/2011/06/MacroKeys070611.pdf (accessed 2 February 2012).

UNDP (2011) *Human Development Report 2011: Sustainability and Equity – A Better Future for All*. New York: UNDP.

UNESCAP (1995) *Municipal Land Management in Asia: A Comparative Study*. New York: United Nations.

UNFPA (2007) *State of World Population 2007: Unleashing the Potential of Urban Growth*. New York: United Nations.

UNFPA (2011) *State of World Population 2011: People and Possibilities in a World of 7 Billion Report*. New York: United Nations.

UN-Habitat (2008) *State of the World's Cities 2008/2009: Harmonious Cities*. London: Earthscan.

UN-Habitat (2011) 'Governing Council of the United Nations Human Settlements Programme – Provisional List of Participants', UN Doc. No. HSP/GC/23/INF/8. Nairobi: United Nations Human Settlements Programme.

Van der Molen, P. and Tuladhar, A.M. (2007) 'Corruption and Land Administration', International Federation of Surveyors. Online. Available at www.fig.net/pub/monthly_articles/march_2007/march_2007_vandermolen_tuladhar.pdf (accessed 2 February 2012).

Wilkinson, R. and Pickett, K. (2010) *The Spirit Level: Why Equality is Better for Everyone*. London: Penguin Books.

Williams, S.M. (2008) *Improving Access to Urban Land Markets Through Less Conventional Land Policy Instruments: Literature Review*. Washington, DC: World Bank.

World Economic Forum (2013) 'Global Risks 2013'. Online. Available at http://reports.weforum.org/global-risks-2013 (accessed 2 February 2013).

Wright Mills, C. (1956) *The Power Elite*. Oxford: Oxford University Press.

3

THE NEW POLITICAL ECONOMY OF AFFORDABLE HOUSING FINANCE AND URBAN DEVELOPMENT

Bruce Ferguson, Peer Smets and David Mason

Introduction

Until very recently, affordable housing in developing and emerging countries mainly seemed to be governments' responsibility. Mortgage finance of developer-built units served a small upper-middle class. The remaining population appeared marginalized from economic growth and unable to afford commercially produced housing. Governments first responded by building a small number of complete housing units. As urbanization and slum formation accelerated, the public sector turned to building less expensive slum-upgrading, sites-and-services, and core-expandable-unit projects. The global shift to markets of the early 1980s convinced donors and governments to shift from building housing projects directly to 'enabling housing markets' mainly through providing mortgage finance and subsidies to private developers. All of these approaches have reached only a lucky or well-connected few, leaving out most of the population.

The only viable home ownership option for most households remains the self-help process (alternately, called 'incremental' or 'progressive' housing). Turner (1976) and other advocates of incremental housing reached this broad conclusion in the late 1960s and clarified this practice in the 1970s. Most households greatly prefer to improve their existing housing unit and neighbourhood located close to jobs, friends, and relatives rather than move to government-subsidized housing projects typically of uneven quality on the distant urban fringe. However, both the advocates of self-help housing and its critics (e.g. Burgess 1978; Davis 2006) have failed to translate these insights into widespread affordable housing. Practice has moved beyond the academic debate over the past 40 years on whether self-help housing is a problem or a solution. Decades of programmes and studies have now shown that incremental housing presents the only alternative for billions of people and can work well if appropriately supported. However, incremental housing ends up costing households and government far more than formal-sector development when unassisted by efficient private and public-sector organizations. Retrofitting most informal settlements with a rational road network along with water and sewerage (i.e. comprehensive upgrading) costs much more than building new formal-sector development (Abiko *et al.* 2007), which for large slums implies enormous costs of many types. Successfully housing the mass market requires adding value to incremental housing and getting ahead of demand for affordable shelter and infrastructure to counter slum formation. The traditional policy argument for slum upgrading and affordable housing finance and development programmes rests on the social and economic benefit to slum dwellers (Luengas and Ruprah 2009), positive externalities that benefit health and welfare beyond these neighbourhoods, and increasing the economic efficiency of urban areas (Freire and Polese 2003). However, rapid growth in effective demand for affordable housing now overshadows the public-policy perspective.

Over the past decade, rising real household incomes have made affordable housing a huge new market opportunity for the private sector more than a public-sector responsibility. Vast new cohorts have joined the urban lower-middle class. This income group now comprises the majority of the population in most middle-income Latin American and Asian cities and will soon account for the bulk of humanity. The new urban lower-middle class currently numbers approximately 2 billion people and is projected to grow to 4.9 billion of a total world population of 8 billion by 2030 (Stephens 2012). Substantial evidence shows that owning an adequate home with secure tenure holds much more importance to people in emerging countries than in advanced high-income nations (Luengas and Ruprah 2009). This growing lower-middle class both demands and can afford some sort of market-rate home.

Simply enabling housing markets through government provision of conventional mortgage finance and intermittent housing subsidies – the main approach of the past 25 years – shows little potential for reaching the lower-middle class and the poor (the base of the income pyramid – 'BOP'). This chapter will discuss the enabling-housing-markets paradigm, and its failure to serve the BOP in an increasingly complex urban context characterized by urban land shortages, natural disasters, the ecological and energy crisis, rising physical violence and crime, and financial crisis. This examination proposes a new paradigm of affordable housing characterized by a wide range of innovative financial products, diverse physical housing solutions, corporate/citizen-sector partnerships for affordable housing products and services for the BOP, and a new affordable housing entrepreneurship.

The enabling-housing-markets paradigm

With the fall of the Soviet Union and the global shift to markets and deregulation in the early 1980s, the World Bank largely abandoned serviced-sites and slum-upgrading projects, declaring them to be unsystemic without concerted evaluation (Buckley and Kalarickal 2006). In other words, the serviced-sites and slum-upgrading projects were seen as being excluded from the housing market. Instead, the World Bank advocated 'enabling housing markets' (Mayo and Angel 1993). Governments should shift from mainly producing housing to enabling housing markets through reforms. Angel (2000) details further the components and methods of the enabling-housing-markets approach. This paradigm assumes that conflict with formal market efficiency results in declining investments and housing that is less affordable and of lower quality, and a lower-quality residential environment (Mayo and Angel 1993: 3).

Instead, governments should guide the housing sector. The seven major enabling instruments consist of strengthening of legal property rights, development of mortgage finance, the rationalization of housing subsidies, the provision of infrastructure for residential land development, the regulation of land and housing development, the organization of the building industry, and the creation of a national institutional framework for managing the housing sector (Mayo and Angel 1993: 4–5).

The enabling-housing-markets strategy has had a profound if uneven impact. Although many governments greatly reduced the relatively simple approach of direct production of affordable housing projects of various types, some continued to do so, such as India. The complexity of reforming each of the seven components of the housing sector and then integrating them has proved daunting for even the most competent governments. Not surprisingly, performance at enabling housing markets has varied widely.

In Latin America, most governments have largely stopped direct housing production. Instead, they have funded mortgages at below-market rates supplemented by direct-demand subsidies[1] and provided land for free or at discounted rates to private developers to build affordable housing. Middle-class households, large homebuilding firms, and the mortgage-finance industry have benefited from the subsidies embedded in mortgage finance and direct-demand subsidy systems, rather than the BOP. This approach has avoided the worst distortions resulting from direct government production and finance to families.[2] However, it has performed unevenly in developing sustainable housing finance and development markets.

For the World Bank, enabling housing markets mainly meant virtually abandoning sites-and-services and slum-upgrading projects for two decades in favour of funding national mortgage systems with loan terms of typically 20 to 30 years for the middle and upper-middle classes. In this respect, Buckley and Kalarickal (2006: xi) observed that '83% of lending and … 70% of the projects for the entire 34 years since 1972 of shelter lending have had satisfactory outcomes, one of the highest satisfaction rates of any sector in the Bank'. These mortgage-finance projects also often attempted to push this mechanism downmarket (e.g. Buckley and Kalarickal 2006: 5). The typical World Bank mortgage-finance project makes disbursal of tranches conditional on policy reforms to improve the enabling environment of borrowing countries.

Various middle-income developing countries have created massive housing-finance funds that account for the great bulk of mortgage lending (see Table 3.1) and drive a growing homebuilding industry. These national housing finance vehicles usually come in two types: provident/housing funds and second-tier liquidity facilities.[3]

The world's largest economies (China, the United States, and – more recently – Japan) have devalued their respective currencies to gain a competitive edge in international trade and stimulate their economies with low interest rates, flooding many financial institutions paying higher yields in major developing countries with liquidity. These liabilities are typically quite short term – one year or less. Extending long-term mortgage finance funded by demand accounts[4] and short-term certificates of deposit creates a dangerous mismatch that grows with the mortgage volume. Governments of major emerging countries have complained vigorously of the resulting 'currency wars', but without result.

Latin America has a long history of runaway government spending and hyperinflation that periodically destroys national mortgage systems. The most recent episode occurred in the 1980s, the lost decade for this region. As a result of this historical memory and relatively low savings rates, real mortgage interest rates are often high relative to inflation and the rate of appreciation of housing, except during real property price booms. In Brazil and Mexico, for example, real interest rates on private unsubsidized mortgages have seldom dropped below 8 per cent per annum. Traditional amortization of large long-term mortgages concentrates the real value of repayment in the first years, greatly reducing the number of households that can

TABLE 3.1 Mortgage finance as a share of GDP

Country	Mortgage finance as share of GDP		
Argentina	4% (2001)	1.3% (2011)	
Bolivia	8.6% (2001)		
Brazil	2% (2002)	4.1% (2011)	
Chile	10.8% (2001)	17% (2011)	
China	<1% (1998)	15% (2008)	
Colombia	7% (2001)	4% (2009)	
Egypt	0.3% (2007)		
European Union	42.6% (2008)		
India	9.8% (2007)	7.1% (2008)	
Indonesia	3% (2007)	1.97% (2008)	
Malaysia	33.7% (2006)	26% (2008)	24.7% (2011)
Mexico	10.6% (1995)	7.9 % (2000)	9.7% (2010)
Nigeria	2% (2006)	1% (2011)	
Panama	24.4% (2002)	22% (2009)	
Peru	2.9% (2001)	2.9% (2011)	
Thailand	17% (2008)		
United States	79.6% (2008)	71.8% (2010)	
Uruguay	7% (2006)	5% (2010)	

Sources: Galindo and Lora (2005); Unitus/Lehman Brothers (2007); Nenova (2010); Hofinet (2012).

afford a traditional mortgage loan and reducing the loan size. Some countries have experimented with double-indexed mortgages[5] that spread the real value of payments more evenly over the term of the loan. Although these double-indexed mortgages may work well for a limited period, they implode with the persistent, high macro-financial volatility that has often characterized Latin America as well as many other emerging countries – when inflation and yearly interest rates rise from 10 to over 30 per cent. Macro-economic and fiscal reform during the 1980s and 1990s succeeded in stabilizing inflation and interest rates in most emerging economies over much of the last decade.

From 2005 to 2011, mortgage interest rates declined and the mortgage lending volume increased dramatically from a small base in the most dynamic emerging economies (e.g. China, India, Chile, Brazil, and parts of East Asia). The flood of money into urban housing in cities suffering from serious supply bottlenecks – particularly in urban land – led to spectacular increases in home prices. 'Urbanization abetted by cheap credit growth' has fuelled a property boom in the more dynamic emerging economies (*Financial Times of London* 2011a). In turn, the real property price boom further inflated the volume of mortgage finance. However, mortgage finance as a share of GDP has remained negligible (less than 1 per cent of GDP in most of Africa and the non-oil-producing countries of the Middle East), stagnant, or shrunk in less dynamic countries and regions (e.g. Argentina, Uruguay, Central America with the exception of Panama, and the United States[6]).

Table 3.1 shows that mortgage loan volume as a share of GDP has increased dramatically and steadily in only two of the countries examined – China and Chile. Idiosyncratic stories involving many economic/financial factors and urban/housing/land conditions lie behind these numbers. The conventional wisdom is that mortgage finance of commercial homebuilding steadily increases with a country's level of household income and size of its economy. This data indicates that the importance of national mortgage markets more often fluctuates modestly due to myriad factors.

Overall, mortgage finance of developer-built units has housed the upper-middle class and fuelled the commercial homebuilding and mortgage-finance industries. In effect, this approach has proved more of a short-term economic stimulus rather than a housing policy. However, it has failed and shows few prospects for housing the BOP. The World Bank (Buckley and Kalarickal 2006) and UN-Habitat (UNCHS 2005) have concluded that governments' heavy focus on mortgage finance of commercial homebuilding has proved an irrelevant diversion from solving the housing problems of most families.

Given the lack of interest of large corporations in the 1980s and 1990s in the mass market for housing, the enabling-housing-markets strategy ended up leaving most families to informal high-cost suppliers of housing inputs and urban services, which Buckley and Kalarickal (2006) call 'savage markets'. From this perspective, the enabling-housing-markets approach came 25 years ahead of its time and focused almost exclusively on a housing finance and production mode exported from the United States and Western Europe poorly suited to the BOP of developing and emerging countries.

Programmes and policies that enable housing markets have failed to improve or worsened shelter and urban conditions for the BOP in many countries (for Latin America, see Ruprah 2010), largely because of urban land bottlenecks (Payne *et al.* 2009). As regards direct demand housing subsidy programmes promoted by the Inter-American Development Bank throughout Latin America for 20 years, Ruprah (2010) concludes: 'on average, the existing size of the voucher would have to be increased by 304% and 374% … to avoid induced indigence and poverty'. In other words, the government subsidy per poor family is only one-third to one-quarter the amount necessary for adequate housing. No wonder that direct demand subsidy programmes have served mainly the upper-middle class and have failed to work for the poor.

Although governments and donors have attempted to drive conventional housing finance downmarket to the BOP for 30 years, the results are disappointing (e.g. Smets 1997, 2004). The bottom 60–80 per cent of the population continues to obtain adequate housing mainly through incremental housing.

Incremental housing achieves affordability through staging the cost of house construction, upgrading tenure, and basic urban services over time; it also reduces the cost of construction through self-contracting, self-building, and innovative lower-cost technologies (e.g. Smets 2004, 2006; Ferguson and Smets 2010). Moreover, these communities lobby governments to pay for regularizing tenure and urban services (i.e. upgrading).

Progressive housing and its finance

Progressive housing offers an alternative that accounts for most housing investment in most emerging countries. This process involves labour by the family and/or small contractors, using a wide variety of types of materials including factory-built components. Finance comes from a wide range of sources, mainly the household's savings. Many families use small credits to supplement their savings in order to complete major phases of the process – such as purchase/regularization of a lot, construction of additional bedroom(s), and building additional units on the property to rent or to house relatives.

The sources of small private loans for incremental housing vary in type and importance among countries including: families, friends, informal lenders, microfinance institutions, pawnshops, savings and credit associations, pension accounts, credit cards, consumer credit from building materials manufacturers/retailers and commercial banks for the purchase of building materials, and even micromortgages in some cases. In some countries, government has got involved, typically providing a very small volume of highly subsidized housing microfinance.

Until roughly 2000, most incremental housing credit came from informal sources rather than financial institutions. Flooded with liquidity, the largest commercial banks have discovered this market and now fund a large portion of this 'unsecured' home credit through a wide variety of vehicles (via building materials retailers/hardware stores, microfinance institutions, credit cards, and through direct unsecured personal loans and, much more rarely, micromortgages for account holders).

Similarly, the terms of private credit for incremental housing differ tremendously. A micromortgage may be available at around 15 per cent per annum in parts of Latin America and India for home construction/remodelling for lower middle-income households. At the other end of the spectrum, informal and payday lenders can charge effective rates of 1,000+ per cent per year. The effective annual interest rate is virtually never divulged to households. For example, microfinance institutions (MFIs) often advertise microcredit at a monthly 'flat rate' without disclosing the impact of compound interest month-to-month on the annual rate; as a result, a monthly flat rate of 5 per cent results in an annual effective interest rate of 80 per cent (rather than 60 per cent as many households would think by multiplying 5 per cent by 12 months).

Good data on this complex ecosystem of small credits for incremental housing is usually quite difficult to acquire. While governments, financial institutions, and banking authorities keep records of mortgage lending, no one tracks the volume of home credit funded by informal sources. Even the volume of home microcredit offered by MFIs and retail credit from banks and stores for the purchase of building materials is murky, although estimates can sometimes be made.

For this reason, a relatively recent quantitative analysis of annual housing investment in Brazil is particularly striking (see Table 3.2).

The composition of these categories of finance and production is revealing. Most progressive housing is self-financed, although government contributes funding, too. Until recently, private-sector financial institutions have had a small role in most countries. In contrast, industrialized construction (formal homebuilding) is financed by the government, the private sector, and households. In terms of markets, self-financed progressive housing accounts were responsible for 62 per cent of new Brazilian housing investment in 2005. Much of this self-financed progressive housing development occurred in the informal sector. In comparison, mortgage finance of developer-built units accounted for 3.2 per cent of new housing investment per annum.[7]

Similarly, the Reserve Bank of India estimates that mortgage lending accounts for less than one-quarter of total housing investment in India as of 2011. In sophisticated, large middle-income countries such as India and Brazil, mortgage finance of developer-built units makes a modest contribution to total housing investment. In most sub-Saharan African countries, less than 1,000 mortgages are originated each year and modern homebuilding firms do not exist.

TABLE 3.2 Methods of production and financing of new Brazilian housing per annum

	Progressive housing	Industrialized construction	Totals
Self-financed by household	R$48 billion (62%) 700,000 units (64%)	R$22 billion (30%) 100,000 units (9%)	R$70 billion (92%) 800,000 units (73%)
Private sector finance	R$0.7 billion (0.9%) 20,000 units	R$0.4billion (0.5%) 50,000 units (5%)	R$1.1 billion (1.4%) 70,000 units
Public sector finance	R$3 billion (4.1%) 130,000 units (12%)	R$2 billion (2.7%) 100,000 units (9%)	R$5 billion (6.8%) 230,000 units (21%)
Totals	R$52 billion (67%) 850,000 units (77%)	R$24 billion (33%) 250,000 units (23%)	R$76 billion (100%) 1.1 million units (100%)

Source: Booz Allen Hamilton (2005).
R$: Brazilian real; R$1 = US$0.49 (August 2012).

Contemporary threats to affordability

Throughout emerging countries, homebuilders and housing agencies complain that the scarcity and high price of suitable land parcels present the largest obstacle to affordable housing development. The economic literature on housing and urban development has long shown that land is the trickiest issue for ongoing housing affordability (George 2006; Freire *et al.* 2007). Urban land is like a treadmill: the faster the economy grows and real household incomes rise, the greater the price appreciation of suitable parcels for residential development in major cities. Without strong countervailing measures, rising land costs in dynamic metropolitan areas of capitalist economies eventually drive housing prices to levels only affordable to the upper-middle class and above.

Housing the BOP on a sustainable basis requires establishing a strong multi-pronged urban land policy that balances the interests of stakeholders (e.g. peasants that own land on the urban fringe, urban housing consumers, government, and developers). These measures typically include: a real property tax applied progressively (at higher rates) to parcels on the urban fringe and to land only rather than land plus buildings; eminent domain law that allows government to purchase urban land at pre-speculative prices for affordable housing development; mandatory land pooling/readjustment on the urban fringe; widespread application of land use instruments that create land/space at affordable prices sufficient to accommodate projected population growth; and levies that capture a substantial share of the appreciation in property values created by public investments (Ferguson and Smith 2010).

These measures combined with analytic techniques such as a land budget, a housing-needs assessment, and a regulatory audit (Cities Alliance and Municipality of São Paulo 2008) constitute urban land reform. East Asia, Western Europe, and the United States have long applied some combination of these measures to capture a substantial portion of the increase in real property values generated by government investment; an annual urban property tax of 1 per cent per year of assessed value (a rough norm for Europe and the United States) typically generates public revenue of 15–18 per cent of the property's total value over time. In general, Latin America and the Caribbean, South Asia, and Africa have lost control of urban land use and fail to recoup appreciation from urbanization and government investments.

Another threat to sustainable and affordable development involves increasing vulnerability to natural disasters and climate change, urban sprawl, and poor-quality habitat. As urbanization continues, informal settlement occurs on more marginal areas such as steep hillsides, floodplains, inappropriate soils, earthquake faults, aquifers, parks, and greenbelts. Large cities typically spread haphazardly over enormous geographic areas at low densities. Urban densities and form often resemble the car-dependent sprawl of Los Angeles rather than the compact, public transport-centred development of Amsterdam.

Masonry and concrete construction have a high energy and carbon content. Urban sprawl requires long commutes to jobs and services (e.g. Urry 2011). Sprawl and high energy/carbon construction greatly increase the cost of housing and urban development. Market prices fail to include most of the externalities of energy, carbon emissions and global climate change, and the public action necessary to fix these broken settlements. These factors make cities highly vulnerable to natural and man-made disasters. The recent record of floods, mudslides, earthquakes, droughts, and tsunamis highlights the rising exposure of cities and their housing stock to disasters in advanced as well as emerging countries (e.g. New Orleans and the New Jersey shore as well as Bangladesh, most of Central America, Pakistan, and the low-lying coastal areas of East Asia). Accelerating climate change ensures that such disasters will increase in frequency and severity.

Large, dense slums also incubate violence and crime. International gangs have taken over increasing portions of urban areas in Latin America, in particular. Largely as a result, Honduras, El Salvador, and the city of Rio de Janeiro have the highest intentional homicide rates in the world. Household surveys show that physical insecurity has become the top concern in Latin America.

The new complexities of housing impact on public and private investment. For example, extending a home-improvement loan without technical assistance in construction that results in poor-quality building in an environmentally hazardous area does much more harm than good. The family may well repay the loan on time. Nonetheless, the resulting habitat is a potential time bomb. Eventually, natural disasters, violence, and/or rising energy prices will likely detonate this explosive mix.

The public sector, alone, clearly lacks the capacity to meet the low/moderate-income shelter challenge. Ruprah (2009) calculated that Latin American governments would have to increase the size of housing programmes 14 times on average to eliminate the housing shortage by 2015!

The shelter challenges of the twenty-first century are driving a radical transformation in the creativity and scale of private market-based affordable housing in collaboration with government. The BOP contains many submarkets. Some can afford consumer credit for extremely basic improvements such as tiling dirt floors. Others want microloans to build extra bedrooms. More prosperous segments of the BOP may qualify for a small mortgage to purchase an existing half-completed unit or build a basic house on their serviced lot, or the cement roof of a one-storey structure on which the household has air rights. The poorest typically require subsidy. One size will not fit all. A spectrum of physical housing solutions and methods of finance accompanied by construction technical assistance services must be packaged and priced appropriately to capture the huge effective demand of the different segments of the BOP.

Populating the affordable housing continuum

The enabling-housing-markets paradigm emerged when deregulated capitalism prevailed in the world economy in the early 1980s. The current context could not be more different. The

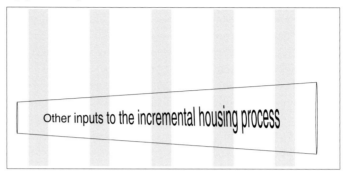

FIGURE 3.1 The affordable housing finance continuum.

US subprime mortgage lending meltdown and housing bust has spread across the globe and sparked a meta-crisis for global capitalism. Most informed experts now recognize that markets must be shaped and made to produce useful outcomes. The private sector in collaboration with government and citizen-sector organizations are the key actors in this fundamental task.

Figure 3.1 broadly illustrates a new approach evolving from many directions for housing and urban development in emerging countries. This image contains two poles. At one end is mortgage finance for large projects of developer-built complete units. At the opposite end, clandestine land subdividers charge a small down payment and a monthly instalment to poor households that purchase their raw unserviced lots. Each point on the continuum corresponds to a specific type of housing solution, a housing credit product, and a series of other inputs to incremental housing.

Housing microfinance (HMF) consists of the wide range of home credit types suited to this spectrum – from small home-improvement loans to micromortgages for projects of core expandable units. HMF, however, is only one of a package of inputs necessary for most of the BOP to develop their home incrementally. The lower the household income, the more additional inputs must be combined with HMF for incremental housing to work well. Figure 3.1 illustrates the increase in width from left to right illustrates the increasing demand for other inputs to incremental housing as household incomes decrease.

A new breed of housing entrepreneurs is packaging these inputs into affordable housing products that add value. Typically, no individual organization can efficiently provide all the missing elements. Collaboration between large corporations, citizen organizations, and government is essential. The strands of a new emerging paradigm of affordable housing and urban development are discussed below.

Housing microfinance

Many MFIs have developed small home-improvement loan products on a limited basis since 2000. Small serial credits, largely for building materials to improve a homeowner unit – which has come to be called 'housing microfinance' – began expanding a decade ago mainly because of synergies with the microfinance industry. By this time, roughly 200 MFIs worldwide had become commercially viable (Robinson 2001). Increasing competition had caused microenterprise-loan markets to tighten in countries such as Bolivia, Bangladesh, and Guatemala. Home-improvement lending and savings products appeared useful next steps for leading MFIs and their intermediaries in these contested markets. Housing microfinance also fit well with the transformation of many MFIs from NGOs into regulated financial institutions that take deposits from the public.

MFIs often offer or require some level of technical assistance in construction and design along with HMF. Much less frequently, they also package other inputs to the incremental-housing process through collaboration with suppliers, including affordable-home developers and building-materials retailers.

The interest rate on housing microloans typically approximates that on microenterprise loans. As MFIs have become increasingly commercial and replace a 'double bottom line' concerning commercial and social development objectives with only one goal – making money – they have come under fire. As a result, some governments have put interest rate caps on MFI credit (Kazmin 2010); e.g. the Indian state of Andra Pradesh (M-CRILL 2011), which accounts for roughly one-third of India's US$7 billion in outstanding MFI loans. HMF interest rates range from a minimum of 20 to 100 per cent per annum depending upon country and region.

The de facto existence of huge market demand for housing microfinance also argues for a favourable cost/benefit ratio under some circumstances. No study, however, analyses an HMF portfolio from the cost/benefit perspective of the borrowers. More typically, housing microfinance borrowers, as MFI clients in general, show little awareness of the effective annual percentage rate or even the nominal interest rate of the microcredit.

BOP products and new affordable housing entrepreneurship

Large modern corporations have started to view affordable housing in dynamic emerging economies as a business worth pursuing. As emerging countries have become the main engine of global economic growth, the academic and business literature has also begun emphasizing opportunities for satisfying their mass markets (Prahalad 2006; Sullivan 2007).

These corporations approach low-income housing systematically, starting with market studies followed by the creation of pilot products before expanding to scale. The Patrimonio Hoy programme of CEMEX, the giant Mexican cement manufacturer, is the most famous. However, many other modern companies have now tackled the affordable housing market, frequently in collaboration with citizen-sector organizations and other private-sector entities (Samaranayake et al. 2011; Bredenoord and Cabrera Montiel, Chapter 15 in this volume).

Affordable housing entrepreneurship is gathering momentum. Anderson and Beck (2012) and Samaranayake et al. (2011) analyse key examples of specific products/projects developed by private-sector organizations with no or little government subsidy and, thus, with the potential to reach massive size.

Corporate building-materials manufacturers and retail chains and the new breed of affordable housing developers offer the most powerful institutional platform with the greatest ability to reach mass markets. Relative to MFIs, building-materials manufacturers and suppliers and affordable-land/home developers have a much more compelling interest in housing microfinance. These corporations must frequently offer credit for their main products to their clients to compete, particularly in large, contested markets. These home suppliers may well come to dominate HMF markets in large, dynamic emerging economies (Ferguson and Smets 2010).

International citizen-sector organizations – particularly Ashoka – have encouraged the involvement of modern corporations in serving low-income markets, including housing, through applied research and pilot projects (Schmidt and Budinich 2006). From a social entrepreneurship perspective, Ashoka has applied the notion of 'hybrid low-income value chains' to affordable housing in emerging countries. In brief, packaging a series of inputs to progressive housing holds the key to turning potential into effective demand and reaching scale (Ferguson 2008; Ferguson and Smets 2010). Ashoka also emphasizes that modern corporations must partner with community organizations to reach low-income communities.

From the perspective of the private sector, modern management methods, particularly a value-chain approach, appear eminently well-suited to organizing, streamlining, and squeezing the costs out of the incremental housing process (Ferguson 2008). The value chain (Porter 1985) categorizes the value activities of an organization or process including: inbound logistics, operations (production), outbound logistics, sales and marketing, service (maintenance), administrative infrastructure management, human-resources management, research and development, and procurement. The costs and value drivers are identified for each value activity. The ultimate goal is to maximize value creation while minimizing costs. The delivery of a mix of products and services to the end customer mobilizes different economic actors. Creating new packages of products along the value chain can bypass intermediaries such as many of those that create the high costs of unassisted progressive housing.

This first generation of BOP initiatives provides key insights for expanding market-based affordable housing finance and development (Samaranayake et al. 2011; Anderson and Beck 2012). These lessons vary by type of organization, such as a commercial bank, MFI, second-tier housing-finance liquidity facility, real estate developer, citizen-sector organization, building-materials manufacturer/retailer, utility company, local government, and national government:

First, first-mover advantage can build an economic moat difficult for competitors to bridge. Positioning a company as a first mover in facilitating high-quality construction creates opportunities for additional sales through vertical and horizontal expansion.

Second, create a dedicated autonomous unit or new company to serve BOP housing markets. Avoid both the mainstream business model geared to the middle class and the symbolic corporate 'social responsibility' programmes that generate good publicity but fail to grow to scale.

Third, stakeholders must work together to package the products and services required for solving the housing problem of diverse BOP segments. The lead organization must partner with others to acquire the missing pieces of the package product.

Fourth, involve neighbourhood citizen-sector organizations to develop trust, market the package product, pre-screen households, organize individual households into groups, and troubleshoot. Formal public- and large private-sector organizations often have little understanding and access to low-income communities; however, they can hire and pay capable community organizations to reach the poor. In turn, these citizen-sector organizations must develop and train networks of promoters (usually neighbourhood women sales representatives), focus on the services useful to business partners, and aggregate demand for the product.

Fifth, local governments must ensure the provision of serviced land. Local governments can exercise control over many of the factors that determine the price and availability of secure tenure to serviced urban land. National governments should encourage a wide variety of housing finance through guarantees, subsidies, appropriate regulation, and other means.

Sixth, technological innovation in low-cost housing construction and basic services has taken a quantum leap. Until recently, technological innovation has played little role in house construction. Local governments typically create a complex web of rules that throttles high-density residential development and discourages creativity in technologies for home construction and infrastructure provision. These stultifying norms include high-cost building, zoning, and subdivision regulations (Bertaud and Douglas 1989), and complicated slow procedures for approving residential development. With the cost of energy skyrocketing, new technologies for homes and communities have become a growth industry. Examples are factory-built elements and basic services – including potable water, solar electricity, off-grid/on-site ovens, low-cost non-polluting stoves, decentralized catchment of rainwater, and cellphone banking (Sullivan 2007).

Numerous innovators are exploring solutions to this nexus of problems. The NGO Habitat for Humanity International is building durable bamboo houses in Nepal, has developed a detailed two-volume toolkit for housing microfinance, and partners with MFIs to create and spread HMF products. Idealab, a consultancy, is on the verge of unveiling a US$2,500 house that will be mass-produced in factories, sold in kits, and feature breakthroughs in ventilation, lighting, and sanitation. Philips has produced the 'Chula', a cheap stove that eliminates the soot that kills 1.6 million people a year worldwide from indoor cooking. The Solar Electric Light Fund is demonstrating a new low-cost product that provides poor families with solar power for roughly the same cost as old but dirty standbys such as kerosene and candles. Echale a Tu Casa rents a brick-making machine to groups of 30 neighbouring Mexican households to compress the mud from their site into eco-blocks at a fraction of the cost and energy content of retail masonry products, and guides these groups in assembling two-bedroom homes that cost half the amount of comparable developer-built units. The Harvard Business School has challenged the multinational corporate community to develop a high-quality house costing no more than US$300 for emerging countries, received numerous entries, and a website disseminates this information (Govindarajan and Sarkar n.d.).

Applying progressive housing to multi-storey buildings and large structures at high density presents additional challenges. One option could be to build a large external skeleton within which individual families construct their unit. The Chilean architectural firm Elemental has designed two-storey row-houses sharing exterior walls that achieve densities comparable to multi-storey condominiums that households can build progressively, and these are now common throughout the country (Syrkett 2013).

Convergence of these new technologies can greatly improve quality and reduce the cost of housing. The first applications are likely to be special, urgent or temporary situations: natural disasters, refugee housing, and slum rehabilitation. The severe problems presented by violence and crime, insecure tenure, and the price and availability of urban land, however, constrain these technologies. If there is no secure place to put a US$300 house, building technology is useless.

Governments, large developers, public mortgage finance systems, and housing and land subsidies are creating a habitat disaster for much of the population in many emerging countries. Rapidly rising real property prices in many dynamic cities caused by attempting to inject more housing credit and subsidies into an urban system constrained by serious supply bottlenecks, particularly in urban land, are leaving the low/moderate-income majority behind.

Only a decade ago, few financial institutions and modern corporations had any interest in affordable housing in emerging countries. In the aftermath of the implosion of the great real property/housing debt bubble in Western Europe and the United States, the tables have now turned. The next huge global boom/bust cycle involves home lending that has flooded emerging markets, much of it at very high rates. Brazil, India, and China experienced an urban real property price boom during much of the first decade of the twenty-first century. A real property bust accompanied by high levels of household debt – much of it for home-related expenditures – is now underway in these countries.

Most dismaying, China currently has 64 million vacant housing units (*Financial Times of London* 2011a) – a level of overbuilding unprecedented in world history (*Financial Times of London* 2011b)! Spurred by local governments that depend on leasing urban property for new housing projects for the bulk of their revenue, this country has built 11 large 'ghost cities' that lie largely unoccupied (Miller 2012). This huge investment appeared a good bet when the national growth rates exceeded 10 per cent per annum prior to 2007; now that China's economic growth and urbanization rates have slowed, the debt incurred in its city/homebuilding super-boom threatens to cause a global economic catastrophe. Many of these vacant units may never be occupied and become slums.

In sum, the current real property bust in these large emerging economies contributes to the meta-crisis of global capitalism. This threat as well as the opportunity presented by the housing mass market in emerging country cities (US$3 billion-plus) call for a new affordable housing entrepreneurship led by the modern private sector, combined with multipronged strong urban land reform by the public sector.

Conclusion

The enabling-housing-markets paradigm succeeded in spreading mortgage finance for the top 20–30 per cent of the income distribution of countries around the globe, saturating the housing market for the top 1 to 2 income deciles. However, the formal system produces only a small fraction of units necessary for the bottom 80 per cent.

A radically new urban context has contributed to making the enabling-housing-markets paradigm largely obsolete. Building affordable housing for the mass market has become much more complicated in the context of the growing threats posed by natural hazards, urban violence and crime, the energy crisis, and financial crises.

The housing market opportunities are equally enormous. Satisfying the mass market requires a continuum of products that add value while reducing costs. Housing affordability now depends much more on local responsiveness, collaboration among stakeholders, and incremental building and finance than on central government mortgages, subsidy systems, large homebuilding firms, and national policies. These opportunities and threats require reshaping progressive housing and its finance. In short, this study has shown that the new political economy of affordable housing finance is characterized by a kaleidoscope of local initiatives against the background of multiple contemporary developments on a global scale.

Notes

1 A portable voucher for home ownership.
2 Including the creation of enormous housing bureaucracies, poor-quality distant housing projects, and corruption.

3 A second-tier liquidity facility obtains equity capital from the central government and sometimes from multilateral donors and the private sector. These liquidity facilities on-lend these funds to intermediary financial institutions such as banks that in turn lend to clients (Magowan 2008: 191).
4 Demand accounts are cheque and savings accounts from which the account holder can withdraw money at any time.
5 Double-indexed mortgages are usually indexed to inflation in combination with an amortized loan with a short-term market interest.
6 In the US, refinance of existing mortgages for purposes other than housing investment now constitutes the bulk of mortgage volume.
7 Brazil's mortgage finance and real property boom from 2006 to 2010 and subsequent bust have changed these numbers somewhat, but not altered the basic picture.

References

Anderson, S. and Beck, R. (2012) *The Big Idea: Global Spread of Affordable Housing*. Next Billion and Ashoka Full Economic Citizenship.

Angel, S. (2000) *Housing Policy Matters: A Global Analysis*. Oxford: Oxford University Press.

Abiko, A., Cardoso, L.R., de Rinaldelli, R., and Haga, H.C.R. (2007) 'Basic costs of slum upgrading in Brazil', *Global Urban Development Magazine*, 3(1).

Bertaud, M.A. and Douglas, L. (1989) *Land Use, Building Codes, and Infrastructure Standards as Barriers to Affordable Housing in Developing Countries*. Washington, DC: World Bank.

Booz Allen Hamilton (2005) *Construção Civil – Evolução e Desafios*, presentation at Forum Nacional da Sustentabilidade da Construção Civil Brasileira. ABRAMAT. Sao Paulo, 21 November.

Buckley, B. and Kalarickal, J. (2006) *Thirty Years of World Bank Shelter Lending: What Have We Learnt?* Washington, DC: World Bank.

Burgess, R. (1978) 'Petty commodity housing or dweller control? A critique of John Turner's view on housing policy', *World Development*, 6(9/10): 1105–1133.

Cities Alliance and Municipality of São Paulo (2008) *Slum Upgrading Up Close: Experiences of Six Cities*. Washington, DC.

Davis, M. (2006) *Planet of Slums*. New York: Verso.

Ferguson, B. (2008) 'A value chain framework for affordable housing in emerging countries', *Global Urban Development Magazine*, 4(2).

Ferguson, B. and Smets, P. (2010) 'Finance for incremental housing: current status and prospects for expansion', *Habitat International*, 34: 288–298.

Ferguson, B. and Smith, D. (2010) *Financing Housing for the Poor for Slum Upgrading and Prevention*. Learning note for the World Bank Institute.

Financial Times of London (2011a) 'Urbanization abetted by cheap credit fuels growth', 23 May.

Financial Times of London (2011b) 'Chinese property; a lofty ceiling reached', 14 December.

Freire, M. and Polese, M. (2003) *Connecting Cities with Macroeconomic Concerns: The Missing Link: Do Local Public Services Matter? A Case Study of Five Cities*. Washington, DC: World Bank.

Freire, M, Ferguson, B., Cira, D., Lima, R. and Kessides, C. (2007) *Land and Urban Policies for Poverty Reduction*. Volumes 1 and 2. Washington, DC: World Bank.

Galindo, A. and Lora, E. (2005) 'Foundations of housing finance', in Inter-American Development Bank (ed.) *Unlocking Credit: The Quest for Deep And Stable Bank Lending*. Washington, DC: IADB.

George, H. (2006) *Progress and Poverty: Why There Are Recessions, and Poverty amid Plenty and What To Do About It!* New York: Robert Schalkenbach Foundation.

Govindarajan, V. and Sarkar, C. (n.d.) *The $300 House*. Online. Available at www.300house.com/concept.html (accessed 15 May 2013).

Hofinet (2012) Housing Finance Information Network Website. URL: http://hofinet.org/ (accessed July 2012).

Kazmin, A. (2010) 'Microfinance backlash grows', *Financial Times of London*, 8 December.

Luengas, P. and Ruprah, I.J. (2009) *Does Owning Your House Make You Happier? Evidence from Latin America.* Washington, DC: IADB.

Magowan, J. (2008) 'Capital-market funding of affordable housing finance in emerging countries: the business case', *Global Urban Development Magazine*, 4(2): 182–194.

Mayo, S.K. and Angel, S. (1993) *Housing Enabling Markets to Work.* Washington, DC: World Bank.

M-CRIL (2011) 'Anatomy of a crisis', *Microfinance Review.* Gurgoan: M-CRIL.

Miller, T. (2012) *China's Urban Billion.* London: Zed Books.

Nenova, T. (2010) *Expanding Housing Finance to the Underserved in South Asia: Market Review and Forward Agenda.* Washington, DC: World Bank.

Payne, G., Durand-Lasserve, A. and Rakodi, C. (2009) 'The limits of land titling and home ownership', *Environment and Urbanization*, 21(2): 443–462.

Porter, M. (1985) *Competitive Advantage: Creating and Sustaining Superior Performance.* New York: Free Press.

Prahalad, C.K. (2006) *The Fortune at the Bottom of the Pyramid.* Upper Saddle River, NJ: Pearson.

Robinson, M.S. (2001) *The Microfinance Revolution.* Washington, DC: World Bank.

Ruprah, I.J. (2009) *The Housing Gap in Latin America: 1995–2015.* Washington, DC: IADB.

Ruprah, I.J. (2010) *Do Social Housing Programs Increase Poverty? An Empirical Analysis of Shelter Induced Poverty in Latin America.* Washington, DC: IADB.

Samaranayake, S., Budinich, V. and Kayser, O. (2011) *Access to Housing at the Base of the Pyramid: Enabling Affordable Housing Markets.* Arlington: Ashoka.

Schmidt, S. and Budinich, V. (2006) *Housing the Poor by Engaging the Private and Citizen Sectors: Social Innovations and "Hybrid Value Chains".* Arlington: Ashoka.

Smets, P. (1997) 'Private housing finance in India: reaching down-market?', *Habitat International*, 21(1), 1–15.

Smets, P. (2004) *Housing Finance and the Urban Poor.* Jaipur, New Delhi: Rawat.

Smets, P. (2006) 'Small is beautiful, but big is often the practice: housing microfinance in discussion', *Habitat International*, 30(3), 595–613.

Stephens, P. (2012) 'The great middle class power grab', *Financial Times of London*, 27 April.

Sullivan, N.P. (2007) *You Can Hear Me Now; How Microloans and Cell Phones are Connecting the World's Poor to the Global Economy.* San Francisco: Jossey-Bass.

Syrkett, A. (2013) *Architectural record. Newsmaker: Alejandro Aravena.* http://archrecord.construction.com/news/2013/02/130215-Newsmaker-Alejandro-Aravena.asp (accessed 15 May 2013)

Turner, J. (1976) *Housing by People: Towards Autonomy in Building Environments.* London: Marion.

UNCHS (2005) *Financing Urban Shelter: Global Report on Human Settlements 2005.* London: Earthscan.

Unitus/Lehman Brothers (2007) *Identifying Trends for Housing Microfinance.* Presentation December 2007.

Urry, J. (2011) *Climate Change and Society.* Oxford: Polity.

4
BACKING THE SELF-BUILDERS

Assisted self-help housing as a sustainable housing provision strategy

Jan Bredenoord and Paul van Lindert

Introduction

Today's rapidly urbanizing countries of the Global South are faced with huge challenges to provide affordable housing for their many low-income families. Over the past few decades many countries in Africa, Asia and Latin America have been confronted with substantial increases in their housing deficits. These deficits have both quantitative and qualitative components and they are most notable in the cities. According to UN estimates, the urban population of the developing world alone will increase from 2.7 billion in the year 2011 to 5.1 billion by 2050 (UN 2012). Although such population projections may well be open to debate, it is obvious that millions of new and upgraded houses will have to be provided in order to accommodate a rapidly growing urban population. Besides the provision of new and 'decent' housing, attention must be paid to the improvement of the existing housing stock, especially in slums and squatter settlements.

The World Bank and UNCHS/UN-Habitat were the major international institutions which from the 1970s onward recognized the vital role of self-help housing in providing affordable housing solutions to the urban poor. Indeed, even today the cities in the developing world have been mainly built on the basis of informal self-building activities (Bredenoord and Van Lindert 2010: 281). Based upon such recognition of the enormous potential and capacity of self-builders in meeting the urgent housing challenges, these international institutions started developing tools for public housing policies to be targeted at the urban poor. National and local governments also adopted the notion of assisted self-help housing, by accepting rather than completely clearing squatter settlements and by facilitating the incremental self-build processes in such neighbourhoods. Incremental house construction implies a stage-wise informal building process, realized by individual families, only if and when their financial situation allows them to take further steps in the building process. This approach has the advantage of excluding the risks of long-term financial obligations in the form of mortgages. On the other hand, it means that the entire process of finishing a self-build house may take a long time (Greene and Rojas 2008; Wakely and Riley 2011). The adoption of policies supporting incremental self-help housing meant a major breakaway from earlier common practices, which often involved the eviction of the illegal inhabitants and the demolition of their provisional shacks in squatter settlements.

This chapter focuses on various vital elements and forms of assisted self-help housing and public housing policies in the developing world. We start with a brief elaboration on the use of common vocabulary and the current discourse around low-income housing. What then follows is a concise overview of the main modalities of housing provision for the urban poor in the developing world. The vital role of incremental, self-help housing processes stands out in most (informal and so-called hybrid) kinds of housing supply. This then leads us to make a plea for a differentiated approach in assisted self-help housing policies, meaning that various forms of outside support may be pertinent to cater to the needs of different categories of households. Such policy packages may range from, for example, the provision of land with basic services, core houses on plots within a sites-and-services scheme, to technical assistance with self-help and housing microfinance schemes. After that, three limitations of self-help housing are presented briefly.

Self-help housing semantics

Whereas the early self-help advocates of the 1970s (Abrams 1964; Mangin 1967; Turner 1967) considered decent housing essentially as a basic need for everyone, the Habitat Agenda, adopted at the City Summit of 1996, formally proclaimed the principle of universal *right* to adequate shelter (UNCHS 1997). According to the rights-based approach to do-it-yourself housing, one of the prime responsibilities of the state (as a duty bearer) is to create the conditions under which the citizens (as right claimers) can fully develop their potential to build and gradually upgrade their own houses in a safe and dignified way. Thus, the national and local governments must enable citizens to develop their own living environments by facilitating or assisting their self-build initiatives (Wakely and Riley 2011).

In this chapter, no conceptual distinction will be made between self-help and self-managed construction. In its purest form, the self-help notion suggests that an owner-occupier of a plot or house performs all construction tasks by himself, possibly with additional help from family members and friends, but not from paid contractors. He also collects the necessary materials and tools needed for the construction. Self-managed construction implies that an owner-occupier of a plot or house manages all building activities by himself, including the purchase of construction materials, the contracting of specialized craftsmen for masonry, plumbing, painting among others, as well as the provision of equipment. As a rule, he will also actively partake in construction activities himself, but this is not always the case. As a matter of fact, at some stage of the incremental building process most self-builders will also commission parts of the construction activities to informal building contractors or to craftsmen who are part of their social network. That is why we prefer to use the notion of self-help or self-build for all construction activities that are operated by owner-occupiers of plots or houses, regardless of whether or not paid labourers are contracted by them.

Table 4.1 presents some of the distinctive characteristics and differences in the *modus operandi* of formal, institutional housing construction and informal, incremental self-build housing. First, it should be noted that the conventional logic of formally produced housing follows the planning–servicing–building–occupation sequence (Baross 1987). Self-build housing in informal settlements usually follows a reversed sequence, starting with the occupation of a plot and the subsequent building of a provisional dwelling unit. The following stages comprise the

TABLE 4.1 Formal versus informal housing provision

	Formal housing provision	Informal (self-help) housing
Development cycle	Planning	Occupation
	Servicing	Building
	Building	Servicing
	Occupation	Planning
Commissioning of construction	State housing institution	Owner-occupier
	Local government	Housing cooperative
	Private real estate developer	Community group
	Building company	
	Housing cooperative	
Funding	Banks (loans, mortgages)	Family (savings and loans)
	Government funding (loans and tax incentives)	Microfinance institutions (loans)
		NGOs (donations and loans)
	Government subsidies	Charity organizations, churches, etc. (donations)
	Employer organizations (loans)	
	International organizations (donations or loans)	Loans by private parties
		Savings and credit associations
Payment	Rents	Short-term instalment for plot purchase
	Payment in instalments (mortgages)	Savings for expansion/improvement of the self-build house
		Microfinance
Construction	Construction companies (often non-local)	Family, friends
		Construction workers (from household's network)
		Informal building contractors (local)

Source: authors' own.

gradual provision of basic public services and infrastructure, which will then involve a range of retro-planning and retro-fitting activities (Berner 2012).

The main stakeholders of the institutional housing sector are both the public sector and private actors such as land developers, banks and construction companies. The prime actors of the self-build sector are the actual owner-occupying households themselves. Usually they operate individually, but they may also be part of a housing cooperative or community-based organization (CBO). Owner-occupiers invest in house construction once they have accumulated sufficient savings for the next phase of the incremental building process. Alternatively, they may get loans from relatives or from microfinance institutions and sometimes from private money lenders. NGOs and grassroots organizations (e.g. faith-based) may also provide technical or financial support to self-builders. Additionally, other civil society organizations can actively support the (often undocumented) residents of self-build settlements by fostering their organizational capacity and supporting their claims for settlement upgrading (Riley et al. 1999).

The distinction between institutional housing and self-build housing in developing countries is a very common way of conceptualizing the contrast between the two modes of housing production. Some have used other labels to mark the differences, including *conventional* versus *unconventional* (Drakakis-Smith, 1981) and *formal* versus *informal* housing. As for the labels of the self-build settlements, adjectives such as spontaneous, irregular, popular and squatter are being used, again in addition to the more pervasive use of informal settlements.

Especially in international housing policy circles, perhaps the most frequently used term to underscore the low quality of living conditions in self-build settlements is slums. UN-Habitat (2006) developed five so-called shelter deprivation indicators for the definition of slum housing: poor structural quality of housing; insufficient living space; lack of access to safe drinking water; lack of access to adequate sanitation; and insecure residential status. In the Millennium Development Goals (MDGs) of the United Nations, Goal 7, Target 11 aims to improve the lives of at least 100 million slum dwellers and to reduce the proportion of urban population living in slums. In connection to that, the principal slogan of the UN and the World Bank-led Cities Alliance campaign became 'Cities without Slums' (Cities Alliance 1999).

Despite the good intentions of MDG 7–11 and the Cities without Slums campaign, various authors have recently pointed to the collateral damage which they are causing (Huchzermeyer 2011; Meth 2013). They discuss the new managerial approach of various national and city administrations which aim to raise their cities into the World Class City league by placing a focus on urban competitiveness and foreign direct investment. Although the Cities without Slums campaign was meant to support policies to improve the quality of life for slum dwellers, for example by *in situ* upgrading, in some countries the local adaptation of the Cities Alliance slogan evolved into that of slum-free cities; this often led to forced eviction of slum dwellers and the demolition of slum houses. Gilbert (2007) also criticizes the labelling of substandard housing as slum housing, which he qualifies as dangerous especially because of the 'series of negative associations that the term conjures up, the false hopes that a campaign against slums raised and the mischief that unscrupulous politicians, developers and planners may do with the term' (Gilbert 2007: 701). The adoption and promotion of the slum-free cities and the shack-free cities mottos as the official banners for housing policies in countries like India and South Africa are a living proof of the dangers mentioned by Gilbert.

Modalities of affordable housing provision

With the above critique in mind, it is more helpful to rely on the more generic term of informal housing, which in itself again includes a wide variety of housing conditions and an array of local expressions for such informal settlements (e.g. *barriadas*, *pueblos jóvenes*, *favelas*, *bustees*, *kaatchi abadis*, *goths*). Although informal settlements worldwide and across time show huge differences in *inter alia* housing standards, living conditions, servicing and connectivity, usually they share one common characteristic: that is, the majority of their housing stock was built incrementally and on the basis of self-help initiatives. The photographs presented in Figure 4.1 illustrate this process of ongoing consolidation of dwelling and neighbourhood improvement for a typical self-built neighbourhood in La Paz, Bolivia.

Acioly and French (2012) present an instructive portrait of the great variety of housing provision modalities in the developing world, ranging from informal to formal, with a so-called informal–formal hybrid modality in between (see Table 4.2). The virtue of the scheme is that it does much more justice to reality than simple binary-based divisions of formal–informal. We have adapted slightly their model in order to demonstrate that most of the modes of housing supply include a vital role for self-build processes. With the exception of categories

10 (public housing schemes) and 11 (private sector companies), all other modes (at least to some degree) are dependent upon the self-build (and often self-organizing) capacities of the residents in informal settlements.

The housing provision continuum shows that self-help processes never develop in splendid isolation from the wider institutional context. Most obviously, this is the case when governments facilitate serviced plots of land through 'sites-and-services' schemes to selected families who then are expected to start building their own homes (see Table 4.2, category 5) (see Figure 4.2). Sometimes, such sites-and-services schemes also include a basic housing unit (often just a 'wet wall') which the owners then use as their core unit that they expand and improve over time. The functional linkages between formal and informal mechanisms are also evident in the various modalities through which some form of state assistance to organized community groups or housing cooperatives is provided (see Table 4.2, categories 6, 7, 8).

Government-led settlement upgrading programmes (see Table 4.2, category 9) focus on regularization of land tenure as well as on the provision of basic services and social and physical infrastructure in informal settlements. The immediate result of such upgrading schemes implying tenure security often is an explosion of self-build activities and ensuing consolidation of informal settlements (see e.g. Strassmann 1984; Choguill 1999; Scott et al. 2013). Depending upon the original design of the dwellings in public housing programmes (e.g. durability, foundations, floor space, plot size) and formal regulations, the inhabitants may also add new rooms (vertically or horizontally) through self-build processes, similar to informal settlement practices (see Table 4.2, category 4). Where such extensions are technically possible and legally permitted, such public housing settlements often experience a rapid and profound transformation (Tipple and Wilkinson 1992; Tipple 2000). In fact this is social housing with the possibility of individual incremental finishing, an upcoming hybrid form of housing.

The first three mentioned categories in Table 4.2 are the informal modalities of housing provision which, by nature, are most affordable to the urban poor. The first one is most typical for many of the cities across the developing world, particularly in Latin American countries where squatting through the illegal occupation of land during many past decades often also was organized for political purposes (and it still sometimes is, especially in election times). The second mode of land supply is driven by private land developers (often also powerful syndicates), who assemble greenfield land and subsequently subdivide it into unserviced plots for sale to prospective owners. Both in Latin America and in some South Asian cities, clandestine land subdivisions mostly take place on the city periphery where rural land is converted into residential urban land. According to Berner (2012) land grabbers may be active with political backing. The subdivision practice opens wide possibilities of bribery, as civil servants may get hold of various well-located plots in return for formal approval of the subdivision (Berner 2012). In the peri-urban areas of major cities in West Africa, unauthorized subdivision often occurs under customary rule (Gough and Yankson 2000; Benjaminsen et al. 2009; Acioly and French 2012).

Also, in West African and Indian cities, sub-dividers and other large-scale land developers target low-income families and produce housing units for rental accommodation (see Table 4.2, category 3). The classic slumlord in South Asian or East African cities typically leases small hutments – or only plots of land – to households (Sivam 2003). China's urban villages have been converted into rental settlements which are virtually the only housing option for poor migrant labourers (Hao et al. 2011). Throughout Africa, Asia and Latin America, self-help builders have gradually expanded their dwellings with new rooms, in the first place to

FIGURE 4.1A The development of neighbourhood Santa Rosa Cinco Dedos in La Paz, Bolivia (1984). Photo by Paul van Lindert.

FIGURE 4.1B The development of neighbourhood Santa Rosa Cinco Dedos in La Paz, Bolivia (1995). Photo by Paul van Lindert.

FIGURE 4.1C The development of neighbourhood Santa Rosa Cinco Dedos in La Paz, Bolivia (2006). Photo by Paul van Lindert.

FIGURE 4.2 Sites-and-services project Nuevo Pachacutec, Ventanilla, Peru. Photo by Jan Bredenoord.

TABLE 4.2 Modalities of housing provision for urban poor and the role of self-help construction

		Modality	Characteristics	Vital role self-build processes Yes	No
Informal	1	Unauthorized owner-occupied self-build	Incremental construction of housing units over many years/decades on land that is (at least initially) occupied illegally	x	
	2	Unauthorized subdivision	Private developers subdivide land into individual plots which are sold on the informal market (without or with housing units)	x	
	3	Rental housing	Construction of units or rooms that are rented to low-income households, outside of formal controls (by rental property developers and by unauthorized self-builders)	x	
Informal–formal hybrid	4	Owner-occupier transformation of social housing	Occupants who have received a government 'social' house incrementally modify and/or enlarge it	x	
	5	Sites and services	Government provision of serviced plots of land on which residents incrementally construct their house	x	
	6	Cooperative housing partnerships	Cooperatives organize themselves (often with support from NGOs), save, obtain land from government and construct houses either communally or individually	x	
	7	Community settlement upgrading and resettlement	Community-based upgrading and/or resettlement; with support from NGOs, local government and/or international funding providers	x	
Formal	8	Legally established community groups	Legally recognized community groups – supported by NGOs – apply for public funding and develop housing on self-management, mutual aid and assisted self-help building processes	x	
	9	Government-led settlement upgrading	Informal settlements are upgraded through infrastructure and service provision and regularization of tenure (by national and local governments, NGOs, CBOs and professionals); fostering housing improvements by the house owners	x	
	10	Direct government 'social housing'	Land and housing developed by the government (sometimes via the private sector) and sold or rented to low-income households (also under rent-to-buy schemes)		x

TABLE 4.2 (*cont.*)

	Modality	Characteristics	Vital role self-build processes	
			Yes	No
11	Private	Profit-seeking developers, often partnering with governments for low-cost housing (public–private partnerships); employer-built housing		x

Source: Adapted from Acioly and French (2012: 424–425).

accommodate their growing families but (at later stages) they also build in order to generate some supplementary income from their tenants.

Broadening the scope of self-help housing assistance

This section focuses on the matter of how both national and local governmental institutions – often in collaboration with other, non-governmental parties – may devise and implement interventions based on that self-build potential by facilitating forms of incremental construction processes, in order to attain affordable housing solutions. By targeting different household categories according to their respective economic conditions, such assisted self-help housing policy packages will vary accordingly, for example in terms of the (initial) quality of the dwelling, plot size, labour input, servicing, costs and finance model among others.

Socio-economic factors – especially households' earning capacity and purchasing power – are to a large degree responsible for the individual differences between self-help housing products in the same neighbourhoods. The national and local policy environments are vital for yet another differentiating force between self-help settlements, in particular because of the key role which government policies play with respect to the provision of public services and infrastructure. Not least of all, the fate of incremental housing through self-help efforts depends also very much on the tolerance towards incremental housing vis-à-vis the ambition of many city administrations to lift their city into the so-called World Class City status category which they often consider incompatible with the growth of informal settlements (Huchzermeyer 2011).

Provided that local governments and politicians are tolerant towards the phenomena of self-help housing and informal settlements, their first task would be to explore and analyse the real housing demand according to the different socio-economic conditions and limitations of their citizens. In various cases, especially in Asia and Africa, and strongly backed by Slum/Shack Dwellers International, national Slum Dwellers Federations and local CBOs have taken up this task through rigorous participatory enumeration and mapping campaigns in informal settlements (see e.g. Karanja 2010; Arputham 2012; Baptist and Bolnick 2012; Makau *et al.* 2012). Such mapping exercises are not only important for gathering necessary information, but also vital 'for all community members to reflect on how they live in the community, how things relate to one another both socially and physically, and to identify the common community problems that concern everyone' (Luansang *et al.* 2012: 506). After documenting and acknowledging the right of their citizens to safe and decent housing, local governments may

TABLE 4.3 Assisted self-help housing options: different components and actors

Basic assistance, with regard to the provision of the plot, house construction and services	Actors
A plot in a suitable urban land development, at affordable price and amortization conditions	Municipality with its institutions and corporations
Tenure security (*de jure* or *de facto*)	Private land developers
An access road and mains infrastructure, including drinking water, electricity and sanitation	Special trust fund (public–private corporation)
	Land bank

Additional assistance, related to the construction and improvement of dwelling and neighbourhood	Actors
Technical assistance (e.g. constructional advice, use of materials, house design)	Municipal advisory team in a housing project
Legal advice (ownership title, building permit, certification and registration of the finished house, etc).	NGOs with housing programmes
	Corporations with housing programmes
	Building materials producers and traders
	Microfinance institutions
Provision of good-quality and low-cost building materials	Community workers
	State institutions
Promotion of microfinance solutions	Young professionals; architects, lawyers, technicians
Support for housing cooperatives	
Support for community-based initiatives	Technical schools

Source: authors' own.

then follow up with the implementation of a variety of measures that can be considered as basic assistance and additional assistance (see Table 4.3).

Basic forms of assistance to self-build processes

As for the basic forms of assistance, a possible model for determining the most suitable continuum of different housing packages for the urban poor may include the following elements:

- Key for all is tenure security (most often confirmed by providing a legal land title).
- Provision of plots with optimal (most efficient) dimensions for urban land use (in most contexts varying between 80 and 120 square metres).
- A core house varying from 20 to 60 square metres that allows for subsequent (horizontal and/or vertical) expansion in the subsequent stages of incremental construction.
- Provision of public services at the neighbourhood level and/or with connections to individual dwellings.
- A choice of cost structures and prices for a range of affordable housing products.

Determining the housing qualities for a mixture of household categories that align with their respective incomes and their options for self-help, self-finance, loans and subsidies will provide a better understanding of the costs and possibilities of assisted self-help housing in new urban expansion plans. Table 4.4 presents a basic framework for a variety of self-help

TABLE 4.4 Assisted self-help housing components: variation in policy packages

Site		Services					
Plot size (m²)	Built-up living space (m²)	Electricity	Piped water*	Septic tank	Paved road	Sewerage	Costs/prices
80	0						Lowest
80	0	x	x				
80	20	x	x				
100	20	x	x	x			⇕
100	40	x	x	x			
120	60	x	x	x	x		
120	80	x	x		x	x	Highest
80–120	80–200†	x	x		x	x	

*Collective or individual taps.
†After vertical expansion.
Source: authors' own.

assistance options for municipal governments which consider new urban land development for the poor. The range of housing products presents different cost structures and prices. The acknowledgement of the necessity of such a differentiated system of housing provision can help in making policies that serve all household categories according to their income-generating capacities. Admittedly some housing specialists and politicians may morally condemn such housing as being inadequate or undignified. But what finally counts is the ability of poor households to improve their housing and living conditions throughout the years, following the argument by Greene and Rojas (2008: 92) that the process of incremental housing can be considered 'a strategy to access housing that can be improved'. The bottom line of the assisted self-help approach is that the facilitation of incremental house construction caters to the needs and priorities of different categories of households who, with time, will gradually expand and improve their dwellings according to their individual requirements and possibilities. In this respect, Ntema (2011: 183) even suggests for South African housing policies that 'emphasis be shifted from concepts such as *dignified size* housing to *people driven housing* and *dweller control*'.

Some components of the total cost structure are crucial for self-builders. Incremental construction means a gradual investment over the years but leaps in construction costs may put the continuation of the process at risk. Some cost leaps are inevitable, for example investments in solid foundations, earthquake resistant and fireproof constructions, or investments in the construction of additional floors and stairs. Other costs are related to land development and the connection to public services. Obviously, it cannot be taken for granted that public utility companies will provide drinking water and electricity connections in informal settlements if the families do not pay their bills. As such, it may be recommended to include the costs of water and electricity connections in the housing packages. At this point it is also pertinent to note that – once the settlement is being serviced with electricity, water, sewerage and garbage collection – the self-built house will more easily become the workplace of home-based entrepreneurs. Many studies underline such combined residential and income-generating functions of self-help housing in informal settlements (e.g. Gough *et al.* 2003; Coen *et al.* 2008; Wiggle 2008; Majale 2008). Thus, self-help support which is geared to the needs and expectations of individual households should also take into account the possibility that the basic dwelling unit may gradually become transformed into a place where households can make a living.

Most components of such basic assistance in support of self-help housing solutions also apply to settlement upgrading policies. Obviously, the exception to this rule is that most self-builders in existing informal settlements already possess a plot and a dwelling. A vital element of settlement upgrading schemes, however, is the regularization of land ownership. As long as tenure insecurity persists, dwellers are not likely to exercise their full potential of self-building efforts, either in terms of financial investment or in terms of labour input. The second basic element of settlement upgrading is the provision of infrastructure and public services, usually starting with extending the city's networks of electricity, piped water, water drainage and sewerage systems. Other improvements can be added, such as the provision of public transport, garbage collection, measures that enhance the resilience of the settlement to natural hazards (e.g. floods and landslides) as well as various kinds of social services such as primary schools, health facilities, playgrounds, community resource centres and the like (Choguill 1999). All such elements of neighbourhood upgrading are realized at the settlement level and are often implemented in partnership with NGOs and CBOs (see Figure 4.3). More often than not, the inhabitants of such informal settlements are expected to also contribute in labour, in order to reduce the costs of the public infrastructure and services.

Additional forms of assistance to self-build efforts

The provision of various kinds of additional assistance which are more specifically tailored to the individual self-builders are also vital prerequisites for broadening the scope of assisted self-help housing policies. Such flanking policies may come in many shapes, for example by giving customized technical or judicial advice; by providing access to good-quality and low-priced construction materials; by granting financial support; or by encouraging the self-builders to collaborate in improving their dwellings and neighbourhood environments.

One way in which local governments and NGOs alike can offer technical, legal and all kinds of other assistance to the residents in informal settlements is through neighbourhood based, low-threshold 'urban resource centres'. The Society for the Promotion of Area Resource Centres (SPARC) in Mumbai and the Urban Resource Centre (URC) in Karachi have set the example for other URCs being replicated, especially across South Asia (Pakistan, India, Sri Lanka) and some other countries in Asia (Riley *et al.* 1999; Hasan 2007). Their main aim, according to Joshi *et al.* (2010: 25), is:

> creating a link between the state government, local government … and the people. They play a dual role, that of bringing information, services and schemes to the people and allowing the service providers (government, corporate, private) to understand specific needs of various target groups.

Other initiatives may be more directly aimed at providing technical assistance for sustainable house construction. The Community Architect Programme in Cuba (Valladares 2013) and the Brazilian house design programme for self-builders (Kowaltowski *et al.* 2005) as well as the work of the Technical Training Resource Centre in Karachi (Ismail 2011) are compelling examples in this respect. Various international associations of professionals and practitioners also engage in participatory training exercises for sustainable urban solutions (see e.g. ISOCARP 2010). The important message from such experiences is that the principle of participation in

FIGURE 4.3 Neighbourhood improvement with playground, San Borja, Lima. Photo by Jan Bredenoord.

design by informal self-builders and their low-threshold access to architects and other technical professionals may lead to the use of building technologies that are especially tailored to the urban poor in terms of affordability, adequacy and functionality. In addition to that, the participatory methodologies applied by community architects often function as a catalyst towards social transformation at the settlement level (Luansang et al. 2012).

Mutual self-help housing provides good development opportunities, such as: knowledge transfer, more quality through specialization and especially, more (common) discipline. Mutual self-help housing can be used to improve cooperation with the local government and other actors like NGOs with housing programmes, public utilities and financial organizations, but basic conditions must be attached. State support for self-managed housing cooperatives has been a reality in, for example, Brazil, for more than a decade (Fruet 2003). The establishment of small housing cooperatives can be promoted by giving them special incentives, such as better access to a building materials bank, combined with microfinance and other forms of (technical) assistance. Successful local and regional experiences with housing cooperatives may be found in various countries such as in the Central American states of Nicaragua and El Salvador, and in Uruguay and India (cf. Ganapati, Chapter 7 in this volume).

Limitations of self-help housing

Because self-help housing is so widespread, the development and availability of adequate 'assistance' to self-builders is needed; this assistance should align not only with land policy, infrastructure and finance, but also with technical assistance designed to improve the quality of housing. In addition, municipal housing policy can be focused on achieving higher housing densities. The activities of housing-NGOs and corporations that support residents in house construction may also contribute to the effective organization of self-builder assistance. Housing stock improvement can be realized by offering technical training for homebuilders, improving technical education and providing advice on sustainable housing, building materials and applications. Because the vital characteristic of self-help housing is home ownership, cooperation from private households concerning the sustainable enlargement and improvement of their homes is required. But self-help housing in an urban setting faces three limitations: the inability to contribute to higher urban densities, poor technical quality, and a lack of sustainable building techniques and building materials. In this section, each limitation is discussed briefly.

Low housing densities and slow pace of construction

While the realization of higher urban densities is a key tenet of sustainable housing and urban planning, the contribution of individual households building on private plots and through self-construction is limited in this respect. In addition, self-help housing may take years to reach consolidation and densification. Households in Lima, Peru and elsewhere have demonstrated the ability to build in three to four layers on plots of 90 square metres; these densities are neither low nor high, but 'middle' (Fernandez-Maldonado and Bredenoord 2010). While high densities can be realized via high-rise apartment buildings, in very high-density projects – such as in China and India – self-help housing is hardly possible. In most countries, the big urbanization challenges require higher densities that give – eventually – good connectivity and proximity to urban services and employment. High-speed housing production is necessary too, given the rapid increase in urban populations worldwide; this cannot be solved by self-help housing alone. A further densification of housing and land use might be achieved when rooms are built for rental purposes, but this happens only if the local housing market takes up such extra dwellings and individual families explore these possibilities. Besides the stimulation of individual densification of houses, there also is a need to increase the social housing production of condominiums, as is being done in countries such as Brazil, India and Ethiopia (UN-Habitat 2010).

Low technical housing quality

Millions of self-help homes feature poor technical quality. Households often opt for a viable and cheap solution rather than for the preferred, stable house construction. Countries vulnerable to seismic activity require earthquake-resilient building designs; this normally cannot be managed by self-builders alone. Giving good information on building techniques and providing (technical) training to homebuilders can make a big difference. The municipal department for building control will have a role to play, with priority for the prevention of home construction in precarious areas such as those that are affected by floods, volcanic eruptions and earthquakes. This is not always easy due to the type of relationship households have with the municipal government. This relationship is in many respects defined by conflicting interests; on one hand residents demand, among other things, public services and assistance with housing, while on the other hand, the municipal government is tasked with control over housing activities. Municipal building control might therefore give priority to safety inspections in order to prevent the dangers related to building collapse and fires. The development of assistance for do-it-yourself builders can help to improve housing quality and prevent residents from making the wrong decisions regarding house construction.

Sustainable house construction and self-help housing

When it comes to self-help housing, sustainable building materials and techniques are generally lacking. This is largely because 'sustainable housing' is a relatively new concept and only marginally introduced in developing countries. Sustainability goes further than 'durable' housing to incorporate targets connected to the protection of the earth and atmosphere, for example by reducing greenhouse gases. Sustainable urban planning measures are: to protect local culture, stimulate social interaction, assist the formation of local communities and complete the ecological functions of landscapes. Other aspects of sustainability are: (1) involving local communities with planning and housing; (2) providing building materials to self-builders; (3) developing building standards; (4) implementing financing mechanisms; and (5) making land available (Ebsen and Rambøll 2000; Choguill 2007). For example, Chen *et al.* (2007) state that houses should be made energy efficient through improved design and construction such as better insulation and reduced wind infiltration, the use of solar energy for day lighting and water heating, as well as solar shading and natural ventilation for summer cooling. Given these definitions, current practices of self-help housing are not always sustainable. A crucial question is whether poor urban households can contribute to sustainable housing initiatives and better neighbourhoods. Theoretically, there is an array of possible solutions for sustainable housing and their corresponding applications that are particularly affordable for low-income households, including new designs and techniques, building materials and sustainable energy solutions (Sullivan and Ward 2012). Nonetheless, certain conditions are needed in order for sustainable housing to become a reality; they include urban planning, and social coherence and development. Social coherence refers to the need to involve households in housing projects, for example within housing cooperatives and other CBOs as described in this chapter and elsewhere in this volume.

Conclusion

Currently, the developing world is witnessing an increase in urban growth rates which correspond with an ongoing urbanization of poverty. So far, the pressing housing needs of the urban poor have in large part been satisfied by the poor themselves. Thus, the power of self-builders is a factor that can be used effectively in pro-poor government housing strategies. However, until now, national public housing policies have only rarely adopted the principles of incremental housing construction (Greene and Rojas 2008; Wakely and Riley 2011). It is to be expected that over the coming decades the role of self-help housing will change depending on the level of economic development of a country, the occurrence of poverty and the intensity of urbanization.

Given the urgency of the urban housing question, new pro-poor housing policies that build upon the power of self-help efforts and that both promote and support initiatives with self-building need to be developed. We make a plea for reintroducing assisted self-help housing as a part of national and local housing policies, and as an acceptable form of self-help. Assisted self-help housing includes both a public (regarding assistance on infrastructure and services) and a private element (regarding home ownership). Assistance for self-help should especially be reintroduced and redeveloped.

In this chapter a distinction has been made between the two main housing provision systems: the formal and the informal. Until now, self-help housing has belonged to the informal sector. Formal housing provision for low- and middle-income households is usually organized by state institutions, among others, although building companies may be involved in the execution. A feature of public (social) housing is that subsidies or subsidized loans are often granted, but there remains a great variety between countries and regions. The opposite of formal housing is informal housing and self-help housing – in a variety of forms – which is normally seen as part of that. Governments often helped with spatial planning and supplying land for housing projects with infrastructures and services in order to provide the basic conditions for self-help housing. Although the help for house building was minimal in many cases (but not always), house construction was exclusively the household's task. In this chapter the main characteristics of the two housing delivery mechanisms are compared on the basis of the following criteria: development cycle, commissioning of construction, funding, payment and construction. Public housing includes the supply of rental housing opportunities, although private home ownership is the most desired form in many countries. However, this might change, especially in big cities. Other developments that have occurred over the past decades include microfinance schemes and the introduction of mixed forms of house construction. Currently, much attention is placed upon the involvement of residents in issues concerning housing and the environment. Small-scale housing cooperatives, where local communities can effectively be involved in upgrading programmes for housing and neighbourhoods, are becoming increasingly prominent in some countries. Most important is that governments become aware of the advantages of self-help housing and that assistance for self-builders might be a good solution for supporting this housing provision mechanism.

While house construction by the do-it-yourself method is still a common practice in many developing countries, one must be aware that self-help housing has at least three limitations, as described. We think that the use of high housing densities eventually excludes self-help housing. Thus, developing assisted self-help housing is an important issue, and offering training programmes for self-builders and improving technical education and vocational training are crucial. While offering technical assistance to self-builders, all kinds of sustainability applications can be implemented in incremental housing practices. Additionally, the development of adequate construction and housing control by local governments – primarily focused on housing safety – is necessary.

Currently, official attitudes on housing themes focus mainly on integrated settlement improvement, which is both a habitat- and city-wide approach. While this is basically an approach with a long-term scope, the urban poor cannot wait that long. The city-wide approach must be accompanied with differentiated and targeted housing policies that support the self-help efforts of the urban poor.

References

Abrams, C. (1964) *Housing in the Modern World*. London: Faber and Faber.
Acioly, C. Jr and French, M. (2012) 'Housing developers: developing world', in S.J. Smith, M. Elsinga, L.F. O'Mahony, O.S. Eng, S. Wachter and R. Ronald (eds) *International Encyclopedia of Housing and Home*. Oxford: Elsevier.

Arputham, J. (2012) 'How community-based enumerations started and developed in India', *Environment and Urbanization*, 24(1): 27–30.

Baptist, C. and Bolnick, J. (2012) 'Participatory enumerations, in situ upgrading and mega events: the 2009 survey in Joe Slovo, Cape Town', *Environment and Urbanization*, 24(1): 59–66.

Baross, P. (1987) 'Land supply for low-income housing: issues and approaches', *Regional Development Dialogue*, 8(4): 29–45.

Benjaminsen, T., Holden, S., Lund, C. and Sjaastad, E. (2009) 'Formalisation of land rights: Some empirical evidence from Mali, Niger and South Africa', *Land Use Policy*, 26(1): 28–35.

Berner, E. (2012) 'Informal housing: Asia', in S. J. Smith, M. Elsinga, L. F. O'Mahony, O.S. Eng, S. Wachter and R. Ronald (eds) *International Encyclopedia of Housing and Home*. Oxford: Elsevier.

Bredenoord, J. and Van Lindert, P. (2010) 'Pro-poor housing policies: rethinking the potential of assisted self-help housing', *Habitat International*, 34(3): 278–287.

Chen, Q., Glicksman, L., Lin, J. and Scott, A. (2007) 'Sustainable urban housing in China', *Journal of Harbin Institute of Technology (New series)*, 14s: 6–9.

Choguill, C. (1999) 'Community infrastructure for low-income cities: the potential for progressive improvement', *Habitat International*, 23(2): 289–301.

Choguill, C. (2007) 'The search for policies to support sustainable housing', *Habitat International*, 31(1): 143–149.

Cities Alliance (1999) *Cities Without Slums: Action Plan for Moving Slum Upgrading to Scale*. Washington, DC: Cities Alliance.

Coen, S., Ross, N. and Turner, S. (2008) '"Without *tiendas* it's a dead neighbourhood": the socio-economic importance of small trade stores in Cochabamba, Bolivia', *Cities*, 25: 327–339.

Drakakis-Smith, D. (1981) *Housing and the Urban Development Process*. London: Croom Helm.

Ebsen, C. and Rambøll, B. (2000) *International Review of Sustainable Low-Cost Housing Projects*. Arhus: Danish International Human Settlements Service.

Fernandez-Maldonado, A. and Bredenoord, J. (2010) 'Progressive housing approaches in current Peruvian policies', *Habitat International*, 34(3): 342–350.

Fruet, G. (2003) 'The low-income housing cooperatives in Porto Alegre, Brazil: a state/community partnership', *Habitat International*, 29(2): 303–324.

Gilbert, A. (2007) 'The return of the slum: does language matter?', *International Journal of Urban and Regional Research*, 31: 697–713.

Gough, K. and Yankson, P. (2000) 'Land markets in African cities: the case of peri-urban Accra, Ghana', *Urban Studies*, 37(13): 2485–2500.

Gough, K., Tipple, G. and Napier, M. (2003) 'Making a living in African cities: the role of home-based enterprises in Accra and Pretoria', *International Planning Studies*, 8(4): 253–277.

Greene, M. and Rojas, E. (2008) 'Incremental construction: a strategy to facilitate access to housing', *Environment and Urbanization*, 20(1): 89–108.

Hao, P., Sliuzas, R. and Geertman, S. (2011) 'The development and redevelopment of urban villages in Shenzhen', *Habitat International*, 35(2): 214–224.

Hasan, A. (2007) 'The Urban Resource Centre, Karachi', *Environment and Urbanization*, 19(1): 275–292.

Huchzermeyer, M. (2011) *Cities with 'Slums': From Informal Settlement Eradication to a Right to the City in Africa*. Claremont: UCT Press.

Ismail, A. (2011) 'The Technical Training Resource Centre (TTRC): building community architects', *Environment and Urbanization*, 23(1): 183–193.

ISOCARP (2010) *Integrating urban communities for sustainable cities*. Young Planning Professionals Workshop of the International Society of City and Regional Planners. 46th ISOCARP Planning Congress (15–18 September), Nairobi.

Joshi, R., Shah, P., Nazareth, K. and Mahadevia, D. (2010) *From Basic Services Delivery to Policy Advocacy – Community Mobilisation in Pravinnagar-Guptanagar, Ahmedabad*. Ahmedabad: Centre for Urban Equity.

Karanja, I. (2010) 'An enumeration and mapping of informal settlements in Kisumu, Kenya, implemented by their inhabitants', *Environment and Urbanization*, 22(1): 217–239.

Kowaltowski, D., Pina, S., Ruschel, R., Labaki, L., Bertolli, S., Borges, F. and Fávero, E. (2005) 'A house design assistance program for the self-building process of the region of Campinas, Brazil: evaluation through a case study', *Habitat International*, 29(1): 95–111.

Luansang, C., Boonmahathanakorn, S. and Domingo-Prics, M.L. (2012) 'The role of community architects in upgrading; reflecting on the experience in Asia', *Environment and Urbanization*, 24(2): 497–512.

Majale, M. (2008) 'Employment creation through participatory urban planning and slum upgrading: the case of Kitale, Kenya', *Habitat International*, 32(2): 270–282.

Makau, J., Dobson, S. and Samia, E. (2012) 'The five-city enumeration: the role of participatory enumerations in developing community capacity and partnerships with government in Uganda', *Environment and Urbanization*, 24(1): 31–46.

Mangin, W. (1967) 'Latin American squatter settlements: a problem and a solution', *Latin American Research Review*, 2: 67–98.

Meth, P. (2013) 'Millennium development goals and urban informal settlements: unintended consequences', *International Development Planning Review*, 35(1): v–xiii.

Ntema, L.J. (2011) 'Self-help housing in South Africa; paradigms, policy and practice', PhD thesis, Bloemfontein: University of the Free State.

Riley, L., Plummer, J., Tayler, K. and Wakeley, P. (1999) *Community Learning and Information Centres as a Tool for Sustainable Urban Development*. Working Paper No. 96. London: GHK/DPU.

Scott, P., Cotton, A. and Sohail Khan, M. (2013) 'Tenure security and household investment decisions for urban sanitation: the case of Dakar, Senegal', *Habitat International*, 40: 58–64.

Sivam, A. (2003) 'Housing supply in Delhi', *Cities*, 20(2): 135–141.

Strassmann, W.P. (1984) 'The timing of urban infrastructure and housing improvements by owner occupants', *World Development*, 12: 743–753.

Sullivan, E. and Ward, P. (2012) 'Sustainable housing applications and policies for low-income self-build and housing rehab', *Habitat International*, 36(2): 312–323.

Tipple, G. (2000) *Extending Themselves: User-Initiated Transformations of Government-Built Housing in Developing Countries*. Liverpool: University of Liverpool Press.

Tipple, G. and Wilkinson, N. (1992) 'Self-help transformation of government-built flats: the case of Helwan, Egypt', in K. Mathéy (ed.) *Beyond Self-Help Housing*. London: Mansell.

Turner, J.F.C. (1967) 'Barriers and channels for housing development in modernizing countries', *Journal of the American Institute of Planners*, 33: 167–180.

UN (2012) *World Urbanization Prospects. The 2011 Revision. Highlight*. New York: UN Department of Economics and Social Affairs, Population Division.

UNCHS (1997) *The Istanbul Declaration and the Habitat Agenda*. Nairobi: UNCHS.

UN-Habitat (2006) *State of the World's Cities 2006/7, the Millennium Development Goals and Urban Sustainability, 30 Years of Shaping the Habitat Agenda*. London: Earthscan.

UN-Habitat (2010) *The Ethiopia Case of Condominium Housing: Integrated Development Programme*. Nairobi: UN-Habitat.

Valladares, A. (2013) 'The community architect program: implementing participation-in-design to improve housing conditions in Cuba', *Habitat International*, 38(1): 18–24.

Wakely, P. and Riley, E. (2011) *The Case for Incremental Housing*. Cities Alliance Policy Research and Working Paper Series No. 1. Washington, DC: Cities Alliance.

Wiggle, J. (2008) 'Shelter, location and livelihoods: exploring the linkages in Mexico City', *International Planning Studies*, 13(3): 197–222.

5
THE RESILIENCE OF SELF-BUILT HOUSING TO NATURAL HAZARDS

Earl Kessler

Introduction

As many natural hazards, often linked with climate change, occur around the globe today, we experience a huge sense of uncertainty and unpredictability. Due to climate change impacts – sea level rise, increased precipitation, rising temperatures and the increase in frequency and intensity of natural disasters – current self-help practices will be challenged (see Urry 2011). Besides these, other natural hazards such as earthquakes and volcanic eruptions can have similar negative impacts on existing urban areas and future urban expansions. Out of necessity, self-help is therefore the principal tool used by low- and middle-income families in developing countries, including urban areas, to address their shelter needs.

The role of self-help is highlighted when thinking programmatically about disaster-responsive slum improvement initiatives. However, the Millennium Development Goal 7 overlooks self-help incremental shelter options as an adaptation strategy; nor is self-help an essential component within the Cities without Slums programmes spearheaded by multinational development banks. Additionally, shelter is judged by the durability of its building materials. Conventional building materials are energy intensive when it comes to production and maintenance and so contribute significantly to climate change. In fact, the built environment is the largest energy-consuming and greenhouse gas-emitting sector because of the combined annual energy required to construct and operate residential, commercial and industrial buildings (Maseria 2011). Efforts to tackle the effects of climate change can bring technology and self-help together through innovative building systems that promote more resilient, greener building materials markets (e.g. EcoMateriales Ecuador 2010; UN-Habitat 2011:79). Any future climate-friendly market for building materials is one that expands the range of choices that families may make to build their homes.

Yet combining climate-friendly technology and self-help is a challenge. First, is there a role for self-help in the new, higher-density, engineered structures that rapid urban growth and climate change are calling for? If so, what are its characteristics and what training requirements and support are needed? Is the definition of durable building materials in need of review? Also, are energy intensive materials the only durable materials? Or can replenishable building materials such as bamboo – made from renewable resources which form a continuum from landscape restoration and plantation to market – play a useful role in improved self-help construction technologies? One thing is certain: information on the durability of renewable building materials will create an awareness of their sustainability.

This chapter presents the evolving resilience of self-built housing to natural hazards. Therefore the first section focuses on disaster response and preparedness initiatives to develop shelter alternatives away from vulnerable sites. Next, the importance of self-help in higher-technology shelter strategies and programmes is highlighted and the role of communities as stakeholders in self-help schemes is discussed. Finally, attention is paid to a climate-friendly building materials market – one that reduces the amount of energy required to manufacture building materials as well as the cost of operations and maintenance of the structures. Here renewable building resources such as bamboo are presented as an opportunity both to reduce the construction industry's carbon footprint as well as to help the industry retain a role in the self-help building process.

Natural hazards and new shelter options

Natural hazards impact on informal settlements in myriad ways including settlement patterns, who builds them and how, as well as the type of building materials used for their construction, expansion and improvement, and the implications of the manufacture of building materials. Whether or not the local environment enables the poor to become active participants in the future growth of cities as well as if the imperatives of climate change are duly reflected in this environment will determine how sustainable the future of urban settlements becomes.

As climate change impacts will affect the security and efficiency of housing, especially in particularly vulnerable areas such as coastal and steep slope areas, new shelter options become a successful adaptation strategy for climate change development programmes. What may be different from past experience is the enhanced role of local government and the strong leadership that mayors can bring towards the creation of sustainable housing options in planned projects that provide an alternative to the informal development of cities as vulnerable, slum settlements. Climate change awareness at the local level is a growing force in urban management. At a conference of mayors in 2009 this was demonstrated by local government associations such as those in the United States that have made climate change mitigation and adaptation a priority. Local governments can initiate programmes to reduce the carbon footprint of cities based on affordability and self-help.

The Solanda self-help shelter programme in Ecuador is presented in Box 5.1. The consolidation of this community is testimony to the potential families have to build and improve their own homes. Unfortunately in the 1980s, multilateral banks and bilateral housing organizations pushed to provide new shelter options through large projects in outlying areas where large, reasonably priced sites were available. But such strategies did not work well since developments were placed away from employment opportunities, services and amenities. A better alternative could have been the use of infill shelter projects using existing infrastructure within the vicinity of employment opportunities. Climate change renews the opportunity to address urban growth through focused urban policies that include new shelter programmes, green shelter delivery systems, long-term financial resources for multi-year shelter programmes, access to credit for low-income families, and building codes that support self-help.

BOX 5.1 THE SOLANDA PROJECT IN QUITO, ECUADOR

The Solanda project in Quito, Ecuador was developed as an alternative to the growth of informal settlements. The project, based on affordability, resulted in an array of incremental housing solutions; each required a family to upgrade and expand through self-help techniques.

In the 1980s, the NGO *Fundación Mariana de Jesus*, the owner of a large flat site in the south of Quito, decided to develop a low-income housing project called Solanda. Solanda offered an alternative to the *Lucha de los Pobres* squatter settlement; this settlement, built on the slopes of the Andes, was vulnerable and in need of resilient construction technologies, site protection and quality control. The project was a unique combination of local government urban services delivery, national government project sponsorship and financing, and the NGO's contribution of land, outreach and beneficiary selection.

Solanda, originally slated to build 4,500 housing solutions, actually built 6,211 housing units that included the following:

1. Sites-and-services: 622 sites-and-services plots with basic infrastructure and a 12 m² sanitary core. As families could not do service provision for themselves, sites-and-services were the most basic solution offered.
2. *Piso-techo*, or floor-and-roof schemes: 2,002 *piso-techo* solutions were simple structures of 24 m² to support a roof and provide a solid floor. The families enclosed the structure with materials of their choice and upgraded them incrementally.
3. Basic core units: 1,527 basic core units were of similar dimensions as the *piso-techo*, enclosed in brick and block walls.
4. Walk-up and other units: 2,060 units of 40–72 m². Walk-up units were also designed to accommodate incremental improvement and expansion.

The planned Solanda population of 15,000–18,000 has grown since 1986 to more than 80,000; 80–90 per cent of the original residents continue to live there. Solanda's vertical expansion, from a mostly single-storey start to the multi-storey community it now is, demonstrates the capacity of and the investment in shelter of the Solanda residents interviewed. All of the interviewees have, over time, invested and expanded their unit through self-help: 4.1 per cent have added one floor; 58.2 per cent have added two floors; 24.5 per cent have added three floors; and 4.1 per cent have added four floors.

A lesson from Solanda is that incremental housing requires structural specifications designed for consolidation and expansion, especially the foundations, to support the densification of settlements that climate change now demands. According to the RTI Institute (2005: 49): 'No new project like Solanda has been initiated by its original government and private sector sponsors, or by anybody else, for that matter. The missing piece is that the Solanda concept was only carried out once. It became one of many one-time-only ideas.' The lesson here is that 'the introduction of reforms and policy changes requires a more sustained support, regardless of how good they are, so they can turn into sustained processes in the future' (RTI Institute 2005: 45).

Source: RTI Institute (2005)

A review of the past 30 years of the World Bank's shelter lending programme concluded that progressive development was the foundation upon which low-income family participation in sites and services, slum upgrading and disaster reconstruction was built. The review found that the World Bank needed to reconsider its urban lending programmes to once again include new shelter options for the poor (Buckley and Kalarickal 2006: 63). The issue was that donors thought in terms of projects. The World Bank's one-off projects did not 'empower the poor and therefore the Bank's approach did not replicate or become institutionalized by the national governments' (Buckley and Kalarickal 2006: 62). Instead, national public sector housing ministries and banks failed to replicate or integrate method. The donors do not provide multi-year support to change the behaviour of the housing institutions that they helped to create. Families, however, did engage and invest. The incremental shelter projects in Ecuador and Panama demonstrate that success.

While the growing awareness of climate change adaptation can encourage local governments to become proactive about the growth of their cities and sustain urban shelter delivery systems, a local information base is essential. This information base needs to identify the demand for new shelter options as well as vulnerable people and places. In addition, safe sites for development and areas that are not suitable for development need to be identified. Informed self-help programming is a potent remedy for existing vulnerabilities and an alternative to slums.

Climate change is responsible for more frequent and intense natural disasters that particularly affect vulnerable communities, especially informal settlements and slums. Thus, the need to upgrade and retrofit the existing built environment is a pressing issue and one that will require improved self-help building skills and construction technologies. Moreover, proactive shelter improvement programmes will need to include access to home-improvement loans. The role of self-help in upgrading existing communities and achieving cities without slums will only grow as access to credit and targeted improvement programmes become part of the donor and local government agenda. Home-improvement programmes, such as those in Panama, are an official programmatic response that addresses the new demands climate change requires including more resilient building systems, the retrofitting of existing structures, and the availability and use of more climate-friendly building materials. Just as the definition of urban infrastructure has to expand to include mitigation infrastructure, so will the definition of disaster response and preparedness have to expand to include new shelter options, site protection and home-improvement programmes that engage self-help techniques.

The devastation of the self-built communities that crumbled in Port-au-Prince, Haiti in the January 2010 earthquake are a lesson to take to heart on local building technologies and practice (see Box 5.2).

BOX 5.2 THE HAITI EXPERIENCE

On 12 January 2010, an estimated 3 million people were impacted when Haiti was struck by a magnitude 7.3 earthquake. According to original estimates, 50–80 per cent of all residential and commercial buildings in the capital and surrounding areas were destroyed or severely damaged. Moreover, up to 300,000 people were killed, 300,000 were injured, and 1.5 million people were made homeless. Shortly thereafter, on 27 February 2010, an 8.8 magnitude earthquake caused 300 deaths in Chile. This significant difference in damage between Haiti and Chile may be explained by the quality of construction and building code enforcement of the Chilean government.

Despite the massive international response that emphasized housing and shelter, OCHA (Office for the Coordination of Humanitarian Affairs) and OIM (International Organization for Migration) estimated that one year after the earthquake 810,000 people – 30 per cent of the metropolitan population – still remained displaced and living in camps (Schwartz *et al.* 2011). Two and a half years later, 390,000 persons still resided in the 575 remaining camps (Sontag 2012). The disaster was horrific and continues to be. Rubble still fills Port-au-Prince and will continue to cause problems as damaged structures are demolished. Families, not wanting or able to wait any longer for a safer home, unfortunately are rebuilding in the same ways that caused the vulnerabilities in the first place.

The Dutch NGO Cordaid (2011) recognized the importance of the Neighbourhood Return and Housing Reconstruction Framework, the approach promoted by the Government of Haiti and the Interim Haiti Recovery Commission. Within this approach, it was clearly recognized that the challenge for Haiti was to marshal the available resources and entrepreneurial capacity of the Haitian people to restore neighbourhoods and improve the quality of life for all those affected by the earthquake. Unfortunately this approach was ignored by donors, many of which had their own agendas.

Self-help is the cornerstone for recovery in Haiti. Yet in conversations with bilateral disaster assistance officials it was recognized that the event was, in fact, a construction disaster made worse by an earthquake. The city was brought down because of the lack of building code enforcement and the faulty building practices that families carried out. Self-help programmes need to demonstrate more technical capacity in order to confront the increased perils and disasters that climate change is expected to bring.

Source: Kessler (2012)

Disaster response and shelter kits

The increased frequency of natural disasters brought on by climate change has spurred disaster relief agencies to reconsider their relief and recovery strategies. Emergency relief all too often relocates victims into temporary housing away from their original community. However, on-site relocation and shelter kits are an alternative self-help approach. In fact, Habitat for Humanity (n.d.) employs the shelter kit concept (see Box 5.3) as the first step in its Pathway to Permanence strategy to support on-site recovery based on self-help. Under the strategy, families move from dependence to participation and from dislocation to re-establishing life's routines on-site. Shelter kits can also be a standard product within relief and recovery strategies to limit competition among donors. Kits are comprised of a set of components to fit the context including tools, supports, and roofing and wall materials configured to suit a family's needs. Box 5.4 describes how shelter kits were successfully employed in the reconstruction of Timor L'Este after its independence.

BOX 5.3 EMERGENCY SHELTER KITS

'Habitat is providing 21,000 Haitian families with emergency shelter kits. Habitat wants to provide the widest range of resources available to help families obtain safe, secure shelter. From experience, Habitat knows that giving families the tools and working alongside them is the best way to improve housing conditions after a disaster.

These kits contain tools to make immediate basic home repairs and construct temporary shelter. All items in the kit have been selected by Habitat's Disaster Response staff and were identified as a priority by USAID's Disaster Assistance Response Team.

Each emergency shelter kit includes:

- (2) five-gallon buckets. These are useful for the removal of concrete and debris and can be used to carry water and other essential supplies.
- (2) contractor-grade tarpaulins, big enough to shelter a family of five. Tarps help families create temporary shelter; they are durable and flexible and can be used in a variety of ways: to create a roof over existing structures or to use in large or small spaces.
- 100 feet of solid braided rope. Used to help secure tarps to posts or trees.
- 100 feet of 14-gauge utility wire. Used to help secure tarps and serve various other functions as needed.
- Roofing nails for attaching tarps and assorted other duties.
- (2) rolls of duct tape. Used to connect two tarps or patch rips.
- (1) 4-pound hammer. Useful for driving in stakes and chipping away concrete, etc.
- Pry bar. For use in salvage and pulling out roofing nails.
- (1) 3-inch mason chisel. For chipping away concrete, blocks and brick in salvage work.
- (1) 8-inch pliers with cutting tool. Used for twisting and cutting wires.
- (10) dust masks. To help protect survivors from the thick dust inherent with cleanup and reconstruction.
- (4) pairs of leather gloves. To help protect hands when working with concrete.
- (4) pairs of safety glasses. For protecting eyes in cleanup and reconstruction.
- (1) 12-inch hacksaw with six replacement blades. For cutting rebar and assorted other duties.
- Folding knife with a steel blade. For cutting rope and assorted other duties.
- Pointed chisel. Used in salvage.

These tools are packed in a container that locks for security. The tote can be converted for a different use later.
*The contents of the Emergency Shelter Kits may vary based on availability and need.'

Source: Habitat for Humanity (n.d.)

BOX 5.4 TIMOR L'ESTE CASE STUDY

A United Nations taskforce and the *Concelho Nacional Resistencia Timor* (CNRT) agreed that the United Nations High Commissioner for Refugees (UNHCR) would be the coordinating body for a reconstruction programme that would distribute shelter kits to 50,000 affected families. An assessment of the reconstruction programme found that the programme offered on-site reconstruction with emergency assistance including distributing shelter kits. Goods distributed included tarpaulins for shelter, as well as blankets, buckets, mats, food staples and other basic household supplies. The relief phase was quickly followed by on-site reconstruction featuring shelter kits. Temporary barracks or refugee camps were not a part of the response strategy. The assessment also found that kits proved to be a valuable resource to families: they provided quick protection to families remaining on their property so they could go on with their daily activities and pursue their livelihoods. Moreover, through self-funded improvements, shelter kits evolved into secure, permanent housing. This is in line with the aim to 'enable affected households to incrementally upgrade from emergency to durable shelter solutions within a reasonably short time and with regard to the constraints on acquiring the additional resources required'.

Source: Weir and Kessler (2006)

The shelter kit programme in Timor L'Este supported sustainable outcomes by way of successfully integrating self-help strategies into its implementation. The result was a clear advantage over off-site temporary shelter. Key characteristics of the shelter kit approach are that it integrates equity that promotes community cohesion and accountability; offers livelihood opportunities in the fabrication of shelter kit components and other related products; operates at scale by providing a single-solution and low-cost starter product to access increased numbers of affected families; and is designed to be upgraded incrementally in a sustainable manner. In the case of Timor L'Este, the shelter kit itself was an equitable, incremental housing solution as community involvement in the selection of partaking families ensured fair distribution, Moreover, the kit's components were used to build a shelter or repair a damaged shelter in a manner appropriate to culture and climate. Shelter improvements were the incubator for local economic activity. In contrast, contract-built projects often ignore the potential for local sourcing of materials and labour as well as the opportunity to build up local skills and business enterprises.

In addition to using a standardized product, the coordination of NGO participation contributed to greater coverage of affected families. Additionally, a programme coordinator formed an integral part of programme implementation and so helped to avoid redundancy, duplication and waste. NGOs were non-competitive because their areas of activity and the shelter kit were clearly defined by the UN provisional government. Concentrating on a single product avoids communities playing one donor or NGO off against the other.

The shelter kit approach fosters accountability; the definition of roles and responsibilities amongst the programme's players allows for the tracking of activities to identify snags in policy and implementation as well as to identify and record lessons learned. In addition, proper tracking and evaluation maximizes the use of resources. Moreover, the shelter kit concept represents a link to mid-term and long-term sustainable development initiatives, the use of improved traditional building materials and capacity building opportunities (Weir and Kessler 2006).

Shelter kit construction programmes can initiate resilient community action planning. For Haiti, as for Timor L'Este, self-help is the key to recovery. How this will fit with future growth strategies in the face of climate change remains to be seen.

Self-help and the new shape of cities

Government-initiated housing projects that translated formal sector shelter policy into self-help initiatives hold important lessons for future urban growth, particularly the successful projects carried out in Ecuador and Panama in the heyday of the sites-and-services boom of the 1980s, as presented in Box 5.1. These cases demonstrate the viability of public sector, self-help shelter strategies. However, the detached, single-family, self-help housing model contributed to urban sprawl; a development strategy that climate change challenges. Yet now, climate change and disaster risk reduction militate for the resurrection of – and new thinking about – public sector self-help shelter programmes that accommodate climate change imperatives. Climate change will reshape cities. As a result, future growth may transition from the urban sprawl that characterizes the expansion of cities now to higher-density development.

In the 1970s, when participation and self-help became the key strategies for the poor to provide shelter for the poor, the technical approach towards solving the housing problem – especially the development of 'Tinker Toy' technologies[1] – was replaced by participatory self-help processes. Gone were the investigations into low-cost technologies that aimed to 'solve' the housing problem; informal settlements changed from slums to new towns of hope. Housing for the poor was left to the initiative of slum developers and self-help builders.

Unless incremental growth of higher-density housing is designed for its users, the demands of climate change will, out of necessity, not only bring technology back into shelter programmes and strategies but also put at risk the role of self-help. To avoid this, small contractors and self-help builders will need to be trained in resilient building methods. Moreover, the low-rise sprawl of both formal projects and informal settlements would become instead integrated, higher-density communities with better access to services and more pedestrian-friendly streets. Nonetheless, linking technology and self-help is a challenge. An example is the search for appropriate earth technologies for housing such as compressed earth blocks (CEBs) and interlocking stabilized soil blocks (ISSBs). This technology, developed in Bogotá, Colombia and used throughout South America, is called the CINVARAM block. This author employed CINVARAM technologies in the new rural town of Puerto Badel located outside of Cartagena, Colombia; this town replaced the old community that flooded each year. While this required the introduction of technological knowledge and training for the local labour forces, soil analysis and the use of low technology soil compressors, this technology can be particularly economical.

The new World Bank Urban Strategy states that:

> Climate change and its impact on developing country cities will require retooling the approaches to urban environmental management. Urbanization if properly managed can also address the climate change agenda through the design of denser, more compact

cities that increase energy efficiency and reduce travel time and costs for urban residents and businesses.

(World Bank 2009: 3)

The World Bank calls for capital investment planning as a multi-year endeavour that includes slum-upgrading at scale and the need for new shelter options, especially sites-and-services (World Bank 2009). This makes clear that the shape of a city in the developing world – its layout and density – is influenced by the lending programmes of multilateral banks and bilateral development agencies. Yet according to Kessler (based on evidence in Haiti, 2012; Guatemala, 1978; and Tsunami Reconstruction Indonesia, 2005), the availability of money for urban development often comes laden with the cultural values and development standards of the lenders. New shelter options should instead depend on the context of the city, its resources, culture and capacity to create and implement shelter programmes.

Addressing climate change will require a stream of resources for long-term initiatives. While private housing finance companies expected to see a market in incremental housing, the administrative costs of small lending were deemed not to be good business. Resources are required for institutional capacity building; for training skilled and unskilled labour in resilient construction technologies; for access to credit; for the development and use of renewable resources for housing; and for retrofitting the existing built environment. Today, local governments can formulate affordable shelter solutions as part of their resilient city strategies.

Partnerships are an increasingly important approach to scale-up growth. The role that the community can play in design and development is an important tool in the climate-friendly development toolkit. Nonetheless, engaging with communities raises expectations of the benefits that will flow to them. Therefore, it is essential that donors, governments and self-help practitioners develop methods to engage with communities and with groups that work with communities. Community engagement also illustrates that there is a shift in donor and government perception alike; communities have transitioned from passive beneficiaries to active partners in a climate-friendly, self-help process. Transparency and consultation are keys towards successful working relationships as well as to create opportunities for communities to engage. Table 5.1 offers an array of activities where self-help and community participation can play significant roles.

New building materials

A climate-friendly industry is one that minimizes the amount of energy consumed in the manufacture of building materials as well as one that promotes efficiency in the operations and maintenance of any resultant structures. Combining the annual energy that is required to operate residential, commercial and industrial buildings along with the embodied energy of industry-produced building materials identifies the built environment as the largest energy-consuming and greenhouse gas-emitting sector (Maseria 2011). In fact, the building industry, including the manufacture of materials, construction processes, and building maintenance and operation, represents 48.7 per cent of energy consumption in the United States. In comparison, the construction industry represents 23.2 per cent while transportation represents 28.1 per cent. Moreover, carbon emissions – not transportation emissions – deriving from the building sector were responsible for nearly half (46.7 per cent) of CO_2 emissions in the United

TABLE 5.1 Climate change participation

Disaster clean-up	Environmental protection	Vulnerable population identification
• Rubble removal and recycling to useful purpose • Site clearing and land conflict resolution • Building materials collection and recycling	• Landscape restitution • Mangrove recuperation • Erosion control • Site protection: retaining walls, dikes and levees	• Mapping vulnerable populations • Identification of the type of care required • Tracking of assistance provided
Shelter approaches • On-site construction – self-help/NGO support • Relocation to a new site – self-help/government • Transitional housing – self-help/government • Retrofit of existing structures – self-help • Temporary shelter – contractor/government with self-help consolidation	**Shelter solutions** • Shelter kits • Sites and services • Core housing • Temporary shelters • Completed housing • High-density, low-rise apartments • Building materials acquisition and market development	**Local economy development** Initiatives for the development of: • Adaptation products design and delivery • Skills development for the community in financial management • Small business development • Basic service delivery • Monitoring and evaluation
Skills training • Improved local building technologies • Environmental restoration, management and site-protection • Sanitation, recycling and composting • Microfinance lending for small business restoration and housing • Training-of-trainers • Trauma mitigation: victim identification, attention and treatment	**Infrastructure retrofit and construction** • Schools, clinics, religious buildings, health and community centres • Community construction management	**Basic services restitution** • Water supply, waste treatment and sanitation • Mitigation and adaptation infrastructure including raised walkways, levees and seawalls • Special requirements of vulnerable groups including women

Source: Kessler (2012).

States in 2009. By comparison, transportation accounted for 33.4 per cent of CO_2 emissions and industry just 19.9 per cent (Maseria 2011). How this plays out in the developing world and in the income sectors that employ self-help is to be seen. Low-income families tend to avoid traditional materials such as bamboo[2] and adobe as they are perceived to be 'poor man's materials'. On the other hand, the concrete block and reinforced concrete frame construction are preferred as a result of their modern image.

Another example comes from bamboo where research and product development are currently changing its image to a multi-purpose, renewable resource. In the following paragraphs, the use of bamboo as a sustainable building material for housing is analysed.

Bamboo offers a range of multi-purpose building qualities; the plant is a seismically resilient building material as well as a tool for landscape restoration and flood and erosion control.

Moreover, with a fast 3–5-year growth cycle, bamboo offers economic opportunities as a cash-crop to small-, medium- and large-scale growers (UN-Habitat 2011).

Although bamboo is not available everywhere, it can be a good alternative to conventional building materials such as wood and concrete. According to Kraul (2011), 'Given the world's environmental imperatives, including climate change, deforestation and endangered aquifers; it is only a matter of time before bamboo makes its own case as a logical replacement for traditional woods in construction projects.'

Training is required to create sustainable bamboo forests as well as to plant bamboo and harvest the mature poles in a sustainable manner. Scaling-up would respond to the demand for construction materials and other value-added industries, using bamboo as the prime material (Kraul 2011). While technical knowledge can be developed locally for the construction of bamboo houses, preservation of the material is crucial; this must be done professionally. Moreover, training of construction workers is necessary to implement technological and construction techniques.

The issue of bamboo shelter has evolved from a focus on better bamboo house designs. Architect Jorge Moran, the director of EcoMateriales at the Catholic University in Guayaquil, Ecuador, has taken the discussion of bamboo housing in a different direction to focus on the development of bamboo building materials and systems to supply self-help construction. Moran's position is that the market for building materials needs to respond to climate change through the development of a reliable supply of building materials that are energy efficient and renewable. Climate-friendly building materials can supply a self-help building components market where each material can be installed manually. The materials include bamboo laminates for floors and wall panels, for moulded roofing sheets and for structural elements. To reflect the viability of renewable resources, the move to materials development carries with it the need for a change in codes and standards. After the 1999 earthquake in Pereira, Colombia, the technical standards for earthquake reconstruction changed to reflect the area's ancient bamboo construction tradition. This resulted in the first-ever, national-level building code that recognized bamboo as a legitimate building material (Asociación Colombiana de Ingeniería Sísmica 1999).

Climate change requires that the choice and production of building materials be seriously reconsidered. Renewable building resources provide the opportunity to reduce the carbon footprint of buildings and the construction industry. These renewable resources also may play a significant role in self-help construction, particularly if they are locally produced and used by local craftsmen and self-builders. Moreover, the construction industry can achieve higher sustainability and thus contribute to local resilience if knowledge developments and training of craftsmen and self-producers is considered.

Currently, the construction model used in developing countries is heavily reliant upon durable materials such as bricks, concrete blocks and steel-reinforced concrete that are produced via energy intensive methods. This makes clear that the building materials supply chain needs to be reformed in order to reduce energy consumption. However, technical issues related to new or newly promoted climate-friendly and self-help materials may be easier to resolve than the change in behaviour and models of progress and modernization. These issues are explored in a series of UN-Habitat reports which focus on Shelter Initiatives for Climate Change Mitigation: sustainable building practices for low-cost housing (SICCMA 2011); a handbook of sustainable housing practices in developing countries (Hannula 2012); and a publication on sustainable housing for sustainable cities (Golubchikov and Badyina 2012).

Conclusions

While self-help will remain the principal strategy for low-income families to develop shelter, self-help construction needs to be made more resilient to potential climate change impacts. But self-help may become a casualty in the course of climate change impacts on city development. Climate variability may change the shape of cities to be more dense with a focus on mixed-use developments intended to limit the urban carbon footprint. How housing for the poor will be developed and by whom, especially in cities where urban growth increasingly is concentrating what was once rural poverty, will not only determine whether self-help will remain the resource it has been, but also determine whether it can realize its potential.

At issue is whether formal housing programmes or informal developers will address the demand for low-cost housing. Cities are recognizing that their informal settlements have become the focus of multilateral and bilateral banks and agencies. But all too often slum upgrading programmes have resulted in the forced resettlement of communities that were not necessarily living in vulnerable areas in order for local governments and developers to reclaim the land for more profitable projects. Communities are relocated to small apartments situated at some distance from employment opportunities, services and community facilities.

Governments are once again beginning to develop new shelter options for the urban poor. In theory, the provision of new shelter options for the urban poor is welcome and a long time in coming. The experience of Solanda in Quito, however, demonstrates how the formal sector could provide self-help housing to the urban poor that is participatory, affordable, sustainable and incremental by design.

Climate change will increase the frequency and intensity of disasters; this requires informal settlements and new shelter development to become more resilient. The case of the 2010 earthquake in Port-au-Prince, Haiti represents just how vulnerable poorly built cities are. In fact, officials engaged in relief and recovery there characterized the event as a construction disaster made worse by an earthquake. While an earthquake is not a result of climate change, the event highlights the need for self-help to develop its technical capacity in order to address the increasing frequency of disaster events that climate change is likely to bring (Kessler 2012).

Climate change might encourage a union between technology and self-help through innovative building systems and a more diverse range of building materials for greener, participatory and resilient urban growth. As self-help home-improvement and retrofitting initiatives promote resilient construction, public sector housing and urban development entities, self-help developers and private builders need to be made aware of the relationship between climate change and the building industry. The definition of durable materials needs to include renewable resources and other more climate-friendly materials. Additionally, access to credit for the development of climate-friendly building materials is now too limited to impact on building materials markets. Greener building technologies and choice of materials requires support and investment so self-help can contribute to reducing the carbon footprint of cities.

Offering a choice of building materials also is especially relevant to disaster recovery and reconstruction programmes. The shelter kit approach (Box 5.3) needs to link temporary shelter solutions with resilient technologies that via self-help techniques can be implemented as part of longer-term shelter delivery systems. Both building codes and normative construction standards need to be modified and enforced to accommodate climate-friendly building.

Future urban growth needs self-help shelter design and settlement planning to incorporate incremental development strategies that are affordable and sustainable. Historic urban areas and basic urban infrastructure also now need to include incremental mitigation infrastructure development and site protection strategies. Climate change will add mitigation infrastructure and site protection to the self-help agenda for resilient communities. After all, as demonstrated in Haiti, investments in site protection turned vulnerabilities into assets to highlight the potential that self-help represents.

Notes

1 Tinker Toys, which contain sticks and joints or nodes that have holes, are toys that allow children to build things. For housing, prefabricated systems of post and beam, and prefabricated panels were thought to solve the housing problem by engineers, planners and others. This technical solution was replaced by the self-help approach to building.
2 The library designed by the architect Jorge Moran for the Catholic University in Guayaquil, Ecuador is an example of the improvements possible in the use of bamboo. Projects such as these have the potential to change the image and clientele of improved traditional building materials and in so doing encourage the widespread use of this traditional building material. Simon Velez, a Colombian architect and advocate of bamboo, promotes new uses of bamboo as a strong, eco-sustainable building material that can substitute for wood and concrete. Velez's projects featuring sophisticated buildings have begun to change the image of bamboo and call attention to its beauty and construction attributes. In 2009, cited for his 'progressive approach to culture and development', Velez won the Prince Claus Award in the Netherlands.

References

Asociación Colombiana de Ingeniería Sísmica (1999) *Manual de Construcción SismoResistente de Viviendas en Bahareque Encementado.* Online. Available at http://web.catie.ac.cr/guadua/usos.htm (accessed 29 April 2013).
Buckley, R. and Kalarickal, J. (2006) *Thirty Years of World Bank Shelter Lending: What Have We Learned?* Washington, DC: The World Bank.
Cordaid (June 2011) Unpublished Job Description for an Urban Planner, Haiti.
EcoMateriales Ecuador (2010) Talleres Ecomateriales.m4v. Online. Available at www.youtube.com/watch?v=tpMhwf9j8VY (accessed 29 April 2013).
Golubchikov, O. and Badyina, A. (2012) *Sustainable Housing for Sustainable Cities.* Nairobi: UN-Habitat.
Habitat for Humanity (n.d.) *Emergency shelter kits*; Online. Available at www.habitat.org/disaster/active_programs/Haiti_emergency_shelter_kits.aspx (accessed 20 July 2013).
Hannula, E.-L. (2012) *Going Green: A Handbook of Sustainable Housing Practices in Developing Countries.* Nairobi: UN-Habitat.
Kessler, E. (2012) 'Katye neighborhood improvement program'. Report of independent evaluation submitted to USAID/OFDA.
Kraul, C. (2011) 'Colombia architect leads bamboo building crusade', *Los Angeles Times*, 29 November.
Maseria, E. (2011) 'Climate change and building'. Online. Available at www.Architecture2030.com (accessed 25 April 2013).
RTI Institute (2005) *LAC Housing and Urban Upgrading Assistance Retrospective.* Honduras and Ecuador. USAID. Online. Available at http://pdf.usaid.gov/pdf_docs/PDACJ073.pdf (accessed January 2014).
Schwartz, T.T., Yves-François, P. and Calpas, E. (2011) *Building Assessment and Rubble Removal in Quake-Affected Neighborhoods in Haiti.* Washington, DC: LTL Strategies.
SICCMA (2011) *Sustainable Building Practices for Low Cost Housing: Implications for Climate Change Mitigation and Adaptation in Developing Countries.* Nairobi: UN-Habitat.

Sontag, D. (2012) 'Years after Haiti quake, safe housing is a dream for many', *New York Times*, 15 August.
UN-Habitat (2011) *Cities and Climate Change: Global Report on Human Settlements 2011*. London: Earthscan.
Urry, J. (2011) *Climate Change and Society*. Cambridge, Malden, MA: Polity.
Weir, S. and Kessler, E. (2006) *Community-Based Disaster Response: Only One Component of an Effective Shelter Framework*. Singapore: Habitat for Humanity.
World Bank (2009) *The World Bank Urban and Local Government Strategy. Systems of Cities: Harnessing Urbanization for Growth and Poverty Alleviation*. Washington, DC: World Bank.

6
RENTING A HOME
The need for a policy response

Alan Gilbert

Renting: a disappearing tenure?

Until the middle of the twentieth century, most urban families were tenants. This included families from every social class – renting was not just the tenure of the poor. In Britain, 89 per cent of households rented accommodation in 1910 and it was not until 1971 that a majority became homeowners. In 2009, 70 per cent of British households owned or were buying their property. Similar changes occurred later in most developed countries and a similar shift towards ownership has been occurring recently in most of the developing world (UN-Habitat 2011a).

Various processes encouraged the shift towards home ownership. The development of rail, tram and bus networks was critically important insofar as it allowed people to live farther from their work. Suburbs, both formal and increasingly informal, began to develop along the new routes. The emergence of mortgage finance systems in some countries allowed the better off to borrow over increasing periods of time. Some governments encouraged home ownership by offering tax relief on mortgage payments. And, as average incomes rose, more and more families could afford to buy. Gradually, strongly encouraged by the propaganda of both governments and the building industry, families became convinced that home ownership was part of their 'culture' and a key indicator of their social position.

At the same time, the rental housing sector was changing. During the twentieth century, more and more governments introduced legislation to control rents and improve the quality of living conditions of tenants (United Nations 1979; UNCHS 2003). This discouraged landlords from investing in rental accommodation and, in any event, new investment opportunities were opening up – including building homes for individual ownership.

In the poorer cities of the world the shift towards home ownership was encouraged by the fact that few governments were able to stop poor people invading land or illegally buying unserviced plots. Many politicians even encouraged the process. As a result, millions of poor people took the opportunity to obtain land on which they could construct a shelter and thereby avoid the need to pay rent. Fuelled by rapid in-migration, urban home ownership grew apace; in Santiago, Chile, for example, the proportion of people living in their own home rose from 41 per cent in 1960 to 73 per cent in 2002.

Of course, there were exceptions to this trend, most notably in Communist states. Home ownership there was discouraged and, in the USSR, two-thirds of households rented accommodation in 1990, mostly in public housing (Hegedüs and Struyk 2005). But when most Communist regimes fell, public housing construction ceased and most governments made social tenants into owners; by 2010, 90 per cent of Hungarian and 84 per cent of Latvian households were homeowners (UN-Habitat 2011b).

However, despite the years of effort and financial expenditure that so many governments have spent in trying to expand home ownership, perhaps 1.2 billion people currently rent accommodation.[1] Indeed, globally probably one-third of all urban dwellers currently live in rental shelter and in some cities, e.g. New York and Zurich, the majority rent (Gilbert 2009).

While the proportion of owner-occupiers has increased in most countries over time, the sheer volume of urban growth, through both migration and natural increase, has led to the numbers of tenants in the cities increasing. Even in cities where the proportion of non-owners has been in rapid decline, the pace of urban expansion has sometimes led to a large increase in the numbers of non-owners. In Mexico City, for example, between 1950 and 2000 the number of tenant and sharer households increased from 484,000 to 3.7 million.

Explaining differences between countries and cities

In broad terms, tenure patterns across countries can be explained in terms of the level of urbanisation, the level of economic development, the dominant form of economic organisation and the ideology of the government.

Even though the better off tend to own and poorer households rent, levels of home ownership in many developed countries are lower than those in most of the developing world. In developed countries, there is actually an inverse relationship between ownership and GDP per capita, with the richest countries tending to have the lowest proportions of homeowners. Affluent Germany and Switzerland have low levels of ownership whereas much poorer Spain and Romania have high rates (Randall 2011: table two). Indeed, worldwide the highest levels of owner-occupation are actually found in very poor countries because most people still live in the countryside. In addition, the incidence of homeowner-occupation is strongly affected by culture, history and, critically, by politics.

Even within the same country, there are often major variations in tenure, not only between urban and rural areas but also between cities. In general, cities with relatively expensive housing and land have high proportions of tenants because many families who would like to own cannot afford to. For this reason, very large cities often have high rates of renting; Los Angeles, New York, Mumbai and Bogotá all have a higher proportion of tenants than most other cities in their respective countries.[2]

In many cities in poor countries, illegal forms of land tenure make access to 'ownership' easier. In most of Africa and Latin America variations in home ownership can be explained in terms of access to cheap or free land. In cities where land invasion or clandestine subdivision has been permitted, thousands and sometimes millions of families have taken advantage. By contrast, where the authorities have been stricter, rates of home ownership tend to be lower. In Ecuador, for example, 64 per cent of households in Guayaquil lived in their own home in 2006 compared with only 48 per cent in invasion-averse Quito.[3]

The nature of the rental housing stock

Rental housing takes many different forms and the rental sector varies considerably both within cities and across countries. UNCHS (1996: 216–217) provides the following list of different kinds of rental accommodation: rooms in subdivided inner-city tenements; rooms in custom-built tenements; rooms, beds or even beds by the hour in boarding or rooming houses, cheap hotels or pensions; rooms or beds in illegal settlements; shacks on rented plots of land; rooms in houses or flats in lower- or middle-income areas; accommodation provided by employers; public housing; and space to sleep rented at work, in public places, even in cemeteries.

Public housing: In many Communist countries most urban housing was provided by the state or by state companies. In Mao's China virtually all urban residents lived in public housing until policy changed in 1988 (Huang and Clark 2002: 9–10). Public housing also contributed substantially to the housing stock in many countries in northern Europe. However, little public housing was ever constructed in most poor countries and, after 1970, very little was available for rent. In Africa, Asia and Latin America, limited budgets combined with the huge demand for housing meant that most families were forced to find their own solution. When governments did build public housing for rent, there were always allocation problems. Too few units meant that long queues developed and privileged groups often gained access to the housing rather than the most deserving. In Venezuela, housing queues were managed according to political criteria, party membership determining access.

To make matters worse, public housing was rarely well managed. Tenants often failed to pay the rent, financial deficits increased, the quality of maintenance fell and social problems began to proliferate in so-called 'sink estates'. The debt crisis of the 1980s and the subsequent need for economic restructuring meant that few governments in Africa or Latin America had money for housing programmes. When some kind of economic recovery began in the 1990s, the new received wisdom was that governments should stay out of the housing arena. If they wished to help poor people, the only suitable policy was to provide up-front capital subsidies for families to buy homes in the market (Gilbert 2004; Held 2000; Huchzermeyer 2003; Mayo 1999). Such a policy would cut government budget deficits, provide the poor with a wider choice of housing and increased efficiency. Few countries have bucked the new approach.[4]

Social housing: After 1980, many governments in Europe transferred responsibility for housing lower-income groups to the social sector and this pattern has been copied in some developing countries. But, with the possible exception of Turkey, Egypt, South Africa and India, housing cooperatives and NGOs seem still to be fledglings in a rather hostile world. In any case, most governments seem more interested in turning the tenants of deteriorated rental housing into homeowners. Cooperatives in Bolivia, Brazil, Peru and South Africa have all improved properties which they have then sold to the former tenants.

Private renting: Most rental housing today is provided by the private sector, increasingly by small investors as large commercial operators have generally forsaken this once vibrant business. Large-scale landlords can still be found in some cities, for example in Bangkok, Kathmandu, Lagos, Nairobi and Mumbai, but in general it is the small landlord who has taken over (Amis 1996; Huchzermeyer 2007; Karki 2002; Kumar 1996). In the consolidated self-help periphery of most Latin American cities, landlords generally have only a couple of tenants (Gilbert 1999). In Asia and Africa, the vast majority of landlords also seem to operate on a small scale (Kumar 2002).

FIGURE 6.1 Mexico City: in the early twentieth century even the well-off lived in rental housing. Photo by Alan Gilbert.

Informal renting of lots: Most tenants rent a room, an apartment or a house directly from a landlord. However, sometimes tenants pay rent for space on which they construct their own, usually rudimentary, dwelling. Such a pattern has been observed in the 'rentyards' of the Caribbean, in the 'lost cities' of Mexico and their equivalents in Lima, in the *bustees* of Calcutta, and in the land rental slum settlements of Bangkok and Calcutta. In South African cities, backyard shelter accommodates a large number of tenants, some of whom have erected their own shacks (Bank 2007; Crankshaw *et al.* 2000; Morange 2002).

A rather different pattern of backyard accommodation developed in the 1980s in Santiago, Chile, when the military regime prohibited the invasion of land. With affordable rental housing in short supply, many fledgling households established homes in their families' backyards (Necochea 1987).

Landlords

In the past, renting was a profitable business (see Figure 6.1). Most rental housing was supplied by those with money to invest and/or land on which to build. Private enterprise produced most of the housing, mainly small-scale investment but with some cases of major institutional investors, even the church.

Gradually, however, the ownership of rental housing changed as private investment became less profitable. The growth of stock markets and other opportunities for investment transformed the commercial calculus. Many former landlords moved into real-estate development for sale, especially when governments began to encourage owner-occupation. In places, increasing state intervention also discouraged landlords from continuing to invest in rental housing. Where rents were held down and it was difficult to evict tenants, rental housing ceased to be a profitable investment. Only in a handful of countries did commercial investment continue.

In most countries, renting became the reserve of the small-scale investor. The limited research published over the past 25 years has shown that most landlords are rather ordinary folk. Unlike the situation in the nineteenth and early twentieth centuries, landlords no longer come from the ranks of the elite and, generally, they have little political influence. Many landlords share the same kind of humble background as that of their tenants. They tend to be former migrants, the landlords differing insofar as they have usually lived in the city longer. Landlords tend to be older than other owners and much older than their tenants. Because of their age, landlords are much more likely to be retired people, to live in larger properties than other families and to have lived longer in their current home. In South Africa, much rental accommodation is created in the backyards of council houses where most of the landlords are themselves tenants and where they have lived for a long time (Crankshaw *et al.* 2000; Morange 2002). Both men and women act as landlords. Most male landlords have a female partner, who often handles the tenants, but many widows and separated women rent out property on their own.

Today, most private landlords operate on a small scale and don't make much money. They would like a higher income from their 'investment' but generally lack the professional skills of the large commercial operators. They do not understand balance sheets or more sophisticated forms of marketing and neither their turnover nor their profits would impress any banker. They extend their property in a piecemeal way, when cash is available, but, because there are so many of them, the rental housing stock expands. They may be invisible to governments, who do nothing whatsoever to help them, but since the 1950s small investors have been responsible for most of the increases in rental housing in Africa, Asia and Latin America (see Figure 6.2).

The tenants

Households choose their tenure from the limited range of options available to them and every city offers a different range of options. In some cities, land is available for free, elsewhere it isn't; some cultures encourage young people to stay with kin, others do not. The varying combination of demand and supply factors, together with different social practices, produces distinctive tenant profiles.

Even within cities, different kinds of family all become tenants. While most tenants are fairly young, different sub-markets contain different age groups. In South Africa, for example, the average age of heads of tenant households is 48 years in government accommodation, 41 years in hostels, 35 years in social housing, 37 years in household rental and 31 years in private formal renting (Martin and Nell Associates 2002). In Mexico City, tenants occupying rent-controlled properties in the central city were much older than other tenants (Coulomb and Sánchez 1991).

In most societies, richer families tend to buy their homes and relatively few rent except at an early stage in their housing career. However, in many cities of Africa, Asia and Latin America it is possible to obtain land cheaply and for very poor families to build their own

FIGURE 6.2 Middle-income rental housing in Bogotá, Colombia. Photo by Alan Gilbert.

accommodation. In such places, most tenants renting in the formal sector are better off than most owners in the informal sector and in per capita terms many young tenants in informal housing earn more than their elderly landlords.

Of course, some governments do not allow poor families to invade land and the poor have to save up to buy plots in informal areas. In Bogotá and Quito the very poor are precluded from de facto ownership and either share with kin or rent accommodation.

Women often find it harder to accede to home ownership, in part because the average female-headed household tends to be poorer. Even ownership in invasion settlements is more difficult insofar as many women lack the skills required in self-help construction.

Most recent arrivals to the city start off as tenants. As Turner's (1968) 'bridgeheader/consolidator' model points out, many migrants to the city seek temporary accommodation in the central city close to where they can find work. Of course, now that the main source of rental accommodation is to be found in the consolidated periphery, the geography of migrant housing has become more complex; fewer recent migrants are to be found near to the city centre.

As people become established in the city and obtain a more reliable source of income, they are more likely to consider home ownership. This is particularly the case for families with children who need more space and who are sometimes less than welcome with landlords. But, even though the majority of people say that they wish to own, not everyone who can afford it actually moves out of rental tenure. Certain households may eschew ownership because they do not want the type of accommodation available to them. Faced with the option of occupying cheap land and building their own home, some poor people will refuse this alternative.

Even if tenants want a home of their own, they may not want to build their own house or to live in a shack without services. Their tenure is in part a choice about lifestyle. Renting may not be wholly desirable but at least it offers a proper roof and access to services. Others feel that such an option is socially unacceptable; some downwardly mobile middle-class people, for example, may feel that living in an illegal subdivision will totally diminish their social status.

For others the question of location reflects a very different set of preferences. In some countries, many people have little wish to own in the city because they actually want to buy, or actually do own property, somewhere else. This is an important consideration in many parts of Africa where many have rural as well as urban ties; the man may work in the city and the family live in the traditional home (Grant 2007). In parts of Asia many people shuttle between periods of work in the city and their 'home' in the countryside.

The rental housing problem

Profitability: Landlords are often accused of making excessive profits and no doubt some do. Certainly, in the slums of Nairobi, some spectacular profits have been reported for landlords offering appallingly inadequate shelter (Amis 1996). This situation has been tolerated because most tenants have no real alternative in that city and because powerful public figures are major landlords.

But, frequently, estimates of the profitability of renting produce surprisingly low figures. In Mexico, landlords in self-help settlements certainly did not make much money in the 1980s and even today landlords in both inner Johannesburg and those renting out backyard accommodation are unlikely to get rich (Crankshaw *et al.* 2000; Morris 1999). However grasping landlords may be, poor people can be exploited only to a certain point. With no alternative use for their accommodation, landlords can only charge poor families what the latter can afford. Such an interpretation is certainly compatible with evidence from Buenos Aires and several Mexican cities over the years; when real incomes fell, rents fell with them.

In any case, economic analysis is in some respects an inappropriate tool to analyse the behaviour of small-scale landlords because few seem to operate on a wholly commercial basis. While every landlord wants some kind of return from his or her investment, the precise motivation for renting is highly variable. As Kumar (2002: 3) points out, renting serves as

> a safety net against precarious employment, meeting household expenditure, housing improvements, a regular source of income when moving from waged employment to own account forms of employment, capital investment and rotation in business, as a form of pension after retirement and old age and as investment for the next generation.

Most landlords rent out rooms or apartments because they need to supplement a meagre income; indeed, for some, it is their only income. Few are going to get rich on what they receive from tenants. They let accommodation because they know of no other way to make money. They do not understand, or indeed trust, most kinds of financial institution, let alone stock exchanges and hedge funds. The virtue of being a landlord lies in the security it offers for the future. After all, large numbers of landlords are old and are living either on their pension or entirely from their rent. But renting out property also helps guard against sudden, unexpected financial difficulties. Unemployment and economic recession are likely to increase potential landlords' willingness to rent.

Affordability: Landlords and their representatives typically argue that rents are too low; tenants and their associations claim that they are too high. Both sides are likely to choose their figures selectively so that it is not always easy to establish the truth. But what is meant by rents being 'too high' or 'too low'? There is no question that some tenants are paying more than they can afford and, over the years, many landlords have no doubt exploited tenants. At the same time, it is equally clear that rents are sometimes too low to attract more investment; a situation particularly likely when rent controls are operating. In practice, research shows that when rents are wholly determined by market forces, they tend to rise and fall in line with real incomes. Faced with generalised poverty, most landlords set low rents because their tenants cannot afford to pay more. But because they are receiving relatively little in rent, landlords cut back on maintenance and investment. In such circumstances rents are simultaneously too low and too high. Landlords do not receive enough to provide adequate accommodation or sufficient to keep their own families out of poverty. At the same time, tenants earning very low incomes are forced to pay a high proportion of their earnings in rent. The problem lies not in rent levels or exploitation by landlords but with the extent of urban poverty.

Rent control: Over the years, many governments have intervened in the housing market, usually in favour of tenants. At the end of the 1980s, rent controls or rent subsidies were being used in about 150 countries in the world (Kalim 1990: 188). However, rent controls have long been less than popular with most economists.

Price controls, even if laboriously tweaked, inevitably produce inefficiencies, reduce supply and cause bad side-effects. Black markets and bribery thrive. Building maintenance is often ignored. Landlords and tenants find themselves in poisonous relationships, since they are linked by law rather than by voluntarily renewable contracts. Unscrupulous property owners go to dangerous lengths to evict tenants in order to get higher-paying replacements; as a result, tenant-protection laws have been enacted that make it almost impossible to evict even a scoundrel (*The Economist* 2003).

This catalogue of sins has convinced increasing numbers of governments to remove rent controls, albeit gradually in order to minimise adjustment costs and to maintain political harmony (Malpezzi and Ball 1991). The principal aim has been to make rental housing more profitable and thereby attract more people to create space for tenants. Unfortunately, removing rent controls rarely seems to have produced the desired effect of stimulating more investment. Real estate companies have generally found building for ownership to be far more profitable. And, ironically in some countries where rent controls have been retained, rental housing has prospered. The majority of Swiss and German tenants are protected from eviction and excessive rent increases but investing in rental property is still profitable (Bourassa and Hoesli 2009; Voigtländer 2009). The lesson seems to be that inflexible rent controls are undesirable, but in well-regulated societies the goals of protecting tenants and encouraging rental housing can be pursued simultaneously.

The quality of rental housing: There can be little doubt that many tenants live in unsatisfactory housing. In Nairobi, 90 per cent of households in rental accommodation in the informal settlements of Nairobi occupy single rooms of between 9 and 14 square metres and each household contains between three and five persons (Syagga *et al.* 2002: 9). While conditions in Nairobi are extreme, inadequate rental accommodation is always associated with poverty. Better off tenants do not live in poor quality housing.

Clearly living conditions in rental housing are not uniformly bad. Much depends on the general state of the housing stock, the rate of migration and the prosperity of the country. And, of course, it is not only tenants who live in poor quality shelter. In poor cities, many tenants are better housed than owners, especially those who live in the newest self-help settlements. While tenants generally occupy less space than owners, the quality of that accommodation is superior (UNCHS 2003). And, while poor owners live in settlements with inadequate water, electricity and education services, most tenants select accommodation in areas that are more established; it is no coincidence that the proportion of tenants increases with the age of a self-help settlement (Gilbert 1999). In Latin America, most tenants at least live in settlements with services.

The quality of rental housing depends on regular maintenance and one of the major complaints from tenants across the globe is that landlords tend to be remiss in responding to their problems. This seems to be true whether or not the landlord lives on the premises. But again it is not only rented property that is poorly maintained. Many owners cannot afford to improve their homes and many family houses in Ghana and Nigeria are in a very poor state because it is in no one's direct interest to maintain them – another example of the 'tragedy of the commons' (Arimah 1997; Arku 2006; Korboe 1992).

Legal issues: In developed countries, the vast majority of tenants and landlords sign written contracts that conform to rules laid down in the rental legislation. In theory, this gives both landlords and tenants the right to go to court in order to seek redress against wrongdoing by the other side. Unfortunately, a great deal of evidence is now accumulating that both landlords and tenants sometimes flout the law because of the inadequacies of the judicial system.

If the legal system often works unsatisfactorily in many developed countries, it works even less well in most developing countries. For a start the majority of landlords and tenants fail to sign contracts. But even if every landlord and tenant signed a written, legally binding contract it would help little because of the tardiness and expense of the judicial system. At present, courts in most countries serve landlords and tenants badly. Even where the courts favour landlords, the legal system is so slow that recalcitrant tenants can stay for years without paying their rent.

Mobility and eviction: Tenant families are often portrayed as living on a knife-edge because they are constantly threatened by eviction. Without denying that many tenants have very limited tenure rights and that some are evicted by their landlords on spurious grounds, many governments have legislated to protect tenants' rights (Malpezzi and Ball 1991; *The Economist* 2003; United Nations 1979; UNCHS 2003). In places this intervention has been so effective that tenants almost never move. In Egypt, Ghana and Mexico some tenants have had more security than owners. Despite the rhetoric, ownership does not prevent eviction, either from foreclosure proceedings or from state intervention. Even where rent controls do not operate, tenants are often protected either by the ambiguity of the law or by weaknesses of the legal system. Tenants do not always have to have legal protection to retain their home. In poorer areas of Cairo, community pressure is often mobilised by tenants against their landlords (Sims 2002).

Research suggests that few tenants move all that frequently. In Latin America and South Africa, the average private tenant household moves every two to three years but in some places they hardly move at all. Even when mobility is rapid, it is not necessarily a sign that tenants are being evicted because some choose to move. Indeed, many tenants favour renting because of the flexibility it brings to their lives. In Alexandra, Johannesburg, many tenants leave on a seasonal basis in order to return to the countryside. Elsewhere employment is casual and temporary and workers have to move around.

Landlord–tenant conflict: Every tenant has a bad story about a landlord. Landlords do not maintain the property, unfairly evict tenants, fail to return deposits, are unsympathetic to temporary economic setbacks, discriminate against certain kinds of family and generally make tenants' lives difficult. Some of these complaints are undoubtedly true but for every vindictive landlord, research shows that many more are benign. At the same time, it is clear that some tenants are a pain; some exploit small-scale landlords by refusing to pay the rent and resort to delaying action in the courts to retain their right to residence. Other tenants move out without having paid what they owe. But, if there have always been awful landlords and terrible tenants, many surveys show that relations between landlords and tenants are far more benign than they are usually portrayed (Cadstedt 2006; Gilbert et al. 1993).

Discrimination: Discrimination of different kinds permeates housing markets throughout the world. In many countries, housing tenure is influenced by race and ethnicity. Insofar as homeowners in the formal sector tend to be more affluent than tenants and income is inversely related to ethnicity, landlords tend to be drawn from certain racial or ethnic groups. But equally important is migration. Insofar as migrants come from a different racial or ethnic group than that of the resident urban population, landlords and tenants are likely to have different ethnic backgrounds.

Race and ethnicity have long complicated relationships between landlords and tenants. Certain ethnic groups may be refused accommodation because of the prejudices of the landlord. Landlords in Surat, India, are reported to be reluctant to accept migrants from Orissa, who have a reputation for drunkenness and for being 'difficult' (Kumar 2002: 102). But in other places, landlords welcome strangers as tenants because they are perceived to be less troublesome; in particular they will leave the premises when asked to, unlike certain members of the family. Admittedly attitudes may change, as in Kenya towards the end of 2001, when an electioneering President Moi advised tenants in Kibera not to pay their rent and the predominantly Luo tenants starting fighting mainly Nubian landlords.

The age, sex and marital status of tenants clearly influence landlords. In India and Mexico, landlords dislike letting to single men; in Bangalore, it is women-headed households, whether widows or single women, who are less welcome (Kumar 2002: 102). And, landlords the world over have always been reluctant to take in large families; in nineteenth-century Britain landlords considered children to be the 'worst despoilers of property' (Englander 1983: 10).

Social polarisation: Today, powerful landlords dominate the rental housing stock only in a few cities around the world and most landlords tend to let property to people from the same social class. Under such circumstances, the rich can hardly be accused of exploiting the poor. In addition, many landlords are themselves poor and are reliant on their rents to survive, particularly in the case of older landlords and widows. Many tenants sympathise with their landlords because they recognise that the latter are similar to themselves. And, of course, most tenants plan to become homeowners one day and perhaps build additional rooms which they will rent out.

The main source of housing inequity today is not caused by poor tenants paying too much rent to rich landlords. Much more important is the growth of home ownership and the perverse incentives which encourage the better off to seek capital gains from buying more expensive property. In the process, rising housing prices exclude the poor from access to home ownership. In some former Communist cities, privatisation of the public housing stock has also contributed to growing inequality (Tran and Dalholm 2005; UN-Habitat 2011b). Social polarisation is even produced among homeowners by the differential rates at which the prices of different kinds of home rise. Property values soar in affluent areas whereas prices in deprived areas tend to rise more slowly and, of course, fall dramatically in times of recession.

The current sub-prime crisis has drawn our attention to the inequities of home ownership and the problems of negative equity and foreclosure.

Government policy

A critical weakness in housing policy across the world is that governments place too much faith in the virtues of home ownership. Following the spiritual lead of the United States and United Kingdom, virtually every government in the world is now attempting to increase the rate of home ownership. In China, 'expanding homeownership underpins the success of housing reforms' (Yu 2006: 297) and a similar approach is common to most parts of East Asia (Groves *et al.* 2007). In Colombia, the governments of Alvaro Uribe promised to create 'a nation of home owners' (see Chapter 17 in this volume) and, in Chile, home ownership has been a key element of housing policy ever since the military regime took power in 1973 (Almarza 1997; Gilbert 2002; Held 2000; Silva-Lerda 1997).

Recent trends in some developed countries suggest there are real limits to the number of families who can afford to buy a home. In the United States, the incidence of home ownership has recently fallen five points below the peak of 70 per cent and rates of ownership among the poor, and particularly those belonging to ethnic minorities, remain at a much lower level (Ross and Yinger 2002). In the United Kingdom, buying a house had become unaffordable for many young and lower-paid households even before the current crisis. Between 1984 and 2004, the proportion of 25- to 29-year-olds owning their home fell from 60 per cent to 50 per cent and among 20- to 24-year-olds from 35 per cent to 20 per cent (Williams 2007: 7).

The growth of home ownership is even in question in some poor countries. First, some of the world's more authoritarian and insensitive governments continue to demolish self-help settlements. In the past ten years, for example, large-scale demolition projects have been common in China, India, Kenya and Zimbabwe. Second, many cities are running out of land, at least in places that are both serviceable and within a reasonable commuting distance (Baross and Van der Linden 1990; Durand-Lasserve and Royston 2002). As a result, in cities as diverse as Bogotá, Kingston, Metro Manila, Port of Spain and Quito, the incidence of renting is increasing (UNCHS 2003; Ballesteros 2004; Clarke 2006).

Given these limits to achieving universal home ownership, it is remarkable how few governments over the past 30 years have developed any kind of rental housing policy. Earlier policies to build public housing for rent have largely disappeared and rent controls are slowly disappearing (UN-Habitat 2011a). Few governments in the 'South' make any mention of renting in their housing programmes. The multilateral development banks and United Nations agencies are little better and nothing in the way of policy seems to have emerged beyond continuing to denounce rent control. Even upgrading programmes seem to ignore any reference to the many landlords and tenants living in shantytowns (Rojas 2010).

Why has rental housing not occupied a more prominent place in policy making? One explanation is that neither landlords nor tenants are such important political actors as they used to be. By turning tenants into owners, governments have greatly reduced tenant numbers and insofar as the more affluent and powerful have grasped the opportunity to own with both hands, it has reduced the likelihood of meaningful lobbying. Landlords are also much less influential than they once were and the big money has typically moved out of rental housing into other kinds of business. Freed from constant political pressure, governments seem to have decided to leave renting alone. Why reform the rent control legislation if that will upset

TABLE 6.1 How to improve the environment for rental housing

DO	DON'T
• Recognise that many urban households live in rental and shared housing	• Ignore non-owners and assume that they all wish to become homeowners now
• Estimate how many rental households and landlords there are	• Attack landlords as a class; large numbers are just as poor as their tenants
• Evaluate whether existing rent control legislation is functioning and is producing desirable results	• Assume that poor households benefit from rent controls; poor landlords most certainly do not, nor do tenants or potential tenants who are not covered by those controls
• Count the tenant families that live in settlements before beginning an urban upgrading project and recognise their special needs	• Demolish or close down poor quality rental accommodation unless it is dangerous to the inhabitants
• Produce simple rental contract templates that can be bought in local stores	• Assume that long contracts are desirable for every kind of tenant
• Set up a cheap arbitration and conciliation service for landlords and tenants that works quickly	• Assume that the court system provides adequate protection for either poor tenants or poor landlords
• Provide credit facilities for poor landlords who wish to extend or improve their accommodation	• Provide subsidies for people to become homeowners while ignoring poor families who continue to rent
• Consider providing subsidies for landlords who wish to improve rental accommodation and install better services	

Source: UN-Habitat (2011a).

tenants and there is so little protest from the landlord lobby? A much better political option is to ignore rental housing and create opportunities for tenants to become homeowners. Many governments have more or less bribed people to become homeowners. In the United States, huge subsidies are offered to homeowners and even in China the government is subsidising the growth of home ownership. In South Africa and increasing numbers of Latin American countries, governments have been offering subsidies to the poor to help them buy a home.

But rental housing is not going to disappear and hence more governments ought to have policies designed to encourage and improve it. This does not mean that they should build public housing for rent, indeed given past experience few are very interested in becoming social landlords. The only sensible approach is to produce an environment more conducive to increasing private and third-sector involvement (see Table 6.1).

Conclusion

Today, almost one in every five households is a tenant. And, if the incidence of formal and informal home ownership is generally rising, the pace of urban growth usually means that tenant households are increasing in number. Little of their accommodation is provided by the state or by social housing associations, the main generator of rental housing being the small-scale private landlord. Because the profits from letting accommodation have been disappointing, most commercial organisations have left the market to smaller-scale operators. In developed countries, it is usually investors with a handful of properties. In poorer countries, it is self-help builders in informal settlements who have created rental space; either they have rooms to spare in their own house or they have been prepared to extend their properties in order to supplement the household income. Some of these landlords exploit their tenants but landlord–tenant relations are generally harmonious. The real problem is the poor quality of the accommodation and services available. Arguably, this is less the fault of the landlords than the result of widespread poverty; poor tenants can only afford to live in poor quality accommodation.

Governments in most poor countries face a choice between allowing the proliferation of self-help ownership, and all of the problems that causes in terms of urban sprawl and infrastructure provision, and improving shelter conditions by encouraging small-scale landlordism. The evidence from many cities is that this alternative is neither exploitative nor socially divisive. In fact, the renting of property by poor landlords to other poor families appears to constitute plain common sense.

Notes

1 Personal calculation from census data.
2 The home ownership rate in Los Angeles was 52 per cent (2010), in New York 50 per cent (2010), in Shanghai 49 per cent (2000), in Geneva 16 per cent (2000) and in Bogotá 46 per cent (2007).
3 Personal communication from Diego Aulestia.
4 In China, the government introduced a public rental housing programme in 1999 targeted at the very poorest families, and South Korea announced plans to build one million public rental units over the decade to 2012. But, even in those countries, official policy continued to emphasise the desirability of home ownership (Guowei 2007; Wang 2007).

References

Almarza, S. (1997) 'Financiamento de la vivienda de estratos de ingresos medios y bajos: la experiencia chilena', *CEPAL Serie Financimiento del Desarrollo 46*, Santiago.
Amis, P. (1996) 'Long-run trends in Nairobi's informal housing market', *Third World Planning Review*, 18: 271–285.
Arimah, B.C. (1997) 'The determinants of housing tenure choice in Ibadan, Nigeria', *Urban Studies*, 34: 105–124.
Arku, G. (2006) 'Housing and development strategies in Ghana, 1945–2000', *International Development Planning Review*, 28: 333–258.
Ballesteros, M.M. (2004) 'Rental housing for urban low-income households in the Philippines', *Philippine Institute for Development Studies Discussion Paper*, DP 2004–47.
Bank, L. (2007) 'The rhythms of the yards: urbanism, backyards and housing policy in South Africa', *Journal of Contemporary African Studies*, 25: 205–228.
Baross, P. and Van der Linden, J. (eds) (1990) *The Transformation of Land Supply Systems in Third World Cities*. Aldershot: Avebury.
Bourassa, S.C. and Hoesli, M. (2009) 'Why do the Swiss rent?', *Journal of Real Estate Finance and Economics*, 24: 286–309.
Cadstedt, J. (2006) *Influence and Invisibility: Tenant in Housing Provision in Mwanza City*. Tanzania, Stockholm: Stockholm University.
Clarke, C. (2006) 'From slum to ghetto: social deprivation in Kingston, Jamaica', *International Development Planning Review*, 28: 1–34.
Coulomb, R. and Sánchez, C. (1991) *¿Todos proprietarios? Vivienda de alquiler y sectores populares en la Ciudad de México*. Mexico City: CENVI.

Crankshaw, O., Gilbert, A.G. and Morris, A. (2000) 'Backyard Soweto', *International Journal of Urban and Regional Research*, 24: 841–857.

Durand-Lasserve, A. and Royston, L. (eds) (2002) *Holding their Ground – Secure Land Tenure for the Urban Poor in Developing Countries*. London: Earthscan.

Englander, D. (1983) *Landlord and Tenant in Urban Britain, 1834–1918*. Oxford: Clarendon Press.

Gilbert, A.G. (1999) 'A home is for ever? Residential mobility and home ownership in self-help settlements', *Environment and Planning A*, 31: 1073–1091.

Gilbert, A.G. (2002) 'Power, ideology and the Washington Consensus: the development and spread of Chilean housing policy', *Housing Studies*, 17: 305–324.

Gilbert, A.G. (2004) 'Helping the poor through housing subsidies: lessons from Chile, Colombia and South Africa', *Habitat International*, 28: 13–40.

Gilbert, A.G. (2009) 'Slums, tenants and home-ownership: on blindness to the obvious', *International Development Planning Review*, 30: i–x.

Gilbert, A.G., Camacho, O.O., Coulomb, R. and Necochea, A. (1993) *In Search of a Home*. London: UCL Press.

Grant, M. (2007) 'Lodging as a migrant economic strategy in urban Zimbabwe', *Development Southern Africa*, 24: 77–90.

Groves, R., Murie, A. and Watson, C. (eds) (2007) *Housing and the New Welfare State: Perspectives from East Asia and Europe*. London: Ashgate.

Guowei, G. (2007) 'Analysis of government policies for solving urban housing problems of poor families in China', *Trialog*, 94: 26–32.

Hegedüs, J. and Struyk, R.J. (eds) (2005) *Housing Finance: New and Old Models in Central Europe, Russia and Kazakhstan*. New York: Open Society Institute, LGI Books.

Held, G. (2000) *Políticas de vivienda de interés social orientadas al mercado: experiencias recientes con subsidios a la demanda en Chile, Costa Rica y Colombia*, CEPAL Serie Financiamiento del Desarrollo 96. Santiago: CEPAL.

Huang, Y. and Clark, W.A.V. (2002) 'Housing tenure choice in transitional urban China: a multilevel analysis', *Urban Studies*, 39: 7–32.

Huchzermeyer, M. (2003) 'A legacy of control: the capital subsidy for housing and informal settlement in South Africa', *International Journal of Urban and Regional Research*, 27: 591–612.

Huchzermeyer, M. (2007) 'Tenement city: the emergence of multi-storey districts through large-scale private landlordism in Nairobi', *International Journal of Urban and Regional Research*, 31: 714–732.

Kalim, S.I. (1990) Rent-control legislation and its impacts in Karachi, in UNCHS (1990) *Rental Housing: Proceedings of an Experts Group Meeting*, Nairobi.

Karki, T.K. (2002) 'Policies to improve the quality of life in the private rental housing of Kathmandu Metropolitan city' (mimeo).

Korboe, D. (1992) 'Family houses in Ghanaian cities: to be or not to be?', *Urban Studies*, 29: 1159–1172.

Kumar, S. (1996) 'Landlordism in Third World urban low-income settlements: a case for further research', *Urban Studies*, 33: 753–782.

Kumar, S. (2002) *Room for Manoeuvre: Tenure and the Urban Poor in India*. Online. Available at www.worldbank.org/urban/symposium2003/docs/presentations/kumar.pdf (accessed 20 May 2013).

Malpezzi, S. and Ball, G. (1991) 'Rent control in developing countries', *World Bank Discussion Papers* 129. Washington, DC: World Bank.

Martin, S.M. and Nell, M. Associates (2002) An assessment of rental housing in South Africa, report for USAID.

Mayo, S.K. (1999) *Subsidies in Housing*, Inter-American Development Bank, Sustainable Development Department Technical Papers Series.

Morange, M. (2002) 'Backyard shacks: the relative success of this housing option in Port Elisabeth', *Urban Forum*, 13: 3–25.

Morris, A. (1999) *Bleakness and Light: Inner-city Transition in Hillbrow, Johannesburg*. Johannesburg: Wits University Press.

Necochea, A. (1987) 'El allegamiento de los sin tierra, estrategia de supervivencia en vivienda', *Revista Latinoamericana de Estudios Urbanos–Regionales (EURE)*, 13–14: 85–100.
Randall, C. (2011) *Housing, Social Trends 41*. London: Office for National Statistics.
Rojas, E. (ed.) (2010) *Building Cities: Neighbourhood Upgrading and Urban Quality of Life*. Washington, DC: Inter-American Development Bank.
Ross, S.L. and Yinger, J. (2002) *The Color of Credit: Mortgage Discrimination, Research Methodology, and Fair-Lending Enforcement*. Cambridge, MA: MIT.
Silva Lerda, S. (1997) *Estudio Analisis de la evolución de la política habitacional chilena: informe final*. Santiago de Chile: MINVU.
Sims, D. (2002) 'What is secure tenure in urban Egypt?', in G. Payne (ed.) *Land, Rights and Innovation: Improving Security of Tenure for the Urban Poor*. London: ITDG Publishing.
Syagga, P., Mitullah, W. and Karirah-Gitau, S. (2002) 'A rapid appraisal of rents in slums and informal settlements, Government of Kenya and UN-Habitat Collaborative Nairobi Slum Upgrading Initiative' (mimeo).
The Economist (2003) 'The great Manhattan rip-off', 7 June.
Tran, H.A. and Dalholm, E. (2005) 'Favoured owners, neglected tenants: privatisation of state owned housing in Hanoi', *Housing Studies*, 20: 897–929.
Turner, J.F.C. (1968) 'Housing priorities, settlement patterns, and urban developing in modernizing countries', *Journal of the American Institute of Planners*, 34: 354–363.
UNCHS (1996) *An Urbanising World: Global Report on Human Settlements 1996*. Oxford: Oxford University Press.
UNCHS (2003) *Rental Housing: An Essential Option for the Urban Poor in Developing Countries*. Nairobi: UNHCS.
UN-Habitat (2011a) *A Policy Guide to Rental Housing in Developing Countries: Quick Policy Guide* series 1. Nairobi: UN-Habitat.
UN-Habitat (2011b) *Affordable Land and Housing in Europe and North America*. Nairobi: UN-Habitat.
United Nations (1979) *Review of Rent Control in Developing Countries*. New York: UN.
Voigtländer, M. (2009) 'Why is the German homeownership rate so low?', *Housing Studies*, 24: 355–372.
Wang, Y.P. (2007) 'From socialist welfare to support of home-ownership: the experience of China', in R. Groves, A. Murie and C. Watson (eds) *Housing and the New Welfare State: Perspectives from East Asia and Europe*. London: Ashgate.
Williams, A. (2007) 'Housing tenure choices among the young', *CML Housing Finance* 06.
Yu, Z. (2006) 'Heterogeneity and dynamics in China's emerging urban housing market: two sides of a success story from the late 1990s', *Habitat International*, 30: 277–304.

7
HOUSING COOPERATIVES IN THE DEVELOPING WORLD

Sukumar Ganapati

Abbreviations

CCU	Centro Cooperativista Uruguayo
CLT	Community land trust
CODI	Community Organizations Development Institute
COTU	Central Organization of Trade Unions
FECOVI	Federación De Cooperativas De Vivienda De Usuarios Por Ahorro Previo
FENACOVI	Federación Nacional de Cooperativas de Vivienda
FUCVAM	Federacion Uruguaya de Cooperetivas Vivienda por Ayuda Mutua
ICA	International Cooperative Alliance
NACHU	National Cooperative Housing Union
NCHF	National Cooperative Housing Federation
SAHCA	South African Housing Cooperative Association
SHF	Social Housing Foundation
UNCHS	United Nations Centre for Human Settlements
UN-Habitat	United Nations Human Settlements Programme

Introduction

Housing cooperatives have had a long history of evolution globally. They emerged in European countries in the late nineteenth century and have since been adopted by countries across other continents. The cooperatives have re-emerged as important organizational elements of housing in the face of the neoliberal policies that swept across developing countries during the early 1990s. The 'enabling' approach emphasized by the World Bank (1993) and the United Nations Centre for Human Settlements (now UN-Habitat) Global Shelter Strategy in 1988 (UNCHS 1996) sought to reduce the scope of the public sector as a provider, while enhancing the role of the private housing markets. With the retreat of the public sector, and the inability of the private sector to cater to low-income groups, third sector organizations like housing cooperatives gained significance in developing countries. This chapter provides an analysis of the role of housing cooperatives across the developing world, specifically in Asia, Latin America, and Africa. The purpose of the analysis is to highlight the common roles played by the cooperatives and to identify the specific institutional conditions that enhance these roles. The analysis is important since there is little systematic examination of the evolution of housing cooperatives across the developing world.

To analyse the housing cooperatives, I differentiate between *organizations* and *institutions* (North 1990). The organizational analysis focuses on the internal organizational characteristics and functions of the housing cooperatives; the institutional analysis examines the broader legal, social, and political economic context in which housing cooperatives evolve. Broadly, housing cooperatives are collective organizations formed for fulfilling shelter-related objectives, such as collective ownership and management, housing finance, building construction, land assembly, etc.

As collective organizations, cooperatives are regaining policy interest in developing countries. Recognizing the significance of housing cooperatives, the UN-Habitat (2000) carried out a broad assessment of cooperative housing strategies in eastern and southern African countries, such as Kenya, South Africa, Tanzania, Uganda, and Zimbabwe. Vakil's (1999) literature review of 30 cases of community-based organizations in Africa and Latin America between 1964 and 1994 shows that an overwhelming majority (22 of them) were organized as cooperatives. Newer forms of collective organizations, such as community land trusts, bear significant synergies with housing cooperatives (UN-Habitat 2012). The United Nations has recognized 2012 as the International Year of Cooperatives. Birchall (2003, 2004) argues that cooperatives are key organizational partners not only for reducing poverty, but also for attaining the Millennium Development Goals. In the housing sector, cooperatives are useful mechanisms for social housing and to foster community action (e.g. by empowering slum-dwellers).

As this chapter shows, housing cooperatives have had an uneven history across the world. At the institutional level, the broader legal and political economic system may or may not be conducive to the growth of housing cooperatives. The legal framework is important for the formation and functioning of cooperatives. Furthermore, institutional structures that support the cooperatives administratively, financially, and technically, including access to land, enhance the ability of housing cooperatives to increase their activities.

The rest of this chapter is structured as follows. The subsequent section highlights the organizational principles of housing cooperatives. Then, the evolution of housing cooperatives in Asia, Latin America, and Africa is examined. Next, the key roles played by housing cooperatives in developing countries are identified. After this, the roles of the institutional framework and the institutional structures in the growth of housing cooperatives are examined. Lastly, the chapter concludes with the institutional conditions for expanding the role of housing cooperatives in the developing world, particularly for low-income households.

Cooperative organizational principles

Cooperatives emerged in European countries in the nineteenth century. In England, consumer cooperative stores began in Rochdale in 1844. Different types of credit cooperatives (e.g. Schulze-Delitzsch, Raiffeisen) emerged in Germany in the 1850s (Guinnane 2001). The cooperatives have diffused across the developing world since then. The International Cooperative Alliance (ICA) formed in 1895 modified and adopted Rochdale principles to define an internationally accepted meaning of the cooperative. Currently, there are seven such cooperative principles: voluntary and open membership; democratic member control; member economic participation; autonomy and independence; education, training, and information; cooperation among cooperatives; and a concern for community. Viewed from their internal organizational principles, cooperatives are voluntary third sector associations (Silver 1991) that are distinct from the first (public) and the second (private) sectors. However, the characteristics of the cooperatives differ between countries based on the institutional context (Ganapati 2010; Ruonavaara 2005).

Two of the above principles are central to most cooperatives: collective ownership and democratic management. Collective ownership entails that members jointly own resources of the cooperative. Members collectively pool their investment resources in the cooperative for achieving certain common objectives. A member's investment is often in the form of share capital, but it could also be in the form of material inputs, labour, or land. Democratic management entails participation of members in monitoring the cooperative. Cooperatives are self-governing organizations, owned and managed by members as a group. Members share the cooperative's benefits. Democratic management implies that members have an equal voice in the decision-making process. That is, decisions are based on the 'one member, one vote' principle, unlike other shareholding firms where decisions are made based on a 'one share, one vote' principle.

In terms of housing, cooperatives entail collective ownership and management of one or more resources according to their housing objectives. In developing countries, generally three types of housing cooperative can be identified based on their housing objectives: tenure, building, and finance cooperatives. Tenure cooperatives are largely for collective ownership and management of housing. In this, cooperative housing is differentiated from condominiums: in a cooperative, the co-op owns the building, and members own shares in the co-op; in a condominium, the individual owns the housing unit. The distinction is, however, ambiguous in developing countries where individual ownership could exist under a cooperative nomenclature. The tenure cooperatives are also called continuing cooperatives since collective ownership is perpetual. Building cooperatives are oriented towards land development and housing construction. They are also called development cooperatives. Finance cooperatives mainly lend money to members for housing purposes. Of course, these three types of cooperative are not mutually exclusive or exhaustive. Hybrid cooperatives could be involved in housing construction, finance, and management as well. Informal cooperatives in developing countries function in similar ways as the formal cooperatives, albeit without formal legal recognition as cooperatives.

The democratic values of the collective lend themselves to mutual self-help in the cooperatives (Lewin 1981; UNCHS 1989). Indeed, cooperatives are important mechanisms for assisted self-help, bringing together state subsidies and individual responsibility through equity participation (Hermanson 1999; Mathéy 1992; Rondinelli 1990). Bredenoord and Van Lindert (2010) argue for assisted self-help, whereby the state could give basic (e.g. access to land) or additional (e.g. technical, microfinance opportunities) assistance. Self-help housing cooperatives could span across the functions of all three types of cooperative. Cooperatives enable self-help in construction, whereby members put in sweat equity for building or supervising the construction. Not paying wages to contractors or other skilled workers reduces the construction costs. In low-income communities, where individuals may have difficulty accessing formal credit, membership in cooperatives helps pool their resources (e.g. for financing, to buy materials) (Rondinelli 1990). Self-help in tenure cooperatives entails that the members collectively manage their housing developments themselves. Member participation in such management is arguably a key stepping stone towards community development and enhancing psychological ownership (Birchall 1988, 2003; Zeuli and Radel 2005).

Housing cooperatives in developing countries

Housing cooperatives in Asia

Housing cooperatives have been active in South Asia since the beginning of the twentieth century. The British introduced Raiffeisen type credit cooperatives as development organizations in the early twentieth century (Rhodes 2012). As Catanach (1970: 3) argues, the cooperatives were, 'to begin with, the creation of the state'. Wolff (1920: 11) observed that these cooperatives were clearly a product of government measures, so that the cooperative's 'character and its objects come to be altogether misunderstood by those for whose benefit it was introduced'. The Co-operative Societies Act passed in 1904 formed the basis of the emergence of credit cooperatives in British India (presently India and Pakistan). It established a key enduring pillar of the cooperative institutional structure – the Registrar's Office. The Registrar was a special government officer who controlled the development of cooperatives in each province. The Registrar's Office gained immense significance over the years and became pivotal for the development of cooperatives.

Housing cooperatives, which were active in mainly a few provinces (e.g. Bombay, Madras) before India's Independence in 1947, have boomed since then (Ganapati 2008). The number of primary housing cooperatives increased from 1,482 in 1950–1951 (Ganapati 2007) to nearly 100,000 in 2010–2011 (CECODHAS Housing Europe and ICA Housing 2012); the membership grew from under 1 million to nearly 7 million during the same period. Cooperatives contributed about 17 per cent of the housing stock during the 10th Five Year Plan period (2002–2007) (CECODHAS Housing Europe and ICA Housing 2012).

The National Cooperative Housing Federation (NCHF) formed in 1969 has been instrumental in establishing a nationwide two-tiered institutional structure of state level secondary Apex cooperatives to mobilize finance for primary cooperatives. The Apex cooperatives helped enhance the growth of primary housing cooperatives, despite the economic liberalization policies since the early 1990s when direct state support to cooperatives waned (Ganapati 2007). The forms of primary cooperatives vary across the states. The tenure cooperatives, also known as *tenant ownership* or *tenant co-partnership* housing societies, are active in Maharashtra and New Delhi. Finance cooperatives are principally in Tamil Nadu. Building cooperatives and other hybrid forms are also distributed across the country. Although cooperatives are active across other Asian countries, they are not as pronounced. In Pakistan, there were over 2,600 primary housing cooperatives with about 1.95 million members in 2011. Based on the township model, the cooperatives established large-scale residential developments on land provided by the state (CECODHAS Housing Europe and ICA Housing 2012). There is no nationwide institutional structure supporting cooperatives; cooperatives have grown to the extent provincial governments have supported them. Moreover, there have been intermittent bans on registration of new cooperatives due to corruption scandals (CECODHAS Housing Europe and ICA Housing 2012).

Cooperatives have been used in divergent ways as instruments of collective financing or land ownership in some East and Southeast Asian countries. In Thailand, the nationwide slum upgrading (*Baan Mankong*) programme, which supported over 1,000 communities, started with encouraging community savings groups and building networks of poor communities. A key aspect of the programme was to promote collective land ownership through community cooperatives that received low-interest loans from the Community Organizations Development Institute (CODI) (Boonyabancha 2009). The programme promoted shelter improvements while maintaining community cohesiveness (Archer 2012). In China, housing cooperatives emerged in the 1980s, but gained traction with housing reforms in the early 1990s. The government encouraged the cooperatives as joint investment mechanisms through the work units (*danwei*) as a part of the Economical and Comfortable Housing (ECH) programme (Deng et al. 2011). In this, individuals and work units invest in the cooperative housing schemes, while the state provides land and tax concessions (Zhang 2006).

Housing cooperatives in Latin America

Among Latin American countries, Uruguay's housing cooperatives are hailed as a model for mutual assistance. Unlike the Asian countries where the state played a key role in setting up cooperatives, the *Centro Cooperativista Uruguayo* (CCU), a non-profit organization founded by Catholic activists, played a catalytic role in Uruguay. Housing cooperatives became a significant social movement in the country, championing public participation, solidarity, and even resisting the state (Canel 2010; Frens-String 2011; Oliver 2012).

The landmark National Housing Law (13.728) of 1968 provided the legal basis for cooperatives to emerge. The CCU strongly influenced the inclusion of cooperatives as means for social housing for workers, which then helped establish a firm place for cooperatives in the country's housing market in the long run. The law enabled collective ownership rights and identified two cooperative models: the *ahorro previo* model for middle-income households to pool their collective savings and construct cooperative neighbourhoods; and the *mutual aid* model of self-help, mutual assistance housing for low-income households (Frens-String 2011). The CCU facilitated the formation of the *Federación Nacional de Cooperativas de Vivienda* (FENACOVI) and the *Federacion Uruguaya de Cooperetivas Vivienda por Ayuda Mutua* (FUCVAM) to support the two types of cooperatives, respectively (Canel 2010).

Housing cooperatives grew remarkably in the early 1970s, contributing over 40 per cent of the housing stock (Khor and Lin 2001). However, the activities of cooperatives were dampened during the civil-military dictatorship between 1973 and 1985, when the regime adopted neoliberal free-market policies, pre-empting collective efforts of cooperatives and labour unions. FENACOVI, for example was dissolved during this period (but it was later reconstituted to become *Federación De Cooperativas De Vivienda De Usuarios Por Ahorro Previo*, FECOVI in 1984). Other constraints on financing and collective ownership rights affected cooperative activities drastically. The share of cooperatives to the housing stock reduced to 10 per cent by 1979 (Khor and Lin 2001). After the military regime ended, cooperatives began to limp back assisted by their political efforts to be included in the national housing strategies.

Despite the challenges, FUCVAM and FECOVI have been actively promoting housing cooperatives in the country. The number of housing cooperatives grew from 365 in 1989 to 581 in 2009 and accounted for nearly half of the cooperatives in Uruguay (Instituto Nacional de Estadística 2009). The FUCVAM model received the 2012 World Habitat Award and has been emulated in Brazil, Paraguay, Bolivia, El Salvador, Nicaragua, Honduras, and Guatemala; it is also being explored in Argentina, Chile, Costa Rica, Cuba, Ecuador, Haiti, Peru, and

Venezuela. Although cooperatives are increasingly adopted by selected communities in these countries, laws enabling cooperatives need to be strengthened (Fruet 2005).

Housing cooperatives in Africa

In Africa, cooperatives emerged in the 1960s when the countries gained independence and sought collective solutions to address development issues. Similar to South Asia, the governments have had a heavy hand in establishing and regulating cooperatives. Economic liberalization with structural adjustment policies during the 1990s sought to emphasize 'enabling' housing policies, reducing government's directive involvement in cooperatives and housing (UNCHS 1996; World Bank 1993). Since then, various international and non-governmental organizations (NGOs) have promoted cooperatives as independent third sector means of development (Develtere et al. 2008). The UN-Habitat (2000) recognized the importance of housing cooperatives within the enabling strategy. The International Labor Office (ILO) initiated the CoopAfrica programme as a regional technical cooperation programme in 2007 to mobilize the cooperatives as self-help mechanisms and to improve their governance, efficiency, and performance. Many African countries have since revised their cooperative laws over the past two decades.

Although uneven, housing cooperatives have increasingly become active in several African countries. In South Africa, housing cooperatives formally emerged only in the late 1990s (Rust 2001). Cooperatives have been increasingly promoted as means of social housing in the post-apartheid era for low- and moderate-income households. A concept similar to housing cooperatives was utilized in the People's Housing Process (PHP), a self-help social housing policy (Marais et al. 2008). The Social Housing Foundation (SHF), a non-profit set up in collaboration with the National Department of Housing in 1997 and funded by international organizations, has been instrumental in promoting the role of cooperatives as a means of collective ownership and secure tenure (SHF 2009). The SHF identified two types of housing cooperative – *continuous* housing cooperatives (which collectively own and govern the housing on a long-term basis, akin to tenure cooperatives) and *development* housing cooperatives (which collectively develop housing for individual ownership, akin to building cooperatives). The SHF helped set up the South African Housing Cooperative Association (SAHCA) in 2004 in order to facilitate primary housing cooperatives, to strengthen support services to them, and to share knowledge among them.

In Kenya, housing cooperatives emerged in the 1980s with the establishment of the National Cooperative Housing Union (NACHU) in 1979 as a technical service organization. Housing cooperatives boomed during the 1990s, from 20 in 1990 to 424 in 2000 (reaching 512 in 2005) (UN-Habitat 2010). Kenya's housing cooperative activities are closely linked with the Apex cooperative. In 2011, NACHU had more than 390 registered housing cooperatives as members (NACHU 2012). NACHU came about through an initiative of the Central Organization of Trade Unions (COTU) which wanted to facilitate improved housing for its members (Alder and Munene 2001). It provides technical services as well as capacity building programmes to its member primary cooperatives. NACHU's main focus is on shelter for low-income communities. Financially supported by international organizations, NACHU has been notably engaged in providing microfinance loans (Houston 2010; Merrill et al. 2007).

Housing cooperatives have had a niche in a few other African countries. In Egypt, housing cooperatives grew from 1,660 in 1996 to 1,987 in 2005, spurred by the government-subsidized loans to housing cooperatives (CECODHAS Housing Europe and ICA Housing 2012; Fahmi and Sutton 2008). Over the past decade, cooperatives have sought more autonomy in the new economic environment and have advocated for new cooperative laws. A similar push for new cooperative laws is also apparent in Ethiopia, where housing cooperatives gained ground under the auspices of the Derg military regime following the 1974 revolution (Tesfaye 2007). Government assistance in terms of access to land and subsidized financing assisted in the cooperatives' growth initially. Housing cooperatives grew from 51 in 1978 to over 3,800 in 2008 (Emana 2009; Fisseha 1987). In Senegal, housing cooperatives grew mainly as a social movement during the 1990s in the face of the decline in housing provided by the state-affiliated housing associations. In 2005, there were over 600 housing cooperatives affiliated with the *Union Nationale des Coopératives d'Habitat*, the national Apex cooperative for housing (Fall 2008). Similar to Senegal, housing cooperatives grew as a movement in Zimbabwe during the 1990s (Kamete 2001, 2006).

Roles of housing cooperatives

As the above section shows, cooperatives play diverse roles in developing countries. Yet, two important and distinctive roles may be highlighted. First, the organizational characteristics of housing cooperatives and their role as social housing mechanisms for low- and moderate-income households should be noted. Second, housing cooperatives are useful vehicles for building community. In particular, cooperatives are used to organize slum-dwellers into informal or formal collectives to obtain group credit and to build self-help housing.

Cooperatives as means for low-income housing

Organizationally, the main emphasis of cooperatives is on the collective organization and management. Housing cooperatives are not specifically oriented towards any income group per se. On one hand, cooperatives have been used by high-income groups for housing exclusivity (e.g. New York; see Maldonado and Rose 1996). On the other hand, cooperatives have been vehicles for social housing, particularly in housing low- and moderate-income households. With the retreat of public housing for low-income households, and the inability of the private sector to accommodate these households, cooperatives have been viewed by developing countries as a mechanism to foster low-income housing (Fruet 2005). Yet, the use of cooperatives across the income groups could be useful in averting the stigma of cooperatives as solely low-income projects. At the same time, the high-income cooperatives may have more capacity to set up institutional support structures.

Can housing cooperatives bring affordable housing solutions in the developing world? Cooperatives hold several advantages for affordable housing to low-income households (Ganapati 2001; Saegert and Benítez 2005). First, cooperatives entail pooling of resources in the collective, which lowers the individual housing costs that each household would otherwise incur. Cooperatives provide a scope for scale economy in land, building materials, construction, financing, management, service provision, and other housing activities. Second, cooperatives entail member participation; the self-responsibility is mutually beneficial for members to reduce their housing costs. Third, credit worthiness of households rises due to collective pooling of resources. While the cooperative can capitalize on the collectively owned land and buildings, individual members can borrow money secured by their cooperative shares. Fourth, cooperatives assist in limiting speculation since the cooperative could potentially limit the capital gains accruing to the member. Limited equity cooperatives, in particular, keep housing affordable by having the first right to refuse the purchase of a unit, by controlling the maximum price, or by putting income limits on the purchasers. Similarly, when members sell a house in cooperative land banks, the cooperative appropriates a part of the sale proceeds for the collectively owned common property; the household obtains the rest of the value, including the value of the housing unit (Turnbull 1983).

Empirically, housing cooperatives have indeed been used for housing low-income households. The cases of India, Uruguay, South Africa, and Kenya show that cooperatives have been used as means of such social housing. Cooperatives directly construct and maintain the housing, or provide finance, or both. However, the cooperatives do not reach down to the very low-income strata. The very low-income households require other public means of housing.

Cooperatives as means for building community

One of the seven core principles of cooperatives is the concern for community. While the cooperative builds internal ties between members, the members are also expected to have solidarity with the broader community. The cooperative principles are amenable to building social capital (Putnam *et al.* 1993). The social capital engendered in the cooperatives is useful on several fronts. The housing cooperatives in Uruguay are particularly good examples of how solidarity formed a basic tenet. Cities around the developing world have adopted housing cooperatives to foster community action. In Mumbai, dilapidated buildings because of rent control have been turned over to sitting tenants for building maintenance (Dua 1991). Public housing programmes in Navi Mumbai have also used cooperatives as a mechanism for collective ownership and management of the allocated housing.

Community land trusts (CLTs), which are often organized as cooperatives, are mechanisms both for affordable housing as well as for fostering community action (UN-Habitat 2012). In CLTs, the land is collectively owned and managed, but members own the houses. The CLT model has been tried out in an informal settlement near Nairobi, albeit with limited success (Bassett 2005). Eco-villages, which are environmentally sustainable communities, are also usually organized as cooperatives (Dawson 2006; Jackson and Svensson 2002).

A notable use of cooperatives is in fostering community action and to ensure tenure security in slums, which are informal settlements where the residents typically do not have title to the land. Since the slum-dwellers do not own the land, they are under a constant threat of being evicted. Security of land tenure is therefore a crucial issue in slums. Slum-dwellers often form a large share (20–50 per cent) of the city's population in developing countries. Cooperatives have increasingly emerged as collective mechanisms to empower slum-dwellers and to give them a voice (Patel *et al.* 2002). Imparato and Ruster (2003) highlight how cooperatives have enabled community participation and slum upgrading in Latin American cities. Cooperatives also enable slum-dwellers to form informal credit groups and microfinance (Oyewole 2010). Such cooperatives assist in the economic advancement of the slum-dwellers, by allowing them to borrow capital for their small businesses (i.e. microenterprise development).

Cooperatives are useful organizational vehicles for self-help housing across the cities in the developing world. In this, cooperatives organize the members into self-help groups. The groups then put their sweat equity into the housing construction to increase its affordability. These self-help groups in slums are used as collective mechanisms for securing cooperative land tenure. Such cooperative land tenure arrangements for slums have been organized across cities in Asia, Africa, and Latin America (Archer 2012; Boonyabancha 2009; UN-Habitat 2011). Mumbai's slum redevelopment policies explicitly envisaged formation of cooperatives among the residents to give them tenure security. The Baan Mankong programme in Bangkok similarly entailed the formation of cooperatives. Similar measures have also been undertaken in Argentina, South Africa, Kenya, Senegal, and other countries.

Institutional context

The institutional level analysis deals with the structural constraints and opportunities in the development of housing cooperatives. Institutions form the matrix of rules that act as *constraints* as well as *opportunities* for organizations like housing cooperatives to evolve. Rules are prescriptions that 'refer to which actions are required, prohibited, or permitted' (Ostrom 1986: 5). The institutional framework forms the incentive structure in which housing cooperatives are embedded (North 1990). Two related aspects of the institutional context can be highlighted for the growth of housing cooperatives. First, the cooperative laws need to ensure the autonomy of housing cooperatives. Second, the cooperative supportive institutional structures could enhance the activities of housing cooperatives.

Political economic environment

In many Asian and African countries, cooperatives gained patronage of the socialist states that had emerged when the countries gained independence after World War II (Birchall 2004). A similar strong state influence persisted in Latin American countries, except in a few countries in the southern cone (Argentina, Chile, and Uruguay, including Brazil) where the European immigrants influenced a more autonomous model of cooperative movement (ILO 2001). The developing country governments encouraged cooperatives through subsidies and other incentives. Housing cooperatives were given preferential treatment. In the process, however, cooperatives were also politically co-opted and acted as parastatals. Cooperatives became state organs, and developed in directions where the states laid an emphasis.

Cooperative laws reflected the role of the state in the developing countries. The laws interfered with the member control and democratic decision-making process, intruding even into the day-to-day operations of the cooperatives. In India, for example, the Cooperative Registrars, who are appointed by the state governments, have been said to be the gods of 'birth, life, and death' of cooperatives. In many countries, the cooperatives were effectively another arm of the state or the ruling party. Cooperatives were top-down, rather than bottom-up social movements (except in Uruguay, where the cooperatives maintained adversarial relations with the state).

With the onset of structural adjustment policies and economic liberalization programmes during the 1990s, government support to the cooperatives diminished across the developing world (Birchall 2004). The cooperatives began to seek more autonomy in their activities for their survival in the competitive environment. Indeed, one of the ICA's cooperative principles – autonomy and independence – emerged in 1995, mainly to be free from government interference in their day-to-day operations. The legal framework to allow housing cooperatives to perform autonomously is a critical requirement for their ability to perform different activities without state interference. Ganapati (2010) argues for embedded autonomy, characterized by a balance between ties with the state and cooperatives' autonomy. Many countries around the world have recognized that cooperatives need autonomy and have begun to revise their laws. India adopted a constitutional amendment in 2011 to provide autonomy to cooperatives. Other Asian countries have similarly revised cooperative laws. In Latin America, the Uruguayan model of housing cooperatives is promoted in other countries by international agencies partly because of their autonomous operations. In Africa, the CoopAfrica programme explicitly promotes cooperative autonomy through Recommendation 193. Several African countries have passed new cooperative legislations over the past two decades.

Supportive institutional structures

Institutional structure refers to the *manifest arrangement of relationships between organizations.* In the context of cooperatives, the cooperative institutional structure refers to the mutually beneficial organizational support systems, such as Apex or secondary umbrella organizations that assist primary cooperatives. The supportive structure enhances the internal organizational strengths, while overcoming the concurrent weaknesses of cooperatives. At the same time, the structure helps in the formation and functioning of housing cooperatives. A supportive institutional structure provides a reinforcing mechanism for organizations to persist and to enhance their activities.

The institutional structure could support development of housing cooperatives in three specific ways. First, the institutional structure could provide administrative, legal, technical, and procedural support, including education to members. Providing such support could enhance the internal strengths while overcoming the internal weaknesses of cooperatives. Administrative support could facilitate primary cooperatives to overcome some of the collective action problems inherent in cooperatives, especially in terms of monitoring and educating the members about management practices. Legal support could reduce the conflicts that arise between members or between members and cooperatives. Technical support is crucial for navigating the real estate market, obtaining building materials, dealing with contractors, and other construction/finance issues. Lastly, procedural support could be in the form of establishing routine procedures for formation and functioning of cooperatives. Such support is crucial for reducing the transaction costs of formation and functioning of housing cooperatives.

Second, the institutional structure could enhance access to finance, which is a key component of housing. As cooperatives are member organizations, they usually raise their finances through their members. However, given the inherent characteristics of the housing market in terms of dedicated assets and lumpy investments, finance raised through members needs to be leveraged with external funding for adequate investment in housing. Cooperatives could also face obstacles in obtaining such finance in the open market, i.e. their transaction costs for obtaining finance could be high. In the absence of external financial support, cooperatives could grow only to the extent they are able to mobilize finance internally for productive housing investments.

Third, the institutional structure could enhance access to land, which is another key component of housing. As the housing market is characterized by a high degree of site specificity, cooperatives typically require large parcels of land for contiguous housing development. Cooperatives could face high transaction costs in access to such large parcels. If such land were unavailable, development of cooperatives may be limited. Thus, both housing finance and land are two critical factors of housing where exogenous institutional support is required to enhance the activities of housing cooperatives.

Three distinct models of the institutional structure could be identified in Asia, Latin America, and Africa. The South Asian model is dominated by the state, whereby the state assists in setting up the support institutional infrastructure. In British colonial countries, the Cooperative Registrars are government appointees who play a crucial role in the development of cooperatives. Additional support structures have a state imprint too. In India, the National Cooperative Housing Federation (NCHF) is a national Apex cooperative established by the Indian government to help set up state level secondary Apex cooperatives in the country. The secondary Apex cooperatives provide financial support to primary cooperatives and their members by mobilizing resources from various other funding agencies (e.g. National Housing Bank, Housing and Urban Development Corporation, etc.). The national institutional structure has helped stimulate the growth of cooperatives nationwide (Ganapati 2007).

In the Latin American model, the cooperatives are a social movement that gathered momentum over time. In Uruguay, the FUCVAM emerged as a secondary cooperative to support the functioning of primary housing cooperatives. It provides technical and financial support to primary cooperatives, including financing social facilities such as gymnasiums, recreation centres, day-care centres, libraries, sports fields, and playgrounds. FUCVAM was initially a product of Uruguay's labour movement, but became a quickly growing autonomous cooperative housing movement. It has also been engaged in political activism, often with antagonistic relationships to the government (Canel 2010).

In the third model of African countries, cooperatives are promoted by national and international agencies and NGOs. The ILO, Canadian Housing Foundation, the Rooftops (a Canadian non-profit), and the Swedish Cooperative Centre are some of international agencies that have promoted housing cooperatives across several African countries. Critics argue that the cooperatives may not be viable after the international NGOs exit, i.e. the cooperatives need to have innate capacity to manage and develop. Yet, in a few countries (e.g. South Africa), local NGOs have also stepped in to promote the cooperatives. A few African countries have national Apex cooperatives to provide support to the primary housing cooperatives. For example, in Kenya, the National Cooperative Housing Union (NACHU) has served as the national Apex body to provide a range of support services to primary cooperatives (financial services, technical assistance, estate management, and advocacy) (UN-Habitat 2010).

Conclusion

Housing cooperatives have grown across South Asia, Latin America, and Africa since the 1990s. The cooperatives' growth since the 1990s is remarkable in the context of economic liberalization policies in general, and the enabling housing policies in particular, which prescribed retreat of the state from being a direct provider of housing. Housing cooperatives have regained significance in the developing world as collective mechanisms to fill the gap left by the public and the private sectors. As collective organizations, the housing cooperatives are not only instruments of collective ownership, but are also mechanisms of housing finance and construction in the developing world.

Although cooperatives are not specifically oriented towards any particular income group, they have demonstrated the potential for low-income households. Such potential is evident in India, Uruguay, Kenya, and South Africa, to name a few countries. Cooperatives are particularly useful in developing countries as collective action mechanisms for self-help housing in slum areas. Local governments in India and Thailand, for example, have provided collective tenure through cooperatives to slum-dwellers. Cooperatives could be effective in limiting speculation by keeping a part of the capital gains within the organization. They could assist low-income households and slum-dwellers in obtaining credit.

Different models of housing cooperative for low-income households or slum-dwellers could indeed be expanded to other countries. The Uruguay model, for example, has been emulated in 15 other countries. Yet, the institutional context matters for expanding the role of housing cooperatives. First, there is a need for cooperative autonomy to expand their activities along different dimensions. Extremes of overt government control or total government neglect of cooperatives stifle their operations; the state–cooperative relations need to be characterized by a balance between ties with the state and cooperatives' autonomy. Second, cooperative institutional structures need to emerge to provide a long-term sustainable environment for housing cooperatives to grow. These structures could provide support to cooperatives in different ways, including administrative, legal, financial, and other types of assistance (e.g. lower labour and material costs). The form of such institutional structures may vary between countries, as illustrated by the broad differences in the structures between Asian, Latin American, and African countries.

References

Alder, G. and Munene, P. (2001) *Shelter Co-operatives in Kenya (Report No. HS/614/01E)*. Nairobi: UN-Habitat.
Archer, D. (2012) 'Baan Mankong participatory slum upgrading in Bangkok, Thailand: Community perceptions of outcomes and security of tenure', *Habitat International*, 36:178–84.
Bassett, E.M. (2005) 'Tinkering with tenure: the community land trust experiment in Voi, Kenya', *Habitat International*, 29: 375–398.
Birchall, J. (1988) *Building Communities the Co-operative Way*. London: Routledge.
Birchall, J. (2003) *Rediscovering the Cooperative Advantage: Poverty Reduction through Self-help*. Geneva: International Labor Office.
Birchall, J. (2004) *Cooperatives and the Millennium Development Goals*. Geneva: International Labor Office.
Boonyabancha, S. (2009) 'Land for housing the poor – by the poor: experiences from the Baan Mankong nationwide slum upgrading programme in Thailand', *Environment and Urbanization*, 17: 21–46.
Bredenoord, J. and Van Lindert, P. (2010) 'Pro-poor housing policies: rethinking the potential of assisted self-help housing', *Habitat International*, 34: 278–287.
Canel, E. (2010) *Barrio Democracy in Latin America: Participatory Decentralization and Community Activism in Montevideo*. University Park, PA: Pennsylvania State University Press.
Catanach, I.J. (1970) *Rural Credit in Western India, 1875–1930; Rural Credit and the Co-operative Movement in the Bombay Presidency*. Berkeley: University of California Press.
CECODHAS Housing Europe and ICA Housing (2012) *Profiles of a Movement: Co-operative Housing around the World*. Online. Available at www.housingeurope.eu/issue/2577 (accessed 10 September 2012).
Dawson, J. (2006) *Ecovillages: New Frontiers for Sustainability*. White River Junction, VT: Chelsea Green Publishing Company.
Deng, L., Shen, Q., and Wang, L. (2011) 'The emerging housing policy framework in China', *Journal of Planning Literature*, 26: 168–183.
Develtere, P., Pollet, I., and Wanyama, F. (eds) (2008) *Cooperating out of Poverty: The Renaissance of the African Cooperative Movement*. Geneva: International Labor Office.

Dua, A. (1991) *Management of Bombay's Housing Renewal Programme (Research Report 27)*. New Delhi: Indian Human Settlements Programme.

Emana, B. (2009) 'Cooperatives: a path to economic and social empowerment in Ethiopia' *(CoopAFRICA Working Paper No. 9)*, Dar es Salaam: International Labor Office.

Fahmi, W. and Sutton, K. (2008) 'Greater Cairo's housing crisis: contested spaces from inner city areas to new communities', *Cities*, 25: 277–297.

Fall, A.S. (2008) 'The Senegalese cooperative movement: embedded in the social economy', in P. Develtere, I. Pollet, and F. Wanyama (eds) *Cooperating out of Poverty: The Renaissance of the African Cooperative Movement*. Geneva: ILO.

Fisseha, W. (1987) 'Analysis and evaluation of housing programs in Ethiopia: 1976–1986', unpublished thesis, Rice University.

Frens-String, J. (2011) 'Revolution through reform: popular assemblies, housing cooperatives, and Uruguay's new left', *Contemporanea*, 2: 11–30. Online. Available at www.geipar.udelar.edu.uy/wp-content/uploads/2012/07/Frens-String.pdf (accessed 10 September 2012)

Fruet, G.M. (2005) 'The low-income housing cooperatives in Porto Alegre, Brazil: a state/community partnership', *Habitat International*, 29: 303–324.

Ganapati, S. (2001) 'Potential of housing cooperatives for low income households: the case of Mumbai, Chennai, and Delhi', *Habitat International*, 25: 147–174.

Ganapati, S. (2007) 'Institutional analysis of growth of housing cooperatives in India', in N. Verma (ed.) *Institutions and Planning*. Amsterdam: Elsevier.

Ganapati, S. (2008) 'A century of differential evolution of housing cooperatives in Mumbai and Chennai', *Housing Studies*, 23: 403–422.

Ganapati, S. (2010) 'Enabling housing cooperatives: lessons from Sweden, India, and the United States', *International Journal of Urban and Regional Research*, 34: 365–380.

Guinnane, T.W. (2001) 'Cooperatives as information machines: German rural credit cooperatives, 1883–1914', *The Journal of Economic History*, 61: 366–389.

Hermanson, J.A. (1999) 'Cooperative housing around the world: examples and experience', *1999 Cooperative Housing Journal: Articles of Lasting Value for Leaders of Cooperative Housing*, 14–20.

Houston, A. (2010) *Housing Support Services for Housing Microfinance Lending in East and Southern Africa: A Case Study of the National Cooperative Housing Union (NACHU)*. Online. Available at www.housingfinanceafrica.org/wp-content/uploads/2012/03/NACHU-case-study1.pdf (accessed 10 September 2012)

ILO (International Labor Office) (2001) *Promotion of Cooperatives*. Geneva, ILO. Online. Available at www.ilo.org/public/english/standards/relm/ilc/ilc89/pdf/rep-v-2.pdf (accessed 10 September 2012)

Imparato, I. and Ruster, R. (2003) *Slum Upgrading and Participation: Lessons from Latin America*. Washington, DC: World Bank.

Instituto Nacional de Estadística (2009) *Censo Nacional de Cooperativas y Sociedades de Fomento Rural, 2008–2009*. Montevideo: Instituto Nacional de Estadística – División Normalización, Investigación y Proyectos. Online. Available at www.ine.gub.uy/biblioteca/censoCoop_2008–2009/Censo-Nacional-de-Cooperativas.pdf (accessed 10 September 2012)

Jackson, H. and Svensson, K. (eds) (2002) *Ecovillage Living: Restoring the Earth and Her People*. Devon: Green Books.

Kamete, A.Y. (2001) 'Civil society, housing and urban governance: the case of urban housing co-operatives in Zimbabwe', in T. Arne, I. Tvedten, and M. Vaa (eds) *Associational Life in African Cities: Popular Responses to the Urban Crisis*. Uppsala: Nordiska Afrikainstitutet.

Kamete, A.Y. (2006) 'Revisiting the urban housing crisis in Zimbabwe: some forgotten dimensions?', *Habitat International*, 30: 981–995.

Khor, M. and Lin, L.L. (eds) (2001) *Good Practices and Innovative Experiences in the South (Vol. 3): Citizen Initiatives in Social Services, Popular Education and Human*. London and New York: Zed Books.

Lewin, A.C. (1981) *Housing Co-operatives in Developing Countries: A Manual for Self-Help in Low-Cost Housing Schemes*, Chichester and Toronto: Wiley and Intermediate Technology Publications.

Maldonado, R. and Rose, R.D. (1996) 'Application of civil rights laws to housing cooperatives: are co-ops bastions of discriminatory exclusion or self-selecting models of community-based living?', *Fordham Urban Law Journal*, 23: 1245–1282.

Marais, L., Ntema, J., and Venter, A. (2008) 'State control in self-help housing: evidence from South Africa', paper presented at the European Housing Network Research Conference, Ireland, 6–9 July. Online. Available at www.hsrc.ac.za/Research_Publication-20686.phtml (accessed 10 September 2012)

Mathéy, K. (1992) *Beyond Self-Help Housing*. London and New York: Mansell.

Merrill, S., Wambugu, A., and Johnston, C. (2007) 'Housing for the poor in Kenya: NACHU's cooperative approach', *USAID MicroNote #38*. Online. Available at http://microlinks.kdid.org/sites/microlinks/files/resource/files/ML5456_mn_38_housing_for_the_poor_in_kenya.pdf (accessed 10 September 2012)

NACHU (National Housing Cooperative Union) (2012) 'About Us'. Online. Available at www.nachu.or.ke/index.php/about-us/about-us-2 (accessed 10 September 2012)

North, D. (1990) *Institutions, Institutional Change and Economic Performance*. Cambridge: Cambridge University Press.

Oliver, M. (2012) 'To buy or not to buy? Mutual assistance housing cooperatives in Uruguay and the challenges of shifting ideologies', *SlideShow and The Inquiry*, 76–86. Online. Available at http://cenhum.artsci.wustl.edu/slideshow-inquiry-2012 (accessed 10 September 2012).

Ostrom, E. (1986) 'An agenda for the study of institutions', *Public Choice*, 48: 3–25.

Oyewole, M.O. (2010) 'Housing development finance through cooperative societies: the case of Ogbomoso, Nigeria', *International Journal of Housing Markets and Analysis*, 3: 245–255.

Patel, S., D'Cruz, C., and Burra, S. (2002) 'Beyond evictions in a global city: people-managed resettlement in Mumbai', *Environment and Urbanization*, 14: 159–172.

Putnam, R.D., Leonardi, R., and Nanetti, R. (1993) *Making Democracy Work: Civic Traditions in Modern Italy*. Princeton: Princeton University Press.

Rhodes, R. (2012) *Empire and Co-Operation: How the British Empire Used Co-Operatives in Its Development Strategies 1900–1970*. Edinburgh: John Donald.

Rondinelli, D.A. (1990) 'Housing the urban poor in developing countries', *American Journal of Economics and Sociology*, 49: 257–269.

Ruonavaara, H. (2005) 'How divergent housing institutions evolve: a comparison of Swedish tenant co-operatives and Finnish shareholders' Housing Companies', *Housing, Theory and Society*, 22: 213–236

Rust, K. (2001) *Shelter Co-Operatives in South Africa (Report No. HS/615/01 E)*. Nairobi: UN-Habitat.

Saegert, S. and Benítez, L. (2005) 'Limited equity housing cooperatives: defining a niche in the low-income housing market', *Journal of Planning Literature*, 19: 427–439.

SHF (Social Housing Foundation) (2009). *Emerging Co-Operative Housing Models in South Africa*. Online. Available at www.rooftops.ca/CMSImages/file/Emerging%20Coop%20Housing%20Models%20in%20South%20Africa.pdf (accessed 10 September 2012).

Silver, H. (1991) 'State, market, and community: housing co-operatives in theoretical perspective', *Netherlands Journal of Housing and the Built Environment*, 6: 185–203.

Tesfaye, A. (2007) 'Problems and prospects of housing development in Ethiopia', *Property Management*, 25: 27–53.

Turnbull, S. (1983) 'Co-operative land banks for low-income housing', in S. Angel, R.W. Archer, S. Tanphiphat, and E. Wegelin (eds) *Land for Housing the Poor*. Singapore: Select Books.

UNCHS (United Nations Centre for Human Settlements) (1989) *Cooperative Housing: Experiences of Mutual Self-Help*. Nairobi: UNCHS.

UNCHS (United Nations Centre for Human Settlements) (1996) *An Urbanizing World: Global Report on Human Settlements*. Oxford: Oxford University Press.

UN-Habitat (2000) *Shelter Co-Operatives in Eastern and Southern Africa, Report No. HS/602/00 E*. Nairobi: UN-Habitat.

UN-Habitat (2010) *The Organisation, Management and Finance of Housing Cooperatives in Kenya*. Nairobi: UN-Habitat.
UN-Habitat (2011) *Affordable Land and Housing in Latin America and the Caribbean*. Nairobi: UN-Habitat.
UN-Habitat (2012) *Community Land Trusts: Affordable Access to Land and Housing*. Nairobi: UN-Habitat.
Vakil, A.C. (1999) 'Problems and prospects of housing CBOs: an analysis of 30 case studies from Africa and Latin America, 1964–1994', *Cities*, 16: 409–422.
Wolff, H.W. (1920) *Indian Cooperative Studies*. Bombay: Oxford University Press.
World Bank (1993) *Housing: Enabling Markets to Work*, Washington, DC: World Bank.
Zeuli, K. and Radel, R. (2005) 'Cooperatives as a community development strategy: linking theory and practice', *Journal of Regional Analysis and Policy*, 35: 43–54.
Zhang, X.Q. (2006) 'Institutional transformation and marketisation: the changing patterns of housing investment in urban China', *Habitat International*, 30: 327–341.

8

THE TRANSNATIONAL EXPERIENCE OF COMMUNITY-LED DEVELOPMENT

The affordable shelter challenge

Beth Chitekwe-Biti, Sheela Patel and Diana Mitlin

Introduction: the challenge of affordability

What are the considered and aggregated experiences of the urban poor in effective shelter delivery, and what does this suggest for housing policy? This chapter will use the experiences of Shack/Slum Dwellers International (SDI) to inform debates on how to address the shelter needs of the 1 billion who are currently lacking safe and secure homes in towns and cities in the Global South. Given the constraints of space, we have chosen to focus on one particularly critical aspect, that of affordability. In this chapter, we discuss how SDI affiliates in the cities of Harare and Mumbai have sought to design housing interventions that enable the participation of even their lowest-income members, blending local action with global support to secure political commitment to pro-poor change.

Shack/Slum Dwellers International is a transnational network of grassroots organizations and federations whose membership now includes 29 affiliates with 17 federations working in 388 cities and involving over 1.1 million savers (UPFI 2011). Membership is made up of primarily informal neighbourhood groups or savings schemes who federate to work at the city and national scale. These local groups are women-led savings schemes located in informal settlements. Activities centre on addressing insecure tenure, basic services and, in some contexts, housing and/or income generation. Savings schemes are constituted by all those who want to save, and savings can be as much or as little as the member chooses; what is emphasized is regularity of savings with the strongest schemes offering the opportunity to save every day. Community savings are used to re-constitute social capital; peer exchanges offer skills, ambition and confidence to the urban poor; and federative structures institutionalize learning and negotiate political deals with local, city and national governments (Appadurai 2001). Multiple experiences with community savings suggest that women find it a more attractive strategy than men (Mitlin *et al.* 2011) and in SDI savings groups, men typically make up only about 10 per cent of the members. Regardless of who saves, savings help to provide a financial contribution to the costs of improved housing. What is remarkable is the rapid spread of SDI's organizing methodologies: ten years ago, there were just six SDI affiliates.

As a network of federations of savings schemes, SDI's work is supported by six international coordinators (two professional and four community leaders), a small secretariat based in Cape Town, a Council of federations that meets every nine months and a Board elected by the Council. The network assists members' activities, manages investment capital through the Urban Poor Fund International (UPFI) (a donor-financed facility) and supports members to have an international voice. Most critically it supports the local actions of savers through horizontal peer community exchanges that teach skills and improve capabilities, assist negotiations with local authorities and simply help as is needed.

SDI affiliates have significant experience in shelter improvements including both greenfield site development and *in situ* upgrading. Shelter improvements are essential for many of their members who face unsafe and insecure housing with uncertain tenure, inadequate infrastructure and basic services, and dwellings which often require temporary repairs to make them habitable. SDI affiliates are anxious to ensure that solutions can go to scale and be inclusive, despite considerable and acute income poverty. For many SDI affiliates, government support is rare and SDI affiliates face a considerable challenge in identifying effective shelter improvement strategies. Savings schemes design solutions that mean they can begin work immediately, but remain conscious of the need for scale and so engage with the complexities of regulatory reform and policy improvements (UN-Habitat 2005). Affiliates are clear that substantive progress necessarily involves the state both for financial subsidies and policy reform (McFarlane 2004). Policy and regulatory reform is needed to reduce costs and enable local communities to control the development process. Savings schemes members know that the most cost-effective and appropriate solutions to shelter will be designed and managed by themselves; but they also recognize that the state has to facilitate the process. To this end, they develop loan funds capitalized by their savings and donors, and sometimes supported by government. Loan funds enable savings schemes to begin incremental housing development (see Figure 8.1). Self-help in this context means that improvements are collectively built and managed, and are undertaken by community groups (primarily savings scheme members). Organizational form is varied depending on the country and the scale of the housing investment: in some contexts, formal housing cooperatives are formed, land may be purchased and a simple housing unit (up to 40 square metres) constructed; elsewhere local groups make incremental improvements to dwellings and/or basic services.

Projects to redesign shelter improvements typically involve a blending of finance. Project finance combines community contributions (savings and in some cases loans) and leveraged resources through dialogue with the state. Donors may also contribute. Government contributions may be through SDI loan funds, project-specific financial commitments and resources in kind. Governments may contribute land and/or incorporate the developments into existing infrastructure upgrading programmes, as well as providing cash.

SDI affiliates face considerable challenges in addressing the scale of need at scale, and one challenge is identifying shelter improvements that are affordable for the majority of members in a context in which incomes are low and state support frequently lacking. Affordable, in this context, means that all members choose to be included and, when included, can afford to make the savings contribution and sometimes loan repayments that are required. In assessing affordability, SDI affiliates do not work with a fixed percentage of income – in part because there are a multitude of circumstances related to livelihood and sources of income and shelter costs. For example, some members work from their homes and have the potential to increase their incomes with improvements; and some may be able to access other contributions to

FIGURE 8.1 Incremental housing construction in Pune, India. Photo by Sparc.

housing from employers and family members if they have the possibility of greater formality. When assessing affordability, affiliates recognize that housing improvements include the costs of access to basic services such as water supplies. Hence affordability is assessed at the local level by savings schemes that methodically collect information with each member completing an affordability form. Current expenditures on rent and services are used as a rough rubric – but the final decision takes into account much other information.

This chapter explores how two federations in two cities, Mumbai (India) and Harare (Zimbabwe), address the challenge of assisting members to secure affordable improvements to secure tenure, access to basic services and housing. These cities have been selected because they represent two alternative economic and political contexts with a considerable difference in the capacity and willingness of the state to contribute to the upgrading of shelter for the urban poor. Both are cities in which the SDI affiliates have considerable experience in testing out and refining solutions.

An introduction to SDI affiliates in Mumbai

Mumbai is the commercial capital of India (although the formal administration is in Delhi). Shelter needs are acute and 60 per cent of the city live in informal settlements, two-thirds of which are notified 'slums'. Just over 50 per cent of formal housing consists of one-room tenements housing five to eight people. Long-standing neglect, a peninsula city and a rapidly growing economy mean that residential densities are now so high and the value of land so great that the solutions that work for low-income people elsewhere are no longer viable.

Aspiring to be a global city, Mumbai has prioritized economic growth (Fernandes 2004). As the authorities expand infrastructure and create open spaces, eviction has become legitimated and routine. Between 2007 and 2017, an estimated 200,000 to 300,000 households will be evicted and relocated due to the investment in public services (expanding the train and road network, improving the airports and redeveloping the port for containerization). Massive resistance by the urban poor plus a high level of organization in informal settlements has resulted in disputes, confrontation and subsequent delays, all of which have imposed costs on these infrastructure projects. As a result, the authorities are now beginning to acknowledge the need to give alternatives to eviction (Patel and Sharma 1998). Meanwhile, construction companies primarily build units of over 93 square metres – unaffordable to even the salaried middle class. The few dwellings that state institutions provide for the low-income families are secured by middle-income households desperate for housing.

The right of those living on the pavements and in other forms of informal accommodation to be treated with dignity has not been accepted. Before the Indian Alliance (SPARC, NSDF and *Mahila Milan*) began its work, many professional civil society organizations tried to use legal strategies to further the needs and interests of the urban poor. In 1980–1981, the Chief Minister of Maharashtra decided to 'clean up' the city and began to evict slum dwellers. *Olga Tellis* v *Municipal Corporation of Mumbai* was admitted as a Public Interest Litigation as city activists protested about this action. In his final judgment, the Lord Chief Justice recognized the difficult conditions that the pavement dwellers faced but he asserted the right of the city authorities to evict them to meet the health and welfare needs of the city as a whole. Despite this judgment the evictions did not take place due to the physical difficulties of removing 30,000 households. This episode illustrates the complexities of shelter improvements: on the one hand, needs are acute; on the other the state has a limited capacity to provide solutions. Over time the work of the Indian Alliance has produced an alternative – that of the right of relocation – which is now the policy framework used by city authorities (SPARC 2011). This experience illustrates the importance of a collective capability to act in the public realm and this theme is returned to below.

The Indian Alliance is the catalyst that led to the formation of SDI as a global movement. In 1984, SPARC, an NGO formed by a group of Indian professional women, began to work with women pavement dwellers to identify the strategies that they wanted to follow to improve their shelter options (D'Cruz and Mitlin 2007). Over the next few years, *Mahila Milan*, a network of women's savings collectives, was formed, and an alliance was made with the National Slum Dwellers Federation (NSDF). The federation had been a grouping of male-led community organizations that contested the eviction of informal settlements. As their leader, Jockin Arputham, observed the work of *Mahila Milan*, he could see the advantages offered by their strategies. The three organizations agreed to collaborate and developed tools that included enumerations and mapping of informal settlements, precedents of required improvements to illustrate practical responses, exchanges between communities to provide new ideas and to consolidate collective action, and the use of savings and loan finance to enable investment at scale. SPARC supported the community federations, helping them network with formal institutions and raising donor finance as required.

By 2011, NSDF and *Mahila Milan* were present in 65 towns and cities, bringing together more than 750,000 savers (SDI 2011). In total they have assisted over 80,000 households with relocation, constructed over 10,000 dwellings and provided over 14,000 toilet seats mostly within community toilet blocks. In the previous year (2010–2011), the Indian Alliance had completed 35 city-to-city exchanges, seven international exchanges, nine state exchanges, established 33 new savings groups, profiled 4,101 settlements in 7 states, mapped 300 settlements, and had 700 houses under construction and over 6,000 toilet seats completed (SPARC 2011). These achievements represent the coming together of new design options combined with innovations in the blending of finance and persistent efforts to negotiate alternative approaches with a range of state agencies.

The challenge of affordable housing in Mumbai

Housing finance

In their initial strategy, the Indian Alliance sought land and access to basic amenities for slum dwellers and sought to demonstrate financial management capacity to banks to encourage them to lend households money to build core houses through loans. However, in Mumbai, high land values led to the government announcing a new approach in 1998 called the Slum Rehabilitation Act (SRA), which designed a process whereby both communities NGOs and conventional developers could use land occupied by slums to build medium-rise housing using increased densities (an additional floor space index or FSI) and hence enabling slum dwellers to secure a market subsidy. Through Transferable Development Rights (TDR) (the increased FSI) additional housing stock is sold in markets to subsidize provision of 25-square-metre dwellings to slum dwellers (see Vaquier 2010). TDRs facilitate the developer of the project to provide high-rise accommodation for low-income households by allowing them to build their higher-income developments at a higher density, i.e. an increase in their FSI.

This changed the strategy of the Alliance in Mumbai from seeking land for self-financed housing to developing a community-driven possibility for slum dwellers to take on their own SRA projects with the support of NGOs. Federation groups now work with SPARC Samudaya Nirman Saharay (Nirman) – an organization established by SPARC to manage building developments – to undertake construction financed through the TDR. This change in strategy was in part due to the banks themselves, who were not ready to lend to slum dwellers. Initial financing for this came through CLIFF, a facility that provides shelter finance to community-driven projects through capital and bank guarantees.

Although the TDR fully subsidizes (or almost fully subsidizes) accommodation, difficulties remain. The federations' experience is that families need up to US$500–1,000 to cover the transition from informal to formal services as they have to cover rates, taxes and service payments. This capital is necessary because if the bills are not paid, the services are cut off. In many instances land was made available to Nirman to build relocation housing for those displaced by infrastructure projects, and these households incurred many expenses due both to the distance from their previous location and the disruption to livelihoods. Although in essence a good strategy, poor governance has meant that many of the previous resettlement units were badly designed and poorly constructed and this has reduced the potential for scale. In this context the work of the Alliance is to demonstrate ways to overcome such challenges.

Shelter design and construction

Inevitably these dwellings are in high-rise blocks and contractor constructed. However, some tasks are subcontracted to the artisanal construction sector. In the contracts that SPARC

FIGURE 8.2 Milan Nagar cooperative housing construction in Mankhurd, Mumbai. Photo by Sparc.

negotiates, the formal contractor company hires workers, puts in the foundations and 'skeleton' of reinforced concrete beams (Figure 8.2). Federation members are given the right to bid for a range of sub-contracts, and organized community groups work with master masons to provide bricklaying, tiling, the making and installation of doors and windows and sometimes electricity. Typically some 10–15 companies are involved in each contract.

In the past, there has been a more substantive role for community design in Mumbai. The federation developed a housing unit with a height of 4.3 metres providing a mezzanine level and additional space for sleeping, enabling an additional 18.5-square-metre area to be available to the household. In the late 1990s, they persuaded the authorities to agree to this design and it was widely used. However, lack of action on housing issues now means that high-rise buildings seem to be the only solution to a lack of housing, and the mezzanine level is no longer permitted due to fire risk. The result is to accommodate low-income households in small tenements with reduced choices. The Indian Alliance has sought to develop designs and layouts that are more community-friendly, but options remain limited within Mumbai: outside of the city, terraced housing is one design alternative.

Community-led development continues in respect of infrastructure provision. Approximately three-quarters of informal settlements do not have access to the city's sewerage and drainage system. Due to a lack of access to adequate supplies of water, households began connecting directly (albeit illegally) and the city has responded with a programme to provide household water connections. However, sanitation remains in crisis and the present ratio is 50 people to one toilet seat. High densities and the small size of many dwellings mean the only viable solution is community toilets. As a result of the work of the Indian Alliance, the authorities now provide funding for community toilets in recognized 'slums'. As the density of informal housing makes household toilets impossible, the federation has designed a communal block that households are proud to use. The women recognized that public toilets were often unpleasant places. Their design includes space for a resident manager (and family) with community meeting rooms above the sanitation facilities. Individual users make a small monthly contribution to the cost. This money is used to pay the manager whose responsibility it is to ensure that the toilets are kept clean, the facilities are not abused and that cleaning materials are available. There is a separate children's toilet area to make it easy for them to use facilities. The Municipal Corporation has approved the design and finances the construction cost of this public toilet; and about 2,000 have been built or are being built by federation women who have organized themselves in construction collectives (SPARC 2011).

Organizational form and self-help

As noted above, high-rise blocks offer few options for the involvement of local residents. To improve their choices, the Indian Alliance has been directly involved in some TDR projects working with construction companies to build for their members (Nirman 2011). The number of projects to be taken up is limited by available project capital. However, the Indian Alliance has benefited from CLIFF support and projects have challenged the designs of many developer-managed projects (Cities Alliance n.d.). The Alliance has also helped women set up enterprises able to bid for toilet construction contracts.

One of the challenges facing informal settlement dwellers in Mumbai is that although free units are provided under the TDR policy, detailed enumerations are required to prove entitlement to benefits, and (as noted above) savings are required to make the transition from informal to formal units. Hence self-help elements remain critical to enabling citizens to acquire these benefits. With respect to enumerations, community-managed surveys are critical to establishing occupation in informal settlements. The Alliance enumerates thousands of households each year (Arputham 2012). With respect to savings, these are organized collectively to support households to contribute and take care of this finance. To date banks have not assisted because they do not want to collect the small change through which the urban poor save. The Alliance continues to have a dialogue with many private and public financial institutions and banks to create secure inflation-proof saving options for the urban poor.

Political negotiation

The history of shelter in Mumbai reflects the success of collective agency to prevent eviction and secure relocation where required and *in situ* upgrading elsewhere. After years of persistent lobbying, extensive organizational capacity-building, and many precedents that showed the capabilities of the federations' members to construct homes and improve services, the government accepted that it needed to provide affordable housing. The federations had to compromise, and accepted that they would receive a unit financed through a market-based cross-subsidy (the TDR) which offered households 25-square-metre tenements. In addition, the federations secured the right of relocation for the pavements dwellers although this is taking place 20–25 kilometres away from their pavement homes. The pavement dwellers reluctantly accepted, recognizing that the alternative is continued evictions and no access to infrastructure and services.

Relocation was only accepted once households recognized that employment would be available at the relocation sites (albeit after some difficult months).

The Indian federations have shown that if the volume of people resisting evictions is small then the state can overwhelm them, but in recent years these numbers have been so large that the state has been forced to negotiate and respond positively. The Indian federations then have to support their members through this process, assessing what is working and what needs to be renegotiated, with new alternatives being illustrated through a further round of precedent-setting investments. The longer the city authorities ignore squatters, the more densities increase and the potential for self-help construction options is reduced.

An introduction to SDI in Harare

For much of its history, Harare (previously named Salisbury) was a colonial administrative centre and this past still dominates its spatial form. Black Africans resided in high-density settlements, often some distance from the town centre. The central area of the city was given over to large plots in low-density neighbourhoods. Medium-density areas were designed for less wealthy but still prosperous white families and medium-rise flats were built during the 1970s to cater for an emerging black professional class. Critical, in terms of future affordability, was the establishment of high infrastructure standards with water-borne sanitation, piped water and concrete block housing (first two rooms, later reduced to one room) being required by building standards (Kamete 2006). Low-income black Africans were denied access to the city. However, as a result of insurgency to secure democratic government, rural dwellers moved to urban centres in the late 1970s to escape the violence in the countryside (Chitekwe-Biti 2009). During this period, households were allowed to rent informally and in some cases squat within high-density suburbs.

Following independence, there was further rural to urban migration and Harare's population doubled between 1980 and 2000 (Government of Zimbabwe 2002). The government, under considerable budgetary pressure, shifted from loan-financed housing ownership to sites and services, with a fixed period of time within which the house had to be constructed to a stipulated standard. Due to a lack of affordability, low-income households consistently failed to comply with building standards. However, numbers of sites and services opportunities were inadequate and the lowest-income households continued to rent backyard shacks or rooms in formal low-income areas, or squatted (despite regular evictions). Holding camps were established for families that had been evicted, many kilometres from the centre of the city and with very rudimentary services and shelters (Chitekwe-Biti 2009). In 2005, Operation Murambatsvina forced hundreds of thousands of informal settlement dwellers from their homes as the government acted to destroy informal shacks.

Massive inequalities remain. In 2002, 10.5 per cent of the city's land was occupied by informal and formal low-income areas housing 76 per cent of the population. High- and middle-income households occupied all but 0.25 per cent of the remaining land. By 2007, there were 236,255 households on the housing waiting list in Harare with an estimated total demand of 500,000.

There is no financial support available from the state for low-income households to improve their shelter. Indeed, the experience of the Zimbabwe Homeless People's Federation is that local authorities are seeking to raise money from housing developments, even those of the lowest-income households. Following a decade of economic crisis, incomes are very low and families struggle to afford their daily living costs. The federation's affordability survey in June 2010 suggests that most members have monthly incomes of between US$50 and US$100. Some of the lowest-income members survive on US$20–30 a month. In November 2011, members estimated that US$150 is the monthly cost of food for a family of six. Monthly room rentals are US$50 in low-income settlements with electricity, and US$35 in informal and under-serviced areas.

The Zimbabwe Homeless People's Federation was launched in 1998. The first savings schemes were initiated in Victoria Falls and Harare following visits from the South African Homeless People's Federation. The encouragement to save whatever amount was possible was an incentive for local residents, many of whom had not joined a housing cooperative (the only option for low-income households) because they could not afford the monthly instalments. Working in alliance with the NGO Dialogue on Shelter (a peer organization to SPARC), the federation grew into a national network. As with the Indian Alliance, the relationship between Dialogue on Shelter and the Zimbabwe Homeless People's Federation is a partnership between an autonomous network of community organizations (the federation) and an NGO, in which the two combine their relative comparative advantages. The Gungano Fund was established shortly after the launch of the federation; Gungano offers shelter and enterprise loans to groups of federation members and has been capitalized by a blend of members' savings and donor grants. It is managed by a committee of federation members.

By 2011, the Zimbabwe federation was present in 53 towns and cities, bringing together more than 47,000 people saving collectively to address their common development needs (SDI 2011). These communities, despite the very adverse economic context, have saved more than US$500,000, secured land for 15,775 families, built 975 houses with a further 1,122 under construction, installed piped water and sewerage on 2,454 plots and raised US$600,000 in capital contributions to Gungano. The federation has memorandums of understanding (MoUs) with the national government and 15 local authorities.

The challenge of affordable housing in Harare

In Zimbabwe, there is no state support to assist the urban poor to improve their housing. In some cases, federation groups in Harare have managed to negotiate the purchase of land at historic development cost which, given the inflation that has taken place, can be a considerable reduction. Federation groups borrow from their loan fund, Gungano, to help cover the costs of development. As in India, in addition to housing, the costs of acquiring formal services are considerable.

In 2005 during a period of hyper-inflation in Zimbabwe, the federation demonstrated its commitment both to affordable solutions and to maintaining the value of its fund when members adopted a suggestion from Gustavo Riofrio, a Peruvian visitor, and switched away from monetary repayments to repayments in building materials. Each group constructing housing received an initial cash loan for a given number of families and would be expected to organize their members to repay these loans in building materials that were given to other members of the group. The initial calculations were that the materials would be fully repaid within four years. Although that did not prove possible, significant materials were repaid. In 2010 with the dollarization of the economy and an end to inflation, Gungano returned to cash repayments.

Affordability is improved by encouraging and enabling loan repayments to be made through small contributions made on a daily basis. In addition, households preparing to build are encouraged to collect building materials like stones, river sand, door frames and windows to reduce the required loan. In many savings schemes, members are only allowed to borrow for cement – to mould bricks and for mortar – and for roofing materials. Unskilled labour is provided by the group of residents who are building together and skilled labour is drawn from trained federation members. With these conditions, a house of 30 square metres required a loan of US$1,000 in 2011.

Affordability is also improved by negotiating the subdivision of plots. In 2003, the federation's lobbying of Harare's city council resulted in the offer of land in Crowborough, a high-density site far from the city centre. The plots were expensive, because they were already serviced, and development would also be costly, because the land was boggy. However, the federation decided to take the land to show the city council what they could do. To reduce costs, they proposed to divide the 300-square-metre plots into two, settling twice as many households and dividing the costs. The local authority planners agreed to the increased densification. The same strategy has been repeated in a more recent Harare development where federation members have agreed to create clusters of five families with each family having a plot of 150 square metres. Clustering of households in this way avoids the council's regulatory requirement for larger (more expensive) plots.

A further strategy to improve affordability is to increase incomes. Gungano has been lending for income generation for some years with mixed results. Members trading in Mbare, the central market area in Harare, have been able to find profitable activities but other savings schemes have struggled to make a success of such projects. However, to assist with repayments, some members have rented a room in their two-room house.

The continuing economic crisis in Zimbabwe and resultant lack of affordability has resulted in a shift away from construction towards tenure security. However, this strategy is constrained as local authorities require housing construction prior to formalizing tenure. Since 2008, the federation has prioritized land acquisition and members have only received a loan sufficient for a shell-house of one room and a bathroom rather than the dwelling that they previously constructed (24–30 square metres including two rooms with a bathroom). Even with this minimal shelter, loans are broken down into components to improve affordability (reducing the amount borrowed at any one time reduces interest charges). The production of building materials is also done by collective self-help to reduce costs and provide a potential source of future income from the skills and capabilities learned in the process.

Self-help construction is increasingly used for services due to the very high costs of local government provision and non-delivery. In Harare, the basic monthly charge from the city council to low-income households in high-density areas to cover the property, council administration, water, sewerage and refuse adds up to US$28 with additional charges for metered water consumption. Households cannot afford to pay and end up sharing connections. With NGO support, federation members have been drilling boreholes. It costs approximately US$4,000 to serve between 80 and 200 households, and households make a monthly contribution of US$1. To provide themselves with low-cost sanitation in areas where there is no sewerage, federation families are constructing sky-loos. These are elevated eco-sanitation toilets that require a loan of US$200–300 to construct. As with housing construction, households provide themselves with river sand and rocks. In one settlement, communal eco-sanitation blocks for 150 households are being constructed. Each block with seven toilets costs US$6,400 with the families contributing US$2 a week to repay loans from Gungano. However, while this option is affordable, Gungano's capital is insufficient to allow it to go to scale.

As is the case in Mumbai, collective efforts to negotiate political alternatives take place alongside practical activities. In December 2005, Zimbabwe celebrated Habitat Day. With thousands still in holding camps from Operation Murambatsvina just a few months earlier, memories of the destruction of their homes were still vivid to federation members. Nevertheless, the federation invited the Minister of Local Government to attend a meeting in Hadcliffe Extension, one of the settlements on the edge of the city with strong federation membership. Once the Minister accepted, members rapidly constructed a house both to prove what they could provide for their members and to advance their own access to services. A federation leader[1] explains the thinking of the federation in engaging the state:

> We will find a solution in negotiating – unlike another organization who goes to the streets to fight. They do not approach someone in an office and explain that these are our grievances. Let us sit. If you shout going around, then they will shout going around and you will never meet and never be resolved … This position has reduced the anger in our members.

In Vancouver, the World Urban Forum in June 2006 provided a further opportunity to engage the Zimbabwe Minister, who was isolated at the Forum because most participants had seen the scenes of the brutal evictions. After discussions, the Minister for Local Government signed an MoU promising the federation members access to 5,000 sites. In 2010, Harare was selected by the Bill & Melinda Gates Foundation to participate in a project to improve conditions for low-income urban residents, and the mayor agreed that the Zimbabwe federation should be a key partner. The project brought the city officials and the federation together. Over time, the officials could see the functionality in their relations with the federation, which could organize people in the neighbourhoods, think of new solutions to old problems, and help them negotiate with other departments in the local authority.

Comparison

SDI's experience across affiliates is that the challenge of affordability is acute. Regardless of the nature of the economy, those living in informal settlements can neither access nor afford commercial loans. As networks encourage savings, provide loans and negotiate for state support, they demonstrate how large numbers can access home improvements. Without alternative incremental shelter designs and a blending of finance, there are few alternatives to demolition and eviction that the state can turn to. In Mumbai, the state has designed a housing programme that provides a full subsidy in recognition that continuing evictions will not solve the shelter programme and that land values require high-rise dwellings; but the costs of formalization mean that residents have to be organized and save collectively for this option to be realizable. In Harare, residents are presently struggling without state financial support – and indeed in a context in which the state exacerbates the affordability problem because of the high cost of basic services.

In both cities, local groups use multiple strategies to help people save for improved shelter and, in the case of Harare, to help households repay loans. Federation groups undertake affordability assessments to help families consider their incomes and assess if they will manage to pay the costs of borrowing and formalization. Local groups encourage savings by visiting households every day. Leaders aggregate information at the group level so that families can see how their savings and loan repayments, and those of their neighbours, are accumulating. Federations help to increase incomes through skill-sharing and enterprise development to sell on construction-related goods and services.

SDI affiliates have been adamant from the beginning of their work that engaging the state is critical to improve the conditions in informal settlements. They are also aware that the need is for generalizable strategies that can offer development opportunities for all. Hence a major challenge is 'raising' the focus of housing interventions to include planning and management at the level of the settlement and city. Without mechanisms to consider urban dynamics and development at appropriate levels and without suitable institutions and processes able to take on this task, shelter needs will not be addressed. As mentioned above, in Mumbai this requires federations to undertake their own enumerations and mapping. This is repeated in Zimbabwe. Upgrading in Epworth, a settlement on the edge of Harare, is being used to develop an upgrading protocol relevant for the country (Chitekwe-Biti *et al.* 2012).

The federations' contribution goes well beyond surveying and mapping to consider shelter solutions themselves. Individualized housing solutions work for higher-income households but do little to assist the lowest-income households who are vulnerable if they are isolated. Collective efforts enable more effective solutions to be identified. In Mumbai, this is the ability for federations to negotiate finance to work with contractors to design and construct TDR-financed dwellings. In Harare, savings schemes and the city federation together negotiate for land, manage community loans, construct infrastructure and assist with housing improvements. The speed and quality of incremental housing construction depends on the strength of the economy, and local groups also support opportunities for income-earning to try to enhance affordability.

In Harare, incremental housing upgrading has been and continues to be the main form of achieving improved shelter, both for housing and amenities. Such upgrading becomes more robust and systematized when supported by collective organization. In Mumbai, there is a continuing emphasis on incremental collective infrastructure in a context in which high densities and limited land availability constrain self-help housing options. In Mumbai, women's enterprises build toilet blocks to a federation design financed by the state. The improvements are considerable and some 10,000 toilet seats have been constructed in informal settlements across the city.[2] In Harare, incremental infrastructure is also important. Increasing emphasis is placed on communal blocks that enable all of the residents (including non-federation members) to benefit from access, not just those able to afford to repay loans for household eco-san toilets. Self-help is also needed due to the council's inability to provide water, so alternatives emerge from collective action. As collective action has demonstrated its effectiveness, the city council have agreed to modify the regulations to legalize the federation's work.

Groups need a strong collective process that can support them to create and then make choices which do not undermine their survival strategies. In both Mumbai and Harare, local groups have negotiated with the state to improve their access to land, even if their rights have not always been recognized. Where required they have formed housing associations or cooperatives, blending these organizational forms with savings scheme activities.

The benefits of collectivity are not just related to the mechanics of construction and loan finance. Working together brings political influence. For example, households are being threatened with eviction in Zimbabwe simply because they cannot afford to build to the timetable required by local authorities. Federation leaders in Kariba have been negotiating for additional time to build. As discussed above, in Mumbai it was organized resistance to evictions that resulted in the authorities offering relocation to pavement dwellers.

Likewise in both cities, despite positive intentions, the international development assistance community is not always helpful and the federation engages with these organizations to improve outcomes. The commitment to human rights led to intense periods of global protest following evictions in Mumbai but such agencies seem to give little consideration to longer-term ramifications of such positioning with the need to negotiate with authorities that waver between hostility and ambivalence (Patel and Mitlin 2009). In Harare, groups faced a very different problem with humanitarian aid providing limited free assistance and saving scheme leaders struggling to put in place alternatives that encourage activism and self-help. Official development assistance programmes may support the state housing programmes but in the experience of SDI affiliates these programmes often have limited relevance for low-income households. An earlier USAID programme to support mortgage finance for housing cooperatives in Zimbabwe, for example, reached few low-income informal sector workers. The strategies outlined here run counter to current policy frameworks of international development agencies, national government policy, real estate conventions and mainstream financial processes, which have favoured individual market-orientated approaches with direct-demand subsidies, the privatization and/or corporatization of basic services, and individual improvements to housing either through capital subsidies or shelter microfinance (Mitlin 2013). In both countries, exchanges and support from the international SDI network have helped to highlight and legitimate the needs of the urban poor, and advance their negotiations with the state.

Conclusions

Self-help is central to the achievement of housing improvements. But self-help does not mean that the state is excluded, government redistribution is ignored and government regulations are disregarded. Rather it means that communities develop the solutions that work for them, and negotiate with the state to achieve improvements at scale. Most notably, self-help remains of central significance as governments scale-up their redistribution, ensuring that improvements achieve scale by being cost-effective in their use of subsidies, that government approaches are relevant to addressing the shelter needs of low-income households because households 'own' and implement the improvements, and that shelter improvements build local organizations ensuring that groups can engage with politicians and officials, and negotiate for further support from a position of strength.

In the absence of incomes, social status or political influence, individual households living in informal settlements throughout the Global South are vulnerable if they are not organized. Emerging alternatives that are bottom-up and led by organized communities need the support of city authorities if they are to be scaled-up. However, despite the significance of local government for the urban poor, the experience of SDI affiliates is that very little attention is given by these authorities to the implications of their policies and programmes for the urban poor if the urban poor are not organized. They are locked into norms and standards that do not fit with the realities of incremental housing. A major focus of the precedents undertaken by SDI affiliates is to reform local authority actions into procedures that facilitate community-led development including negotiated standards. The federation model used by SDI affiliates creates local to national networks so that, as organizational ability and confidence grow, the urban poor can negotiate with the state.

SDI affiliates believe that the ideal solution to achieve inclusion is for the state to finance both the bulk and internal settlement infrastructure systems, and let the people cover the costs of upkeep and maintenance. If the city cannot afford this scale of investment, then at least they should provide the bulk services. It is simply not possible for individual low-income settlements working alone to produce a long-term solution for the management of city-wide infrastructure such as sewerage and water supply. However, with access to bulk infrastructure, communities can do a lot for themselves.

There is an urgent need for city authorities to engage organized citizens, such as the SDI-affiliated community federations, in order to understand how infrastructure installation in informal settlements can take place. As communities innovate both housing designs and the blending of finances to improve affordability, then city officials learn more about the processes through which informal settlements consolidate, and as they work closely with urban residents, more effective development interventions and related norms can be put in place. Innovations take time and considerable trial and error but progress has been made. In Mumbai, the federations believe that they have persuaded the state to offer relocation due to the force of their organization against evictions. But they believe collaborative planning is needed to respect the struggles of pavement dwellers and adjust state procedures to be more supportive. Whatever the attitude of the state, SDI affiliates recognize that, in most circumstances, to achieve scale residents need to cover much of the costs of housing themselves, while the state provides access to land and infrastructure. Identifying affordable solutions is central to addressing the shelter challenge. The ambition of affiliates is to identify and put in place the scaling-up of precedents that enable all of those in need to secure shelter. This means developing options that others can explore, and that cities can adopt and develop. As elaborated above, affordability inevitably means that both citizens and the state have to contribute what they can. Solutions are diverse as they respond to local opportunities and realities. They emerge from the genuine engagement between relevant agencies who share a commitment to finding shelter options that are inclusive and which together offer a prospect of improved shelter for all.

Notes

1 Davious Muvindi, a national coordinator with the Zimbabwe Homeless People's Federation, interviewed on 23 January 2012.
2 Analysis of projects completed to date by SPARC staff.

References

Appadurai, A. (2001) 'Deep democracy: urban governmentality and the horizon of politics', *Environment and Urbanization*, 13(2): 23–43.
Arputham, J. (2012) 'How community-based enumerations started and developed in India', *Environment and Urbanization*, 24(1): 27–30.
Chitekwe-Biti, B. (2009) 'Struggles for urban land by the Zimbabwe Homeless People's Federation', *Environment and Urbanization*, 21(2): 347–367.
Chitekwe-Biti, B., Mudimu, P., Masimba, G. and Jera, T. (2012) 'Developing an informal settlement upgrading protocol in Zimbabwe – the Epworth story', *Environment and Urbanization*, 24(1): 131–148.

Cities Alliance (n.d.) 'The community led infrastructure financing facility'. Online. Available at www.citiesalliance.org/sites/citiesalliance.org/files/cliff-article[1].pdf (accessed 23 March 2013).

D' Cruz, C. and Mitlin, D. (2007) 'Shack/Slum Dwellers International: one experience of the contribution of membership organizations to pro-poor urban development', in R. Kanbur, M. Chen, R. Jhabvala and C. Richards (eds) *Membership Based Organizations of the Poor*. Abingdon: Routledge.

Fernandes, L. (2004) 'The politics of forgetting: class politics, state power and the restructuring of urban space in India', *Urban Studies*, 41(12): 2415–2430.

Government of Zimbabwe (2002) *Annual Census Report*. Harare: Government of Zimbabwe.

Kamete, A.Y. (2006) 'Revisiting the urban housing crisis in Zimbabwe: some forgotten dimensions?', *Habitat International*, 30: 981–995.

McFarlane, C. (2004) 'Geographical imaginations and spaces of political engagements: examples from the Indian Alliance', *Antipode*, 36(5): 890–916.

Mitlin, D. (2013), 'Innovations in shelter finance', in E.D. Sclar, N. Volavka-Close and P. Brown (eds) *The Urban Transformation: Health, Shelter and Climate Change*. Abingdon/New York: Routledge.

Mitlin, D., Satterthwaite, D. and Bartlett, S. (2011) 'Capital, capacities and collaboration: the multiple roles of community savings in addressing urban poverty', *IIED Poverty Reduction in Urban Areas, Working Paper 34*. London: International Institute for Environment and Development.

Nirman (2011) *Annual Monitoring Report on CLIFF Implementation by SPARC Samudaya Nirman Sahayak (NIRMAN)*. Mumbai: Nirman.

Patel, S. and Mitlin, D. (2009) 'Reinterpreting the rights based approach: a grassroots perspective on rights and development', in S. Hickey and D. Mitlin (eds) *Exploring the Pitfalls and Potentials of the Rights Based Approach to Development*. Sterling, VA: Kumarian Press.

Patel, S. and Sharma, K. (1998) 'One David and three Goliaths: avoiding anti-poor solutions to Mumbai's transport problems', *Environment and Urbanization*, 10(2): 149–159.

SDI (Shack/Slum Dwellers International) (2011) *Urban Poor Fund International Financing Facility of Shack/Slum Dwellers International Annual Report 2011*. Cape Town: SDI.

SPARC (Society for the Promotion of Area Resource Centres) (2011) *Annual Review*. Mumbai: SPARC.

UN-Habitat (2005) *Global Report on Human Settlements 2005 Shelter Finance*. London: Earthscan.

UPFI (2011) 'Urban Poor Fund International'. Online. Available at www.sdinet.org/upfi/ (accessed 23 March 2013).

Vaquier, D. (2010) 'The impact of slum resettlement in urban integration in Mumbai: the case of the Chandivali Project', *CSH Occasional Paper No. 26*.

PART II
Asia
Introduction

Peer Smets, Jan Bredenoord and Paul van Lindert

The Asian urban population has increased from 229 million in 1950 to 1.7 billion in 2010; and it is estimated that the number of urban residents in this macro-region will reach 3.3 billion in 2050 (UN Department of Economic and Social Affairs 2012). This development is expected to continue, but South Asia has to face the fastest growth. In addition, economic growth in the region has led to rising land prices. As a result, the pressure on the supply of land and housing is enormous, which forces people to settle in informal settlements. From the 1980s onwards the enabling strategy gained ground, resulting in programmes such as the Million Houses Programme in Sri Lanka (Joshi and Sohail Khan 2010). Although the enabling approach underpins many contemporary Asian housing policies, access to affordable housing for the poorer sections of society is still a big challenge. This is especially because, as the private sector mainly tends to serve the better off, the poorer sections depend more on the informal sector (Majale *et al.* 2011). More than 50 per cent of slum dwellers in the world live in Asia, and 61 per cent of the Asian population lives in slums and informal settlements, a fact that has contributed to Asia's leading position in innovative slum upgrading projects: for example the Indonesian Kampung Improvement Programme (see Chapters 11 and 12) and the Baan Mankong Programme in Thailand. Both focus on the social, economic and environmental factors of slums and informal settlements. Here a stakeholder approach has been used in which the slum dwellers play an important role in articulating shelter needs and priorities (Majale *et al.* 2011). Another good example is a network organization of national slum dwellers organizations, called SDI (Shack/Slum Dwellers International), which works in many Asian cities, but also in Africa and Latin America. SDI aims at capacity building, knowledge sharing and an exchange of key experiences concerning the struggle for adequate and affordable housing through micro savings, women's empowerment, land tenure reform, housing supply and upgrading activities (Majale *et al.* 2011; Smets 2002). Over the past 60 years the main challenges for households have been obtaining access to affordable land and housing finance. Furthermore, governments need to focus on developing a supportive institutional and regulatory framework that facilitates the affordability of housing (Majale *et al.* 2011).

The collection of chapters contained in this second part of the book focuses on the urban housing conditions for lower income groups in India, Pakistan, Indonesia, Sri Lanka and China.

In Chapter 9, *Urmi Sengupta* elaborates on affordable housing provision in India, including new frontiers and challenges. Indian housing is characterized by a huge housing deficit mainly concentrated in the economically weaker section of society. Recent accounts of urban housing have transitioned from welfare to entrepreneurial forms of governance and the swift production of housing in tandem with the rapidly growing Indian economy. This was manifested in a spectacular housing development reflecting a sort of Western concept of design, density and everyday life wherein a proportion of this housing is projected and legitimized as affordable housing. The author explores the factors that led to a market provision of affordable housing and the emerging trend in design, standards and quality to articulate a reinterpretation of 'affordability'. Through the detailed study of a pioneer housing model – 'Sukhobristi' in Kolkata – it is argued that affordability in its broadest sense has evolved to achieve a paradigmatic shift in terms of housing production and consumption. Meanwhile there is a greater recognition among developers for the need to bring affordable housing from the shadow of marginalization into the mainstream – a trickling down to the low-income segment. The current trend also reflects uniformity and standardization in the housing supply.

In Chapter 10, *Arif Hasan*, with a focus on Karachi, describes how the poor currently house themselves in Pakistan where the housing demand–supply gap is considerable. It is estimated that the city requires 80,000 housing units per year but the formal sector can provide no more than 30,000 to 40,000. This demand–supply gap was previously taken care of by developing informal settlements, called *katchi abadis*, on state land on the periphery of the then smaller city (in spatial terms) or even within the city. State land today is increasingly used for middle- and lower-middle-income households and is developed by formal sector builders. Even where it is used for informal settlements, it is too expensive for the very poor. It is also on the periphery of a now huge city and hence too far away from places of work, education, recreation and health facilities. As a solution, existing settlement densification is taking place and, even in informal and/or regularized settlements, people are building vertically. The rental market is developing in inner city low-income settlements. Even low-rise formal settlements are being converted into medium-rise tenements to cater to the needs of lower- and lower-middle-income groups. Karachi has substantial government-owned land resources and a number of well-known community development projects related to the housing sector.

In Chapter 11, *Devisari Tunas and Laksmi Darmoyono* describe the self-help housing practices in Indonesia where housing provision remains one of the most problematic development challenges. Whilst public housing production is increasing by the year, it is still far from sufficient; it also is not really targeting the low-income groups that need it the most. Problems such as limited financial capacity, policy mismatch and poor implementation are pinpointed as the causes of this challenging situation. As a consequence, low-income groups are often left on their own; they frequently have to settle for self-help housing with or without collaboration with a local community and/or an NGO. Self-help housing thus has formed an integral part of the Indonesian housing provision landscape. The authors also elaborate on state housing policies such as the important Kampung Improvement Programme or KIP, which was very successful (see also Chapter 12). KIP focuses mainly on neighbourhood improvement, but not on assistance for individual self-help housing. The authors describe a prominent example of a self-help KIP in Jetisharjo in Yogyakarta. Furthermore, they focus on a self-help component in the state housing programme that introduced 'Swadaya housing'. This gives subsidies for housing improvements, but its impact is limited. Consequently 'affordable' housing is still not reasonably priced for the very low-income group.

By focusing on important experiences from Indonesia and Pakistan, *Florian Steinberg* elaborates in Chapter 12 on community contracting in neighbourhood improvement and housing. Community contracting has become one of the innovative features in housing projects which have been supported by multilateral development agencies like the Asian Development Bank (ADB). While the ADB is committed to supporting community-driven development (CDD) in various sectors, the experience of CDD in neighbourhood improvement or housing is still relatively new, with little reflection so far about its value and contribution. The basic assumption is that through community contracting, beneficiaries will obtain better value for the money spent and that through the mechanisms of their direct control, they may also have sufficient say to decide on what will be created. The ADB has implemented two types of community contracting schemes, namely (1) the community group modality and (2) the individual cash-transfer modality. The experiences of Indonesia and Pakistan illustrate these two modalities of community contracting, and illustrate that participatory processes are essential to achieving good results. These experiences will need to be replicated.

In Chapter 13, *Sharadbala Joshi and M. Sohail Khan* explain the housing situation of the poor in Sri Lanka. Since 1948, the government has introduced housing policies to support public housing or incremental/self-help housing. The Million Houses Programme in the 1980s subsequently influenced, at a global level, assisted self-help housing processes and methodologies. The government's focus is still on pro-poor disaster-related housing, redevelopment and resettlement projects. Most housing programmes have claimed to include the participation of the poor in the upgrading or construction of their houses. Recent significant initiatives such as the Sahaspura high-rise apartment project in Colombo, tsunami housing initiatives and participatory upgrading of settlements have contributed to the revival/establishing of Community Development Councils. The experiences with people's participation provide significant lessons for the future of self-help housing policies, and raise questions about whether the 'People's Process', which evolved in Sri Lanka, has been successfully streamlined into housing. With the desire for higher urban area densities, the demand for single houses is likely to be replaced by a demand for smaller and compact apartments rather than upgrading of underserviced/informal settlements. The government wants to make the high-rise approach more pragmatic through the participation of people, while, at the same time, encouraging their relocation from informal settlements and redeveloping dilapidated areas.

In Chapter 14, *Mingye Li and Jean Claude Driant* describe how during the past two decades, affordable housing policies have played different roles in urban China. This chapter highlights the changing economic and urban context which has affected to a large extent the evolution in housing policy. The introduction of three major programmes for affordable housing in the 1990s facilitated the housing reform and ensured a smooth transition. Then, in the rapid process of housing marketization, policy priority was given to commercial housing rather than to affordable housing. Yet the market failed to meet the needs of socially and economically disadvantaged groups, and housing inequality became an acute problem. Consequently, a renewed emphasis has been placed on affordable housing policy since 2007. This chapter explores the renewed affordable housing policy at a national and local level with the illustration of two case studies. These reflect (1) the current affordable housing policy in the city of Chongqing, which mainly consists of the Public Rental Housing programme, and

(2) a multi-target housing protection system developing with the provision of Low Rental Housing, Economic and Comfortable Housing (ECH) and Public Rental Housing in the city of Nanjing. ECH and Public Rental Housing constitute the major types of affordable housing under the current provision. It is argued that current affordable housing policy is subject to the economic objectives of both the central and local governments.

References

Joshi, S. and Sohail Khan, M. (2010) 'The Million Houses programme – revisiting the issues', *Habitat International*, 34(3): 306–314.

Majale, M., Tipple, G. and French, M. (2011) *Affordable Land and Housing in Asia*. Nairobi: UN-Habitat.

Smets, P. (2002) 'Global habitat policies leading to slum dweller resistance and co-management', in D. Kooiman, E. Koster, P. Smets and B. Venema (eds) *Conflict in a Globalising World: Studies in Honour of Peter Kloos*. Assen: Van Gorcum.

UN Department of Economic and Social Affairs (2012) *Population Division World Urbanization Prospects, The 2011 Revision*. New York: United Nations. Online. Available at http://esa.un.org/unup/pdf/WUP2011_Highlights.pdf (accessed 10 November 2013).

9
NEW FRONTIERS AND CHALLENGES FOR AFFORDABLE HOUSING PROVISION IN INDIA

Urmi Sengupta

Abbreviations

CBO	Community-based organisation
DDA	Delhi Development Authority
EMI	Equated monthly instalment
EWS	Economically weaker section
FAR	Floor area ratio
FDI	Foreign direct investment
GDP	Gross domestic product
HDFC	Housing Development and Finance Corporation
HFC	Housing Finance Corporations
HIG	High-income group
HUDA	Haryna Urban Development Authority
HUDCO	Housing and Urban Development Corporation
INR	Indian rupees
IT	Information technology
JNNURM	Jawaharlal Nehru National Urban Renewal Mission
KMDA	Kolkata Metropolitan Development Authority
LIG	Low-income group
MFI	Microfinance Institutions
MGIs	McKinsey Global Institute
MIG	Middle-income group
NBC	National Building Code
NUHHP	National Urban Housing and Habitat Policy
NGO	Non-governmental organisation
PPP	Public–Private Partnerships
ULCRA	Urban Land Ceiling and Regulation Act, 1976
VAMBAY	Valmiki Ambedkar Awas Yojana
WBHIDCO	West Bengal Housing and Infrastructure Development Authority

Introduction

Affordable housing has become a major policy challenge in urban India (see Table 9.1) over the past few decades. The 11th Five-Year Plan identified the housing deficit in India to be 24.7 million in 2007 – the economically weaker section (EWS)[1] representing the highest housing need with 21.78 million units. To address this the Government of India has initiated reforms in line with international trends of enabling housing to work (World Bank 1993). Primarily, the focus has been on fostering private sector participation in providing affordable housing for the EWS and low-income group (LIG) and instituting mass housing for accelerated housing growth. These changes are altering the landscape of low-to-middle-income housing in terms of consumption and production. Evidence suggests that the affordable housing sector is rapidly becoming the fastest growing segment in the Indian real estate sector.

Concomitantly, the definition of affordable housing is changing to include affordability for a much wider section of the society and, in tandem, there is a visible change in the notion of home, identity and lifestyle. The steadily growing middle class – deemed the most visible urban embodiment of globalisation (Fernandes 2004) – is the largest consumer group of housing, triggering a discernible shift in what constitutes a 'home'. Private developers fashion affordable housing in the templates used for middle-income (MIG) and high-income group (HIG) housing. Indeed, mass housing cannot succeed without the benefit of standardisation and uniformity instilling efficiency in the supply chain, but sweeping generalisation on quality and standards raises two critical questions: first, is the stock that is targeted at low-income households aligned to their needs and expectations? And second, what is affordable housing, how is it defined, whose affordability are we talking about? The answers to these questions provide some insight into the extent to which affordability problems arise from inconsistency in quality, costs and aspirations. While defining affordability in literature, there has been a consistent effort to analyse whether households have an affordability problem because they choose to consume housing that is better quality than affordable stock (Hancock 1993; Hulchanski 1995; Whitehead 1999; Thalmann 2003; Quigley and Raphael 2004). The question that underpins this chapter is whether, paradoxically, they might need to consume this more expensive housing because there is no other housing available.

The chapter investigates the inherent contradictions and paradoxes in the housing 'dream' currently being packaged as affordable homes in India. It provides an overview of the past and current government policies and programmes in order to elucidate the factors that led to the gradual transition of affordable housing from being a state-led to a market provision. This is followed by an analysis of the emerging trend in articulating affordable housing by both government and market and the role of housing standards and guidelines in shaping this trend. The chapter uses an empirical study of a pioneering affordable housing model from Kolkata to highlight the conceptual contradiction associated with the perception and marketability of affordable housing. Specifically, given that privately provided affordable housing could achieve mass housing proportions, it is important to test the notion that the equation between quality, price and affordability is neither simplistic nor straightforward. Rather, it depends on how people in their everyday lives interpret affordability and how the market/developers respond to such interpretation.

The remainder of the chapter proceeds as follows. The next section charts the historical development of affordable housing in India during the pre- and post-1991 eras. This will be

TABLE 9.1 Urban housing shortage in India

	1961	1971	1981	1991	2001
Total population (millions)	439.2	548.2	683.3	846.3	1,028.6
Urban population (millions)	78.9	109.1	159.5	217.5	286.1
Housing shortage (million units)	3.6	3	7	8.2	10.6

Source: Compiled by author based on information from census figures.

followed by a section that presents a contemporary interpretation of affordability in India. Next, attention will be paid to key features of the Sukhobristi model to assess its role and impact on affordable housing in India. The final two sections analyse and conclude.

Policy responses to housing crisis: development of affordable housing in India

Housing since 1947

Broadly speaking, housing for the urban poor has been a politicised, contested and visible cornerstone of welfare provision in India. The welfare link is a no-frills recognition of 'unaffordability' in society, but financial commitment has been patchy[2] and affordable housing provision has centred on targeted subsidies to individuals and loan assistance to governmental agencies through the Housing and Urban Development Corporation (HUDCO). The government focus also lay on fostering partnerships with non-governmental organisations (NGOs), community-based organisations (CBOs), cooperatives and to some extent to the private sector to improve the supply chain. For instance, housing cooperatives in India – identified with public sector activities for their dependence on public sector funds (Renaud 1985) in early years – have grown to 92,000 organisations from 5,564 in 1960 and have an estimated housing output of 2.5 million homes. The movement has now evolved with a strong institutional framework based on the concept of 'self-financing' and diversity in its financial portfolio.[3]

But it is really the two-pronged strategy – sites and services, and public housing – seemingly laden with contrasting objectives that defined the social housing landscape in early years. The former, as a form of progressive development, was quintessentially pro-poor in concept but in practice, owing to the World Bank's involvement, it relied excessively on neoliberal principles of affordability, cost recovery and replicability to succeed, which was ahead of its time. Nationwide output remained poor as difficulties in site assembly and local resource mobilisation made large-scale implementation nearly impossible (Pugh 2001). The principle of progressive development (including those in slum upgrading programmes) ran contrary to local building codes and land use regulations (Buckley and Kalarickal 2006). The latter strategy thus became the primary Indian government approach to affordable housing for many years. Public housing was aimed at income-eligible households at highly subsidised rent. However, low overall output, allocation discrepancy and high maintenance costs made a strong economic case for moving away from this approach (Sengupta 2006). Between 1970 and 2000, public housing production in India averaged 1 unit per 5,000 people. City authorities such as the Delhi Development Authority (DDA) have been criticised for producing rather fewer houses despite having acquired large reserves of land (Payne 2011).

The era, labelled as the 'modernist' period, is marked by the concept of affordability trapped in the dilemma of perception – a 'stereotype' of how people live in shanties and slums. A typical design approach for affordable housing was then to compress a home into a single room with very basic provision. They were built on welfare-state principles with a low commodity value exhibiting a form of slummification (Wadhwa 2007). By the late 1980s, following the international trend and Global Shelter Strategy, in particular, a National Housing Policy was announced in 1987 with government's role firmly established as provider for the poorest group and facilitator for other income groups. The draft also laid the foundation for regulatory reforms, which would benefit the housing industry a decade later.

Housing after 1991

India's housing and real estate market has a relatively short history. It started in 1991 when economic reform led to multi-dimensional reforms in trade, industry and finance sectors including housing and real estate. The country's gross domestic product (GDP) grew to a notable 9.2 per cent in the year 2006–2007 from 5.8 per cent in 2000–2001. The reform paved the way for relaxing regulatory barriers to encourage private sector participation – such as 100 per cent foreign direct investment (FDI) in integrated township development, abrogation of the Urban Land Ceiling and Regulation Act, 1976 (ULCRA) and reduction in stamp duty – designed to boost housing supply and remove red tape. Interestingly, housing and property prices remained stable, despite the global financial crisis, attributed largely to the culture of home purchases through personal savings and other sources of capital outside the banking and mortgage system.

Housing boom and the widening gap in affordability levels

The domestic boom has, however, had a varying impact on different income segments. Owner-occupiers gained most from price inflation. This author's interviews with households in older housing estates such as Kalindi in Kolkata revealed that housing prices have tripled since 2003–2004, which aligns with Chandrasekhara's (2011) observation that housing prices in 2009 were above 2007 levels in Kolkata (up 85 per cent), Mumbai (up 26 per cent) and Delhi (up 13 per cent) after prices rose 30 per cent in 2008. Housing has consistently been seen as performing as well as if not better than other investment portfolios such as bonds, fixed deposits and post office savings. Rapid appreciation of property prices led to higher disposable income raising the purchasing power of a segment of the population, even if it was only 2–5 per cent of the national population. In a country of 1.21 billion, 5 per cent equates to 60 million, roughly the size of the population of the United Kingdom. Further, there has been a dramatic rise of the middle class in India as a consequence of globalisation (Deshpande 1998; Lakha 1999) and their lifestyle and consumption pattern has been a definer of a group with different housing aspirations and attitudes. The steadily growing middle class, currently accounting for 30 per cent of the population, is seen as crucial to sustaining higher-end housing across the country. The residential skyscrapers such as the pair of Imperial Towers in Mumbai or Kolkata's Urbana, Burj Al Hind in Calicut, Kerala, or Gurgaon's DLF Tower have become today's urban housing spectaculars that evoke both the technological and architectural sublime although they sit uncomfortably with affordable housing principles.

The rise of the middle class has been equated with the rise in affordability levels in that homes across the country are more affordable than they were five or ten years ago (Shetty 2012). According to the Housing Development and Finance Corporation (HDFC), the prices of homes may have gone up but median income of average urban households has trebled in the past ten years. The affordability level, measured through the income to price ratio, declined to 4.6 times households' annual income in the year 2012 from 22 in the year 1995 (*Business Standard* 2012). Whilst this is a significant achievement the varied geographic and socio-economic background of the Indian population makes such generalisations problematic. Median household income in metro cities is higher than in secondary cities such as Ahmedabad, Patna, Surat or Jaipur, but their housing predicament can be far worse. Up to 54 per cent of the population in major cities such as Delhi and Mumbai live in slum conditions compared to the national average of 28 per cent (MGI 2010). Moreover, the recent housing boom has been accompanied by a widening income gap across different income groups and resultant decline in housing affordability for the lowest segment of the population.

Overall, there has been good progress in housing supply over the past decade or so. Between 1991 and 2001 the number of housing units grew by about 54 million; housing quality improved; and the number of households living in cramped conditions dropped. In cities the home ownership rate rose from 63 to 67 per cent and in the country by one percentage point to 95 per cent (GOI 2007). New schemes such as JNNURM (Jawaharlal Nehru National Urban Renewal Mission) and VAMBAY (Valmiki Ambedkar Awas Yojana) have led to the production of millions of low-cost homes across India aimed at resettling slum dwellers living below the poverty line. Public–private partnership (PPP) has also been a delivery vehicle for affordable housing through a system of cross subsidy. Since 2007, the National Urban Housing and Habitat Policy (NUHHP) has required up to 10–15 per cent of land in every public and private housing project or 20–25 per cent of floor area ratio (FAR)/floor space index (whichever is greater) to be reserved for EWS/LIG housing through appropriate legal stipulations and spatial incentives. Many proactive development authorities such as Noida and the Haryna Urban Development Authority (HUDA) have imposed limits on the floor area of residential units in a bid to increase the proportion of affordable units in developers' schemes. Despite these concerted efforts, metro cities in India continue to witness both quantitative and qualitative housing problems. PPP, for example, has been criticised for inelastic supply, causing real price appreciation and eventually pricing low-income dwellers out of the system (Sengupta 2006). Due to the lack of any normative framework on affordability, private developers are free to determine what constitutes an affordable range. Between 2009 and 2012, developer-initiated affordable housing across Indian cities was priced between INR 500,000 and INR 1,000,000 (US$9,090–18,181) (Jones Lang Lasalle 2012).

Affordable housing: contemporary interpretation

Historically, the idea of affordable housing has been subject to the vagaries of perception and definitional issues. For the most part 'affordable housing' has been loosely synonymous with low-income housing in all government documents. The idea of inability to pay was rather ideologically viewed and not properly analysed. Affordable housing has also been interchangeably used with 'low-cost' housing; the distinction between the two is now starting to be articulated (Table 9.2). Championed by HUDCO and maverick architects such as Laurie

TABLE 9.2 Low-cost and affordable housing in India

Parameters	Low-cost housing	Affordable housing
Amenities	Bare minimum to none	Basic
Target income class	EWS and LIG	LIG and MIG
Size	<28 m^2	28–112 m^2
Location	Inner city, some in periphery	Inner city
Developer	Government	Private developers, government
EMI* to gross monthly income	>30%	>40%
Finance sources	MFIs	Commercial banks

Source: Compiled from KPMG (2010) and MGI (2010).
*EMI or equated monthly instalment is a fixed payment amount made by a borrower to a lender at a specified date each calendar month. EMIs are used to pay off both interest and principal over a specified period.

Baker, low-cost housing had a strong focus on building materials and technology and catered to the poorest group.

In recent years, efforts to construct and reconstruct perceptions of affordability have been directed to somewhat broadening the definition while remaining within the basic framework of affordability as a ratio of price/rent of housing to household income. The NUHHP 2007, while attempting to chart a path for the nature of state involvement in the housing sector for the future, 'diversified' its definition by treating it as a 'concept' that cuts across income or context bands. It prescribes 'affordable housing for all' as a key element to achieve sustainable urban development, taking the 'affordability' equation out of the exclusive domain of the 'lowest segment' of the population. A task force in 2008 recommended affordability levels (see Table 9.3) for the EWS, LIG and MIG by correlating affordability with income, and these have gained ground. The proposal recognises that the housing cost-to-income ratio differs for different income groups and that lower-income households pay much less than higher-income households. But there are conceptual flaws in such deliberations, which make such interpretations not an end but a means to an end. Affordability defined solely as ability to pay ignores the appropriateness in terms of household size, location or different forms of quality such as amenities. It also excludes transaction costs or the recurring costs such as maintenance and utility or even cost of commuting to a workplace. A practical definition of affordability is hard to determine given differing notions on what comprises affordability and the contextual differences across households and housing markets for a country as diverse as India. There is a good rationale for continued use of the 30/40 affordability rule (meaning those spending more than 30 per cent of their income on housing, while earning in the bottom 40 per cent of the income range) generally because it provides continuity with traditionally used measures and also because it can be easily implemented. However, a clear distinction should be made with reference to the target group(s) for whom affordability is being determined. Housing affordability for an EWS ought to be viewed with the same lens as for the middle or even lower middle class, but then the remaining sum should be enough for meeting other needs without falling below the poverty line.

Housing size has been a barometer for affordability in India and the government has a history of juggling with it to establish affordability levels. The NUHHP 2007 recommended a reduction in minimum standards by legislation to make the cost accessible to different income

TABLE 9.3 Affordability ratio of different income groups

Income group	EMI/Rent to income ratio	Cost of housing to income ratio	Size
EWS/LIG	>30%	>4 times household gross annual income	28–56 m^2
MIG	>40%	>5 times household gross annual income	>112 m^2

Source: Parekh (2008).

TABLE 9.4 Housing categories scenario in India

Housing category	Income class threshold in INR (US$)	Value of homes in INR million	Average space consumption per household (m^2)
EWS	<2000 (US$36)	–	<28
LIG	2,000–5,000 (US$36–90)	0.1–0.2	37–75
MIG	5,000–10,000 (US$90–182)	0.2–0.4	75–93
Higher middle income	10,000–200,000 (US$182–3,636)	0.35–0.8	93–121
HIG	200,000–500,000 (US$3,636–9,091)	0.8–1.7	116–162
Luxury	>500,000	20+	232

Source: KPMG (2010).
Exchange rate US$1 = INR 55.

groups (Kumar 1989). Subsequently the 1990 draft aimed at preventing luxury housing by reducing plot size to 120 square metres. The historical 'space squeeze', as a tool for lowering the cost, has continued in some of the EWS homes under JNNURM and developer homes such as Shubh Griha and Sukhobristi. In essence the market has determined its own interpretation and categories (Table 9.4). Most recently, the task force in 2008 favoured raising the size threshold from 25 to 28–56 square metres for the deprived segment. While this does not represent a significant increase, these normative prescriptions have been perceived to be counter-intuitive to both scale of production and affordability. According to MGI (2010) a 25-square-metre threshold is prohibitively expensive as the average cost of providing such minimal housing is around INR 440,000 (US$8,000) including land and tertiary infrastructure with a lower range of cost involved and where subsidy is not available. The corollary to this view is that for many, despite the modest size, the new housing will still be an improvement from the cramped conditions they live in. The inordinate focus on size has also obscured the potential of innovative design to bridge the imbalance in space use and lower costs.

Most market studies are, however, geared towards identifying market opportunity[4] rather than engaging in any debate on the conceptual or theoretical basis of government interpretation of affordability. Supporting the general thrust of the government's view that affordability can occur at every level, these studies offer far more useful income categories and their market capitalisation is based on the size and build costs (see Figure 9.1). The corollary to this view is

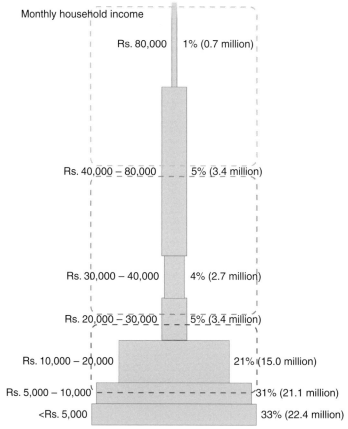

FIGURE 9.1 Urban income pyramid in India.
Source: MGI (2010).

that in Tier 1 cities such as Mumbai, housing shortage encompasses even households earning up to INR 500,000 (US$9,090) a year, assuming an income outlay of 35 per cent (MGI 2010). Such segmentation may be a tool for a more effective targeting of investments and identifying gaps in the market; it is also a carefully crafted argument to cut out distinctive roles for the state and the market. The developers' concentration on providing low- to middle-income housing and include the lowest income bracket confirms this.

The neoliberal interpretation of affordable housing that conveniently establishes itself in the broad mindset of the policymakers as well as private developers has philosophical ramifications. As the national developers such as DLF, Omaxe, Raheja, Ansals and Unitechs plunge into building homes in the affordable range the focus is rapidly moving away from providing housing to the bottom 30 per cent of the housing population which has an income less than INR 5,000 (US$90) a month. 'The brief history of neoliberalism has shown obsession for hyper forms and mega construction and a much reduced appetite on aspects such as affordable housing' (Banerjee-Guha 2009: 105). Furthermore, with the entry of large developers, housing quality and standards are consistently rising and the middle-class 'dream' is being conveniently passed on to the urban poor. Developers seem to be capitalising on the idea that behaviours of the poor tend to follow their affluent counterparts when restrictions on consumption options are removed (Leeds 1971). A survey of some of the upcoming projects in cities as diverse as Mumbai and Rewari in Haryana confirms that the key ingredients of 'middle-class aspirations' commonly associated with homes costing INR 6 million (US$0.1million) have also occupied centre stage in affordable homes costing one-twelfth of that price. Playgrounds, gyms and round-the-clock security systems have all become the norm. These ramifications reflect the start of the great denouement of the stereotype that defines affordable housing in India today even if it is also laden with a high dose of hubris.

The next section explores the Sukhobristi housing development. The information is based on field visits in 2007 and 2011. Some of the numerical details have been obtained from the Kolkata Metropolitan Development Authority (KMDA) and the developer.

The evolution of developer-initiated affordable housing: an example

The Sukhobristi (Shower of Joy) covers about 60 ha in Rajarahat Kolkata. Located approximately 10 kilometres from central Kolkata, it is the largest mass housing project in New Town[5] consisting of 20,000 flats (for an estimated 100,000 population) aimed at lower- and middle-income groups (Figure 9.2). It is a fascinating model not only for being a flagship PPP project but also because it signifies a neoliberal interpretation of mass housing for the urban poor. As a partnership project, it seeks to satisfy both public and private goals. The strategy adopted was to roll out a replicable, contemporary design of homes that is affordable and of acceptable quality. Homes are sold at levels nearly half of market rates, and strikingly, on a freehold basis without any restrictive covenants on the titles, or restriction to maintain affordability to perpetuity. As a result, homes are now available in the second hand market at approximately double the original price. Developed by the group which has constructed higher-end housing such as the 60-storey Imperial Towers in Mumbai – India's tallest residential towers to date – Sukhobristi has the hallmark of lifestyle logic flowing from luxurious apartments offered at an unbelievably low price tag. The following sections examine key features and the extent to which these suggest the emergence of a new affordable housing paradigm.

Housing provision and facilities: middle-class dream exemplified

The project provides two types of apartments in a 60:40 split: one-bedroom units with carpet area of 30 square metres originally sold for INR 285,000–300,000 (US$5,181–5,454) and the two-bedroom units with carpet area of 44.5 square metres for INR 570,000 (US$10,363). As such, housing size stays within the range recommended by the National Building Code (NBC) as minimum standards and is the principal measure of quality, although housing quality is a composite good (Fiadzo *et al.* 2001). Apart from the size, it is the higher density (300 units per hectare) that has led to higher output. The 'low-cost–high-rise' approach contrasts with the traditional practice in India that sees ground plus four-storey as a norm and density band set by the NBC (125–150 units per hectare for metropolitan urban areas). Notwithstanding that development regulations are applied with considerable local and regional variations, their application in Sukhobristi demonstrates radical changes. In terms of house type, the project is a major departure from the government policy of promoting mixed-income housing or the international trend of integrating affordable housing within the market housing (Tiesdell 2004). The high concentration of lower-end housing ensures effective targeting and inhibits

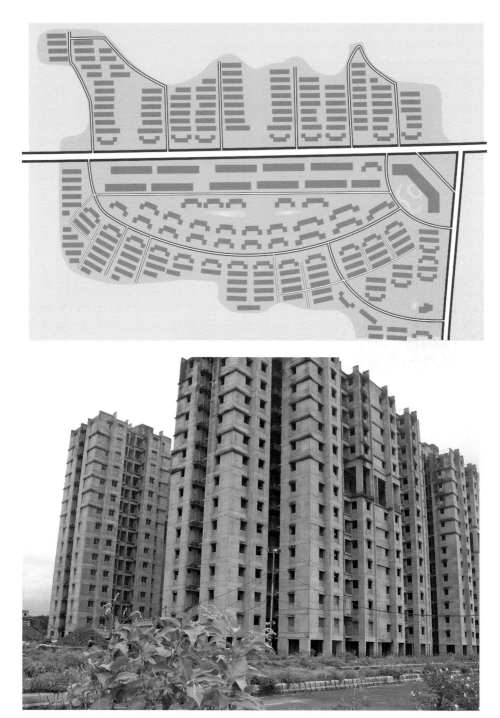

FIGURE 9.2 Sukhobristi Master Plan and building features.

FIGURE 9.2   (cont.)

speculative buyers, but runs the risk of creating areas of deprivation amidst a fairly affluent suburban setting.

Sukhobristi is conceived as a self-contained constellation of residential apartment blocks with shopping malls and entertainment facilities. According to the municipal laws, Sukhobristi falls in the category 'B' municipality complex requiring proper social infrastructure including a health care centre. It consists of 37,162 square metres of shopping floor, speciality retail, banks and a post office. The developer has managed to provide plenty of green spaces and parking. Overall, the facilities provided obscure the differences between Sukhobristi and other middle-tier housing schemes, although variations in the quality and level of these facilities can be found. Tiesdell (2004) observed that development standards between market-rate and affordable units may differ in obvious factors such as garden size and parking provision. In terms of perception, the 'feel good factor' that is associated with the name Sukhobristi is everywhere, from the façade of the most upmarket shopping centre to the humblest rubbish bin. A closer look behind the gates reveals a mimicry of middle- and upper-class lifestyles. The residential blocks may not be post-modern architectural pastiche, or adorned with classical and baroque details, but each block exhibits an individually tailored approach to make the new owners feel privileged. They clearly have a gated feel with a guardhouse, uniformed security men and close-circuit systems. The shopping and entertainment areas are similarly, if less conspicuously, protected. Residents are given the option to use facilities such as fitness clubs and swimming pools. Most residents commute to Central Kolkata for jobs; relatively cheap transport in Kolkata compensates. As such, New Town has been developed as an integrated development (commercial, leisure, residential and light industrial such as information technology (IT) parks etc.). In its facilities and amenities, the Sukhobristi model reinforces middle-class aspirations and values in contemporary India. It provides more than just housing for its residents – a carefully packaged new way of life. Despite being located some 10 kilometres from Kolkata at a rather isolated location and its high-rise mass housing character, built contrary to traditional housing with shops and workshops, and streets where trade, production and social contacts are fostered, Sukhobristi appears to be a feasible solution to the overpopulated country.

Use of subsidy as a catalyst

An ongoing challenge for the government in India has been how best to meet the cost of affordable housing without government direct involvement and by developing and implementing a subsidy mechanism that can be differentially rewarded to the developer. Past PPP projects that focused on HIG subsidising LIG units resulted in lower overall production and an even lower proportion of low-income homes in the project (Sengupta and Tipple 2007), indicating higher cost per subsidised unit. Direct subsidy through land and cross-subsidising housing production have no visible budgetary cost to either party (government or private developer), and are hence popular.

In the first instance the Sukhobristi model could be branded as a single sector, risk-prone model with potential for failure. The model is unique for absence of HIG and an off-site subsidy. Within the framework of direct supply-side subsidy, the West Bengal Housing and Infrastructure Development Authority (WBHIDCO) offered 50 acres of land to the developer in the New Town at a submarket price for developing IT type uses and IT-enabled services on condition that the developer would not compromise with the public goals broadly determined by the government. Public leverage has a particular significance in strategies for disadvantaged communities, and Sukhobristi's outcomes are being keenly watched by policymakers and market. It is beyond the scope of this chapter to debate whether or not public funding has benefited the target group. It is my contention that lower supply and lack of means-testing will always exacerbate the problem. From interviews it was evident that the speculative buying that took place in Sukhobristi was done mainly by small brokers in the lower classes rather than by the organised upper class. For the policymakers, eligibility criteria for affordable housing remain a grey area and it is important that policies are introduced to select the real poor.

Marketing approach

Notwithstanding the converging architectural and lifestyle trends of different income groups, Sukhobristi represents a new way of offering affordable housing for consumption, which attempts to be different from the usual middle-class housing. Distinctions can be detected in the advertisement and marketing rhetoric. First, marketing for affordable housing is grounded not so much on the global identity but on the quintessential Indian and regional (Bengali) identity. Right from the name 'Sukhobristi' (having Sukho – happiness and Bristi – shower in Bengali), marketing brochures claim 'a blend of modernism and the true essence of Bengal'.[6] Second, the distinction can also be made in terms of greater alignment with the needs of the poor. Community facilities provided – especially schools and health centres – are seemingly the most important services that the majority of the urban poor have limited access to. Native design parameters – street side entrance, shaded walkways and a compact design – have been pro-poor. In facing NIMBYism, architects often resort to aligning with high-end counterparts for acceptability (Ahrentzen 2006). Sukhobristi's layout is simple and straightforward and devoid of gimmicks such as open-plan kitchens and level difference within dwelling units. The building façade looks interesting with the use of white, grey and yellowish cream colours.

In sum, the Sukhobristi model has proved that it is important to recognise that affordable housing represents one of several 'spaces of consumption' in which both the housing price and design that draw people need to be increasingly contextualised, and at the same time hybridised, while enabling the consumer to experience them as part of a wider suite of experiences.

Affordable housing: paradigm shift or riding the wave?

An emerging trend in affordable housing in India points to the changing direction in the way it is produced and consumed – from being entirely state-produced, low density, low quality housing to that which is high density, premium quality and low-to-moderately priced. It is also produced by either private or public–private enterprises for consumption by a wider section of society. The new affordable housing projects such as Sukhobristi are unquestionably superior to the large ghettoised 'slum conditions' that blight major cities of India. They provide facilities and amenities that the urban poor are traditionally deprived of. Higher quality and better facilities may eventually engender price rise per affordable unit, will likely endure longer than a public housing project and be better managed. Several factors have contributed to this shift. Broadening of the definition of affordable housing has removed the negativity surrounding the terminology and increased market appeal. The lull in the luxury housing market in India owing to the global economic downturn has forced developers to diversify and explore alternative markets with lower risk and greater return. Concomitantly, middle-class value systems and preferences are rapidly penetrating the mindset of the urban poor – their concept of 'home' now changing from yesteryears' user-initiated incremental building to 'ready to move' flats. Expansion of access to credit facilities to many low-income families has pushed them into the kind of 'home-buying obsession' usually associated with the middle class.

Nonetheless, the 'neoliberal' interpretation of affordability currently being articulated in India is problematic as it fails to satisfy some of the basic conditions essential for a viable, affordable housing market. First, the expression of 'affordability' using income and space thresholds does not work for the diverse context across different cities. For instance, there may be very few households in Mumbai with incomes well below the EWS limit but they still find it impossible to access any type of unsubsidised housing given the exorbitant price tag attached to real estate in Mumbai and will be forced to live as slum or squatter residents. Housing is a location-specific issue, which calls for income limits and affordability levels of EWS, LIG and MIG to be defined at the local level. Second while the building industry will benefit from the lower costs of standardised design, building materials and techniques through higher overall output, the approach is contrary to user compatibility, in terms of quality and sustainability needs. Whether the lower-end affordable housing at INR 300,000 (US$5,455) or the higher-end semi-affordable housing priced at INR 3 million (US$54,545), both are subject to the same entrapment as property developers broadly bracket them as 'one- to three-bedroom apartments' with a pool and a gym, 24-hour water and security back-ups as standard. Quality itself is a dynamic magnitude and incorporates several factors in one single bundle, which represent household preferences and lifestyles and the choice that people make about how much housing to consume relative to other goods (Keare and Jimenez 1983; Lee 1990; Quigley and Raphael 2004). Thirdly, current affordable housing initiatives do not focus on the poorest in society, where housing poverty is mostly concentrated.

There are other important lessons that emerge from Sukhobristi, which point to continued challenges in developing affordable housing. The project shows that given the limited availability of land in urban areas,[7] it may still be unviable for developers to provide affordable housing without some form of state subsidy. In other words, recognition that land provision for social housing is not easily available within the context of the market conditions makes a strong case for government intervention for the provision of land (Whitehead 2007). By the same logic, it would not be economically prudent for the government, which is the supplier of the land, to develop affordable housing in a more centralised location even if it means commuting costs could be a lot lower. The model also shows that the 'off-site subsidy' model instead of the traditional 'on-site cross subsidy' results in better value through higher output. It also helps to reinforce the notion that relaxing regulations positively affects the supply chain resulting in higher overall output. By removing constraints on density, unit size and FAR, it was possible for Sukhobristi to achieve higher output thereby reducing the cost per unit overall. The effects of stringent regulation on 'affordability' have been well documented. Bertaud et al. (2003) found the restrictive limitations on building heights in Mumbai bid up housing costs for lower-income families by as much as 15 to 20 per cent of income. Sukhobristi confirms a positive outcome from what has been termed 'slow but steady progress' to relax these regulations over the past decade or so (Bertaud 2010). It is evident that the private sector will likely capitalise on this to supply homes to the burgeoning middle class in the short term, but the need to accelerate the drive to reduce regulatory barriers persists.

The model also flags up challenges that persist in areas of finance. In the face of limited supply relative to strong pent-up demand, access to finance becomes a determinant for access to housing. Commercial banks typically do not serve low-income groups below the 'viable' threshold to ensure repayment, or who cannot provide collateral for loans,[8] especially given the disproportionate increase in house prices[9] relative to increase in household income observed in recent years. Microfinance institutions have attempted to fill this gap since the 1980s when the need to develop effective financial intermediaries was first identified. But their performance in urban areas has been dismal due to the longer period of housing loans (typically between five and seven years minimum, if not more) and larger amount of loan needed. Smets (2006) laments the big loans that are increasingly becoming the norm, which is contrary to the incremental building practice of the poor. Given that the cheapest affordable unit in Sukhobristi costs INR 300,000 (US$5,454), without access to finance, it is still out of bounds for many. There is a continuing challenge to evolve a system for financing housing loans on a large scale for the lower income groups.

Conclusion

This chapter aimed to capture the contradictions and paradoxes, and the manner in which the concept of affordability is embedded in both discourse and practice in India. On one hand, westernisation, often considered analogous to modernisation, has influenced the consumption and production patterns affecting affordability. On the other, multiple actors have used affordability, as an idea, for various purposes. For policymakers it has been a fertile ground for experimentation. For the market it is an untapped segment of consumers, which can lead to a high degree of profitability using the same design, construction and marketing templates as used for luxury housing. The complexity surrounding the perception and implementation of affordability suggests that there is no single measure for assessing the nature and degree of housing affordability problems.

Sukhobristi as an embodiment of modern day affordable housing helps, at a conceptual level, to initiate a great denouement of the stereotype that defined affordable housing for much of the previous half-century. There is a greater recognition among developers of the need to bring affordable housing from the shadow of marginalisation into the mainstream and through the benefits from globalisation – of high-quality products and services – trickling down to the low-income segment. Current trends also reflect uniformity and standardisation in housing provision, which is not necessarily a bad thing given the country's gigantic need for affordable housing. The Sukhobristi model also helps to reconfirm the importance of land subsidy, regulatory reforms and a widening of access to finance to enhance affordability for the poor.

No doubt Sukhobristi presents an interesting proposition, but questions still remain as to how far it is representative for urban India. Or, for 'affordable housing' in urban India. Does it herald a paradigm shift in affordable housing provision in India? Answers to these fundamental questions lie in the context of where Indian housing is situated – lack of supply and unprecedented demand within the neoliberal context. The neoliberal context itself is inevitably exclusionary through its focus on extending home ownership and the role of the market (Malpass and Murrie 1999: 82). This implies that not need but demand would be the key for housing production and consumption under such conditions. There are numerous detailed matters in Sukhobristi such as maintaining affordability to perpetuity, effective targeting or an intent to target the most needy in society that are still unresolved and they do point to methodological flaws in the basic notions of market development and participation in housing provision. Notwithstanding that these issues make the model far less paradigmatic, its potential to be so cannot be undermined. It is a quintessentially neoliberal model, where state and private sector have played out their envisioned role. It is also a manifestation of the recognition to the target group for affordability, which may or may not be the most needy. It has to be understood that Sukhobristi is just one of the tiny cogs in the much bigger supply chain and that the scheme does not aim to solve the whole housing affordability problem in India. But it is the potential of replicability of a scheme of this nature that gives us hope for solving India's housing problem, eventually. Whether or not the 'Sukhobristi model' survives the test of time, it can be argued that the new policy principles and practices associated with the project will be reshaping the affordable housing policy landscape for the foreseeable future.

Notes

1   Central government in India uses income threshold as a benchmark for prioritising welfare policies: up to INR 1,999 (US$36.36) in the EWS; between INR 2,000 and INR 4,999 (US$36.36–90.9) in the LIG; between INR 5,000 and INR 9,999 (US$90.90–181.8) in the MIG and more than INR 10,000 (US$181.8) in the HIG. State governments have been given freedom to determine their own threshold and as a result there is a considerable variation in practice.
2   For instance, in the first Five Year Plan, 7.4 per cent of the total plan resources were allocated for housing. Its share in the subsequent plan resources ranged between 1.2 per cent and 4.9 per cent.

3 For instance, during the first three years of the Tenth Five Year Plan (2002–2005), the Apex Co-operative Housing Federations raised INR 17.74 billion (US$322 million) from various funding agencies such as LIC (Life Insurance Corporation of India), the National Housing Bank, HUDCO, Commercial and Co-operative Bank.
4 A study (KPMG 2010) puts the housing requirement for the sub-INR 100,000 (US$1,818) income group across seven major cities at 2.06 million units – a market size of INR 3,300 billion (US$60.5 billion).
5 New Town is the first planned satellite town on the outskirts of Kolkata. It covers 3,550 ha and is estimated to provide housing and employment opportunities to an estimated 5 million population.
6 Comparable expressions can be found in Tata's Shubh Griha (the 'nano' home) whose brochures claim 'every feature is inspired by and reminiscent of the cultural splendour of Gujarat'; even though the project was designed by Toronto-based architects.
7 The Town and Country Planning Organization (TCPO) suggests that catering for the demand of the EWS and LIG categories alone would require 84,724 to 120,882 hectares of additional land. Land as a state subsidy is not unique to India.
8 The 'bias' is visible from the fact that over 73 per cent of housing loans extended by HFCs exceeded INR 300,000 (US$5,454) and 93 per cent exceeded INR 100,000 (US$1,818).
9 A recent survey (Lloyds TSB 2012) shows Indian house prices have risen by most since 2001, having increased by 284 per cent in real terms (i.e. after allowing for consumer price inflation) since 2001 – equivalent to an average annual rise of 14 per cent. This is almost six times the 50 per cent rise in real UK house prices over the same period and over 10 times the 23 per cent rise seen in the euro area.

References

Ahrentzen, S. (2006) 'More than just looking good: toward an evidence-based design practice in affordable housing', in ACSA, *Affordable Design: Convening the Conversation*. Washington, DC: Fannie Mae Foundation.

Banerjee-Guha, S. (2009) 'Neoliberalising the "urban": new geographies of power and injustice in Indian cities', *Economic and Political Weekly*, 44(22): 95–107.

Bertaud A. (2010) 'Land markets, government interventions, and housing affordability', Working Paper No. 18. Washington, DC: Wolfensohn Center for Development.

Bertaud, A., Buckley, R. and Owens, K. (2003) 'Has Indian urban policy been impoverishing?' Presented at the World Bank Urban Research Symposium, Washington, DC, 15–17 December.

Buckley, R. and Kalarickal, J. (2006) *Thirty Years of World Bank Shelter Lending: What Have We Learned?* Washington, DC: World Bank.

Business Standard (2012) 'Homes most affordable in 30 yrs, says HDFC', 20 May.

Chandrasekhara, C.P. (2011) 'The housing market and housing finance under liberalization in India', in A. Bardhan, R. Edelstein and C. Kroll (eds) *Global Housing Markets: Crises, Policies, and Institutions*. Hoboken, NJ: John Wiley & Sons.

Deshpande, S. (1998) 'After culture: renewed agendas for the political economy of India', *Cultural Dynamics*, 10(2): 147–169.

Fernandes, L. (2004) 'The politics of forgetting: class politics, state power and the restructuring of urban space in India', *Urban Studies*, 41(12): 2415–2430.

Fiadzo, E.D., Houston, J.E. and Godwin, D.D. (2001) 'Estimating housing quality for poverty and development policy analysis: CQIQ in Ghana', *Social Indicators Research*, 53(2): 137–162.

GOI (Government of India) (2007) *National Urban Housing and Habitat Policy*. New Delhi: Ministry of Housing & Urban Poverty Alleviation.

Hancock, K.E. (1993) '"Can't pay? Won't pay?" or economic principles of "affordability"', *Urban Studies*, 30(1): 127–145.

Hulchanski, D. J. (1995) 'The concept of housing affordability: six contemporary uses of the housing expenditure to income ratio', *Housing Studies*, 10(4): 471–491.

Jones Lang Lasalle (2012) *Affordable Housing in India: An Inclusive Approach to Sheltering the Bottom of the Pyramid*. India: Jones Lang Lasalle.

Keare, D. and Jimenez, E. (1983) *Progressive Development and Affordability in the Design of Urban Shelter Projects*. Washington, DC: World Bank.

KPMG (2010) *Affordable Housing – A Key Growth Driver in the Real Estate Sector?* India: KPMG.

Kumar, A. (1989) 'National housing policy – the implications', *Economic and Political Weekly*, 24(23): 1285–1294.

Lakha, S. (1999) 'The state, globalisation, and the Indian middle-class identity', in M. Pinches (ed.) *Culture and Privilege in Capitalist Asia*. London: Routledge.

Lee, M. (1990) 'The affordability criteria: inefficient, inequitable and immoral?', in M. Raj and P. Nientied (eds) *Housing and Income in Third World Urban Development*. London: Aspect Publishing.

Leeds, A. (1971) 'The concept of the "Culture of Poverty": conceptual, logical, and empirical problems, with perspectives from Brazil and Peru', in E.B. Leacock (ed.) *The Culture of Poverty: A Critique*. New York: Simon and Schuster, 226–284.

Lloyds TSB (2012) *Emerging Markets Top Global House Price League over the Past Decade*. UK: Lloyds TSB.

Malpass, P. and Murrie, A. (1999) *Housing Policy and Practice*. London: Macmillan.

MGI (McKinsey Global Institute) (2010) *India's Urban Awakening: Building Inclusive Cities, Sustaining Economic Growth*. New Delhi: McKinsey and Company.

Parekh, D. (2008) *Report of the High Level Task Force Affordable Housing for All*. India: GOI.

Payne, G. (2011) '*Social Housing in a Globalising World, Built Environment and Sustainable Development*'. Havana, Cuba: MACDES conference (December).

Pugh, C. (2001) 'The theory and practice of housing sector development for developing countries, 1950–99', *Housing Studies*, 16(4), 399–423.

Quigley, J.M. and Raphael, S. (2004) 'Is housing unaffordable? Why isn't it more affordable?', *Journal of Economic Perspectives*, 18(1): 191–214.

Renaud, B. (1985) *Housing and Financial Institutions in Developing Countries*. Chicago, IL: International Union of Building Societies and Savings Associations.

Sengupta, U. (2006) 'Liberalization and the privatisation of public rental housing in Kolkata', *Cities*, 23(4): 269–278.

Sengupta, U. and Tipple, A.G. (2007) 'Performance of public sector housing in Kolkata in the post reform milieu', *Urban Studies*, 44(10): 2009–2027.

Shetty, M. (2012) 'Homes become more affordable in last 10 years', *Times of India*, 2 May.

Smets, P. (2006) 'Small is beautiful but big is often the norm: housing microfinance in discussion', *Habitat International*, 30: 595–613.

Thalmann, P. (2003) '"House poor" or simply "poor"?', *Journal of Housing Economics*, 12(4): 291–317.

Tiesdell, S. (2004) 'Integrating affordable housing within market-rate developments: the design dimension', *Environment and Planning B: Planning and Design*, 31(2): 195–212.

Wadhwa, K. (2007) *Affordable Housing for Urban Poor*. Delhi: National Resource Centre, School Planning and Architecture.

Whitehead, C. (1999) 'The provision of finance for social housing: the UK experience', *Urban Studies*, 36(4): 657–672.

Whitehead, C. (2007) 'Planning policies and affordable housing: England as a successful case study?', *Housing Studies*, 22(1): 25–44.

World Bank (1993) *Enabling Housing to Work*. Washington, DC: World Bank.

10

HOW THE POOR HOUSE THEMSELVES IN PAKISTAN TODAY

Arif Hasan

Abbreviations

CDGK	City District Government Karachi
HBFCL	House Building Finance Company Limited
KAIRP	Katchi Abadi Improvement and Regularization Programme
KSDP	Karachi Strategic Development Plan
LDA	Lyari Development Authority
MDA	Malir Development Authority
OPP	Orangi Pilot Project

Glossary

Bisi	*Bisi* committee is a savings group whose collective savings rotate periodically between the members of the group
Goth	Village
Katchi abadi	Settlement without tenure
KIBOR	Karachi Interbank rate set by the State Bank of Pakistan. For details see www.investopedia.com/terms/i/interbankrate.asp#ixzz1r4D9R7Bs
Pugri	Good will money which the tenant pays and as a result it gives him the freedom from being evicted and from paying high rent
Pukhtoon	Residents of the Khyber Pukhtoonkhawa Province of Pakistan which borders on Afghanistan

Introduction

With an estimated population of 177.1 million in mid-2011 (Government of Pakistan 2011), Pakistan is the sixth most populous country in the world. In 1947, when the country was created, its population (excluding East Pakistan, which later became Bangladesh) was only 32.5 million. Because of this phenomenal increase, housing has been one of its most pressing problems. To tackle some of the housing related issues the federal government enacted the National Housing Policy in 2001. The policy document estimated an annual housing demand of 570,000 units against a supply of 300,000. Thus there was at that time a backlog of 270,000 units per year (Government of Pakistan 2001).

The policy document proposed a number of strategies to reduce the housing demand–supply gap. These policies included removing bottlenecks in identifying and providing state land for low-income housing, land acquisition, land registration and land disposal. A more liberal framework for financing housing through mortgage loans, savings and loans schemes, pension and provident funds, and introduction of microfinance schemes was also proposed. The private sector, and finance and building industies were given incentives to invest in housing activities. Another proposal was aimed at improving the ongoing Katchi Abadi Improvement and Regularization Programme (KAIRP) (Government of Pakistan 2001).

Paperwork for most of the proposals has been carried out. However, matters related to disputed land ownership and encroachments have not been documented. This is because of pressure from the developer's lobby which the government agencies are not able to withstand or because the agencies have compromised their positions by accepting benefits from the developers. As such, attempts at implementing the proposals have been made with varying success. However, in spite of these measures the housing supply gap has increased. This is because the reforms, except of KAIRP, are unaffordable and/or inaccessible for the poor, who depend almost entirely on informal processes for acquiring land and finance for meeting their housing needs (Hasan *et al.* 2013). For instance, acquiring a loan from the housing banks requires a formal job, ownership of a plot of land or initial payments made in a housing/apartment scheme. This is something almost none of the poor in Karachi possess.

Karachi is the largest city of Pakistan. Its 2010 population was estimated at 15.4 million and its 2015 population has been estimated at 18.04 million. In 1941, it had a population of 450,000 (City District Government Karachi 2006). Based on these figures, 9 per cent of Pakistan's total population, and 24 per cent of the country's urban population, live in Karachi. In addition, the city generates 15 per cent of the country's gross domestic product (GDP) and provides 25 per cent of the revenues for the federal government (City District Government Karachi 2006). Housing policies in Karachi are similar to those in the rest of Pakistan inasmuch as the poor are expected to access the market and the housing banks for ownership of a formal housing unit. However, there have been fairly large subsidized schemes in Pakistan for rehabilitating earthquake and flood victims.

In spite of Karachi's revenue-generating capacity, the city has not been able to cater to the housing needs of the huge influx of poor families from the rural areas and as refugees from the various regional conflicts and natural disasters. Many attempts at providing and/or facilitating housing have been made from time to time but due to governance and political conflict related issues their success has been limited (Hasan *et al.* 2013).

The Karachi housing demand is estimated at 80,000 units per year and formal sector supply at about 32,000 housing units with an additional 32,000 being built in *katchi abadis* (estimated by the author). Meanwhile, 75.5 per cent of Karachiites are classified as poor and as such they constitute the majority of the unmet demand (City District Government Karachi 2006).

In 2001, the City District Government Karachi (CDGK) replaced the old colonial bureaucratic system. In 2007, the CDGK had its Karachi Strategic Development Plan (KSDP) 2020 approved by the City Council. The KSDP 2020 has made a number of proposals for promoting housing for low- and lower-middle-income groups. These include strengthening of

KAIRP and notifying additional informal settlements for regularization; completing ongoing site and services projects on a priority basis; converting sites for single unit houses into apartment complexes; commercializing the main arteries of the city by permitting high-rise apartment construction on them; and promoting incremental housing development schemes on the Saiban model (City District Government Karachi 2006). Briefly, Saiban is a Karachi-based non-governmental organization (NGO) that develops initially unserviced plot settlements (see Saiban n.d.). The residents make shacks and pay for the land in instalments over a five-year period. They get together to develop their own neighbourhood water and sewage infrastructure and build their homes incrementally. For this, they are provided with technical assistance by Saiban on the Orangi Pilot Project (OPP) model (see OPP n.d.). Meanwhile, Saiban with payment received from the plot owners develops the trunk infrastructure and gets NGOs to develop the social infrastructure such as schools, health clinics, parks and community centres. With its links with government organizations and transporters, it helps in establishing transport facilities for the settlement. Land for the Saiban schemes has been provided by the government and paid for in instalments by the residents.

Meanwhile, the CDGK continues to prepare plans for developing land and auctions parcels to developers for building of sites and services, apartment houses and/or single unit housing schemes. Through this process the middle-, and to some extent, lower-middle-income groups benefit from these schemes. The main beneficiaries, however, are the developers and builders, who also benefit from the more liberal loan and mortgage programmes promoted by federal government policies which their clients can now access for purchasing their products.

None of the above programmes have the possibility of reaching the poor except for KAIRP and the incremental housing schemes on the Saiban model. The latter have been abandoned since no land is being provided to Saiban by the city government. This is because the city government is only providing land to supporters of the political party that controls the city government. So the question that emerges from this discussion is 'how do the poor house themselves in Karachi today?' This chapter tries to address this question.

The structure of the chapter is as follows. After a short introduction to the background of Karachi's housing problems, the development of the informal land and housing sector is discussed as well as the response of the state to it through the KAIRP process. Next, the chapter discusses the physical and social changes that have taken place in Karachi's informal settlements and tries to relate them to the new requirements and aspirations of their residents. Then the focus will be on the question of how the poor house themselves in the city today. Three processes are described: the transformation of villages into low-income urban settlements; densification of existing settlements; and the impact of a more liberal policy on the availability of mortgage loans. Finally, the chapter discusses issues of sustainability of the existing policies.

Background

Before 1947, Karachi had no major housing related problems. Density in the working-class areas was very low and there was sufficient open space in and around them to expand. But then, in August 1947, the partition of the subcontinent happened and Pakistan was created as an independent state. As a result of the Partition agreement, forced and agreed transfer of populations took place. Karachi was flooded by refugees from India and its population of about 450,000 increased within a few months to over a million. The scale of the change was enormous. In the intercensal years of 1931–1941, Karachi's population increased by 135,088 or by 44.91 per cent. Between 1941 and 1951 on the other hand, it increased by 632,572 or

TABLE 10.1 Population of *katchi abadis*

	1970s (1978)	1980s (1985)	1990s (1998)	2006 (projection)
Population	2,000,000	2,600,000	4,901,067	8,540,000
Number of households	227,000	356,000	700,152	1,200,000
Percentage of population	55%	43%	50%	61%

Sources: Dowall 1989; World Bank 1990; Master Plan Group of Offices 2007.

by 145.12 per cent (Government of Pakistan 1931, 1941, 1951). This was the beginning of Karachi's housing problems. The solution to these problems could not be found through formal sector development schemes, though many were attempted (Hasan *et al.* 2013). Informal processes took over and were aided by the fact that the land around Karachi was owned by government agencies and consisted mainly of desert and pasture land used by the herders living in the villages around the old city.

Development of the informal sector and the state's response

Initially, unorganized invasions occupied available government land within and around the immediate vicinity of the then city. Demolitions of some of these settlements by the state in the early 1950s led to the emergence of informal developers who created subdivisions with the informal support of government officials, police and whenever possible, politicians. This development was cheap and affordable to poor families. An added attraction was that the settlements were not too far away from the work and industrial areas of the city. House construction was supported by small contractors and material suppliers. Expenses on house building came from savings through the *bisi* committees (Hasan 2000). This pattern of development became common for subsequent migration to Karachi from other parts of Pakistan.

By 1978 the informal settlements (*katchi abadis*) of Karachi had a population of two million or 55 per cent of the city's population. It was at this stage that the KAIRP was launched. Of these informal settlements, 89 per cent have been marked for regularization – estimated by the author – and as such, in theory, they are secure unless their land is required for infrastructure development. If it is required, it can be acquired through the Land Acquisition Act which in theory guarantees compensation at market rates to all regularized land and property owners. Those without land title, however, are not entitled to compensation, though in recent evictions (last 10 years), they have been provided by the government with an 80-square-yard plot on the city's periphery and Rs 50,000 (US$556) as compensation.

In spite of the KAIRP, the population of *katchi abadis* increased continuously from 55 per cent (or 227,000 households) of the city's total population in 1978 to 61 per cent (or 1.2 million households) in 2006 (Dowall 1989; World Bank 1990; City District Government Karachi 2006). This is shown in Table 10.1. The major problem has been the setting of a cut-off date for the regularization of the *katchi abadis*. The cut-off date has changed with time and political pressure generated through the election process. Currently, it is 20 December 1997.

Physical and social changes in informal settlements

Most of the pre-1990 settlements have changed over time. Unlike before, their new leadership is young and educated. They are no longer purely working-class settlements. A sizeable minority of residents are white-collar workers, college and school teachers, or entrepreneurs in the informal sector with strong links with formal sector industry and the services sector. They have shed their flowery feudal vocabulary; they contain beauty parlours, video halls, private schools and privately run health facilities. They also contain an increasing number of women working in formal sector industries or as contract labour within their homes or at work centres in their neighbourhoods (Hasan 2010).

As a result of these changes, these settlements have new middle-class aspirations. However, due to recession, inflation, absence of affordable technical education (which the job market requires) and cutting of subsidies on health, education and utilities (as a result of structural adjustment and neoliberal reforms), these aspirations cannot be met easily. The newer settlements have similar but more serious monetary constraints. Consumerism has also invaded the sociology of the more affluent of these settlements. As a result of the above observations, families have little or no savings left. Also, the cost of land in well-located informal settlements is exorbitantly high as compared to 20 years ago when compared to the daily-wage for unskilled labour then and today (Hasan 2008). Given these realities, families looking for a home have only two options. One, to shift to the periphery of the city where land is cheap but far from the workplace, or two, densify the house by building upwards.

How the poor house themselves today

Transformation of villages into urban settlements

Karachi is lucky in that it has large tracts of government-owned land on its periphery. This government land is dotted by 2,173 listed *goths* or small villages although the figure is disputed. Most of them form part of what was previously known as the rural district of Karachi. In 1987, the government launched the Gothabad (Goth Development) Schemes under which land title was given to the residents of the *goths*. Under the Sindh Local Government Ordinance 2001, the *goths* of Karachi district became 'urban' and as a result, the villagers became owners of 'urban land' (OPP n.d.; *Express Tribune* 2012).

However, the process of regularization of a *goth* is not easy. Only *goths* that existed before March 1985 can be regularized. The burden of proof that the villages existed before that date falls on the residents themselves. This proof can be in the shape of birth and death certificates, identification cards bearing the address of the *goth*, a stamped letter envelope or any other relevant document (*Express Tribune* 2012). This requires collective action and in the case of the rural areas the elders of the traditional clan leadership organize the whole process. Very often, they are unable to organize it effectively. In addition, informal payments to the officials in government agencies are also required to initiate and/or complete the process. Sometimes, these payments are so high that a village cannot afford them. Due to these constraints, middlemen, backed by formal and informal developers, step in and form a 'joint venture' with the *goth* elders. They make the payments, take responsibility for the process and the *goth* leadership, against payments (while protecting certain land parcels), transfer the land, including community pasture land, to the developers. The developers then subdivide the land and sell it formally and/or informally (Hasan *et al.* 2013).

In the case of formal development, schemes are submitted to the Malir Development Authority (MDA) and Lyari Development Authority (LDA), in whose areas the *goths* are located (Hasan *et al.* 2013). Advertisements for such schemes are made in the press. They usually consist of 80- and 120-square-yard plots and the price varies between Rs 40,000 (US$445) and Rs 120,000 (US$1,334) for raw land. Development charges are in addition to this. They are paid in instalments for the provision of electricity, water, road and sewage infrastructure. Depending on the location, the schemes become habitable in five to ten years.

In the case of informal development, there is no approval from any authority though sometimes the literature for the promotion of the scheme mentions an MDA or LDA approval. By paying the MDA or LDA authorities, the developer sees to it that they do not challenge this statement. In the case of informal development, people can move in immediately onto their plots and build their housing. Development comes slowly through lobbying with politicians and utility agencies, self-help and technical and managerial support from NGOs and by using the community's ethnic and clan based linkages. It is estimated that over 100,000 plots (formal and informal) have been developed on the peripheries of the city over the past decade (OPP n.d.; Hasan *et al.* 2013).

The development on the periphery is viewed differently by different actors in this development drama. Studies show that living on the periphery has serious problems for the residents since they are far from their places of work, better quality schools and health facilities, entertainment and recreation options. Their transport costs increase considerably as a result and, due to the distances involved, their women can no longer access work in the neighbourhood. There are social costs as well. Because of long hours of travelling to and from work, the head of the household does not spend time with the family and is also exhausted when he arrives home. This adversely affects family relations and the behaviour patterns of his children (Urban Resource Centre 2004; Ghous *et al.* 2012).

Developers disagree with the contention that living far from the city is a negative. They argue that environmental conditions on the periphery are better in terms of air and noise pollution. They also say that it is less costly living far away. The wife does not have the opportunity of going shopping and wasting money. One can always excuse oneself from socializing in the city or attending events on the basis of being so far away. They also argue that living near the rich is psychologically disturbing for the poor, especially the younger generation which is already exposed to so much consumerism and attractive advertisements (Hasan *et al.* 2013).

Whatever the opinion, the Gothabad Scheme and related developments have produced enough lots of land to satisfy the needs of Karachi's low-income groups (at least for those who can afford them) for the next five years. The lower-middle-income groups are also attracted to these schemes and have made purchases both for building and for speculation. Formal sector developers working in the city proper feel that these housing schemes on the periphery have lowered the cost and demand of formal sector housing (Hasan *et al.* 2013). However, costs of transport have almost doubled in the past five years and there is pressure from the transporters' lobby to increase them further. There is evidence to suggest that there is now a trend of low-income communities preferring to rent accommodation within the city rather than live on the periphery due to the rising costs of transport.

Densification

Not all Karachiites whose family members are increasing can afford the cost of the developments on the periphery. Many of them also do not wish their younger generation to go through the same process of incrementally building their homes and acquiring services through self-help and lobbying. The younger generation is also different from them inasmuch as it has acquired middle-class values and white-collar jobs and businesses. In addition, many of them are not willing to live far away from their places of work, relatives and better social facilities. Such families have slowly built upwards, often without permission, and as a result densified their settlements. This process of densification is continuing in almost all of the older *katchi abadis* and is being carried out through three different processes, which are explained below.

The first process is the building upwards by the family. Research establishes that most house owners wish to keep at least one of their sons and his family with them. Construction is incremental. Case studies of settlements in the inner city areas of Karachi and previously peripheral settlements show that their densities have increased from 600 persons per hectare to 4,000 persons per hectare and from 200 persons per hectare to 1,195 persons per hectare, respectively. In the case of the inner city settlements, the high densities have created a number of physical and social problems. The number of persons per room sometimes exceeds 10. There is no private space for newly wed couples. Because of congestion, the father often sleeps on the street or does not come home. Children cannot be supervised and so they form gangs and take to drugs (Hasan *et al*. 2010).

The second process is simply an increase in the number of persons per apartment. In the case of apartment complexes built in 1974, the number of persons per room varied from 10 to 15 in 2010. When the apartments were occupied initially, their population consisted of young married couples with one or two children. Now the children have grown up, married and have children of their own, but due to cash constraints and a lack of affordable loans they cannot purchase apartments or plots of land as additional accommodation (Hasan *et al*. 2010).

The third process of densification is increasing rapidly in the old city areas which have become for the most part low- and lower-middle income but with a small, politically well-connected and rich entrepreneurial class dealing in port related activities, land and property. Many of them have homes in the upper-middle and elite areas of the city as well, where their children study. History tells us that probably after a generation they will no longer live and work in these areas.

In these old areas of the city, almost all houses consisted of one or two storeys and were built of stone. Today they are being converted into four-to-six-storey apartment blocks. The process is that a developer buys the plot of land on which the house stands. He converts it into an apartment block and in addition to the payment for the land, he gives the owner one or two apartments as well, free of cost. Most of these apartments are two-room affairs and are rented out through the *pugri* system. A *pugri* of Rs 700,000 (US$775) to Rs 750,000 (US$834) is demanded, after which the rent of the apartment comes down to Rs 200 (US$2.3) per month. Without *pugri* the rent is Rs 3,000 (US$34) per month. In both cases, an increase of 5 per cent per year in rent is agreed upon. In this way, the developer recovers more than 100 per cent of his costs and at the same time establishes an income for himself (Hasan *et al*. 2013). This sort of development is carried out in many cases without formal approval from the Sindh Building Control Authority whose permission is necessary before construction can take place. The clients of these builders are normally middle- or lower-middle-income groups.

Most of the neighbourhoods of the old city are ethnically homogeneous. The older residents, especially those who are politically and/or socially active, resent the development that is taking place because they claim that outsiders are moving in through the densification process made possible by converting houses into apartments. They are afraid that their ethnic and/or linguistic group will become a minority in their neighbourhood and their tangible and intangible cultures will be ruined (Hasan *et al.* 2013).

Impact of the liberalization of provision of mortgage loans

As a result of the government's aggressively promoted neoliberal policies, there have been no public sector housing schemes for low-income groups over the past two decades. This is in sharp contrast to the 1970s and 1980s when the state developed over 110,000 plots (Hasan 2000) for low-income groups in addition to the development of 26,000 acres (1,040 hectares) as sites and services with a majority percentage, at least in theory, for low-income groups (Karachi Development Authority 1989). Realizing the seriousness of the housing situation, the government has provided incentives to the private banking sector to create mortgage finance schemes and also to liberalize the loan conditions so as to help a larger number of families to access the housing market. Though this has provided relief to families that own plots and have formal sector jobs, it has not really been able to service the needs of the majority of the poor in Karachi.

To give a boost to its policies, the government-owned House Building Finance Corporation has become a private company called the House Building Finance Company Limited (HBFCL n.d.). In addition, there are micro-credit banks that also lend small loans for house improvement. Another important development is the Islamic banking system where instead of credit and interest rates, there is a joint ownership of the house between the 'owner' and the bank till the loan is repaid. Over the past decade, the ceilings for grant of loans have also become far more flexible. As a result of these reforms, housing finance availability increased by 400 per cent to Rs 3.5 billion (US$39 million) in 2003. However, in January 2004, it was estimated that there was still an unmet demand of Rs 70 billion (US$778 million) (*Daily Dawn* 2004).

It has been established that for building a house on a plot of land in a formally planned area, a low-income family requires Rs 500,000 (US$5,556). This does not include the cost of land, which the family has to purchase from its own resources. A similar sum is required to purchase an apartment in a developer built complex. Monthly repayments over a 15-year period for a family that earns Rs 15,000 (US$166) per month should not exceed Rs 5,000 (US$56) (Hasan *et al.* 2013), whereas repayment for such a loan works out as more than Rs 10,000 (US$112) per month over a 15-year period because of the high rate of interest. Also, the most important requirement of low-income groups is funding for the purchase of a plot of land in a formal sector scheme, which banks do not provide. Also, they do not provide funds to plot owners in informal settlements.

In spite of theses change in policies, the housing backlog in Pakistan increased from 4.33 million in 1998 to 7.57 million in 2009 (Nenova 2010). Apart from a shortage of funds available with the banks, there are other serious problems as well. For one, none of the banks offers loans for the purchase of land without which a loan is not available except for the purchase of an apartment, which is not a preferred choice for the vast majority of poor families for both affordability related and socio-economic reasons (Hasan *et al.* 2010). Repayment on loans is affordable for families earning Rs 20,000 (US$223) or more. The problem is not with the interest charged by the housing banks themselves but with the high rate of KIBOR, which is currently 12 per cent per annum.

Then there are other problems as well. For getting a loan the applicant must give evidence of income and property. Both should be verifiable. This means ownership documents, which the vast majority of residents living in informal settlements do not possess. The process of acquiring a loan is also cumbersome and people very often engage middlemen at a cost to help them out. However it must be said that the housing banks have done everything possible to inform their prospective clients through their websites on their requirements and how to meet them (Hasan *et al.* 2013). They also inform their prospective clients on the process and documents required for purchasing a house, apartment or a plot of land in the different jurisdictions of the city. But this knowledge is only available to the better off among the poor who have access to the internet.

The most attractive loan packages are offered by the Islamic banking system (Hasan *et al.* 2013). However, here also documentation of ownership of land, income and tax-paying businesses is required for getting a loan. The advantage of the micro-credit banks, on the other hand, is that they offer small short-term loans of Rs 50,000 to Rs 500,000 (US$556 to US$5,556) which can be used for house improvements such as laying a proper roof, building a toilet or acquiring utility connections. Here again, the problem of verifiable property and income related documents arises. It is worth noting that 24 per cent of applications for construction, 11.5 per cent for purchase of property and 7 per cent for land are rejected due to an absence of proper documentation (Asia Foundation 2008).

Issues of sustainability

As discussed above, the credit options for sustainability can only work if a major reform is carried out, interest rates are lowered and/or subsidized, loans are provided for the purchase of land and land for low-income groups is made available. Karachi has a booming real estate development in both the formal and informal sectors with adequate skilled manpower and entrepreneurship and also substantial state-owned land resources. However, the problems the city faces make it difficult to cash in on this potential. This is because, apart from the issues raised in the above discussion, Karachiites face other housing related problems as well that overshadow many of the concerns expressed in the earlier sections. These relate to regional and local conflicts that have made it difficult for government institutions to function. These conflicts are explained below.

During the Afghan war against the Soviets, supplies for the war effort went through Karachi. Again, in the war of attrition that followed, the supply route was through Karachi. In the present Afghan war, Karachi has been the main source of supplies to the NATO troops and also for the Afghan transit trade. As a result, it has become the headquarters of rival interests in the Afghan war and the rivals have also found local supporters, some of whom are proxies for the different international and regional players involved in the war. Heroin trafficking partly financed the war effort, and much of it exited through Karachi port and was also used locally. Guns were an essential part of the drug trade. This was the beginning of what Karachiites call the 'drug and Kalashnikov' culture. It was also the beginning of large-scale investments, whose sources were undeclared and 'unknown', in land and real estate business. It also led to a further weakening of an already deteriorating governance system. In the early 1990s, gun power first came to be used to settle land disputes and to forcibly occupy land and property. Through a system of bribes and coercion, the formal governance system became 'informalized' and violations of land related laws, rules, regulations and procedures became common (Hasan *et al.* 2013).

Karachi has various ethnicities and the major ethnicity is of Urdu speakers who constitute 48 per cent of the population of the city. They are represented by an important political party (Muttahida Quomi Movement or MQM as it is referred to). However, Sindh, the province of which Karachi is the capital, is Sindhi speaking, unlike the city. As such, there is conflict between the province and the city. There are also strong *Pukhtoon* interests in trade, transport and businesses. In such a situation, decentralization carried out under the Sindh Local Government Ordinance 2001, which brought the MQM to power, increased ethnic tensions and initiated turf wars between rival ethnic groups in which the land suppliers and financers are important players. In these turf wars 14 estate agents were killed in two years (2010 and 2011) by what Karachiites call the 'land mafia' (Hasan *et al.* 2013). As a result of these conflicts, decisions regarding the structure of local government for Karachi remain undecided, with various civic agencies being pressurized by conflicting ethnic groups represented by their political affiliations.

As a result of these turf wars, an increasing number of settlements and apartment complexes are becoming uni-ethnic and so are various neighbourhoods of new townships, and in some cases, the townships and complexes are being planned for specific ethnic and/or religious groups (Hasan 2011). Security as such is a major consideration in the purchase or renting of property. In addition, the local governance systems have become helpless and corrupt. Bribes to the development and utility agencies are common and developers feel that in the absence of these informal payments they could reduce prices by 18 to 25 per cent. Due to the system of corruption, people use middlemen or their ethnic connections to fulfil the requirements of land and property purchase and/or for fulfilling the requirements needed to get documentation (Hasan *et al.* 2013).

Given the present situation, the majority of Karachiites have no option but to densify their homes or live in settlements on the periphery and develop them through collective efforts. There are other options but they require political will to develop and implement a reform agenda for local governance and financial institutions. One option is developing public housing on government land within the city. Such land exists in considerable quantity but is hoarded for commercial returns and speculation by the land owning agencies. They do not want to have poor settlements or apartments on this land for this would lower land values in the neighbourhood and deprive them of revenue. However, if this land is treated as a subsidy, housing can easily be made affordable through loans and through subsidies from commercial development at these locations. The other option is the initiation of a massive, transparent and efficient programme of giving formal land titles to the residents who at present do not have them or are not entitled to them. On the basis of these titles, loans for building incrementally could be made available to them, provided the state and the banks have the necessary funds. Yet another option would be to support the expansion of community-based NGO programmes which have shown that the lower income groups can afford the cost of land, its development and their homes, if they pay for them incrementally (Saiban n.d.). Financial support for the expansion of these efforts could upscale them. But it must be understood that NGO efforts alone cannot deal with the enormity of the problem. And also, that without bringing down the interest rates to 6 per cent or less, lower income groups earning Rs 12,000 (US$134) to Rs 15,000 (US$167) per month cannot be serviced.

Given the political and regional situation described in this section, the reforms proposed above will not be implemented for the foreseeable future. However, there are other reasons as well. There is a massive anti-poor bias in policy making and planning. Much of this bias is related to the conventional training of professionals and bureaucrats and the class biases of these two groups.

Conclusions

Karachi's housing demand has always outstripped supply. The gap was previously taken care of through the formation of *katchi abadis* on state land on the periphery of a relatively smaller, in spatial terms, city. As discussed in the chapter, *katchi abadis* are history because they are being used for an increasingly middle-income market. Even in informal settlements, they have become far too expensive for the poor to afford. The other option is being provided by the urbanization of the villages on Karachi's periphery. However, living far away from the city has immense transport and social costs of which the long journey times and discomfort of travelling are not the least. As a result, old settlements are densifying; rentals in informal settlements nearer to the city are becoming a preferred option for an increasingly large number of families, and old houses in the inner city are being purchased by developers and being turned into lower-middle- and lower-income tenements. Although, the state has carried out reforms to make housing loans available for lower income groups, and has tried to facilitate the process of acquiring them, the loans are failing to reach the target group. This is because of loan conditions, such as, the ownership of a plot of land on which to construct; high interest rates that make the loan unaffordable for those who earn Rs 15,000 (US$56) or less, which is the income of the majority of the poor; and the requirement that the applicant for the loan should have a formal job, which very few of the poor do.

The reform agenda discussed in the previous section is doable but unlikely to be carried through. The major constraint in implementing reform is related to Karachi's ethnic conflict and the spin-offs of the Afghan war. These conflicts have turned land into an instrument of power and control over turf. To contain the growing conflict, discretionary powers of politicians and government officials have been increased and are used for the political and financial interests of powerful developers, many of whom have dubious origins and ethnic affiliation. As a result of these conflicts and turf wars, already unclear land titles have become even more unclear; and manipulation of the market by pressure and targeted killings of estate agents and property dealers have made an already inefficient system of justice in land and property related issues almost ineffective. Because of the ethnic and regional conflict, Karachi's governance system also remains undecided. Because of these issues, the will for reform and change has been sapped.

The end of the Afghan war will be followed by a war of attrition. Hopefully, things will change after the war of attrition fizzles out. However, to really overcome the governance crisis, Karachi's ethnic parties will have to work out a consensus on living together. For this they will have to behave as statesmen and rise above the politics of 'constituencies' and 'votes' in the larger interests of the city and the province. One hopes that this will happen sooner rather than later.

References

Asia Foundation (2008) *Consumer Financing in Pakistan: Issues, Challenges and the Way Forward*. Islamabad: Consumer Rights Association of Pakistan.

City District Government Karachi (2006) *Karachi Strategic Development Plan 2020*, Karachi: City District Government.

Daily Dawn (2004) News report, 25 January, Karachi.
Dowall, D. (1989) *Karachi Land and Housing Study.* KDA-Master Plan Department (MPD), Karachi: Karachi Development Authority.
Express Tribune (2012) News report 16 February: '800 years on a battle for survival resurfaces for Karachi's old villages', Karachi.
Ghous, K., Ahmed, N., Sidat R. and Areeb, T. (2012) *Gender Dimensions of Development Induced Displacement and Resettlement: The Case of the Lyari Expressway.* Karachi: Social Policy and Development Centre.
Government of Pakistan (1931) *Population Census Reports.* Islamabad: GoP.
Government of Pakistan (1941) *Population Census Reports.* Islamabad: GoP.
Government of Pakistan (1951) *Population Census Reports.* Islamabad: GoP.
Government of Pakistan (2001) *National Housing Policy 2001.* Islamabad: GoP.
Government of Pakistan (2011) *Pakistan Economic Survey 2010–11.* Islamabad: Economic Advisor Wing, Finance Division.
Hasan, A. (2000) *Housing for the Poor.* Karachi: City Press Karachi.
Hasan, A. (2008) 'Housing security and related issues: the case of Karachi', unpublished paper for UNESCAP.
Hasan, A. (2010) *Participatory Development.* Karachi: Oxford University Press.
Hasan, A. (2011) 'Karachi violence: a summary of what 14 persons in affected areas say', note prepared for consultation at the Pakistan Institute of Labour Education and Research, Karachi, 26 August 2011 and subsequently published by the Human Rights Commission of Pakistan.
Hasan, A., Sadiq, A. and Ahmed, S. (2010) *Planning for High Density in Low Income Settlements: Four Case Studies from Karachi.* London: IIED.
Hasan, A., Raza, M., Ahmed, N., Sadiq, A., Ahmed, S. and Sarwar, M.B. (2013) 'Land ownership, control and contestation in Karachi and implications for low income housing', Urbanization and Emerging Population Issues Working Paper 10. London: IIED.
HBFCL (n.d.) 'Eligibility' Online. Available at www.hbfcl.com/nc_eligibility_criteria.html (accessed 10 October 2013).
Karachi Development Authority Master Plan Group of Offices (1989) *Karachi Development Plan 2000.* Karachi: KDA.
Master Plan Group of Offices (2007) *Karachi Strategic Development Plan 2020.* City District Government Karachi.
Nenova. T. (2010) *Expanding Housing Finance to the Underserviced in Asia.* Washington, DC: World Bank.
OPP (n.d.) Online. Available at www.oppinstitutions.org (accessed: 10 October 2013)
Saiban (n.d.). Website Saiban. Online. Available at www.saibanpakistan.org (accessed 20 October 2012).
Urban Resource Centre (2004) *Livelihood Substitution.* Karachi: Ushba Publishing International.
World Bank (1990) *Shelter for Low Income Communities: Inception Report on Sindh*, October. Washington, DC: World Bank.

11
SELF-HELP HOUSING IN INDONESIA

Devisari Tunas and Laksmi T. Darmoyono

Abbreviations

APBN	National Budget
BTN	National Mortgage Bank
CSR	Corporate Social Responsibility
FLPP	Housing Finance Liquidity Facility
GDP	Gross domestic product
KIP	Kampung Improvement Programme
KPR	National Mortgage Credit
NGO	Non-governmental organization
PERUMNAS	National Housing and Urban Development Corporation
Repelita	Five-Year Development Plan
SoE	State-owned enterprise

Introduction

Housing delivery is one of the toughest development challenges in Indonesia. In 2011, the housing shortage in Indonesia was estimated to be more than 8 million units (Kristopo 2011); if counting the inhabitable but substandard housing units, the number would be 13 million (Kusumaputra 2011). While the government is planning to reduce this number in the coming 20 years, the local capacity is far from sufficient (Pikiran Rakyat 2012). The government is not yet able to fulfil the annual new housing demand of 735,000 units (UN-Habitat 2006). At the same time there are still 54,000 hectares of slums in 10,000 locations across the country, which house close to 18 million people (Indonesian Ministry of Housing 2009). With classic problems such as lack of financial, institutional and legal capacity, the housing shortage in the country is likely to increase even more.

Data from the National Statistical Bureau (BPS 2010) shows that 67.9 per cent of the urban population live in their own houses while 21.5 per cent live in rented or leased homes. In Indonesia there is a strong tradition of home ownership. Owning a house is not only deemed to be a necessary investment scheme, it is a sign of prestige. However, around 17.2 per cent of urban households do not have any legal certification of property ownership (BPS 2010). Households either have tribal land ownership (that is yet to be legally recognized) or they occupy illegal housing; this situation brings a sense of insecurity for many households, particularly those located in urban areas.

In practice, the government has developed many housing policies and programmes to provide low-income housing for its citizens. These include the Settlement Upgrading Programme (the Kampung Improvement Programme, or KIP), the National Housing Programme, policies on land provision and lately housing funding based upon Housing Finance Liquidity Facility (Fasilitas Likuiditas Pembiayaan Perumahan or FLPP) which involves close collaboration between the public (government) and the private sectors (banking, SoE, and other corporations). Although the implementation of these regulations was not unsuccessful, in reality, due to many factors such as high interest rates and policy mismatch, 'affordable' housing is still not affordable for low-income groups. Furthermore, for institutional-related reasons, not everybody has access to housing schemes. As a consequence, a local form of self-help housing called *kampung* continues to sprout in many urban areas across the country. Considering the given conditions, self-help housing seems to be the only alternative for low-income people at the moment.

In this chapter, we first discuss the housing situation in Indonesia in terms of its policies, regulations and delivery systems as well as the conditions that led to the emergence of self-help initiatives. Next we discuss the self-help housing experience in Indonesia illustrated by the case of a self-help *kampung* improvement project in Yogyakarta, which illustrates a self-help success story.

A brief overview of housing development in Indonesia

The Indonesian housing sector has come a long way. Chronologically, it can be divided into three periods of development: the old regime period (1945–1965), the new regime period (1966–1998) and the decentralization period (1998–present). Within each period, the housing programmes and policies focused on different agendas; while the old regime dealt mainly with the post-independence population explosion and short-term urban development projects, the new regime focused more on public housing provisions as part of a more general and long-term social development programme. For example, the first national public housing programme, called PERUMNAS (see the section entitled 'The emergence of urban *kampungs* as self-help housing under the new regime'), was a product of this particular era. The decentralization period on the other hand focuses more on the shift of housing provision responsibility from central government to the regional and local government levels.

Housing production and delivery in the country can be divided into the usual two sectors: public and private. While the public sector focuses more on the low- to lower-middle-income groups, the private sector targets the more lucrative mid- to high-income groups. Recognizing the absence of the public sector in housing provision in this market segment, the private sector took the lead in this area not only by capturing a massive housing demand from this segment, but also by governing the trends of its development in terms of its location, typology and distribution. Thanks to the 1990s economic deregulation that enabled private developers to seek foreign capital and investment credit, the country experienced a massive property boom.

New town developments, driven by the private sector, sprang up all over major Indonesian cities. These enormous developments of low-density, landed-residential housing estates have swallowed vast amounts of rural and peri-urban agricultural lands. The private land developers created a dream lifestyle for an urban population who yearn for an ideal (landed) family house with a garden. This trend has shifted many inner city people, belonging mostly to middle- to upper-income groups, to the suburbs. Meanwhile, the decline of agriculture activities in the rural and peri-urban areas has triggered more migration to big cities, contributing to the densification of low-income urban settlements.

Early attempts to provide housing for the population under the old regime

Right after independence, the country witnessed an unprecedented population explosion. Driven by the lack of employment in rural areas and attracted by the bright lights of the cities, millions of rural migrants came to the big cities. This massive migration contributed to the burgeoning of informal urban settlements. This situation forced city authorities to look for public housing alternatives. For example, in the 1950s and with a garden city concept, Jakarta municipality developed a satellite city named Kebayoran Baru a few kilometres away from the city centre (Kompas 2006). However, due to rapid population growth, after several years the capacity of the satellite city was insufficient to accommodate the ever-growing population.

Since then, the government has created a number of policies, regulations and action plans. Realizing the financial potentialities of the private sector, the government ratified Act no. 1/1964 on 'Housing Basics' that encouraged active engagement of the private sector and the state-owned enterprise (SoE) to support the provision of public housing. Under this scheme, the government 'forced' big enterprises to provide housing for their employees. Some large SoEs, mostly related to the mining and oil industries, then developed thousands of housing units (with basic infrastructure and facilities) for their employees in their operational areas, often rural or remote locations. Though to a certain extent the programme was able to reduce the housing deficit at that time, it did not offer any housing solutions for those who were not employed by those enterprises. By allocating industrial areas in rural or remote locations, the government expected to stimulate local economic development that could in turn help to reduce the flow of migration to big cities. Though successful in some areas, as a whole this strategy was not very successful as rural–urban migration continued to escalate.

The emergence of urban *kampungs* as self-help housing under the new regime

While the old regime fixated on a campaign of nation building characterized by grand urban development, the new regime under Suharto focused more on economic improvement to bring long-term socio-economic and political stability to the country. Although the previous regime had delivered various housing provision programmes, they were still not sufficient to meet the ever-growing housing demand. With the unstoppable flow of rural–urban migration (city authorities in response even proclaimed Jakarta a city closed to migrants) and an insufficient stock of low-income public housing in the cities, informal settlements sprouted across vacant urban lands including illegal areas such as along railway tracks, river banks and in brownfield sites. In these informal settlements, low-income groups created their own housing. With limited financial capacity they built their own houses out of makeshift building materials such as reclaimed wooden boards, cardboard and used metal, and with low sanitation standards; this type of settlement is known in Indonesia as an urban *kampung*. Urban *kampungs* are commonly understood as non-formal, high-density settlements for low-income groups that usually occupy vacant urban lands. These settlements usually have limited or no access to basic infrastructure and public facilities. In many cases, they also are prone to environmental hazards (Handayani 2009; Tunas and Peresthu 2010). Mostly self-initiated both individually and collectively, the urban *kampung* in this case can be considered to be one form of self-help housing in Indonesia.

Urban *kampungs* have continued to provide housing (and sources of employment) for the urban poor for many years. Recognizing the importance of self-help housing, and knowing the limited financial capacity of low-income people, the government initiated a programme to improve housing and environmental conditions in urban *kampungs*. One of the best-known approaches is the KIP, which was initially introduced in the 1960s. This programme marked the government's acceptance of *kampungs* as one of the available forms of low-income housing.

The first KIP, targeting a number of urban *kampungs* in the city, was implemented in Jakarta under the framework of the Mohammad Husni Thamrin project. The project involved a number of implementation stages based on the priority of each *kampung*. Through the KIP approach, the government helped low-income groups gain access to basic infrastructure and public facilities such as clean water and sanitation, garbage disposal, drainage, roads and green open space, among others (Dhakal 2002; Juliman 2006; Kuswartojo *et al.* 2005) that are required to improve the physical and spatial qualities and create a healthy living environment for *kampung* residents. Thus the KIP in this sense can be considered to be a formal self-help housing initiative in which the government shows a level of institutional support.

As it greatly improved physical conditions in many *kampungs* in the city, this programme showed positive results after five years (1969–1974) of implementation (Juliman 2006). The KIP was then further implemented in a number of other big cities in Indonesia. In fact, during the first ten years, it managed to help over 3.3 million *kampung* inhabitants at a cost of only US$118 per person (Werlin 1999).

The second KIP was implemented under Repelita II or the National Five-Year Strategic Planning Programme (GoI 1978) in Surabaya. At this time, Surabaya, the second biggest city in Indonesia, was struggling with rapid growth of slum areas. Due to the successful KIP implementations in Jakarta and Surabaya, this programme was eventually adopted as part of the national development programme.

Starting with Repelita III (GoI 1979), the KIP was expanded to 190 cities across Indonesia (GoI 1984). During Repelita IV, the KIP was further carried out in an additional 400 cities around the country. At this stage the programme started to adopt a community participation approach which encouraged more active community engagement in settlement upgrading activities (GoI 1984). This approach was deemed necessary for communities to develop a sense of ownership and responsibility – aspects that are crucial for the success of KIP projects. Until Repelita V (GoI 1989), the KIP managed to improve a vast number of *kampungs* in 470 cities across Indonesia through a community participation approach (GoI 1995).

Repelita VI, the last five-year planning programme under the new regime, focused on slum area improvement for 125 cities countrywide. However, Repelita VI was not only based on physical development; the programme also included social and economic improvement through the Tribina programme that involves a three-fold approach as an integrated part of *kampung* improvement projects: physical development, social improvement and economic improvement (Kuswartojo *et al.* 2005). With this development, the KIP was transformed from a programme that focused solely on physical development to a more elaborate programme that included empowerment of the local community through the introduction of basic education and micro-scale economic programmes. The new programmes were expected to provide some basic knowledge on the importance of a healthy living environment and sustainable livelihood. With increased understanding and new skills, the community was expected to be more proactive and able to 'help' themselves. Moreover, with this new direction the programme was expected to change its top-down course to a more bottom-up approach.

After more than 30 years, with active community participation the KIP succeeded in improving both the physical and non-physical conditions in many urban *kampungs* in the country. Nonetheless, although the KIP positively contributed to self-help housing improvement, there are still several challenges that the government and low-income groups must face. Limited public financial capacity, insufficient land provision, lack of political will and legal enforcement, and unclear housing regulations and policies are only a few of the problems.

Apart from the Settlement Upgrading programme, the new regime also established a national public housing programme. Compared to other Asian countries, Indonesia started rather late; it was not until 1974 that the government eventually launched the first public housing programme under the National Housing Corporation or PERUMNAS. PERUMNAS was initially designated for civil servants but later also targeted low-income groups in general. In addition, a financial scheme supported by the National Bank, National Mortgage Credit (KPR), was also introduced to support the programme. Nowadays KPR is also supported by the private sector through the 'Corporate Social Responsibilities' scheme. Under KPR, the government and the National Mortgage Bank (BTN) provide financial support for low-income groups to build or improve their housing by means of a soft-loan mechanism. This scheme is supported by a number of financial resources such as international loans, APBN (the National Budget), short-term funds and others (Sudana and Winarso 2005). As it provides many households with the possibility to own a house, KPR yields some positive results. However, the bank faces many difficulties in financing housing development since it has to deal with long-term loans while at the same time provide immediate construction credits for developers (Sudana and Winarso 2005).

Housing development under the decentralization period

In 1998 and 1999, Indonesia faced both political turmoil and an economic crisis that culminated in the dismantling of the new regime. In 1999 the new government introduced a decentralization system that aimed to 'bring the government closer to the people' (Hofman and Kaiser 2002). Under this new system, where the one-size-fits-all policy is deemed to be both unsuitable and unresponsive to local conditions, the central government distributes responsibilities to local government (municipality or regional) to develop their own regulations or policies based on the local context. Local government thus is (or will be) responsible for developing its own development agendas, including those of housing. The rationale behind this policy is that the central government recognizes the importance of more contextual local policies and development programmes. Nonetheless, though the local government is free to develop its own housing agenda, it still has to adhere to the general strategic plan set by the central government.

The existing national public housing programme has not been successful in meeting the ever-growing housing demand. Up until 1998, it was only able to provide 50 per cent of annual total demand. One of the problems associated with the lack of housing stock is the fact that public housing investment in Indonesia is very low; it comprises only 1.5 per cent of the total GDP (gross domestic product), while in other countries it commonly ranges from 2 to 8 per cent. Additionally, mortgage finance in Indonesia is only 3 per cent of the GDP, while in Malaysia for example it is 25 per cent (Hoek-Smit 2002).

The decentralization policy was expected to be able to address the problems. Implementation, however, is not supported by the local conditions. Policy mismatch and the lack of local capacity and institutional support are identified as key reasons why the decentralization policy has failed to stimulate local development. To address this failure, a new policy that clarified and specified the task divisions in terms of housing delivery between the central and local government was issued in 2011. Its impact, however, is still to be evaluated.

Conflicting and mismatching policies are well-known themes in the narrative of Indonesian housing development. These issues therefore deserve special attention in light of decentralization as they often hinder the process of housing delivery. One recent example is the new housing financial scheme and the newly updated housing regulation No. 1/2011. The financial crisis that hit Indonesia in mid-1997 greatly limited the government budget for housing credit. One of the biggest problems in the Indonesian housing credit system is maturity mismatch. While most banking institutions provide only short-term housing credits under the KPR scheme, in reality most of KPR's targets are lower- to lower-middle-income groups who have limited financial capacity. This situation has greatly limited the access to housing credit. To address this mismatch and to support the KPR scheme, the government introduced a secondary housing mortgage under Presidential Decree No. 19/2005 on Secondary Housing Mortgage. This new institution is responsible for facilitating the flow of medium- and long-term funds from the capital market to the housing sector through the KPR agency (PT. SMF 2011). Apart from the secondary housing mortgage, the government also introduced a financial mechanism (FLPP, or Housing Finance Liquidity Facility) in 2010, which was designed to support housing finance for lower-middle- and low-income people through low-cost, long-term funding. The FLPP scheme, falling under the authority of the Ministry of Housing, is managed by a public service agency – the Housing Financing Centre – which collaborates with banking institutions. The FLPP receives financial support from SoEs, banks and other resources; one is from SMF through the banking sector (PT. SMF 2011).

However, the implementation of this new scheme still requires some adaptation and adjustment in order to align with the existing national housing context. Concerns have been raised over a number of issues, for example administration procedures and house pricing. Many low-income people cannot fulfil the administration requirements since most do not hold an identity card or tax registration number. This situation has rendered them ineligible to apply for a mortgage. House pricing on the other hand is considered unrealistic compared to the market conditions (Suara Merdeka 2013). Under housing regulation no. 1/2011 on Housing and Settlement, which acts as an overarching policy to all housing policies in Indonesia, the government is to provide a subsidy for 36-square-metre-house units that are priced at not more than Rp 70 million (around US$7,070, tax free). However, in reality, due to high land value and construction costs, a house of that size would cost much more. As a consequence

TABLE 11.1 PERUMNAS housing production from 2000 to 2010

Housing types	Numbers in 2000	Numbers in 2010
Shop house	0	658
Flats	120	1,402
Simple housing	1,637	2,135
Core housing	1,785	546
Very simple housing	2,926	5,781

Source: BPS (2010).

only limited numbers of houses are eligible for this subsidy. The new financial scheme highlights clearly the mismatch between policies and realities.

To make matters worse, the update of regulation no. 1/2011 defines 36 square metres as the minimal size of 'healthy and proper' housing. The existing low-income housing programme has 21-square-metre houses as their smallest units, and they have been constructed and sold in great numbers (many of them are still in construction or currently on the market). The new law, however, states that units smaller than 36 square metres are considered 'a non-proper living unit' and therefore are not eligible for subsidy. As a consequence developers are suffering great financial losses since they are not able to sell such houses (according to Indopos (2012), there are approximately 43,023 unsold units on the market). As a result, it becomes difficult for developers to reinvest money to build more low-income housing units. Moreover, low-income groups accordingly cannot afford the 36 square metre units that are not only more expensive, but also often unsubsidized. As a result, the Indonesian Real Estate Association and local associations of private developers are currently lobbying for the withdrawal of the regulation update (Latief 2012).

The gap between supply and demand

Since its establishment in the 1970s, PERUMNAS, the programme under which SoEs provide housing for lower-middle- to low-income people, has produced only 500,000 housing units across the country (PERUMNAS 2013); this is a very small number compared to the size of the country's population. Moreover, with its current capacity to cater to only 50 per cent of the annual housing demand, the existing large housing deficit, and the mismatch between the credit scheme policy and its implementation, self-help housing continues to be the main alternative for the urban poor. The price of simple housing units is also much too high for the target group. Therefore, even though there has been an increase in production from year 2000 to 2010 (see Table 11.1), the programme does not really cater to the intended group: the urban poor. The housing unit price, which starts at 75 million rupiah (or roughly US$7,900) for the smallest apartment, is simply not affordable for the low-income group, most of whom do not have regular jobs and incomes (see Table 11.2). Rental units would actually be a better option for low-income groups as these would fit their income levels and employment patterns better. Unfortunately, since the government focus is largely on ownership rather than rental units, many low-income groups do not have sufficient formal or public options for this type of housing. This situation has raised much criticism of the government's commitment to solving the housing problem as a whole.

TABLE 11.2 Comparison of flat price, income and housing credits

Income (million Rp per month)	Max floor area (m²)	Flat price (million Rp)	Subsidy for down payment (million Rp)	Interest rate per annum
1.2–2.5	21	75	7	5
2.5–3.5	30	110	6	3.5
3.5–4.5	36	144	5	2.5

Source: Housing Ministry Regulation (2007).

Rp 1 million = US$1,000, Bank Indonesia, 26 November 2012.

Self-help housing experiences in Indonesia

In Indonesia, self-help housing takes a number of forms (see Table 11.3). The first is based entirely on local initiative and is associated with informal settlements such as urban *kampung* and squatter settlements which are mostly located in vacant urban lands and brownfield areas, as well as along river banks or railway tracks. The second form of self-help housing is based on collaborations between NGOs (which are mostly non-profit) and local inhabitants. For example, there are several instances of self-help housing led by both pro-poor religious and non-religious organizations. The third form is organized by for-profit organizations as part of their employee welfare programme or more general social programme; the Borromeus hospital housing corporation in Bandung, who pioneered housing provision for its low-income employees, is a good example. The fourth form is assisted by the government in collaboration with the local community. The government would normally help with the provision of basic infrastructures and public facilities, and/or relevant financial instruments.

While the first form is normally devoid of a planning process (though not uncoordinated) and often organically formed, the second, third and fourth forms may involve some degree of planning.

Whatever the form, self-help housing relies on a community's capacity to initiate and develop housing by way of personal financial and social resources. Self-help housing involves complex social processes to establish community collaboration and a collective sense of responsibility and awareness to improve and maintain the quality of the living environment, all within limited resources and capacity. Self-help also shows the community's capacity to adapt to and deal with daily challenges through individual or communal action based on the given culture, values and needs. Therefore, in order to gain an understanding of the social mechanism of self-help housing, this section analyses, by using Sustainable Livelihood Analysis, some basic factors that influence a community's capacity and ability to deal with those challenges.

Through Sustainable Livelihood Analysis, the connection between five basic factors that are fundamental to supporting the continuity of the self-help housing mechanism under shocks and stresses can be examined: natural capital, social capital, physical capital, economic (or financial) capital and human capital (Majale 2002; Morse *et al.* 2009; Odero 2006; Scoones 1998). Natural capital refers to a community's capacity to manage natural resources that are significant to the environment and the community. Meanwhile, social capital encompasses the community's capacity to collaborate with other community members and parties to achieve common goals; this involves a communal arrangement between individuals and organizations

TABLE 11.3 Different forms of low-income self-help housing in Indonesia

Type	Stakeholders	Source of funding	Examples
Entirely self initiative	Local community: individual or collective	Own funding (personal saving and/or informal loans)	Informal settlement
Collaborative	Local community and NGOs	Own funding (personal saving and/or informal loans) Donations (from individuals or institutions)	Pro-poor self-help housing projects
Private housing corporation	Private sectors (companies/ for-profit organizations), local community (and certain degree of government involvement)	Funding from private sector, own funding, bank credit	Cooperative
Assisted self-help housing	Government, local community and NGO	Government subsidy, own funding	Sites-and-services projects

by means of which values and norms are exchanged through negotiation processes. Physical capital refers to the physical assets of the community – such as housing, basic infrastructure and facilities – that can support improved living conditions and well-being. Economic (or financial) capital refers to a community's capacity to secure sustainable funding for self-help efforts through micro-economic activities, such as small-scale enterprises. Finally, human capital describes a community's capacity to improve living conditions through creativity, innovation and knowledge. All of these factors are significant in supporting self-help housing initiatives in Indonesia.

In the past few decades, the self-help concept in the housing sector has become popular in Indonesia especially within the low-income group. To some extent, the government should also receive some credit for their own self-help support programme called Swadaya, outlined in Box 11.1.

BOX 11.1 GOVERNMENT INITIATED SELF-HELP PROGRAMME: SWADAYA

The government has also included a limited self-help component in their housing programme by introducing Swadaya housing, which gives subsidies for housing improvements. This programme was intended to help low-income households, which earn no more than 1.25–2 million rupiah (US$132–210) per month (depending on the cities where they live), living in substandard housing, and it falls under the responsibility of the provincial government. This programme includes not only individual housing improvements but in some cases also infrastructural and public facilities development. The selection of subsidy recipients is done by the municipality and local district authority based on certain socio-economic priorities. Each provincial government has to propose this home-improvement funding to the housing ministry based on their own necessity and priorities. Though critics have heavily scrutinized the less than transparent subsidy distribution, the programme was said to be able to help more than 160,000 poor households in 2012 across the country (Nuraisyah Dewi 2012). From 2012 to 2014 the government is targeting implementation of 1.25 million housing improvement projects (Kredit Properti 2012).

For another example of self-help housing in Indonesia see Box 11.2. The case of Kampung Jetisharjo, a self-help *kampung* improvement initiative in Yogyakarta, Central Java, highlights a community initiative, commitment and engagement in self-help to improve their living conditions. It also emphasizes the importance of basic infrastructure provision as a precondition to living improvement in general. In the Jetisharjo case, the self-help housing effort was preceded by a basic infrastructure upgrading project that subsequently created funding opportunities for the housing project.

BOX 11.2 SELF-HELP *KAMPUNG* IMPROVEMENT IN JETISHARJO, YOGYAKARTA

A few decades ago Jetisharjo was effectively uninhabitable. The riverbank that was located next to the settlement was an area for public toilets and garbage dumping. In the early 1990s the river, which was the settlement's only source of water, became so heavily polluted that it was no longer possible for the local community to get clean water. Facing such a grave situation with no government support, the local community was forced to seek its own alternative source of clean water. This was the starting point of the self-help initiative in Jetisharjo.

Fortunately for the community the *kampung* was close to a number of water springs which were located along the adjacent riverbank. Using their own resources and relatively low technology (to extract and purify water), the community started to utilize these springs as their source of clean water. In 1991, using a simple water distribution system, they started distributing clean water across the neighbourhood. This effort was finally recognized by the local (public) water provider who eventually supported the initiative. In order to manage the clean water distribution effectively, a small-scale enterprise called Usaha Air Bersih (UAB) Tirta Kencana was established. This enterprise is managed by and for the community, and so far it has been successfully providing clean water not only for the local inhabitants but also to those of surrounding areas. Through time, the profit generated also helped to finance the upgrading of local houses in the *kampungs*. The improvement of living conditions in the area created a positive trickle-down effect in which it stimulated the development of the local economy through the establishment of a number of small-scale enterprises and home industries.

Kampung Jetisharjo presents a success story as a self-help *kampung* improvement project. There are a number of learning points that may be drawn from this case. First, the case emphasizes the importance of recognizing existing potential natural capital that can

> be developed for the benefit of a community. By mobilizing and developing the existing natural capital (spring water and river), the *kampung* inhabitants eventually improved their human capital (capacity and capability to manage and coordinate the local community), social capital (capacity and capability to develop collaboration with other parties, thus expanding their social network) and human capital (capacity and capability to develop and manage small-scale enterprises and home industries, etc). All of these types of capital are crucial not only to support further physical capital development (the improvement of the living conditions) in the *kampung*, but also to aid the community in achieving long-term goals and dealing with future challenges.
>
> Second, the case shows that infrastructure provision could also be based on (or at least initiated by) a self-help initiative. In situations where there are limited provisions such as in Jetisharjo, sometimes the local community may have to find their own solution. Jetisharjo owed its success to strong engagement of the *kampung* inhabitants and good multi-stakeholder collaboration (with local government and also other stakeholders, i.e. the academics who helped them to design the water distribution system).
>
> Experience from this *kampung* showed that the local capacity to manage multi-stakeholder collaboration, and to create and capture added value from the existing natural capital should not be undermined. However, despite its success stories, Jetisharjo is still facing another challenge. The sustainability of a long-term self-help initiative depends largely on the willingness and the commitment of the local community to carry out the missions and share the responsibilities. This necessitates certain levels of investment in time and social relations. Without proper leadership succession such an initiative would be difficult to maintain.
>
> (Based on authors' in-depth interviews with residents in Jetisharjo: with Mr Totok and Mr Musmo in 2010 and with Mr Nugroho in 2012.)

From an economic perspective, self-help includes possibilities for the community to develop micro-economic activity that can support and help the community members, such as *koperasi*, a local form of small-scale enterprise. In fact, some cases show that the micro-economic activity inspired by self-help initiatives can provide additional income for community members which could in turn be reinvested to improve their living environment.

Additionally, self-help initiatives also may build social capital. Self-help initiatives strengthen the social bonds among community members and encourage them to work together as a team to reach a common goal; this is known as *gotong royong* in Indonesia. *Gotong royong*, which can be defined as a collaborative effort to reach a common goal, serves as the building block of community life in both urban and rural areas of Indonesia. Self-help initiatives also rely on strong social capital in other ways: community members can mobilize gains from alliances and social networks in order to self-provide. As a certain degree of negotiation with other co-inhabitants or a mediator is required, trust is an important factor.

The case study demonstrates how the idea of self-help implies a capacity to mobilize and strategically manage one's human, financial or natural resources and creates a sense of self-authority. It generates a feeling of belonging and responsibility to one's living environment. The experience from the case study shows the following key factors in such self-help initiatives:

- *Social capital*: The Kampung Jetisharjo community show great capacity to organize themselves to initiate, plan and launch the project. This requires a certain degree of social cohesion through which the negotiation process is facilitated. Without a strong sense of community bonding and vision for a common goal, it would be difficult for the community to implement the project. Also significant in this process is strong leadership.
- *Financial capital*: The demand for clean water from the surrounding area created an opportunity for the local community to strengthen their financial capital. This has served as a rather stable source of funding to further develop the local clean water-supply enterprise. At the same time, the improvement of water infrastructure in the area created more opportunities for some of the inhabitants to establish home industries.
- *Natural capital*: In Jetisharjo, the community was able to benefit from the river and the water springs. The community managed to use these natural assets to improve their quality of living and subsequently their economic conditions.
- *Physical capital*: The basic infrastructure improvements in Jetisharjo (road construction, sewage and waste management, and basic public facilities provision) are examples of physical capital development which supports the continuity of the local livelihood.
- *Human capital*: The community empowerment programme in this *kampung*, organized by the water enterprise, can help to increase the level of human capital not only by providing the community with some useful skills, but also by encouraging them to be more proactive and responsive in solving local problems. In short, it enables people to 'help themselves' and prepare to face future challenges.

The capacity to manage the five basic types of capital is crucial; it is an outcome of a continuous process where every involved agency (community, government, volunteers and other stakeholders) actively participate to develop strategies not only for survival, but most importantly to support longer-term goals. During this process, *kampung* inhabitants are expected to develop new skills such as how to manage inter-organization between all stakeholders for environmental protection, how to run small-scale enterprises to secure funding for the *kampung* inhabitants and how to deal with unpredictable conditions in the future. Leadership is another aspect that is essential to support self-help housing. Good, visionary leadership is needed to ensure the sustainability of such programmes.

Conclusion

Housing development in Indonesia has come a long way since the country's independence. It is unfortunate that local governments did not foresee the drastic urban development and population growth in its early days, hence the absence of a long-term public housing plan. As a result, authorities were unprepared to cope with the development consequences, including those of housing. Current existing national housing projects and programmes are serving more as 'patch up' work rather than those implemented by way of a long-term, holistic plan. It seems likely that the central government will not be able to cope with national housing issues in the near future.

In a situation where the local government is not able yet to provide proper housing for all, self-help housing should be considered as a viable alternative. However, there should be limits: self-help housing consolidation should be based on a long-term vision and clear socio-economic and environmental considerations. Not every form of self-help housing in Indonesia should be considered as a housing alternative; while it is proper to consolidate and formalize some of them, those that are located in illegal and hazardous areas have to be removed with some assistance.

Additionally, self-help housing should be developed as a formal housing alternative assisted by proper strategies, planning and guidelines. As it relies on grassroots involvement, self-help housing could potentially address the problems that really matter. Strong community commitment and involvement are key aspects in this matter. However, the role of NGOs is also equally important to mediate the process and guide a project in the right direction. At the same time, the government should be able to accommodate and facilitate the process through institutional, social and financial support.

Self-help housing should be considered not only as a mechanism for self-catered housing provision, but also as an opportunity for long-term social and economic learning for the local inhabitants. The self-help concept emphasizes one's ability to manage social, economic and environmental resources and use them to improve housing and living standards. Self-help projects in general, therefore, involve a learning process that empowers and helps a local community to develop social-financial capital. Through a process of trial and error, a community can learn valuable lessons to achieve their long-term goals as well as a sustainable future. Kampung Jetisharjo illustrates how a community can develop creative solutions through the use of local resources as well as implementing and funding projects. Self-help projects are time-consuming, however, as they involve complex social processes. Continuous negotiations to reach consensus are essential to ensure smooth implementation throughout the whole period. In Jetisharjo, it took approximately ten years before the inhabitants could help themselves in supporting their social, economic and physical development in a sustainable way.

Though self-help housing seems to work at the moment, the government is still ultimately responsible for providing low-income housing units. Thus, the government should have a stronger presence in the mechanism of low-income housing provision. However, due to financial problems the government has a limited capacity to provide housing for citizens, and collaboration with the private sector – including housing developers – is necessary. The recent decentralization policy is expected to boost housing development at the local level. By transferring responsibilities and planning authority to the local level, it is expected that the local government would be able to adjust national policy to be in line with local needs, including those of low-income housing.

Acknowledgement

The authors would like to express their gratitude to Pak Totok, Pak Musmo and Pak F. X. Eko Nugroho from Kampung Jetisharjo and UAB Tirta Kencana, Yogyakarta; Allis Nurdini and Dory Purnawarman from ITB; the Napitupulu family (Bang Erwin and Vinon); and Mia Ariani and family for providing valuable information for this research.

References

BPS (2010) *Statistik Perumahan Indonesia*. Jakarta Biro: Pusat Statistik Indonesia.

Dhakal, S. (2002) *Comprehensive Kampung Improvement Program in Surabaya as a Model of Community Participation*, Working Paper, Urban Environmental Management Project, Kitakyushu: Institute of Global Environmental Strategies.

GoI (1978) *Pelaksanaan Tahun Keempat Repelita II*, Departemen Penerangan Republik Indonesia.
GoI (1979) *Laporan Repelita III (1979–1984)*, Pemerintah Republik Indonesia.
GoI (1984) *Laporan Repelita IV (1984–1989)*, Pemerintah Republik Indonesia.
GoI (1989) *Laporan Repelita V (1989–1995)*, Pemerintah Republik Indonesia.
GoI (1995) *Laporan Repelita VI (1995–1999)*, Pemerintah Republik Indonesia.
Handayani, Sri (2009) *Penerapan Metode Penelitian Particpatory Research Apraisal Dalam Penelitian Permukiman Vernakular* (Permukiman Kampung Kota), Seminar Nasional Penelitian Arsitektur – Metoda dan Penerapannya Seri 2, Semarang: UNDIP.
Hoek-Smit, M.C. (2002) *Implementing Indonesia's New Housing Policy: The Way Forward*. Kimpraswil: Government of Indonesia and the World Bank.
Hofman, B. and Kaiser, K. (2002) *The Making of the Big Bang and its Aftermath: A Political Economy Perspective, Can decentralization help rebuild Indonesia?* Conference paper, May 2002, Atlanta: Georgia State University.
Housing Ministry Regulation (2007) Permenpera no. 7/PERMEN/M/2007.
Indonesian Ministry of Housing (2009) 'Indonesia's housing policies and programmes', a presentation at the Workshop on Housing Finance in South Asia. Jakarta, 26 May 2009.
Indopos (2012) UU No 1/2011 Dipersoalkan di MK, 23/03/2012. Online. Available at www.indopos.co.id/index.php/arsip-berita-nasional/75-nasional-reviews/23170-uu-no-12011-dipersoalkan-di-mk.html/ (accessed 2 September 2013).
Juliman, D. (2006) *The World's First Slum Upgrading Programme*, World Urban Forum III, An International UN-Habitat Event on Sustainability, Vancouver, Canada.
Kompas (2006) Kebayoran Baru, Riwayatmu Dulu, 29 July 2006.
Kredit Properti (2012) Kredit Property Website. Online. Available at www.kreditproperti.com/ (accessed 2 September 2013).
Kristopo (2011) Menpera: Data BPS Evaluasi Backlog Perumahan. Online. Available at www.infobanknews.com/2011/01/menpera-data-bps-evaluasi-backlog-perumahan/ (accessed 3 September 2013).
Kusumaputra, R.A. (2011) Eddy: Apersi Bangun Perumahan Murah Terpadu, Kompas, 25 March 2011. Online. Available at http://kompas.com/read/2011/03/25/07482595/Eddy.Apersi.Bangun.Perumahan.Murah.Terpadu (accessed 3 September 2013).
Kuswartojo, T. *et al*. (2005) *Perumahan dan Permukiman di Indonesia*. Bandung: Penerbit ITB.
Latief, M (2012) Masyarakat Desak UU Perumahan Dicabut. Online. Available at http://properti.kompas.com/read/2012/03/26/11153569/Masyarakat.Desak.UU.Perumahan.Dicabut/ (accessed 1 September 2013).
Majale, M. (2002) *Towards Pro-Poor Regulatory Guidelines for Urban Upgrading, Intermediate Technology Development Group (ITDG)*. Rugby: Schumacher Centre for Technology and Development.
Morse, S., McNamara, N. and Acholo, M. (2009) *Sustainable Livelihood Approach: A Critical Analysis Theory and Practice*, Geographical Paper No. 189. West Berkshire: University of Reading.
Nuraisyah Dewi, S. (2012) Perumahan Swadaya: Butuh Rp14,1 Triliun, Pemda Diminta Berikan Dukungan, Bisnis Indonesia, 12 June 2012.
Odero, K. (2006) 'Information Capital: 6th Asset of Sustainable Livelihood Framework', *Discovery and Innovation*, 18(2): 83–91.
PERUMNAS (2013) PERUMNAS. Online. Available at http://perumnas.co.id/perumahan-landed-house/ (accessed 1 May 2013).
Pikiran Rakyat (2012) *Angka Backlog Rumah Pasti Membengkak*, 20 February 2012. Online. Available at www.pikiran-rakyat.com/node/177606 (accessed 2 June 2013).
PT. SMF (2011) 'Mengalirkan Dana Pasar Modal ke Sektor Perumahan', Report 2011.
Scoones, I. (1998) *Sustainable Rural Livelihoods: A Framework for Analysis*, Working Paper 72. Brighton: Institute for Development Studies.
Suara Merdeka (2013) 'Pengembang enggan buat rumah murah'. Online. Available at http://m.suaramerdeka.com/index.php/read/cetak/2013/06/19/228152 (accessed 19 June 2013).

Sudana, I. and Winarso, H. (2005) Peluang Pengembangan Institusi Pengelola Dana Pembangunan Perumahan Nasional, Yayasan Soegijanto Soegijoko – Urban and Regional Development Institute.
Tunas, D. and Peresthu, A. (2010) 'The Self-Help Housing in Indonesia: The Only Option for the Poor?', *Habitat International*, 34(3): 315–322.
UN-Habitat (2006) *Enabling Shelter Strategies: Review of Experience from Two Decades of Implementation*. Nairobi: UN-Habitat.
Werlin, H. (1999) 'The slum upgrading myth', *Urban Studies*, 36(9): 1523–2534.

12

COMMUNITY CONTRACTING IN NEIGHBOURHOOD IMPROVEMENT AND HOUSING

Indonesia and Pakistan

Florian Steinberg

Abbreviations

ADB	Asian Development Bank
BKM	Badan Kelompok Masyarakat
BRR	Badan Rehabilitasi dan Reconstruksi (Aceh and Nias Agency for Rehabilitation and Reconstruction)
CDD	Community-driven development
EEAP	Earthquake Emergency Assistance Project
ERRA	Earthquake Reconstruction and Rehabilitation Authority
ETESP	Earthquake and Tsunami Emergency Support Project
IADB	Inter-American Development Bank
IUIDP	Integrated Urban Infrastructure Development Programme
KIP	Kampung Improvement Programme
MDB	Multilateral development bank
NGO	Non-governmental organization
NUP	Neighbourhood Upgrading Plan
NUSSP	Neighbourhood Upgrading and Shelter Sector Project
SEWA	Self-Employed Women's Association
SWM	Solid waste management
UN	United Nations

Introduction

Over the next 40 years, an additional 2.6 billion people will double the planet's urban areas, 90 per cent of which will happen mostly in emerging country cities. Most of these new urban residents will have low to moderate incomes. According to the World Resources Institute, the unsatisfied market for affordable housing, which is growing explosively, totals US$331 billion and is located mostly in emerging countries (Hammond *et al.* 2007).

Various multilateral development banks (MDBs), like the World Bank and the Inter-American Development Bank (IADB), observed that most government-funded or government-sponsored mortgage and subsidy programmes have instead helped the richest one-third of the population to buy developer-built units, leaving the urban poor and inhabitants of informal settlements to fend for themselves (Buckley and Kalarickal 2006). Most households build their homes incrementally (and informally) through self-help to afford home ownership because modern corporations have largely ignored this massive market. Future infrastructure upgrading of unassisted, incremental housing and unplanned neighbourhood developments tend to be dysfunctional and more costly than formal developments. However, informal income earners in the developing world are unable to access existing mortgage, finance markets, and land supply schemes, neither is it possible for them to graduate into the formal supply system. Self-help housing, therefore, becomes the norm.

Aided self-help housing was introduced as a government approach towards inclusive development in the 1980s. Since then, many governments or government supported programmes have adopted and mainstreamed self-help and incremental housing. With the adoption of housing microfinance, even the poorest now have access to finance which is adjustable to their needs and payment capacities. This is an improvement over the conventional housing finance system.

This chapter will dwell on the experiences of Indonesia and Pakistan which were supported through the Asian Development Bank (ADB) funded Neighbourhood Upgrading and Shelter Sector Project (NUSSP) in Indonesia; the Aceh-Nias Housing Reconstruction or Rehabilitation in Indonesia, under its Earthquake and Tsunami Emergency Support Project (ETESP); and the cash-transfer assistance programme in Pakistan under the Earthquake Emergency Assistance Project (EEAP).

Experiences of the Asian Development Bank in mainstreaming self-help housing

During the 1960s, the ADB's housing assistance was initially directed at public housing in Hong Kong and South Korea, and, later, Indonesia. With the start of the self-help housing debate, more low-cost options were being sought. The ADB participated in Indonesia's large-scale efforts to provide area-based upgrading assistance in the context of Indonesia's Kampung Improvement Programme (KIP). The nation-wide KIP existed from the early 1980s to the late 1990s, and received wide donor support, including from the World Bank and the Asian Development Bank.[1] When the KIP was incorporated into the nation-wide Integrated Urban Infrastructure Development Programme (IUIDP) during the 1980s and 1990s, many of the ADB-supported urban projects in Indonesia supported infrastructure improvements in informal urban low-income neighbourhoods (*kampung*) (Asian Development Bank 1997, 2010a; World Bank 2003).

The IUIDP covered eight major urban service components: (1) spatial urban planning; (2) water supply; (3) sewerage and human waste; (4) solid waste management (SWM); (5) drainage and flood control; (6) urban roads; (7) market infrastructure improvement programme; and (viii) housing (i.e. KIP; core housing and sites-and-services schemes; urban renewal and resettlement; new settlements; urban land provision and guided land development; public housing; and rental housing) (Van der Hoff and Steinberg 1992).

The evolution of community contracting is also inspired by other successful community-driven development (CDD) experiences in urban housing. In the 1990s, many innovative housing finance programs led by non-governmental organizations (NGOs) emerged. For instance, in Ahmedabad, India, the Self-Employed Women's Association (SEWA) Bank offered microfinancing for housing (Bhatt 2001). The Bangladeshi Grameen Bank offered similar microfinance for housing schemes (Bornstein 2005). Other programs started to work on a more systemic and city-wide approach. The Indore and Ahmedabad Slum Networking Programs (Asnani 2001; Parikh 1996; Tripathi n.d.), as well as city-wide slum improvement programs of the Community Organizations Development Institute in some 200 towns in Thailand (Boonyabancha 2005; 2011), also indicate the massive shift in support for community-based development programmes that incorporated the incremental infrastructure improvements and forms of self-help or self-managed housing.

Innovation driven by dialogue with partners

In institutions like the ADB, the international discourse on self-help housing was unknown, and remains largely unknown today since it is rather academic. However, in response to requests from its developing member countries, the ADB adopted innovative thinking into its urban practice. While housing remains low on the ADB's list of priorities and comprises at best only about 5 per cent of its urban operations,[2] some governments such as those of Indonesia, India, Mongolia, Pakistan, the Philippines and Sri Lanka have driven the agenda by incorporating innovative schemes in their loan programme designs, some of which may not have been possible in the 1970s. Highly ideologically centred and polarized discussions on the merits and potentials of self-help housing in the circles of academics (Ward 1982) and development specialists (Mathéy 1991) may have had little impact on MDBs like the ADB, but they did have some indirect impact on the demand by developing member countries to seek support for community-driven projects.

Self-help, in the context of ADB-assisted projects, refers to community participation and self-management, rather than actual hands-on construction. The following section will provide brief descriptions of the three ADB-supported projects that included community contracting for neighbourhood and housing improvements. This chapter, however, does not include other examples of ADB-supported self-help housing and neighbourhood improvement projects in India, Kyrgyzstan, Mongolia and the Philippines which embody the ADB's community-driven development model that aims for sector-wide impacts, sustainability and replicability (Asian Development Bank 2009, 2010a; Government of Mongolia/ADB 2007; Jorgensen and Dasgupta 2011; Steinberg 2011).

Community contracting – its importance and potentials

Communities are defined by the physical territory they reside in, and the ethnic or socio-economic patterns which determine their existence. The modality of community contracting, as defined by the ADB, attempts to establish small and manageable contract units. The ADB's standard for community contracts is US$30,000 per contract. This is lower than similar contracts being used by UN-Habitat for community contracting, which can reach up to US$70,000 per contract. The small size of these contracts makes it necessary that in a given community there will be many such small contracts in order to implement sizable infrastructure or housing investments. Community contracts can cover infrastructure, home improvements and new house building.

Thus, community contracting is a procurement modality in which the community is put in charge of designing and organizing purchases of goods, or the contracting and supervision of services and civil works. The legal representative of registered community organizations will sign the contracts. The representatives can be male or female. In some of the ADB-supported projects all legal documents are being signed by both males and females of a household in order to ensure full ownership rights to both partners. Community contracting will strive to settle conflicts amicably as otherwise such conflicts will become counterproductive. This is important as communities often are rather heterogeneous.

The community contracting modality is a partnership arrangement where communities play the roles of three actors – promoter, engineer and contractor. In this perspective it differs starkly from the conventional modality of public sector or agency-driven procurement. The legal status of such a community contract is fully binding and mutually acceptable to private sector vendors or service providers. Community members will jointly manage the community contract, and their association or community group will become accountable to the government and the funding agency. The advantage of community contracting is that it leads to more cost-effective and more responsive civil works. One of the prime assumptions of community contracting is that stronger ownership will produce better civil works, at lower cost, or more value for money. Since communities will be required to undertake a much bigger effort, it enhances community cohesion and empowerment. On the other side, it means that local governments or technical agencies will have reduced workloads, and reduced control over decisions of contract awards. The disadvantage of community contracting is its labour-intensive nature. For relatively small amounts there is a lot of paperwork to be done. Politicians and government officials will have less influence, and this can contribute to a change in local 'patron–client' relationships.

Community contracting was introduced in Sri Lanka by the National Housing Development Authority in 1987 in response to the failures of the conventional tender and contract system. Since 1987, community contracts have become common for many agencies in Sri Lanka, and across Asia and Africa. They have been applied by the World Bank, the Japan Bank for International Cooperation and UN-Habitat (Jayaratne 2003; Sohail and Cotton 2000; Yap 1994).

Community contracting represents an innovation in procurement and project implementation. The ADB has been using community procurement since 2002. Although it also signifies an important step towards community empowerment, the labour-intensive nature of document and fund management often makes it necessary to assist this process. ADB assessments of the CDD experiences clearly indicate that the community contracting process needs quite substantial inputs from community facilitators who regularly work with communities. In cases where the intensity of community participation was less than actually required, such facilitation has been crucial to sustain the administrative efforts (Asian Development Bank 2012).

In particular, community contracting schemes have promoted good governance through transparent planning, procurement, disbursement and implementation based on jointly agreed procedures, and strengthened local institutional arrangements; and helped to create transparent mechanisms for transferring investment funds to bank accounts of communities or individual beneficiaries.

The cash transfer modality is a variation of the community contracting system, but without the community commitment. Nevertheless, depending on the local conditions it may involve a similar community process. The cash transfer modality may appear to be easier to administer, but it requires intensive monitoring and supervision.

The application of community contracting in neighbourhood improvement and housing in ADB-supported schemes has so far been limited to projects that were grant financed by the government. In the case of the NUSSP and EEAP the loans to the governments of Indonesia and Pakistan were converted into grants to the communities. In the case of the ETESP the whole emergency assistance to Indonesia was provided in the form of a grant. But, in principle, the application of community contracting should also be possible in situations where communities become the borrowers under a government-sponsored scheme. And there are a good number of cases that support the hypothesis that community groups can be responsible for amortization requirements under loan schemes,[3] as has been demonstrated in the ADB-supported 'STEP-UP' project in Manila (Steinberg 2011).

Indonesia – neighbourhood upgrading

Neighbourhood upgrading has been a long-term human settlements programme of the Government of Indonesia (Steinberg 1991). In 2003 the ADB approved a US$68.6 million loan (including a concessionary loan of US$13.89 million) for the Neighbourhood Upgrading and Shelter Sector Project (NUSSP) (Asian Development Bank 2003). The purpose of the project was to upgrade slum tenements and provide new housing for beneficiaries. Its overall goal was to help improve living conditions among the urban poor by getting the beneficiaries to benefit from the development of infrastructure and housing facilities through their participation. Beneficiaries were required to participate in managing and financing the initiative in a way that both expanded their asset base and improved their overall level of well-being.

A participatory, community-driven process was used to address weak beneficiary ownership of works. Beneficiary communities were required to prepare their own neighbourhood upgrading plans (NUPs), which were used to formulate specific project investments. The targeted communities were requested to form community self-help groups (*badan kelompok masyarakat* – BKM), and facilitators were employed by the project to assist communities and their BKMs in preparing and implementing their NUPs. With their NUPs in place, they received funds in 'block grants' that partially financed implementation of their NUPs; the beneficiaries or the local governments provided the balance through cash or in-kind contributions. With these funds allocated, the participating communities were able to sign civil works contracts for the construction of facilities, and signed contracts between the BKM and the city public works project managers. In accordance with the ADB procedure for community contracts, each contract had to be limited to US$30,000.

By the end of 2009, 803 NUPs were completed, and more than 3,000 civil works contracts were awarded and implemented by the beneficiary groups. The number of beneficiaries totalled about 3.1 million people living in 783,123 households, of which 350,000 families (40 per cent) were officially categorized as poor.

The project, which the ADB rated as highly efficient (Asian Development Bank 2011), was implemented in 32 cities across 17 provinces. Project components included (i) improving site planning and management systems for establishing new sites for the urban poor, as well as upgrading existing sites; (ii) improving access to shelter finance for the poor through a central financial institution and local financial institutions; (iii) upgrading of low-income neighbourhoods and new site development; and (iv) strengthening of institutions responsible for programme delivery.

Under the project, approximately 6,832 hectares of slum settlements spread over 32 urban areas were provided with water supply and sanitation facilities (630 public standpipes; about 28 km of water pipelines; 2,620 public toilets or communal sanitation facilities), drainage and footpaths (1,100 km), solid waste collection facilities (386 units of temporary waste disposal; 1,470 waste collection carts; 5,220 communal bins and 7,360 household bins) and street lighting (16,000 street lights). Beneficiaries enjoyed a better quality of life with an increased number of healthy days and decreased health-related expenses. Easier access to safe water and sanitation facilities reduced the amount of time required to obtain safe water, freeing additional time for income-generating activities. Cleaner water and improved hygiene, as well as better drainage, lowered the incidence and severity of waterborne diseases. More efficient drainage reduced flooding and, consequently, property destruction due to floods. Improved street lighting reduced petty crime and violence. Although provision of microcredit for home improvement was part of the project scope, this component was dropped during implementation since other microfinance institutions provided cheaper credit.

The NUSSP was able to reach out to 3.1 million people (783,123 households) because of the cost-efficiency of the initiatives undertaken. Ultimately, it demonstrated that there is significant demand for settlement upgrading in Indonesia's urban areas. It also proved that city-wide planning with highly participatory arrangements enables local governments and residents to collaborate in improving their physical environment. Despite the evident cost-efficiency of neighbourhood improvement, a limitation of the programme has been the low level of physical standards, which will limit the lifetime of the investments. From the government and community perspective, community contracting has been much appreciated since it has produced results faster than the conventional contractor-led process of civil works.

Indonesia – community contracting in Nias[4]

In April 2005, shortly after the Asian tsunami of December 2004, the ADB approved the ETESP, providing a US$290 million grant for rehabilitation and reconstruction needs in Aceh Province and Nias Island (Asian Development Bank 2005a). Some US$74 million of the grant was dedicated to housing reconstruction. The overall objective of the housing programme was to provide housing for those made homeless by the earthquakes and tsunami so that people could re-establish their lives. Secondary objectives were to provide land tenure security for residents, which would assist in economic recovery and provide a healthy and sanitary living environment.

Multilateral agencies, like the ADB, collaborated with the Government of Indonesia's Aceh and Nias Rehabilitation and Reconstruction Agency to develop a housing reconstruction and rehabilitation programme. The anticipated number of units for housing reconstruction was 14,000 at appraisal and 8,000 during the change in scope in March 2006. Housing rehabilitation was anticipated at 10,000 units during appraisal. As of April 2009, the ETESP housing programme had reconstructed about 6,000 housing units and rehabilitated 1,109 partially damaged homes. This reduced output was caused by the increase in unit cost that resulted from price increases, quality improvements, and implementation and land constraints (Asian Development Bank 2010b).

Housing rehabilitation was implemented at a considerably lower scale. While the verification process was too labour-intensive, many potential beneficiaries realized it was more beneficial for them to completely demolish left-over structures and request maximum reinstatement under the government's capped housing replacement entitlement policy for the tsunami victims. Nevertheless, 834 on-budget and 275 off-budget housing rehabilitations were realized and implemented through the community contracting mechanisms.

The project utilized innovative approaches and introduced new technology to its beneficiaries. In non-traditional villages, the reconstruction of houses produced an important contribution to earthquake-resistant construction; the typology applied was copied by the Badan Rehabilitasi dan Reconstruksi (BRR; Aceh and Nias Agency for Rehabilitation and Reconstruction) and a few NGOs. In Nias, on-budget housing rehabilitation was a major success in terms of rehabilitating heritage structures in a culturally sensitive context. Restoring earthquake-damaged housing in traditional villages in southern Nias posed challenges that were addressed in an unprecedented manner. What was first considered a highly complex and problematic combination of on-budget and community contracting proved highly successful. Community contracting encouraged maximum participation, which overcame building material supply problems and ensured that historic architecture was sustained while building technology innovations were carefully introduced. With the support received, the residents had the option to renovate or reconstruct their houses, while about 30 per cent of residents increased investments by 50–100 per cent through their own financial contribution.

Community contracting proved a viable alternative to commercial contracting, particularly for small-sized housing and housing rehabilitation contracts (for groups of six to eight houses). However, this approach was less practical for neighbourhood infrastructure works, despite the community's interest in participating in this type of work. The skills limitations of both community groups and the local – mostly small-scale – contractors hampered the implementation of both types of contractual arrangements. Prior to deciding the type of contracting to be used, such limitations should have been carefully considered. Community contracting appears the most suitable and beneficiary oriented approach. However, for future post-emergency situations, in-field assistance should accompany community contracting to monitor quality compliance and ensure that progress payments are only made after documented progress on site. A limitation of the community contracting process has been the local culture of strong individualism. Not all community members found it easy to appreciate the collective nature of community decisions. This has made community facilitation at times a very complex and complicated process.

Pakistan – cash transfer and self-help housing reconstruction

Another modality of community contracting emerges when project beneficiaries and participants receive cash assistance, as was recently applied in Pakistan. In 2005, an earthquake wreaked havoc in Pakistan's Azad Jammu and Kashmir, and Khyber Pakhtunkhwa, killing more than 50,000 people and damaging thousands of buildings; 462,546 houses were completely, and 101,091 partially damaged. The ADB committed US$1 billion for earthquake emergency assistance under its Earthquake Emergency Assistance Project (EEAP) (Asian Development Bank 2005b) for education, health, power, transport, housing, livelihood and governance. While all activities were coordinated through the Earthquake Reconstruction and Rehabilitation Authority (ERRA), the housing component was implemented through the self-help efforts of each household.

The ADB funded US$417 million for the reconstruction of more than 600,000 houses. Cash grants, which were administered by the ERRA and UN-Habitat, were transferred to the bank accounts of beneficiaries (ERRA 2008). UN-Habitat assisted the self-help construction effort by monitoring construction quality and adherence to the technical requirements of earthquake resistance.[5] In an effort to make sure houses were built to be earthquake resistant, the ERRA opened Housing Reconstruction Centres. The centres provided training and technical assistance to partner organizations which had mobile teams that directly assisted and provided information to people reconstructing their homes. In September 2012, 436,486 housing units had been completed (see www.erra.pk/sectors/housing.asp).

Where feasible, the ERRA encouraged beneficiary families to work together in community groups, and jointly manage the procurement, transport and construction process. Group surveillance was encouraged and supported through awareness and capacity-building programmes to validate and evaluate compliance with earthquake-resistant building standards. Thus, the reconstruction process was owner-driven and fully participatory (ERRA 2006). Some 700,000 persons got trained in seismically safe reconstruction.

Much can be learned on disaster management and reconstruction work through Pakistan's experience in massive self-help housing. The cash transfer programme is considered a great success due to its simplified and highly efficient administrative work. The work included a rigorous identification of deserving beneficiaries, and the registration of beneficiaries as owners of bank accounts to which cash transfers could be made. The programme was assisted by NGOs and UN-Habitat which monitored physical progress and, on the basis of physical completion benchmarks, authorized payments. The cash transfers allowed community members to control their own reconstruction programme, and brought substantial amounts of cash payments into the local construction industry, creating employment and local economic benefits (Heltberg 2008; Jha *et al.* 2010). The limitation of the individual cash transfer system was that each and every transaction needed to be monitored, which turned out to be a labour-intensive challenge for the external monitoring agents.

Impacts of ADB projects

The above experiences have triggered continued demand for other similarly inclusive urban development projects. Indonesia's request for more neighbourhood upgrading combined with guided land development and Mongolia's request for an inclusive peri-urban development in Ulaanbaatar City's informal settlement (*ger*) areas indicate the continued importance of the habitat agenda. India and Bangladesh are also requesting habitat improvement projects, with more countries expected to follow as urbanization accelerates.

Sustained practices through community-based approaches, including self-help and community contracting, are needed to meet the challenges of upscaling efforts. The decline of government roles in the production of housing commands more innovative solutions to facilitate housing demand. More regulatory interventions in land and finance will be expected, while private involvement will be relied on to cover market segments that have remained outside the scope of formal market operators.

Looking ahead: more community-driven development and private solutions

Community contracting cannot be the panacea for housing of the urban poor. But it has the potential to become an important instrument to make aided self-help neighbourhood improvement and housing schemes a reality. Donor support can become more effective and bring large resources into the fold of community control. The combination of community efforts with a decentralized procurement mechanism is a powerful innovation which can go a long way.

In 2010, Harvard's Business Review website published the idea of Govindarajan and Sarkar of a US$300 ready-made house (Echanove and Srivastava 2011) that could improve the lives of millions of poor people around the world. According to the website, a vast US$424 billion market for cheap homes exists which represents the 1.413 billion urban poor households. And this market is largely untapped. However, replacing existing incrementally built houses with those that are ready-made is an idealistic solution all too common in the field of social entrepreneurship. This top-down, market-based solution to massive urban housing may appeal to some. However, there is doubt on whether this can be successfully tailored to the dynamics of urban communities in different countries with varying contexts.

Instead, there is a need for creative and inclusive market-based approaches given the growing consensus that government-initiated housing, settlement improvements and urban renewal programmes will not be able to finance the vast amount of urban interventions. Rather than handling large housing provision programmes, governments should concentrate more on efficient land administration and housing finance system reforms, while making these accessible to all citizens, including urban dwellers that work and live in the informal sector. Long-term mortgage-based financing or alternative collateral forms (employment-based or community guarantee funds) will be required.

In many poor countries, there exists a vast unsatisfied market for housing and basic habitat-related services. Affordable housing solutions that meet the needs of urban poor households are in demand. Private developers and service providers need to formulate services and products that add value and allow access to formal solutions by cutting costs for this target group. Developers and financial institutions need to create housing credit products that can properly implement these service packages. Households can act as their own general contractors who can hire skilled labour or subcontract at various stages of the building process. There is also a need to establish support services for land regularization; tenure and titling; construction design; technical assistance; and construction materials supply at bulk prices. Further, the support system should include low-cost mortgage credit, shorter-term credit, and banking products that can accommodate group credit or microfinance products (with low or no collateral requirements) for home improvement or incremental building.

The majority of urban poor households could buy a well-crafted product today, but they require more accessible housing finance. Product innovation and reforms in finance are needed to include populations that have been marginalized for lack of collateral or lack of formal employment. This implies that governments need to forge partnerships with financial institutions, such as microfinance institutions, which are experienced in working with poor customers. NGOs have many comparative advantages in marketing and identifying creditworthy households, which should be used more widely. They, therefore, need to cultivate trust in the capacity of urban poor households and forge household savings programmes in low-income communities. The fact that there is a well-articulated demand for affordable housing initiatives should be enough incentive for NGOs and private providers to engage in the vast housing sector. Community contracting can play an important role to make housing innovations happen.

Notes

1   In recent years the World Bank has supported the implementation of the Urban Poverty Project, which is similar to the ADB's Neighbourhood Upgrading and Shelter Sector Project, as described below.

2   This is an estimate by the author, based on data presented in the only comprehensive analysis of the ADB's urban work to date (Asian Development Bank 2006).
3   Recovery of loan funds is used as a mechanism to operate a revolving fund.
4   This section draws from Steinberg and Smidt (2010). See also Asian Development Bank (2010a, 2010b).
5   However, some 0.5 per cent of housing may have been built on the fault lines, or unsuitable sites which are in danger of land slide.

References

Asian Development Bank (1997) *Impact Evaluation Study on the Bank Assistance to the Urban Development and Housing Sector*. Manila: ADB.
Asian Development Bank (2003) *Loans 2072/2073-INO: Neighborhood Upgrading and Shelter Sector Project*. Manila: ADB.
Asian Development Bank (2005a) *ETESP Grant 0003-INO: Indonesia: Earthquake and Tsunami Emergency*. Manila: ADB.
Asian Development Bank (2005b) *Islamic Republic of Pakistan: Earthquake Emergency Assistance Project*. Manila: ADB.
Asian Development Bank (2006) *Urban Sector Strategy and Operations – Evaluation Study*, Operations Evaluation Department SST: REG 2006–03. Manila: ADB.
Asian Development Bank (2009) *Mongolia: Housing Finance (Sector) Project,* Project Completion Report. Manila: ADB.
Asian Development Bank (2010a) *Indonesia: Has the Multi-Subsector Approach been Effective for Urban Services Assistance?* Independent Evaluation Department. Manila: ADB.
Asian Development Bank (2010b) *Earthquake and Tsunami Emergency Support Project – Housing Component*, Project Completion Report. Manila: ADB.
Asian Development Bank (2011) *Neighborhood Upgrading and Shelter Sector Project*, Project Completion Report. Manila: ADB.
Asian Development Bank (2012) *The Neighborhood Upgrading and Shelter Sector Project in Indonesia, Sharing Knowledge on Community-Driven Development*. Manila: ADB.
Asnani, P.U. (2001) 'Slum Networking Project – Ahmedabad', in UNCHS, *Good Urban Governance Campaign*. New Delhi: Government of India.
Bhatt, B. (2001) 'Ahmedabad Parivartan Program', in UNCHS, *Good Urban Governance Campaign*. New Delhi: Government of India.
Boonyabancha, S. (2005) 'Baan Mankong: going to scale with "slum" and squatter upgrading in Thailand', *Environment and Urbanization*, 17(1): 21–46.
Boonyabancha, S. (2011) *Trusting that People Can Do It, Design with the Other 90 percent: Cities*. New York: Smithsonian Coopera-Hewitt National Design Museum.
Bornstein, D. (2005) *The Price of a Dream: The Story of the Grameen Bank*. New York: Oxford University Press.
Buckley, R. and Kalarickal, J. (2006) *Thirty Years of World Bank Shelter Lending: What Have We Learned?* Washington, DC: World Bank.
Earthquake Reconstruction and Rehabilitation Authority (2006) *Building Back Better: Rural Housing Reconstruction Strategy of Earthquake Hit Districts in NWFP and AJK*, March. Online. Available at www.erra.pk/sectors/housing.asp (accessed 12 December 2011).
Earthquake Reconstruction and Rehabilitation Authority (2008) *Compliance Manual*, Guidelines for the Construction of Compliant Rural Houses. Islamabad: UN-Habitat.
Echanove, M. and Srivasatava, R. (2011) 'Hands-off our houses', *International Herald Tribune*, 2 June.
Government of Mongolia/ADB (2007) *Mongolia: Housing Finance (Sector) Project – Implementation Outcomes*. Ulaan Baatar: GoM.
Hammond, A., Kramer, W.J., Tran, J. and Katz, R. (2007) *The Next 4 Billion: Market Size and Business Strategy at the Base of the Pyramid*. Washington, DC: Courtland Walker.

Heltberg, R. (2008) 'The World Bank's experience with cash support in some recent natural disasters', *Humanitarian Practice Network*, Issue 40, October 2008, Online. Available at www.odihpn.org/humanitarian-exchange-magazine/issue-40/the-world-banks-experience-with-cash-support-in-some-recent-natural-disasters (accessed 20 April 2012).

Jayaratne, K.A. (2003) 'Community contracting as a means of improving the livelihoods of the urban poor in Sri Lanka', *ASSIST Bulletin*, No. 15, ILO, Switzerland.

Jha, A.K., Barenstein, J.D., Phelps, P.M., Pittet, D. and Sena, S. (eds) (2010) *Safer Homes, Stronger Communities: A Handbook for Reconstructing after Natural Disasters*. Washington, DC: World Bank.

Jorgensen, A. and Dasgupta, S. (2011) 'India: ADB's involvement in slum rehabilitation', in F. Steinberg and M. Lindfield (eds) *Inclusive Cities*, Urban Development Series. Manila: ADB.

Mathéy, K. (ed.) (1991) *Beyond Self-Help Housing*. Munich: Mansell; London, New York: Profil Verlag.

Parikh, H.H (1996) 'Slum networking', *Architecture and Design*, 13(4), 18–23.

Sohail, M. and Cotton, A. (2000) *Performance Monitoring of Micro Contracts for the Procurement of Urban Infrastructure*. Leicestershire: WEDC, Loughborough University.

Steinberg, F. (1991) 'People's participation and self help in the Indonesian Kampung', in K. Mathéy (ed.) *Beyond Self-Help Housing*. Munich: Mansell; London, New York: Profil Verlag.

Steinberg, F. (2011) 'Philippines: strategic private sector partnerships for urban poverty reduction in Metro Manila', in F. Steinberg and M. Lindfield (eds) *Inclusive Cities*, Urban Development Series. Manila: ADB.

Steinberg, F. and Smidt, P. (eds) (2010) *Rebuilding Lives and Homes in Aceh and Nias, Indonesia*, Urban Development Series. Manila: ADB.

Tripathi, D. (n.d.) *Slum Networking in Ahmedabad: The Sanjay Nagar Pilot Project*. UCL, DPU Working Paper No. 101.

Van der Hoff, R. and Steinberg, F. (1992) *Innovative Approaches to Urban Management: The Integrated Urban Infrastructure Development Programme in Indonesia*. Aldershot: Avebury.

Ward, P.M. (ed.) (1982) *Self Help Housing – A Critique*. London: Alexandrine Press, Mansell.

World Bank (2003) *Cities in Transition: Urban Sector Review in an Era of Decentralization in Indonesia*, East Asia Urban Working Paper Series, Dissemination Paper 7. Washington, DC: World Bank Infrastructure Department, Urban Sector Development Unit.

Yap, K.S. (1994) *The Community Construction Contract System in Sri Lanka*. Nairobi: UNCHS.

13

HOUSING FUTURES

Housing for the poor in Sri Lanka

Sharadbala Joshi and M. Sohail Khan

Abbreviations

ACCA	Asian Coalition for Community Action
ACHR	Asian Coalition for Housing Rights
CAP	Community action plan
CDCs	Community Development Councils
CLAF-Net	Community Livelihood Action Facility Network
HCDC	Housing and Community Development Committee
LEI-CDP	Lunawa Environmental Improvement and Community Development Project
MHP	Million Houses Programme
NGOs	Non-government organisations
NHDA	National Housing Development Authority
PAFs	Project-affected families
RADA	Reconstruction and Development Authority
SLR	Sri Lankan rupees
STP	Sustainable Townships Programme
SUF	Slum Upgrading Facility
TAFREN	Task Force for Rebuilding the Nation
UDA	Urban Development Authority
UN	United Nations
UNICEF	United Nations Children's Fund
USUP	Urban Settlement Upgrading Programme

Introduction

Since the mid-1950s, governments in countries of South Asia have attempted to meet the housing demand of the poor, and introduced housing policies often backed by public finance to support public, subsidised and incremental/self-help housing. With rapid urbanisation, rising real estate prices, transition to market-driven housing finance systems and focus on slum-free cities, governments are implementing redevelopment projects for central districts of cities. Recently, new housing stock is being created under reconstruction and resettlement projects in areas affected by environmental disasters and civil unrest.

The legal ownership of a house is important in Sri Lanka – an island nation situated north of the equator and off the south-eastern coast of India. The island covers an area of 65,610 square kilometres and, except for the south-central mountainous region, is covered by coastal plains (GoSL 2012a). Over 54 per cent of the total population of 20,277,597 lives in 7 of 25 Districts with Colombo District having a population of 2,323,826 (GoSL 2012b).

The urban housing stock comprises single, attached and row (terraced) houses, apartments, line-rooms[1] and shanties. The preference for single houses is evident since over 92.5 per cent of occupied houses are single houses, 3.4 per cent are line-rooms, 0.9 per cent are attached houses, 0.7 per cent are apartments and 1.6 per cent are shanties (GoSL 2012c). The higher income groups have houses on individual or cooperative society plots, while the poor often live in rented or self-owned houses with limited tenure. While the estimated annual demand for new houses is around 50,000 to 100,000 units, the supply is increasing gradually with the involvement of the private sector, and improved housing finance options (GoSL 2011).

Since independence in 1948, the government has been active in the housing sector as a policy maker, regulatory authority, administrator, lender, developer and landlord. Successive governments have coordinated land and housing policies, and introduced policies for managing mortgages, land use, rental rates, taxes, building material prices, etc. The needs of different income groups for autonomously built, cooperative, group or rental housing, extensions and upgrading have been addressed through national housing programmes and sub-programmes. The approach to assisted self-help housing evolved after its introduction under the Hundred Thousand Houses Programme and extensive promotion under the Million Houses Programme (MHP). This subsequently influenced the processes and methodology for assisted self-help housing globally. The Sri Lankan experiences therefore offer a unique longitudinal retrospective on assisted self-help housing during periods of peace, war and emergencies.

This chapter explores housing policies and programmes in Sri Lanka in a chronological order. The four sections include an overview of the housing situation, housing policies and evolution of the self-help approach, efficacy of housing policies, community-centred initiatives and the processes, tools and structure that evolved for enabling community participation. The chapter concludes with implications for governments and stakeholders involved in housing, urban planning and urban management.

Housing policies and aided self-help

The legislative authority and urban land and planning policies in Sri Lanka can be traced to colonial laws and ordinances. The government got powers for compulsory acquisition of privately owned land under the demarcated public land (1840), Town Improvement (1915) and Town and Country Planning (1946) ordinances (Wakely 2008). After formation of the Ministry of Housing and the National Housing Department, the National Housing Act 37 (1954) provided the legal framework for housing development. As slums and shanties proliferated, legislation for sites-and-services and housing programmes was passed, and housing investment was significantly increased. For middle- and lower-middle-income groups, the National Housing Department provided land, infrastructure and apartments in government housing schemes on a rent–purchase basis; that is, rather than being tenants in perpetuity, the 'tenants' could opt to own the rented apartment at the end of a predefined period.

This changed from 1971 when the newly elected government initiated a social welfare approach and passed the Land Reform Act (1972), which controlled land ownership amongst individuals and allowed nationalisation of land owned by foreign companies. In 1973, the Common Amenities Board Law recognised the existence of under-serviced settlements, while the Ceiling on Housing Property Law regulated ownership (number of properties that individuals and corporates could own), and house sizes and construction costs. The Acts enabled appropriation of 'excess' houses, and land acquisition from landowners and private developers (Chularatne 2000). The Protection of Tenants (Special Provision) Law No. 7 (1972) strengthened the rights of house occupants and enabled redistribution of housing assets, while Rent Act No. 7 (1972) controlled rents that property owners could levy, and included financial assistance for tenants wanting to purchase surplus houses. Later amendments attempted to strike a balance between the rights of landowners and tenants. Significantly, the 1999 amendment to the Apartment Ownership Law (1973) enabled individual ownership of condominium property and regularisation of occupants in government owned apartments (MUDCPU 2001).

From the 1970s, coinciding with changes in ruling parties, housing policies changed from welfare to provider to 'aided self-help' to market-based and self-financing approaches. In some cases, instruments such as permission to reside or use land, or designate 'special project areas', were used to improve access to housing. In 1977, the ruling party adopted policies of economic liberalisation and invested heavily in a national housing programme. It established the Urban Development Authority (UDA) and the National Housing Development Authority (NHDA) for coordination, promotion and implementation of all housing programmes, and introduced the UDA and NHDA Acts in 1978. The Acts gave the government extensive powers for acquisition and transfer of land for low-income housing and redevelopment of slums and shanties (Dolapihilla 2000). Further, new housing banks were established and long-term subsidised loans introduced for house construction and upgrading, and development of sites and services using self-help and community support.

Nevertheless, in the absence of an overarching housing policy, the housing programmes have been negatively influenced (GoSL 2011). The government has expressed its commitment to developing a national housing policy through participatory consultations. However, the lack of political will and changes in policy have hindered efforts to finalise the current draft policy.

Post 1970: emphasis on housing and improvement programmes

In 1978, the UDA developed a Slums and Shanty Improvement Programme (1978–1984) for provision of basic common amenities in Colombo and other towns. It field-tested new planning, administrative and operational procedures, including waiver of planning and building bylaws in areas declared 'special project areas' (Woodring 1984; Sevanatha 2001). Some families were granted legal ownership of houses, while those in areas with no high priority land use were given 30-year leases. Concurrently, the Urban Basic Services Improvement Programme (1978–1986) was introduced in Colombo for improving amenities and empowering residents to organise themselves into Community Development Councils (CDCs) (Dayaratne and Samarawickrama 2003). This systematising of community participation through CDCs influenced future UNICEF programmes and community-led interventions.

The Hundred Thousand Houses Programme (1978–1983) marked a shift to a state-dominated provider approach for public housing. The programme, which aimed to build 100,000 houses and provide families living in extreme poverty with free housing and an opportunity to become landowners and homebuilders, comprised three sub-programmes: aided self-help (50,000), direct construction (36,000) and housing loans for self-help housing (14,000). Under the self-help sub-programme, the NHDA provided families with land, loans, information, management guidance and 'housing kits' comprising a house plan, building manual and building materials. People could decide the house location and orientation, adjust house plans to accommodate socio-cultural and climatic requirements, pool labour and build at their convenience (Redman 2009). Although the approach was cost-effective and implementable, there were shortages of building materials and cost recovery was poor – partially because there was no policy for recovering loans when the Programme was launched (Woodring 1984).

In 1979, previous subsidies and rationing for the poor were replaced by food and kerosene stamps for families with monthly incomes of less than SLR 300 (US$19) (Morrison and Arreaga-Rodas 1981). The government also revised its Public Investment Plan due to worldwide recession, slowdown of internal economic growth and escalation in cost of construction/building materials. From allocation of approximately 10 per cent of public investment to housing in 1980–1981, the allocation for housing and urban development was reduced to 3 per cent in 1984–1985. Subsequently, the United States Agency for International Development provided a Housing Guarantee loan to strengthen public mortgage institutions and commercial banks with the objective of improving shelter and services through appropriate policies and programmes (Kane 1994).

From 1983, the government invested in countrywide housing programmes, administrative reforms and poverty alleviation programmes (Sirivardana 2004). In 1983, the MHP, which represented a paradigm shift in housing approaches, was announced. The programme aimed to extend financial and technical assistance to one million families through six sub-programmes, with emphasis on decentralised implementation, community engagement and development, use of traditional building materials and revival of low-cost construction methods. The urban and rural housing sub-programmes focused on the poor and self-help options. The urban sub-programme comprised *in situ* upgrading, relocation, sites-and-services projects and soft loan options for purchase of plots, house construction or improvements.

For decentralised management, effective disbursement of resources to beneficiaries and devolution of responsibilities, the Urban Housing Division of the NHDA and its 23 Administrative Districts were made responsible for implementing these sub-programmes. From being an implementer, the NHDA's role changed to being a provider of loans with designs of houses, bills of quantities, pre-designed material packages, and technical assistance for individuals and community groups. Rural and urban Housing Options and Loan Packages were prepared, setting the loan limits and conditions for each option. The credit for construction of a basic dwelling was issued in three instalments and additions were financed by the house builder (Wakely 2008). The CDCs and an apex inter-sectoral and inter-agency forum at the municipal level were institutionalised as structures through which communities could prioritise their needs and decide on what they wanted done. On termination of the MHP in 1989, the 1.5 Million Houses Programme was initiated for housing people in all sectors. The achievements of the programmes are reflected in the 2001 census, which showed that while 329,221 enumerated houses were constructed during 1970–1979, 1,323,206 were constructed during 1980–1994 (GoSL 2001).

In 1994, the new government reverted to state housing provision by direct construction, and in 1998 the Real Estate Exchange Limited – a government-owned company – and the Urban Service Improvement Project were established. The Sustainable Townships Programme (STP) was introduced in Colombo with the objective of releasing over 60 per cent of plots in commercially viable locations, relocating families without land titles to compact townships and recovering relocation costs of project-affected families (PAFs) through the sale of assembled and redeveloped land (Deheragoda 2011). Contrary to expectations, the PAFs who relocated into 'Sahaspura', the first STP high-rise complex, identified several planning and management problems. Some families did not vacate the original sites and hence the original plots could neither be developed nor sold to raise capital to cover resettlement costs and start a revolving fund. The company therefore remains dependent on external funding for STP implementation (Wakely 2008).

In 2008, the government established the Urban Settlement Development Authority to undertake participatory upgrading and/or development of slum and shanty areas and housing, infrastructure and urban services development projects. This was followed in 2010 with the 'Janasevana' Housing Programme that aims to provide adequate housing for poor families by 2015 – that is, about 663,069 new houses and 866,963 houses requiring repairs. Janasevana includes 11 sub-programmes and options for providing land and title deeds. The programme, to be implemented by the NHDA, involves CDCs in decision-making and encourages use of local building materials (GoSL 2011).

Currently, based on lessons learnt, the government is supporting construction of 46,000 houses under the owner-driven North-East Housing and Reconstruction Programme, and is committed to improving housing access by: (i) enhancing and encouraging private sector participation; (ii) redeveloping government land, and using the proceeds for constructing houses for the poor and displaced; and (iii) maximising use of existing housing stock through upgrading and services provision (Nenova 2010).

Decentralisation and community participation

The key achievements of the housing programmes in Sri Lanka were decentralisation, institutionalising of the participatory process, formalising of the community action plans (CAPs) methodology, and the introduction and development of community contracting as a procurement system.

Decentralisation and Community Development Councils

An important factor for the success of the aided self-help approach is decentralisation through a three-tier system of representation. The settlement level CDCs, which are the dominant and accepted community-based organisations, are responsible for improving (planning, implementing and monitoring) the physical environment and social aspects of a settlement; maintaining relationships with non-government organisations (NGOs)/civil society groups; and conducting and keeping records of regular meetings. The District Housing and Community Development Council, chaired by the district medical health officer, is responsible for conducting monthly meetings for discussing and deciding on CDC proposals. The Housing and Community Development Committee (HCDC), presided by the mayor, is responsible for making policy decisions on CDCs, monitoring services provided by municipal departments and implementing citywide health, education, social, environmental and housing programmes

(Sevanatha 1999). Over the years, although the number of CDCs has reduced either because they are less active or non-functional, they are represented in the HCDCs that continue representing and responding to the needs of the poor.

Community action plans

The CAP methodology evolved as a means for community capacity building and as a management tool as lessons from the field were incorporated in the implementation of the MHP. CAPs involve approaching people as initiators, collaborators and resources, supporting them in organising themselves, involving them in reflecting on and understanding their situation, and identifying socio-economic and physical problems, needs and assets. The community is then supported in building a shared vision, prioritising community needs, developing strategies that are contextually appropriate and achievable through collective effort, identifying short- and medium-term actions, articulating the action plan, deciding on the monitoring mechanism, and finally in presenting the CAP to the community and other stakeholders. This is followed by issue-specific workshops based on community requirements.

Community contracts

Community contracts are awarded to community organisations for carrying out small-scale infrastructure works that are identified and prioritised in a CAP. Compared to conventional contracts, community contracts optimise use of available resources, retain investments within communities and support people in becoming productive. The drawbacks of community contracts include hidden costs on staff time for community training, auditing of financial records and inspections of work constructed under community contracts; inadequate capacities of CDCs; and procedural delays in reimbursing communities based on work-progress (United Nations 2005). In Colombo, 158 community contracts were issued to CDCs by various agencies during 1986–2004 (United Nations 2005).

In January 2012, the government recognised community contracts as a standard procurement system. This enabled government institutions and ministries to offer contracts valued up to SRL 1 million (US$64,220) directly to 13 types of eligible community-based organisations without following normal tender procedures.

Capacity building

The importance of training and information dissemination under aided self-help initiatives is highlighted by the outcomes under the MHP. The NHDA's training division conducted training to enable a common understanding of programme objectives and procedures, and enhance skills for participation of implementing staff and community members (Lankatilleke 1986). This led to the preparation of implementation guidelines, 'A Trainers Guidebook', detailing of procedural steps, and formalising of the CAP methodology and community contracts (Sirivardana 1986).

Land tenure

The government has enabled housing access to people having leasehold titles, illegal tenure and user permits/enumeration cards that are used as 'tenure entitlement certificates' and evidence of stay in Colombo (Vélez-Guerra 2005). About 12,150 entitlement certificates recognising a right of occupancy were awarded during 1985–1989 to households in 80 settlements in Colombo. According to Sevanatha (2003), the occupants of 45 per cent of under-serviced settlements have freehold rights, 19 per cent have leasehold rights, 30 per cent have user permits and 6 per cent are unauthorised occupants. The 20-year tenancy leases issued under the MHP were extended to 30 and then 50 years, and finally in 2006, the leaseholders were issued freehold titles (Wakely 2008). Currently, owner-occupied houses predominate in urban (74.2 per cent) and rural (88.5 per cent) areas (GoSL 2010).

Influence of self-managed and incremental housing

From the late 1980s, multiple stakeholders in countries across Africa and Asia, including funding agencies, the Asian Coalition for Housing Rights (ACHR), international NGOs and UN agencies have adapted and/or incorporated CAP, community contracting and community financing. UN-Habitat, which refers to the overall process from community mobilisation to community involvement in construction as the 'People's Process', has successfully introduced it for housing, settlement upgrading, and for recovery and reconstruction in post-disaster and post-conflict situations (UN-Habitat 2007).

In Colombo, the impact of national housing programmes has been significant. A study of 1,614 informal settlements found that housing was permanent in 80 per cent of settlements, semi-permanent in 14 per cent and temporary in 6 per cent (CMC and Sevanatha 2002). The Women's Bank and some professionals who were involved in the implementation of the MHP have been instrumental in facilitating CDC participation, CAPs and community contracts, preparation of the Colombo poverty profile (1994), and in upgrading, resettlement and reconstruction. The overview of these initiatives highlights the benefits of governments taking a lead in promoting self-help in reconstruction and resettlement processes.

After the 2004 tsunami, over 200 organisations were involved in donor-driven reconstruction under the tsunami housing programme across Sri Lanka. By December 2005, only 4,299 houses had been built; 10,707 were under construction, and construction of 14,500 houses was pending (GoSL 2005). The delays were attributed to the flawed buffer zone policy[2] and uncertainty caused by its revisions, lack of coordination and transparency in allocation of aid resources leading to oversupply of houses in some regions, severe shortage of technical skills in government, implementing agencies and the construction industry, and difficulties in reconciling commitments and progress at national and district levels (Nissanka and Rameezdeen 2008). The effectiveness of agencies, including the Task Force for Rebuilding the Nation (TAFREN) in coordinating reconstruction efforts was limited because of its changing mandates, inadequate organisational links, and lack of clarity regarding its and the line ministries' policy-making powers. In November 2005, with the change in government, a decision was taken to amalgamate the various coordinating agencies into the Reconstruction and Development Authority (RADA), which was given wide powers by an Act of Parliament (Bhattacharjee *et al.* 2007). The situation improved after the government withdrew some controls, drafted the tsunami housing and development policies (Shaw and Ahmed 2010), and issued an Extraordinary Gazette (1632/26) that required every council to promote social inclusivity, civil society participation and partnerships (CLGF 2011). For donor-funded houses, requirements of a minimum house size, water and toilet facilities, and land and house ownership titles were specified. By 2010 when the programme ended, the owner-driven initiatives were more successful than contractor-built houses supported by donors.

The Lunawa Environmental Improvement and Community Development Project (LEI-CDP), completed in December 2010, aimed to mitigate flood damage and improve drainage and canal systems by developing basic infrastructure around Lake Lunawa. It included a community upgrading sub-Programme for 441 households in 15 settlements (Perera 2006). The LEI-CDP strategy of giving equal importance to social mobilisation and the technical components, and involving two well-known NGOs for social marketing and community mobilisation, contributed substantially to its success. The involvement of 514 PAFs in the finalisation of a comprehensive, equitable and inclusive 'Resettlement Package' as per government guidelines for involuntary resettlement helped address problems of distrust towards public agencies and eased the relocation process (Perera 2006). The main project office and a Community Information Centre were located in an NGO's office in the field where joint monthly coordination meetings were held, resulting in better communication, coordination and relations amongst stakeholders and other projects, efficient use of resources and reduced politicisation of the process. CAPs were prepared, and a housing advisory unit established for providing planning and design support. Further, new CDCs were created, existing CDCs strengthened and 'community contracts' issued in project areas.

UN-Habitat, under its Slum Upgrading Facility (SUF), aimed 'to test and develop new financial instruments and methods for expanding private sector finance and public sector involvement in slum upgrading' (UN-Habitat 2009). In February 2006, UN-Habitat entered into a Memorandum of Understanding with Moratuwa Municipal Council, the Women's Development Bank Federation and Slum Dwellers International to undertake pilot upgrading, redevelopment, and relocation projects. The partners collaborated with an NGO (Janarukula) to establish the Moratuwa Urban Poor Fund and obtained a loan from HSBC Bank for a pilot slum upgrading project. Further, the Lanka Financial Services for Underserved Settlements facility was established to provide credit enhancement to upgrading/redevelopment projects. The SUF approach was found to be unsustainable because to make two apartment buildings affordable the buildings were built to lower standards and 20 beneficiary households received a subsidy of around US$2,900 each – US$900 from the government and US$2,000 from SUF 'seed money' (UN-Habitat 2011).

After the tsunami, the Women's Cooperative and Sevanatha established the Community Livelihood Action Facility Network (CLAF-Net) with other civil society organisations and ACHR assistance under which shelter and livelihood improvement programmes are being implemented in 12 urban areas. The partners are also implementing the Urban Settlement Upgrading Programme (USUP), which aims to tackle problems of land, infrastructure, housing and social and economic development (ACCA/ACHR 2012). The Asian Coalition for Community Action (ACCA) Programme supports community-led citywide upgrading in 153 cities in 19 Asian countries. The process involves supporting communities to improve their shelter and livelihoods, and in savings groups forming Community Development Funds with local governments. The CLAF-Net passes funds to Community Development Funds as a first step towards establishing city-based funds, while the Women's Cooperative has expanded elements of housing, land tenure and settlement upgrading in its programmes, and is thereby contributing towards making the USUP a national process. Four hundred and eighty-eight households in eight settlements in Moratuwa have already been given freehold land titles (Samarasinghe 2012).

Reflections for the future of self-help housing policies

The experiences from Sri Lanka reveal that despite varying political commitment for the self-help approach, the government has allocated substantial funds for national housing programmes. It has changed institutional arrangements and management processes for decentralised decision-making, adapted the step-by-step decision process for community involvement in upgrading projects, delineated the roles and responsibilities of stakeholders, and encouraged use of tools and methodologies for participatory decision-making. Although the number of families resettled/relocated under the tsunami housing programmes, STP and LEI-CDP is lower than those reached under the MHP, the owner/PAF-driven initiatives were more successful than conventional approaches that were ongoing at the same time. The NGOs and experts who facilitated community participation mobilised communities and assisted them in forming CDCs, and in securing and managing loans, government services and infrastructure. They also provided technical advice and training in financial management, etc.

The experiences of decentralised implementation under the MHP, the tsunami housing programmes, the LEI-CDP and USUP show that the success of self-help programmes depends on the commitment of governments and leaders, supportive policies and structures, capacity building, and continual attention and support that enable corrections and changes in response to conditions on the ground. They reveal that upgrading, resettlement and housing projects involving 200 to 500 families are more likely to succeed with the support of NGOs who facilitate community participation.

Conclusions

This chapter has described aided housing programmes, related policy directions and legislation, and the role of funding agencies, government and grassroots organisations in promoting self-help for resettlement, redevelopment and rehabilitation programmes. It has highlighted how favourable policies, financial and technical assistance, standards and regulations can contribute to successful partnerships among government, experts, funding agencies, NGOs and communities, and in programme implementation.

The experiences also show that community-centred approaches require consistent and high-level political commitment, clear communication of policies, institutionalising of the roles of CDCs and appropriate management systems, involvement of financing institutions that focus on the poor and capacity building support. In addition, they entail interdependence amongst collaborators, as well as 'enabling partners' who mobilise and enable community participation in the process of visioning, strategising and changing settlement situations, and facilitate the linkage between individual households and financing institutions. Thus, to house the poor successfully, the government needs to have a comprehensive housing policy and an integrated approach to settlement planning, housing finance and institutional arrangements.

Assisted self-help is appropriate in an environment where the demand for single houses is rising and where communities have social capital but do not have adequate shelter, or need new shelters because of environmental disasters, conflicts or for resettlement of PAFs. With the changed economic scenario in developing countries, and high densities of urban areas, the demand for single houses is likely to be replaced by a demand for smaller and compact apartments rather than upgrading of under-serviced/informal settlements. This is true in Sri Lanka where, despite problems with the Sahaspura scheme, the government wants to make the high-rise approach more pragmatic through participation of people, encourage relocation from informal settlements and redevelop dilapidated areas. In this context, the nature of support for housing and community participation would be different since apartments are not built for specific end-users. It will require greater facilitating support from NGOs, experts and planners.

Acknowledgement

The authors are thankful to K. Jayaratne who provided invaluable insights, comments and data; Diane Deacon and the Building and Social Housing Foundation, UK for financially supporting the research on which the paper is based; and to Lalith Lankatilleke and Susil Srivardana for their comments. The opinions expressed and any errors or omissions are the authors.

Notes

1 Line-rooms are single rooms of about 10 × 12 feet in a long barrack building consisting of 10–12 rooms fronted by an open veranda. Barracks with back-to-back housing can contain as many as 24 households.
2 Nearly three months after the tsunami, the government announced the creation of a 100 m buffer zone in the south and a 200 m buffer zone in the north within which heavy restrictions were imposed on rebuilding. While the occupants of undamaged and slightly damaged houses were allowed to remain in the buffer zone, new constructions were not permitted within it. Further, the restriction presented the challenge of creating alternative livelihood options for those occupied in fisheries, tourism and trade. Ultimately, under public pressure, the government relaxed the rule in October 2005 and scaled down the buffer zone to about 50 m in a limited number of districts.

References

ACCA/ACHR (2012) '11th ACCA Programme Committee Meeting', 17 March. Quezon City: ACCA.
Bhattacharjee, A. et al. (2007) *Final Evaluation of CARE Australia supported tsunami response in Trinco and Batti Districts of Sri Lanka*. Final Report for CARE Australia and CARE Sri Lanka, May 2007.
Chularatne, H. (2000) 'Land tenure issues and improvement of urban low income settlements – experiences of Colombo, Sri Lanka', paper presented at the Regional Workshop on Settlements of the Urban Poor: Challenges in the New Millennium at Dhaka, Bangladesh, 18–19 February.
CLGF (2011) 'Sri Lanka local gtovernment profile', in *Commonwealth Local Government Handbook 2011/12*. CLGF.
CMC and Sevanatha (2002) *Poverty Profile: City of Colombo. Urban Poverty Reduction through Community Empowerment*. Colombo: CMC/Sevanatha.
Dayaratne, R. and Samarawickrama, R. (2003) 'Empowering communities in the peri-urban areas of Colombo', *Environment and Urbanization*, 15(1): 101–110.
Deheragoda, K. (2011) *The Rehousing Option for Colombo's Poor*. Gangodawila: University of Sri Jayewardenepura.
Dolapihilla, S. (2000) 'Public sector housing development in Sri Lanka, with special reference to urban informal resettlements in Colombo', *Lund University Alumni Papers*. Lund: Lund University.
GoSL (2001) 'Census of Population and Housing 2001. H6. Year of Construction', Colombo: GoSL.
GoSL (2005) 'Report on National Post Tsunami Lessons Learned and Best Practices Workshop', Colombo, 8–9 June 2005. Colombo: GoSL.
GoSL (2010) 'Household Income and Expenditure Survey (2009/10), Final Report', GoSL: Department of Census and Statistics. Online. Available at www.statistics.gov.lk/HIES/HIES2009_10FinalReport.pdf (accessed 28 January 2013).

GoSL (2011) 'Conference Proceedings, Janasevana – Housing For All', National Housing Symposium, Ministry of Construction, Engineering Services, Housing and Common Amenities, 22–23 March 2011, Colombo: Sri Lanka Foundation Institute.

GoSL (2012a) 'About Sri Lanka'. Online. Available at www.gov.lk/gov/index.php?option=com_content&view=article&id=52&lang=en (accessed 28 January 2013).

GoSL (2012b) 'Preliminary Report (Provisional) – 1, Census of Population and Housing 2011, Population of Sri Lanka by District', Colombo: GoSL Department of Census and Statistics.

GoSL (2012c) 'Census of Population and Housing 2011. Hh61 – Occupied housing units in districts and Divisional Secretary's Divisions by type of housing unit', Colombo: GoSL.

Kane, H.W. (1994) 'Concept Paper: Sustainable housing finance for low-income shelter, 383-HG-004 (Second Tranche)', Colombo: USAID.

Lankatilleke, L. (1986) 'Training and information for institutional development for the implementation of the Million Houses Programme of Sri Lanka', *Habitat International*, 10(3): 109–129.

Morrison, T.K. and Arreaga-Rodas, L. (1981) *Economic Liberalization in Developing Countries: Some Lessons from Three Case Studies – Sri Lanka, Egypt and Sudan*. AID, Bureau for Programme and Policy Coordination.

MUDCPU (2001) *Sri Lanka Country Report, Istanbul+5. June 2001*. Colombo: Ministry of Urban Development, Construction and Public Utilities.

Nenova, T. (2010) *Expanding Housing Finance to the Underserved in South Asia Market Review and Forward Agenda*. Washington, DC: World Bank.

Nissanka, K. and Rameezdeen, R. (2008) 'Study of factors affecting post disaster housing reconstruction', in K. Keraminiyage, S. Jayasena, D. Amaratunga and R. Haigh (eds) *Post Disaster Recovery Challenges in Sri Lanka*. Manchester: University of Salford.

Perera, L. (2006) 'Resettlement of people through consensus, Proceedings of APEN International Conference on Practice change for sustainable communities: Exploring footprints, pathways and possibilities', 6–8 March, at Beechworth, Victoria, Australia.

Redman, S. (2009) 'A study of support-based housing and community participation in the Million Houses Programme, Sri Lanka 1977–1989', Research Report. Online. Available at http://architectureinsights.com.au/media/uploads/resources/FINAL_MILLION_HOUSES_PROGRAMME_Sonya_Redman.pdf (accessed 25 September 2013).

Samarasinghe, R. (2012) *ACHR/ACCA City Wide Settlement Upgrading Program, Sri Lanka Country Report – 2012*.

Sevanatha (1999) *Role of Community Based Organizations in Provision of Municipal Services, Urban Management Programme-Colombo City Consultations*. Colombo: Sevanatha.

Sevanatha (2001) *Regulatory Guidelines for Urban Upgrading: Case Study of Colombo, Sri Lanka*. Colombo/Loughborough: Sevanatha and WEDC.

Sevanatha (2003) 'The case of Colombo, Sri Lanka: understanding slums', Case study prepared for the *Global Report on Human Settlements 2003*. Nairobi: UN-Habitat.

Shaw, J. and Ahmed, I. (2010) *Design and Delivery of Post-Disaster Housing Resettlement Programs: Case Studies from Sri Lanka and India*. Melbourne: The Royal Melbourne Institute of Technology.

Sirivardana, S. (1986) 'Reflections on the implementation of the Million Houses Programme', *Habitat International*, 10(3): 91–108.

Sirivardana, S. (2004) 'Innovative practice amidst positive potential for Paradigm Shift: the case of Sri Lanka', in P. Wignaraja and S. Sirivardana (eds) *Pro Poor Growth and Governance in South-Asia, Decentralisation and Participatory Development*. New Delhi: Sage.

UN-Habitat (2007) *People's Process in Post-Disaster and Post-Conflict Recovery and Reconstruction*. Fukuoka: UN-Habitat.

UN-Habitat (2009) *Innovative Approaches for Involuntary Resettlement: Lunawa Environmental Improvement & Community Development Project*, project brochure. Fukuoka: UN-Habitat.

UN-Habitat (2011) *Evaluation Report 4/2011, Slum Upgrading Facility, Pilot Programme, End-of-Programme Evaluation*. Nairobi: UN-Habitat.

United Nations (2005) *Improving the Lives of the Urban Poor: Case Studies on the Provision of Basic Services Through Partnerships*. New Delhi: UN-ESCAP.

Vélez-Guerra, A. (2005) *Land Tenure and the Urban Poor's Environmental Burdens: A Case Study of Four Settlements in Colombo, Sri Lanka*. Ottawa: IDRC.

Wakely, P. (2008) 'Land tenure in under-served settlements in Colombo', *IDRC Urban Poverty and Environment Report Series* 6. Ottawa: IDRC.

Woodring, M.D. (1984) *Evaluation of 383-HG-001: First Phase of Housing Guarantee Program, Sri Lanka*. Washington, DC: National Councils of Savings Institutions.

14
AFFORDABLE HOUSING POLICIES IN URBAN CHINA

Mingye Li and Jean-Claude Driant

Abbreviations

ECH   Economic and Comfortable Housing
HPF   Housing Provident Fund
PIR   Price-to-income ratio

Introduction

Housing policy in China has changed significantly since the housing reform of the 1980s in which socialist welfare housing provided by state-owned institutions and municipal governments was replaced with a market provision system (Wang and Murie 1996, 2011; Zhao and Bourassa 2003). This reform led not only to an increase in the demand for housing in urban areas but also to an improvement in living conditions. For example, the average floor space per inhabitant in urban areas increased from 3.6 square metres in 1978, to 32.7 square metres in 2011 (National Bureau of Statistics 2012). However, during the rapid process of housing marketization, serious housing inequality resulted because affordable housing policies were not developed adequately. In response, the Chinese government placed a renewed emphasis on affordable housing polices in 2007.

This chapter examines the introduction, evolution and relaunch of affordable housing policies during the past two decades by situating these policies within the economic and urban context of China and with an emphasis on the implementation of the renewed affordable housing policy. In the first section China's housing reform is briefly reviewed, and the three major affordable housing programmes introduced in this period as well as their role in the transformation of the housing system are discussed. The following section assesses the process of housing marketization as well as the changes in the affordable housing policy that made housing inequality an acute problem. As it is argued that the current affordable housing policy is subject to the economic objectives of both central and local governments, we examine the renewed affordable housing policy at both the national and local level with the illustration of two case studies. The last section provides an overview of the chapter's contents.

China's housing reform

From public housing to a market-oriented system

China's housing reform, launched in the 1980s, constitutes the major context of the development of affordable housing policies during the past two decades. Prior to the reform, housing provision in Chinese cities was characterized by the dominance of socialist public housing with work units[1] playing a key role in the housing allocation process. Under this system, public housing was part of the welfare provision whereby employees received work units in exchange for a very low salary (Wu 1996; Huang and Clark 2002; Zhao and Bourassa 2003). However, serious problems which questioned this system were identified. In sum, an acute housing shortage resulted from the heavy financial burden placed upon the government; this also led to an unfair distribution under the mechanism of the planned economy (Wang and Murie 1996, 1999; Wu 1996; Logan *et al.* 2009).

In the 1980s, according to the policy of Reform and Opening up, the government took the initiative to search for new ways of housing provision. Following a gradual and pragmatic approach (Wu 2002), transitional policies were introduced to encourage private housing ownership, such as the sale of public housing at a low price. It was not until 1998 that the central government made a decision to ban the allocation of public housing, which amounted to the end of the public housing system.

Introduction of the affordable housing policy

During the transitional period in the 1990s, an affordable housing policy was introduced. It consisted of three programmes: Economic and Comfortable Housing (*jingji shiyong fang*), Low Rental Housing (*lianzu fang*) and the Housing Provident Fund (*zhufang gongjijin*). On one hand, these programmes served to promote the housing reform and reduce the conflicts caused by the termination of the public housing system; on the other, they formed the basis of the affordable housing system in China.

The Economic and Comfortable Housing programme (jingji shiyong fang)

The circular letter of the State Council (1998) announced the establishment of a housing provision system mainly underpinned by the Economic and Comfortable Housing, or ECH programme. ECH is designed for low- and middle-income urban households who are unable to purchase a home at the going market rate. Accordingly, ECH ambitiously set out to cover the needs of 70–80 per cent of urban households (Wang 2000). ECH differs from previous socialist public housing initiatives in two ways. First, ECH units are developed for sale, not for rent. Second, most ECH units were built by for-profit real estate developers and sold to eligible families through market transactions (Deng *et al.* 2011). In terms of financing, local governments are expected to provide free land to developers as well as reduce or even waive various development fees and taxes. In exchange, local governments regulate the sales price to around 50–60 per cent of that of commercial housing (National Bureau of Statistics of China 2009), keeping the profit margin to no more than 3 per cent.

The Low Rental Housing programme (lianzu fang)

The Low Rental Housing programme is intended for urban households with the lowest incomes. The programme consists of two parts: a rent allowance as the primary means of protection as well as a direct supply of low rental housing as a supplementary measure. The direct supply of low rental housing, due to low availability, is especially intended for urban households facing particular difficulties such as families with sick, elderly or disabled household members. While housing provision under the Low Rental Housing programme is exclusively for rent, the rent income is very low. Financing depends completely on local government subsidies. In practice, instead of building new low rental housing units, many local governments used old public housing units to accommodate eligible households.

The Housing Provident Fund programme (zhufang gongjijin)

The Housing Provident Fund programme (HPF) is a compulsory savings programme in which both employers and employees contribute a certain percentage of the employee's salary, initially set at 5 per cent per month, to a special account administered by the management centre of each local government. In return, employees can not only withdraw their savings from their own account but also get low-interest mortgage loans from the pool of money for qualified housing purposes such as a home purchase or home improvement. Theoretically, public institutions, state-owned enterprises, urban collective enterprises, private enterprises and foreign-funded enterprises are involved in the programme.

The three housing programmes played an important role in facilitating the transformation of China's housing system. ECH formed a hybrid vehicle towards urban household home ownership in which private developers were allowed to participate in the housing development process and thus alleviated the burden of investment costs from local governments. The HPF allowed work units to contribute a cash subsidy in lieu of companies directly building public housing units for their employees (Wang 2001). Employees were then expected to purchase market-priced housing using their Housing Provident Fund savings and loans, along with their other financial resources (Deng et al. 2011). As for the Low Rental Housing programme, despite its scarcity, it is to some extent a continuation of the public housing system.

Housing marketization and disadvantaged groups

After the 1997 Asian financial crisis, the Chinese government made a great effort to stimulate housing consumption and promote the marketization of housing (Deng et al. 2011; Wang and Murie 2011). In 2003, a State Council circular letter marked a turning point in China's housing policies. The letter proclaimed that the real estate sector constituted 'the pillar industry of the national economy' and that 'commercial housing rather than ECH was designated as the type of housing available for the majority of urban households' (State Council 2003). Consequently, the process of housing marketization was further promoted during the years that followed. The real estate market became prosperous with the dramatic increase both in the value of investment and in housing prices. Meanwhile, the development of affordable housing declined. Some scholars estimated that the marketization reform pushed the housing system from one extreme to the other, causing 'over-marketization'. This meant that the housing market was increasingly inadequate in providing housing for socially and economically disadvantaged groups (Ye et al. 2010).

Rising housing prices and lack of housing affordability

The pent-up demand for housing has been released by the accelerated process of commercialization. The newly established real estate market experienced a period of prosperity until the financial crisis in 2008. The floor space of commercialized residential buildings (not including ECH) rose from 66.5 million square metres in 1997 to 666.3 million square metres in 2007 (National Bureau of Statistics of China 2008). Accordingly, the price of housing continued to rise; a total increase of 92.9 per cent was noted between 1998 and 2008. The rate of increase was more significant in large cities. For example, the average price of new commercial housing increased by 144 per cent in Beijing and 168 per cent in Shanghai during the same period (National Bureau of Statistics of China 2009). Moreover, speculation in housing based on the positive expectation of the real estate market has also pushed up house prices.

Housing affordability is commonly measured by the price-to-income ratio (PIR) or the ratio between median housing price and median income.[2] According to the Centre for Urban Development and Land Policy of Peking University – Lincoln Institute, the average PIR at the national level in China was estimated to be 5.56 in 2007; this is higher than the international standard of 3 to 5 suggested by the UN-Habitat (Ren and Man 2010). The cities with the highest PIR are located in coastal areas, such as Xiamen (10.42), Nanjing (10.00) and Shanghai (9.81). The cities with a PIR below 4 are located in the hinterland including Chongqing (4.46), Yinchuan (4.67) and Hohhot (4.72) (Ren and Man 2010). Besides the regional disparity, the income gap is another key factor preventing affordable housing. The same research shows that the PIR of the first decile group of urban households with the lowest incomes is three times higher than the PIR of the tenth decile group of urban households with the highest incomes.

Decline in the development of affordable housing

The boom in commercial housing came at the expense of affordable housing development. As shown in Figure 14.1, between 2000 and 2008, the investment in ECH units sharply declined. The proportion of residential building floor space devoted to newly started ECH shifted from more than 20 per cent in 2000 to less than 7 per cent after 2005. Up to 2005, only 6.5 per cent of urban households had benefited from this housing programme (National Bureau of Statistics of China 2005); this is significantly lower than the 70–80 per cent initially expected.

Despite the decline in the development of ECH units, there were no restrictions on the generous household income limits allowing access to ECH units. As a result, many eligible low-income households could not afford ECH units while upper-income households largely benefited from the programme. Moreover, in some cities, in order to facilitate the process of urbanization, priority was given to families affected by urban renewal and redevelopment schemes regardless of low-income status.

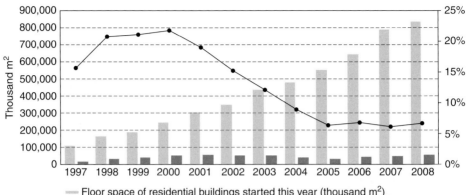

FIGURE 14.1 ECH floor space and total residential building proportion in China (1997–2008). *Source*: National Bureau of Statistics of China (2009).

In the case of Low Rental Housing, the coverage rate remained very low. Beneficiaries of this programme accounted for about 329,000 households in 2005; this represented less than 0.2 per cent of the total number of urban households (Ba and Wang 2010). Most local governments were reluctant to develop new low rental housing schemes due to the potentially heavy investment and low rental revenue.

The third housing programme – the HPF – has progressed steadily since its creation in the 1990s. By 2007, 71.9 million employees were covered by the programme, representing 68.5 per cent of the total number of registered employees. However, the programme suffers from marked disparities between employees from different types of enterprises. The majority of beneficiaries are employees of state-owned enterprises, public institutions or large companies. In contrast, many employees working in small businesses with short-term contracts are excluded from the programme.

As illustrated, the affordable housing programmes introduced in the 1990s did little to reduce housing inequalities during the decade that followed. In the course of over-marketization, upper-income urban households and privileged 'insiders' have improved their housing conditions while socially and economically disadvantaged groups have been subjected to market prices.

'Urban village' – informal affordable housing for migrants

Migrant workers, among the most socially and economically disadvantaged populations in China, usually face difficulties with housing. Migrants are the product of China's urbanization movement, which has provoked a massive rural–urban migration since the late 1970s (Song *et al.* 2008). In 2009, the number of rural migrants working in cities and towns reached 150 million (China Science Center of International Eurasian Academy of Sciences *et al.* 2010). The majority of migrant workers, usually employed in low-paid sectors, cannot afford housing on the formal market. Moreover, under China's urban–rural dualistic social and economic structure caused by the household registration system,[3] people with agricultural household

FIGURE 14.2 ECH housing units in Nanjing (top) and Low Rental Housing units in Chongqing (bottom). Photos by Mingye Li.

registration – the case for most migrant workers – are excluded from the urban social security system, including affordable housing programmes.

In this context, 'urban villages' (*ChengZhongCun*) emerged in many large coastal cities. In the course of rapid urbanization, a great number of villages situated on the city fringes have been swallowed by urban developments. Yet, some existing residential areas escaped total urbanization for various reasons. For example, local governments were unwilling to pay the high compensation amounts demanded by affected villagers. Hence, urban villages resulted – villages that did not become full-fledged urban areas but are nevertheless swallowed by urban sprawl (Lin *et al.* 2011).

Although urban villages are surrounded by an urban landscape, their governance remains under the rural administrative system. Rural land is owned collectively rather than by the state.[4] Native villagers, as members of a rural community, are entitled to an equal share of the collectively owned land and are allowed to build their own houses on it. The construction of buildings is not controlled by an urban-area application. Thus, native villagers are able to build substandard housing units with extra floor space for lease to migrant workers. As migrants need to minimize their expenses and only seek very limited living space, the low rent drives the majority of migrants to settle in urban villages. This results in high density and overcrowding which raise public health and safety concerns (Song *et al.* 2008; Lin *et al.* 2011). Nevertheless, the poor living conditions do not have an impact on the attractiveness of urban villages for migrants.

The urban village is the outcome of both China's urbanization processes and the dualist urban–rural social and economic structure. Urban villages play an important role in providing migrant workers with affordable rental housing in cities. However, this type of housing could hardly be included within the framework of affordable housing. This is because most urban village housing construction is 'illegal' and associated with many problems such as overcrowding, chaotic land use and intensified social disorder (Song *et al.* 2008). In response to these problems, local governments usually adopt redevelopment programmes, most of which have focused on demolishing villages, resettling native villagers and encouraging real estate companies to take part in the redevelopment projects. Nevertheless, little attention has been given to migrant workers. The only way for them to survive in cities is to seek low rental housing in other urban villages.

The relaunch of an affordable housing policy and its productivist characteristics

Commercial housing price increases as well as increased housing inequality have led to growing dissatisfaction among the people. To make amends, the central government declared its intention to reform the affordable housing policy in 2007 (State Council 2007). At the end of 2008, in order to cope with the global financial crisis, the state announced a 4 trillion yuan stimulus package[5] (US$640 billion), in which about 7 per cent was dedicated to affordable housing investment. During the following years, the objective of affordable housing development has become more and more ambitious. The programme went from aiming to protect 7.5 million low-income urban households with housing difficulties in 2009 (People's Republic of China 2009) to a scheme to build 10 million affordable housing units in 2011; between 2011 and 2015 a total of 36 million affordable housing units are due to be built (National People's Congress 2011). The following section examines this policy at both the national and the local level.

Affordable housing policy at the national level

As mentioned earlier, the real estate sector was said to be the pillar industry of the national economy in 2003. Indeed, its status has not changed since. This sector contributed approximately 1–2 percentage points of the country's gross domestic product (GDP) growth rate, which has varied between 8 and 11 per cent in recent years (Zhang and Xuan 2011). To combat the rise in housing prices, the central government had to resolve a dilemma. On one hand, it sought to cool the overheated market and to calm social unrest caused by soaring house prices; on the other hand, the government was concerned about the stability of the real estate sector, which constitutes the driving force of the national economy.

The renewed affordable housing policy with its large-scale construction component provides a way to solve this dilemma. According to the Ministry of Housing and Urban-Rural Development, the affordable housing policy aims to achieve several economic and social objectives: first, to stimulate domestic demand and to maintain steady economic growth; second, to improve people's living conditions and to share the achievements of the Reform and Opening-up; and third, to promote social equality and political stability. In the Government Work Reports for the period 2009–2011 (People's Republic of China 2009), the policy concerning affordable housing development was included in the measures to promote a healthy and steady development of the real estate market. This means that the provision of affordable housing is deemed to be a housing price regulation tool used to cool down the overheated residential property markets, since its provision is expected to reduce the demand for housing. Meanwhile, the large-scale investment in affordable housing could be a new driving force to further economic growth, especially during the global crisis. This explains one of the reasons why bricks and mortar subsidies rather than housing allowance have been chosen at a national level. Moreover, since 2010, the central government has taken tough actions to regulate the overheated real estate market. Consequently, the price increase has slowed down and the volume of transactions has fallen since early 2010. The substantial investment in affordable housing development was expected to compensate for the decline in the property market. From this perspective, the new affordable housing policy is closely related to the economic circumstances, which is consistent with the productivist welfare model prevailing in other East Asian countries (Holliday 2000).

Concerning the typology of affordable housing and the corresponding target group, two measures have been taken at a national level. First, a new housing programme called Public Rental Housing (*gonggong zulin fang*) was introduced in 2010. Second, the income limits of each type of housing programme were adjusted. Thus, the new affordable housing system is composed of three programmes designed for three household groups: Low Rental Housing intended for the lowest- and low-income urban households, affordable housing for low-income urban households and the Public Rental Housing for lower-middle-income urban households as well as for new employees including migrant workers if the local financial situation permits. At the political level, affordable housing has become more comprehensive with the multi-level protection system and its consideration for migrant workers.

In practice, 'affordable housing' is actually a broad term which includes not only the three 'formal' housing programmes; it also includes the renewal of shanty areas. According to a scheme of the National Affordable Housing Development in 2011 (Ministry of Housing and Urban-Rural Development 2011), among a total of 10 million housing units to be built this year, housing provided for under the shanty area renewal scheme accounted for 41.5 per cent

TABLE 14.1 Principal characteristics of Chongqing and Nanjing

	Administrative status	Population (2010)	Urban population (%, 2009)	Area (km²)	Urban population average income (per capita, 2009)	GDP (2010)
Chongqing	Direct-controlled municipality	28.8 million	51.6	82,300	18,729 yuan (US$2,986)	585 billion yuan (US$93 billion)
Nanjing	Sub-provincial municipality, capital of Jiangsu Province	7.7 million	77.2	6,598	28,278 yuan (US$4,508)	417 billion yuan (US$66 billion)

Source: Nanjing Municipal Bureau Statistics (2009–2011); Chongqing Municipal Bureau Statistics (2011).

of the total. This was followed by Public Rental Housing at 22.7 per cent while ECH and Low Rental Housing accounted for only 11.0 per cent and 16.5 per cent, respectively. The priority given to housing under the shanty area renewal scheme can be understood in the context of rapid urbanization in China as is discussed in the following case studies.

Affordable housing policy at the local level: evidence from Chongqing and Nanjing

Decentralization in the course of economic reform has transformed China's local governments from passive agents of the central government into key actors pursuing local development and ensuring the application of various urban policies (Zhu 2004). To understand in greater detail the implementation of affordable housing policy, two case studies have been chosen for our analysis: Chongqing, a direct-controlled municipality in central and western China; and Nanjing, a provincial capital in the prosperous lower Yangtze region. This choice allows us to contrast different policy options adopted by these two cities with respect to position in the administrative hierarchy, size and location of the city, and the level of economic development and structure of the economy. Such variations determine to a large extent the kinds and amounts of resources a city can mobilize as well as the willingness of the city to undertake substantial affordable housing projects (see Table 14.1). First-tier cities like Beijing and Shanghai have not been chosen for our study since they have been addressed by most urban research in China. Moreover, their special status cannot represent the general situation in the country.

BOX 14.1 CHONGQING

In implementing affordable housing policy, Chongqing is considered to be a model city. The city introduced ECH in 1998 and Low Rental Housing in 2002. In 2009, the municipal government became the pioneer of the Public Rental Housing programme with the aim of achieving the largest Public Rental Housing stock in the country. In 2010, this objective started to take shape through an ambitious scheme to build 40 million square metres of Public Rental Housing within three years. In addition, according to the municipal government, Low Rental Housing and ECH were to be integrated into the Public Rental Housing system by setting different rent levels. This means that the current affordable housing policy in Chongqing consists mainly of the Public Rental Housing programme.

Compared to national-level policy, the Public Rental Housing programme in Chongqing has a broader target covering not only registered urban households but also the migrant population as well as recent graduates with housing difficulties who also possess an employment contract. In this case, the criteria should be simplified to 'holding a job, with no accommodation'. The municipal government has even set quotas for each type of population: urban residents account for 30–40 per cent of the total target population, recent graduates for 10–20 per cent and migrant workers for 50 per cent (Liu et al. 2010).

Two types of Public Rental Housing can be identified in Chongqing: the first is a residential area open to all of the three groups of applicants; the second is Public Rental Housing intended for migrant workers and located in industrial parks. The former is characterized by a large community (about 50,000 dwellers for each area), moderate apartment size (between 30 and 80 square metres) and high density (high-rise blocks with over 20 floors). The latter is actually a collection of dormitories rather than a real residential area. While the level of comfort is generally low, the conditions of Public Rental Housing are better than those in rental housing in urban villages. Moreover, proximity to the workplace allows employers to better manage their staff who often work long hours.

The affordable housing policy in Chongqing emphasized accommodation for migrant workers who had long been excluded from the urban security system. On one hand, this policy does reduce the housing inequality by resolving the housing difficulties of migrant workers; on the other hand, it aims to attract migrant workers who constitute the major labour force of Chongqing. This consideration is related to the city's industrial development strategy.

In 1997, following the National Western Development Plan,[6] the city of Chongqing was separated from Sichuan province to become the fourth direct-controlled municipality of the country. In this context, Chongqing has become the driving force in the development of central and western regions of China. However, with a large rural population and a tradition of heavy industry, Chongqing's GDP per capita and average income per capita of urban households amount to only 40 per cent and 66 per cent, respectively, of those of Nanjing (see Table 14.1). In order to narrow the economic gap that exists with coastal cities, the municipal government adopted an industrial upgrade strategy aiming to move away from traditional heavy industry to modern light industry following consumer demand such as the production of electronic devices. Since these activities are highly labour-intensive, the provision of migrant worker Public Rental Housing could attract more low-cost labour forces from rural areas. Thus, the development of Public Rental Housing for migrant workers in the city has been thriving.

BOX 14.2 NANJING

The city of Nanjing introduced an affordable housing policy in 2002. Today a multi-target housing protection system has been developing with the provision of Low Rental Housing, ECH and Public Rental Housing. In 2010, the municipal government launched four mixed affordable housing schemes with a total floor space of 10 million square metres, composed of 61,000 units of ECH, 10,000 units of Public Rental Housing and 5,000 units of Low Rental Housing. Moreover, between 2011 and 2015, the government aims to build 90,000 units of Public Rental Housing and 80,000 ECH units. From these programmes, we can see that ECH and Public Rental Housing constitute the major types of affordable housing under the current provision.

The Low Rental Housing system is designed for the poorest households in Nanjing. However, the coverage rate remained very low; in 2010, only 2.2 per cent of urban households in the city benefited from the system.

ECH is the dominant affordable housing programme in Nanjing. From 2002 to 2010, more than 100,000 housing units have been provided. Indeed, since 2004, a large part of ECH has been assigned to land-expropriated rural households (about 80 per cent) and house-expropriated urban households (about 15 per cent), while the non-expropriated low- and middle-income beneficiaries accounted for a very small share (less than 10 per cent).[7] Moreover, among the 61,000 units of ECH programmed in the four affordable housing projects, 35,000 units were designated for land-expropriated rural households, 16,000 units for house-expropriated urban households and only 10,000 for low- and middle-income households.

The priority given to land-expropriated rural households can be explained by the rapid urban expansion of Nanjing. In the process of urbanization, the municipal government, which holds the power of expropriation, has been zealous in transforming vast rural areas into industrial parks and new towns. Yet expropriation of farmlands and rural household land constitutes a precondition of such projects. In order to promote urban development and to avoid social unrest, the municipal government undertook the task of relocating the land-expropriated rural households.

The expropriation in urban areas is driven by urban renewal and development. In Nanjing, as in many other Chinese cities, a large number of urban renewal projects are underway. The municipal government, utilizing instruments of urban planning, is masterminding the transformation of urban space. Old dilapidated downtown homes are being expropriated and original residents are relocated to peripheral areas where land is much cheaper. Land use rights of downtown areas are transferred to real estate developers for more profitable projects, such as office buildings or high-quality residences. This has provided the municipal government with substantial transfer income,[8] one of the greatest sources of revenue for the local exchequer.

The Public Rental Housing programme was introduced in Nanjing in 2010. In terms of target group, besides lower- to middle-income urban households, the groups called 'highly qualified professionals', 'young talents' and migrants have been introduced. Among the 90,000 units of Public Rental Housing programmed between 2011 and 2015, 10,000 units were designated for 'highly qualified professionals' and 50,000 for recent graduates (including young talents) and migrant workers. The redefinition of the target group for Public Rental Housing corresponds to the local development strategy of Nanjing.

According to the 12th Five-Year Plan in Nanjing, the city aims to become one of the National Innovation Cities by 2015 as well as to transform 'Made in Nanjing' into 'Innovated in Nanjing'. One of the measures is to promote high-tech industries such as information and communication. To do this, the municipal government carried out human resource plans supporting this strategy which aims to attract more than 220,000 highly qualified individuals by 2015. The investment in Public Rental Housing for young talented people is also part of the plan.

The two case studies of Chongqing and Nanjing (see Box 14.1 and Box 14.2) show that local governments are granted the right to adapt to their local situations and introduce their own measures while respecting the overall orientation of affordable housing policy determined by the central government. Generally speaking, large-scale construction of affordable housing is underway in each city. Yet due to different levels of economic and urban development, the municipal governments place emphasis on different groups. In Chongqing, Public Rental Housing units are assigned not only to lower- and middle-income urban households but also to migrant labourers who are needed for the city's industrial upgrade strategy. In Nanjing, newly built, affordable homes are largely used to ensure a smooth running of urbanization and urban renovation so as to increase local land revenues and to enhance the city's competitiveness. Meanwhile, a highly qualified workforce and young talented people have been included in the target to support the city's human resource plans.

Conclusion

During the past two decades, affordable housing policies have played different roles in urban China. This chapter highlights the changing economic and urban contexts which affected to a large extent the evolution of housing policy. The introduction of affordable housing programmes in the 1990s facilitated the housing reform and ensured a smooth transition. Then, in the process of housing marketization, policy gave priority to commercial housing rather than affordable housing. Yet the market failed to meet the needs of socially and economically disadvantaged groups. Housing inequality became an acute problem. As a result, there has been renewed emphasis on affordable housing policies since 2007.

Indeed, this chapter explores the renewed affordable housing policy at both a national and local level. At the national level, the central government is deeply involved in the national economy via its institutional forces. The affordable housing policy has been given a regulatory role for the residential property market and has been used to stimulate national economic growth during the global crisis. It is undeniable that large-scale investment in affordable housing will improve the housing conditions of urban households facing difficulties. Nevertheless, because of the fluctuation in the orientation of affordable housing policy in the interest of the state's economic strategy, we can still identify the productivist nature of the policy.

At a local level, China's municipal governments are no longer passive agents of the central government. Instead they have become key actors pursuing local development. Under this mechanism, stimulating economic growth and expanding the revenue base, including the land transfer income and industrial tax, have become top priorities of local governments (Shen 2007). Other urban policies also are used to support key goals. Therefore, affordable housing policy at the local level plays a role that goes beyond the basic sense of social security which aims to assist the deprived population. First, newly built, affordable homes are largely used to ensure the smooth running of urbanization and urban renovation processes so as to increase the local land revenue and to enhance the city's economic competitiveness. Second, Public Rental Housing units are assigned not only to lower- and middle-income urban households but also to migrant labourers, a highly qualified workforce and young talented people. In other words, the productive working groups are privileged in affordable housing programmes so as to support local industrial development. However, several concerns arise from this productivist model of affordable housing development. First, intensive schemes in peripheral areas could result in social polarization and segregation. Moreover, as the targeting determined by the productivist concept is not always consistent with a social objective, social injustice could result.

Notes

1 In the context of state socialism, a work unit or *Danwei* generally refers to a specific kind of workplace that acts as an extension of the state apparatus to undertake the function of social control.
2 The method called 'Median Multiple' is widely used for evaluating urban housing markets; the method has been recommended by the World Bank and the United Nations and is used by the Harvard University Joint Center on Housing (Demographia 2013).
3 In 1958, the household registration system was officially promulgated by the Chinese government to control the movement of people between urban and rural areas. Individuals were broadly categorized as 'agricultural' or 'non-agricultural' residents.
4 China adopted a dual land tenure system under which land ownership is independent of land use rights. Urban land, called 'State Land', is owned by the state, while rural land, called 'Collective Land', is owed by rural collectives.
5 A decision on a stimulus package estimated at 4 trillion yuan (about US$640 billion) was announced by the State Council on 9 November 2008. It would be spent over the two following years to finance programmes in ten major areas, one of which concerns affordable housing (China View 2008).
6 The National Western Development Plan is a policy launched by the central government of the People's Republic of China in 2000. It aims to improve the level of economic and social development of the western half of China, which severely lagged behind the eastern half (*People Daily* 2001).
7 One of the authors was involved in the discussion with the agents of the Municipal Bureau of Social Protection and Home Ownership of Nanjing in August 2011. The data in this paragraph were collected from unpublished policy documents.
8 Municipal governments, delegating the ownership of state land, assign the land use rights to land users, who in turn pay fees for the assignment thereof to the state (People's Republic of China 1990).

References

Ba, S. and Wang, Z. (2010) 'Capital, system reform and international experience: about public low rental house', *Reform*, 193: 80–85.
China Science Center of International Eurasian Academy of Sciences, China Association of Mayors and UN-HABITAT (2010) *The State of China's Cities (2010–2011)*. Beijing, China: Foreign Languages Press.

China View (2008) 'China's 4 trillion yuan stimulus to boost economy, domestic demand'. Online. Available at http://news.xinhuanet.com/english/2008–11/09/content_10331324.htm (accessed 29 September 2012).

Chongqing Municipal Bureau Statistics (2011) *Chongqing Statistical Yearbook 2009–2011*. Municipality of Chongqing.

Demographia (2013) 'The 9th Annual Demographia International Housing Affordability Survey'. Online. Available at www.demographia.com/dhi.pdf (accessed 28 October 2012).

Deng, L., Shen, Q. and Wang, L. (2011) 'The emerging housing policy framework in China', *Journal of Planning Literature*, 26(2): 168–183.

Holliday, I. (2000) 'Productivist welfare capitalism: social policy in East Asia', *Political Studies*, 48: 706–723.

Huang, Y. and Clark, W.A.V. (2002) 'Housing tenure choice in transitional urban China: a multilevel analysis', *Urban Studies*, 39(1): 7–32.

Lin, Y., De Meulder, B. and Wang, S. (2011) 'Understanding the "Village in the City" in Guangzhou: economic integration and development issue and their implications for the urban migrant', *Urban Studies*, 48(16): 3583–3598.

Liu, K., Huang, H. and Tang, Y. (2010) 'The logic of Chongqing, Observation'. Online. Available at http://news.xinhuanet.com/politics/2011–07/18/c_121682722.htm (accessed 20 September 2012).

Logan, J.R., Fang, Y. and Zhang, Z. (2009) 'Access to housing in urban China', *International Journal of Urban and Regional Research*, 33(4): 914–935.

Ministry of Housing and Urban-Rural Development (2011) Discourse of M. Jiang Weixin Minister of Housing and Urban-Rural Development in the 23th session of the eleventh Standing Committee of the National People's Congress. Online. Available at http://news.xinhuanet.com/politics/2011–10/25/c_111123514.htm (accessed 23 September 2012).

Nanjing Municipal Bureau Statistics (2009–2011) *Nanjing Statistical Yearbook 2009–2011*, Nanjing. Online. Available at www.njtj.gov.cn/2004/2011/index.htm (accessed 15 August 2012)

National Bureau of Statistics of China (2005) 'Census of 1 per cent of population in 2005', Beijing. Online. Available at www.stats.gov.cn/tjsj/pcsj/rkpc/dwcrkpc/ (accessed August 25 2011)

National Bureau of Statistics of China (2008) *China Statistical Yearbook 1998–2008*, Beijing. Online. Available at www.stats.gov.cn/tjsj/ndsj/2008/indexeh.htm (accessed 23 September 2013).

National Bureau of Statistics of China (2009) *China Statistical Yearbook 1999–2009*, Beijing. Online. Available at www.stats.gov.cn/tjsj/ndsj/ (accessed 20 August 2012).

National Bureau of Statistics of China (2012) *China Statistical Yearbook 1996–2012*, Beijing. Online. Available at www.stats.gov.cn/tjsj/ndsj/ (accessed 20 August 2012).

National People's Congress of the People's Republic of China (2011) *China's 12th Five-Year Plan (2011–2015)*. Online. Available at www.gov.cn/2011lh/content_1825838.htm (accessed 9 September 2012).

People Daily (2001) 'The National Western Development Plan'. Online. Available at www.people.com.cn/GB/channel3/21/20001228/364518.html (accessed 20 September 2012).

People's Republic of China (1990) 'Interim regulation of People's Republic of China concerning the assignment and transfer of the right to the use of the state-owned land in urban areas 1990'. Online. Available at www.mlr.gov.cn/zwgk/flfg/tdglflfg/200601/t20060119_642175.htm (accessed 25 September 2012).

People's Republic of China (2009) *Government Work Report 2009–2011*. Online. Available at www.gov.cn/test/2006–02/16/content200719.htm (accessed 8 October 2012).

Ren, R. and Man, Y. (2010) 'A research on housing affordability in China', Policy report no. 1, Centre for Urban Development and Land Policy of Peking University-Lincoln Institute. Online. Available at http://plc.pku.edu.cn/publicationsdetails.aspx (accessed 27 August 2012).

Shen, J. (2007) 'Scale, state and the city: urban transformation in post-reform China', *Habitat International*, 31: 303–316

Song, Y., Zenou, Y. and Ding, C. (2008) 'Let's not throw the baby out with the bath water: the role of urban villages in housing rural migrants in China', *Urban Studies*, 45(2): 313–330.

State Council of People's Republic of China (1998) 'Further reform of urban housing system and speeding up housing development', circular letter, Beijing.

State Council of People's Republic of China (2003) 'Promoting a continuous and healthy development of the real estate market', circular letter, Beijing.

State Council of People's Republic of China (2007) 'Suggestions of the State Council on solving the housing difficulties of urban low-income households', Beijing.

Wang, Y.P. (2000) 'Housing reform and its impacts on the urban poor in China', *Housing Studies*, 15(6): 845–864.

Wang, Y.P. (2001) 'Urban housing reform and finance in China: a case study of Beijing', *Urban Affairs Review*, 36(5): 620–645.

Wang, Y.P. and Murie, A. (1996) 'The process of commercialization of urban housing in China', *Urban Studies*, 33(6): 971–989.

Wang, Y.P. and Murie, A (1999) 'Commercial housing development in urban China', *Urban Studies*, 36(9): 1475–1494.

Wang, Y.P. and Murie, A. (2011) 'The new affordable and social housing provision system in China: implications for comparative housing studies', *International Journal of Housing Policy*, 11(3): 237–254.

Wu, F. (1996) 'Changes in the structure of public housing provision in urban China', *Urban Studies*, 33(9): 1601–1627.

Wu, F. (2002) 'Real estate development and the transformation of urban space in China's transitional economy, with special reference to Shanghai', in Logan, J.R. (ed.) *The New Chinese City: Globalization and Market Reform*. Oxford, Malden: Blackwell Publishers.

Ye, J., Song, J. and Tian, C. (2010) 'An analysis of housing policy during economic transition in China', Research Center for Land Policy, Renmin University of China, *International Journal of Housing Policy*, 10(3): 273–300.

Zhang, J. and Xuan, W. (2011) 'Urban housing in China 2009: a brief review', *City Planning Review*, 35(1): 40–45.

Zhao, Y. and Bourassa, S.C. (2003) 'China's urban housing reform: recent achievements and new inequities', *Housing Studies*, 18(5): 721–744.

Zhu, J. (2004) 'Local developmental state and order in China's urban development during transition', *International Journal of Urban Regional Research*, 28(2): 424–447.

PART III
Latin America
Introduction

Jan Bredenoord, Paul van Lindert and Peer Smets

The macro-region of Latin America (inclusive of the Caribbean), with an urban population of 75.5 per cent, is already highly urbanized. It is estimated that this proportion will reach 85 per cent in 2030. Moreover, the quality of urban housing and the surrounding environment is sometimes so low that one can speak of 'slums'. But many neighbourhoods, being part of the (big) cities in Latin America – at first probably also described as 'slum areas' – illustrate a certain positive impact of self-help housing by the poor, at least in the provision of land and housing. One of the most influential development advisers, from the 1960s onwards, to impact local housing policies in Latin American countries and its discourse is John Turner (1976). He showed that incremental housing production and consumption took place mainly in the informal sector. Although there are many tenure modalities in Latin America, the most widespread form is individual home ownership. In fact, approximately 17 per cent of total households in the region (inclusive of the Caribbean) rent their dwellings (Bouillon 2012: 90). Latin America is the continent where many initiatives – especially engaged by urban social movements on housing and land issues – have been developed over the past decades (McBride and French 2011). Hot-button issues include the discussions surrounding too much bureaucracy, as well as land titling issues (De Soto 1989, 2001). Another Latin American development is the emerging availability of 'ABC mixed housing finance', which was started in Chile and replicated and implemented in other countries such as Ecuador, Costa Rica, Colombia, El Salvador, Peru and Uruguay (see e.g. Klaufus 2010). Additionally, an important development that also impacts on liveability in informal settlements is participatory budgeting. First developed in the municipality of Porte Alegre in Brazil (Shah 2007), participatory budgeting has been copied and introduced in many other countries and municipalities in Latin America.

The collection of chapters in this third part of the book elaborate on the urban housing conditions for the lower income groups in six Latin American countries: Mexico, Brazil, Colombia, Peru, Ecuador and Nicaragua.

In Chapter 15 *Jan Bredenoord and Lorena Cabrera Montiel* describe the changes in Mexico's housing market for the urban poor. Since the early 1970s there has been a considerable transition from rental to owner-occupied housing, powered by (1) various sorts of self-managed housing and (2) institutional low-cost housing. The irregular self-help housing gradually changed towards individual incremental housing, while public housing institutions have changed their approaches and working methods considerably. Today, Mexico's urban housing market for the poor has widened its scope and shows, for example, new finance for home renovations and also hybrid forms of housing, including self-managed as well as social housing. However, the growth of the urban population goes hand in hand with an increased demand for cheap housing for the (very) low-income brackets. Currently, interest in urban renewal, neighbourhood upgrading and individual home improvements is becoming central, while sustainable urban development becomes a main issue connected to social housing reform. Institutional housing has been developed adequately in Mexico, but the availability of large amounts of vacant houses in 2013 is alarming.

In Chapter 16 *Suzana Pasternak and Camila D'Ottaviano* describe both the early and more recent housing provision policies in Brazil and the significant changes. Between the mass public construction programmes of the 1960s and 1970s and the more recent My Life My House Programme of 2009, Brazil went through periods of low investment in social housing. As a result, the 'housing' landscape of Brazil's cities is deeply marked by irregular land subdivisions and self-help construction as a primary form of housing access for the lower income classes. Initially, self-help housing mainly occurred on individual lots that were purchased by households in peripheral areas, slums and squatter areas. The authors describe São Paulo's attempts to rectify this situation through innovative self-construction experiments (e.g. São Paulo's Municipal Self-Management Housing Provision Programme of 1989–1991), which have been supported by the São Paulo state. Together with a supportive loan programme, the institutionalization of self-management became a fact. Moreover, since the 1990s, the role cooperatives play in Brazil has increased significantly. Over the past two decades, self-help and grassroots task forces have been steadily incorporated into governmental housing programmes.

In Chapter 17 *Alan Gilbert* critically reviews the evolution of housing policies in Colombia. While successive governments implemented a variety of policies and institutions, a shift was made from direct provision of housing to sites and services; subsidies are now provided in the form of low interest rates for low- and middle-income families. In Colombia, around half of the population lives in accommodation created through self-help. Successive policies were not able to reach the lowest income groups; in general, programmes were too expensive. The central mortgage bank lent only to (upper-) middle-class families. Housing corporations did not reach low-income people sufficiently, but the housing agency of that time, INURBE, implemented a housing policy based on granting subsidies, targeted at the poorest families but not at the required scale. In 2012 the government planned to give 100,000 houses to very poor families. According to the author, the government would do better to place more emphasis on implementing genuinely pro-poor policy measures, such as supplementing family incomes; providing better health care; or offering free education to children. Among other things, the government should also think about expanding the supply of rental housing for those who are unable to purchase a dwelling.

Ana María Fernández-Maldonado describes in Chapter 18 the ineffectiveness of state involvement in housing matters during the past decades of economic recession and political instability, and the related importance of self-help housing in Peru. As a consequence of rapid population growth in Peruvian cities, especially in Lima, housing deficits have continuously increased. Since 2003 the Peruvian housing sector has experienced a growing dynamism, partly triggered by a housing reform that established programmes and finance mechanisms to reconcile the demands of the poor and the supply of affordable housing. Housing policies are mostly geared toward the delivery of new homes and not toward assisting incremental housing. The housing programmes have delivered more new homes than ever before, but they are still insufficient to confront the huge housing deficit. Despite the pro-poor rhetoric of successive governments, the objective of building homes for the poor does not seem feasible in the present circumstances. The lack of cheap land to develop and the preference of large construction firms in targeting middle-income households partly explain this situation. The situation is further aggravated by the lack of effective planning and coordination between housing policies and local development plans.

In Chapter 19 *Christien Klaufus and Laura Cedrés Pérez* describe the changing housing-policy paradigms in Ecuador. Here former policies that aimed at the production of small standardized houses for the poor have had to be replaced by programmes that integrate housing policies into large-scale urban planning. The starting point for this chapter is the question of what role incremental housing and related self-help solutions could still play in the supply of affordable housing. Under the title 'Buen Vivir' or Good Living or Collective Wellbeing, the left-wing Correa government introduced a new state philosophy in 2008, which created a new political landscape with specific programmes and actors. This ambitious plan has had various consequences for the housing sector. In this chapter the authors analyse the targets and the outcomes regarding housing as well as the role of the (new) actors within the sector. They conclude that the increased state budget for housing and upgrading has had positive consequences, especially since the production of affordable new housing solutions has risen significantly. But the 'task' of improving the existing (self-built) housing stock was not taken up in profound ways, partly because the theoretical integration of various habitat-related policy fields did not result in practically coherent policy instruments. For example, no attention was paid to the demand for cheap rental houses in cities. During the second term of the Correa government (2013–2017), a necessary broadening of the policy for public housing will hopefully give attention to the aforementioned shortcomings. Consequently, the role of incremental housing in Ecuadorian society within the context of the new policy paradigm is still under discussion.

In Chapter 20 *Jan Bredenoord and Bart van der Meulen* describe the vast self-help housing practice in Nicaragua. After Haiti, Nicaragua is the second poorest country in the Americas. The bad socio-economic situation of the population and the inability of the government to generate sufficient financial means for public housing are the main causes. Many low-income households have limited access to housing finance for house construction and a large number of low-income households live in houses of poor quality; in Managua this is 57 per cent. The authors describe the roles of main actors in social housing in Managua and León, including national and local governments, non-governmental organizations, community-based organizations (CBOs), and private actors such as developers and banks. The issues of housing typology and costs of housing are analysed in order to give insight into the affordability of low-income housing. Moreover, a new public housing finance system for low-income households is being created (2012) by the Ortega government, with help from the Inter-American Development Bank. At the end of 2012 in the cities of Managua and León, there are various irregular land occupations, which is a sign of a remaining demand for sites-and-services schemes. The stimulation of housing cooperatives is occurring in the country, which is promising. Yet due to political strategizing, the role of CBOs in Nicaragua turns out to be a complicated one. As the government opts for the status quo on housing production, there necessarily will be more focus on the improvement of houses. This will most likely provide an extra stimulus to the existing practice of incremental housing.

References

Bouillon, C. (ed.) (2012) *Room for Development: Housing Markets in Latin America and the Caribbean*. New York: Palgrave Macmillan.
De Soto, H. (1989) *The Other Path*. New York: Harper & Row Publishers.
De Soto, H. (2001) *The Mystery of Capital: Why Capitalism Triumphs in the West and Fails Everywhere Else*. London: Black Swan.
Klaufus, C. (2010) 'The two ABCs of aided self help housing in Ecuador', *Habitat International*, 34(3): 351–358.
McBride, B. and French, M. (2011) *Affordable Land and Housing in Latin America and the Caribbean*. Nairobi: UN-Habitat.
Shah, A. (2007) *Participatory Budgeting*. Washington, DC: World Bank.
Turner, J. (1976) *Housing by People: Towards Autonomy in Building Environment*. London: Marion.

15

AFFORDABLE HOUSING FOR LOW-INCOME GROUPS IN MEXICO AND URBAN HOUSING CHALLENGES OF TODAY

Jan Bredenoord and Lorena Cabrera Montiel

Abbreviations

CFE	Federal Commission of Electricity
CIDOC	Centre of Housing Research and Documentation
CONAVI	National Housing Commission
CORETT	Commission for regularization of land ownership
DUIS	Sustainable integrated urban development
FONHAPO	National Fund for Low-Income Housing
FOVI	Fund of Operation and Finance for Housing
FOVISSSTE	National Housing Fund of the Institute of Security and Social Services for State Workers
GoM	Government of Mexico (Federal)
IMSS	Mexican Social Security Institute
INEGI	National Institute of Statistics and Geography
INFONAVIT	Institute of the National Housing Fund for Workers (private)
ISSFAM	Military Housing Fund of the Social Security Institute for the Mexican Armed Forces
IVNL	Housing Institute of Nuevo León
ONAVIS	National housing organizations
PEMEX	Mexican Oil
PSV(A)	Social Housing Production (Assisted)
SEDATU	Secretariat of Agrarian, Territorial and Urban Development
SEDESOL	Secretariat of Social Development
SHF	Federal Mortgage Society
SOFOL	Limited object financial society
SOFOM	Multipurpose financial society

Introduction

Housing for low-income groups in Mexico is provided by two housing delivery systems: self-help housing and social housing. Both are or must be affordable for low- and middle low-income groups. Self-help housing is widespread, but families self-construct their homes less often than they did in the past and contract out more work to professional construction workers. In 1972 social housing production (i.e. subsidized low-cost housing for owner-occupiers and not for renters) started growing significantly with the introduction of support from the federal government. This made home ownership possible for many people with permanent employment. Policies for urban land development were created with *reservas territoriales* (public land reserves) which included access to *ejido* land (land collectively used by farmers). Since 2000, social housing production has received a significant second stimulus and the government is focusing on promoting the construction of new houses, the purchase of existing homes and home renovations (Bredenoord and Verkoren 2010).

In Mexico, housing practices underwent several paradigm shifts: from rental housing to home ownership, from irregular urban developments to more regulated expansion plans and from massive standard-housing to a broad offer of (mixed) housing. Meanwhile, the housing sector in Mexico has become complex with many public and private actors working together to execute a variety of housing programmes.

Before 1960, low-cost housing demand in Mexico was normally solved by urban rental markets. In the early 1960s, however, many poor townspeople and rural–urban migrants began making their homes in self-built areas located adjacent to cities. Modest houses were built there by poor households. These non-regulated urban developments, which sometimes turned into slums at the fringes of cities, caused many environmental problems. Regulation of land use and provision of services were promoted sporadically by some politicians and later by government programmes.[1] In due course, many neighbourhoods were consolidated, a process coupled with the gradual introduction of public services and the promotion of security of tenure. In the consolidated neighbourhoods, citizens replaced initial building materials with more durable ones. Later on they often built extensions, added storeys and used internal spaces adjacent to streets as (work)shops.

Furthermore, the nature of self-help housing has changed gradually; in the beginning there was self-help housing within irregular/illegal neighbourhoods, and later this was replaced with self-managed housing where households hire skilled construction workers (for parts of construction) within improved urban areas. Self-managed housing is a more developed form of self-help housing. In 2003, of a total of 24.13 million housing units, 62.9 per cent were houses produced through self-help; 23.6 per cent were social houses financed by housing institutions (between 1963 and 2003); and 13.5 per cent were realized by private initiatives (Coulomb 2010). According to another source, in 2008, 74 per cent of the total housing stock was built through self-production processes: 65 per cent in urban areas and 92 per cent in rural areas (PUEC-UNAM 2013: 32). These figures illustrate the importance of self-help housing.

Social housing policy in Mexico has been developing for four decades and currently it is intended to benefit low-income families. One can still find a huge amount of individual self-help housing. In addition, well-organized one-family houses and in the cities three- to five-storey housing complexes were realized by developers. In a number of cases one can find hybrid house construction, such as small houses in organized projects with the possibility of incremental finishing and mixed housing finance. The housing practice in Mexico faces a number of challenges, for example with sustainable housing (a policy that started only a few years ago), the social housing production (a policy that started several years ago) and finally the existence of many uninhabited houses.

This chapter begins with an overview of urban development in Mexico since the 1960s and how low-quality self-built neighbourhoods were gradually consolidated and incorporated into cities. This is followed by a discussion of the government initiatives (in 1972 and 2000, respectively) to increase housing production. This stimulus resulted in a broadened scope of housing finance and typologies. The chapter also covers some aspects of sustainable housing and planning, which are becoming increasingly relevant in Mexico's social housing production. We conclude by discussing aspects of the current challenges facing housing and urban planning, including social housing production and uninhabited housing.

Urban development and housing since 1960

From 1960 to 2010 the total population of Mexico grew from 35 to 112 million (INEGI 2010). Simultaneously, the level of urbanization rose from 32 to 75 per cent, while the number of metropolitan areas (with more than 1 million inhabitants) rose from 2 to 12 per cent (INEGI 2005a). In the same period the population of Mexico City itself grew from about 5 to 20 million people. During the 1950s and 1960s, Mexican urban growth combined with a constant demand for low-cost housing from the lowest income groups (INEGI 2005b) caused a large-scale urbanization of poverty. Poor families began to self-build on an ad-hoc basis, leading to an immense growth of spontaneous suburbs, mainly in non-regulated neighbourhoods or slums. Ongoing rural–urban migration induced the government to develop a new strategy for urban growth that included social housing.

During and after the 1960s, the Federal Government of Mexico (GoM) gave assistance to self-managed urbanization by implementing urban planning and offering infrastructures such as roads, in order to avoid the creation of future slums. A prominent example of this phenomenon can be found in Nezahualcóyotl (Figure 15.1), a municipality with over 1.1 million residents, which is part of metropolitan Mexico City. Self-construction of houses started here in the 1950s, through squatting and purchases of land by private developers, who made a profit by selling plots to individual households. Eventually, the area was developed according to public planning with avenues, by interventions of the State of México (adjacent to the Federal District). Descriptions of the development of this vast self-help housing area, which is comparable to other areas in Mexico, can be found in Ribbeck (2002), Municipality of Nezahualcóyotl (n.d.), Connolly (2003) and Bredenoord and Verkoren (2010).

Since the early 1970s, the government has stimulated social housing by the establishment of public housing institutions, which has led to substantial social housing production. In those early years of massive urban growth many new areas with standard houses were urbanized according to new basic standards of urban planning. The neoliberal government policies of the 1990s had consequences for the social housing production. For example, there was a temporary increase in investments by banks. Another temporary consequence was that the market for housing shifted from low-income households to middle-income households. In due course, it became clear that there was, and is, a constant need to focus on the housing requirements of low-income groups. The number of Mexicans living in poverty in 2010 was estimated at 46.2 per cent of Mexico's population.[2] Earlier, Connolly (2006) pointed out that policymakers

FIGURE 15.1   Self-built housing in Nezahualcóyotl. Photo by Jan Bredenoord.

needed to recognize the importance of self-help housing for this group and to incorporate it into housing policies.

After 2000, social housing production increased significantly. Between 2001 and 2009 there were more than 9 million housing finance subsidies and loans, and yearly there were over 1 million housing finance actions (CONAVI 2010a). Currently, housing and urban planning in Mexico are at a new crossroads, as new visions of sustainable housing and urban planning are emerging (GoM 2012). The governmental focus since around 2010 has been on sustainable urban development, for example through new policies and DUIS projects, as described in this chapter.

Government interventions on housing

Housing policy in Mexico has gone through different stages (see Table 15.1). Before the 1970s, the federal government's involvement with house construction was limited and mainly focused on investments in infrastructures such as main roads and streets, with a special focus on Mexico City. The first housing agency, the Fund of Operation and Finance for Housing (FOVI), was established as early as 1963. Between 1947 and 1970 an average of only 9,500 dwellings per year were built by public housing institutions in the entire country (Landaeta 1994: 194).

In 1972, cooperation between government, labour unions and employers started a new phase of public housing production. A charge of 5 per cent on salaries created public funds

TABLE 15.1 Housing policies and financial stages

	Before 1972	1972–1992	1992–2000	2000 to present
		Benefactor and interventionist state	State facilities and deregulation	Financialization
Housing policy	First federal agencies	• First housing funds • Federal Housing Law (1984) • ONAVIS – technical control	• Reform LFV (1997) • ONAVIS leave technical control • Benefits to private promoters	• Reform LFV (2004, 2006, 2011) • ONAVIS only financial functions • Ensure demand to promoters • CONAVI (2001), coordinate housing agencies
Social financial capital		Low + middle income, employed • INFONAVIT (1972), private • FOVISSSTE (1972), public • FOVIMI-ISSFAM, CFE, PEMEX • Public promoters Low income, unwaged • INDECO (1970–1981) • FONHAPO (1981) • Fiscal resources • Social promoters	• Reform ONAVIS (1992) • Changing loans conditions • Increased investments, loans (employer contribution + SAR) • Private promoters • FONHAPO (until 1997) • Fiscal, own, World Bank resources • Reduced social subsidies • Public and social promoters	• INFONAVIT, FOVISSSTE, mortgage bank/savings fund • Participation in BMV • FONHAPO (reappears 2001), purchase, improvement, self-production or PSV subsidies
Private financial capital	Legal reserve to banks (3%) for housing Middle income • PFV, FOGA • FOVI (1963)	Middle income • FOVI • Fiscal resources • Public promoters Middle + upper income • Employers' contribution (5%) • Banking nationalization (1982) • Liberalization – increase mortgages	• FOVI-PROSAVI (1997) • Fiscal, own resources • World Bank loan (2000) • Private promoters • Banking re-privatization (1988–1994); new multiple banks, SOFOLs (1995) • Market fragmentation – increasing resources	• SHF (2001-prior FOVI), development bank/mortgage financing/guarantees financial institutions (private, public) • Commercial banks • SOFOLs – SOFOMs • Bridge loans/mortgage loans • Private developers
Co-financing			Extend loans to lower-income • FOVISSSTE + bank (1989–1997)	ONAVI + ONAVI/bank/SOFOL/ Private developer

Source: Lorena Cabrera Montiel, own research at Institute of Geography, National Autonomous University of Mexico.
BMV: Mexican Stock Exchange; FOGA: Guarantee and Support Fund for Housing Loans; LFV: Federal Housing Law; PFV: Housing Finance Program; PROSAVI: Special Programme of Loans and Grants for Housing; SAR: System for Retirement Savings.

that were to be used for social housing for workers in certain sectors. The establishment of such public housing funds as INFONAVIT, the fund for private sector workers, and FOVISSSTE, the fund for public sector workers, was a milestone in Mexican social housing history. Other public agencies (e.g. CFE, IMSS, ISSFAM and PEMEX) arranged mortgage financing for their employees too. This finance model has been investigated and described, for example by UN-Habitat (2011a) and Bouillon (2012: 204). Housing production for low- and middle-income groups increased through a huge supply of plots with a basic or core dwelling, but access to subsidized housing remained restricted to heads of households earning at least two to four times the national minimal wage. Thus, a large part of the populace was (still) not served. In response to this, the government developed additional programmes for the many households that lacked permanent employment and were thus denied access to social housing. From 1981 to 1997, the National Fund for Low-Income Housing (FONHAPO) was the government institution responsible for granting housing subsidies for low-Income households without formal jobs. Later on, other agencies, such as the Secretariat of Social Development (SEDESOL) and the National Housing Commission (CONAVI), resumed or expanded this national policy.

In 1992, the restructuring of the main housing agencies initiated a new stage that significantly changed their role. While initially they had been initiators, organizers and executors, after 1992 they became solely policymakers and financers, leaving production in the hands of private and social developers.

The private financial sector had participated in granting mortgage loans for middle- and higher-income groups, resulting in residential housing. The private sector also offered resources to other money lenders, such as housing corporations. After the financial crisis of 1994, commercial banks stopped providing housing loans; their share in housing finance declined from 54.4 per cent in 1994 to 6.3 per cent in 1997 (BBVA Research 2002) and to 2 per cent in 2000 (Temiño 2007). Other specialized, non-banking financial companies took their place, mainly SOFOLs (limited object financial societies), which emerged in 1993 since it was a requirement for Mexico to sign the NAFTA (North American Free Trade Agreement) to have similar financial organizations to those existing in the United States, such as single purpose or limited purpose financial intermediaries, diversifying the housing finance sector.

After 2000, new changes in housing policies took place. For example, responsibility for implementing new housing policies began to shift from the federal government to states and municipalities. In 2001 FOVI was incorporated into the Federal Mortgage Society (SHF), and it became the new housing finance institution for low-income households (Bouillon 2012: 196). The SHF took over the support and regulation of SOFOLs, which were virtually the only private institutions that financed social housing, providing 21 per cent of new housing loans (Temiño 2007). Between 2000 and 2004, banks came back in housing finance, due to macro-economic stability and new credit schemes, partnering with SOFOLs. After the financial crisis of 2008, SOFOLs went through serious difficulties and despite government aid, some of them collapsed. Regardless, the SOFOLs' authorization was due to end in July 2013 (Berrospide et al. 2012), and this has now happened. Consequently, some were liquidated and others became SOFOMs (multipurpose financial societies), oriented possibly towards new segments: low-income families without access to mortgages, and new financial intermediaries such as cooperatives (PUEC-UNAM 2013: 95).

Over the past four decades INFONAVIT's and FOVISSSTE's housing production has grown very significantly. This growth occurred after they became housing finance institutions where beneficiaries have their accounts (amounts not being used for housing can be used for pensions). INFONAVIT increased gradually from an average yearly production of 25,360 housing units in the initial period (1973–1976) to 475,000 housing finance actions in 2010 and 501,000 in 2012 (CONAVI 2012). In 2004, INFONAVIT started participating in the Mexican Stock Exchange and mortgage finance was strengthened through co-financing, extending loans to lower-income groups and allowing access to higher value homes. Even though public institutions involved in housing finance hold more than 90 per cent of the national mortgage portfolio (BBVA Research 2012) – INFONAVIT represents 60 per cent and FOVISSSTE 10 per cent (Chiquier and Lea 2009) – the housing policy was diversified. Thus, construction firms, project developers, specialized and publicly supported finance institutions and municipalities might give credit for housing projects. Since 2000 a new finance system has emerged, through combining several resources for social housing such as saving, subsidies and credit (mixed financing), which was a breakthrough in Mexico. The new Housing Law (GoM 2006) and the Social Housing Programme 2007–2012 were intended to consolidate the Federal Subsidies Programme.

Housing production boost from 2000 onwards

Since 2000 housing policy has been renewed and this has increased the diversity in home ownership, including self-construction and mortgages or public credit for housing. These new policies have given low-income families broader financing possibilities, such as smaller loans and mixed housing finance, increasing all together home ownership by low-income families. CIDOC-SHF (2006, 2009) stated that between 2006 and 2012 more than 5 million dwellings would be needed, of which the public sector might realize 50 per cent.

In Mexico a housing typology has developed over time. Some institutional sources work with the categories basic, social, economic and medium houses. In 2009 the SHF worked to develop a comparable classification system for types of housing (UN-Habitat 2011b). An evaluation in 2003 revealed that the supply of *basic* housing (accessible for households earning up to three times the minimum wage) represented less than 1 per cent of homes offered in the market, while the effective demand was 40.9 per cent for this income group (Coulomb 2010: 577). This meant that there was a large gap between supply and demand. Since April 2010, the housing sector has used the Classification Approved Housing Value, which was agreed upon by INFONAVIT, SHF, CONAVI, financial institutions (banks and SOFOLs), FOVISSSTE, Softec (private consultancy) and the Mexican Mortgage Association. Furthermore, there is the classification of housing by average price, which is based on the (federal) housing building code. Currently, the sector is using the following terms: Economic, Popular, Traditional, Medium, Residential and Residential Plus. Table 15.2 gives price ranges of current housing types, necessary incomes, construction areas and estimated numbers of rooms per type.

Over time, the average plot size has become smaller for single-family homes, varying from 60 to 140 square metres. Construction of housing in rows on small plots of 100–120 square metres is still the standard, but some plots are even smaller than 40 square metres. Housing prices vary between around US$10,000 and US$35,000. Measured in terms of the necessary amount of income, families must earn between US$600 and US$1,000 per month to afford a home. A large percentage of Mexican families earn less than this amount and houses built by housing institutions are not available to them.

TABLE 15.2 Housing types in the Mexican subsidized housing market

Housing types	VSMMDF* Income brackets	Price ranges in Mexican pesos in 2012	Price ranges in US$ in 2012	Average floor space area in m^2	Number of rooms
Economic	<118	<223,590	<17,042	30	3
Popular	118–200	223,591–378,966	17,042–28,885	42.5	4
Traditional	200–350	378,967–663,191	29,885–50,548	62.5	5
Medium	350–750	663,192–1,421,124	50,548–108,317	97.5	6
Residential	750–1500	1,421,125–2,842,248	108,317–216,635	145	7
Residential Plus	>1500	>2,842,248	>216,635	225	8

Source: CONAVI (2010c).
*VSMMDF: times the minimum salary (monthly) for the Federal District of Mexico = 1,894.8 pesos or US$144.4. In January 2012, the minimum daily salary for the Federal District of Mexico was 62.33 pesos (US$4.75).

FIGURE 15.2 Housing complex El Cortijo in Tlalnepantla. Photo by Jan Bredenoord.

The housing developers Casas GEO and Homex, as well as many others, build economical and popular houses, but they produce residential housing and expensive apartments as well. Private building companies and developers do not offer cheap basic houses or starter houses.

In the supply of social housing, multi-storey houses and apartment buildings are becoming more and more common in large metropolitan areas (Figure 15.2). The housing building code (CONAVI 2010c) developed a typology: one-family house; duplex or double house; multi-family housing; horizontal condominium; vertical condominium; and mixed condominium.

BOX 15.1 SOCIAL HOUSING FINANCE IN MEXICO

In 2000 the federal government developed a large-scale poverty reduction programme (Hábitat), which transferred a significant amount of financial resources to the local governments. At the same time, the housing policy changed, partly as a result of the Housing Law (GoM 2006), which honoured self-managed housing (article 4 VIII), an important policy change. Since 2006, SEDESOL (Secretariat of Social Development) has supported the construction of 1.9 million concrete floors in 1,328 municipalities, an investment of around US$1 billion (CIDOC/SHF 2011). The government focused further on social housing, as a consequence of the targets of the National Housing Programme 2008–2012 PNV (GoM 2008). The social housing policy focuses on the poorest segments of the market through the programmes and schemes offered by FONHAPO, CONAVI and SHF.

FONHAPO is a federal trust fund, coordinated by SEDESOL. The 'Borrow and Subsidy' programmes for housing are *Tu Casa* (Your Home) and *Vivienda Rural* (Rural Housing); they provide grants for the construction of new homes, the purchase of existing homes, and home improvements. FONHAPO is aimed at municipalities with a low human development index, where the fight against urban poverty is most needed and in areas struck by natural disasters. Funding is provided on the condition that the state or municipality provide additional housing finance and a small deposit is made by the receivers. For the possibilities for subsidies, see FONHAPO (n.d.).

- Purchase or construction of basic housing units in urban areas, up to US$4,000 (40,000–53,000 pesos); which can be the basis for (later) incremental expansion and improvement.
- Home enlargements in (sub)urban areas up to US$1,500 (15,000–20,000 pesos).
- Home renovations in (sub)urban areas up to US$1,000 (10,000–15,000 pesos).

In 2007 a federal funding programme for housing was created called 'Esta es tu Casa' (This is your House). The programme, carried out by CONAVI, focuses on households with incomes less than five times the minimum wage for the purchase, construction or improvement of a dwelling. The programme can be used to subsidize or fund the purchase of a plot and the self-construction on it. Mixed housing finance provides grants and loans and asks participants to contribute a small deposit (5 per cent). The grant provides from US$1,000 for home improvement to US$3,000 for the self-construction of a dwelling and up to US$4,500 for the purchase of a new or existing home. The funding is implemented through 'executive bodies', such as municipalities, banks, SOFOLs or housing institutions. The maximum value of a property for which funding can be requested is set at US$20,000 (CONAVI 2009).

SHF is the Mexican 'Federal Mortgage Society'. SHF does not directly address credit applicants (builders/developers of new/used housing, or people who need a loan to buy/

> build/remodel a home). It offers the following schemes and products through financial intermediaries such as SOFOLs, SOFOMs and banks:
>
> (1) *Individual housing funds* (loans to improve/expand/remodel a home; loans for assisted self-help housing; loans for house purchase; co-financing with INFONAVIT/ FOVISSSTE; and credit that incorporates the subsidy programme 'Esta es tu Casa' by CONAVI).
> (2) *Funds for housing production* (bridge loans; equity and debt financing with private/ institutional capital).
> (3) *Insurance/coverage* (credit risk sharing with private/financial institutions; swap UDIs to minimum wages; certainty of timely compliance; coverage for credit risk of portfolios for underserved populations; see SHCP n.d.) (Investment units (UDIs) are value units based on price increase, used to fund obligations of mortgage loans or any commercial act. They were created in 1995, in order to protect banks, largely focused on mortgage loans; Banco de México n.d.)

Table 15.3 shows the number of housing finance operations; total numbers are far over 1 million and peak to 1.769 million in 2008. However, for one house a household might obtain finance from different sources.

Sustainable housing and planning

Since 2010, policymakers have been reconsidering the nationwide housing policy. The policy has increasingly focused on sustainable housing and urban development, a responsible decrease in the housing backlog and, finally, better regulation of urban housing. Furthermore, policymakers are trying to develop integral urban development and address sustainability issues by involving all the necessary disciplines and stakeholders and encouraging the participation of communities. They are implementing strategies such as: sustainable integrated urban development, urban rehabilitation and densification, and promoting eco-technologies through a housing finance instrument that encourages the use of sustainable applications on housing. Other connected targets are control of urban sprawl and mobility, and the promotion of improved quality of life for all residents. Government parties and the private sector also recognize the importance of social housing production to solve the housing needs of low-income populations and propose new financing schemes for social housing production. The goal is to promote projects that incorporate sustainable urban solutions with community participation (CIDOC/SHF 2012).

The government is focusing on housing re-densification in the inner-city (CONAVI 2010b) and the control of urban sprawl. Individual households and private and public developers are densifying their properties too, with the latter parties increasing their production of multi-storey housing such as apartment buildings. Currently, new government scenarios and instruments for housing are available. Since 2010, governmental institutions have been developing integrated approaches to housing through DUIS. This certification system is based on orderly growth of cities and development of sustainable urban environments with well-designed housing. One authorized DUIS project involving integrated spatial planning will

TABLE 15.3 Overview of housing finance operations in Mexico, 2006–2011

Housing finance providers	2006	2007	2008	2009	2010	2011
Financial entities	92,763	112,913	63,607	53,055	36,672	10,763
ONAVIS	539,712	591,913	712,593	585,978	602,099	600,646
State organizations	23,228	94,628	65,671	37,733	34,833	20,508
Other organizations	20,889	18,504	18,768	17,174	11,084	11,566
Federal subsidies	500,612	286,433	908,530	727,771	798,113	722,879
Totals	1,177,204	1,104,379	1,769,169	1,421,711	1,482,801	1,366,362

Source: CONAVI (2012).

facilitate urban expansion plans for approximately 312,000 households, in an area of about 9,242 hectares, which will benefit 1,250,000 people. In addition, 11 potential projects in 9 states are under evaluation, which would provide over 200,000 new homes (CIDOC/SHF 2012).

Making urban policies that implement sustainability goals is a challenge in Mexico. These goals include higher densities and the use of sustainable building materials. As urban density increases, the compact city is becoming an important catchphrase. High urban density has serious consequences for low-cost housing since it reduces the possibilities for self-help housing (GoM 2012).[3]

Another stimulus for sustainable housing that has been in effect for several years is 'green mortgages', which enable the purchase of sustainable housing with ecological and technological solutions for energy efficiency and renewable energies, such as solar heaters, energy-saving lamps, water-saving valves, thermal insulation, high-efficiency air conditioners, etc. (CIDOC/SHF 2011). In 2011 INFONAVIT issued 376,815 green mortgages (INFONAVIT 2012).

Housing and urban planning challenges of today

Mexico's social housing policy encourages private home ownership. Rental dwellings are rarely promoted and often rental complexes are dated. Rental housing is mainly offered by private parties, for example by families in older suburbs. The extent and quality of rental stock has not been sufficiently investigated and policy herewith is lacking. In 2000, the rental housing stock amounted to only 13 per cent of the total housing stock (Coulomb 2010). The stimulation of rental housing is necessary to help those who cannot afford the (subsidized) purchase of a house or a self-help housing solution, such as people with disabilities, students and the elderly.

In 2013, land-for-housing, which involves the purchase of land for urban social housing, was not a primary focus of housing policy, probably because the federal government's main goal was to increase the number of housing finance 'actions' to over 1 million annually. Land-for-housing is a difficult issue because it is not easy to find new land in the vicinity of cities and develop it by public means, while land prices are increasing considerably. One can find some public and public–private land developments in several states. Some of these have a special trust fund, which in Mexico is called a *fideicomiso*. But land-for-housing remains a complicating factor for the planning of Mexican cities. Over the next 25 years 553,000 hectares will be needed to satisfy the demand of the housing market (an average of 22,121 hectares annually). SEDESOL estimates that 70 per cent of the land-for-urban-growth during the coming years will be provided by *ejido* land (CIDOC/SHF 2012). For better articulation of housing policy the Secretariat of Agrarian, Territorial and Urban Development was established (formerly the SRA). It is responsible for coordinating CONAVI, CORETT and FONHAPO, and signing agreements with INFONAVIT. Its mission is to provide and improve housing for low-income households (DOF 2013).[4]

The national housing policy pays little attention to new forms of savings and building structures, or to the promotion of small housing cooperatives and the sustaining of technical assistance for self-builders, but there are some small-scale examples of these developments (Ortiz 2012). While the government's focus since 2000 has been on growing housing finance actions, its attention to other housing issues such as typology, land and construction costs has slackened. New forms of multi-storey housing in the urban context are becoming more common, such as duplexes with two storeys and apartments with three or more storeys. These types of housing need more political attention in view of the upcoming compact city policy.

Box 15.2 provides examples of assisted self-help housing. We think that more research on the best ways to assist self-builders may be crucial for future housing quality because self-help housing is still common.

BOX 15.2 EXAMPLES OF ASSISTED SELF-HELP HOUSING IN MEXICO

Assisted self-help housing is widespread but not fully institutionalized, possibly because self-help housing has only been seen as acceptable since around 2000. Self-help (now often self-managed housing) is still very common and therefore we focus on some significant examples. Private actors are making a positive contribution in this field.

An example of a municipality that supports self-help housing is Nuevo Laredo, where a trust fund in 1999 was founded for Land Reserve in favour of people with low incomes, to prevent illegal settlements from arising elsewhere in the municipality. The trust fund bought 343 hectares of land; the area was developed, and afterwards plots were sold to families (Gobierno y gestión local n.d.). This is an illustration of a land-for-housing programme (it is one of the many *reservas territoriales*, as are the DUIS projects).

A housing project for 70 social housing units was realized in Monterrey, Nuevo León (Santa Catarina). The project has homes with a ground floor and two more storeys, as well as duplex homes. Both types of homes, after completion by individual families, can be enlarged. The ground floor homes can be enlarged from 40 to 58 square metres and the duplex homes from 40 to 76 square metres. This is a hybrid housing solution in which phasing out by self-help is integrated into the housing design. It is developed by Elemental Architects from Chile (Aravena and Iacobelli 2012; IVNL n.d.).

The cement company CEMEX developed a social aid programme that offers building materials and technical assistance to self-builders and credit for home renovations. Their award-winning programme *Patrimonio Hoy* benefited more than 250,000 households in 22 Mexican states (Bouillon 2012: 224; CEMEX n.d.). Another cement company, Holcim

Apasco, introduced its 'Mi Casa' scheme, helping people self-construct homes to an acceptable standard by providing affordable construction materials. By 2008, Holcim Apasco had set up more than 1,100 standardized *Mi Casa* building materials centres, offering technical assistance too (Holcim Apasco n.d.).

Social housing production (see text below) is growing, due to the efforts of the housing institutes. In addition, public housing institutions such as FONHAPO, CONAVI and SHF have stimulated the implementation of social housing. Other parties, including a range of non-govermental organizations (NGOs), social project developers, construction companies, and state/regional and local actors have provided a significant share of the financing for social housing and improvements. One of the prominent examples is Habitat for Humanity Mexico, which operates in 18 states throughout Mexico, and has served 165,000 people in 1,000 communities (Habitat for Humanity Mexico n.d.).

Besides the challenges of adequate urban planning and sustainable housing, two additional housing challenges that are very relevant for the future of social housing production in Mexico will be described below.

Social housing production is becoming a vision

Social housing production contributes to the production of affordable housing, including private self-help housing. Additionally, non-profit NGOs play an important role in meeting the housing needs of low-income groups (CIDOC/SHF 2012). Social housing production involves various actors: self-help entities (mutual aid cooperatives, civic associations and social entrepreneurs); specialized non-profit producers (housing cooperatives, housing-NGOs, technical corporations linked with social movements, philanthropic organizations, etc.); and institutions supporting social housing production and habitat (federations of housing cooperatives, socially responsible companies and social developers). CONAVI facilitates Assisted Social Housing Production (PSVA), through Social Executors and Social Housing Developers, which support individual or collective social self-producers by giving them social, technical, financial, administrative, legal and/or accounting assistance (Ortiz 2012). PSVA is beginning to consolidate as a public policy. Since 2010 CONAVI, in partnership with other agencies, has organized basic training workshops for different actors involved with social housing production (CIDOC/SHF 2012).

Uninhabited housing: a potential threat

In 2010 there were nearly 5 million uninhabited houses out of a national total of 35 million homes, which is about 14 per cent (INEGI 2010). This is 4.5 times the annual housing demand of 1.1 million in 2011 (CIDOC/SHF 2011). A substantial part of the uninhabited housing is located in the northern states of Mexico and the lowest proportion is located in the Federal District (8 per cent). The phenomenon is associated with several factors, including the crisis and economic adjustments, international migration, and the violence and insecurity prevailing in some cities in the north (Sanchez and Salazar 2011). It is also linked with long distances to work, a lack of services, low housing quality, the possibilities to purchase a second home (INFONAVIT 2011) and the overproduction of new housing as a consequence

FIGURE 15.3A Uninhabited row-houses in Galaxia La Calera, Puebla. Photo by Lorena Cabrera Montiel.

FIGURE 15.3B Uninhabited apartments in Villa San Carlos, Puebla. Photo by the authors. Photo by Lorena Cabrera Montiel.

of federal policy (BBVA Research 2011; Sanchez and Salazar 2011). This alarming situation is probably a result of public agencies offering too many new houses. In the first quarter of 2007, 85.7 per cent of INFONAVIT mortgage loans were used to purchase new housing units (UN-Habitat 2011b). Municipalities with large numbers of uninhabited housing also received more public funds and built more new housing (BBVA Research 2011).

The failure of the housing policy is apparent in the current situation of major homebuilders. These companies benefited from federal policy in the past decade and now are dominating the market. In 2012 four companies, which were producing 30 per cent of all the housing nationally (PUEC-UNAM 2013: 74), were confronted with cash problems and increasing debts, due to low sales, rising construction costs and cessation of mortgage payments (of inhabited houses). Despite continued public housing actions, many people are still homeless and the housing stock of low-income families has significant shortcomings. This increases environmental damage, the disintegration of urban and social structures, and insecurity. Moreover, the number of overdue mortgages is growing. Figures 15.3a and 15.3b show uninhabited houses in Puebla (row-houses and apartments, respectively).

Conclusion

Between 1972 and 2012 the Mexican housing market underwent several changes. We mention the transformation from rental to owner-occupied housing in the 1960s and 1970s and, during the following four decades, the development of public support schemes for housing including finance for self-building. Public housing institutions, such as INFONAVIT, that were established in 1972, are still functioning but have changed considerably in scope and approach. Since around 2000, Mexico's urban housing market for the poor started widening its scope and, powered by an array of new kinds of housing finance, currently offers hybrid forms of housing that combine social housing with self-managed finishing.

The development of housing typology in Mexico indicates that there are two dominant building forms: (1) the individual incremental building method, which results in each plot having a house with its own outside walls; and (2) the project-based housing, which has led to the production of large numbers of subsidized housing. Within the last building form, there are two types that can be distinguished: projects with small family homes on private plots and complexes with apartment buildings with three, four or five floors that are usually in a compact setting where houses cannot be extended individually. We think that in the future researchers should pay more attention to condominium housing, its manifestations and its construction costs because in the future more condominiums will be built, especially in metropolitan areas.

For some years, one of the government's new objectives has been to make housing more sustainable, as demonstrated by government publications (GoM 2008, 2012). The objectives for sustainable housing clearly go a step further than simply creating 'durable housing', since goals for protecting the earth and the climate are also taken into account. Consequently, the government promotes, for example, 'green buildings' and the use of sustainable building materials and construction technologies. The financial sector already provides green mortgages for the financing of sustainable applications for homes. In the next few years, sustainable housing should be further developed in Mexican cities, for example by striving for adequate city planning, and sufficient and well-designed public spaces such as parks and squares.

For several years policymakers have been developing the 'social production of habitat' in Mexico as a policy concept. Other countries could benefit from this accumulated knowledge. Because social housing production can be affected by economic depressions and political dialogue concerning 'decent housing' for low-income households, the affordability of housing solutions will be an ongoing discussion. We hold that self-help housing gives households more independence and more flexibility concerning the expansion of dwellings than the housing built by institutions. Social housing production in Mexico is becoming a government policy, and self-help housing is seen as an important part of that. Consequently, the land-for-housing issue must be investigated too.

The growth of urban populations still goes hand in hand with a huge demand for cheap housing for the lowest income brackets. In the near future, new urban expansion plans will still be necessary, but attention to urban renewal, neighbourhood upgrading and home improvements is already present in current policies. Private letting and subletting occur in various forms, but are not officially monitored.

The presence of many uninhabited houses in Mexico is alarming and a possible threat for the housing market and for social coherence and public safety in neighbourhoods. The causes in various parts of the country may be different, but most likely include the overproduction of subsidized dwellings and apartments. We think it is wise to examine this phenomenon thoroughly, in order to avoid adverse effects for the housing market.

Notes

1 Government programmes are e.g. CORETT (Commission for regularization of land ownership), PROCEDE, Programme of certification of *ejido* rights and titling, and PISO Firme, a programme of SEDESOL (Secretariat of Social Development).
2 Extreme poverty (those living on less than US$76 a month in urban areas and less than US$53 in rural areas) reduced slightly to 10.4 per cent (World Bank 2013).
3 One may assume that in multi-storey housing, e.g. duplex, multi-family housing, vertical condominium, the self-help housing part is still limited, compared to traditional self-help housing.
4 Other actions have been implemented to solve housing problems: minimum standards through ISA (*Accredited Satisfaction Index*) and ICAVI (*Housing Quality Index*) executed by INFONAVIT, and the INV (National Housing Inventory) by INEGI.

References

Aravena, A. and Iacobelli, A. (2012) *ELEMENTAL Manual de Vivienda Incremental y Diseño Participativo*. Ostfidern: Hatje Cantz Verlag.
Banco de México (n.d.) Information on Banxico. Online. Available at www.banxico.org.mx/ayuda/temas-mas-consultados/udis--unidades-inversion-.html (accessed 6 February 2014).
BBVA Research (2002) 'El financiamiento a la vivienda y sus participantes', *Situación Inmobiliaria*, April: 14–23. Online. Available at www.bbvaresearch.com/KETD/fbin/mult/0204_SituacionInmobiliariaMexico_05_tcm346–178684.pdf (accessed 2 September 2013).
BBVA Research (2011) 'La vivienda deshabitada en México', *Situación Inmobiliaria*, July: 25–34. Online. Available at www.bbvaresearch.com/KETD/fbin/mult/1107_SituacionInmobiliariaMexico_20_tcm346–262669.pdf (accessed 2 September 2013).
BBVA Research (2012) 'Mirando atrás: lo bueno y no tan bueno de la política de vivienda', *Situación Inmobiliaria*, July: 31–34. Online. Available at www.bbvaresearch.com/KETD/fbin/mult/1207_SituacionInmobiliariaMexico_Jul12_tcm346–348280.pdf (accessed 2 September 2013).

Berrospide, J., Herrerias, R., Lopez-Gallo, F. and Mier-y-Teran, A. (2012) *Non-Bank Finance-Companies in Mexico: The Rise and Fall of an Industry*. Online. Available at http://daac.itam.mx/sites/default/files/nonbank_credit_crunch_mexico_dec2012.pdf (accessed 2 September 2013).

Bouillon, C. (ed.) (2012) *Room for Development: Housing Markets in Latin America and the Caribbean*. New York: Palgrave Macmillan.

Bredenoord, J. and Verkoren, O. (2010) 'Between self-help – and institutional housing: a bird's eye view of Mexico's housing production for low and (lower) middle-income groups', *Habitat International*, 34(3): 359–365.

CEMEX (n.d.) 'Programa Patrimonio Hoy'. Online. Available at www.cemexmexico.com/DesarrolloSustentables/PatrimonioHoy.aspx (accessed 20 May 2013).

Chiquier, L. and Lea, M. (2009) *Housing Finance Policy in Emerging Markets*. Washington, DC: World Bank.

CIDOC/SHF (2006) *Estado Actual de la Vivienda en México 2006*. Mexico City: GoM.

CIDOC/SHF (2009) *Estado Actual de la Vivienda en México 2009*. Mexico City: GoM.

CIDOC/SHF (2011) *Estado Actual de la Vivienda en México 2011*. Mexico City: GoM.

CIDOC/SHF (2012) *Estado actual de la Vivienda en México 2012*. Mexico City: GoM.

CONAVI (2009) *Programa federal de Subsidios de Vivienda*. Mexico City: GoM.

CONAVI (2010a) *Estadísticas de Vivienda*, Housing Actions 1973–2010. Mexico City: GoM.

CONAVI (2010b) *Guía para la Redensificación Habitacional en la Ciudad Interior*. Mexico City: GoM. Online. Available at www.conorevi.org.mx/pdf/taller/Guia_para_la_Redensificacion.pdf (accessed 20 May 2013).

CONAVI (2010c) *Código de Edificación de Vivienda 2010*. Mexico City: GoM.

CONAVI (2012) *Programa Anual de Financiamientos para Vivienda*. Mexico City: GoM.

Connolly, P. (2003) *The Case of Mexico City*. Online. Available at www.ucl.ac.uk/dpu-projects/Global_Report/pdfs/Mexico.pdf (accessed 20 May 2013).

Connolly, P. (2006) '¿Política de vivienda o política de construcción?', in A. Borjas Benavente and M. Bucio Escobedo (eds) *La vivienda en México: construyendo análisis y propuestas*. Mexico: Centro de Estudios Sociales y de Opinión Pública. Online. Available at www3.diputados.gob.mx/camara/content/download/28775/126415/file/La_vivienda_en_Mexico_construyendo_analisis_y_propuestas.pdf (accessed 20 May 2013).

Coulomb, R. (2010) 'Evolución reciente y situación actual del derecho a la vivienda', in G. Garza and M. Schteingart (eds) *Los Grandes Problemas de México. II Desarrollo Urbano y Regional, México*. Tlalpan: El Colegio de México.

DOF (2013) Diario Oficial de la Federación, February 11. 'SEDATU', Mexico City: GoM.

FONHAPO (n.d.) General information, Mexico City: GoM. Online. Available at www.fonhapo.gob.mx (accessed 20 May 2013).

Gobierno y gestión local (n.d.) 'Nuevo Laredo Tamaulipas Programa reservas territoriales'. Online. Available at www.premiomunicipal.org.mx/p2009/pa_tamaulipas.php (accessed 7 October 2013).

GoM (2006) *Ley de Vivienda 2006*. Mexico City: GoM.

GoM (2008) *Programa Nacional de Vivienda 2008–2012: Hacia un Desarrollo Habitacional Sustentable*. Mexico City: GoM.

GoM (2012) *Sustainable Housing in Mexico (SHF, INFONAVIT, CONAVI)*. Mexico City: GoM.

Habitat for Humanity Mexico (n.d.) General information. Online. Available at www.habitatmexico.org (accessed 20 May 2013).

Holcim Apasco México (n.d.): *Iniciativa de vivienda pagable 'Mi Casa'*. Online. Available at www.holcim.com/en/case-studies/holcim-apasco-mexico-affordable-housing-initiatives-mi-casa.html (accessed 20 May 2013).

INEGI (2005a) *Delimitación zonas metropolitanas de México, 2005*. Online. Available at www.inegi.org.mx/prod_serv/.../DZMM_2005_0.pdf (accessed 20 May 2013).

INEGI (2005b) *Mexican Population and Household Census 2005*. Online. Available at www.inegi.org.mx/prod_serv/contenidos/espanol/bvinegi/productos/geografia/publicaciones/delimex05/DZMM_2005_0.pdf (accessed 20 May 2013).

INEGI (2010) *Censo General de Población y Vivienda 2010*. Mexico City: GoM.
INFONAVIT (2011) *Plan Financiero 2011–2015*. Online. Available at www.boletin.dseinfonavit.org.mx/051/doctos/PF_2011_2015.pdf (accessed 20 May 2013).
INFONAVIT (2012) *Housing, Mexico's Strategic Driving Force. 2011 Results & Institutional Outlook*. Mexico: Presentation INFONAVIT for Mexico housing day 2012.
IVNL (n.d.) Instituto de la Vivienda de Nuevo León. Online. Available at www.nl.gob.mx/?P=inst_de_vivienda (accessed 20 May 2013).
Landaeta, G. (1994) *Strategies for Low-Income Housing: A Comparative Study on Nicaragua, Mexico, Guatemala, Cuba, Panama, Costa Rica and El Salvador*. Lund: Lund University.
Municipality of Nezahualcóyotl (n.d.) Historia del municipio. Online. Available at www.neza.gob.mx (accessed 20 May 2013).
Ortiz, E. (2012) *Producción social de la vivienda y el hábitat: Bases conceptuales y correlación con los procesos habitacionales*. Mexico: Habitat International Coalition.
PUEC-UNAM (2013) *México, Perfil del sector de la vivienda*. Mexico: UN-Habitat, CONAVI, PUEC-UNAM. Online. Available at www.economia.unam.mx/cedrus/descargas/perfil_sector_vivienda_digital.pdf (accessed 20 May 2013).
Ribbeck, E. (2002) *Die informelle moderne spontanes bauen in Mexiko-Stadt*. Stuttgart/Heidelberg: Awf-Verlag.
Sanchez, L. and Salazar, C. (2011) 'Lo que dicen las viviendas deshabitadas sobre el censo de población 2010', *Coyuntura Demográfica*, 1: 66–72.
SHCP (n.d.) Information on SHF. Online. Available at www.shcp.gob.mx/POLITICAFINANCIERA/banca_desarrollo/programas_institucionales/Paginas/SHF.aspx (accessed 20 May 2013).
Temiño, I. (2007) *El mercado hipotecario en Latinoamérica. Una visión de negocio*. Madrid: ESIC.
UN-Habitat (2011a) *Affordable Land and Housing in Latin America and the Caribbean*. Nairobi: UN-Habitat.
UN-Habitat (2011b) *Housing Finance Mechanisms in Mexico*. Nairobi: UN-Habitat.
World Bank (2013) Mexico Overview. Online. Available at www.worldbank.org/en/country/mexico/overview (accessed 20 May 2013).

16
HALF A CENTURY OF SELF-HELP IN BRAZIL

Suzana Pasternak and Camila D'Ottaviano

Abbreviations

BNH	National Housing Bank
CDHU	São Paulo State Urban and Housing Development Agency
FDS	Social Development Fund
FGTS	Worker's Severance Compensation Fund
FUNACOM	Self-Management Housing Provision Programme
FUNAPS	Sub-Standard Housing Dwellers Support Fund
INOCOOP	Guidance Institute for Housing Cooperatives
MCMV	My Life My House Programme
MCMV-E	My Life My House Entities Programme
PCS	Solidarity Loan Programme
PRODEPO	Economic Centres Development Support Programme
PROFILURB	Land Development Financing Programme
PROMORAR	Sub-Standard Housing Eradication Programme
SEHAB	Municipal Housing Secretariat

Introduction

During the past half-century, housing provision policies went through significant changes in Brazil. From programmes of mass construction in the 1960s and 1970s, coordinated by the National Housing Bank (BNH – established in 1964 and abolished in 1986), until the recent My Life My House Programme (MCMV), Brazil has gone through periods of low investment in social housing production. As a result, the Brazilian city is deeply marked by irregular land subdivisions and self-help construction – the primary means for the lower income classes to access housing.

The types of dwellings that are predominant among low-income groups in Brazil vary according to both the city and the time period. Historically, four basic types of dwellings stand out: *cortiços* (slums and poor tenements), *favelas* (shanty towns and squatter settlements), large public housing projects and, finally, urban developments located on the outskirts of the city where residents build upon their own properties.

Within the urban outskirts of Brazil's larger cities– *the favelas*, *cortiços* and areas where squatters live in empty buildings – self-built houses typify the type of dwellings found. In fact, self-built homes have been one of the few available housing alternatives for the low-income population.

In 2011, the total number of dwellings in the country was 61,470,054 of which 53,210,429 were located in urban areas. The urban housing deficit was estimated as 8.55 per cent of the total stock, or more than 4.5 million units. In the city of São Paulo, which has more than 3.6 million housing units, the deficit in 2010 was about 412,000 units. In 2010, an estimated 6 per cent of Brazil's population lived in *favelas*. In some metropolitan capitals the percentage is even higher. For example, over 20 per cent of the municipal populations of Salvador, Recife and São Luis lived in *favelas*; in Belém this proportion exceeds 50 per cent. In 2010, 11 per cent of São Paulo's population lived in *favelas*.

Not all *favela* houses are counted as part of the housing deficit; only 13.5 per cent of the units – units built with poor materials or with a density exceeding 3 persons per bedroom – contribute to the housing shortage figure. As Brazilian policy allows squatter upgrading and land regularization, a great number of housing units in *favelas* can be improved and maintained.

Due to high levels of poverty and inequality, the paradigms guiding housing policies and interventions in Brazil as a whole and in São Paulo in particular have changed. Up until 1940, the private sector took the lead role. Intervention was fragile and based on encouraging the private sector to build rental houses in working-class neighbourhoods. Then, between the 1940s and mid-1960s, the predominant paradigm was characterized by a certain degree of state and parastatal intervention that started with the Low Class Housing Foundation federal agency and the financing of houses for members by the Retirement and Pension Institutes. The next guiding paradigm was typical for the military dictatorship between 1964 and 1985. During this time, housing interventions became stronger through the 'enterprising state' model. This model was central developmentalist, authoritarian and centralizing. The BNH centralized all resources and disseminated a standard procedure for the whole country. Nonetheless, the intervention paradigm started to change once again at the end of the1970s, and after the return of democracy and the enactment of the new constitution in 1988, housing policy became decentralized and municipality based. Awareness about informality, segregation and poverty took on a new dimension. Until the 1980s, the *favelas* were simply removed or, at most, had occasional urban intervention to minimize the permanence of their inhabitants (including parks workers in Rio de Janeiro, as well as the inhabitants of villages and temporary housing units in Sao Paulo); *favela* suppression was always the goal. Gradually, *favela* upgrading projects and policies began to predominate over this approach and the right to remain in a *favela* settlement was recognized. Moreover, the possibility of using existing housing investments changed the paradigm of intervention; this resulted in allowing physical improvements to be made in *favelas* as well as increased social policies geared toward *favela* inhabitants. Similarly, building contractors no longer had exclusivity over the construction of large housing projects. There was a growing awareness that self-construction in the urban outskirts had much more to do with low urban salaries than with a choice based on rural collectivism.

This chapter shows how this change in paradigm occurred as well as when and how new types of interventions in Brazil's housing sector came into being, particularly in São Paulo city. However, except for a few major federal programmes, it is difficult to analyse housing interventions throughout the country. After the constitution of 1988, Brazilian housing policy was decentralized and became a municipal function. As a result, there are several specific municipal programmes.

The focus upon São Paulo to illustrate housing policy in Brazil is not trivial: São Paulo is the largest and richest Brazilian city and the only state capital that relies on federal, state and municipal housing funds. Additionally, the city has been the host of innovative experiences in *favelas*-upgrading, interventions in *cortiços* and self-constructed housing policy. São Paulo also is the focus of the current federal housing construction policy – which partly has brought back the old practice of entrusting the construction of housing projects to large contractors.

This chapter is organized into five sections. The first section illustrates the evolution of Brazilian housing policies over the past two decades as well as their turning points. This is followed by two sections describing São Paulo's innovative self-construction experience, which has been appropriated and expanded by the state government through the São Paulo Self-Help Programme. The fourth section describes the current federal low-income housing programme MCMV and its effects on the housing deficit and urban landscape. The last section provides an analysis of the paradigms of Brazil and São Paulo's housing policies.

The evolution of Brazilian housing policy

During the military dictatorship, especially in the first half of the 1970s, the government launched a large number of infrastructure and housing projects. State intervention in the housing sector reflected a central developmentalist, authoritarian and centralizing 'enterprising state', in which users and society as a whole did not participate. The National Housing Bank set a paradigm for the sector by centralizing all resources and by disseminating a standardized type of intervention across the nation whereby the construction of huge housing projects created a monotonous landscape in the urban outskirts. These undertakings had no concern for design or project nor did they enable the participation of the community in the management of the construction site or in the drawing up of the project plans. The standard procedure was the direct financing of the producers and buyers of the new units. The prevailing notion at the time was that mass construction, aided by industrial forms of production, would solve the urban housing deficit problem.

It was only in 1975 that a second generation of social housing programmes called 'reformist options' started to appear. The first self-construction incentive policy appeared with the creation of PROFILURB – or the Land Development Financing Programme. The loans were destined for the production of serviced plots, the acquisition of construction material and for homebuilder technical assistance. The programme was a response to the increasing pressure for popular participation in public housing programmes.

In 1979, PROFILURB was replaced by PROMORAR – the Sub-Standard Housing Eradication Programme. The new goal was to keep *favela* populations in their sites and to regulate land occupation. PROMORAR was the first federal infrastructure upgrading programme for urban settlements. At the time land tenure was not yet a goal. Whilst PROFILURB aimed to prevent the expansion of *favelas* by offering *favela* residents sites and services as an alternative, PROMORAR acknowledged the existence of these settlements and the impossibility of resettling their populations. In 1984, the Self-Construction National Programme (or the

TABLE 16.1 Housing loans granted by BNH (1964–1985)

	Programmes	Loans granted	%
Popular (low-income) market*	Conventional programmes (COHABs)	1,235,409	27.7
	Alternative programmes (PROMORAR, João de Barro, FICAM and PROFILURB)	264,397	5.9
	Total	1,499,806	33.6
Economy (budget) market†	Cooperatives	488,659	10.9
	Other programmes (Institute, Mortgage, Venture for Pron, Prosin)	299,471	6.7
	Total	788,130	17.6
Middle (average) market‡	SBPE	1,898,975	42.5
	Other programmes (Recon, PRODEPO)	280,418	6.3
	Total	2,176,393	48.8
Total		**4,467,329**	**100**

Sources: Saches (1999); Moreira (2009: 42).
*Popular market – designed for new residential unit construction in partnership with housing companies (municipal or state) in general in large peripheral areas, for families with income between 0 and 3 minimum wages.
†Economy market – designed for families with income between 3 and 6 minimum wages, operated by housing cooperatives.
‡Middle market – designed for households with incomes exceeding 6 minimum wages, operated by private agents.
COHAB: housing agency; PROMORAR: Sub-Standard Housing Eradication Programme; FICAM: social housing improvement and construction financing programme; PROFILURB: Land Development Financing Programme; Prosin: Labour Workers National Housing Programme; SBPE: Brazilian Savings and Loan System; Recon: Building Materials Financing or Refinancing Subprogramme; and PRODEPO: Economic Centres Development Support Programme.

João de Barro Programme) institutionalized assisted self-construction as a public housing policy. João de Barro was a government-assisted self-construction programme for collectives or individuals. Only families with monthly incomes up to 1.5 minimum wages could qualify for assistance. The loans (which at the time were 120 UPC – or capital standard unit – about US$700) were for the acquisition of construction materials. The land was provided by the state or municipal governments while the labour came from the interested population. Loan payments were initially less than 10 per cent of the monthly minimum wage. However, the João de Barro Programme achieved modest results; only 6,971 loans were provided between 1984 and the first half of 1985 (Andrade and Azevedo 1982). Despite being a cheaper form of federal government intervention in the housing sector, as shown in Table 16.1, the alternative programmes received only 5.9 per cent of total investment.

The 1980s, known as the 'lost decade' in Brazil, were marked by a worsening of the economic crisis, an acceleration in urban land prices, land invasions organized by housing movements and a reduction in BNH investments which culminated in the bank's closure in 1986 (Arretche 1990).

The replacement of the National Housing Bank with the Federal Savings Bank in 1986 did not change federal housing policy concepts. After 1992, decentralization and the subsequent dismantling of the central developmentalist model became an issue. Incentives began for setting up state and municipal funds and councils; these were to be responsible for producing social housing through a decentralized system that included popular management.

By the end of the 1980s, the city of Recife had introduced pioneering experiments in poor settlement areas that occupied over 100 hectares and were under the control of the Pernambuco Housing Agency and Recife Urbanization Agency (Souza 2007). In those areas, the legalization process was already underway and priority was given to Social Interest Special Areas. This resulted in the Social Purpose Land Tenure Plan; this was the management instrument implemented by the municipal government for the legalization and urbanization of precarious neighbourhoods.

In 1995, the federal government's housing policy was changed through a restructuring of the financing system. A new system, called the Real Estate Financing System, established new forms of funding directly in the capital market (such as real estate funds and securitization of receivables, among others). Priority was shifted from producer loans to direct consumer loans through what were called 'letters of credit'. Over ten years (1995–2004), the Loan Programme granted some 300,000 loans (Valença and Bonates 2010).

During this period, land occupation and the number of clandestine and irregular developments kept growing in Brazil's major cities. Two types of city were being built: the formal, legal city, and what was referred to as the 'real city' – an informal settlement where low-income populations settled. The notion that the real city had to be accepted alongside the formal one started to feature in the urban mindset. As a result, alternative solutions were again discussed.

Consequently, there was a growing emphasis placed on community participation, the need to come to terms with the real city, and the development of new types of management – such as self-management and co-management – through partnerships with non-governmental organizations. This process accelerated especially during late 1980s and after the 1988 constitution increased the municipalities' decision-making powers and financial capacity. Under this scenario, the first self-management policy experiments, which occurred largely on a municipal level – and in the case of São Paulo, on a state level too (Bonduki 2004, 2008) – were born.

FUNAPS-comunitário – São Paulo's innovative experiment

The housing cooperatives experience started in Brazil in 1965 during the National Housing Bank period with the Guidance Institute for Housing Cooperatives or INOCOOP. INOCOOP, comprised of municipal and state institutes, was part of the Brazilian Housing Finance System designed to unionize workers who needed professional technical, administrative, social and financial support for housing production and purchase. This institute provided advisory services to cooperatives, building societies, associations and municipalities. A large part of INOCOOP was linked to Catholic entities responsible not only for organizing the groups and housing construction, but also for mediating between organized groups and the National Housing Bank. Since the cooperatives had tax benefits that could be transferred to the borrowers, they also worked towards achieving cheaper units than those built by construction companies.

INOCOOP brought together union workers with family incomes between three and eight minimum wages. After 1986 and the closure of the National Housing Bank, INOCOOP continued for a while to operate mainly through self-financing. The institution then became much more consortium-oriented than a cooperative, but it was soon dismantled.

According to Federal Law 5764/1971, cooperatives are not subject to state control. Members are responsible for cooperative activities and accounts. Additionally, at the start, housing cooperatives were not related to self-help or collective task force initiatives. However, cooperatives have traditionally facilitated collaboration between the state and the community in order to provide lower-income populations with access to public housing funds. A housing cooperative could be established from a neighbourhood group (in order to obtain property titles), a resident's association comprised of squatters, or renters settled in a given location or from a cooperative union (Fruet 2005). Since the 1990s, the role cooperatives play in Brazil has increased significantly.

Between 1982 and 1985, São Paulo state had its first pioneering housing construction experiments, implemented through self-Help task force building programmes. These programmes allowed the participation of families in the development of projects and the construction of housing units. The first experiences were conducted with public resources (from the municipal housing company and/or the State Housing Development Agency) as well as technical assistance from outside professionals.

The most important experiences at this initial stage were Vila Nova Cachoeirinha (1982), a residential project built in the northern area of São Paulo city; Recanto da Alegria (1983), an intervention project in a *favela* in the south of the city; and Vila Comunitária (1985) in São Bernardo do Campo, in São Paulo metropolitan region.

These first experiences were mostly the result of certain professionals' personal involvement and community associations; each tried to reproduce the Uruguayan cooperative experience in Brazil, even if only on a temporary and experimental basis. According to Moreira (2009: 47):

> The novelty of these pioneering experiences lies in the participation of professionals who sought to break with the movements' particular actions and demands by introducing, not without resistance from the public authorities, new elements found in Uruguayan housing policy: the housing units production by cooperatives users through invested resources self-management, and mutual aid construction process.

In 1984 and based on the initiatives of the professionals who acted in the São Paulo and São Bernardo do Campo task force building programmes, the First Housing Movements Meeting was held with the theme of 'Mutual and Self-Help Cooperatives'. The event was organized by the associations responsible for the housing programmes in the São Paulo metropolitan region and representatives from Uruguay's Mutual Help Cooperatives Federation. This meeting was the first attempt to draw up an alternative proposal for a centralized federal housing policy. A second meeting in 1985 created the Housing, Mutual Help and Self-Help Movements Cooperation, whose main principles of self-management, mutual aid, solidarity and common property were based on the Uruguayan experience.

1987 and 1988 were marked by large occupation movements, particularly in the eastern area of São Paulo city. These movements were spurred by the creation of the São Paulo Housing Movements Union and by the vigorous actions of the Urban Reform National Movement, which culminated with the enactment of the new constitution in 1988. According to Moreira (2009: 51):

> Involvement in this process, which resulted in the drawing up of the Popular Constitutional Amendment on Urban Reform, enabled popular movements to incorporate new concepts about the city, participative management and other mechanisms that could strengthen their organization and actions.

In 1989, after the election of a mayor from the Workers' Party (PT), municipal housing policy changed drastically. The new Municipal Housing Secretariat (SEHAB) set up a technical group involved in urban reform and popular self-help movements. Between 1989 and 1992, the new administration adopted as an active principle the acknowledgement of the real city and its peculiarities. In order to deal with urban and housing problems in accordance with their specificities, the new administration developed an action programme, which included the following: the upgrading and land regularization of squatter settlements, the verticalization of *favelas*, housing improvements and interventions in *cortiços*, the production of new housing units, access to and on regular neighbourhoods as well as secure land ownership.

This scenario, as well as increased pressure from the Catholic Church and popular housing movements, led to the creation of the Sub-Standard Housing Dwellers Support Fund – or the FUNAPS Programme (FUNAPS) in 1979 as a solution to the increasing demand from housing movements for a self-help housing programme. It was designed to meet the demand coming from the segment of São Paulo's population that lived in poor quality housing and earned less than four minimum wages a month. As the resources could be invested in a non-refundable fund, this municipal programme was used as an alternative for those with no access to regular loans.

FUNAPS was SEHAB's main funding source and was used to implement other initiatives such as FUNACOM, or the Self-Management Housing Provision Programme, as well as interventions in at-risk *favela* areas and *favela*-upgrading on public land. The FUNACOM Programme was conceived by the São Paulo Municipality in partnership with 108 construction community associations and 24 technical advisory entities to benefit about 60,000 people (Bonduki 1996: 180). FUNACOM instituted a process of housing production through government and organized society partnership in a system that Bonduki (1996: 183) called non-state public management. The São Paulo municipality participated by financing the operation through FUNAPS while resident associations (formed exclusively by residents) ran the undertaking. Service entities drew up the designs and helped with the construction work.

FUNACOM was a pioneering programme in Brazil, in which community associations signed an agreement with FUNAPS for funding and the promotion of construction. The associations were responsible for the selection and hiring of technical advisory services, resource management and jobsite construction, including the organization and hiring of all cooperative and skilled labour up to the limit of 10 per cent of funding. In addition, São Paulo municipality established rules that guided the process; technical assistance payment could not exceed 4 per cent of the funding. The focus given to the task force work rule (whereby only 18 per cent of the total funding could be expended on contracting external help such as masons) was emphasized by using 82 per cent of funds in the purchase of construction materials.

In three and a half years, 93 partnerships built 12,351 housing units through this self-help building task force system (Ronconi 1995). Besides the quantitative results, São Paulo's experience with FUNACOM inspired the consolidation of a new type of housing provision made possible by public authorities and by strengthening certain housing movements.

The São Paulo model went beyond the local scope and became a parameter for new national policies. Based on the housing movements' actions, the São Paulo state government created the Self-Help Programme, a state building task force programme which subsequently became São Paulo's State Self-Help Programme. After the end of the PT administration in 1992, the Self-Help Programme was responsible for maintaining self-management programmes. The plan was to combine public, social and non-profit aspects of state action with the private sector's agility and efficiency. Moreover, public authorities would no longer be solely responsible for social programmes.

São Paulo's State Self-Help Programme and supportive loan programme – the institutionalization of self-management

The housing policies both in São Paulo state and São Paulo municipality have special characteristics whereby the pioneering municipal self-management experiences such as the São Paulo State Urban and Housing Development Agency's (CDHU) Self-Help Programme and the São Paulo State Self-Help Programme have become important references.

Since its origin in 1984 in São Paulo state, the CDHU has been responsible for a significant part of housing provision in cities outside the capital. With financial support obtained from 1 per cent of the state goods tax, São Paulo is the only Brazilian state with secured funds for housing initiatives.

In 1995, the São Paulo State Self-Help Programme was created. The programme 'aimed at encouraging the population to organize itself and at reducing production costs and deadlines' (Royer 2002: 103). From a quantitative viewpoint, the units produced under the building task force system did not exceed 6 per cent of the total. However, a preliminary assessment conducted by CDHU at the end of the programme's first year confirmed (Royer 2002: 109):

> (1) the appointment of the participating associations by Housing Movements Union; (2) the selection of the families based on internal criteria; (3) the hiring of technical aides without any interference from CDHU, and the association's freedom to choose the architectural projects; (4) the construction of housing units with area and/or finishing standards above those adopted by CDHU (these upgrades in scale were obtained through the management of the construction works).

CDHU's Self-Help Programme has been active for over two decades. Although the investment volume destined for the programme is still far below the sums allocated for traditional construction works, it remains an important housing access tool, especially in bigger cities where housing movements are better organized and land value is significantly higher.

In 1996, besides the individual loans awarded at the federal level, the cooperative credit letter, a housing loan for cooperatives and groups, was established. However, unlike the São Paulo experience, individuals participating in this federal programme were the final beneficiaries instead of the housing cooperatives. There were local government cooperative credit letter initiatives in Minas Gerais state where, between 1991 and 2005, within the state capital of Belo Horizonte 11 projects benefited 1247 families; 684 units were also constructed in Ipatinga. In addition, such projects occurred in Fortaleza, Goiânia, South Mato Grosso, Rio de Janeiro (where only 143 units were produced) and Porto Alegre. As all of these projects were local government initiatives, access to the most significant federal funds was unavailable.

In 2004, during the first term of the Lula government, the creation of the PCS or the Solidarity Loan Programme represented a real possibility for a national expansion of self-help housing programmes. The programme was intended for low-income families (earning up to three minimum wages a month) that were organized into associations; it was not necessary to be linked to a housing movement. The PCS's main goals were, according to the Cities Ministry (Ministério das Cidades 2012):

> to offer the low-income population, unable to save money, access to regular housing through special and subsidized credit; ... to give priority to families earning less than three minimum wages a month ...; to encourage the housing cooperative system and the mutual aid principle, through popular participation and by empowering the community to come up with solutions for its common housing problems, in accordance with local needs, characteristics, customs and habits.

Although regarded as an important achievement by the housing movements, PCS cannot draw from Brazil's main housing fund: the Worker's Severance Compensation Fund (FGTS). Pressure from building companies and bankers forced PCS to use existing resources instead from a little-used fund called the Social Development Fund (FDS). Although limited, these resources were cheaper than the FGTS and allowed loan amortization instalments to incur no interest charges. Although used on federal programmes for the first time, this was a timid beginning for subsidy-guided housing.

Per programme criteria, each contract is made directly with the borrower. Associations are responsible for project management and supervision. Projects range from 50 to 200 housing units; while small housing complexes are emphasized, it is possible to produce dispersed units and housing renewing. The PCS undertakes both land acquisition and construction as well as renovation or expansion. In addition, the programme employs various methods including self-help, task force, direct administration (where the housing movement is responsible for construction administration) and global contract (where an external company administers construction). For example, some interesting experiments were carried out including possession transfer and Social Security National Institute building recovery in the city centre in Porto Alegre and *cortiço* improvement in the central area for 113 families in Santos. In total, between 2005 and 2011, 476 million Brazilian reals, or roughly US$260 million, was invested in 21,600 housing units, with resources from the FDS (Ministério das Cidades 2012).

In quantitative terms, the average of just over 3,000 housing units per year is insufficient given both Brazil's size and shortage of housing. Further, when analysing the programme's territorial distribution it becomes clear that units are mainly located in small towns in the south region and in the state of Goiás in the midwest; little has been built in the larger cities where housing shortages are more severe. Nonetheless, the PCS is symbolic because it is the first time that the Brazilian government not only recognized housing cooperatives and associations as partners in housing production, but also provided a subsidy for low-income families.

On the other hand, the programme's design was based on excessive bureaucracy. Short deadlines for project approval coupled with individual financing have discouraged cohesiveness between association members. Moreover, low borrowing limits have forced cooperatives to seek partnership with local and state governments, diminishing cooperatives' autonomy. For example, the sole São Paulo project is a complex with 200 units divided among ten buildings that were only built with additional funding provided through state grants (Ronconi 1995).

Nevertheless, the PCS represents an important change in the Brazilian housing policy model which has evolved from temporary pilot projects to a nationwide self-management programme (Moreira 2009).

Programa minha casa minha vida entidades – the latest policy

In 2009, big changes in Brazil's national housing policy were set in motion. Through Law 11,977 of 7 July, the federal government launched MCMV, which set a production target of 1 million new housing units. Amid an economic crisis, the programme set out to tackle two distinct issues. The first was to lower the housing deficit, which at the time was close to 5.5 million homes. The second aim was to boost the construction industry through job creation and increased capital flow. Similarly to BNH, the programme's main priority was to promote economic growth during a period of international economic crisis.

The programme, still in operation, is funded by federal budget resources which include the Workers Unemployment Fund and the Guarantee Financing Fund of the FGTS. Despite officially being a stand-alone programme, MCMV can be viewed as a policy with different outreach strategies aligned according to a population's income band. In other words, of the 1 million housing units foreseen in the programme's first stage, 40 per cent were destined for families earning between zero and three minimum wages a month while another 40 per cent was destined for families earning between three and six minimum wages a month. Finally, 20 per cent was destined for families earning between six and ten minimum wages a month. The loans also fitted a geographical criterion based on the housing deficit calculated by the João Pinheiro Foundation in 2008.

As a result, the funding ranges for the acquisition or construction of new properties under MCMV vary according to the region and municipality size. The definition of the financed property value also varies according to region, as shown in Table 16.2.

By the end of 2010, the programme had contracted 1,005,128 housing units while the total investment reached R$53.16 billion (about US$25.3 billion); this included resources from the federal budget in subsidies as well as those from FGTS.

As shown in Table 16.3, of the initial targets, only the first income band was exceeded; 571,000 contracted units were constructed which is 43 per cent more than initially projected. In the other two income bands, the volume of contracted units reached 70 per cent of the target.

With the creation of MCMV, all other housing programmes have either been incorporated into it or terminated. PCS was converted into an MCMV sub-programme called My Life My House Entities (MCMV-E). MCMV-E is structured similarly to the Solidarity Loan Programme, including the target public (families earning up to three minimum wages a month), the ways to access the programme (through organized housing bodies) and the funding source (FDS).

For the first time, in a differentiated manner and according to income band, a considerable subsidy has been allocated into a non-refundable fund for the construction of social housing units for very low-income groups. Moreover, the small subsidy embedded in PCS expanded and became explicit under the programme. In addition, the law decreeing the programme also foresees specific instruments to facilitate land regulation. In fact, Chapter 3 of MCMV is entirely dedicated to this issue. The main instrument for land tenure, Urban Demarcation, is still being implemented by some Brazilian municipalities.

Nonetheless, despite some advancement, financing is limited to new properties and the programme makes no provisions for the secondary market or socially oriented rental housing sub-programmes. Moreover, the possibility to include building rehabilitation financing is especially lacking. It is also important to note that access to well-located land and adequate

TABLE 16.2 Subsidies per income band for the acquisition or construction of new properties in MCMV (2009–2010)

	Income group (in monthly minimum wages, MW)			
	Up to 3 MW	3–4 MW	4–5 MW	5–6 MW
Municipalities of São Paulo, Belo Horizonte and federal district metropolitan regions	R$23,000 US$10,132	R$16,000–20,000 US$7,948–9,692	R$9,000–16,000 US$3965–7048	R$2,000–9,000 US$881–9.965
Municipalities with a population of at least 100,000, capital, or metropolitan regions	R$17,000 US$7,489	R$10,000–17,000 US$4,405–7,489	R$3,000–10,000 US$1,323–4,405	R$2,000–9,000 US$881–3,965
Municipalities with a population of 50,000–100,000	R$13,000 US$5,727	R$6,000–13,000 US$2,643–5,727	R$2,000–6,000 US$881–2,643	R$2,000 US$881
Municipalities with a population of 20,000–50,000	R$8,000 US$3,524	R$2,000–8,000 US$881–3,524	R$2,000 US$881	R$1,500 US$661
Municipalities with a population of less than 20,000	R$7,000 US$3,084	R$2,000–7,000 US$881–3,084	R$1,500 US$661	R$1,000 US$441

Source: Ferreira (2012: 43).
Monthly minimum wage in 2009 was R$465,00 (US$205).

TABLE 16.3 Housing units contracted according to income band (2009–2010)

Income band (number of minimum wages)	Contracted housing units	Target MCMV (housing units)	% of the contracted target
0–3	571,321	400,000	143%
3–6	284,772	400,000	71%
6–10	149,035	200,000	75%
Total	1,005,128	1,000,000	101%

Source: Ministério das Cidades (2010).

urban infrastructure remains a problem. Builders keep buying land in peripheral areas, especially on the outskirts of cities where land is cheaper. In larger cities, this means an increase in the urban perimeter and an ever-increasing periphery.

Another problem is that public subsidies also benefit families earning between three and six minimum wages a month. Many experts claim that this measure will benefit those earning between three and six minimum wages a month, as investors and real estate developers end

TABLE 16.4 Housing units contracted, 0 to 3 minimum wages (2009–2010)

Programmes	Total housing units	%
MCMV – FAR	404,407	71%
MCMV-E FDS	9,395	2%
PNHR	5,167	1%
Municipalities with fewer than 50,000 inhabitants	63,772	11%
FGTS	88,580	16%
Total	571,321	100%

Source: Ministério das Cidades (2010).
MCMV–FAR: My Life My House Programme with funding from Residential Leasing Fund; MCMV-E FDS: My Life My House Entities Programme with funding from Social Development Fund; PNHR: Rural Housing National Plan; FGTS: Worker's Severance Compensation Fund financing.

up acquiring urban pieces of land that are better located than those acquired by lower income groups. These groups are thus unable to remunerate their investment and therefore are pushed further to the peripheral fringes. MCMV has undoubtedly warmed up the Brazilian construction market largely by increasing competition for land as well as by creating a strong demand for labour. In fact, this has created labour shortages and salary increases which are reflected in construction prices.

Above all, by encouraging private housing production for low-income groups, the MCMV Programme allows for high levels of subsidy (between 60 and 90 per cent of property value), yet it does not interfere on the construction site nor in project definition. Company projects are approved by the appropriate bodies and then sold to the Brazilian Federal Savings Bank. Buyers pay subsidized benefits to the Bank which in turn promptly provides the total purchase cost to the constructor. For private building companies the sale is guaranteed with no risk of default or vacancy and without spending on marketing and related costs. This is significant as the state bank assumes all the risk while there is a real estate subsidy having social demand as a justification (Arantes and Fix 2009).

As programme targets are based on the housing demand, divided into income range and region, even with the large-scale production occurring over the last three years there is no sign of housing overproduction. Table 16.4 shows the division of the 571,000 units contracted within the zero to three minimum wages a month band, based on existing sub-programmes. MCMV-E has contracted 9,395 housing units – which is only 2 per cent of the total for this income band within a total investment of 440 million Brazilian reals or roughly US$210 million (Ministério das Cidades 2010).

Throughout the MCMV Programme, MCMV-E was responsible for 1 per cent of total housing units. In other words, the chosen model is a global undertaking, without resident participation; residents are treated instead as consumers rather than process participants. Unlike participative programmes, architectural and urban results are mediocre, without any recovery of project quality or architectural variety. As a result, large and repetitive housing complexes spread once again around the periphery of cities.

In 2011, a second phase of the programme was approved, with a new target of 2 million new residential units to be built between 2011 and 2014. Of the total amount, 50 per cent

TABLE 16.5 MCMV-E Programme by September 2012

Units contracted	Investment in R$	Units delivered	Units finished
15,484	446,754,815	1,477	2,615

Source: Ministérios das Cidades (2012).

went to the zero to three minimum wages band; 6 per cent of the total investment was allocated to MCMV-E.

According to data from the Cities Ministry, MCMV-E has contracted 15,484 units through a total investment of almost 447 million Brazilian reals, or roughly US$270 million since its launch in 2009 (see Table 16.5). Although modest, if we take into consideration the amount invested, there was a significant increase in the resources allocated to MCMV-E between the first and the second rounds of MCMV.

Final considerations

Past state interventions in the housing sector were in line with a central developmentalist, authoritarian and centralizing entrepreneurial state, characterized by a lack of participation of both user and the wider society. It was only in 1975 that a second generation of Brazilian social housing programmes started to appear with the so-called 'reformist options'. These include PROFILURB in 1975, PROMORAR in 1979 and João De Barro in 1984. Simultaneously, traditional solutions characterized by high financing costs, housing projects built on the city outskirts, and the subsequent segregation and isolation problems as well as the political costs resulting from the destruction of spontaneous settlements spurred the search for alternative solutions to the housing shortage. Throughout the 1980s, these solutions were based on three premises:

- The acknowledgement of *favelas* as part of the real city and thus the possibility of integration and formalization.
- The choice of cheaper solutions, such as sites-and-services upgrading, to replace the exclusive production of large housing projects.
- A return to incremental housing and the introduction of self-construction as a valid and cheap means of house ownership as well as a path to citizenship through solidarity work.

Between 1989 and 1992, more than 12,000 housing units were constructed under São Paulo Municipality's Self-Management Housing Provision Programme, led by the Municipal Housing Secretariat. In quantitative terms this is a small number, in view of the city's real needs. However, in qualitative terms, the architectural projects were exemplary as larger units with higher construction standards were built at a lower cost. As the material purchases were made directly by the residents' associations involved in the project, they were able to choose better materials at lower prices. Additionally, an on-site technical aide ensured efficient management of the works, better use of paid labour and a more effective construction process overall. According to the promoters of the self-help building task forces, the development of communal and solidarity activities within the process also led to advances in community organization and citizenship status.

Despite some significant differences, such as subsidy amounts, the selection of borrowers from a municipalities' register, and a clear separation between the demands from the low-income population and the other income bands, MCMV has signalled a return of the developmentalist state. It has also spurred the construction of housing projects on the city outskirts where land is cheaper, especially for the lowest income band (up to three minimum wages). On the other hand, the recent important increase in housing with targeted subsidies is a goal that has to be considered in Brazilian housing policy.

Furthermore, this policy does not imply an end to building task force programmes. In addition to MCMV-E, they still occur through state government financing in São Paulo. Nor does it mean the end of *favela* upgrading policies; these are currently being adopted nationwide.

Although of minor significance in numerical terms, the self-management housing provision experiences of the 1980s and 1990s have established a paradigm. Programmes such as the Solidarity Loan Programme and MCMV-E have proven to be feasible alternatives, especially in large cities. Moreover, improved architectural design and construction quality of the housing units built under the self-management system over the past 30 years is noticeable, as is the social mobility prompted by the self-management process.

The significant increase in the number of people living in *favelas* in the past decade combined with a growing housing deficit has posed an important challenge towards the large-scale building of housing units with more desirable architectural designs, construction and urban services. Bearing this in mind, self-management could be a good example to follow.

References

Andrade, L.A.G. and Azevedo, S. (1982) *Habitação e poder – Da Fundação da casa popular ao Banco Nacional da habitação*. Rio de Janeiro: Zahar.

Arantes, P.F. and Fix, M. (2009) *Minha Casa, Minha Vida*. Online. Available at www.observatoriodasmetropoles.net/download/gthab/text_ref_outros/fixe_arantes_MCMV.pdf (accessed 16 July 2013).

Arretche, M. (1990) 'Intervenção do Estado e Setor Privado: o modelo brasileiro de política habitaciona', *Espaço e Debates* 31. São Paulo: Núcleo de Estudos Regionais e Urbanos.

Bonduki, N.G. (1996) *Habitat: práticas bem-sucedidas em habitação, meio ambiente e gestão urbana nas cidades brasileiras*. São Paulo: Studio Nobel.

Bonduki, N. (2004) *Origens da habitação social no Brasil*. São Paulo: Estação Liberdade.

Bonduki, N. (2008) 'Política habitacional e inclusão social no Brasil: revisão histórica e novas perspectivas no governo Lula', *Revista eletrônica de Arquitetura e Urbanismo*, 1: 70–104. Online. Available at www.historiaestudio.com.br/wp-content/uploads/2012/10/Deficit Habitacional-II.pdf (accessed 16 July 2013).

Ferreira, J.S.W. (ed.) (2012) *Produzir casas ou construir cidades? Desafios para um novo Brasil urbano. Parâmetros de qualidade para a implementação de projetos habitacionais e urbanos*. São Paulo: LABHAB/FUPAM.

Fruet, G.M. (2005) 'The low income housing cooperatives in Porto Alegre, Brazil: a state/community partnership', *Habitat International*, 29: 303–324.

Ministério das Cidades (2010) *Posição de contratação PMCMV (0–3 Salários Mínimos): 04/05/2010*.

Ministério das Cidades (2012) Programas e Ações. Programa Crédito Solidário. Online. Available at www.cidades.gov.br/index.php/programas-e-acoes/519-programa-credito-solidario (accessed 16 July 2013).

Moreira, F.A. (2009) '*O lugar da autogestão no Governo Lula'*. Dissertação de Mestrado. São Paulo: FAUUSP.

Ronconi, R. (1995) *Mutirões autogestionados: levantamento de obras 1989–1995*. São Paulo: FASE-SP.
Royer, L. de O. (2002) *A Política Habitacional no Estado de São Paulo: estudo sobre a Companhia de Desenvolvimento Habitacional e Urbano do Estado de São Paulo, CDHU*. Tese de Doutorado, São Paulo: FAUUSP.
Saches, C. (1999) *São Paulo: políticas públicas e habitação popular*. São Paulo: EDUSP.
Souza, M.A. de Almeida (2007) 'Política habitacional para os excluídos: o caso da Região Metropolitana do Recife', in A.L. Cardoso (ed.) *Habitação Social nas metrópoles brasileiras*. Porto Alegre: Coleção Habitare-Finep.
Valença, M.M. and Bonates, M.F. (2010) 'The trajectory of social housing policy in Brazil: from the National Housing Bank to the Ministry of the Cities', *Habitat International*, 34(2): 165–173.

17
HOUSING POLICY IN COLOMBIA

Alan Gilbert

Abbreviations

AFC	*Cuentas de ahorro para el fomento de la construcción*; Savings accounts for the development of construction
Camacol	*Cámara Colombiana de Comercio*; Colombian Chamber of Commerce
CAVs	*Corporaciones de Ahorro y Vivienda*; Corporations for Savings and Housing
CCFs	*Cajas de Compensación Familiar*; Family Assistance Funds
DTF	*Dépositos Término Fijo*; 90 day average interest rate
FONVIVIENDA	*Fondo Nacional de Vivienda*; National Housing Fund
ICT	*Instituto de Crédito Territorial*; Institute for Territorial Credit
INURBE	*Instituto Nacional de Vivienda de Interés Social y Reforma Urbana*; National Institute for Social Interest Housing and Urban Reform
POT	*Plan de Ordenamiento Territorial*; Territorial ordering plan
UPAC	*Unidad de Poder Adquisitivo Constante*; Unit of constant purchasing equivalent
UVR	*Unidad de Valor Real*; Unit of constant value.
VIP	*Vivienda de Interés Prioritario*; Priority Interest Housing, intended for those earning 0–2 minimum salaries
VIS	*Vivienda de Interés Social;* Social Interest Housing, intended for those earning 2–4 minimum salaries

Introduction

Every country in Latin America faces a major housing problem and Colombia is no different. In 2010, 3.8 million households or 36 per cent of all families in the country lacked adequate shelter (Pinto 2010). Of these, one-third did not have their own home and the rest lived in poor quality housing, defined as that lacking services, built of inferior materials or providing too little space. Around two-thirds of those living in inadequate housing earned less than four minimum salaries, a threshold that 82 per cent of Colombian households fail to meet. Poor housing conditions, therefore, are predominantly a symptom of low incomes.

Colombian housing ranges from the luxurious to the most rudimentary of shacks. The formal housing stock varies from high-quality housing, increasingly in gated communities and high rise apartment blocks in the largest cities, to decent but rather small social housing units. Private formal housing is financed by a mortgage system that is well developed by Latin American standards but which struggles to reach less affluent households. The state used to provide public housing but now provides subsidies to poor families and subsidises the interest rate of others. However, perhaps half of the population lives in accommodation created through self-help processes. In the countryside most homes have been constructed by their inhabitants and in urban areas the proportion varies by city but is rarely less than half of the total stock. In the nation's capital, Bogotá, 54 per cent of the homes built between 1993 and 2005 were constructed informally (Florián 2011). The quality of this accommodation is variable. New self-housing is inevitably flimsy and lacks any kind of service but over time Colombians have proved themselves capable of building substantial homes, sometimes with as many as four storeys. Fortunately, the servicing agencies in the larger cities are very effective and the provision of water and sewerage in Bogotá and Medellín is virtually universal. In the smaller cities and particularly in the countryside the servicing situation is much more precarious; in 2011 only 12 per cent of rural homes had access to any sewage connection.

In 2011, 51 per cent of Colombian families owned, formally or informally, or were buying their home (DANE 2012). Rates of ownership were higher in those cities where the authorities have tacitly allowed public, and occasionally private, land to be invaded. Such land provides poor families with the space to construct flimsy, unserviced accommodation. In the Andes, where land is generally more expensive and is more often privately owned, invasions are discouraged strongly. Here so-called pirate urbanisers subdivide land and sell it to poorer people (Gilbert 1981). For the very poor the cost of buying even an unserviced plot is unaffordable and they tend to rent or share accommodation. As a result, some 46 per cent of families in Bogotá rent, many of whom find rooms in areas of consolidated self-help housing (Gilbert 1999) (see also Figure 17.1).

Over the years, the government has devised a whole string of policies to improve the housing situation. These policies have been similar to those in most of Latin America. For years a state bank offered mortgages to middle-income groups for buying housing, and the government also provided a limited amount of social housing through state agencies, introduced rent control legislation and allowed most of the population to house itself in self-help shelter. Later, it strongly encouraged formal private home ownership, adopted a supply-side capital subsidy programme for the poor, did little for rental housing and began to regulate and service informal settlements.

This chapter will explain the development of Colombian housing policy. It will show that while progress has been made, no housing policy can be wholly effective in such a poor and unequal country, with a growing population and rapidly expanding cities. In addition, for decades Colombia has suffered from a great deal of civil strife and many natural disasters, principally earthquakes and floods. The result has been that the housing deficit has increased over time.

FIGURE 17.1 Bogotá: now consolidated shelter but building self-help housing on a hillside is not easy. Photo by Alan Gilbert.

A brief history of Colombian state housing intervention to 1990

Housing for the poor: The Spanish flu epidemic that struck many parts of the world between 1918 and 1920 badly affected Colombia. Frightened that this disease would spread further, the national government attempted to improve living conditions for the poor. Unfortunately, little happened in practice.

The first real effort to provide housing for the poor came with the establishment of the *Instituto de Crédito Territorial* (ICT) in 1939. During its 50-year life it built or financed some 700,000 housing solutions most of which were concentrated in the country's largest cities (Torres 1996: 61). Unusually for its time, it never built housing for rent (Laun 1977: 311). For many years, the institute was a technical leader in the social housing field in Latin America and build some quality estates (Gutiérrez Cuevas 1989: 11). However, it became increasingly obvious that its programmes were too expensive for the poor and it responded after 1958 by concentrating on sites and services, and mutual help solutions (Laun 1977: 298). Then the increasing cost of capital and building materials, perhaps combined with poor management of the self-help options, led to financial difficulties and increasing criticism from Camacol (*Cámara Colombiana de Comercio*), the construction industry's main lobby group. This conjuncture led the agency to return to building finished housing. It tried to cheapen the cost of the houses by building on the unserviced edge of cities and not paying municipal taxes, something that caused major conflicts with the planning authorities in Bogotá in 1976. Even so, by the 1970s, it was clear that few poor families had sufficient savings with which to put down a deposit for an ICT house. In response, presidential candidate Belisario Betancur came up with an apparent solution – to offer popular housing to families without a down payment. When he became president in 1982 he increased the agency's resources, and the demand for ICT housing was so great that beneficiaries had to be selected by lottery. Unfortunately for the agency, many beneficiaries did not meet their monthly repayments and, because it was politically impossible to evict them, part of each loan was turned into a subsidy. During its final 15 years, the ICT was giving subsidies worth 70 per cent of the value of the house (Giraldo 1997: 182). In 1991, the agency was declared technically bankrupt and closed down.

While the ICT was the principal social housing agency, similar kinds of agency were also operating at the municipal level. Such agencies were strengthened in 1942 when the national government encouraged local authorities to develop popular housing and authorised the Finance Ministry to lend them money to build 'model popular neighbourhoods'.

Housing for the middle classes: In 1926 three overseas mortgage companies began lending for housing but as a result of the 1929 crash, the government was forced to intervene. It set up two new institutions to offer mortgages: the *Caja de Crédito Agrario* in 1931 and the *Banco Central Hipotecario* (BCH) in 1932. The BCH raised the amount of bank lending to the building sector and helped Colombia through the world recession of the 1930s. It was the only institution to offer long-term credit and between 1968 and 1973 the BCH was responsible for three-quarters of all loans for private housing construction (Jaramillo 1982: 16). Its main failing from a societal viewpoint was that it lent only to middle- and upper-middle-class people, offering them very generous terms (Jaramillo 1985).

National governments had long understood how building homes could contribute to Colombia's economic growth and in 1970 housing became the key plank in the 'Four Strategies' plan of President Misael Pastrana Borrero. Building on the ideas of Lauchlin Currie, the plan introduced a new housing funding system, which it was hoped would generate the resources to invest massively in the construction of formal housing. Such investment would create jobs and raise land values, which could be taxed in order to finance the provision of infrastructure and services. When combined with innovative urban planning, specifically the creation of 'cities within the city', the quality of urban life would be improved. And by encouraging faster migration from the countryside it would help raise living standards in the rural areas. It was a recipe both for economic growth and for the redistribution of wealth (Currie 1961, 1982).

The government issued a decree permitting the establishment of *Corporaciones de Ahorro y Vivienda* (CAV). These would attract savings and issue mortgages at rates adjusted for inflation – *Unidad de Poder Adquisitivo Constante* (UPAC). By the late 1970s, the CAVs were responsible for two-thirds of all housing finance while the contribution of the BCH fell from 80 per cent in 1970 to 3 per cent in 1984 (Giraldo and López 1990: 24). In practice, the system failed to greatly expand housing production. The scheme also provided little in the way of finance for low-income housing because few among the poor could afford the cost of a mortgage.

The urban reform of 1989: Law 9 was supposed to provide the means through which the state could provide decent living conditions in the country's cities (Giraldo 1989). Municipalities were required to produce development plans and were given the means to obtain land on which to develop housing or public projects. New taxes were established on capital gains from property and on luxury housing, and value-added tax was extended to sales of cement. In addition, the law gave the municipalities power to expropriate, without compensation, the land of 'pirate urbanisers' (the developers of illegal settlements which they sold to families who built their own homes). Giraldo and López (1990: 30) believe it was one of the most significant pieces of legislation in the previous 25 years, providing the means 'to plan for the development of our disorganised cities' and to accelerate the pace of construction. Unfortunately, it proved very difficult to implement and few local authorities were sufficiently competent to use it properly. The result was that they failed to control the rising cost of urban land (Giraldo 1999: 89), which discouraged formal housing construction and encouraged the proliferation of self-help solutions.

The neoliberal transformation (1990–1994)

In 1990 a new government came to power promising to transform the country's development model. César Gaviria wanted to follow the lessons of Chile and Washington and his 'Pacific Revolution' aimed to liberalise trade, reform labour legislation and sweep away government controls on financial and capital markets (DNP 1991). Housing policy was reformed along neoliberal lines with the aim of suppressing the specialised housing banks and transforming the UPAC system. It gave more responsibility to the municipalities, dismantled the old state model of direct construction moving to a demand-based subsidy system and targeted government spending on the poorest section of the population (Giraldo 1997: 181). The housing programme aimed to construct 539,000 solutions between 1991 and 1994, of which 72 per cent would be 'social interest' units (DNP 1991). It would encourage private investment in the housing sector, both by offering subsidies to the poor willing to buy and through obliging the finance system to invest more in low-cost housing. In future, the state would not build homes; it would only act as a facilitator to encourage the private sector to enter the social housing field. The policy later became known across Latin America as the ABC policy, based as it was on the triple element of savings (*ahorro*), subsidy (*bono*) and credit (*crédito*) (see Figure 17.2). The bankrupt ICT was replaced by a more modest agency, *Instituto Nacional de Vivienda de Interés Social y Reforma Urbana* (INURBE), which would offer subsidies to the poor, shifting from the supply-side model followed by the ICT to a demand-led approach.

The inspiration for this shift came from the experience of Chile (Gilbert 2002, 2004). Colombia offered lower subsidies than the Chileans because it had a stronger financial sector, many more poor people to subsidise and fewer resources to dedicate to the task. Colombia also opted for a fixed subsidy, whatever the value of the social housing unit, which would encourage the poor to buy cheaper housing units. Prior savings, a key plank of the Chilean programme, were nearly ruled out because the incoming minister thought that this would exclude poor Colombians from inclusion in the subsidy programme. Eventually, however, prior savings were retained but only as one of the criteria for selection. The new programme offered subsidies to those earning less than four minimum salaries, without their own home or those whose accommodation was poorly constructed or overcrowded, lacked a title deed or was without services. The subsidy could be supplemented by UPAC-denominated mortgage loans from private lenders. The beneficiary of the subsidy decided how to use the subsidy but never received it directly.

Some 100,000 social interest units were constructed each year between 1990 and 1994 compared to only 37,000 per annum under the ICT during the 1970s, and the private sector's share of investment in social interest housing increased from nothing between 1987 and 1990 to 62 per cent (Hommes *et al.* 1994: 162). The housing subsidies were also better directed than previously, 58 per cent going to families earning up to four minimum salaries (DNP 1994b: 22).

FIGURE 17.2 ABC housing for sale in Bogotá. Photo by Alan Gilbert.

However, the programme suffered from several serious problems. First, the programme was so popular that the INURBE was overwhelmed with applications and a queue developed consisting of 150,000 families awaiting decisions (Salazar 1994: 32; Giraldo 1997: 185). Second, only 73 per cent of beneficiaries used their subsidies because: they could not afford one of the available housing solutions; they could not find a satisfactory housing solution; and/or they could not obtain a loan (DNP 1994a: 3). For many, the loan was the critical constraint because the banks did not accept applications from independent or informal sector workers and loans from the CAVs required a deposit of 30 per cent, a sum way beyond the budget of most low-income families. Third, even though cheaper upgrading and sites-and-services components had been included, few local authorities were able to provide developers with enough serviced land. As a result of these difficulties, only 6 per cent of the subsidies that were actually used went to the poorest 10 per cent; most of the subsidies went to those in the middle income bands and 8 per cent went to the richest one-fifth (Giraldo 1997).

More emphasis on the poor (1994–1998)

The Samper administration that took over in August 1994 continued to offer subsidies for social interest housing (DNP 1994a: 3). However, it also modified housing policy in several important ways. First, it promised to increase the number of beneficiaries from the 211,000 distributed between 1991 and 1994 to 500,000 over the next four years (DNP 1994a: 1). Second, it changed the procedure for selecting beneficiaries to speed up the allocation process. In future, local committees of interested parties would identify deserving communities, those where at least 70 per cent of the households were living in precarious conditions or lacking decent homes (DNP 1994a: 4).[1] Third, 82 per cent of all subsidies would be aimed at households earning less than two minimum salaries and settlement upgrading would take priority over financing new housing. Sites-and-services projects would be discontinued because it was unacceptable to offer families only a plot of land; most new solutions would take the form of 'basic units' and 'progressive housing' (DNP 1995: 134).

The Samper government considered the shortage of urban land to be a major barrier to housing the poor and gave priority to urban reform. In 1997, Congress approved Law 388, which built on its 1989 predecessor and required municipalities to create *Planes de Ordenamiento Territorial* (POTs) which would establish long-term goals for urban development. It also laid down ways through which the state could oblige landowners to use their land for social purposes.

The succeeding government was blunt in its evaluation of Samper's programme. It had relied far too much on settlement upgrading (DNP 1998: 524) and had neglected the provision of cheap housing units for the poor. The shortage of urbanised land and the excessively complicated and slow process of issuing building licences had slowed construction (Budinich et al. 1999: 5). It also noted how poor families had had great difficulty in obtaining credit. Samper's attempt to allocate more subsidies through collective application processes was badly flawed by fraudulent claims and clientelism (Cárdenas et al. 1999).

Responding to disaster and economic crisis (1998–2002)

President Andrés Pastrana wanted to revive the economy and bring peace to a highly unequal and violent country. The government's housing programme aimed to increase long-term financing opportunities, to improve the poor's access to credit, alleviate the housing debt problem and generate jobs through the construction programme. However, four major factors complicated implementation during the government's term in office: the Asian financial crisis of 1997, which hurt the national economy and increased poverty; the increase in guerrilla activity; the earthquake that hit the coffee zone on 25 January 1999, and left around 250,000 people homeless; and a surprising decision by the country's Constitutional Court that led to the demise of the UPAC system (see below).

The government promised to deliver 420,000 social housing units of which 242,000 would be subsidised. The emphasis would be on formal sector construction, and the previous government's emphasis on urban upgrading was abandoned. The government reintroduced the prior savings requirement, dropped by the previous administration, on the grounds that prior savings encouraged families to contribute to their own housing solution and helped them obtain credit (DNP 1998: 525). To compensate for this change very poor families would be eligible for a double subsidy: local governments or non-governmental organisations would contribute an additional 10–20 per cent to families who lacked savings or access to credit (Budinich et al.1999: 23).

The new eligibility criteria were certainly more transparent and better focused, with 75 per cent of beneficiary households falling into the bottom three deciles of the income distribution (Ministerio de Hacienda et al. 2002: 19). However, the high priority given to women-headed households created a problem insofar as an astounding 62 per cent of all INURBE subsidies went to this group (Budinich et al. 1999: 91, 95).

The savings requirement was effective in encouraging large numbers of people to save and, by January 2002, 630,000 accounts had been opened (Ministerio de Hacienda et al. 2002). However, the growth in savings accounts encouraged larger numbers to apply for subsidies and the system could not cope; one newspaper claimed that 'one hundred thousand families were chasing 3,300 subsidies' (*El Tiempo* 2000a). The number of subsidies allocated during this period was actually lower than that assigned during the previous administration.

If the pace at which subsidies were being delivered was widely criticised, so too was the poor quality of so many of the social housing units being produced. A subsequent report claimed that some 15,000 social housing units had such severe structural problems that they might have to be demolished (*Semana* 2005). Questions were also raised about the destination of the subsidised homes. A survey conducted in late 2001 found that only 38 per cent of households were occupying the house for which they had obtained a subsidy, 37 per cent of the subsidised houses were empty and 15 per cent were being rented to other families (Ministerio de Desarrollo Económico y DNP 2002: 9).

Over and above the problems facing the subsidy programme, the government was confronted by a major crisis in the wider housing finance system. The neoliberal reforms of 1990, and the efforts to make the financial sector more competitive, had put the UPAC system under increasing pressure. To allow the CAVs to compete against the ordinary banks, the basis for calculating savings and mortgage repayments was tied increasingly to the short-term deposit rate (DTF), rather than to consumer prices (Urrutia-Montoya and Namen-León 2011). While these modifications sustained the system for a while, they undermined the long-term nature of UPAC lending (Giraldo and López 1990; Mutis-Caballero 1997: 8; Echeverry *et al.* 1999: 2). The system's fragility was finally exposed in 1997 when the authorities decided to increase interest rates rapidly so as to sustain the external value of the *peso*. Rising interest rates raised the cost of UPAC mortgages and hit borrowers just when house prices had begun to fall rapidly. By the end of 1998, 140,000 out of 800,000 mortgage borrowers surrendered their units because they could not afford their monthly payments (Persaud and Ortíz 2003: 339).

The crisis threatened to bring down the whole financial system and was only partially resolved in 1999 by compensating middle-income families in default on their mortgage payments. Nevertheless, several institutions went out of business and those that survived became ordinary banks.

The UPAC system came to an end in 1998 when the Constitutional Court decreed that it was unconstitutional to tie mortgage rates to the DTF rather than to consumer prices. In June 2000, the government was forced to create the *Unidad de Valor Real* (UVR), which tied future rises in mortgage rates to the consumer price index. Urrutia-Montoya and Namen-León (2011: 19) argue that the Court's decision was made on political grounds and, while it saved many debtors from losing their homes, it damaged the banks and cut the supply of mortgage credit for years to come (*Semana* 2001). It was also very costly for the government, which was now responsible for paying the difference between the UVR rate and the UPAC rate up to US$50,000 per loan. Persaud and Ortíz (2003: 339) claim that debt relief for some 800,000 families eventually cost about US$1.8 billion. Serrano (2011: 65) also claims that the UVR system has failed for while the value of mortgages issued in pesos more than tripled between 2007 and June 2011, the value of UVR-based mortgages fell by 25 per cent.

Towards a nation of homeowners (2002–2010)

Like most of his predecessors, President Alvaro Uribe wanted to improve the distribution of income, accelerate the pace of economic growth and protect the most vulnerable groups in society (DNP 2003). A key component of his national plan was to increase the rate of home ownership, a goal that was to be achieved through greater emphasis on subsidised social housing, protecting the middle class through the issue of UVR loans, and continuing to offer tax relief to savers through *Cuentas de ahorro para el fomento de la construcción* (AFCs) (MAVDT 2004).[2] The INURBE was wound up on the grounds that it was inefficient and arguably corrupt. The *Fondo Nacional de Vivienda* (FONVIVIENDA) was created to take over some of the INURBE's responsibilities and the *Cajas de Compensación Familiar* (CCFs) were given more responsibility for recommending households for subsidies.

A target of 400,000 social housing units was set and the number of the subsidies to be distributed was reduced. The new approach was widely criticised, especially when in March 2004 the government cut the subsidy from 23 minimum salaries to 17, the equivalent of US$740 (Navarro-Wolf 2004: 44; *El Tiempo* 2005). The cut would allow benefits to be distributed to a larger number of poor families but critics complained that as a result the poor had neither the savings nor sufficient access to credit to buy social housing. The main CCFs soon reported a large fall in applications and the government was forced to raise the value of the subsidy available to affiliates of the CCFs and to allow independent workers to apply for subsidies.

The limited availability and cost of credit continued to be a problem throughout the administration, although it did manage to increase the allocation of subsidies and more or less achieved its target of providing 400,000 social housing units. However, it failed to eliminate the large number of fraudulent applications and a later evaluation revealed that only one-third of the interviewees were actually living in the house acquired through the subsidy (DNP 2007b: 27).

Alvaro Uribe was re-elected in 2006. The housing programme remained largely unchanged and aimed to prevent the formation of new informal settlements, to upgrade existing marginal areas, to increase the role of the private sector in financing housing and to encourage the development of an efficient and competitive building sector. The main change was a promise to deliver 828,000 social housing 'solutions' – albeit only 400,000 as subsidised units, the rest a mixture of distributing legal titles (323,000) and providing loans (104,000) (DNP 2007a: 186).

The distribution of subsidies was improved but the programme was hampered by the fact that less than two-thirds of FONVIVIENDA subsidies were actually taken up (Pinto 2010). The explanations for this were familiar: the subsidy was too small, the two-year period to take up the subsidy was too short, the house did not meet expectations or was not built in time and, of course, the beneficiaries' lack of resources to support a loan (Pinto 2010). The consequence of the failure to distribute the subsidies was made worse by the arrival of increasing numbers of displaced people in the major cities. By 2010, around 3.5 million people had fled from the violence in the countryside (Acción Social 2011). These people had already become a matter of real concern and 70 per cent of FNA subsidies were being directed to these families. This was also a belated response to the Constitutional Court's decision in 2004 which declared that the government had a duty to provide housing subsidies to this group (Chirivi *et al.* 2010).

The economic recession that hit the country in 2009 did not help. Bank lending plummeted and the rate of housing construction only picked up when the government agreed to subsidise the mortgage interest rate (Uribe 2011). A further problem facing the housing programme was the shortage of serviced land. Builders claimed that the local authorities were often slow in approving projects, less than efficient in servicing the land and sometimes demanded bribes. The government attempted to address that problem in 2007 through establishing 'macro projects' for social housing in any part of the country. The law allowed the central government to expropriate land without consulting the local authorities (*El Tiempo* 2007; MAVDT 2008). Several schemes were established in a number of major cities but, in

2010, the Constitutional Court decreed that urban planning was a local responsibility and the nation state was prohibited from overriding the local authorities.

Prosperity for all (2010–2014)

President Manuel Santos's national plan, 'More employment, less poverty and more security', was similar to many earlier plans although it was much more optimistic about the future, something permitted by rising world prices for the country's exports and increasing inflows of foreign direct investment. Housing, along with mining, agriculture, infrastructure and innovation, was one of the five 'locomotives' that the government hoped would drive the economy. And, to demonstrate the importance of the sector, a new Ministry of Housing, City and Territory was created. One million new homes would be built, 80 per cent more than during the previous administration. The supply of social housing would be increased through the implementation of 'second generation macro-projects'. To stimulate demand, the temporary device of subsidising the interest rate was continued; a measure that was considered to have been so successful that funding was doubled (*Viva Real* 2010).

The government planned to give out 500,000 subsidies; 300,000 through the FONVIVIENDA and the rest through the CCFs. The number of subsidies being disbursed was increased to help deal with the increasing numbers of displaced people. To add to those displaced by violence, some half a million were made homeless by the disastrous floods that hit the country towards the end of 2010 (DNP 2011: 419).

The government was well aware that too few of the assigned housing subsidies were ever used and announced a whole range of measures to improve take-up. These included widening the voluntary savings programme to include new groups, strengthening microfinance institutions, increasing access of independent workers to credit and introducing an unemployment insurance scheme. Perhaps the most significant innovation was that subsidies would be approved only when a family had obtained mortgage finance. However, it was doubtful whether this would overcome the principal problem facing poor households: how to marshal the savings to put down a deposit and thereby obtain a mortgage (Pinto 2010). Perhaps that was why in April 2012, the government announced a radically new approach. The 1.3 million Colombian households classified as being extremely poor would be entitled to apply for one of 100,000 homes that would be available free from July 2013. The programme will cost US$224 million and will be financed from the increasing tax returns being generated by the buoyant economy. How the beneficiaries will be selected is still not clear but is likely to incorporate a lottery system. While many observers have applauded the initiative, and Congress approved the measure unanimously, the measure worries many others (Gilbert 2014; Giraldo 2012; Molina 2012; *Semana* 2012). First, because there are so many very poor families only one in 13 will obtain a free home. Second, the government will select the builders and given the low price, the quality of construction may well be poor. Third, the failings of the mass popular building schemes in Brazil and Mexico may be repeated – lots of homes being constructed in areas far from places of work and lacking adequate public services. Fourth, giving the very poor their own home runs the risk that the beneficiaries will be unable to pay for the costs of public services and maintenance. Fifth, it is unclear how this programme will affect the standard ABC system. Finally, many fear that the programme is too populist, motivated by the wish of the president to gain support for his bid to win re-election in 2014.

Reflections on Colombian housing policy

The housing deficit: The authorities in Colombia regularly publish figures about the size of the housing task facing them. Unfortunately, this task seems to be getting stiffer; between 1973 and 2010 the housing deficit increased from 2.2 to 3.8 million (Gaitán and Piraquive 1990; Pinto 2010). Admittedly the housing deficit fell from 75 to 36 per cent of the country's households, mostly due to a reduction in the qualitative deficit, the result of improving access to public services. However, if Pecha-Garzón (2011: 45) is correct in estimating that it will take 102 years to eliminate Colombia's housing deficit, it suggests that either the government's approach is misguided or, given the extent of poverty and inequality, eliminating the housing deficit is an impossible task.

Improved servicing: Over the years the quality of servicing in Colombia has improved markedly. Between 1985 and 2005, for example, access to potable water improved from 58 per cent to 83 per cent and sewerage connection from 47 to 63 per cent. Such progress represents a major step forward in improving housing conditions – and the current government intends to maintain recent progress by bringing water to 2.8 million more people and sewerage to a further 4.5 million (Mora 2011). This appears to be a more effective and probably cheaper route to improving housing conditions than building more *Vivienda de Interés Social* (VIS) and *Vivienda de Interés Prioritario* (VIP) units.

Subsidy and credit: Mortgage lending as a proportion of gross domestic product in Colombia is low by international standards (Torres 2011: 308). Given that 60 per cent of Colombian households in 2008 earned less than 2.5 minimum salaries and 80 per cent of the population spent more each month than they earned, only a minority of Colombians are able to save for a deposit on a house (Pinto 2010). As such, any subsidy policy that relies on savings and loans is bound to fall short. The current government has clearly accepted that logic in offering free homes to some of the poor.

Housing tenure: A long-established goal of housing policy in Colombia has been to turn every family into a homeowner. However, the high cost of housing in the big cities means that the policy has been less than successful; home ownership rose from 53 per cent in 1973 to 64 per cent in 1993 only to fall to 54 per cent in 2005 (*El Tiempo* 2004). Despite this inconvenient fact, no government has done much to develop a rental housing policy. The rental housing law of 2003 failed to generate much more commercial investment and the only help given to tenants in recent years has been to offer displaced families a short-term rental subsidy.

Land: Despite the optimism generated by the two urban reform laws, they have failed to match expectation (Fique Pinto 2006: 105). Betterment taxes are thin on the ground and in most parts of the country property taxes are too low. At least some effort is now being made to accelerate the supply of serviced land through the development of macro-projects, even if this approach worries many local housing experts. In Bogotá, the authorities created a land bank, Metrovivienda, which has had some success but which has failed to produce serviced land in sufficient quantities (Gilbert 2009).

The quality of social housing: Over the years there have been consistent complaints about the quality of social housing. Some homes have had structural faults and some projects have been built in environmentally risky areas or on unstable land (*El Tiempo* 2000b). In cities like Bogotá where land prices are so high, social housing has sometimes been built illegally, on lots as small as 21 square metres (Mora 2008). Many of the homes have been poorly designed and most have offered very little in the way of space (Tarchópulos and Ceballos 2003: 48; Maldonado

FIGURE 17.3 Not much space in ABC housing for sale in Bogotá. Photo by Alan Gilbert.

2003: 8; Ballén 2009: 163). The benefits of living in a 36-square-metre apartment on the sixth floor of a block with no lift have to be questioned (see Figure 17.3). With the introduction of a free housing programme this kind of problem may become worse.

Conclusion

Over the past two or three decades a succession of Colombian governments have used housing to stimulate economic growth and reduce the level of unemployment. While this has worked to a degree, policy has seldom acted anti-cyclically and the country has suffered from a series of housing booms and slumps. Constant tinkering with the credit and the subsidy systems suggests that something is wrong with the model.

The aim of creating a nation of homeowners has been flawed. Homeowners have benefited through tax rebates, cheap credit and subsidies, but it has been the better off who have gained most from the system. Colombia's efforts to provide social housing through a combination of subsidies and credit have been simplistic. Most of the problems stem from a simple problematic equation: too many Colombians are too poor to buy their own formal house even when they receive a subsidy. Constructors faced with a shortage of serviced land and sometimes using less than efficient building methods cannot provide decent housing at the price specified by the government. If there is one lesson across the world about housing, it is that if you build cheaply you are likely to obtain a poor product. This has unfortunate knock-on effects on everyone – inhabitants, constructors and the state. The current government's plan to give houses to 100,000 very poor families may worsen this problem as well as creating new ones: how best to select the beneficiaries and how to avoid the creation of social ghettoes as has occurred in Chile (Rodríguez and Sugranyes 2011).

Ultimately, much depends on the state's willingness to give higher priority to housing. While the Colombian constitution decrees that housing is a human right, unlike liberty or security, it is regarded as 'a second generation right'. This lower constitutional priority is reflected in the government's traditionally low expenditure on housing. Between 1995 and 2006 spending on INURBE-FONVIVIENDA subsidies, as a proportion of total government investment, averaged 1.77 per cent and only once exceeded 2 per cent (Pecha-Garzón 2011: 27). The current government has reacted by increasing spending substantially; we will have to wait to see how successful that strategy will prove.

But perhaps the Colombian state should proceed in a different direction. If it really wishes to help the poorest it might be advised to help them in other ways: by supplementing their income, providing better health care or offering wholly free education to their children. It should certainly not assume that every family at a given point in time either needs or wants to be a homeowner and it should think about expanding the supply of rental housing to accommodate the young, migrant and temporarily employed households that are in no position to buy.

This critical conclusion is not meant to suggest that Colombia has got everything wrong. Its housing policy is certainly superior to that of many of its neighbours and the quality of its housing stock has improved over time. Indeed, the efforts to improve the quality of servicing and infrastructure have been impressive, and particularly so in Bogotá and Medellín. While it has failed to reduce the housing deficit, shelter conditions have certainly not deteriorated. And, because poverty in the country has been declining that is bound to help improve housing conditions in the future.

Notes

1 The problem of the 127,000 housing queue was resolved somewhat arbitrarily in January 1995 by stopping any more families applying directly for subsidies.
2 The government also made an ineffective effort to encourage the private sector to produce housing for rent, and the *Ley de Arriendos* was introduced in June 2003 under pressure from the building and real-estate lobbies.

References

Acción Social (2011) Registro único de población desplazada, SAPD. Online. Available at www.accionsocial.gov.co/Estadisticas/SI_266_Informacion%20PAG%20WEB%20(4-08-2010)%20ver%202. htm (accessed 15 August 2011).
Ballén, S.A. (2009) *Vivienda social en altura: tipologías urbanas y directrices de producción en Bogotá*, Universidad Nacional. Online. Available at www.facartes.unal.edu.co/otros/tesis_habitat/vivienda_social_altura. pdf (accessed 15 August 2011).
Budinich, E., Contrucci, P., Paúl, L.H. and Ubilla, R. (1999) 'Informe final: Programa de vivienda de interés social; Política de vivienda urbana período 1999–2002 Colombia', 20 October (mimeo).
Cárdenas, R.E., Escobar, D., Pedraza, B. and Zapata, J.G. (1999) *Pobreza y vivienda de interés social en Colombia: los programas de vivienda urbana de la Red de Solidaridad Social*. Bogotá: Ediciones Uniandes.
Chirivi, E., García, D. and Montoya, V. (2010) '¿Y dónde están los subsidios? Un balance sobre el subsidio familiar de vivienda en Colombia', *Informe Económico* 25, Camacol.
Currie, L.L. (1961) *Operación Colombia: un programa nacional de desarrollo económico y Social*. Bogotá: Departamento Administrativo de Planeación y Servicios Técnicos.

Currie, L.L. (1982) 'La política de vivienda', *Desarrollo y Socieda*, 4: 3–9.
DANE (2012) *Encuesta Nacional de Calidad de Vida 2011*. Bogotá: Departamento Nacional de Estadística.
DNP (1991) *La Revolución Pacífica*. Santafé de Bogotá.
DNP (1994a) 'Política de vivienda social urbana', Consejo Nacional de Política Económica y Social (CONPES), Documento 2729.
DNP (1994b) 'La Revolución Pacífica: programa de vivienda', *Revista Camacol*, 58: 20–27.
DNP (1995) *El Salto Social: Plan Nacional de Desarrollo: ley de inversiones 1994–1998*. Santafé de Bogotá: DNP.
DNP (1998) *Cambio para Construir la Paz: Plan Nacional de Desarrollo 1998–2002: síntesis*. Bogotá: DNP.
DNP (2003) *Hacia un Estado Comunitario: Plan Nacional de Desarrollo 2002–2006*. Bogotá: DNP.
DNP (2007a) *Estado Comunitario: desarrollo para todos, Plan Nacional de Desarrollo 2006–2010*. Bogotá: DNP.
DNP (2007b) *Programa de Vivienda de Interés Social Urbana: Impactos en la calidad de vida y evaluación del proceso de focalización*. Bogotá: DNP.
DNP (2011) *Plan Nacional de Desarrollo 2010–2014: Vivienda y ciudades amables*. Bogotá: DNP.
Echeverry, J.C., Gracia, O. and Urdinola, B.P. (1999) 'Upac: evolución y crisis de un modelo de desarrollo', *DNP Archivos de Macroeconomía*, Documento 128.
El Tiempo (2000a) 'Subsidios para VIS en 30 días', 1 April.
El Tiempo (2000b) 'Grietas en vivienda social', 24 August.
El Tiempo (2004) 'Ahora hay menos colombianos con vivienda propia', 5 August.
El Tiempo (2005) 'Editorial: Y del techito, nada', 26 June.
El Tiempo (2007) 'Programa de macroproyectos permitirá expropiar lotes y construir vivienda social', 26 June.
Fique Pinto, L.F. (2006) *Vivienda social en Colombia: políticas públicas y habitabilidad en los años noventa*. Bogotá: Universidad Nacional de Colombia.
Florián, A. (2011) '¿Para donde vamos en vivienda social?', *Razón Pública*, 29 August.
Gaitán, F. and Piraquive, G. (1990) 'Indicadores de déficit cuantitativo y cualitativo', *Revista Camacol*, 45: 41–52.
Gilbert, A.G. (1981) 'Pirates and invaders: land acquisition in urban Colombia and Venezuela', *World Development*, 9: 657–678.
Gilbert, A.G. (1999) 'A home is for ever? Residential mobility and home ownership in self-help settlements', *Environment and Planning A*, 31: 1073–1091.
Gilbert, A.G. (2002) 'Power, ideology and the Washington Consensus: the development and spread of Chilean housing policy', *Housing Studies*, 17: 305–324.
Gilbert, A.G. (2004) 'Learning from others: the spread of capital housing subsidies', *International Planning Studies*, 9: 197–216.
Gilbert, A.G. (2009) 'The rise (and fall?) of a state land bank', *Habitat International*, 33: 425–435.
Gilbert, A.G. (2014) 'Free housing for the poor: an effective way to address poverty?', *Habitat International*, 41: 253–261.
Giraldo, F. (ed.) (1989) *Reforma urbana y desarrollo social*. Bogotá: Camacol.
Giraldo, F. (1997) 'Las políticas de vivienda en los noventa', *Desarrollo Urbano en Cifras*, 3: 177–229.
Giraldo, F. (1999) *Ciudad y crisis: hacia un nuevo paradigma?* Bogotá: Tercer Mundo Editores.
Giraldo, F. (2012) 'El nuevo plan de vivienda "gratis": la apuesta de Santos y Vargas Lleras', *Razón Pública*, 6 May.
Giraldo, F. and López, H.F. (1990) 'Los ciclos de la edificación en Colombia: 1950–1990', *Revista Camacol*, 44: 10–38.
Gutiérrez Cuevas, C. (1989) 'ICT: 50 años cumpliendo con Colombia', *Revista Camacol*, 39: 10–22.
Hommes, R., Montenegro, A. and Roda, P. (eds) (1994) *Una apertura hacia el futuro: balance económico 1990–1994*. Bogotá: Ministerio de Hacienda y Crédito Público and Departamento Nacional de Planeación.
Jaramillo, S. (1982) 'La política de vivienda en Colombia ¿hacia una redefinición de sus objetivos?', *Desarrollo y Sociedad*, 4: 11–26.

Jaramillo, S. (1985) 'Entre el UPAC y la autoconstrucción: comentarios y sugerencias a la política de vivienda', *Controversia*, 123–124, Bogotá: CINEP.

Laun, J.I. (1977) 'El estado y la vivienda en Colombia: análisis de urbanizaciones del Instituto de Crédito Territorial en Bogotá', in C. Castillo (ed.) *Vida urbana y urbanismo*. Bogotá: Instituto Colombiano de Cultura.

Maldonado, M.M. (2003) '*Al encuentro social y urbano'*, *U.N. Periódico* 53, Bogotá: Universidad Nacional.

MAVDT (Ministerio de Ambiente, Vivienda y Desarrollo Territorial) (2004) *Camino hacia un País de propietarios con desarrollo sostenible – Plan Sectorial 2002–2006*. Bogotá: MAVDT.

MAVDT (Ministerio de Ambiente, Vivienda y Desarrollo Territorial) (2008) *Macroproyectos: Paso histórico en Vivienda de Interés Social*, 30 November. Online. Available at www.minambiente.gov.co/contenido/contenido.aspx?conID=2910&catID=818 (accessed 23 August 2012).

Ministerio de Desarrollo Económico y DNP (2002) *Evaluación del programa de subsidio familiar de vivienda de interés social, 1999–2002*, CONPES 3178, 15 July 2002.

Ministerio de Hacienda y Crédito Público, Ministerio de Desarrollo Económico y DNP (2002) *Bases de la política de vivienda 2002–2006: ajustes al programa de subsidio familiar de vivienda e incentives de oferta y demanda para créditos de vivienda en UVRS*, Documento CONPES 3200, 30 September 2002.

Molina, I. (2012) 'Vivienda gratuita para pobres: ¿Continuidad o ruptura en la política?', *Razón Pública*, 29 April.

Mora, C.P. (2011) 'La Prosperidad Democrática a través de agua y saneamiento para los más pobres: Los retos del cuatrienio', Presentación al XIII Congreso Nacional de Andesco, Medellin, 22–24 June.

Mora, I.M. (2008) 'Ni espacio para caminar queda en Viviendas de Interés Social porque sus medidas no son las de ley', *El Tiempo*, 19 April.

Mutis-Caballero, S. (1997) 'Los créditos de vivienda a 30 años', *El Tiempo*, 5 July.

Navarro-Wolf, A. (2004) 'VIS ceversa', *Cambio*, 6 September.

Pecha-Garzón, C. (2011) *Programa de Vivienda de Interés Social de Colombia: Una Evaluación*, Oficina de Evaluación y Supervisión, Banco Interamericano de Desarrollo.

Persaud, T. and Ortíz, A. (2003) 'Urban development', in M.M. Giugale, O. Lafourcade and C. Luff (eds), *Colombia: The Economic Foundation of Peace*. Washington, DC: World Bank.

Pinto, M.E. (2010) 'Propuestas para la nueva política habitacional', II Foro de Vivienda, ASOBANCARIA, 3 de diciembre.

Rodríguez, A. and Sugranyes, A. (2011) 'Vivienda privada de ciudad', *Revista de Ingeniería*, 35: 100–107.

Salazar, S.E. (1994) 'Vivienda social', *Revista Camacol*, 61: 28–32.

Semana (2001) 'Aquí quién manda?', 16 August.

Semana (2005) 'La casa en el aire', 30 April.

Semana (2012) 'El plan es Germán', 28 April.

Serrano, J. (2011) 'Financiamiento para la adquisición de vivienda, presentation to the fórum on "La vivienda en América Latina: revisando estrategias"', Bogotá: Universidad de los Andes, 13 October.

Tarchópulos, D. and Ceballos, O.L. (2003) *La calidad de la vivienda dirigida a los sectores de bajos ingresos en Bogotá*. Bogotá: Central Editorial Javeriano.

Torres, J.E. (1996) 'Colombia: estudio de caso programa de subsidios a la damanda de vivienda', in F. Conway, M. Michelsons, M. Valera and J.E. Torres (eds) *A Review of Demand Side Housing Subsidy Programs: The Case of Latin America*. Washington, DC: The Urban Institute.

Torres, J.E. (2011) 'Estudio sobre el mercado de arrendamiento de vivienda en Colombia: informe final', Bogotá (mimeo).

Uribe, J.D. (2011) 'Informe de política monetaria y rendición de cuentas', Banco de la República, 1 August.

Urrutia-Montoya, M. and Namen-León, O.M. (2011) 'Historia del crédito hipotecario en Colombia', *Documentos CEDE* 008729, Universidad de los Andes.

Viva Real (2010) 'Vivienda, una de las prioridades del gobierno de Santos', 28 June.

18
INCREMENTAL HOUSING IN PERU AND THE ROLE OF THE SOCIAL HOUSING SECTOR

Ana María Fernández-Maldonado

Abbreviations

ABC (scheme)	Ahorro-Bono-Crédito; Savings-Subsidy-Credit
Banmat	Banco de Materiales; Construction Materials Bank
BFH	Bono Familiar Habitacional; Housing Family Subsidy
CAPECO	Cámara Peruana de la Construcción; Peruvian Chamber of Construction
COFOPRI	Commission for the Official Registration of Informal Property
CONFIEP	Confederación de Empresarios del Perú; Peruvian Federation of Entrepreneurs
FMV	Fondo Mivivienda; Mivivienda Fund
FONAVI	Fondo Nacional de Vivienda; National Housing Fund
PNV	Plan Nacional de Vivienda; National Housing Plan

Introduction

Since the mid-1950s, rapid urbanization processes have skewed urban development in Peruvian cities. On one hand, since the Peruvian state was hardly involved in housing supply, the 'formal' development process was led by the real-estate market and mainly based on land speculation. On the other hand, stimulated by permissive national policies, the massive and 'informal' development of peripheral areas was led by poor settlers. This has produced a centre–periphery urban structure in which the conventionally built central districts are surrounded by large extensions of substandard housing areas. This informal pattern of urban development causes great economic disadvantages to the city in the long term; it is now known that it is more economical to prevent informal settlements than to upgrade them (Bouillon 2012).

Consequently, after Nicaragua and Bolivia, Peru has the third largest housing deficit in Latin America (Bouillon 2012). Figures from the 2007 Census of Population and Housing (INEI 2008) show that the total housing deficit increased by 82 per cent since the previous 1993 census – from 1.02 to 1.86 million homes at the national level. Table 18.1 shows that while the quantitative deficit decreased slightly, the qualitative deficit increased by 135 per

TABLE 18.1 Peruvian housing deficit according to the national census of 1993 and 2007

	Quantitative deficit	Qualitative deficit	Total
1993 census	397,756	624,427	1,022,183
2007 census	389,745	1,470,947	1,860,692

Source: INEI (2008); Rojas (2011).

cent, suggesting the prominence of *autoconstrucción* (literally, self-construction). In this text, we refer to this phenomenon as incremental housing.

Since 2003, the Peruvian housing sector has experienced a growing dynamism triggered in part by a housing reform which established programmes and finance mechanisms to assist the poor as well as increase the supply of affordable housing. While the housing programmes have delivered more new homes than ever before, the reforms are still not sufficient to resolve the huge housing deficit. In fact, the supply is not even enough to tackle the annual demand coming from newly formed households (Fernández-Maldonado and Bredenoord 2010). As a result, two out of three new homes in Peru are still built through incremental housing schemes (BBVA Research 2011).

The main objective of this chapter is to discuss the role and position of incremental housing within Peruvian housing policies as well as the achievements and limitations of these policies. The main questions guiding this inquiry are: To what extent are the current policies useful in overcoming the existing housing deficit? Which programmes or schemes address incremental housing within current policies? What are the main housing policy achievements and limitations regarding the housing conditions of the poor? The methods used to answer these questions are both quantitative and qualitative. As is usual in developing countries, the former have methodological limitations. Nonetheless they provide useful insight into the main trends and features.

The chapter is organized into four sections. The first section describes the singularities of incremental housing processes in Peru. The next two sections present the main features of the Peruvian social housing system as well as examining the main outcomes of almost ten years of social housing programmes within two different periods corresponding to the Toledo and García administrations. The last section discusses the main achievements and challenges facing the current social housing system in effectively providing affordable housing to the poor.

Incremental housing in Peru

Barriadas are areas that exhibit an informal, reversed process of urban development: households settle on the land before it is developed, after which basic services are deployed and the dwellings are built (Figure 18.1 illustrates the difference between conventional and informal ways of urban development). Within *barriadas*, each household is in charge of the construction of its own dwelling; this process is called *autoconstrucción*[1] in Peru. By providing technical support to settlers of peripheral *barriadas* since their origins in the mid-1950s, Peruvian authorities were pioneers in assisting housing processes.

In several Latin American countries, rapid urbanization resulted from a huge migration stream due in part to processes related to the demographic transition. In Peru, thousands of migrants from the Andes, attracted by the incipient process of industrialization taking place

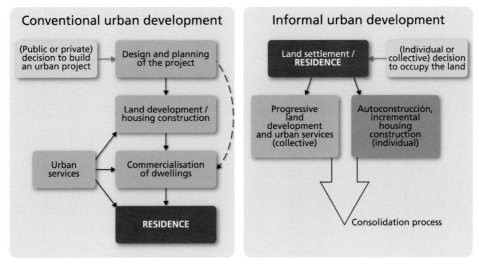

FIGURE 18.1 Conventional and informal ways of urban development.

in cities, left the countryside. This was especially the case in Lima, where peripheral *barriadas* developed faster and more extensively than in any other Latin American city.

These processes would inspire Turner's self-help approach. Turner (1968) claimed that supporting progressive housing processes, as Peruvian authorities did, was a more realistic way to tackle the housing deficit in poor countries. Arguing that the poor prefer large unfinished dwellings which can be gradually enlarged and improved (rather than the standard, finished units offered by conventional projects), he concluded that Peruvian squatters had followed the most appropriate housing strategy. By building progressively and according to their circumstances, squatters could save up to 50 per cent of the total housing costs (see Figure 18.2).

In February 1961, the Peruvian government passed a pioneer policy which recognized the legal status of existing informal settlements. The aim of the policy was to integrate existing *barriadas* into the city by means of incremental housing whereby the physical improvement and the legalization of *barriadas* were coupled in a process called 'physical and legal regularization'. The process began by legalizing the settlement, a crucial step towards providing collective tenure security and encouraging home improvement investments. Next, basic services such as roads, electricity, water and sewerage were delivered. In the final stages of integration residents received property titles (Riofrío 1991).

During the 1960s and 1970s, *barriadas* expanded hugely and became the most common form of urban development in Lima and other Peruvian cities, although the commitment of successive governments towards technical assistance varied greatly. During the 1970s, assisted self-help was promoted heavily by the government. This stimulated neighbourhood upgrading, providing connection to basic services and roads. In 1971, an innovative type of *barriada* was born in Lima, Villa El Salvador, in which both the government and the organized population played important roles in settlement development.

In 1979, a National Housing Fund (FONAVI) was established to fund national housing programmes through the mandatory contributions from the salary of all workers. However, its creation did not lead to the actual construction of new homes for low-income households as in other Latin American countries. FONAVI contributed to assisted self-help by funding the

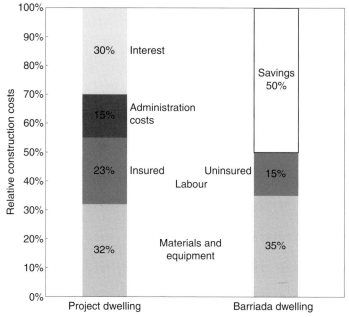

FIGURE 18.2 Relative construction costs of a project dwelling and a *barriada* dwelling.
Source: Mangin and Turner (1968).

Banco de Materiales (Banmat), created in 1980 as a revolving fund to provide low-interest-rate loans on building materials. Since 1985, however, FONAVI has been used for other objectives than housing, becoming a tax rather than a contribution[2] (Calderón 2005).

The situation in Peru in the 1980s was very unsettling. Hyperinflation led to widespread poverty and unemployment while terrorist groups gradually took control of a great part of the country's territory through political insurgency. As political violence escalated, the economic recession worsened; a vicious circle of poverty and violence paralysed the economy. Public support to *barriadas* halted.

To break the economic deadlock, a shock therapy of privatization and liberalization processes was applied in July 1990. This was framed within a set of political measures aimed at reducing the state's role in most social and economic sectors. As a result, the state withdrew from the housing sector in 1992 when the Ministry of Housing, the Central Mortgage Bank, the Housing Bank, housing cooperatives and public programmes for land delivery were dismantled (Ministerio de Vivienda 2006b). Housing was accorded lower priority in the allocation of resources and the right to adequate housing was removed from the constitution during its 1993 revision (Fernández-Maldonado 2010).

In 1996, a national programme to provide property titles to residents of informal settlements was established according to De Soto's ideas. Called COFOPRI (Commission for the Official Registration of Informal Property), it was assumed that regularizing property would facilitate the integration of both formal and informal housing markets into a citywide real-estate market. COFOPRI, considered the world's largest programme of its type and a model to other countries, granted more than 1.8 million land titles up to 2009, mostly in Lima. However, designed merely as a legal process, COFOPRI has been completely divorced from housing improvement and neighbourhood upgrading housing policies (Calderón 2009b).[3]

In 1999, the government established the Mivivienda Fund (Fondo Mivivienda, or FMV) with an initial capital of US$514 million left over from the liquidation of FONAVI (UN-Habitat 2008). Its purpose was to help finance the acquisition of affordable homes (with values of less than US$30,000) for households who could not afford mortgage credit. During the first two years, FMV granted only 548 loans.

The new social housing policy

In July 2001, the new government made a complete turnaround from the neglectful attitude of the Fujimori government towards housing issues. The Ministry of Housing was re-established and the government elaborated a new housing policy according to the recommendations of the World Bank and the Inter-American Development Bank, following the principles of Chilean housing policy. This policy was also implemented in Colombia, Costa Rica, Mexico and Brazil. The reform was based on the so-called ABC scheme, which refers to the three keywords of the financial scheme: Ahorro-Bono-Crédito (Savings-Subsidy-Credit). To purchase a house under this scheme, a household first makes a down payment with its own savings (*ahorro*). Next, the household receives the subsidy (*bono*). Finally, the household receives credit from a financial institution (*crédito*) to finance the rest of the debt. In this way, private construction firms could produce affordable housing while the state would provide direct subsidies to assist the poor.

FMV and Banmat were appointed as the main institutions of the housing sector. FMV organizes housing supply through commercial banks whereby the state subsidizes the interest rate to bring it under market level. For households that did not qualify for bank credit, Banmat offered (public) credit for new homes and for self-help activities.

FMV has two main programmes: Mivivienda Credit and Techo Propio. The first one targets middle-class households while the latter targets low-income households. Under these programmes, the household makes an initial down payment of 10 per cent of the value of the house with its own savings. Next, the household is awarded a subsidy after which it receives credit from a financial institution. The amount of the subsidy – called the Bono Familiar Habitacional (Housing Family Subsidy or BFH) – varies according to the programme or construction type (Fernández-Maldonado and Bredenoord 2010).

The policy was initially implemented through a National Housing Plan (PNV) (2003–2007), which established different social housing programmes for segments of the population unable to afford a home through a commercial bank mortgage. While the government organized the scheme, the private sector was to be the engine of the system, responsible for organizing the majority of activities involved in the production of new homes. Figure 18.3[4] illustrates the public and private sector roles in each phase of the housing production chain as specified by Mivivienda's director.[5]

In view of the programme's poor results, local critics argue that this policy was not intended to meet the housing needs of the poor. It instead had a broader economic logic as the core of an economic programme supporting the financial and construction sectors, which were still suffering from the 1998 economic crisis. A strengthened construction industry would reduce unemployment and reactivate the local economy. The policy was designed in close consultation with the CONFIEP (Peruvian Federation of Entrepreneurs) and CAPECO (Peruvian Chamber of Construction); each made several demands to guarantee enough profitability for the construction sector and lessen risks for the financial sector.

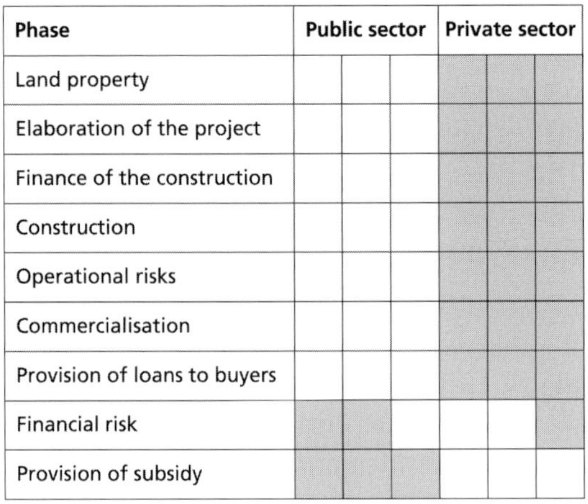

Phase	Public sector	Private sector
Land property		▒
Elaboration of the project		▒
Finance of the construction		▒
Construction		▒
Operational risks		▒
Commercialisation		▒
Provision of loans to buyers		▒
Financial risk	▒	
Provision of subsidy	▒	

FIGURE 18.3 Main phases of the social housing projects and the sector responsible for their implementation.
Source: Rojas (2011: 17).

To activate the system, many of these demands were met and building standards were relaxed to reduce the production costs of new homes (Calderón 2009a) in 'acceptable' (i.e. central) areas of Lima. In 1999, the government waived payment of the General Sales Tax (or value-added tax (VAT)), which was around 18 per cent at the time) for new homes of up to US$30,000. In 2001, a new regulation established that the taxable amount of VAT on the sale of new homes would exclude the value of the land; this allowed new homes of up to US$35,000 to be built in central areas (Calderón 2009b). To calm financial fears, the government established an additional rule to increase the participation of households who did not qualify for bank loans; thus the Mivivienda Fund (FMV) guaranteed two-thirds of each mortgage loan provided by financing institutions (Calderon 2009b).

Figure 18.4 shows how the Peruvian housing supply has been organized between the state, private sector and dwellers since August 2012. It is difficult, however, to completely separate state-enabled and assisted self-help housing as they overlap.

As the figure illustrates, there are four types of state involvement in housing: (a) supply of new homes within ABC schemes; (b) construction of a home or home improvement (in informal areas) within ABC schemes; (c) micro-finance programmes assisting households who cannot qualify for a commercial mortgage (this replaces Banmat which ceased operation in August 2012); and (d) legalization of informally settled property. The last is done through COFOPRI, whose impact in terms of housing is very limited since it provides no advantages to beneficiaries in gaining access to formal credit. COFOPRI provides only titles and is not linked to neighbourhood upgrading.

There are also commercial and non-profit micro-finance schemes involved in self-help housing. While the latter are negligible, the former are significant. Micasa from Mibanco is worth mentioning as it is the second largest commercial micro-finance institution in Latin America. Originally established to provide micro-finance to entrepreneurs, Micasa now provides loans of up to US$10,000 for housing-related activities to be paid within two to five years. Due to the high interest rates, loans are paid on average in 20 months. From December 2000 to May 2006, Micasa supplied more than 180,000 loans and had very few arrears (Gwinn 2006).

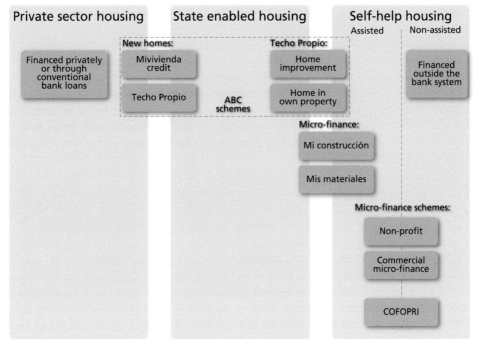

FIGURE 18.4 Current types of state involvement in housing in Peru.

The availability of funds for social housing and the establishment of a clear policy with specific programmes and subsidies propelled the housing sector. The reactivation of Peru's economy, which started to grow significantly from 2002, increased the availability of public and private resources. This, in the context of the huge and contained housing demand, contributed to the dynamism of both the construction and the financial sectors. Increased private real-estate investments eventually triggered a process of urban development commodification which is transforming Lima and other large Peruvian cities. Real estate became a hot business and the construction sector one of the pillars of the economy.

One of the most important challenges of the Peruvian housing situation, however, is the disconnection that exists between housing policies and local planning issues. The Ministry of Housing recognizes that one of the characteristics of Peruvian urban management is the isolated and even contradictory intervention of public agents or sectors in urban processes (Ministerio de Vivienda 2006b). Housing authorities generally have sectoral visions of the housing problem, which is seen to be an isolated and quantitative problem to be tackled through national policies and technical means. They generally share the private sector vision that local governments are sources of conflicts and barriers rather than the body responsible for planning and guiding the growth and development of cities at the district and metropolitan levels. This is not exclusively a Peruvian problem; this trend has been observed at the wider Latin American level where, due to the weaknesses of local planning, there is little awareness of the implementation consequences of sectoral policies in city development. Due to the traditionally formalistic type of planning, there is no clear vision to orient the growth and development of cities.

The overall neglect of urban planning has been, however, more dramatic in Peru than in other Latin American countries. Local plans may have existed on paper, but due to laissez-faire political attitudes, the city has expanded without control. As a result, central government considerations were more important than local plans; higher-level government officials have imposed top-down, sectoral policies and spatial interventions when they considered it necessary. Municipal autonomy was very much weakened during the Fujimori administration in the 1990s. According to Crot (2006: 44): 'While the districts regained their autonomy after Alejandro Toledo's election in 2001, the ten previous years of uncoordinated spatial policies and non-existent metropolitan agenda have frustrated urban planning and become engraved onto the city's territorial organization.'

To improve coordination between urban planning with housing interventions, the 2003 Municipalities Law granted responsibilities for housing planning and management to local (i.e. municipal) authorities. But due to the weakness of local governments and the lack of a planning culture at the local level, this mandate has hardly been fulfilled. The absence of an articulated urban policy to orient and order metropolitan development has been denounced by local researchers (Calderón 2009a; Joseph 2009). In fact, Calderón (2009a: 49) states that: 'In practice, local governments lack the tools to allow them to orient the growth of cities. Their functions, in terms of authorizing new developments, limit themselves to the formal city, they lack control and management of public land.'

Housing policy implementation 2001–2006

An examination of the results of social housing programmes during the Toledo administration (July 2001 to July 2006) showed several problematic trends. In spite of the reactivation of the national economy and the construction sector, only 100,000 new homes were built in the formal construction sector (both social and commercial) during the five-year period (*El Comercio* 2006); this represents an average housing production of 20,000 new homes per year. This is a small fraction of the estimated 130,000 new homes needed to reduce the housing deficit (*El Comercio* 2012).

Additionally, most social housing – 33,000 units – was built for middle-class households (Mivivienda); only 6,000 homes were built for low-income households (Techo Propio). Despite the availability of funds for subsidies, Techo Propio stagnated (Fernández-Maldonado and Bredenoord 2010). The private sector was not interested in building for Techo Propio due to the lower returns that large construction firms receive from building homes for low-income segments. This has produced a mismatch between housing supply and demand, which remains until now. The extent of this mismatch can be observed in CAPECO's 2011 data on Metropolitan Lima housing. Illustrated in Table 18.2, the large, unmet demand in the lower price categories becomes clear.

A third issue was the exclusive focus on the supply of new homes and lack of approaches related to self-help housing activities during this period. This is obviously related to the 'housing as product' approach of the Peruvian reform. During this period, self-help processes were viewed very negatively, both by politicians and CAPECO representatives. Assistance to self-help was, consequently, not important in the initial housing plan.

The fourth problem was the inclination towards the preferred locations of high- and middle-income segments. As a result, there has been a preference for Metropolitan Lima over other cities (see Figure 18.5), and for central areas over peripheral ones. However, this trend is gradually

TABLE 18.2 Supply and demand of housing units in Metropolitan Lima in 2011

Home prices in US$	Existing demand of households	Supply of housing units	Unsatisfied demand of households	
4,000–20,000	192,171	51	192,120	49.08%
20,001–60,000	167,528	5,786	161,742	41.32%
>60,000	47,781	10,209	37,572	9.60%
Total	407,480	16,046	391,434	100%

Source: CAPECO (2012).

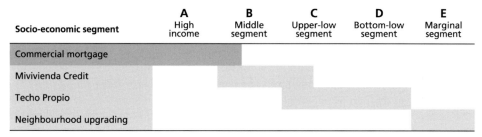

FIGURE 18.5 Housing finance system according to socio-economic sector (NSE).
Source: Ministerio de Vivienda (2006a: 36).

evolving due to the increasing difficulty of finding adequate land to build upon. Thus, areas outside of the centre are being slowly subsumed into real-estate expansion dynamics.

But there is a positive aspect that should be highlighted: the indirect effects of FMV activities during this period have been more important than the few loans granted under the scheme. FMV, as a catalyser of home building activities, pushed property prices downward and allowed the redirection of private real-estate investment to income segments previously considered unprofitable (Calderón 2009a). Thus, the new housing programmes were very successful in that: (a) they increased housing supply; (b) they spurred property price reduction; (c) they promoted the growth of the mortgage market; and (d) in Lima, they produced a process of 'return to the centre' of middle-income households.

Housing policy implementation 2006–2011

The previous section described how, despite successfully activating the construction and financial sectors, the social housing system mainly served middle-class households during the initial years. While the Toledo administration (2001–2006) was characterized by economic austerity measures and growth without redistribution, the García government, inaugurated in July 2006, claimed that the fight against poverty would be its main goal and thus established sectoral programmes with names suggesting redistributive aims. These included Educación para todos (Education for all), Agua para todos (Water for all) and Vivienda para todos (Housing for all).

Under World Bank and multilateral agency recommendations, housing policy was modified to include the creation of a new programme for lower-income households, an increase in the maximal home value for Techo Propio beneficiaries as well as the modification of the

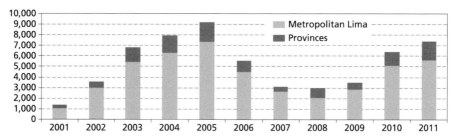

FIGURE 18.6 Number of Mivivienda Credits granted, 2001–2011.
Source: Ministerio de Vivienda (2012).

requirements and simplification of procedures for homes under US$10,000 (*El Comercio* 2006). The new National Housing Plan (2006–2011) specified the targets for each socio-economic segment (Figure 18.5 illustrates each Nivel Socio-Económico, or NSE[6]). For example, since extremely poor households (belonging to segment E) are unable to afford a home, the state only assists them through neighbourhood upgrading.

This structure was later changed to introduce Mi Hogar as a sub-programme of the FMV for the C sector. In this way, each socio-economic level or NSE had a dedicated programme inside the FMV: Mivivienda Credit for the B sector, Mi Hogar for the C sector and Techo Propio for the D sector. After a few years, Mi Hogar ceased.

Statistics of the Peruvian Ministry of Housing have been used to examine the main trends within each of the three different social housing schemes of Mivivienda Credit, Techo Propio and Banmat during the García administration (2006–2011). Figure 18.6, showing the evolution of Mivivienda Credits, illustrates a decrease in the total number of credits during the 2006–2011 period but an opposite trend during the later years. The figure also shows the strong preference for locations in Metropolitan Lima, as during the previous period.

There was a significant increase in the number of subsidies granted through Techo Propio during the 2006–2011 period. Techo Propio has three modalities: 'new homes', 'building on own property' and 'home improvement'. They do not imply self-built or self-managed processes, but rather the construction of a small home (33 m^2) or part thereof (generally a concrete slab roof) by private construction firms in informal areas (see Figure 18.7). However, it is evident that these dwellings will be expanded or adapted through self-help activities. It is also clear that even if this type of modality may help individual households to address their immediate housing problem, it does not benefit the city as a whole because there is no accompanying neighbourhood upgrading process.

During the 2006–2011 period, most Techo Propio grants went to the 'building on own property' modality (see Figure 18.8). However, since 2009, a clear reduction in the number of subsidies has been observed, related to a conflict between FMV and the Ministry of Economy, which provides the funds for the subsidies. In July 2009, the Ministry did not want to transfer US$60 million to FMV when the funds for Techo Propio subsidies were exhausted. A temporary stop of Techo Propio was announced and FMV's goal to grant 50,000 subsidies that year could not be achieved (Quispe 2009). After several months of discussion, the housing subsidies were restructured. The subsidy level was linked to the income level of the household and the Ministry of Economy was put in charge of checking income levels to approve subsidies.

FIGURE 18.7 Dwelling built through Techo Propio 'building in own property' in Collique, Comas. Photo by Ana María Fernández-Maldonado.

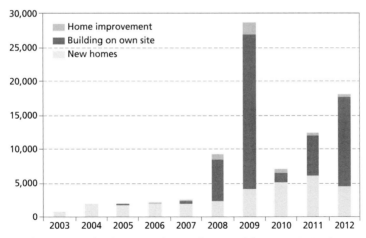

FIGURE 18.8 Techo Propio subsidies granted in its three modalities, 2003–2012.
Source: Ministerio de Vivienda (2012).

The situation of Banmat deteriorated during the 2006–2011 period. The number of granted loans diminished annually to only 3,111 in 2011. A scandalous allocation of new homes to affluent people caused the closing of Banmat's programme for new homes. Other corruption affairs – repeated amnesty of repayments to 'extreme' poor, fraud in the acquisition of building materials, etc. – heavily undermined Banmat's reputation and produced huge arrears that led

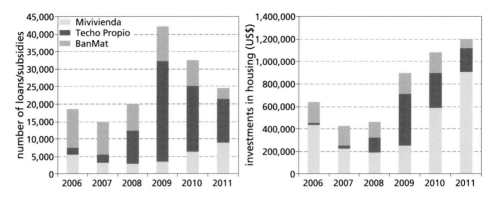

FIGURE 18.9 Number of loans and subsidies (left) and amount of money they represent (right) in the three social housing programmes, 2006–2011.
Source: Ministerio de Vivienda (2012).

to its financial breakdown. Banmat finally ceased in August 2012. After compiling Mivivienda, Techo Propio and Banmat credits (see Figure 18.9, left side), a clear declining trend in Techo Propio and Banmat subsidies and loans can be distinguished as well as a modest growth in the number of Mivivienda Credits. This goes against the rhetoric of national authorities which repeatedly claimed during that period to be reorienting the social housing policy in favour of the C (middle-low-income) and D (low-income) segments. Figure 18.9 (right side), illustrating the amount of money spent in the each of the three schemes, gives a clear picture of the preference for Mivivienda Credit in the allocation of funds. More than two-thirds of total funds were spent on this scheme in 2011.

Comparing the trends of this period with those of the previous government administration we can state that:

- the number of annual promoted homes increased slightly during this period but was still insufficient to tackle the huge housing deficit;
- the favouritism towards middle-class groups diminished in the first three years of this period but increased again during the last three;
- the preference for Lima over other Peruvian cities, especially in the Mivivienda Credit scheme, was maintained; and
- although the rhetoric towards self-help schemes changed, the statistical data indicates very little orientation towards incremental housing.

The Humala government, inaugurated in July 2011, aims to focus on increased housing in poor urban and rural areas as well as on making more funds available towards this end. This is the first time that rural housing has been taken into account in the housing policy. These measures, however, are still in the making. On the other hand, the housing sector in general continues to expand; the number of homes offered by the social and commercial housing sectors reached 35,636 units in 2011, 40 per cent more than in 2010 (*El Comercio* 2012). Moreover, the granting of commercial mortgage credits grew steadily during 2012. The expansion includes projects built outside the central areas as well as in provincial cities.

Conclusion: challenges of the current social housing system

The previous sections described how assistance to incremental housing processes fit within Peruvian housing policies. These policies closely follow the housing reform model implemented in Chile and later replicated in several other Latin American countries. These policies have not only effectively increased the availability of housing credit, they produced a construction boom by meeting the stated goal of strengthening the construction and financial sectors. At the aggregated level, the policy has increased housing supply, reduced housing prices and extended mortgage credits to middle-income and, through direct subsidies, to middle-low-income groups. But the goal to tackle the housing deficit of low-income households has not been met. The city keeps on growing through *barriadas*.

Poverty levels and the preference of large construction firms for middle-income households partly explain this situation. According to UN-Habitat (2008: 4): '[T]he source of the housing problem in Peru is to be found in low affordability conditions and a mismatch between existing demand and available supply, rather than in an outright lack of housing construction activity'.

That developers and financial institutions of the formal private sector satisfy only a portion of the housing demand is a common, but difficult to overcome, occurrence in developing countries (Ferguson and Navarrete 2003). Indeed, this is the case in Peru. During 2011, 39,870 homes were offered in Lima within the formal sector (both social and commercial); of these only 4.37 per cent were offered for under US$30,000 (CAPECO 2012) and therefore affordable for poorer households. These figures suggest the pronounced ineffectiveness of the housing policies in addressing the housing demands of the poor. This examination into incremental housing within the wider housing policy has shown that while the Toledo administration was neglectful, during the García administration programmes were implemented through Techo Propio and Banmat. Yet despite the pro-poor rhetoric during the García period, Techo Propio funds gradually reduced after an initial impetus, while Banmat suffered a fatal financial breakdown. Nonetheless, Mivivienda, now in charge of all state-supported housing, claims that the financial support for the acquisition, building and improvement of housing in poor areas will be increased; this implies a renewed push for incremental housing.

Peru's housing policies have also resulted in land use intensification. The need for lower housing costs has led to moderate land consumption activity; newly built homes in the formal sector (both social and commercial) are smaller, and moreover, 93 per cent of them are apartments (CAPECO 2012). In a city characterized by a horizontal pattern of urban growth – by way of one-family houses on single parcels of land – these trends seem very auspicious. This change in mind-set and of accepting multi-family housing solutions is a step in the right direction for sustainability.

Nonetheless, the crucial issue for sustainable development is effective planning and coordination between housing policies and local development plans. After all, intensification of land use was hardly envisioned to result from current urban policies, and as such may be considered as 'spontaneous' and unplanned as the *barriadas* themselves. There is an increasing awareness that Peruvian cities cannot continue to grow through *barriadas*. But due to insufficient housing alternatives, the poor continue to build upon and occupy increasingly distant, dangerous and steep land. As it is 7.5 times cheaper to prevent the formation of *barriadas* than to build neighbourhoods (Bouillon 2012), such a pattern of growth is not only economically unsustainable, it is also environmentally unsustainable given the amount of land required. This growth pattern is also socially unsustainable due to the obvious disadvantages related to the socio-spatial segregation of communities. However, there is still no clear vision on how to organize urban growth in a structured way so that horizontal growth and inefficient land use patterns are discouraged.

The Peruvian experience suggests that the housing problem cannot be solved through real-estate business projects made possible by state-supported credit. Since most Peruvian households use incremental housing to gain access to shelter, improving this process is essential. The Peruvian social housing system is still in its infancy; the system needs to become more sophisticated to adapt itself to the nature of the national housing deficit. To overcome the current constraints, new mechanisms – especially addressed to poor households – should be implemented to complement the current financial schemes for building new homes.

A sensible housing policy will need to pay careful attention to several issues which are gradually emerging in the Latin American housing debate. These include the sustainable finance of housing programmes, the production of low-cost, serviced land, the finance of the externalities of new developments, efficient programmes for progressive housing, land value capture instruments and, especially, the coordination of the housing policy with urban policies and plans.

Notes

1 Processes of *autoconstrucción* may also occur on land that has been previously developed; however, it is not common.
2 In the 1990s, President Fujimori used the FONAVI fund at his own discretion and for clientelistic purposes (Calderón 2005).
3 Despite its international success, local empirical studies have refuted De Soto's assumptions (Fernández-Maldonado 2007).
4 The list enumerates the phases of the construction of the (architectural) project, but does not mention its urban aspects, which are evidently provided by (public) agencies.
5 Commercialization of the dwellings is in the hands of the private sector for Mivivienda Credit, but not for Techo Propio. Here beneficiaries must register in FMV offices and deal with FMV officials.
6 NSE or Nivel Socio-Económico – socio-economic levels – is a category based on variables related to the possessions and consumption habits of households, as: level of education of the household head; (way of) access to the medical system; tenure of household equipment and services; level of home crowding; and home building materials. Households are then distributed across five categories: high segment (A), middle segment (B), upper-low segment (C), bottom-low segment (D) and marginal segment (E), whose average household incomes were (in Lima, in 2009) US$3,573; US$997; US$473; US$343; and US$243 respectively. They represented 5.2 per cent, 17.7 per cent, 33.1 per cent, 30.2 per cent and 13.8 per cent of the total households, respectively (Campodónico 2010).

References

BBVA Research (2011) *Situación inmobiliaria Peru Año 2011*. Santiago de Chile: BBVA Research Latam.
Bouillon, C.P. (ed.) (2012) *Room for Development: Housing Markets in Latin America and the Caribbean*. Inter-American Development Bank, New York: Palgrave Macmillan.
Calderón, J. (2005) *La ciudad ilegal. Lima en el siglo XX*. Lima: Fondo Editorial de la Facultad de Ciencias Sociales, Universidad Nacional Mayor de San Marcos.
Calderón, J. (2009a) 'Títulos de propiedad, mercados y políticas urbanas', *Centro-h, Revista de la Organización Latinoamericana y del Caribe de Centros Históricos*, 3: 47–62.

Calderón, J. (2009b) 'El efecto Mivivienda: Política de vivienda para la clase media y diferenciación social', *Sociológica, Revista del Colegio de Sociólogos del Perú*, 1: 1.
Campodónico, H. (2010) 'La pirámide socio-económica limeña', *La República*, 5 November.
CAPECO (2012) *El Mercado de Edificaciones Urbanas en Lima Metropolitana y el Callao*. Lima: Cámara Peruana de la Construcción.
Crot, L. (2006) '"Scenographic" and "cosmetic" planning: Globalization and territorial restructuring in Buenos Aires', *Journal of Urban Affairs*, 28(3): 227–251.
El Comercio (2006) 'Gobierno se enfocará en promover viviendas en los sectores C, D y E', 13 October.
El Comercio (2012) 'Constructoras ejecutarán unos 20 megaproyectos en Lima este año', 26 January.
Ferguson, B. and Navarrete, J. (2003) 'New approaches to progressive housing in Latin America: A key to habitat programs and policy', *Habitat International*, 27(2): 309–323.
Fernández-Maldonado, A.M. (2007) *Fifty Years of Barriadas in Lima: Revisiting Turner and De Soto*. Presented at the ENHR International Conference on Sustainable Urban Areas, Rotterdam.
Fernández-Maldonado, A.M. (2010) *Recent Housing Policies in Lima and Their Effects on Sustainability*. Presented at the 42nd ISOCARP Conference: Sustainable City/Developing World, Nairobi.
Fernández-Maldonado, A.M. and Bredenoord, J. (2010) 'Progressive housing approaches in the current Peruvian policies', *Habitat International*, 34(3): 342–350.
Gwinn, W.B. (2006) 'Vivienda', in M. Giugale, V. Fretes-Cibils and J. Newman (eds) *Perú: la oportunidad de un país diferente. Próspero, equitativo y gobernable*. Lima: World Bank.
INEI (2008) *Censo de Población y Vivienda 2007, Datos de Vivienda*. Lima, Instituto Nacional de Estadística e Informática.
Joseph, J. (2009) 'La fragmentación y articulación de la ciudad', in J. Calderón Cockburn (ed.) *Foro urbano: Los nuevos rostros de la ciudad de Lima*. Lima: Colegio de Sociólogos del Perú.
Mangin, W. and Turner, J. (1968) 'The Barriada movement', *Progressive Architecture*, 5: 154–162.
Ministerio de Vivienda (2006a) *Planes nacionales de vivienda y saneamiento 2006–2015*. Lima: Ministerio de Vivienda, Construcción y Saneamiento.
Ministerio de Vivienda (2006b) *Plan Nacional De Desarrollo Urbano- Territorio Para Todos, Lineamientos de Política 2006–2015*. Lima: Ministerio de Vivienda, Construcción y Saneamiento.
Ministerio de Vivienda (2012) *Compendio estadístico 2011*, Online. Available at http://fenix.vivienda.gob.pe/compendio2011/ (accessed 29 March 2012).
Quispe, M. (2009) 'Dejan sin fondos a Techo Propio', *La República*, 19 July.
Riofrío, G. (1991) *Producir la ciudad (popular) de los '90: Entre el mercado y el estado*. Lima: DESCO, Centro de estudios y promoción del desarrollo.
Rojas, J. (2011) 'Fondo MIVIVIENDA', presentation at the 41 Asamblea General de ALIDE, Asunción, 20 May.
Turner, J. (1968) 'Housing priorities, settlement patterns, and urban development in modernizing countries', *Journal of the American Planning Association*, 34(6): 354–363.
UN-Habitat (2008) *Housing Finance Mechanisms in Peru*. Nairobi: UN-Habitat.

19
FROM SHORTAGE REDUCTION TO A WELLBEING APPROACH

Changing paradigms in Ecuadorian housing policies

Christien Klaufus and Laura Cedrés Pérez

Abbreviations

BEV	Ecuadorian Housing Bank; Banco Ecuatoriano de la Vivienda
BIESS	Ecuadorian Social Security Bank; Banco del Instituto Ecuatoriano de Seguridad Social
COOTAD	Organic Code for Territorial Organization, Autonomy and Decentralization; Código Orgánico de Organización Territorial, Autonomía y Descentralización
CSV	Social Contract for Housing; Contrato Social por la Vivienda
GADs	Decentralized Autonomous Governments; Gobiernos Autónomos Descentralizados
IESS	Ecuadorian Social Security Institute; Instituto Ecuatoriano de Seguridad Social
INEC	National Institute of Statistics and Censuses; Instituto Nacional de Estadística y Censos
JNV	National Housing Junta, predecessor of MIDUVI; Junta Nacional de la Vivienda
MIDUVI	Ministry of Urban Development and Housing; Ministerio de Desarrollo Urbano y Vivienda
SENPLADES	National Secretary of Planning and Development; Secretaría Nacional de Planificación y Desarrollo
SIV	Housing Incentives System; Sistema de Incentivos para la Vivienda
SNI	National Information System; Sistema Nacional de Información

Introduction

Ecuador usually has been seen as a small but oil-rich Andean nation that struggles with poverty, indigenous claims and slow development. In addition the unorthodox approaches of its left-wing government have possibly given the country a reputation of political rebel without

TABLE 19.1 Housing shortages in Ecuador, 2010

	Rural		Urban		Total	
Total housing stock	1,357,420		2,391,499		3,748,919	
Qualitative housing shortage	480,108	35.4%	761,526	31.8%	1,241,634	33.1%
Quantitative housing shortage	436,750	32.3%	271,051	11.3%	707,801	18.9%
Total housing shortage	916,858	67.5%	1,032,577	43.2%	1,949.435	52.0%

Source: INEC (2011a); SNI (2011a).

a cause. Many older studies stress the country's political instability, economic crisis, sustained poverty and social inequality, which resulted in a massive outflow of Ecuadorians in the late 1990s and 2000s (e.g. Jokish and Pribilsky 2002; Whitten 2003). However, not much has been written about the sweeping societal changes under the Correa government 2007–2013. Ecuador has been ruled by five presidents since 2000. The only president finishing his term was Rafael Correa. Since the start of his government attempts have been made to develop the country in more sustainable ways and reduce social inequality. A reduction of housing shortages and simultaneous reforms of urban planning and territorial policies became a priority again. With a housing deficit of almost two million housing units (SNI 2011a), this is an urgent political topic. Housing shortages have been reduced since 2007. Yet, an important part of the assumed shortage reduction from 75.5 per cent in 2005 (INEC 2006) to 52 per cent in 2010 (SNI 2011a) can be explained by the politics of redefining 'housing shortage'; therefore those figures need to be handled with care.[1] Besides, as Table 19.1 shows, 33.1 per cent of the total housing stock still needs to be improved (qualitative housing shortage) and 18.9 per cent needs to be replaced (quantitative shortage). This chapter scrutinizes the new housing paradigm and discusses the role of incremental housing within a context of profound policy changes.

An historical overview of Ecuador's housing policies starts in the 1960s with the founding of an Ecuadorian Housing Bank (BEV), followed a decade later by the founding of an executive organization named Junta Nacional de la Vivienda (JNV). During the 1960s and 1970s, national housing shortages were tackled through a top-down programme for the production of cheap, standardized but physically unattractive housing units of 36 square metres financed by the state and constructed by private parties. This approach proved inefficient due to relatively high costs, high levels of abuse of state finances, and low production numbers outside the two metropolitan areas Quito and Guayaquil. In the second half of the 1990s, the JNV was integrated into the new Ministry of Urban Development and Housing (MIDUVI) and the BEV changed from a direct financer of housing solutions to a second-tier bank. The state changed its housing programmes according to the Chilean model of market-based incentives (1978), which was later implemented in several other countries (see Held 2000). As a result, the Housing

TABLE 19.2 Housing types in existing housing stock in Ecuador, 2010*

	Rural	Urban	Total
Single-family home of durable materials	74.9%	67.6%	70.5%
Family apartment	2.6%	17.6%	11.7%
Room(s) (rented out to families)	1.4%	6.8%	4.7%
Small family home of adjacent rooms without hallway	7.9%	3.5%	5.3%
Coastal house made from cane, wood, mud or straw	8.6%	3.1%	5.3%
Temporary shack made of non-durable materials	2.0%	0.7%	1.2%
Highland house made of mud-bricks and straw	2.0%	0.1%	0.9%
Other types	0.5%	0.5%	0.5%

Source: INEC (2011a).
*The housing typologies used in the 2010 census do not correspond to tenure categories, except for the housing type 'rooms', which are always rental units.

Incentives System (SIV), financially supported by the Inter-American Development Bank, was introduced in 1998.

In this incentives system, low-income families could apply for a subsidy and an additional loan provided they had savings in the bank. The ABC formula of *ahorro* (savings), *bono* (grant) and *crédito* (loan) was used to promote the programme. Over the years the SIV programme was continuously adapted, but the basic assumptions remained the same. Overall housing shortages were reduced. Additional effects of the SIV policy were sought in the development of local financial markets and construction sectors (Klaufus 2010). By improving the national Gini coefficient, the programme was believed to benefit the countries' economic outlook. With that goal in mind, most housing grants were again channelled to Quito and Guayaquil, where the sheer quantity of informal settlements negatively influenced the Gini index (Neira Rizzo 2011: 43).[2] The territorial bias was seen as a necessary evil (Mejía Granizo 2011: 37).[3] From the start in 1998, the increase in the amount of granted subsidies looked promising as it suggested an overall improvement of the housing stock (see Frank 2004). Table 19.2 shows that according to the 2010 census, 70 per cent of the housing stock was qualified as (more or less) permanent single-family homes. However, micro-research on the actual destination of the grants showed that financial abuse remained a problem and that the number of targeted families that profited was lower than the number of granted subsidies or the increase in permanent single-family homes suggested (see Klaufus 2010).

From the late 1990s until 2007 neoliberal influences resulted in a diminished role of the state in spatial planning and housing provision. With the change of administration in 2007, state responsibility for affordable housing provision across the national territory became a priority again. Acknowledging that the historical bias towards Quito and Guayaquil had not balanced out national development and the fact that urban growth increasingly took place in smaller cities without well-equipped planning departments forced the state to rethink its territorial administration (Neira Rizzo 2011: 43). The government defined it as their aim to improve local-level governance and tackle housing and land problems 'closer to home' through an integrated land–habitat–housing approach. The paradigm changes were profound on all levels of society, raising the question of what role incremental housing and related self-help solutions could still play in the supply of affordable housing. This question forms the starting point for this chapter. In the next sections, the policy changes will be discussed first.

Then the actors participating in the new political landscape are described, followed by an analysis of the role of incremental housing in Ecuadorian society within the context of the new policy paradigm.

Constitutional change for a harmonious society

The new government's first act was the creation of a new constitution in 2008 based on the notion of *Buen Vivir* in Spanish or *Sumak Kawsay* in Quechua (Registro Oficial 2008). The principle of Buen Vivir, which can be translated as 'living well', 'harmonious cohabitation' or 'collective wellbeing', undergirds a National Development Plan for sustainable development, in which not neoliberal economic growth but a well-balanced quality of life should be central. Although Buen Vivir is said to be of indigenous origins, the intellectual legacy of Amartya Sen is noticeable throughout the constitution's philosophical underpinnings. Within 'left turn' Latin American governments, Buen Vivir appeals to politicians who propagate a pluri-national society, such as Rafael Correa but also Evo Morales in Bolivia. To make spatial and urban development more sustainable, the administrative territorial organization was drastically transformed based on the Spanish and – again – Chilean administrative models. Until 2008 the national territory was divided into provinces and cantons, subdivided into urban and rural areas. That division was based on capital flows and resulted in a prioritization of the two main cities Quito and Guayaquil (López Castro 2010). The 2008 constitution laid the foundation for decentralization through the creation of extra administrative layers: regions (in between the national and provincial governments); special regimes; and local rural governments.[4] In this division the implementation of Buen Vivir development is attributed to administrative clusters called Gobiernos Autónomos Descentralizados or GADs. The GADs are entities that comprise regions as well as provincial, cantonal and rural governments. Analogous to the Ley 388 in Colombia, each GAD has to effectuate the spatial organization of the territory and present a development plan. However, unlike Colombia the legal definition of the rights and duties of governance bodies, comparable to the Ley 388, has not yet been developed. Neither the 2008 constitution nor the Organic Code for Territorial Organization, Autonomy and Decentralization (COOTAD) defines which entities constitute the intermediate and local governmental levels. Each administrative level will operate through participatory councils similar to the Brazilian participatory planning model. The elaboration of the new Land Management and Territorial Organization Law (under revision in 2013) is seen as a crucial precondition for the territorial and development plans that each GAD has to implement (Neira Rizzo 2011: 49) (see Figure 19.1).

Yet reality proves complicated. After the ratification of the constitution, President Correa thwarted the National Development Plan's objective to achieve sustainable habitats by approving a mining law in 2009 and by proposing the partial privatization of water in a controversial law in 2010. Some authors are therefore sceptical about the outcomes. Walsh (2010) questions the reinforced role of the state, arguing that the inherited power inequalities inhibit the aim to achieve equal development for all. She also questions the Buen Vivir principle as the white and *mestizo* upper classes might not be susceptible to a concept presented as an indigenous ancestral notion. Moreover, ideas about sustainable development are not specifically Ecuadorian but resemble the Quality of Life and Wellbeing approaches in Western development thought. The discursive recognition of Buen Vivir could therefore be regarded as Western development thinking in indigenous disguise (Walsh 2010). Another doubt has been phrased in terms of

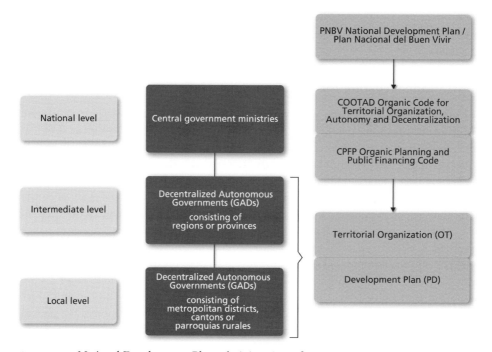

FIGURE 19.1   National Development Plan: administrative reforms.
Source: SENPLADES (2009: 355–359); López Castro (2010); elaboration by the authors.

legal jurisdictions, as the GADs will have to work without clear information (cadastral systems) regarding land ownership, which can cause overlapping territorial rights (Egas Reyes 2011; Mejía Granizo 2011; Neira Rizzo 2011).

Parties involved in new housing and habitat policies

Prior to the Correa government, a collective of approximately 33 concerned social organizations, companies, groups and individual professionals joined forces in 2005, in response to the decision of the preceding government to abolish the national housing subsidies. They started operating under the name 'Social Contract for Housing' (CSV) (Ruiz Pozo and Pinto 2010: 293). Pressured by their protests against a lack of political interest in housing policies on the part of the former government, that government reinstalled the subsidies. In continuation, the Correa government acknowledged the need to revitalize the social housing programmes in 2007, stating that 'A dignified house for everybody … That is revolution!' Whereas the three preceding presidents had allocated US$24 million to reduce housing shortages, the Correa government would contribute US$660 million – almost 30 times as much. According to the literature, the increase was possible thanks to Ecuador's booming oil economy (Conaghan 2008: 55). National sources, however, state that the 'oil boom' had existed for decades; only this time oil money was spent on social projects.

The CSV became involved in the formulation of the new constitution and the National Development Plan, and later in the design of new laws on housing and human settlements (SENPLADES 2009; Ruiz Pozo 2011). Because of their involvement, the constitution explicitly mentions the 'right to a habitat and a dignified house' (Registro Oficial 2008: Art. 30) and 'the right to the city' (Registro Oficial 2008: Art. 31), determining that the Ecuadorian state 'improves precarious housing, supplies shelter, public spaces and green areas, and promotes renting out under special regulations' (Registro Oficial 2008: Art. 375). Assisted self-help housing is an implicit aim of the CSV, and for several actors this is an accepted and valuable solution for the existing housing problem; a viewpoint they expressed at the 2011 Latin American Meeting on Habitat and Housing (Empresa Quito Vivienda 2011). As governmental institutions, MIDUVI and SENPLADES (National Secretary of Planning and Development) are central to the new policies. As part of the Ecuadorian Social Security Institute (IESS), a financial-institutional counterpart, the Ecuadorian Social Security Bank (BIESS) was created in 2009 to facilitate mortgages and invest in real-estate development (BIESS 2012). The participants in the CSV thus deal in different settings with the national governmental entities. The government in turn deals with international counterparts such as the Inter-American Development Bank that finances housing programmes.

To synchronize policies for housing, upgrading and urban spatial planning within MIDUVI, a department for Habitat and Human Settlements was created parallel to the Housing department. The Housing department was specifically involved in the SIV applications. The Habitat department has to develop urban planning and land management policies and offer technical assistance to municipalities. It also aims to tackle juridical loopholes. One such juridical problem of 'legal informality' is caused by partial usufruct of land or housing: users of partial properties can obtain partial ownership through a court decision. Often, partial ownership results in lots with sizes smaller than those allowed by the municipal regulations, yet municipal authorities are unable to block the court procedure. To prevent land speculation, accumulation of unused land and urban sprawl, the Habitat and Human Settlements department develops instruments for land management that can be used by municipalities, for example to expropriate and redevelop land, or to apply progressive tax systems. It also offers support to municipalities with Territorial and Development Plans. The synchronization of municipal land registries will be established through a national system of land registries.[5]

Self-help housing

In former national housing programmes, people from the urban periphery and rural areas were often discouraged from applying for a grant. First, they faced restrictions on the house design; second, they had to open up a bank account; and third, they were required to provide free labour for the construction of basic infrastructure (Klaufus 2010). In practice, people in need of better housing often preferred to be financially independent, opting for self-help solutions. Nowadays, MIDUVI (n.d.) offers assistance to self-help housing (*autogestión*) by selling 'technical assistance services, laboratories for the production of concrete, soil studies, design and planning of housing projects to the public and private sector (housing cooperatives, municipalities and others)'. As is known from previous attempts to commercially steer self-help housing, many of the offered services will be too expensive for the urban poor. For them, more elementary forms of self-help housing continue to be the most obvious solution.

Formal numbers regarding the self-built housing stock in Ecuador do not exist, but similar to other Latin American countries self-help housing was overrepresented in rapidly growing cities such as Quito and Guayaquil. Although the growth index of those metropolises has flattened out since 1990, new settlements do still appear. Some databases give estimations about formal and informal housing, without specifying the self-help component. An unpublished evaluation study suggests that approximately 53 per cent of the housing solutions built in Quito in 2006 were informal against 56 per cent in Guayaquil (Ospina and Erazo Espinosa 2009: 51). In combination with data from the Municipality of Quito about the legalization of 41,643 housing lots in informal settlements between 2001 and 2007 (Ospina 2010: 112), it can be deduced that self-help housing is still dominant in the segment of low-cost houses (defined as houses under US$35,000; Ospina and Erazo Espinosa 2009). Quito has tried to tackle the large number of unregistered self-help housing units in informal settlements with the creation of a municipal legalization unit in 2001. They succeeded in legalizing 196 informal settlements between 2001 and 2007 (Ospina 2010: 112), yet the total number of informal settlements also increased by 100, as new settlements were created exactly because families hoped that their neighbourhoods would be legalized by the municipal legalization unit. Some authorities therefore concluded that the policy to legalize informal settlements at that time 'generated more informality than it solved'.[6] The situation in Quito's informal settlements, where families live in crowded concrete-block houses on the Andean slopes, is not comparable with Guayaquil's poor families who live dispersed in huts or shacks in the unhealthy swamps of the lowlands. The specific geographical and cultural situations have forced both municipalities to find local solutions for upgrading and regularization. Yet the run on urban land continues, as was shown in 2010 in Guayaquil when President Correa declared a large area with informal settlements to be a 'Reserved Security Area', offering inhabitants the opportunity to be relocated to new formal housing in Ciudad Victoria (see Box 19.1). Once the announcement was made, the number of invasions increased drastically. Images of the military trying to dismantle the bamboo shelters appeared in newspapers across the country, stirring up the debate about formalization and relocation policies.

BOX 19.1 CIUDAD VICTORIA, GUAYAQUIL

On 28 December 2010, President Rafael Correa passed a decree to protect the land where the major Hydraulic Plan of the Aqueduct of Santa Helena was planned. Through that decree an area of more than 9,000 hectares was declared to be a Reserved Security Area. However, as some 444 hectares of the security area were inhabited by settlers living in provisional shelters, the president sent a military garrison to take control of the area and initiate a resettlement operation. As soon as the rumour spread that the state would finance the resettlement and the costs of new housing, other households, largely families from other parts of Ecuador's coastal area, started to settle in the protected area in the hope of receiving a new home in the resettlement area. As a result, the entire resettlement operation descended into chaos. To solve the problem, MIDUVI, in collaboration with local authorities and the non-governmental organization Hogar de Cristo, produced a detailed map based on satellite images taken before and after 28 December in order to identify relocation-eligible households. Initially, a total of 1,208 households were placed on the list and 112 hectares in the La Ladillera sector were selected as the relocation area. 'Ciudad Victoria' was designed to offer housing to approximately 6,000 to 8,000 families. New homes ranged in size from 40 square metres (at a cost of roughly US$12,500) to 50 square metres (roughly US$18,500). In addition, some 3,700 households from the invasion area would receive a MIDUVI grant of US$5,000. This could be supplemented by a

> credit of at least US$7,000 with a monthly pay-off of US$50 to US$70 over 12 years. The first 420 houses were inaugurated by President Rafael Correa in July 2012.
> *Sources*: *El Universo* (2011); Hogar de Cristo (2011); *El Telégrafo* (2012).

Parallel to low-cost self-help housing in informal urban settlements, self-built and self-generated villas started to appear in increasing numbers in the urban peripheries, often financed with remittances from transnational migration. The opulent 'arquitectura de remesas' first appeared in the southern provinces Azuay and Cañar and later in other regions too. The houses became non-verbal communications of the (imagined) economic success and social mobility of low-income households that had long been marginalized (Pribilsky 2007; Klaufus 2011; cf. Piedrasanta 2010). The authorities of Ecuador's third city, Cuenca, slowly acknowledged this new trend in informal self-help solutions:

> This other recent architecture, which might relate to migration, (does) not address the Cuencan identity theme, since they are far more interested in enhancing their profile in the city, as a powerful economic sector. ... These migrant houses in the city, as well as in the countryside, ignore the former aspects of Cuencan architecture. It is a social sector unwilling to be embedded in a tradition. It is a new social sector that aims to stress its presence and to set itself apart from the rest, indicating a clear distinction: 'this is my architecture, this expresses who I am, and what my status is, like a new social status.' This social sector was long marginalized. Now they want to show they have economic power. Later they will advance to political power. *Architect and head of a cultural institute in Cuenca 21.11.02.*
>
> (Klaufus 2012: 206–207)

Once the popularity of large villas spread across the urban peripheries and the countryside, they became catalysts of more migration and more construction activities, which resulted in land speculation and elevated costs of construction materials and labour (due to labour scarcity as many construction workers had migrated) (Kyle 2000; Pribilsky 2007; Klaufus 2012). Critics said that adverse economic effects were not the only outcome; the quality of the rural landscape was said to degrade because the designs were inadequate for the rural surroundings in which they appeared and many villas were not built in compliance with local rules and regulations. Furthermore, the increase in the number of unoccupied homes triggered real or imagined waves of social insecurity (Pribilsky 2007).

In two focus-group sessions held with residents from Sigsig, near Cuenca, several members of transnational families admitted that they had been drawn into what could be called a 'dream-house competition', and that a lack of professional involvement resulted in financial losses and unfinished or inadequate housing.[7] Box 19.2 presents a personal statement of a returned migrant who was drawn into the competition. An attempt to regulate that trend was made with the government programme 'Bono del Migrante'. Coordinated by MIDUVI with support from the Secretaría Nacional del Migrante (SENAMI), the programme tries to strengthen transnational ties between migrants abroad and their families in Ecuador (Pinto and Ruiz 2008: 86), to influence the investment of foreign currencies in local financial, real-estate and construction sectors (Ospina and Erazo Espinosa 2009; Hall 2010). Simultaneously, the programme aims to stimulate formal housing solutions, offering migrant families a large array of turn-key houses in urban areas. Project developers can sell housing units up to US$60,000 (land prices included). Remittance-receivers can also build a house on land they own or improve an existing house as long as remittances are used as collateral. Families who want to obtain houses in *rural* areas are not eligible for this grant.

Housing projects being built across the country as part of the various MIDUVI programmes have been partially listed by MIDUVI. One list shows considerable differences with regard to the size and number of projects per city or province: Quito heads the list with over 8,300 single-family homes and approximately 3,200 apartments; the province of Guayas (where Guayaquil is situated) follows with almost 6,400 single-family homes but no apartment buildings, whereas in Cuenca 622 apartments were being developed against some 400 houses (MIDUVI 2010). The prices of housing units in the two metropolitan areas vary from US$10,000 to US$60,000, whereas in Cuenca costs are higher since no houses or apartments are offered below US$20,000. Although the list can only be read as an indication, the metropolitan bias seems to continue. On the one hand, the government's decision to open up their housing programmes to the urban middle class has induced the real-estate sector and BIESS to construct fully serviced residential areas. On the other hand, the list of projects signals a lack of integrated habitat policies, which might paradoxically induce informal self-help solutions. It should be noted that MIDUVI does have a subsidy for individuals to obtain land titles, yet municipalities are responsible for the regularization of informal settlements as a whole. Even though MIDUVI tries to formalize all self-help housing solutions, the financial costs for individuals to receive support and a strong emphasis on the development of middle-class turn-key housing can thus be expected to steer families without access to loans towards self-help housing solutions – as they have done for decades.

BOX 19.2 THE 'DREAM-HOUSE COMPETITION' IN SELF-HELP HOUSING

A returned migrant, a middle-aged man named José who had lived and worked in the United States from 2000 to 2012, had engaged in the symbolic competition to build the nicest 'dream house' in Sigsig. He discovered the financial and social consequences of his house-building project. On one hand, the self-generated housing solution offered him the cultural capital to solicit social prestige:

> I tell you, in my case I'll make my house the way I like it, not because I see another house that I want, let alone I would want to copy another one, no, but only because I am going to live there and I want to feel good in my house. It will be for me, not for other people. But I have seen friends who went to have a look at other houses and said 'make mine exactly the same'. They have come to my house and told me that it was beautiful, but I wouldn't like it if they copied it because everyone has to have his own style. (José, Focus group session, University of Cuenca/VLIR, Sigsig 2 May 2012)

> On the other hand, the project became a financial and social liability:
>
> When I left this country, I left behind a workshop that I owned for about four or five years. I had considerable debts, many, primary materials, machines, all that. I was really affected by that and for that reason I felt obliged to leave the country to move forward. With the jobs I've had I improved the workshop, with tools. I have not invested 100 per cent but a small amount in the workshop and in a car, which is the fundamental tool of the workshop. I have improved the workshop with the remittances I've sent and with another part of the remittances I've built a rather large house. But I did not receive any good advice, I don't know, I did not get that over here, and now the house is abandoned and I cannot even fully finish it. Now I don't know what to do, I am thinking about selling it. I don't know, I have another house where I am living, and that other house is in a spot where nothing is produced. In any case it is costing me a lot to pay taxes and all that. So, I wrongly invested in those things. (José, Focus group session, University of Cuenca/VLIR, Sigsig 2 May 2012)

Housing and habitat policies, a discussion

We started this chapter explaining that Ecuador has seen improvements in the amount of low-cost housing available between 2005 and 2010, yet part of those results can be explained by a change of definition. In 2005, houses made of all kinds of non-durable materials were considered inadequate. Five years later houses were counted as inadequate only when the construction materials included 'uncoated cane walls' or 'earth floors' or anything of lesser quality (INEC 2011b: 6), meaning that self-built adobe houses were now considered to be adequate again. Furthermore, the share of households living in physically unsuitable houses was still 45 per cent and of households living in overcrowded houses 17.5 per cent (SNI 2011a). The numbers implied an improvement, but not as radical as the figures suggested at first sight.

Notwithstanding the definitions, the increased budget destined for housing and the upgrading did and does have an impact. In the first four years of Correa's presidency over 190,000 housing units were built, half of which were new houses in rural areas (see Table 19.3). Although the government aimed to improve the quality of the existing self-built housing stock through upgrading programmes, that change has not been effected and the emphasis is still on new housing. Real-estate developers either build centrally located apartment buildings or suburban single-family houses not accessible for the urban poor. A second point of attention concerns rental housing. In the National Development Plan the housing problem was only described in terms of 'not owning a house', something that affects one in three households (SENPLADES 2009: 191), yet it did not address the improvement of rental housing, which might be over a fifth of the housing units (INEC 2011a). Paradoxically, the high value attributed to home ownership so often associated with neoliberal governments has been included in Rafael Correa's 'Citizens' Revolution'. Fortunately, some of the discriminatory regulations from the former versions of the SIV programme that affected people in the urban periphery and rural areas have been straightened out. Yet rural applicants still face the restriction that their houses need to be designed with 'local materials' and according to 'traditional technologies' in participatory sessions under MIDUVI's guidance, so a paternalist stance towards the inhabitants of the urban periphery and rural areas can still be detected.

TABLE 19.3 Paid grants for new housing and home improvement during former and current government terms, 2011

MIDUVI	Former governments						Correa government				Total	
Programme	2002	2003	2004	2005	2006	2007	2008	2009	2010		2007–2010
Urban												
New	4,999	3,193	4,041	5,685	1,826	5,705	12,512	14,210	3,287		35,714
Improvement	3,903	3,605	5,316	4,511	2,727	3,410	7,750	7,380	552		19,092
Urbano-marginal												
New	3,518	3,631	1,059	54	1,287	2,713	5,124	1,558	700		10,095
Improvement	619	1,339	47		110	932	1,391	88	4		2,415
Rural												
New	9,184	6,863	7,470	6,495	7,698	14,476	61,999	15,374	3,523		95,372
Improvement	2,392	1,344	1,256	866	1,854	1,742	4,938	1,331	413		8,424
Middle-class projects	0	0	0	0	0	0	0	0	11,492		11,492
Projects for disabled people	0	0	0	0	0	0	0	0	2,290		2,290
Resettlement and emergencies	0	0	0	0	0	0	5,136	435	1,641		7,212
Total number of grants	24,615	19,975	19,189	17,611	15,502	28,978	98,850	40,376	23,902		192,106
Investment in US dollar	19,678,352	15,938,068	16,288,550	17,659,658	10,550,550	90,094,000	361,375,480	150,969,047	114,496,487		716,935,014

Separate projects for rural and urban teachers as well as the SAV-BID and INTI projects have been integrated into the table according to their geographical location.
Sources: www.miduvi.gob.ec and www.habitatyvivienda.gob.ec/p/; data processed by authors.

At the start of 2013, the second term of the Correa government ended. Policy outcomes gave evidence of reduced housing shortages, but not of more integrated housing and habitat policies as projected. Correa was elected again and has a third term for his 'Citizens Revolution'. First versions of the Land Law that is under review have proposed the creation of a Superintendent of Territorial Organization to supervise territorial planning and land use. Yet, as lawyers have remarked, there is a risk of creating unclear jurisdictions which can obstruct the coherence of the programmes (Mejía Granizo 2011; Neira Rizzo 2011). In addition, the government has recently defined a scenario for 'ordered cities': with over 60 per cent of the population living in urban areas, the government aims to develop an urban agenda that strengthens social housing programmes and policies, and simultaneously integrates those policies into the urban and land planning schedules to put into practice the model of a 'polycentric' Ecuador as envisioned in the National Development Plan. To conclude, the housing problem has been addressed by reducing numbers, as was done before, but not necessarily by giving citizens more control to decide over their habitats (Cedrés Pérez 2012). Whether the Buen Vivir approach results in better housing solutions for all thus remains to be seen in the four years Correa has left to govern.

Notes

1 In the 2005 Life Conditions Survey, a housing unit in Ecuador was considered 'spacious enough' when it contained more than two rooms for a household of maximum five people (INEC 2006: 6). Complementary to this, qualitative housing shortages were measured along three dimensions: 'adequate construction materials' of floors, walls and roof; 'overcrowding', i.e. when more than three people share a bedroom; and access to electricity, drinking water and sanitation (INEC 2006: 8–10). According to that survey, 72 per cent of the housing stock was inadequate based on the construction materials alone (adobe, cane and wood). In the 2010 census, the 'qualitative housing shortage' was defined as the number of houses 'considered as recoverable based on the combination of predominant materials of floor, walls and roof and on the state of those materials' (SNI 2011b). The 'quantitative housing shortage' was defined by the same indicators as the number of 'unrecoverable houses' (SNI 2011c). In 2010, Ecuador had almost 14.5 million inhabitants in 3.8 million households that occupied 3.7 million housing units, resulting in less than four people per housing unit on average (INEC 2011b).
2 Architect J. Morales, MIDUVI, interview 12 March 2011.
3 Lawyer A. Mejía, MIDUVI, interview 12 March 2011.
4 Regions are administrative collaborations between two or more adjacent provinces. Special regimes form an extraordinary administrative category which includes Autonomous Metropolitan Districts; the Galapagos islands; and acknowledged indigenous, afro-Ecuadorian, ancestral or pluri-national districts.
5 Lawyer A. Mejía, MIDUVI, interview 12 March 2011.
6 Lawyer A. Mejía, MIDUVI, interview 12 March 2011.
7 The focus group sessions were part of the Belgium VLIR-IUC funded Project 'Migración Internacional y Desarrollo Local' carried out in collaboration with the Universidad de Cuenca.

References

BIESS Banco del Instituto Ecuatoriano de Seguridad Social (2012) Online. Available at www.biess.fin.ec/index.php/la-institucion (accessed 14 March 2012).

Cedrés Pérez, L. (2012) 'La participación ciudadana en la construcción de hábitat incluyente y sostenible: hacia la materialización del derecho a la ciudad', in T. Bolívar and J. Erazo Espinosa (eds) *Dimensiones del hábitat popular latinoamericano*. Quito: FLACSO, CLACSO, Instituto de la Ciudad, 187–207.

Conaghan, C. (2008) 'Ecuador: Correa's plebiscitary presidency', *Journal of Democracy*, 19(2): 46–60.

Egas Reyes, P. (2011) 'La propiedad en la Constitución del Ecuador', *Fórum de Direito Urbano e Ambiental*, 10(57): 13–33.

El Telégrafo (2012) 'Presidente Correa entrega viviendas en Guayaquil', 24 July, Online. Available at www.eltelegrafo.com.ec (accessed 7 August 2013).

El Universo (2011) '120 familias, primeras en Ciudad Victoria', 18 December, Online. Available at www.eluniverso.com (accessed 8 March 2012).

Empresa Quito Vivienda (2011) 'Encuentro latinoamericano sobre habitat y vivienda', Municipio del Distrito Metropolitano de Quito. Online. Available at www.noticiasquito.gob.ec (accessed 6 December 2012).

Frank, D. (2004) 'A market-based housing improvement system for low-income families – the Housing Incentive System (SIV) in Ecuador', *Environment and Urbanization*, 16(1): 171–184.

Hall, J. (2010) *Ten Years of Innovation in Remittances: Lessons Learned and Models for the Future*. Independent Review of the Multilateral Investment Fund Remittance Portfolio. Washington, DC: Inter-American Development Bank.

Held, G. (2000) *Políticas de vivienda de interés social orientadas al mercado: experiencias recientes con subsidios a la demanda en Chile, Costa Rica y Colombia*. Serie Financiamiento del Desarrollo No. 96. Santiago de Chile: United Nations/CEPAL.

Hogar de Cristo (2011) *Boletin Virtual*, Enero 2011, 1–8, Online. Available at www.hogardecristo.org.ec/boletinesok.html (accessed 15 March 2012).

INEC (Instituto Nacional de Estadística y Censos) (2006) *Las condiciones de vida de los Ecuatorianos: resultados de la encuesta de condiciones de vida quinta ronda – vivienda*. Quito: INEC.

INEC (2011a) 'Resultados del Censo de Población y Vivienda 2010', SPSS database, Instituto Nacional de Estadísticas y Censos, Online. Available at www.inec.gob.ec/cpv/ (accessed 9 December 2012).

INEC (2011b) 'Resultados del Censo de Población y Vivienda 2010', printed summary, Online. Available at www.inec.gob.ec/cpv/index.php?option=com_remository&Itemid=96&func=startdown&id=35&lang=es (accessed 6 December 2012).

Jokisch, B. and Pribilsky, J. (2002) 'The panic to leave: economic crisis and the "New Emigration" from Ecuador', *International Migration*, 40: 75–101.

Klaufus, C. (2010) 'The two ABCs of aided self-help housing in Ecuador', *Habitat International*, 34: 351–358.

Klaufus, C. (2011) 'Arquitectura de remesas: "demonstration effect" in Latin American popular architecture', *Etnofoor*, 23(1): 9–28.

Klaufus, C. (2012) *Urban Residence: Housing and Social Transformations in Globalizing Ecuador*. Oxford, New York: Berghahn.

Kyle, D. (2000) *Transnational Peasants: Migrations, Networks, and Ethnicity in Andean Ecuador*. Baltimore: The Johns Hopkins University Press.

López Castro, J. (2010) 'El derecho del Buen Vivir: Hábitat y Vivienda en la Constitución de La República y en el Proyecto de Ley de Organización Territorial', thesis, Universidad Autónoma de Quito – UNAQ.

Mejía Granizo, A. (2011) 'Planificación del desarrollo, ordenamiento territorial y gestión de suelo en Ecuador: Nuevos paradigmas y reforma legal en Ecuador', *Fórum de Direito Urbano e Ambiental*, 10(57): 35–41.

MIDUVI Ministerio de Desarrollo Urbano y Vivienda (2010) 'Registro de proyectos de vivienda: sistema de incentivos para vivienda enero-octubre 2010', www.MIDUVI.gob.ec/index.php?option=com_content&view=article&id=250&Itemid=333 (accessed 14 March 2012).

MIDUVI (n.d.) 'Habitat y Vivienda.' Online. Available at www.habitatyvivienda.gob.ec/p/ (accessed 5 December 2012).

Neira Rizzo, J. (2011) 'Panorama normativo sobre el marco normativo en materia de planificación del desarrollo y ordenamiento territorial en el Ecuador', *Fórum de Direito Urbano e Ambiental*, 10(57): 43–49.

Ospina, O. (2010) *Dolarización y Desarrollo Urbano: Mercado de Vivienda Nueva en Quito*. Quito: FLACSO and Abya Yala.

Ospina, O. and Erazo Espinosa, J. (2009) 'Dolarización y generación de vivienda formal: su lectura en Ecuador', *Ecuador Debate*, 76: 29–53.

Piedrasanta, R. (ed.) (2010) *Arquitectura de las Remesas*. Exhibition and book. Guatemala City: AECID/CCE Guatemala/CCE El Salvador/CCE Honduras.

Pinto, V. and Ruiz, L. (2008) *Migración, Remesas y Vivienda: Una mirada desde las administraciones zonales Eloy Alfaro y Calderón del Distrito Metropolitano de Quito*. Quito: CIUDAD.

Pribilsky, J. (2007) *La Chulla Vida: Gender, Migration and the Family in Andean Ecuador and New York City*. Syracuse, NY: Syracuse University Press.

Registro Oficial (2008) The Constitution, 20 October, No. 449.

Ruiz Pozo, L. (2011) 'Actores sociales, incidencia política, fortalecimiento y capitalización: La ampliación del margen de maniobra del colectivo "contrato social por la vivienda"', paper presented at N-AERUS XII Internacional Conference, 20–22 October, Madrid.

Ruiz Pozo, S. and Pinto, V. (2010) 'El contrato social por la vivienda – CSV en Ecuador', in A. Sugranyes and C. Mathivet (eds) *Ciudades para Todos: Por el Derecho a la Ciudad; Propuestas y Experiencias*. Santiago: Habitat International Coalition, 293–300.

SENPLADES Secretaría Nacional de Planificación y Desarrollo (2009) 'Plan Nacional para el Buen Vivir 2009–2013: Construyendo un estado plurinacional e intercultural'. Quito: SENPLADES.

SNI (Sistema Nacional de Información) (2011a) Indicadores de vivienda y hogar, SNI online database, section 'Información Vivienda y Hogar', Gobierno Nacional de la República del Ecuador, Online. Available at http://indestadistica.sni.gob.ec/QvAJAXZfc/opendoc.htm?document=SNI.qvw&host=QVS@kukuri&anonymous=truehttp://indestadistica.sni.gob.ec/QvAJAXZfc/opendoc.htm?document=SNI.qvw&host=QVS@kukuri&anonymous=true&bookmark=Document/BM05 (accessed 3 June 2013).

SNI (2011b) Ficha Técnica: Déficit Habitacional Cualitativo, SNI online database, section 'Información Vivienda y Hogar', Gobierno Nacional de la República del Ecuador, Online. Available at www.sni.gob.ec/documents/10156/984d15e9-4443-4564-9ffa-6222fbe8c53c (accessed 3 June 2013).

SNI (2011c) Ficha Técnica: Déficit Habitacional Cuantitativo, SNI online database, section 'Información Vivienda y Hogar', Gobierno Nacional de la República del Ecuador, Online. Available at www.sni.gob.ec/documents/10156/99db94c8-6c19-433f-b14a-93b3a15a34d6 (accessed 3 June 2013).

Walsh, C. (2010) 'Development as *Buen Vivir*: Institutional arrangements and (de)colonial entanglements', *Development*, 53(1): 15–21.

Whitten, N. (ed.) (2003) *Millennial Ecuador: Critical Essays on Cultural Transformations and Social Dynamics*. Iowa City: University of Iowa Press.

20
SELF-HELP HOUSING AND UPCOMING POLICIES FOR AFFORDABLE HOUSING IN NICARAGUA

Jan Bredenoord and Bart van der Meulen

Abbreviations

ACENVI	Inter-American Association of Housing
CADUR	Nicaraguan Chamber of Project Developers
CENCOVICOD RL	Nicaraguan Centre of Housing Cooperatives with Mutual Help
CPC	Council of Citizen Power
ENACAL	Nicaraguan Water and Sewerage company
ERAMAC/BdMM	Municipal Company for Housing and Building Materials in León
FOSOVI	Social Housing Fund (Government)
FSLN	Sandinista National Liberation Front (political party)
FUCVAM	Uruguayan Federation of Housing Cooperatives with Mutual Help
GoN	Government of Nicaragua
IDB	Inter-American Development Bank
INIDE	National Institute of Development Information (Government)
INSS	Nicaraguan Institute of Social Security (Government)
INVUR	Nicaraguan Institute of Urban and Rural Housing (Government)
MCN	Nicaraguan Community Movement
PNV	National Housing Plan

Introduction

For a long time, self-help housing in Nicaragua was a matter of great importance. The occurrence of self-help or self-managed housing is the result of two factors: (1) the public sector has insufficient financial means to build a large number of social houses, and (2) the very bad socio-economic situation of the population means that many families have too little money to buy, build or renovate their house. Moreover, a large number of households with low incomes live in houses of poor quality. For example, in Managua this is 57 per cent of all households while 43 per cent of households cannot afford a dwelling on a 100-square-metre plot (Bouillon/IDB 2012). In 2012, a new government system for social housing was introduced.

However, for many low-income households there are few financing possibilities for house construction. Nicaragua is the second poorest country in the Americas,[1] after Haiti. The country has 6,071,045 inhabitants (as of June 2012), of which 58 per cent live in urban areas. Over 60 per cent of the population lives in the western part of the country, bordering the Pacific Ocean. At more than 70 per cent, the population is mainly urban in this area. The capital of Managua is the country's biggest city, with over one million inhabitants. On the outskirts of this extended city one can find many spontaneous human settlements where approximately 30 per cent of the city's population lives. Managua mostly has low densities and one can speak of 'marginal areas' near the city's outskirts. In other cities one can find similar situations, but at a smaller scale. Besides migration towards Managua, one can find 'migration out of the city' of up to 20 kilometres, which leads to suburbanization in the nearby rural parts. The second largest city in Nicaragua is León, with approximately 200,000 inhabitants, where suburban development is occurring through planned city expansion (see Box 20.1).

BOX 20.1 LEÓN SOUTH EAST

The urban expansion plan León South East (LSE) in the municipality of León is a significant development plan. Started in 1999, the plan originally aimed to produce 5,000 plots in order to facilitate self-help housing. This largest sites-and-services scheme in Nicaragua is based upon the practice of self-construction; since 2000, 6,000 plots have been developed.

Under LSE, the local government bought land for housing and developed it with funding from the city link between León and Utrecht in the Netherlands. Plots were sold at low prices, initially at only US$250 to families with low incomes. In the period 2003–2005, approximately 600 houses were built annually through subsidies from the government and given through INVUR/FOSOVI (Bredenoord 2005). NGOs especially showed interest and within three to four years hundreds of houses were built with their help. Later on the prices of plots increased; however, this did not impede the selling of plots. By 2009 the first 5,000 plots were sold, the majority of them on the basis of payment by instalments. However, self-construction within León South East did not fulfil original hopes and a significant number of plots were not built upon. We have estimated that as of May 2013 about 2,800 houses were built on 5,600 plots (or roughly 50 per cent of the plots) (see Figure 20.2).

No measures were taken to stimulate plot owners to start the construction process. According to Tijssen (2011), some owners who have not yet built upon their plot argued that the plot 'is too far away from the city', 'the situation over there is miserable and there is no security' and 'we bought [the plot] for later on'. As a result, some neighbourhoods are abandoned and overgrown with plants. Moreover, community building is difficult according to the social workers and there are problems with public safety.

One can conclude that that the sites-and-services concept in León is not functioning as it once did. As a result, the municipality is trying to establish a strategy in order involve the private sector in the construction of houses for middle- and low-income households. This has been successful and various developers offer complete houses outside the

> original LSE zone, albeit at isolated locations. Although in its initial phase, one developer had already sold 167 houses within the León South East zone in 2012.
>
> Nonetheless, the municipality still faces certain challenges. For example, since the end of 2012, 650 invaders have illegally occupied land within a green zone. With high-voltage cables nearby, this dangerous situation forces the municipality to displace the settlers to new plots outside of the zone. According to Mario Balladares, General Manager of the Municipality of León, the families do not want to leave the dangerous area in spite of the municipality's offer of plots at accessible prices and with favourable loans from the municipality (*El Nuevo Diario* 2013).

Often, local governments in Nicaragua do not operate under effective urban planning that anticipates land use changes or the huge demand for land and housing. A growing population needs urban services such as streets with pavements, sewerage, electricity, drinking water, as well as access to schools and public health services among others; within the marginal urban areas there are many arrears in these aspects. Housing quality in marginal urban zones is mainly low: sometimes there are overcrowded houses, and houses have leaking roofs, earth floors, noise nuisance and an absence of privacy. Income levels differ quite significantly; this is illustrated in Table 20.1, which displays the five income classes of monthly income per household. Monthly costs for buying or renting a house normally cannot be above 20 per cent of a household's income, an indication given by the government.

The housing deficit in Nicaragua was estimated by the national government (INVUR) at 400,000 houses in the year 2005 (GoN 2005). Another source informs of a deficit of 745,000 houses, composed of a qualitative deficit of 420,000 houses and a quantitative deficit of 325,000 houses (ACENVI/SNV 2012).

In this chapter attention is paid to a housing typology for low- and middle-income households. This was considered necessary in order to gain insight into the construction costs low- and middle-income households face when building a dwelling. To collect this data, the authors held interviews in 2012 with several housing specialists in Nicaragua.[2] Furthermore, a series of housing activities in Managua and León were investigated, expecting thus to obtain an initial glimpse of the current practice of social housing in Nicaragua which might be an alternative to self-help housing. The results give an overview not only of the types of homes and construction prices but also of which party is building or offering the housing. Nonetheless, while the housing market for cheaper and affordable houses in Nicaragua comes into focus, further research is needed.

The chapter is organized as follows: in the next section the main characteristics of Nicaraguan self-help housing are described, followed by government housing policies at both the national and local levels. After that, contributions from the private sector, non-governmental organizations (NGOs) and other stakeholders are presented briefly. The urban housing challenges of Nicaragua are presented thereafter: housing typology, housing quality and future densification of housing. Finally, in the conclusion it is stated that self-help housing remains important in Nicaragua and that improved technical assistance for self-builders might improve the quality of housing. This is a realistic policy option for the time being, given the bad economic situation.

TABLE 20.1 Housing classification per income category in Nicaragua

	Monthly income in US$	Part of the population (%)	Housing classification
Extreme poverty (E)	≤58	11.7	Without access to a decent house or property
Poverty (D)	58–150	35.8	Sites with services or simple house
Medium low (C)	150–350	33.7	Houses of US$5,000–10,000
Medium (B)	350–700	13.0	Houses of US$10,000–15,000
Medium high/high (A)	≥700	5.8	≥US$15,000

Source: GoN (2005); adapted by the authors.

Self-help housing versus public housing

Self-help housing in Nicaragua is very common, not because people are fond of building their own homes, but rather due to the high level of poverty in the country. There are three types of self-help housing: (1) autonomous self-help housing constructed by the dwellers, (2) self-help housing in which the users hire qualified craftsmen for construction and (3) assisted self-help-housing (Ortiz 2004). In fact, according to the PNV (National Housing Plan), 85 per cent of actual housing production is realized by the mode of self-construction and self-financing (GoN 2005). Housing in Nicaragua was influenced – after the 1979 revolution – by changes in state policies. In one period the emphasis was placed on social housing projects and in another on sites-and-services schemes. During the first decade after the revolution, the government tried to set up social housing programmes but the outcome was not at scale. At that time international help, focused for example on low-income housing, was present in Nicaragua. We mention the many city-to-city and country-to-country cooperations, and the various international organizations giving help, including housing provision, in the fight against poverty.

One might assume that the massive execution of government housing programmes would diminish self-construction, but that is not the case in Nicaragua. In the 1960s, the institute INVI (nowadays known as INVUR, or the Nicaraguan Institute of Urban and Rural Housing) set up housing programmes through which entire neighbourhoods were created, for example the *Colonia Maestro Gabriel*, an urban expansion of Managua; this expansion was consolidated completely 50 years after its construction (see Figure 20.1). INVI sold 120-square-metre plots with basic houses to families. Without exception the inhabitants have expanded their houses, up to 100 square metres, leaving a patio of 20 square metres. This was initially modest housing for first-time homeowners; the households expanded and finished their houses in due course. Through the years, many houses were sold to other families. Nowadays this *Colonia* is a safe and quiet neighbourhood; some houses have two floors while some have rooms available to let.

In the 1980s the government initiated a plan to offer houses to low- and middle-income households. However, the number of built houses was too small and therefore municipalities – after 1985 – offered land-for-housing to families, usually with the consequence that families

FIGURE 20.1 Street view in Colonia Maestro Gabriel, Managua. Photo by Jan Bredenoord.

obtained non-serviced plots. Self-help housing was the main housing provision mechanism, but many households benefited from the help of aid organizations such as housing NGOs which offered construction materials and technical assistance. Sometimes there was even a building materials bank for provision of materials at reasonable prices.

After 2000, the Bolaños government started a programme by which subsidies were given, making possible the construction of a large number of houses from 2002 to 2005. There are indications that self-construction since then has diminished because of initiatives by private parties and the state programme. In self-construction everyone acts individually, and occasionally this might go on for years. Sometimes it is characterized by a long renovation process due to limited family incomes or responsibilities related to caring for children, parents and other family members.

Obtaining official data related to self-construction is difficult; there is no structural investigation on the housing stock. Nonetheless, according to housing specialists one can assume that the majority of low-income households still construct and renovate their own houses.[3] In 2012 and 2013, it was possible to obtain loans for housing self-construction and renovation through a programme of FOSOVI (the Social Housing Fund). Although the government – with the help of international funds – tried at regular intervals to invest in social housing programmes, their impact has always been too low given the huge housing demand. Additionally, the government gives priority to home renovations, meaning that small subsidies and loans can be used for that. One can say that self-help housing is still an important housing production factor in the country, often connected to poverty. As a result, the quality of housing in Nicaragua is particularly low.

FIGURE 20.2 Cooperative housing in León South East. Photo by Jan Bredenoord.

We postulate that organized housing provision in Nicaragua, whether by the government or other organizations, usually was only temporarily available and so did not offer a structural and durable solution to resolve the housing demand. This is why self-help housing is still a main factor in housing provision and home renovation.

Government housing policies

The role of the national government

Nicaragua's total housing stock is 1,116,540 units (INIDE 2005). Taking into account that there are 6,071,045 inhabitants (INIDE 2012), the average number of residents per house is 5.43. A considerable portion of the housing stock is in bad condition; these houses (about 400,000 or 40 per cent of the total stock) must be replaced or renovated drastically as, for different reasons, they do not comply with the minimum standards. However, there are some factors negatively influencing adequate housing in Nicaragua, such as: insufficient public investment in the construction sector; frequent natural disasters; social, political and economic instability; rural–urban migration; and the constant increase in new, poor families. While poor families, who fall into two wealth conditions of 'extreme poverty' (11.7 per cent) and 'poverty' (35.8 per cent) (see Table 20.1), are willing to build or renovate their house, they often depend totally on themselves. As such, it often takes these families years to finish construction; those living in extreme poverty have little ability to change their lives, and finding a formal job is extremely difficult. These households live in modest, self-built

FIGURE 20.3 Modest housing in Barrio Granada, Managua. Photo by Jan Bredenoord.

houses or in rented houses that are often in bad shape. The proportion of rented houses in Nicaragua is only 5–6 per cent, the lowest of any Latin American country (Bouillon/IDB 2012: 93).

The National Housing Plan 2005–2025 (PNV) contains objectives for increasing the production of housing. According to the PNV, roughly 40,000 units should be produced annually; however, current production is hardly 25 per cent of that amount. At the moment the PNV is under revision, given a changing political vision on housing and the limited financial resources of the government. After the Housing Law (Nr 677) was approved in 2009, low-income households could obtain grants and credit for housing (GoN 2009a). Since 2012, FOSOVI subsidies of US$1,500 are available for the construction of a new house; smaller subsidies are also available for home renovations. Additionally, under the Regulations of the Housing Law, conditions are defined for obtaining a subsidy or loan (GoN 2009b). Implementation of the law and regulations is controlled by the National Housing Council, an advisory agency, as well as by executive administrations such as INVUR and FOSOVI.

State housing policy consists of the following programmes:

- *Plan Techo* supplies corrugated roof sheets to poor households with leaking roofs.
- *Vivienda Solidaria* provides social housing for people with very low incomes.
- *Casa Mejor* is a credit for renovation programme within local communities that provides access to low interest loans of 7 per cent.

- *Crédito Justo*, aimed at social housing construction, provides commercial bank loans (for a maximum unit price of US$20,000) at a standard interest rate of roughly 8 per cent by way of a fiscal subsidy interest rate diminished to 5.5 per cent.

Based on the vision of INVUR/FOSOVI (n.d.) and an interview held with a representative of this government organization, the following aspects of housing policies were reviewed by the end of 2012:

- The establishment of a land bank in order to help the poorest people in obtaining a plot either on state property or on private land within (sub)urban zones.
- Stimulation and facilitation of small housing cooperatives; currently there are 300 housing cooperatives in the country, most of them in the establishment phase.
- Stimulation of private sector cooperation including banks, builders and developers.
- A refocusing of housing production on the effective demand, so that production is not oriented on what is necessary, but instead on what is possible and what people can afford.
- Stimulation of home renovations and focus on their funding.

From the beginning of 2013, families may receive small subsidy amounts of around US$650 for housing repair or up to US$2,500 for the construction of modest houses between 21 and 36 square metres. Funding by the IDB (Inter-American Development Bank) makes this possible. The government has chosen to supply built houses for the lowest income groups; these houses are donated to families that do not have the capacity to pay but urgently need housing. Selection of the poorest people demands a careful process, which is executed within the scope of programmes like *Plan Techo* and *Vivienda Solidaria*; these are government donations by intervention of the CPC (Council of Citizen Power). Currently, mixed housing funding (savings–subsidy–loan), copied from practices in other Latin-American countries, is present in Nicaragua (MacDonald and CEPAL 2005). The IDB and INSS (Nicaraguan Institute of Social Security) both help the government with funding in order to facilitate the execution of tasks within the social housing scope. Without these possibilities it would be very difficult to carry out the housing policies.

Nonetheless, the government and private producers together will not be able to generate more than 10,000 new houses per year – this does not meet the current housing demand. Limiting factors, indicated by INVUR/FOSOVI, include: (1) the majority of families in Nicaragua cannot afford to buy a house, regardless of how modest it might be, (2) the construction sector does not have sufficient capacity to raise production significantly, (3) the production of construction materials is insufficient and a significant increase is not foreseen.

The role of local government

Local governments can execute tasks related to housing construction in order to sell or rent them to families belonging to certain social groups. While not very common, this might be done by a municipal housing company. In fact, according to Article 6 of the Municipal Law, a local government is allowed to execute some tasks related to housing (GoN 1988). The construction of houses is not included, but it is possible to establish a municipal bank for building materials. The installation and maintenance of the sewer and drinking water systems are tasks of ENACAL (the local water company). Local governments are normally responsible for the physical planning, by which urban space is designated for various functions such as housing, industry, recreation and transport, among others. The municipal planning system of León has, since 1995, been developed at two levels: the city level and the neighbourhood level (Bredenoord 2005). In 2012 the guiding municipal-level document was the Municipal Plan for Territorial Planning and Development – draft November 2012 (Municipality of León 2012). Municipalities registered with INVUR can build (or have built) houses as well as request subsidies from the government. When a municipality wants to build houses, a municipal housing company could be helpful. For example, the municipality of León has done so with ERAMAC/BdMM (Municipal Company for Housing and Building Materials) in León South East, where 157 social houses were built between 2007 and 2012 and where 350 loans were issued for renovation of individual houses (ERAMAC/BdMM 2012).

Already in the 1980s, houses with various floors were being built in León within the 'Fundeci' complex through interventions of the Ministry of Housing Affairs (formerly MINVAH) and the municipality of León. In the same period the municipality of Managua built comparable housing with two floors within the 'San Antonio' complex. After 1990, similar housing projects, with up to three floors, have not been executed, although there is a demand for small houses from those wishing to enter the housing market; people usually rent a house or rooms through private parties.

In general, local governments do not have sufficient funds for the establishment of housing companies. However, outsourcing housing production, through alliances with NGOs and the private sector, is an option; often housing-NGOs have access to external funds while the private sector may be able to obtain capital. Cooperation between the public and private sectors will hopefully increase in the future, necessarily leading to the development of housing projects in cooperation with community-based organizations (CBOs). Local governments can, like NGOs, promote the establishment of housing cooperatives within their territory. The organization CENCOVICOD RL, or the Nicaraguan Centre of Housing Cooperatives with Mutual Help, is the umbrella organization that helps housing cooperatives to work on a mutual basis (CENCOVICOD RL 2012) (see Figure 20.2).

Contributions of NGOs and the private sector

In addition to public involvement in housing there are important private sector activities in Nicaragua, including the contributions of NGOs as well as of private building corporations, developers and banks. In this section, we focus briefly on the contributions of these private organizations. In most cases one can speak of cooperation between residents in a certain area, NGOs, a local government and contractors, among others for the execution of public works. Regarding housing, cooperation between residents, NGOs, CBOs and housing corporations and banks is essential too, as described elsewhere in this chapter.

Contribution of NGOs

It is obvious that NGOs in Nicaragua play an important role in providing affordable houses for low-income families. Often the NGOs administer funds provided by international organizations and donors. Important NGOs with a housing agenda, which operate throughout the country, are, among others: CEPRODEL, Habitat for Humanity, Habitar and PRODEL.

Based on the FUCVAM model in Uruguay, CEPRODEL (Centre for the Promotion of Local Development) specializes in the establishment of cooperatives and small housing cooperative assistance on the basis of mutual help. The FUCVAM concept was developed in Nicaragua with the help of external funders, local governments and international city links. Over the course of several years the operational mode of CEPRODEL with housing cooperatives has been improved (CEPRODEL 2012). Habitat for Humanity Nicaragua executes a programme for the construction of houses as well as for increasing the availability of affordable housing in various cities. This NGO supports the social production of habitat and, by way of local leadership, capacity development. It works with low-income families who earn less than US$350 a month, as well as providing support for self-construction through building the capacity of and providing technical assistance to homebuilders (Habitat for Humanity n.d.). Habitar (Centre for Studies and Promotion of Housing) specializes in the integral improvement of the housing situation in underdeveloped communities. Habitar often cooperates with local governments (as is the case in Managua, see Box 20.2) and locally organized communities. PRODEL (Programme for Local Development), an international initiative to improve the life of poor people in the northern and western parts of the country, was established in 1993. Since 2003, PRODEL has financed loans for home improvements through a loan from the IDB (US$3 million). The NGO operates like a bank to cooperate with organizations in microcredits for small communities and individual families for housing improvement (UN-Habitat 2011). It also offers technical assistance to families for home renovations. These NGOs take into account the following factors: (1) affordability, (2) the local context, (3) subsidy or donation conditions and (4) the potential level of self-help input of the residents. In addition to the NGOs outlined above, there are various other NGOs with housing programmes. Housing NGOs depend heavily on the subsidy system of the government; if the state subsidy programme is limited – which was the case between 2006 and 2011 – NGO housing programmes are limited too. Nonetheless, Nicaraguan NGOs have been overall very effective in obtaining international resources to provide housing for the poor.

BOX 20.2 ANEXO BARRIO GRENADA, SECTOR 17: A NEIGHBOURHOOD ON THE OUTSKIRTS OF MANAGUA

In this Managua suburb with 1,260 residents, the NGO Habitar executed a community project in cooperation with the municipality. The neighbourhood – located on the city's outskirts in the south – has been densified significantly since the 1980s.

Between 2006 and 2009 the situation in the neighbourhood was investigated and on the basis of the results partial improvement projects were started. For example, in order to prevent houses as well as soil from falling into the sewage canals, one project aimed to improve the walls of the open sewer that pass through the neighbourhood. To facilitate this, Habitar organized instructive workshops. A community house was constructed and garbage collection was organized. Another project is the legalization of property. Of the 286 plots with houses, 54 have been legalized (till November 2012). The project management obtained funding from the municipality of Managua and a Spanish donor.

> This programme is described by Habitar as an example of 'public social cooperation'. Additionally, some neighbourhood houses have been built with the help of government programmes; these are modest houses called *vivienda solidaria* and *vivienda semilla* (seed dwellings) that are sometimes donated by the government (see Figure 20.3).
>
> Alley improvement and the construction of new houses is also occurring in Anexo Barrio Grenada. Thanks to the Chilean NGO SELAVIP, individual households can receive assistance with home repair. Moreover, by way of a small subterranean canal and bacteriological treatment, waste water is directed safely to the open sewer canal. Within this small land development, Habitat for Humanity and Habitar are cooperating to bring about a small-scale expansion. Under this scheme, Canadian volunteers, in the form of a building brigade, helped the future inhabitants. Habitar purchased the land while Habitat for Humanity built houses of 24 square metres (at a cost of US$2,500 per unit); the residents in turn pay US$10–15 per month (to own). The project also included organized instruction workshops to encourage responsible water use. To execute this integral renovation of the neighbourhood, a significant number of external parties were involved.
>
> *Source*: Interviews held by the authors; see Note 2.

Contribution of the private sector

Nicaragua has a significant number of developers focused on the housing market. Currently, households looking to construct a house valued below US$20,000 can receive a subsidy of US$1,500 from INVUR/FOSOVI. In response to this limit, the umbrella organization representing the interests of developers (CADUR) asked the government to raise the cost limit for social housing construction from US$20,000 to US$26,500 (CADUR 2012). However, the limit does not seem to deter developers. While up until a few years ago developers only built houses for the medium- and high-income groups, lately a switch in focus has taken place. This is a result of the limited market for higher-income housing. Instead, there is a massive demand for the construction of houses for low-income families. Developers take this reality into account by offering houses valued between US$15,000 and US$25,000. In fact, in 2012 developers almost exclusively built modest, one-floor family houses, but only about 4,000 units. However, the quality of the construction process is not always adequate. For example, as a result of the first modest rainfall, about six neighbourhoods in Managua – built by private developers – were flooded. The (Housing) Department of Managua soon found itself in serious trouble (*La Prensa* 2013a).

In addition to housing developers, there are other private companies helping families to construct or improve their houses. An example is CEMEX, a large cement company that has the programme Patrimonio Hoy, through which it participates in the social production of housing and provides training to self-building families. Another example of corporate involvement can be found in León, where the Arnecom company built 330 employee houses with the help of the NGO Cáritas (Bredenoord 2005).

In general, banks have hardly participated in the provision of social housing in the past; during the past few years, however, this has started to change. Currently there are four national banks that devote funds to the finance of social housing: BANPRO, BAC, BANCENTRO and BDF. This occurs under an agreement with the INSS, which provides these banks with capital for social housing. Through the INSS contribution, the government gives – indirectly – a subsidy for the interest payment on mortgages in housing construction. The banks administer a fund of US$90 million; US$45 million is provided by the banks and the other half by the INSS. However, as the government recently announced that it will not renew the subsidy in 2014, it is very likely that interest rates and home prices will increase (*La Prensa* 2013b). The BDF is administering a new scheme, with funds provided by the IDB, through which it can finance rental housing with the option of future ownership (*El Nuevo Diario* 2012).

Contribution of CBOs

In Nicaragua the model of the community organizations emerged in the struggle against the Somoza dictatorship of the 1970s. Out of the *Comités de Defensa Civil* and later on the *Comités de Defensa Sandinista* (in the 1980s) emerged the Nicaraguan Community Movement (MCN) in 1988, which was organized at national level and had developed from a covert organization of the Sandinista National Liberation Front (FSLN) into an independent one. After the Ortega government came to power in 2007, the FSLN established the CPC, a group of organizations with a mandate to serve residents' interests at the neighbourhood level. However, results of various investigations show that these organizations often implement FSLN interests instead (Prado 2008; Serra Vázquez 2010). As a result, problems sometimes emerge between the neighbourhood committees of the Community Movement and the CPC. In this polarized environment, housing activities for neighbourhood renovation might suffer severe problems (Mansuri and Rao 2004). Although it is necessary to involve residents in the development of housing projects, both types of CBOs do not always operate together successfully. In order to avoid this, a (new) group of residents may prefer to cooperate instead with an NGO, which will organize the target group and involve the municipality in the execution of works and housing (see Box 20.2). Nonetheless, the contribution of CBOs to housing is indirect. While they sometimes take the initiative, they normally do not have capacity to invest. As a result, CBOs must be involved in social housing programmes.

Urban housing challenges

In this section, we briefly present some important urban housing challenges in Nicaragua. Research on the housing types in the country is under-studied. There is also insufficient insight into corresponding construction costs and aspects of land use. Some current solutions, which can be described as particularly 'suburban', concern small houses; this is understandable given the existence of so many low-income families. Finding urban solutions for low-income families in any future urban setting is challenging in Nicaragua. Future urban solutions demand the economical use of land and higher densities, which has consequences for housing typology. A second challenge is to create affordable housing solutions within the urban Nicaragua of tomorrow. A third concern is the need for renovation and transformation of existing urban areas in order to bring higher-quality housing as well as higher urban densities within reach. In 2013 this was still quite theoretical for Nicaragua.

Development of housing typologies

In this chapter we focus on a housing typology within the low- and medium-income groups. As a result, housing types include very simple, temporary, incremental and basic up to (modest) housing for the middle class, which is mostly residential. To establish the characteristics of each, indicators are used such as the amount of floor space and the costs of construction (sometimes including the price of the plot). In Nicaragua, different concepts are used to refer to a house of a certain quality. *Vivienda semilla* (literally 'seed dwelling') is an incremental house that ranges from 9 to 24 square metres while *vivienda solidaria* is a very simple house which is donated to poor families. *Vivienda básica* is a regulatory concept for a house of 36 square metres. Finally *vivienda económica* is a middle-class house. Over time, concepts related to housing have changed. The concept of 'social housing' is important, because the state determined the maximum house price limit for obtaining a subsidy – both plot and construction – at US$20,000. Table 20.2 outlines the social housing solutions offered in 2012 to households in Managua and León.

Table 20.2 gives an overview of all dwelling types located in well-organized suburban housing projects offered to residents in Managua and León. All types are for households looking to obtain or expand a property. Obtaining external help, through the work of volunteers, donations and subsidies, is for the most part possible. However, rental housing is not addressed in these projects.

One can find that very modest 'housing solutions' for incremental housing, solidarity housing (donations by the government) or House 'Roof' ('Techo', formerly 'Techo para mi país') were offered to households – Income Category E – by housing NGOs or the government,. These solutions were found mainly in Managua at the city edges. All other solutions were found in the urban expansion plan León South East, in the municipality of León. There the municipality is offering – through the involvement of the Municipal Building Materials Bank (BdMM) – houses with a floor space of either 42 or 53 square metres and construction costs between US$6,000 and US$8,000 (not including the plot). Most other basic housing types as well as more houses are being offered by private housing developers; building costs, which include the plot as well as a septic tank or a connection to the sewer system, range between US$10,000 and US$20,000. The Union of Teachers (*Ánden*) also sells houses to its members.

All housing types and applications for Income Category E are modest and affordable for low-income households (monthly costs US$10–20). With donations, monthly costs are almost zero, although these are limited in number. Nonetheless, housing solutions on offer for lower income groups are adequate, at least in León where households can purchase houses at a monthly cost of between US$70 and US$123 (November 2012 prices). This means that only households in the medium-low Income Category C – with incomes between US$150 and US$350 per month – are able to buy such houses there. As such, these households depend on donations and subsidies too. In general, the offer of houses between US$10,000 and US$20,000 is not sufficient for households in Income Category D. One can find similar schemes in other cities; however, not all cities have effective land-for-housing programmes comparable to León South East.

Future research in Nicaraguan housing should also contain aspects of housing typology, construction costs, costs of land and sanitary solutions, among others in order to be able to determine the suitable housing type per income group. This is, after all, essential information for the formulation of affordable housing policies.

Between 2003 and 2005, individual house plots in León ranged between 160 and 200 square metres. In 2012, smaller plots of 120 square metres could be found in León South East. Plot sizes in Managua are comparable but certainly not smaller. As such, research on housing typology – with characteristics such as plot size, living space, sustainable applications and

TABLE 20.2 Typology of social housing solutions in Managua and León (November 2012)

Housing type	Floor space (m²)	Construction costs (US$)	Monthly costs (US$)	Characteristic	Offered by
Incremental house	9	1,500	10	Expansion of existing house	NGO 'SELAVIP', Managua
Incremental house	18	2,500	10–15	Core house	NGO 'Habitar', Managua
Incremental house	24	3,500 built by volunteers	15	Core house	NGO Habitat for Humanity, Managua
Solidarity house	20–40	Unknown	Donation	Metal construction; plates of Plycem	National government, Managua
'Roof' (modest house)	About 20	Unknown; built by volunteers	Donation	Wooden house	NGO 'TECHO', Managua
Basic house	42	6,000 exclusive plot	Unknown	Small house, septic tank	Municipality of León (BdMM)
Basic house +	53	8,000 exclusive plot	Unknown	Medium house	Municipality of León (BdMM)
Basic house +	36	9,900 including plot and septic tank	68	Small house	Developer CastelNica, León
Basic house ++	44	13,990 including plot and septic tank	80 (estimate)	Small house	Developer CastelNica, León
Basic house ++	48	14,400 including plot and septic tank	100 (estimate)	Medium house	Developer CastelNica, León
Basic house ++	50	18,000 including plot and sewerage	80	Medium house, sustainable	Union of teachers, León
Basic house ++	42	18,500 including plot and sewerage	114	Small house, sustainable	Developer REALNISA, León
Basic house ++	50	19,990 including plot and sewerage	123	Medium house, sustainable	Developer REALNISA, León

Source: the authors' own compilation on the basis of information obtained by housing institutions and corporations (see column to the right) and from INVUR (interview).

services – should include other aspects of housing such as local market characteristics. A focus on future condominium housing in the cities is necessary also, for example regarding the fact that current housing densities in Managua are relatively low.

Improvement in the quality of the housing stock

According to experts, the quality of the housing stock in Nicaragua is generally low. This is understandable since a large part of the housing stock was built through the self-help efforts of a population with limited financial means. We believe that setting up programmes that provide homebuilders with technical assistance and small credits for individual home improvement is one of the options to improve the quality of the housing stock.

Urban renovation and urban densities

Because of a relatively high degree of urbanization in the western region of Nicaragua, some subjects about future cities are discussed here. Two types of migration exist in Managua: migration towards the city by poor people on one hand, and out-migration toward the city outskirts by middle- to high-income households on the other hand. Managua currently is characterized as low density; the majority of houses have only one floor. However, households independently enlarge their houses, leading to higher densities, for example by building a second floor. If Managua keeps on growing, structural solutions might be found for intensifying land use. It is quite difficult to obtain centrally located urban space in order to develop housing and commercial functions at reasonable prices.

For some parts of the city and certain target groups, the development of housing complexes with several floors will create higher density conditions, while public areas can be improved qualitatively by making space for parks and other green areas. The Inter-American Association of Housing (ACENVI) (ACENVI/SNV 2012) designed a plan for urban renovation in District II of Managua, near the city's centre, with an initial phase called *Parques de Santa Ana*. The starting point is the construction of 220 apartments in medium-high, four-floor buildings and the installation of public spaces with squares and green areas. In total, some 5,000 apartments might be built in District II. In 2012, ACENVI offered this study project to the government. Given these developments, more research on urban densification and new housing types is necessary in the near future.

Conclusions

As a result of the prolonged unfavourable economic situation in Nicaragua, houses often continue to be built via self-help. Since the beginning of 2013, within and around the cities of Managua and León as well as other cities, various illegal land occupations are occurring; this is an outcome of the lack of government policy for low-cost housing for low-income families. However, for the past few years and after a period of low public production, government housing policies have focused on stimulating the social housing sector (e.g. the government directly donated simple houses to very low-income families). Moreover, via subsidies and loans the government made a step towards a mixed housing finance system; current funding by loans of IDB and INSS are advantageous. However, the government is not able to stimulate strongly the social production of new housing because of a lack of sufficient funding and the low capacity of the population to pay for decent housing. Foreign aid organizations are active in Nicaragua, but these entities cannot solve the huge housing shortages on their own. There are many national NGOs focusing on social housing too, but current activity is rather low as they are dependent on external finance and public subsidies.

In this chapter some housing policy challenges are described. First is how to develop an attitude for research on decent and affordable housing types for low-income groups. Thus, insight into a housing typology and solutions for small-scale home renovations and related costs are essential for future housing policies. Second is how housing policy and practices can be developed, while involving the potential of self-help with house construction and home renovation, within the limited economic situation in the country. Finally, how can urban problems, such as a lack of urban land for housing and the demand for urban housing in higher densities, be tackled given the economic constraints? Housing research should be focused too on the prominent role of self-help housing and its potential for the improvement of the housing stock in the country. The development of housing policies is a matter of concern for the national government as well as the local government. Local governments might develop their own policy in cooperation with their local stakeholders (Municipality of León 2007).

There is a discussion about the role of the municipalities as a potential housing provider for targeted social groups. It is indisputable that municipalities may assist via initiatives such as providing technical assistance to self-constructors. Additionally, the stimulation of housing cooperatives is occurring and that is promising. The role of CBOs in Nicaragua turns out to be a complicated one, due to political practices (as outlined regarding the politically motivated CPC). Moreover, banks can be involved in the social housing theme; there are signs that this is beginning to work. The government continues to opt for the status quo on housing production, and focuses more on the improvement of houses.

Notes

1 In Nicaragua, GDP per capita (2005) is PPP $2,430. Online. Available at http://hdrstats.undp.org/en/indicators/20206.html (accessed 18 June 2013).
2 Interviewed housing specialists are: Stalin Peña Solis (ACENVI); Bernarda López (Ánden – Syndicate of teachers); Yilver Guerrero and Fabricio Munguía (Municipality of León); Ninette Morales and Cony Rosales (Habitar); César Sandino and Tito Castillo (CADUR); Faníz Jirón (CENCOVICOD RL); Dalila González and Rigoberto Hernández (Ceprodel); Ananieth Cano Ocampo (Cooperativa de Vivienda La Esperanza, Estelí); Stewart Hadacre (Habitat for Humanity, Canada); Guillermo Arana Campos (INVUR/FOSOVI – National Government); Julio Denis Jaleano (Poder Ciudadana Managua); Tomás Donaire, PRODEL, León; Modesto Jarquín (National Council of City Links between Nicaragua and The Netherlands).
3 The authors have spoken with the mentioned housing specialists; according to them it is estimated that at least 70 per cent of households in Nicaragua still construct their house by self-management.

References

ACENVI/SNV (2012) 'Construyendo una Ciudad Sana. Proyecto de renovación urbana, Distrito II Managua', Primera Etapa Parques de Santa Ana, Version 16 February 2012, Managua: Acenvi.
Bouillon, C. and IDB (ed.) (2012) *Room for Development*. New York: Palgrave Macmillan.
Bredenoord, J. (2005) *Estrategias de desarrollo urbano en León, Nicaragua, bi-lingual*. Amsterdam: Dutch University Press.

CADUR (2012) 'Propuesta para el Fortalecimiento del Programa Nacional de Vivienda', Managua: Cámara de Urbanizadores de Nicaragua.
CENCOVICOD RL (2012) 'Cooperativas de vivienda; Construyendo comunidades con la Ley 677', Propuesta de Financiamiento para Proyecto habitacionales en Lotes Concentrados, ejecutados por Cooperativas de Vivienda por Ayuda Mutua, Version: 6 October 2012, Managua: CENCOVICOD RL.
CEPRODEL (2012) *Documentos normativos. Colección: Gerencia Social – Cooperativas de Vivienda por Ayuda Mutua*. Managua: CEPRODEL.
El Nuevo Diario (2012) 'BDF con novedoso programa de viviendas'. Online. Available at www.elnuevodiario.com.ni (accessed 20 June 2013).
El Nuevo Diario (2013) '16 propiedades ocupadas en León'. Online. Available at www.elnuevodiario.com.ni (accessed 20 June 2013).
ERAMAC/BdMM (2012) *Presentación Banco de Materiales 2007–2012*. León: Municipality.
GoN (1988) *Ley de Municipios*. Managua: National Government.
GoN (2005) *Plan Nacional de Vivienda de la República de Nicaragua 2005–2025*. Managua: National Government.
GoN (2009a) *Ley especial para el fomento de la construcción de vivienda y de acceso a la vivienda de interés social*. Managua: National Government.
GoN (2009b) *Reglamento de la Ley No. 677*. Managua: National Government.
Habitat for Humanity (n.d.) Information on Nicaragua housing. Online. Available at www.habitatnicaragua.org (accessed 20 June 2013).
INIDE (2005) *VIII Censo de Población y IV de Vivienda*. Managua: National Government. Online. Available at www.inide.gob.ni (accessed 20 June 2013).
INIDE (2012) *Población Total, estimada al 30 de Junio del año 2012*. Managua: National Government. Online. Available at www.inide.gob.ni (accessed 20 June 2013).
INVUR/FOSOVI (n.d.) *Information on Nicaragua housing*. Managua: National Government. Online. Available at www.invur.gob.ni (accessed 20 June 2013).
La Prensa (2013a) 'Dueños de casas están indefensos'. Online. Available at www.laprensa.com.ni (accessed 26 June 2013).
La Prensa (2013b) 'Subsidio a viviendas no se renovará'. Online. Available at www.laprensa.com.ni (accessed 26 June 2013).
MacDonald, J. and CEPAL (2005) *La otra agenda urbana. Tareas, experiencias y programas para aliviar la pobreza y precariedad en las ciudades de América Latina y el Caribe*. Santiago de Chile: United Nations.
Mansuri, G. and Rao, V. (2004) 'Community-Based and -Driven Development: a Critical Review', *The World Bank Research Observer*, 19: 1, Washington, DC: World Bank.
Municipality of León (2007) 'Plan de Acción de Vivienda León 2008', document of the City link León – Utrecht, León: Municipality.
Municipality of León (2012) *Plan Municipal de Ordenamiento y Desarrollo Territorial,* document of the City of León, draft November 2012, León: Municipality.
Ortiz F, E. (2004) *Notas sobre la producción social de viviendas; elementos básicos para su conceptualización e impulso*. Mexico DF: Casas y Ciudad.
Prado, S. (2008) *Modelos de participación ciudadana y presupuestos municipales,* Entre los CDM y los CPC. Managua: CEAP.
Serra Vázquez, L. (2010) 'Los retos de la participación ciudadana a nivel municipal en Nicaragua', *Colección OSAL*, Clacso XI (27): 98–115, Buenos Aires: CLACSO. Online. Available at bibliotecavirtual.clacso.org.ar/ar/libros/osal/osal27/10Serra.pdf (accessed 6 October 2013).
Tijssen, J. (2011) 'To move or not to move: opportunities and challenges for low-income households to build a house in León Southeast, Nicaragua', Master thesis, Utrecht University.
UN-Habitat (2011) *Affordable Land and Housing in Latin America and the Caribbean*. Nairobi: UN-Habitat.

PART IV

Africa
Introduction

Paul van Lindert, Jan Bredenoord and Peer Smets

Africa is still a predominantly 'rural' continent, but projections for the coming decades forecast a rapid urban transition. Although only 40 per cent of Africa's aggregate population is defined as urban, most population increase already occurs in cities. Some of the chief cities in the continent boast huge rates of population growth, but the biggest amount of urban growth is concentrated in the smaller and medium-sized towns (Majale et al. 2011; UN-Habitat 2014).

The regional difference between the countries north and south of the Sahel region is huge. While the northern African countries have markedly above average urbanization levels (54 per cent) compared to the sub-Saharan African countries, they also are characterized by their lower demographic growth patterns. With the exception of some countries, most notably South Africa, the sub-Saharan African region struggles with high fertility rates (Parnell and Walawege 2011). These and other characteristics – such as poor health care, low levels of education, vulnerable livelihoods and high rates of poverty – reflect the differences in economic development between North Africa and sub-Saharan Africa. In the academic debate surrounding sub-Saharan African urbanization, the rare phenomenon of rapid city growth without economic development in the cities has been typified as a form of 'African exceptionalism' (McGranahan et al. 2009; White et al. 2008). Although the economies of many sub-Saharan African countries have recently shown sustained patterns of growth, much of this growth is still based on the export of primary products without significant industrialization in the cities.

While North African cities saw their absolute numbers of slum dwellers decrease over the past two decades, the corresponding trends for sub-Saharan African countries are gloomy. Majale et al. (2011) explain the different trends by pointing to the large-scale implementation of housing programmes across the North African region. They also draw attention to the fact that the quality of housing in low-income settlements in sub-Saharan African cities is extremely low – in fact, much lower than in comparable settlements in Asia or Latin America. A very important reason for such extreme housing deficiencies is lack of land tenure security, which also limits the self-help incremental housing potential.

The collection of chapters in this final part of the book elaborate on the urban housing conditions for the lower income groups in five African countries: Egypt, South Africa, Nigeria, Kenya and Ghana.

In Chapter 21, *Ahmed Soliman* presents a critical review and analysis of Egypt's massive housing programmes during the past 40 years. Such housing programmes are, by and large, embedded in policies to develop many new towns in the desert areas of northern Egypt. His review of the various housing programmes that were implemented throughout the years provides a detailed account of the different modalities of housing provision, distinguishing between the formal, informal and hybrid modes of supply. Most of the more recent housing programmes and projects that target Egypt's urban poor can be considered as 'hybrid'. This follows from the dominant forms of housing policies through which land is being allocated by the state; private parties are involved for the development of land while labour is provided by the low-income settlers. Soliman's account is, in essence, the story of Egypt's successive public housing programme failures. In it, he reveals how well-intentioned policies to develop the country and to house the urban masses have led to unaffordable and unsustainable results. Time and again, these programmes have failed to meet the effective demands of the poor. In addition to being unaffordable to the poor, most of these new housing options are also situated in remote desert areas or in distant new towns, which makes it difficult for people to earn a living. As a result, many poor families resort to informal housing on agricultural lands near the cities, thus contributing to the loss of food production areas. The distortions that have been created in the housing market have led to massive housing vacancies, while investment in the rental market was curbed.

Marie Huchzermeyer elaborates in Chapter 22 on the housing policies of post-apartheid South Africa. Her analysis points to the substantial distortions and disparities of the South African housing market. These are attributed both to the spatial-economic legacy of 46 years of apartheid policy and the particular way in which post-apartheid urban and housing policies have engaged with this reality. The main mechanism that has been applied steadily to provide housing to South Africa's urban poor was based on the supply-side, once-off capital subsidy to land developers who produce estates with small, free-standing houses. Since 1994, this grant mechanism has been the main ingredient of the state's housing assistance programmes to the poor, who could achieve ownership of such standardized housing units for free. Typically, the locations of such housing projects are in the peripheries of cities or in some cases are even more remote, which contributes to an exacerbation of poverty because of the resulting disconnection from urban labour markets. There is an urgent need to shift away from the free delivery of houses to a more diverse, productive and participatory housing approach that focuses on incremental housing through assisted self-help programmes and informal settlement upgrading. Although it is recognized now that the state should reform its housing delivery and allocation policies, Huchzermeyer describes the many political, ideological and bureaucratic hurdles of such policy change. Most revealing is her perspective on the government's 'slum eradication' focus, instead of 'slum upgrading', which has encouraged provinces and municipalities across South Africa to set informal settlement eradication targets.

Nigeria is another country that is known for its eradication of informal settlements. In Chapter 23, *Uche Cosmas Ikejiofor* explains how recent demolitions of settlements in Lagos and Abuja were motivated by modernist planning concepts which favour mega-projects and do not take into account informal city development. As in Egypt and South Africa, the land issue is the main bottleneck for the urban poor to house themselves. With no other alternative than to rent, most poor squat on vacant lands at the peripheries of the cities. Against that background, and with the aim to use scarce public resources efficiently, Nigeria's new housing policy shifted to increase the involvement of real estate developers, building companies and mortgage institutions by way of engaging them in public–private partnerships (PPP). The policy aims to unleash the potential of the private sector, households and community organizations. Ikejiofor's critical assessment of the new policy discloses the main bottlenecks, which include a diversity of institutional and managerial weaknesses and issues of deception in the private and the public sectors. So far, the PPP experience in Nigeria has shown that such partnerships do not lead necessarily to sustainable housing that is affordable to the neediest citizens. The PPP strategy in housing delivery has been largely implemented as a solely formal sector strategy, resulting in high delivery costs and very limited impact for the lower income groups. The author argues that approaches likely to make significant impact on urban low-income housing supply on a sustainable basis must involve informal sector housing producers made up of private householders and small-scale producers.

In Chapter 24, *Bob Hendriks* discusses low-income housing and housing policies in Kenya. While presenting a detailed account of housing delivery mechanisms and the impacts of housing policies on the urban poor, he is particularly interested in discovering innovative ways of governance. His assessment of conventional state housing provision policies is that these have had only limited impacts on the poor. Some of the reasons for limited impact include institutional constraints, exclusionary allocation procedures and occupation by the better off. Housing cooperatives, trusts and societies have recently grown substantially in Kenya and the author considers the emergence and impact of such institutions as promising. These and other community-led initiatives can make the difference for Kenya's urban poor. Most projects focus on securing land tenure, assisting self-help incremental housing and settlement upgrading. Another interesting housing practice described by Hendriks is the phenomenon of so-called 'dweller-initiated transformations' of formally built dwellings in middle-class estates in Nairobi by the owners, who extend their homes informally. This hybrid form of housing provision offers reasonably affordable rental housing for low-income groups.

Paul Yankson and Katherine Gough highlight the important role of rental accommodation in compound housing for Ghana's urban poor in Chapter 25. Such housing provides the type of low-cost accommodation which, in most other contexts, is found in the self-build settlements. The chapter starts with an overview of public housing policies since Ghana's independence. The impact upon low-income households has been minimal; the state typically acts as facilitator of private sector-led housing and the resulting housing units are only affordable to the middle and upper income segments of the population. The authors then explain the different land allocation systems in Ghana. The urban land market has different segments, which operate side by side: Parallel to the modern land market there is a traditional market of customary lands, although the latter also is increasingly commoditized. That makes it ever more challenging for the poor to obtain access to land. The problematic land issue is the main reason for the importance of rental housing in urban Ghana. The authors further elaborate on the nature of landlordism, tenancy dynamics and tenant/landlord relationships.

References

McGranahan, G., Mitlin, D., Satterthwaite, D., Tacoli, C. and Turok, I. (2009) *Africa's Urban Transition and the Role of Regional Collaboration*, Human Settlements Working Paper Series, Theme: Urban Change 5. London: IIED.

Majale, M., Tipple, G. and French, M. (2011) *Affordable Land and Housing in Africa*, Adequate Housing Series 3. Nairobi: UN-Habitat.

Parnell, S. and Walawege, R. (2011) 'Sub-Saharan African urbanisation and global environmental change', *Global Environmental Change*, 21 (supplement 1): 12–20.

UN-Habitat (2014) *The State of African Cities: Re-imagining Sustainable Urban Transitions*. Nairobi: UN-Habitat.

White, M.J., Mberu, B.U. and Collinson, M.A. (2008) 'African urbanization: recent trends and implications', in G. Martine, G. McGranahan, M. Montgomery and R. Fernández-Castilla (eds) *The New Global Frontier: Urbanization, Poverty and Environment in the 21st Century*. London: Earthscan.

21
PATHWAYS TOWARDS SELF-HELP HOUSING INNOVATIONS IN EGYPT

Ahmed M. Soliman

Abbreviations

CAPMAS	Central Agency for Public Mobilization and Statistics
GOPP	General Organization for Physical Planning
ISDF	Informal Settlements Development Facility
NGO	Non-government organization
NHP	National Housing Project
NSHP	National Social Housing Programme

Introduction

After the 1973 war, the Egyptian government initiated an ambitious development programme to build a series of new towns in the desert and to redevelop the Suez Canal cities. The policy, based on massive housing programmes and involving assisted self-help techniques, aimed to tackle the country's acute housing shortage. However, this chapter illustrates that the urban housing crisis in Egypt is a problem not of scarcity but instead one of a distorted housing market whereby an accumulation of ill-conceived and inadequate policies led over time to a mismatch between supply and demand as well as to severely curtailed private sector investment in housing construction. The government's failure to ensure affordable, viable housing for the urban poor has led many to build homes – semi-legally or illegally – on privately owned agricultural land that skirts urban areas.

This chapter, based upon previous research (Soliman 1991, 2012a) as well as a more recent ethnographic study which employed official document review and informal interviews with stakeholders,[1] critically reviews the debate on self-help housing techniques and their relation to the transformation of Egypt's urban housing policies during a period of socio-economic and political transition. It analyses the impact of such policies in selected new towns, and then focuses on communal self-help housing occurring on agricultural land located at the urban fringes which now accounts for 35–40 per cent of total housing production. The study shows that there are diverse and complex mechanisms behind housing informality in Egyptian cities including at the local level 'technical enablement', or informal housing governance which facilitates cooperation among various actors. Here it was predicted that economic and governance reforms, with contributions from grassroots organizations, would facilitate communal self-help housing as a sustainable and innovative housing solution. Finally, the extent to which the Mubarak National Housing Project facilitated access to housing for the urban poor is also examined.

The chapter is organized into five parts. The first part outlines the current housing situation in Egypt while the second describes the evolution of self-help housing. Next, self-help housing within the framework of Egypt's new towns is discussed. The fourth part examines the Mubarak National Housing Project both before and after the revolution. Finally, the last section provides recommendations for future action.

The housing situation in Egypt

Egypt's population, currently approaching 92 million (CAPMAS 2013), is expected to reach 151 million by 2050; 62.4 per cent of this population will live in urban environments. Satellite images already reveal substantial informal housing developments on agricultural land as belts of poverty surrounding Egyptian cities. The result is a growing divergence between the *old* and the *new* parts of the urban agglomeration, a 'great divide' between 'establishing', 'struggling' and 'emerging' urban spaces (Soliman 2012b). The first space is the domain of the new gated communities of society's elites while the second is the formal city which symbolizes a community that obeys prevailing laws. The final emerging space of housing informality is the domain of the urban poor.

While urban housing production is controlled by the state, the market and the community-based systems, housing development in Egypt occurs within both formal and informal systems. The difference between formal and informal housing relates to the legality of tenure, the level of workforce segregation, the use of waged labour, the significance of the means of production and the purpose for acquiring the housing unit. These different forms of housing production, based on supply, demand and manner of construction, are interrelated.

Formal housing can be divided into three subgroups: private, public and slum housing located in the city centre.[2] Each is considered formal because it

- is built by affluent groups and organized institutions either by individual or mass production;
- uses a capitalist form of production;
- obeys the prevailing law, including local building codes and regulated styles of construction.

Informal housing is subdivided into three sub-typologies: squatter, semi-informal and hybrid housing (Soliman 1989, 2004). These, in turn, are linked to various forms of capital by which different types of informal housing development can be identified:

- Squatter housing, often constructed using self-help techniques, involves the illegal occupation of mostly publicly owned land.
- Semi-informal housing or housing informality relies on communal self-help housing; this is a process of informal housing construction featuring individual innovations that

are not developed through regulated procedures or with the help of recognized housing institutions. Housing informality follows the same steps as formal housing but at a smaller scale, with variation in the capital involved (in terms of semi- and petty capitalist) as well as backing through the covert role of legal institutions. Its mode of construction depends on the requirements of middle-income groups and of the urban poor. Communal self-help housing exists in the Egyptian informal landscape on agricultural land whereby social networks are important elements for producing a commodity in a short time and at the lowest cost. Nonetheless, illegally constructed semi-informal housing has legality of tenure. Many factors have facilitated or constrained the expansion of semi-informal housing nationally.
- Hybrid housing sits in-between housing informality, which is primarily for use and exchange value, and squatter housing, which is for use value.

During the inter-census period from 1986 to 1996, the average annual growth rate of urban housing construction in Egypt (at 3.6 per cent) far surpassed the urban population growth rate (at 1.9 per cent). In the subsequent inter-census period from 1996 to 2006, the number of urban housing units produced annually grew to 263,838. Of these, 55.6 per cent were formal and 45.4 per cent were informal. By 2007, an estimated 8.5 million informal housing units held at least 21.2 and 12.8 million Egyptians in urban and rural areas, respectively. In 2006, the total number of housing units in urban areas reached 14,282 million units; this amounted to almost double the number of urban households (7,844 million), which resulted in a housing surplus of 6,438 million units. Within this figure, 3,428 million units were vacant, 1,102 million units were unavailable because of a lack of basic services and 1,908 units million have been kept unused for future speculation (CAPMAS 2006). Units are traditionally kept vacant with the expectation that children will inhabit them after marriage, as well as for speculation purposes. Another explanation is that the sustained rapid construction over the past 25 years and the relative lack of alternative investment avenues made real estate an inflation-proof savings and investment mechanism, even without a rental yield. Continued uncertainty about the enforceability of the new rental law makes many owners hesitant to let their unoccupied units.

These statistics reinforce the argument that the urban housing crisis in Egypt is a problem not of scarcity but instead one of a distorted housing market whereby an accumulation of ill-conceived and inadequate policies led over time to a mismatch between supply and demand and to severely curtailed private sector investment in housing construction. The government's failure to ensure affordable, viable housing for the urban poor has led many to build homes – semi-legally or illegally – on privately owned agricultural land. This phenomenon is called *ashwaiyyat*, or housing informality. Thus, housing informality on agricultural land inevitably became one type of housing delivery system to accommodate the urban poor. In fact, approximately 40 per cent of the inhabitants of Egyptian cities now live this way.

There are three mechanisms for carrying out low-income housing projects: formal, organized (in the form of sites-and-services and upgrading programmes) and informal. While the first is a finished product, the latter two involve the self-help technique. It is also important to distinguish between self-help and self-build. Self-help is independent of others, while self-build is dependent on the cooperation of a second party. Self-help and self-build housing techniques are defined as the economic use of effort and sweat equity by an individual or a group; each depends on either external and/or internal help without using formal housing institutions (for example, through the financial assistance of family members). As stated previously, communal self-help housing is a process of informal housing construction that employs a community-based approach; many factors facilitated or constrained its expansion nationally. Assisted self-help housing is a construction method dependent on the cooperation or involvement of the state and a third party.

The construction of formal housing is subject to approval from several national to local governmental agencies, including the Ministry of Housing, while the construction of organized low-income housing projects needs official approval from the responsible institutions. These projects face several barriers including scarcity of funds, long and complicated procedures for project approval, and an extended period of implementation. On the other hand, the mechanisms used to construct informal housing are remarkably fast. They take no more than a few weeks and cost less than the official methods. Low-income groups have often relied on communal self-help housing as a community-based approach to accelerate their access to housing. Moreover, various actors participate or cooperate – informally, formally or both – in formulating, accelerating and encouraging the construction of informal housing. These include public bodies via a covert role (facilitators) and governmental agencies (organizers or regulators) that permit the relaxation of privileging law, allow the installation of basic services and accept the status quo of urban informality. In addition, small proprietors (providers) who own small land plots on a city's periphery or private enterprises (operators) that own large plots of land in key parts of agricultural areas as well as prospective customers supplied by the operators and intermediaries who regulate the exchange of goods and services among the beneficiaries also participate. Finally, informal credit institutions (the *Gamaiyyat*) which provide the necessary funding for goods and services also participate in the production of informal housing. All of these actors combined have facilitated housing informality and created housing market forces that accommodate the incomes of the urban poor (Soliman 2010).

Based upon a communal self-help approach, the urban poor have converted agricultural land into informal urban areas. In fact, housing informality is often developed in advance of the principal lines of urban growth and road networks and is often based upon the following factors. First, housing informality is developed on agricultural land where the landowner has some sort of legal tenure such as a formal occupation permit (or *hiyazah*). Moreover, the possibility of improved services and economic status as well as the ability to start a small enterprise at home are also important factors. Second, informal housing is built in close proximity to job opportunities, social community networks and amenities. Third, residents often incrementally adopt local planning conventions (see Soliman 2010) to provide themselves with suitable shelter without the burden of restrictive regulations and procedures. Instead, plot size, housing type, quality and level of investment and improvements to housing construction vary according to the level of secure tenure and the residents' needs and resources. Finally, the urban poor rely upon an informal credit system called *ghameyhia* that exists through cooperation between all stakeholders including the household, an intermediary, the landowner and an informal contractor (Soliman 2010). This collective monetary system operates in such a way that each stakeholder's needs in the agricultural land development process are met. Under this system, a certain amount of money from each group member is collected on a monthly basis; the total collected amount of money is paid once for each member on an alternating basis. In general, housing construction costs are paid on an incremental basis, with a down payment of between 25 and 30 per cent of the total cost; the rest is repaid on a monthly basis over three to five years.

As soon as the informal areas are consolidated and approved by the relevant authority, housing informality offers residents the possibility to change from illegal occupation status to legal residence status. This not only grants residents the opportunity to become owner-occupiers, it enables localities to become part of a formal city. Thus, unit designs and standards within housing informality are customized according to the residents' needs and requirements. Housing informality therefore offers a wide range of plot sizes with the conservation of local planning conventions as well as providing considerable flexibility in designing layouts. In addition, land plots can be used as an asset to protect residents from inflation and to facilitate the development of home-based enterprises, as well as to give residents attractive financial returns. Housing informality also enables the imbalance between demand and supply to be corrected (Soliman 2010).

Housing informality continues to be a response to the shortage of affordable housing, the scarcity of land for the urban poor, the relaxing of law enforcement and the weakness of urban planning. Therefore, housing informality is not developed through established or state-regulated procedures, and it does not utilize the recognized institutions of housing and housing finance, but rather relies on the system of communal self-help housing. The government is unable to compete with the preference for housing informality either in the implementation process or in the local credit system.

The evolution of self-help housing in Egypt

The evolution of the self-help approach and its impact on the housing policies in Egypt can be explored in five phases (Soliman 2012b). The first phase was the post-World War II period (1945–1952) which entailed the uprooting of entire communities. At this time, a policy using self-help was introduced, albeit on a limited scale (Fathy 1973).

The second phase was the period of extensive production from 1952 to 1970. Under Nasser's rule, the state acted in favour of low-income groups to gain political and popular support to sustain the regime's control over society. A massive public housing project was constructed during this time. In the early 1960s, a resettlement programme to develop certain areas in the prime urban agglomerations was established. Scattered core housing schemes using self-help housing were introduced in Cairo and Alexandria. Due to defeat during the 1967 war, serious economic disruptions occurred in Egypt, diverting all national resources towards the investment on military forces, halting public expenditure on housing and reducing foreign exchange reserves, all of which had major effects on the rate of housing production during that era.

The third phase (1970–1980) was a period of active but ad hoc state intervention. After the 1973 war, the open door policy, or *infitah*, was implemented in 1974 and the government intervened more positively in the housing market. Rebuilding the Suez Canal cities was a first step towards providing housing for rural immigrants. The government also recognized the role private developers could play in tackling the shortage of housing. As a result, this era witnessed various experiences in public housing, sites-and-services, core housing and upgrading schemes in both the new and old towns of Egypt. The urban poor, those on limited incomes and the self-employed were hit the hardest by the *infitah* policy. In the early 1980s, the state adopted an arbitrary role in the form of an unclear strategy in housing policy by facilitating the flow of housing components, but benefits of the effort were diverted erroneously to the middle and upper classes of society and away from the urban poor.

The fourth phase, beginning in the mid-1980s, was characterized by a slowdown of private formal and informal housing production combined with increased housing prices. During this phase, there was no clear policy to accommodate the urban poor.

The final phase began in the 1990s and lasted until 2010. To combat social instability and domestic terrorism, in May 1993 Mubarak's government announced a national programme to upgrade the informal areas of Egypt through the allocation of a total of 550 million Egyptian pounds, or roughly US$104 million, up to the year 2002. Nonetheless, attempts to further the enablement approach using sites-and-services and self-help techniques failed to tackle the urban poor housing shortage (Soliman 1995). In 2008, the government took an important step towards institutionalization by upgrading informal settlements through the creation of the Informal Settlements Development Facility (ISDF). However, little progress was made as the programme does not include self-help as an approach for upgrading the unplanned areas. Rather, the ISDF relies on a cost recovery approach in which housing is treated as an asset. Since Mubarak's resignation in 2011, little has been done on the ground for the urban poor. On the contrary, urban sprawl on agricultural land at the periphery of urban areas has flourished. It is estimated that during the 18 months following the 2011 uprising, Egypt has lost between 100,000 and 120,000 *faddan*, or roughly between 42,000 and 50,400 hectares, of agricultural land to informal housing. Therefore, agricultural land is being lost at an estimated monthly, daily and hourly rate of 25,666,666, 855,555 and 35,648 square metres, respectively.

Self-help housing within the framework of Egypt's new towns

After the October 1973 war, a policy for new towns was planned. The policy sought to develop new communities to absorb the rapid urban population growth of 1.5 million people in Cairo and Alexandria within 20 years of the establishment of these new communities, as well as to decentralize the population within the major urban areas and to reconfigure Egypt by establishing a new demographic scenario. After the introduction of the *infitah* policy in 1974, over a dozen new towns were built in what became known as the first generation. Later, second and third generations, comprised of 31 new towns dispersed throughout Egypt, were developed (see Figure 21.1).

From 1974 to 1981, authorities implemented several housing policies using self-help techniques within the reconstructions of the Suez Canal cities of Suez, Ismailia and Port Said. Among these policies were upgrading and sites-and-services programmes in the *El Heker* project in Ismailia city (Davidson 1981, 1984),[3] core housing in Suez city (Stewart 1981) and a three-story, low-cost housing block in Port Said city (Welbank and Edwards 1981). Learning from the experience gained from the rebuilding of the Suez Canal cities, the Egyptian government implemented sites-and-services and core housing policies in the first generation of new towns including Tenth of Ramadan, Sadat and Bourg El Arab.

These policies aimed to modify current housing policies through the inclusion of self-help housing techniques in order to minimize governmental housing costs, to release the government from having to provide complete housing and to stimulate individuals to participate in building their own homes. Several criteria guided these policies: the provision of serviced housing plots of various sizes for the urban poor in new towns; offering a wide-ranging choice regarding the type of housing plots, location and price; encouraging self-help housing techniques in the construction to reduce the average cost per unit; and land tenure opportunities for all income levels of employed residents. Finally, the policy encouraged a piecemeal process

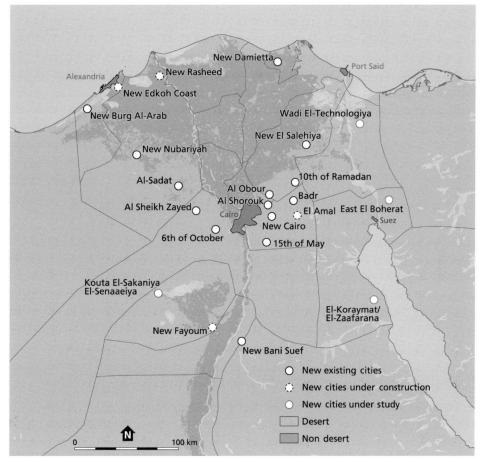

FIGURE 21.1 New towns in Upper Egypt.

that could adapt to the changing needs of a family resulting from *inter alia* different stages of the family life cycle, increasing incomes and changes in household size.

Policy implementation faced many challenges. Initially, sites and tenure allocation in the new towns were poorly designed. Criteria for land ownership and utilization of land for shelter were unclear. Management failed to provide housing plots to most of the industrial employees who worked in the new towns as well as for the self-employed. Three alternatives were available to the cities' civil servants, who were on fixed incomes: owner–occupier, a rental unit in the industry's own township or a plot of land allocated to those who lived, worked or were born within the city's jurisdiction. In all cases, certain restrictions were imposed on land allocations. For example, 25 per cent of the total price of the land plot was to be paid in advance with the remainder to be paid over ten years at subsidized interest rates with monthly payments amounting to 25 per cent of the employee's salary.

Another restriction was the stipulation that the housing unit had to be constructed within two years. As most urban poor are not formally employed, their access to credit facilities is reduced. This prevented many of them from obtaining a plot of land in the new towns. Moreover, for a variety of reasons, the urban poor also faced many problems in the construction process such as a lack of cheap building materials, an insufficiency of basic services (e.g. water and electricity supplies, and a sewage system) and a lack of flexibility within the housing unit to make changes to the interior or exterior spaces.

Self-help housing in the new towns also faced financial limitations. The few public mortgage institutions that exist in Egypt suffer from a lack of funds largely due to an overdependence on government subvention and an inability to mobilize and generate internal funds, as well as loan recovery problems. These problems hampered the operations of the few existing mortgage institutions including housing and development banks and cooperative housing associations, among others. At the same time, lending policies regarding down payments, interest rates, lending to building ratios, loan amounts and bureaucratic procedures were inappropriate for the working class. Institutional obstacles of urban governance and its effectiveness on self-help housing were noticeable.

The new towns could have experimented with new forms of government and reformed existing ones. Instead, institutions set up for the management of new towns appeared to be ad hoc interventions rather than deliberate efforts to create a viable administrative structure. The failure of self-help techniques in new towns as well as the inappropriate housing policy for the urban poor led people, particularly those looking for cheap shelter, to seek out alternative solutions. Among these alternatives were 'hand claim'[4] (or *wadaa' yed*), squatting in desert areas, erecting houses on agricultural land or on top of existing buildings, squeezing into cemetery sites at the 'Cities of the Dead' (Soliman 2004) or living in garbage dumps (Famhi and Sutton 2006).

The national housing project before and after the January revolution

In 2005, the Mubarak administration launched the National Housing Project (NHP) to provide 500,000 housing units within six years at an estimated cost of US$6.23 billion (GOPP 2010). Half of these units were to be located in old cities and half were to be built in new cities. The NHP was based on the seven principles shown in Table 21.1. It was estimated that 209,373 total housing units were built in 2008–2009; 92,378 units, built by the private sector, comprised 44 per cent of the total units while 105,578 units, built according to the low-cost housing projects in governorates and new cities, comprised 50 per cent of the total units. Finally, 11,408 units, comprising 6 per cent of the total units, were implemented by the government in both rural and urban areas. The deficit of the NHP constituted around 58 per cent of the total target units.

As shown in Table 21.1, the introduction of the NHP options enhanced housing market diversification for the urban poor. Housing options varied in size between 30–40 m^2 per rental unit for those with the lowest incomes and 63 m^2 per ownership unit. To encourage home ownership, the larger-sized units were reserved for those with the ability to provide a down payment. The NHP introduced the concept of 'Build Your House' or '*Ibni Beitak*' via a self-build technique; this aspect constituted around 18 per cent of the proposed project. The scheme, allocated in 34 sites and distributed across 13 new towns, offered 88,889 plots of land each measuring 150 m^2. The participants in the scheme had to obey certain regulations; the built-up area could not exceed 50 per cent of the allocated land plot and the maximum building height was three floors (see Figure 21.2).

Moreover, a financial subsidy of US$2,830 with a zero interest rate was paid to the applicant over 20 years and on an incremental basis according to the ground floor construction

FIGURE 21.2 *Ibni Beitak* scheme in Sadat City. Photo by Ahmed Soliman.

progress (Figure 21.3). The aim was to launch the project and create a core housing development which would encourage other people to settle on the site. The cost of the construction of the other two floors was dependent on the financial resources of the settler; construction was not to exceed five years. Another innovative step offered by the NHP for the owners of *Ibni Beitak* land was to provide, for those able to qualify and willing to build a second floor, access to a second National Housing subsidy of US$2,830 per unit.

Significant cost was covered and significant efforts were made by the government to enhance the subsidy mechanisms to reach the targeted groups. The total direct subsidy for each single plot within the original 88,889 housing plots was estimated at 57,000 Egyptian pounds or roughly US$10,755. Yet after accounting for other subsidies under this programme, the beneficiary of a scheme such as *Ibni Beitak* receives the largest direct subsidy amount per unit. Another concern is affordability, since some axes of the NHP (such as the private sector axis) require a contribution by the urban poor beyond their financial means. This is combined with the fact that the mortgage loan, a main channel towards acquiring financial support apart from a direct government grant, is constrained by a stipulation that restricts monthly repayments to 25 per cent of household income, which would not cover the principal. Unless the affordability constraint is resolved, it is likely that there will be a leakage of units towards higher-income households. Thus there definitely would be a growing pressure to increase subsidies in order to keep the units affordable for less affluent target groups in any future housing programme adopted by the government.

As explained above, while the NHP looks good in theory, in practice it failed to meet the requirements of the urban poor. The share of the *Ibni Beitak* scheme comprised 17.78 per

TABLE 21.1 The National Housing Project (NHP) under the Mubarak Election Program (2005–2011)

Aims	Type of housing	Number of units - Targeted	Number of units - Actual	Rate of implementation %	Actual rate of target units (% of total targeted units)
Providing ownership of residential units with an area of 63 m² in Governorates and new cities	Public	268,756	105,587	39.3	53.75
Aiming to implement a number of housing units with an area of 63 m² in new cities; 105,000 units thereof have already been delivered to applicants, and the remainder are currently under delivery according to the plan					
Providing plots of lands with small areas in new cities to the project of 'Build your House' or *Ibni Beitak* scheme	Private	88,889	76,852	86.5	17.78
Around 88,800 plots of land of an area 150 m² per plot were allocated for those who met the conditions of the NHP/Build Your House, with the aim to build a residential building consisting of ground floor and two floors (three units) with an average area of 63 m² for each unit, priced at LE 70 per square metre, and in the event of complete building of three residential units, the citizen is fully exempted from the price of the land					
Building housing units by investors	Private	35,469	14,642	41.3	7.09
Providing lands in new cities to investors to build housing units (63 m²) and facilitating ownerships to the beneficiaries. 6,675 *faddan* in 14 new cities were allocated to 141 companies with the purpose of implementing 35,400 residential units within the framework of the NHP					
Building the family house in 6th of October City and providing ownerships for families	Private	3,020	884	29.3	0.60
3,000 residential units were implemented in 6th of October and delivered to applicants, and utilities such as schools and markets are currently under implementation					

Description		Type			
Renting small housing units with area of 30–40 m² for the very poorest people	The project aims to facilitate housing units, with an area of 42 km² per unit, for more needy citizens who cannot afford down payments. Around 13,000 units are currently being implemented in 6th of October and 1,500 units have already been delivered	Public	74,958	3,449	4.6	14.99
Syndicates and housing co-ops. Renting 63 m² housing units in the Governorate and new cities	Aims to provide 20,216 residential units with an area of 63 m² per unit for members of housing co-ops and syndicates	Public	20,216	3,831	19.0	4.04
Building and providing ownerships of the 'Rural House' in the Governorate and its surrounding desert area (Back Desert)	Aiming to implement a number of housing units with an area of 63 m² in the Governorate and Back Desert	Public	8,692	4,128	47.5	1.74
Total			500,000	209,373	41.9	100.0

Source: Ministry of Housing, Utilities and Urban Development (MHUUD), 2009, adapted by the author.
LE: Livre Egyptien (LE 5.3 = US$1 in 2008–2009).
1 *faddan* = 0.42 hectare.

FIGURE 21.3 Incremental house construction in Sadat City. Photo by Ahmed Soliman.

cent of the total target units, while the people living below the poverty line in Egypt reached around 55 per cent of the total population (World Bank 2011). In addition, the scheme has not been applied in a way that suits the local environment. For example, government low-cost housing programmes are situated in the distant new towns or in remote desert areas, making it more difficult, if not impossible, for the urban poor to earn a living. Also, the NHP's pledge of 83,300 units per year would cover only roughly 50 per cent of the estimated need. Without the formal sector catering to the remaining 50 per cent, policy reforms must be put in place to remove the distortions in the housing market – distortions that not only have kept a large number of units vacant but have also stifled investment in the rental sector (see 'The housing situation in Egypt' section, above). In addition, the NHP failed to account for future price increases of various housing components. Nor did it consider the rate of inflation occurring in local and international markets. A lack of funds and the absence of services installation (including sewage systems, and water and electricity supplies) caused a delay in the implementation processes which only aggravated the price increase. Finally, restrictive procedures for housing and land allocation have discouraged people from moving into the new cities. Therefore, government policy creates dwellings without dwellers in remote areas and dwellers without dwellings in urban areas.

The shortage of affordable housing for the urban poor was one of the main causes of the recent revolt where Egyptians rose up in January 2011 to achieve the noble objectives of 'bread, freedom, dignity, and social justice'. Two months after the revolt, more than one million people had applied for housing to the Ministry of Housing and Urban Development. To absorb the people's anger, the multiple transitional governments responded to this huge demand for housing in three ways: turning a blind eye to illegal construction on existing residential buildings, continuing the laissez-faire attitudes towards illegal residential development on agricultural land and finally by introducing the National Social Housing Programme (NSHP) to build one million housing units within the next five years to meet the immediate demand for housing.

The NSHP is based on two principles: (1) allocating plots of land of 300–400 m² in the new towns to private developers who are able to finish the construction process within two to three years, and (2) continuing the '*Ibni Beitak*' scheme in new towns. This plan recalls the previous scheme, the NHP, in its size and ambition. However, an analysis of the NHP revealed that the government achieved barely 42 per cent of the total target units. Comparing the NSHP to what has already been implemented on the ground, the picture is unclear. Assuming that each 400 m² plot will contain 16 housing units with an average height of four floors and four units per floor, a residential area of 25 km² is required to hold one million housing units. In addition, 50 per cent of the area will need to be allocated for roads, services and open spaces, bringing the total area needed to meet the requirements of the NSHP to 37.5 km². This area constitutes 60 and 40 per cent of the total sizes of the new cities of Sadat and Tenth of Ramadan, respectively. It also represents 11 and nearly 50 per cent of the total serviced built-up area (349.166 km²) and the total housing production (571,770 housing units) of 17 new towns, respectively, in the year 1990. Moreover, the total cost of land and infrastructure installation under the NSHP will be around US$5 billion while the total cost of housing construction will be around US$16.66 billion. The total cost of the NSHP will be around US$21 billion. However, an annual estimated sum of US$4.2 billion will be needed to implement the NSHP. This constitutes around three and a half times the total subsidy amount for NHP housing which was dispersed over six years and not even completed. Moreover, it also constitutes the loan amount that the Egyptian government is currently negotiating with the International Monetary Fund to fund the economic reform programme.

Conclusion

It has been argued that, in the prevailing conditions of socio-economic and political transitions and market imbalance in Egypt, it is not possible for the urban poor to employ formal state or market supply mechanisms to access affordable housing – whether at a project level (e.g. sites and services) or a programme level (e.g. targeted subsidies, self-help techniques and urban development programmes). In the first generation of Egypt's new towns during the 1980s and 1990s, housing development via self-help techniques was seen as a significant investment engine to accelerate the development of the new towns. However, it did not meet the requirements of the urban poor. Thus, housing informality on agricultural land with the cooperation of various actors using communal self-help housing was a practical mechanism for meeting the urgent housing requirements of the urban poor. This process relied on a cost recovery basis in order to meet the costs of construction as well as land prices in a short period of time rather than depending on a formal subsidy scheme. As local residents have enough knowledge about affordable housing themselves to meet their requirements either through housing production or in the reproduction of capital, they have been innovative in a number of specific aspects. For example, the urban poor conceived a number of standards, including the freedom to shape their own built environment, an incremental construction process without restricted regulations, and the possibility to improve services and economic status incrementally. Once the urban poor implemented these aspects they could then break out of their poverty traps, take control of their destinies, and achieve economic and social 'lift-off' to housing development. In addition, a sort of informal credit system has flourished to match both the economic circumstances as well as the social dimensions of the urban poor. Therefore, Egypt's housing policy should provide for those standards in the housing process rather than relying on self-help techniques alone. All of this underscores the suspicion that the government's policy of encouraging self-help techniques is no more than artificial fluff. Rather than relying on self-help housing alone, housing components and simplified building procedures are the main ingredients of housing construction. Therefore, one lesson learned from housing informality is that it needs to be comprehensively re-planned, re-modelled, and re-coordinated not only so that better guidelines for future housing policies are formulated, but also to finally help the urban poor to break out of the vicious circle of poverty.

The real estate market of housing informality and the communal laws surrounding property rights take the form of a 'cultural struggle' thus benefiting both the underprivileged and the elites equally. The former scramble for their rights to housing and the latter promote an underlying economic and speculative mechanism serving only the financial sector and landowners. Nonetheless, both have created an informal economy by which urban informality flourishes in converted agricultural areas. Although this is a great loss for the national economy, the same mechanisms should be employed on desert land by involving private developers to replicate what has proceeded on agricultural lands. The government should continue to allocate large swathes of desert land in the new towns, albeit facilitated with social amenities and low cost public transport to serve as an appropriate economic base with special incentives to encourage private developers to invest in and develop these areas in a sustainable way. Moreover, developers should be given the freedom to re-subdivide the land according to the needs of the urban poor. Additionally, standards should be promoted to accelerate the housing development process to increase housing production for the urban poor. This mechanism has achieved great success for affluent groups in the gated communities surrounding Cairo city.

Under various administrations, conservative politicians and lawmakers have supported the status quo by way of outdated land and property laws, turning away even temporary use of fallow and unused land for occupation. Speculators and lawmakers hijack the production of housing for large-scale, profit-oriented mechanisms by colluding under the pretension of constitutional rights. The failure of Mubarak's institutions and the subsequent transitional governments prior to the Egyptian revolt of 2011 to suspend or disrupt this mechanism leads to more imbalanced housing conditions – a market flooded with unaffordable housing for the poor and abandoned luxury apartments for the wealthy.

Notes

1 Stakeholders include local municipal officials, residents, planners, NGOs, real estate agents and land developers.
2 These are old areas located in the city centre, having legality of tenure and constructed through the prevailing system, which have deteriorated over time.
3 A critique of this policy is discussed in Soliman (1988).
4 Hand claim or *wadaa' yed* means that a person can squat on a piece of land for a certain period of time.

References

CAPMAS (2006) *General Statistics for Population and Housing: Population Census*. Cairo: Central Agency for Public Mobilization and Statistics.

CAPMAS (2013) *General Statistics for Population and Housing: Population Census*. Cairo: Central Agency for Public Mobilization and Statistics.
Davidson, F. (1981) 'Ismailia: from master plan to implementation', *Third World Planning Review*, 3(2): 161–178.
Davidson, F. (1984) 'Ismalia: combined upgrading and sites and services projects in Egypt', in G. Payne (ed.) *Low-Income Housing in the Development World: The Role of Site and Services and Settlement Upgrading*. Chichester: John Wiley.
Famhi, W. and Sutton, K. (2006) 'Cairo's Zabaleen garbage recyclers: multi-nationals' takeover and state relocation plans', *Habitat International Journal*, 30: 809–837.
Fathy, H. (1973) *Architecture for the Poor*. London: The University of Chicago Press.
GOPP (2010) *Ibni Beitak Scheme*. Cairo: General Organization for Physical Planning.
MHUUD (2009) *The National Housing Project under the Mubarak Election Program (2005–2011)*. Cairo: MHUUD.
Soliman, A. (1988) 'Housing the urban poor in Egypt: a critique of present policies', *International Journal of Urban and Regional Research*, 12: 65–86.
Soliman, A. (1989) 'Housing mechanisms in Egypt: a critique', *Netherlands Journal of Housing and Environmental Research*, 4: 31–50.
Soliman, A. (1991) 'New town development as a means to housing solution: the Egyptian case', in P. Merlin and M. Sudarskis (eds) *From Garden City to Urban Reconstruction: A New Towns Perspective*. The Hague: INTA Press.
Soliman, A. (1995) 'A tale of informal housing in Egypt', in B. Aldrich and R. Sandhu (eds) *Housing the Urban Poor: Policy and Practice in Developing Countries*. London: Zed Books, pp. 295–315.
Soliman, A. (2004) *A Possible Way Out: Formalizing Housing Informality in Egyptian Cities*. Lanham: University Press of America.
Soliman, A. (2010) 'Rethinking urban informality and the planning process in Egypt', *International Development Planning Review*, 32(2): 119–143.
Soliman, A. (2012a) 'Tilting at pyramids: informality of land conversion in Cairo', paper delivered at the 6th Urban Research Symposium, Rethinking Cities: Framing the Future, Barcelona, 8–10 October.
Soliman, A. (2012b) 'The Egyptian episode of self-build housing', *Habitat International Journal*, 36(2): 226–236.
Stewart, R. (1981) 'The development of the city of Suez', *Third World Planning Review*, 3(2): 179–200.
Welbank, M. and Edwards, A. (1981) 'Port Said: planning for reconstruction and development', *Third World Planning Review*, 3(2): 143–160.
World Bank (2011) *Was growth in Egypt between 2005 and 2008 pro-poor? From static to dynamic poverty profile*. Policy Research Working Paper 5589, Washington, DC: World Bank.

22
CHANGING HOUSING POLICY IN SOUTH AFRICA

Marie Huchzermeyer

Abbreviations

ANC	African National Congress
BNG	Breaking New Ground
CLC	Community Law Centre
DHS	Department of Human Settlements
DoH	Department of Housing
NGO	Non-governmental organisation
NPC	National Planning Commission
NUSP	National Upgrading Support Programme
PHP	People's Housing Process
RDP	Reconstruction and Development Programme
RSA	Republic of South Africa
SACN	South African Cities Network
SERI	Socio-Economic Rights Institute of South Africa
StatsSA	Statistics South Africa
UN	United Nations

Introduction

Since South Africa's first democratic elections in 1994, a capital subsidy for individually owned, free-standing housing units has dominated state housing delivery to the poor in this country. Unlike the capital subsidy systems in Colombia, Chile and Costa Rica, which consist of demand-side subsidies disbursed in the form of a voucher with elaborate means-testing, a savings requirement and linked to credit (Richards 1995; Jenkins and Smith 2001; Gilbert 2004), the South African capital subsidy is a supply-side grant. The state disburses batches of capital subsidies (a fixed amount per household) to developers who produce estates with small houses. Provincial governments then allocate these units to qualifying beneficiary households for free, though often overriding the official allocation criteria (Tomlinson 2011: 423). Within this approach, beneficiary choice and participation are minimal.

Much criticism has been levelled at the peripheral location, segregated nature and top-down process of these fully subsidised housing developments. The state's acceptance of the shortcomings of this approach has gradually increased. In its own uncomfortable estimations, the housing backlog continued to grow from 1.5 million units in 1994 (DoH 1994) to 2.1 million units in 2012 (NPC 2012). Eighteen years after the advent of a constitutional democracy in South Africa, the African National Congress (ANC)-led government had begun seriously reassessing the direction of its housing policy. With impetus from the Treasury, which questions the financial sustainability of the state's expenditure on capital subsidies for formal housing, for the first time there is the prospect of a departure from the once-off, supply-side capital subsidy for the 'free-of-charge' acquisition of house ownership by poor households as the dominant housing assistance programme. The new, if still ambiguous, political and fiscal will within government to change the course of state housing assistance comes eight years after the official introduction of a policy shift termed *'Breaking New Ground': A Comprehensive Plan for the Development of Sustainable Human Settlements* (DoH 2004a) (officially abbreviated to 'BNG') in 2004. It also follows the renaming, in 2010, of the national Department of Housing (DoH) as the Department of Human Settlements (DHS). BNG itself stemmed from the ANC-led government's review of its first ten years of rule in 2003, which resulted in the first official acceptance of criticisms of the state's housing delivery approach. However, BNG (originally a five-year plan) and the renaming of the department did not themselves change the dominant course of housing delivery in South Africa in any significant way. This was largely due to the bureaucratic machinery built around the dominant housing delivery programme, opportunities for corruption and political promises made in relation to free housing delivery (CLC and SERI 2013).

The international social policy literature has long pointed to the difficulties of achieving policy change that involves termination of a programme (Nakamura and Smallwood 1980). 'If criticism of and opposition to a policy become sufficiently strong that the policy-makers feel impelled to take action, a policy is more likely to be altered than terminated' (Anderson, 2003: 274). Anderson (2003: 276) lists the following factors that 'may contribute to the termination of policies' – 'ideology, the urge to economise, altered political conditions, and clear policy failure'. However, the termination of a policy is 'difficult to accomplish', in part because of the political support under which it was first proposed and adopted (Anderson 2003: 274). Further, the severity and 'unpleasant consequences' of policy termination must be anticipated – '[i]t has an undertone of admitting failure' (Anderson 2003: 275).

While recent state-commissioned reviews in South Africa have unanimously revealed the necessity for change in housing policy, as I will show in this chapter, Anderson (2003: 276) observes that '[m]ost commonly … systematic evaluation has not been a critical element in policy termination'. Indeed, very few evaluations actually lead to fundamental policy change (Nakamura and Smallwood 1980). A common position, instead, would be to argue for more resources to be allocated to a programme before taking seriously recommendations for termination (Dye 1978).

This chapter reviews the difficult process of housing policy change in South Africa. Towards this end, it locates housing state assistance within a wider political commitment to social grants, as well as in the context of socio-economic and demographic change. The chapter points to the limited way in which incrementalism has been accommodated within shifts in housing policy since its introduction in 1994 and provides evidence of growing (and for the state increasingly legitimate) calls for a more fundamental departure from this policy.

The socio-economic context of state housing assistance in South Africa

South Africa's housing situation must be understood within a challenging socio-economic setting. The state's housing subsidy system in turn is part of an extensive system of social spending by the state, which seeks to respond to this context. The South African state's economic policy since 1996 has prioritised economic growth in order to capture resources for redistribution. This limited the housing budget when an increase in budget was needed to reach the state's housing goals (Baumann 2003). This macro-economic approach has not reduced inequality in any significant way. In 2009, 30 per cent of households in South Africa were reported to be spending below R 800/US$80 per month, whereas 68.8 per cent were reported to be spending under R 2,500/US$250 per month (to qualify for a capital subsidy for 'free' housing, a household may earn up to R 3,500). At the other end of the scale, 6.7 per cent were reported to be spending over R 10,000/US$1,000 per month (StatsSA 2010).

While the state argues that data collection methodologies (particularly from 2000 to 2006) changed to the extent that it cannot be conclusively inferred that inequality in South Africa has increased in the last decade, it does acknowledge that 'inequality remains high' (RSA 2010: 28). The expansion of the social spending, then, has merely enabled the state to manage, but not overcome, the country's high level of inequality.

One contributing factor to persistent inequality, no doubt, is the HIV/Aids pandemic, and the state's denialist approach to this disease from 1994 through to 2007. HIV/Aids is reported to be the cause of 40.3–43.6 per cent of all deaths from 2001 to 2011, and in 2011 it was estimated that 10 per cent of the total population (5.38 million people) was living with HIV (StatsSA 2011). Of these, 1 million are now receiving antiretroviral treatment (StatsSA 2011), at a considerable cost to the state. One of many ways in which HIV/Aids contributes to inequality is the far-reaching repercussions of the loss of an income earner for poor households (Butler 2010). The other contributing factor to high inequality, in the state's own analysis, 'is the high unemployment rate and low labour force participation rate in South Africa' (RSA 2010: 38). Unemployment is 'hovering around 25%, going slightly below at times of boom, and marginally above in the recession' (RSA 2010: 39). In 2000, it was found that 5.2 per cent of people employed were earning under 1 dollar per day (RSA 2010: 31). While the state's social spending has advanced functional literacy levels in the 15- to 25-year age group from 83.4 per cent in 2002 to 93.1 per cent in 2009 (RSA 2010: 43), the economic policy has not succeeded in translating this into higher labour force participation. Instead, the state has had to expand its social support system.

The number of people receiving income support stood at 14.1 million people in 2010. The reach of this programme rose substantially from only 2.6 million people in 1994, an increase from approximately 6.4 per cent of the total population to 28.6 per cent. The income grants, which include pensions, child support and disability grants, have resulted in a reduction in absolute poverty. Simultaneously, the provision of free basic services to indigent households increased. Despite these gains, the prevalence of underweight children increased from 1994 to 2005, and food security has become a central concern (RSA 2010).

Of relevance to housing is that household size decreased, with a reduction in fertility rates from 2.95 children per woman in 2001 to 2.35 in 2011 (StatsSA 2011). Cross (2008: 10) notes a further contributor to decreasing household size, namely that grant income to individuals allows them to split away from larger households and form new, though vulnerable and often female headed, households. This in turn increases the housing demand. In addition, migration flows within South Africa increase the housing demand in cities. While migration in South Africa is often misrepresented as a flood of foreigners entering through porous borders, far larger flows of internal migration have shaped South Africa's cities, with the highest outflow of people from the least urbanised provinces (Eastern Cape and Limpopo) and the largest inflows into South Africa's most urbanised provinces (Gauteng and the Western Cape) (StatsSA 2006, 2011). While '[t]he largest metropolitan areas have grown fastest', migration has not always followed economic growth (Todes *et al.* 2010: 5), understandably so as much of this growth has not created new employment opportunities. Analyses of migration found that movement of poor households between rural areas, small towns and cities is often 'in search of housing or services' (Todes *et al.* 2010: 5).

By 2009, 2.94 million houses fully subsidised by the post-apartheid government 'were completed/under construction' in a steady line of increase from zero in April 1994 (Gordon *et al.* 2011: 25). For the year 2009, StatsSA (2010: 22) reported that '12.8% of South African households were living in … [a] state subsidised dwelling' (this translates into 1.77 million households), whereas 13.5 per cent (or 1.86 million households) 'had at least one household member on a demand database/waiting list for state subsidised housing' (StatsSA 2010: 22). Around 13.4 per cent of all households (1.85 million households) were reported to be living in 'informal dwellings' (StatsSA 2010: 21), an indicator generally used in South Africa to determine the housing backlog. In Landman and Napier's (2010: 305) words: '[t]oday's land invasion is tomorrow's housing backlog'. Of concern to the state too is that 14.9 per cent of subsidised housing beneficiaries reported their roofs as leaking, and 16.1 per cent that their walls 'were weak or very weak' (StatsSA 2010: 23).

Cross (2008: 7) explores the interface between social grants and housing delivery, suggesting that '[m]any or most' newly formed households in Johannesburg's poor settlements

> include very little human capital, and have few if any members in a position to enter the labour market or earn income. These brittle grant-supported households seem to be appearing in proliferating numbers, making additional problems for the government assault on shack housing through accelerated delivery.

Cross (2008: 10) further points out that the cost of living in or maintaining formal subsidised housing cannot be sustained on grant income alone.

The picture I present might suggest a state doing its utmost in reaching out to the poor in the context of economic forces beyond its control. However, critics have pointed to corruption, dysfunctionality in state departments, limited commitments to service delivery and a state carrying out 'rituals that have little bearing on what actually happens inside the state and even less impact on the needs of the people, no matter how pleasing they might be to progressive policy advocates' (von Holdt 2010: 259). In relation to housing delivery, corruption, fraud and waiting list confusion are widespread (CLC and SERI 2013). One outcome of the state's ritualised expenditure on housing subsidies has been the exacerbation of poverty by means of increased peripheralisation of the poor from the urban economy through relocation to distant subsidised estates. As Baumann (2003: 85) put it, '[t]he overall impact of non-credit-linked (i.e. subsidy only) housing projects may be negative for the "very poor", because of its impact on their survival strategies'. The idea of a state locked into meaningless rituals speaks to the inability over the past decade or more to change in any significant way the interface between housing budget and the reality of poor urban households.

Shifts in South Africa's housing delivery and allocation system

From 1994 to 2004, the first decade of ANC rule in South Africa, the political focus was squarely on delivering large quantities of houses. In the first democratic elections in 1994, the ANC and its alliance partners promised 1 million houses in their first five years in government. The alliance articulated this promise in its election manifesto, the Reconstruction and Development Programme (RDP) (ANC 1994). While discarding most tenets of the RDP and instead conceding to a negotiated housing policy modelled to a large extent on the late apartheid sites-and-services framework with the addition of a minimal 'top-structure' or house (Bond 2000; Huchzermeyer 2001), over time the term 'RDP house' came to be adopted for fully subsidised houses. The new government achieved its target of 1 million houses in its second five-year term, and celebrated the delivery of 2 million houses during its third term.

Provincial governments manage the housing application and allocation processes according to a shortlist of qualification criteria covering income, age, dependants, prior benefit from the subsidy system, resident status and fitness to enter into a contract (DoH 2000). Formal queues or 'housing demand database' lists may entail over a decade of 'waiting', compounded by increasing corruption in the allocation process (CLC and SERI 2013). Housing subsidised under this programme is allocated under freehold title, with the intention 'to support further accumulation through household self-investment over time' (Cross 2008: 4). However, the legally complicated process of title registration is often delayed. Of '2.94 million houses reported as being completed or under construction' in 2009, only 1.44 million or 51 per cent 'are registered in the Deeds Registry' (Gordon *et al.* 2011: 25). An interesting insight into the scale of South Africa's housing delivery is that the 1.44 million registered subsidised houses are believed to make up 24 per cent of South Africa's formally registered property market (FinMark Trust 2011).

As a result of delays and exclusions in relation to the formal delivery system, alternative forms of accommodation remain necessary for both qualifying applicants and for poor households or individuals who do not meet the qualification criteria. Such housing is predominantly in informal settlements (both owner occupation and rental), in the backyards of formal low-income housing (informal backyard rental), and in those cities whose centres have experienced disinvestment such as Durban and Johannesburg, informally converted inner city buildings (informal rental or informal occupation) (see Figures 22.1, 22.2 and 22.3). All of these are inadequate, particularly in terms of tenure security and access to basic services. From the point of view of both those in the queue and the state, the only form of legitimate housing for the urban poor is the fully subsidised and state-allocated house with freehold tenure. Alternative forms of housing are considered temporary (Landman and Napier 2010), and their incremental improvement is understandably not recognised as a worthwhile investment. Those not qualifying for the formal subsidised housing largely see themselves as excluded and needing to get by on informal, temporary terms.

Housing policy since 1994 'has evolved over the years into a complex multifaceted entity with many components' (Charlton and Kihato 2006: 252). This evolution included the introduction of institutional subsidies for non-profit rental or so-called 'social housing', the establishment of a number of housing agencies with functions ranging from credit guarantees to social housing support and the introduction in 1998 of a 'People's Housing Process' (PHP). A number of urban development non-governmental organisations (NGOs) lobbied policy-makers for initially the inclusion and later the expansion and revision of state support for self-help

FIGURE 22.1 The Isiqalo informal settlement in Philippi – Cape Town, 2012. Photo by Marie Huchzermeyer.

FIGURE 22.2 Backyard rental shacks in Tembisa, Johannesburg/Ekurhuleni, 2012. Photo by Gauteng City-Region Observatory (GCRO), with permission.

FIGURE 22.3 Neglected inner city buildings in Johannesburg provide opportunities for informal occupation. Photo by Marie Huchzermeyer, 2013.

housing (Carey 2009). However, with the housing bureaucracy focused on meeting delivery targets, state-supported incremental or self-help housing under the PHP remained sidelined. It applied mainly to households who had received a serviced site from the development agencies of the late apartheid government, or for whom special deals were brokered with different tiers of government by the NGO People's Dialogue. Neither sat comfortably with the perceived beneficiary entitlement to a complete product or house (Baumann and Bolnick 2001).

For the period from 2002 to 2010, the state sought to incentivise beneficiary appreciation and investment in its subsidised houses by requiring a savings contribution of R 2,479/US$323 (DHS 2010). Those contributing sweat equity through a PHP programme were exempt from this contribution. As with the income criteria for subsidy qualification, the beneficiary contribution was never adjusted to inflation. The savings requirement, however, boosted the PHP for a short period. In the absence of any savings scheme to assist households to come up with the cash, beneficiary take-up of subsidised housing dropped. At that point, the Ministry attempted to mainstream the PHP. However, municipalities, provinces and developers, still focused on numbers, circumvented the time-consuming participatory processes of the PHP and invented what came to be known as 'managed/contractor driven PHP', in essence no different from conventional housing delivery, avoiding the savings requirement (DHS 2010).

Following a review, in 2009 an Enhanced People's Housing Process (EPHP) was included under 'Incremental Interventions' in the national Housing Code of 2009 (DHS 2009). Another programme under this section of the Housing Code is Upgrading Informal Settlements (DHS 2009), first introduced as Chapter 13 of the national Housing Code in 2004 (DoH 2004b). This new subsidy programme was introduced through the BNG policy. Building on a 'managed research process aimed at providing new policy direction and establishing a research agenda to inform and support policy decision-making' (Charlton and Kihato 2006: 259), BNG called for quality subsidised housing on well-located land with social amenities, in addition to informal settlement upgrading (DoH 2004a). BNG's emphasis on securing well-located positions in the city for its housing programmes related to a new commitment to break with the segregated nature of so-called RDP housing by encouraging mixed-income and compact or medium density developments, ensuring links to livelihood opportunities (DoH 2004a). Tomlinson (2011: 420) explains that BNG

> reveals a fundamental shift away from simply delivering RDP housing units to the delivery of 'sustainable human settlements'. BNG requires 'complex demand driven processes' to be carried out and therefore a much more sophisticated institutional response on the part of local government, than was previously the case.

Tomlinson further explains that, 'these increasingly complex responsibilities, coupled with insufficient capacity to adequately carry them out, have resulted in an inability of local authorities to adapt successfully to their new role' (Tomlinson 2011: 420). This is exemplified by the state adopting but never promoting its Upgrading of Informal Settlements programme. While the City of Cape Town led with the first submission for funding under the programme in 2008 for the Hangberg informal settlement, this remained the only project for several years and at the time of writing in 2012, no upgrading projects under this programme had reached Phase 4. As Tissington (2011: 9) notes, 'we have yet to see one successful and properly executed *in situ* upgrade of an informal settlement in Durban, Cape Town or Johannesburg'.

However, the reasons for non-implementation of the Upgrading of Informal Settlements programme go beyond the complexity of the challenge and insufficiency of state capacity. Its adoption into official policy clashed with a substantial political shift in relation to housing around 2000. This was captured initially by the Minister of Housing in 2001: 'Then it was where to build new houses; today it's how to eradicate informal settlements' (Mthembi-Mahanyele 2001). The state attributed this shift in priority towards achieving the complete eradication of all informal settlements (not their incremental upgrading) to its commitment in relation to the UN's Millennium Development Goals (Sisulu 2005). The United Nations (UN) promoted the Millennium Development Goal target to significantly improve the lives of at least 100 million 'slum' dwellers (or 10 per cent of the world's 'slum' population at the time) by 2020, through the slogan 'Cities Without Slums' (UN 2000: 5). Already in 2001, the DoH understood itself as being mandated to achieve shack-free cities by 2014, the end of the ANC's fourth term in government (Huchzermeyer 2004). In 2004, as Minister Lindiwe Sisulu was handed the reins of the Housing Ministry, the 'slum eradication' focus gained political momentum, and provinces and municipalities were encouraged to set eradication targets (Pithouse 2009; Huchzermeyer 2011).

The state maintained its housing waiting lists or 'demand databases'. However, under pressure to meet the informal settlement eradication target, increasingly houses financed through the capital subsidy were prioritised for relocation of households from informal settlements earmarked for eradication or clearance (CLC and SERI 2013). Informal settlement households qualifying for the once-off capital subsidy were offered, and often forcefully relocated to, completed units in distant housing developments. Alternatively, they were moved to temporary relocation areas and their informal settlements deemed 'eradicated' (Huchzermeyer 2011).

Prospects for more far-reaching policy change?

Despite persistent inequality and the increasing need for and dependency on social and income grants in South Africa, as set out at the beginning of this chapter, the South African government one decade into the new millennium was optimistic about its ability to move beyond this situation. In 2009, it committed to a *Medium Term Strategic Framework* for its fourth term in office, 2009 to 2014 (The Presidency 2009). This spells out a set of cross-sectoral goals. The overarching goals involve halving poverty and unemployment by 2014; ensuring that the benefits of economic growth are distributed more equitably while also reducing inequality; improving health and skills while ensuring that access to basic services is universal; freeing the nation of 'racism, sexism, tribalism and xenophobia'; and reducing crime and corruption and thereby improving citizens' safety (RSA 2010: 16). Among the ten 'Strategic Priorities and Programmes' of the Medium Term Strategic Framework is one that speaks directly to the way the state subsidises and delivers housing: 'Strategic Priority 2: Massive programme to build economic and social infrastructure' (The Presidency 2009:16). Mirroring the objectives of BNG, this commits the state to achieving 'suitably located low-cost and affordable housing', capacity building to double the rate at which housing is provided and 'enabling the country to meet the Millennium Development Goal in respect of informal settlements' (The Presidency 2009: 17). A further commitment is the 'provision of housing to all income levels and mixed-income housing' (The Presidency 2009: 17). This priority further speaks to the challenge of housing in suitable locations by committing to a break with the perpetuation of 'apartheid spatial planning and the marginalisation of the poor from economic opportunities and cultural amenities' (The Presidency 2009: 17).

The current, fourth term of ANC government (2009–2014) has seen some important shifts in political commitment to housing. The target of eradicating or eliminating informal settlements by 2014 was dropped from high level political statements, although performance reporting against this target continued at provincial level (Huchzermeyer 2011). The Presidency instead promoted a new target to upgrade informal settlements as part of a new 'outcomes approach' (The Presidency 2010a). This saw the Presidency articulating 12 'outcomes' for the term up to 2014 spanning basic education, health, safety, skills, infrastructure, rural communities, human settlements, local government, environment and public services. Each outcome is translated into 'performance agreements' between the President and his respective Ministers, and subsequent to this 'delivery agreements' signed with relevant implementing partners (The Presidency 2010a). While the outcomes broadly coincide with entrenched policy intents, they may be seen as a high level attempt at breaking out of the meaningless rituals of the bureaucracy mentioned above and which in the housing sector have churned out free standardised units on the urban periphery.

Outcome Eight, 'Human Settlements', has the following outputs:

- upgrading 400,000 units of accommodation within informal settlements;
- improving access to basic services;
- facilitating the provision of 600,000 accommodation units within the gap market for people earning between R 3,500 and R 12,800;

- mobilisation of well-located public land for low-income and affordable housing with increased densities on this land and in general (The Presidency 2010b).

The first output, which requires implementation of the Upgrading of Informal Settlements Programme, is combined with a requirement to deliver 20,000 affordable rental units per year in good locations (The Presidency 2010b). 'Affordable' here speaks to the need for housing alternatives for poor households in informal settlements not qualifying for subsidised housing under freehold title and not earning enough to qualify for rental housing provided by housing associations through the Social Housing programme. The outcomes approach does not call for an end to fully subsidised or capital subsidy housing. Instead it seeks to impose new priorities. Within the DHS, the National Upgrading Support Programme (NUSP) has the mandate to assist in the achievement of the target to effect upgrading for 400,000 households in informal settlements. Given the time pressure of the target, the NUSP sees its role largely as working pragmatically within the state housing delivery machinery, therefore supporting provinces and municipalities in dealing with informal settlements through the application of conventional procedures, standards and requirements designed for greenfield housing delivery, rather than treating '*in situ* upgrading' as fundamentally different as would be the case in the international upgrading practice.

Beyond its outcomes approach, the Presidency further proceeded in setting up a National Planning Commission (NPC) consisting of independent expert commissioners with the task of conducting a high level analysis or diagnostic and of developing concrete recommendations. The Commission had the 'license to be honest, bold, cut through the silos of government and take on board the views of all South Africans' (Manuel 2011). The Commission produced its National Development Plan in 2012. This recommends that human settlement development be focused on attaining spatial justice, spatial sustainability, spatial resilience, spatial quality and spatial efficiency (NPC 2012: 276). Similar to the preamble of BNG of 2004, it states that '[u]nwittingly, post-apartheid housing policy had reinforced apartheid spatial geography', neglecting public infrastructure, tending to locate housing on cheap land and in a uniform manner, not meeting diverse needs and in particular the need for rental housing (NPC 2012: 268). However, taking its licence to be bolder than previous policy statements, it recommends to '[u]rgently review the existing grant and subsidy regime for housing' towards greater diversification including state funding for public spaces and public infrastructure (NPC 2012: 287). It suggests a facilitating rather than providing role for the state in relation to housing. The Commission further recognises 'the role played by informal settlements' and recommends enhancing 'the existing national programme for upgrading informal settlements by developing a range of tailored responses' (NPC 2012: 289).

A similar approach was expressed in the South African Cities Network's 2011 *State of the Cities Report* (SACN 2011). The Cities Network represents South Africa's nine largest municipalities, many of which have maintained a ritualised drive to eradicate informal settlements, in conjunction with their provinces (Huchzermeyer 2011). The National Planning Commission (NPC 2012: 273) refers to this tendency only indirectly, as 'ambivalence across government towards how to address the upgrading of informal settlements'. The State of the Cities Report speaks more strongly to this reality. It urges bureaucracies to recognise informal settlements 'as important reception areas because of their low barriers to entry into the urban labour market – an accessible location to search for employment and a relatively low cost of living … A policy of slum eradication or replacement by formal housing in these areas is unhelpful'

(SACN 2011: 69). A development finance review commissioned by the DHS has gone further to recommend that 'the current subsidy should be phased out over time', setting out scenarios for this process (DHS 2011: 12).

Conclusion

South African civil society, NGOs, academics and progressive housing practitioners are currently asking whether a substantial housing policy change is imminent. Will the state succeed in discontinuing its standardised housing delivery with its standardised capital subsidy funding mechanism, with long waiting lists of understandably impatient beneficiaries? Will the state mainstream support for diversification, innovation and incrementalism in the form of participatory informal settlement upgrading, the release of well-located land for auto-construction of housing and the encouragement of different tenure forms? Policy reviews led to the introduction of new policy programmes in 2004 and a shift in the official policy aims. However, the state machinery has not followed this through, instead largely continuing the mass delivery of standardised housing on the urban periphery. Current high level expert advice commissioned by the Presidency points towards the need for a shift away from or even termination of the capital subsidy programme allocating poorly located housing free of charge to qualifying beneficiaries. However, it remains uncertain whether the fiscal and ideological pressure and the evidence of inappropriate outcomes are sufficient to entice the ruling ANC with its alliance partners to politically abandon this form of social support in their fourth term in government.

Acknowledgements

Compilation of this chapter benefited from conversations with Philip Harrison, Sarah Charlton, Steve Topham, Mark Misselhorn and students in the MBE (Housing) programme in the School of Architecture and Planning at the University of the Witwatersrand, Johannesburg.

References

ANC (1994) *Reconstruction and Development Programme: A Policy Framework*. African National Congress (ANC), Johannesburg.
Anderson, J. (2003) *Public Policymaking*, 5th edn. New York: Houghton Mifflin Company.
Baumann, T. (2003) 'Housing policy and poverty in South Africa', in F. Khan and P. Thring (eds) *Housing Policy and Practice in Post-Apartheid South Africa*. Sandown: Heinemann.
Baumann, T. and Bolnick, J. (2001) 'Out of the frying pan into the fire: the limits of loan finance in a capital subsidy context', *Environment and Urbanization*, 13(2): 103–115.
Bond, P. (2000) *Elite Transition: From Apartheid to Neoliberalism in South Africa*. London: Pluto Press.
Butler, A. (2010) 'Consolidation first: institutional reform priorities in the creation of a developmental state in South Africa', in O. Edigheji (ed.) *Constructing a Democratic Developmental State in South Africa: Potentials and Challenges*. Cape Town: Human Sciences Research Council (HSRC) Press.
Carey, S. (2009) *Success at a Price: How NGO Advocacy led to Changes in South Africa's People's Housing Process*, Planact, Good Governance Learning Network and Rooftops Canada, Johannesburg. Online. Available at www.planact.org.za/images/stories/documents/research_reports/success_at_a_price/PHP%20Advocacy – lessons%20for%20NGOs%20final.pdf (accessed 12 April 2012).
Charlton, S. and Kihato, C. (2006) 'Reaching the poor? An analysis of the influences of the evolution of South Africa's housing programme', in U. Pillay, R. Tomlinson and J. du Toit (eds) *Democracy and Delivery: Urban Policy in South Africa*. Cape Town: Human Sciences Research Council (HSRC) Press.

CLC and SERI (2013) *'Jumping the Queue', Waiting Lists and other Myths: Perceptions and Practice around Housing Demand and Allocation in South Africa*. Johannesburg: Community Law Centre (CLC) and Socio-Economic Rights Centre of South Africa (SERI).

Cross, C. (2008) 'Housing delivery as anti-poverty: where's the bottom line?', Draft paper. Pretoria: Centre for Policy, Economy and Growth, Human Sciences Research Council. Online. Available at www.hsrc.ac.za/Document-3213.phtml (accessed 7 April 2012).

DHS (2009) The National Housing Code. Pretoria: Department of Human Settlements.

DHS (2010) *People's Housing Process*. Pretoria: Department of Human Settlements. Online. Available at www.dhs.gov.za/Content/Spotlight/People%20Housing%20Process.htm (accessed 7 April 2011).

DHS (2011) 'Human Settlement Sector: Development Finance Review: Strategic Analysis, Conclusion and Recommendation', presented to the Financial and Fiscal Commission. Shisaka Development Management Services, October. Online. Available at www.ffc.co.za/index.php/component/doc-man/doc…/70-shisaka.html (accessed 4 April 2011).

DoH (1994) *White Paper: A New Housing Policy and Strategy for South Africa*. Pretoria: Department of Housing.

DoH (2000) *National Housing Code*. Pretoria: Department of Housing.

DoH (2004a) *'Breaking New Ground': A Comprehensive Plan for the Development of Sustainable Human Settlements*. Pretoria: Department of Housing.

DoH (2004b) 'National Housing Programmes: Upgrading of Informal Settlements', Chapter 13 of the *National Housing Code*. Pretoria: Department of Housing.

Dye, T. (1978) *Understanding Public Policy*. Englewood Cliffs, NJ: Prentice-Hall.

FinMark Trust (2011) 'One quarter of South Africa's property market is government-subsidised stock', FinMark Trust Press Release, 1 December.

Gilbert, A. (2004) 'Helping the poor through subsidies: lessons from Chile, Colombia and South Africa', *Habitat International*, 28(1): 114.

Gordon, R., Bertholdi, A. and Nell, M. (2011) *Housing Subsidy Assets: Exploring the Performance of Grant Subsidised Housing in South Africa*. A research initiative sponsored by FinMark Trust, Urban LandMark, National Department of Human Settlements, Western Cape Department of Human Settlements, South African Cities Network and FB Heron Foundation, Johannesburg: Shisaka Development Management Services.

Huchzermeyer, M. (2001) 'Housing for the poor? Negotiated housing policy in South Africa', *Habitat International*, 25(3): 303–331.

Huchzermeyer, M. (2004) 'From "contravention of laws" to "lack of rights": redefining the problem of informal settlements in South Africa', *Habitat International*, 28(3): 333–347.

Huchzermeyer, M. (2011) *'Cities with "Slums": From Informal Settlement Eradication to a Right to the City in Africa'*. Cape Town: University of Cape Town (UCT) Press.

Jenkins, P. and Smith, H. (2001) 'An institutional approach to analysis of state capacity in housing systems in the developing world: case studies of South Africa and Costa Rica', *Housing Studies*, 16(4): 485–507.

Landman, K. and Napier, M. (2010) 'Waiting for a house or building your own? Reconsidering state provision, aided and unaided self-help in South Africa', *Habitat International*, 34: 299–305.

Manuel, T. (2011) 'Foreword', in National Planning Commission: *National Development Plan Vision for 2030*. RP270/2011, Pretoria: National Planning Commission, The Presidency.

Mthembi-Mayanyele, S. (2001) 'Budget speech by the Minister of Housing, Ms Sankie Mthembi-Mahanyele', National Assembly, 19 June. Online. Available at www.info.gov.za/speeches/2001/010619245p1992.htm (accessed 14 August 2008).

Nakamura, R. and Smallwood, F. (1980) *The Politics of Implementation*. New York: St Martin's Press.

NPC (2012) *National Development Plan 2030: Our Future – Make it Work*. Pretoria: National Planning Commission, The Presidency.

Pithouse, R. (2009) 'A progressive policy without progressive politics: lessons from the failure to implement "Breaking New Ground"', *Town and Regional Planning*, 54: 1–14.

Richards, B. (1995) 'Poverty and housing in Chile: the development of a neo-liberal welfare state', *Habitat International*, 19(4): 515–527.

RSA (2010) *Millennium Development Goals Country Report 2010*. Pretoria: Republic of South Africa.

SACN (2011) *Towards Resilient Cities: A Reflection on the First Decade of Democratic and Transitional Local Government in South Africa 2001–2010*. 2011 State of the Cities Report, Johannesburg: South African Cities Network (SACN).

Sisulu, L. (2005) 'Speech by L.N. Sisulu, Minister of Housing, on the occasion of the tabling of the Budget Vote for the Department of Housing for the 2005/06 financial year', Cape Town: National Assembly, 17 May. Online. Available at www.info.gov.za/speeches/2005/05051715451004.htm (accessed 14 August 2008).

StatsSA (2006) *Migration and Urbanisation in South Africa*. Report no. 03-04-02 (2006), Pretoria: Statistics South Africa.

StatsSA (2010) *General Household Survey 2009 (Revised Version)*. Report no. P0318, Pretoria: Statistics South Africa.

StatsSA (2011) *Mid-Year Population Estimates 2011*. Statistical Release P0302, Pretoria: Statistics South Africa.

The Presidency (2009) *Together Doing More and Better. Medium Term Strategic Framework. A Framework to Guide Government's Programme in the Electoral Mandate Period (2009–2014)*. Issued by the Minister in the Presidency: Planning, Pretoria: The Presidency, Pretoria. Online. Available at www.info.gov.za/view/DownloadFileAction?id=103901 (accessed 7 April 2012).

The Presidency (2010a) *Guide to the Outcomes Approach*. 27 May, Pretoria: The Presidency. Online. Available at www.thepresidency.gov.za/dpme/docs/guideline.pdf (accessed 7 April 2012).

The Presidency (2010b) 'Outputs and Measures. Outcome 8: Sustainable Human Settlements and an Improved Quality of Household Life'. Draft. Pretoria: The Presidency. Online. Available at www.thepresidency.gov.za/dpme/docs/outcome8.pdf (accessed 7 April 2012).

Tissington, K. (2011) *A Resource Guide to Housing in South Africa 1994–2010. Legislation, Policy, Programmes and Practice*. Johannesburg: Socio-Economic Rights Institute of South Africa (SERI).

Todes, A., Cross, C., Kok, P., Wentzel, M. and van Zyl, J. (2010) 'South African urbanisation after apartheid', *Trialog*, 104: 4–8.

Tomlinson, M. (2011) 'Managing the risk in housing delivery: local government in South Africa', *Habitat International*, 35: 419–425.

Von Holdt, K. (2010) 'The South African post-apartheid bureaucracy: inner workings, contradictory rationales and the developmental state', in O. Edigheji (ed.) *Constructing a Democratic Developmental State in South Africa: Potentials and Challenges*. Cape Town: Human Sciences Research Council (HSRC) Press.

UN (2000) 'Resolution adopted by the General Assembly: 55/2. United Nations Millennium Declaration'. New York: United Nations.

23

DASHED HOPES?

Public–private partnership and sustainable urban low-income housing delivery in Nigeria

Uche Cosmas Ikejiofor

Abbreviations

BUMPAN	Building Materials Producers' Association of Nigeria
CBO	Community-based organization
FHA	Federal Housing Authority
FMBN	Federal Mortgage Bank of Nigeria
FMHUD	Federal Ministry of Housing and Urban Development
ILO	International Labour Organization
NBRRI	Nigerian Building and Road Research Institute
NBS	National Bureau of Statistics
NGOs	Non-governmental organizations
NHF	National Housing Fund
NPC	National Population Commission
PPP	Public–private partnership
REDAN	Real Estate Developers' Association of Nigeria
UNCHS	United Nations Centre for Human Settlements

Introduction

The deepening housing crises in most developing countries, particularly at the lower-income segment of the urban housing market, have attracted the attention of analysts for some time. According to UNCHS (1996), between the United Nations Conference on Human Settlements in Vancouver in 1976 (Habitat I) and the City Summit in Istanbul in 1996 (Habitat II), there was no evidence of improvement in the housing conditions of lower income groups in terms of affordability, tenure, standards and access to services. In Nigeria, the urban low-income housing situation is definitely worse now than a decade earlier due largely to increasingly high urban growth rates and worsening economic and political climates. These have adversely affected both governments' capacity to make significant new shelter investments, and the real incomes of urban households and their ability to make any substantial savings from which housing investments (in new construction or improvements) can be made. Massive urbanization in contexts of extreme poverty and limited state capacity, together with intense competition for resources, has perpetuated enormous deficiencies in both the quality and quantity of housing. Current indicators show that the problems are not about to abate.

In an attempt to devise approaches to urban housing delivery that are suited to a period of scarce public resources and enormous housing needs, analysts agree that public authorities need to look beyond the problem of carrying out individual projects and find ways to improve the workings of the housing market as a whole (Okpala 1992; Rakodi 1992; Ikejiofor 1999; Ogu and Ogbuozobe 2001).

A basic theme in much of the current thinking is that public agencies can make the greatest contribution to the supply of housing, not by building houses – an effort which, in the best of cases, meets only a tiny fraction of the need – but by improving the efficiency of the housing market so that more housing of the right kind is produced on a large scale by formal and informal private sectors (World Bank 1987; Ikejiofor 2005; Oruwari 2006; UN-Habitat 2006). A well-functioning public–private partnership (PPP) in housing delivery, therefore, is one that uses knowledge about how housing markets work, that serves the needs of all stakeholders in housing delivery, that mitigates past housing market distortions and that is sustainable (Sa-Aadu 1998: 40)

The overall aim of the chapter is to evaluate the ongoing PPP regime in housing delivery in Nigeria with a view to determining whether it has been able to cater for the needs of urban low-income earners and to explore alternative approaches that offer better prospects in the pursuit of this goal. To achieve this aim, the objectives to be pursued are three-fold:

- to document existing housing delivery options as well as highlight current practices through which the urban poor house themselves in Nigeria;
- to trace the evolution of the PPP as the officially preferred housing delivery strategy in Nigeria and carry out a preliminary evaluation of Nigeria's performance in its implementation, particularly as it affects urban low-income housing supply; and
- to explore some alternative approaches that hold better prospects for tackling the daunting challenge of sustainable urban low-income housing supply.

In this introductory section, an attempt has been made to explain the basis as well as the basic concepts of the PPP paradigm in housing delivery and to articulate the overall aim and objectives of the chapter. The section that follows presents a review of existing housing delivery options in Nigeria. This is followed by a brief overview of how the urban poor house themselves in Nigeria at the moment. An attempt to locate the origins as well as highlight some potentials of the PPP strategy as the preferred housing delivery policy option in Nigeria is then made, followed by a preliminary evaluation of some outcomes of the implementation of this policy. The chapter wraps up by exploring some alternative approaches that hold better prospects for tackling the daunting challenge of sustainable urban low-income housing supply. It is based on empirical evidence as well as a review of relevant literature and documentary sources.

Housing delivery options in Nigeria

Existing housing delivery options in Nigeria can be broadly categorized into two: public sector produced and private sector produced. The evolving trend in direct public sector involvement in housing provision in Nigeria can be characterized as a three-stage sequence: government-built public housing; the aided self-help programme (sites and services); and the 'support approach' policy. The first stage took off with the launching of Nigeria's Third National Development Plan (1975–1980) and involved the initiation of ambitious public sector programmes for the construction of dwellings mostly for civil servants and the lower income groups. At the federal level, the most widespread example of this occurred during the civil administration (1979–1983) of then President Shehu Shagari – hence the name 'Shagari Low-Cost Housing Estates', which can be found in every state of Nigeria. At the state level, almost all state governments have embarked on one housing development programme or another, usually through their housing development corporations. Even in the current regime of PPP, the construction of complete dwelling units for sale has continued to be adopted by governments under a variety of names, such as 'the proto-type housing scheme' – a pilot scheme where government builds and sells house types it considers appropriate for particular socio-economic groups with the hope that the larger society will replicate such examples.

The aided self-help (sites and services) phase witnessed the extension of state aid to low-income groups to build and improve their houses. This strategy took off in the mid-1980s, promoted by the World Bank. Practical difficulties have been reported with targeting beneficiaries, corruption in the allocation of plots, and determining the appropriate level of subsidies to build into schemes to make them affordable to target groups and at the same time replicable. Onibokun et al. (1995: 51) define affordable shelter in the Nigerian context as where charges must be small mortgage repayments not generally exceeding 20 per cent of the income of the beneficiary.

In the 'support approach' phase (which commenced with the launching of the 2002 National Housing Policy and includes the ongoing PPP strategy), a consensus appears to exist that the principal role for government should be the support and facilitation of the development of private sector institutions and markets. This flows from the proposition that free markets allocate resources more efficiently than any other allocative device. Government activities in this phase will be highlighted subsequently in the section 'Implementation of the PPP strategy in Nigeria' where the scorecard of the PPP strategy comes under scrutiny.

In the recent past, governments (particularly at the federal level) have been attempting to promote a new housing delivery strategy targeted at low-income earners. The Federal Mortgage Bank of Nigeria (FMBN) launched the 'Informal Cooperative Housing Scheme' in December 2011. The scheme is tailored towards integrating the informal low-income sector (including artisans, roadside mechanics, market traders and farmers) into the National Housing Fund (NHF) scheme.

To participate in the scheme, an informal sector operator is required to become a member of a cooperative society duly accredited by the FMBN. This informal sector operator then makes contributions to the NHF scheme through the cooperative society, thus qualifying to purchase subsidized housing through an affordable mortgage loan that can be repaid from his/her informal enterprise proceeds.

Private sector housing production in Nigeria involves a continuum comprising:

- the fully conventional (as found in most small- and large-scale production by the capitalist private sector);
- the semi-conventional (as found in housing where rights to land are either legal or based on traditional tenure systems, but buildings on such land are without building or planning approval because they do not satisfy extant building or planning codes – as found in

most central city tenements and rooming houses; and housing which satisfies the building codes but is built on illegally occupied and/or subdivided land); and
- the unconventional (where housing does not satisfy the building codes and is also built on illegally occupied and/or subdivided land).

Older studies show that categories two and three above are produced mostly by the small-scale informal sector and account for over 80 per cent of all housing production in Nigeria's urban areas (Ikejiofor 1997; Arimah and Adeagbo 2000). Most self-help and self-managed housing production is included in these two categories. This situation conforms somewhat to the typology of housing provision for the urban poor in Third World countries as illustrated by Drakakis-Smith (1979: 23).

The official concept of the informal sector in Nigeria is based on the relationship between enterprises and state regulation (Onyebueke and Geyer 2011: 66). Hence, the informal sector in the Nigerian context can be defined as comprising those economic activities in which government is not functionally cognizant of the activities carried out. The Nigerian situation conforms to a large extent with the terms used by the International Labour Organization (ILO 1975: 18) to define the sector, i.e. reliance on indigenous technology, small-scale operations and labour-intensive adaptive technology.

It is noteworthy that non-governmental organizations (NGOs) and community-based organizations (CBOs) do not play significant roles in housing delivery in Nigeria at the moment. But this might change in the future, especially if the current efforts by the government to promote cooperative housing succeed.

How the urban poor house themselves in Nigeria

In the following paragraphs, I shall make brief comments on the methods employed by the urban poor in Nigeria to access land and build the houses they live in, as well as the technical quality of the houses so produced. It is my belief that understanding current realities will shed some light on such concepts as affordability and sustainability as they relate to urban low-income housing production, as well as the reasons behind the recommendations made in the section 'In search of workable solutions'. It should be pointed out that renting and sharing of dwelling units are other strategies through which the urban poor access housing (Ikejiofor 1998a) but these are not our concern here.

It is generally agreed that of all the ingredients of housing, land is the most critical. This is easily attested to by the fact that wherever land has been made available, even the urban poor have been able to provide themselves with some form of housing. With regard to access to urban land in Nigeria today, the poor fall under two categories: a tiny minority who are members of the indigenous land-owning communities in an urban centre and a vast majority who are migrants to the urban centre mostly from the hinterlands (Ikejiofor et al. 2004). While it is still possible for the former to access land through such non-commercial channels as inheritance and free allocation from increasingly depleting communal holdings, the latter have no option but to rent or buy (where this is possible) from the emerging land markets or, in the majority of cases (as seen in all major urban centres), squat on any unoccupied land usually at the periphery of the city where development is yet to reach (Fadare and Mills-Tettey 1992; Ikejiofor 1998b; Ikejiofor et al. 2004).

The urgent need for shelter, lack of funds and absence of tenure security over such invaded land has a direct bearing on the form and the technical quality of the housing initially produced.

There is general disorder and neglect with respect to buildings, streets and other structures, overcrowding, low sanitation standards, use of unconventional and often substandard materials and construction techniques, and absence of facilities or amenities in the neighbourhoods that subsequently emerge (Fadare and Mills-Tettey 1992; UN-Habitat 2003). Figures from the National Population Commission (NPC 2010) indicate that such housing provides accommodation for up to 60 per cent of about 80 million urban residents in Nigeria. The ubiquity of such informal settlements in Nigeria's vast urban landscape is partly explained by a large and rapidly growing population and the fact that the country's performance in key human development indices has been declining for some time. The National Bureau of Statistics (NBS 2012) reports that Nigeria's poverty rate rose from 69 per cent in 2010 to 71 per cent in 2011 and that unemployment also increased from more than 12 million to over 14 million within the same period.

Duke-Lucio *et al.* (2010) examined a variety of housing related experiences of the urban poor regarding amenities and structure, stability, money outlays and neighbourhood characteristics and concluded that these experiences have latent and sequential costs that involve lack of safety, poor physical health, poor mental health, decreasing social capital, hopelessness, poor education and diminished life opportunities, all of which have important financial and non-financial implications for families.

The usual source of funds for such housing investment is the personal savings of the would-be homeowner who may sometimes enjoy trade credits from local artisans and materials dealers. Because of the limited funds available, the housing package is usually delivered piecemeal starting with a core unit (which is immediately occupied upon completion) through self-building or self-managed building. This makes the whole process affordable to the would-be homeowner. There is considerable evidence that both the quality of the materials used for construction and finishing and the size of the dwelling units improve gradually over time in tandem with settlement consolidation (Fadare and Mills-Tettey 1992; Ikejiofor 1997; UN-Habitat 2006).

The 2002 national housing policy as the origin of the PPP strategy in housing delivery in Nigeria

The main outcome of the 2002 housing policy was the government's acceptance of the need to move away from the direct construction and sale of houses. According to the policy document, construction would be private sector driven, with government providing an enabling environment.

The Real Estate Developers' Association of Nigeria (REDAN) and the Building Materials Producers' Association of Nigeria (BUMPAN) were created as umbrella organizations for the articulation and implementation of private sector initiatives in housing production. It was believed that the activities of these bodies (which the government intended to facilitate), together with functional mortgage institutions, would result in more houses being produced at a faster rate for Nigerians. The regime shift embraced by government in the new policy aimed to use scarce public resources to unleash the energies of the private sector, households and community organizations to increase the supply of affordable housing.

The thrust of the 2002 housing policy as it affected land delivery was the alignment of the 1978 Land Use Decree with the policy of putting housing provision in the mainstream of a free market economy. The proposed amendments to the decree were expected to result in unimpeded and speedier land transactions. In view of the anticipated rise in the volume of land transactions, the policy proposed that an easy land titling and registration process be put in place to facilitate quick mortgage transactions. Land registries were to be modernized and computerized, and established in state capitals and local government headquarters. A central land depository covering the whole country was to be created. Federal and state governments were to make land available to developers for the construction of houses on three- to five-year development leases, with certificates of occupancy issued to the purchasers of the houses by the appropriate authority. These developments marked the emergence of the PPP as the preferred housing delivery policy option in Nigeria.

More than ten years down the line, what does the scorecard of this policy regime look like? This forms the focus of the following section.

Implementation of the PPP strategy in Nigeria: a preliminary evaluation of outcomes

The worsening housing deficit shows clearly that the 2002 policy has failed to achieve its objectives and that the PPP strategy in housing delivery has not performed satisfactorily. Speaking at the annual conference of the Mortgage Banking Association of Nigeria in October 2012, the Managing Director of the FMBN noted that at a conservative rate of 2 million nairas (US$12,500) per unit, a whopping sum of over 34 trillion nairas (US$212.5 billion) would be required to bridge the housing deficit of 17 million units in the country (US$1 = 160 Nigerian nairas as of 31 January 2013).

A comparative cost analysis carried out by the Nigerian Building and Road Research Institute (NBRRI 2012) shows that the conventional house type that falls within the cost range referred to by the FMBN Managing Director (excluding the cost of land and services installation) is a two-bedroom semi-detached bungalow consisting of two bedrooms, one sitting room, veranda, kitchen, water closet and bathroom, with a total floor area of about 75 square metres and built with cement-stabilized compressed laterite interlocking blocks and zinc sheets as roof covering. It will be shown in the following subsection that even this house type will pose affordability problems for the lower income groups who constitute the bulk of the Nigerian population.

It was against this backdrop that a committee was set up by the Minister of Lands, Housing and Urban Development in 2011 to revise the 2002 policy with a view to addressing observed constraints and shortcomings. The committee recognized that the urban low-income housing delivery challenge has remained intractable. It recommended, among other things, a mixed mass housing delivery approach consisting essentially of public–private partnership as the main policy thrust, supported by cooperative and social housing strategies. The revised policy was presented to the Federal Executive Council for adoption by the Minister in June 2012. I have argued elsewhere (Ikejiofor 2012) that these approaches will be neither equitable nor sustainable in addressing the urban low-income housing delivery challenge under the present socio-economic circumstances in Nigeria. The PPP strategy has been bogged down by the following challenges.

The weak roles of the public and private sectors

The various housing programmes that have been commissioned by the three tiers of government since the commencement of the PPP regime have, without exception, been implemented as solely formal sector programmes involving the government and the formal private sector. This has resulted in the usual high delivery costs and limited impact. Where developers have managed to complete their projects, the PPP strategy has become synonymous with the production of expensive dwellings by the capitalist private sector for sale to wealthy individuals. This has created serious accessibility challenges and equity concerns as regards meeting social needs.

A situation has arisen where houses produced under PPP programmes are derisively referred to by the populace as 'diaspora houses' – meaning houses that can be afforded only by those few lucky Nigerians working and earning foreign currency wages outside the country. It is noteworthy that many innovative products and housing models from the United States, Malaysia, Singapore and South Africa currently being employed by various developers (from Hydraform and prefab technologies to row housing) have, so far, proved incapable of delivering low-cost houses in the Nigerian context.

Table 23.1 summarizes case studies of selected PPP projects in major cities from the three regional blocks in Nigeria showing, among other things, on-site facilities as well as the selling prices of completed house types.

Many reasons can be adduced to explain this state of affairs, one of which is the unrestrained profit motive on the part of the corporate private sector involved. This has led to the high-income group being chosen as the preferred target beneficiaries of such programmes and, arising from this, a conventional definition in which the housing package is viewed as comprising a decent house and all services and infrastructures required in it, each meeting certain minimum physical standards of design and construction determined by the government. Tied to this is the conception of housing as a product that has to be completely finished before use. Experience has shown that in a bid to meet these set standards (which are often tailored along the lines of those of the industrially developed countries) all at once, such conventional housing delivery inevitably becomes capital-intensive while the final product is mostly beyond the means of the low- and middle-income groups. It is noteworthy that there are currently no specific efforts to target low-income urban dwellers in PPP housing projects in Nigeria.

Notwithstanding the fact that the monthly minimum wage of public sector workers in Nigeria was increased from 8,000 nairas (US$50) to 18,000 nairas (US$112.5) in 2011, it is clear that all houses produced through the PPP strategy at present fall far beyond what middle- and low-income families can afford. A simple analysis shows that at 18,000 nairas (US$112.5) per month, the total annual salary of the lowest paid public sector worker at the moment is 216,000 nairas (US$1,350). The cost of the cheapest PPP-produced housing unit as shown in Table 23.1 is 10 million nairas (US$62,500). Hence, it will take the lowest paid public sector worker about 46 years to save enough money for the cheapest PPP-produced house if the entire salary is utilized for nothing else but that purpose. For the NBRRI-proposed two-bedroom bungalow referred to earlier, which has a production cost estimate of 2 million nairas (US$12,500) (excluding cost of land and infrastructure installation), the lowest paid public sector worker would need to save the total annual salary for more than nine years to be able to afford such a housing unit. It is easy to conclude, therefore, that none of the existing or proposed official housing options is affordable to the vast majority of Nigerians who fall into the lower income segments. It is for this reason that, in the opinion of this author, the sites-and-services approach (with core housing) remains the most viable solution to sustainable urban low-income housing delivery, as will be argued in the section 'In search of workable solutions'.

TABLE 23.1 Summary of case studies of selected PPP projects showing on-site facilities and selling prices of house types

	Project/Location	Developer	House type/selling price	Facilities provided
1	Haven Homes Estate, Lagos (South West Nigeria)	Haven Homes Limited	Detached 3-bedroom duplex at N 65 million (US$406,250)	Mezzanine levels, galleries, atriums, roof-top terraces, indoor gardens
2	Platinum Rows Estate, Lekki, Lagos (South West Nigeria)	Ibile Holdings Limited	4-bedroom terrace bungalow plus 1-room boys quarter at N 50 million (US$312,500)	Tarred internal roads, concrete drainage and underground utility ducts
3	Carlton Gate Estate, Ibadan (South West Nigeria)	Megamound Investment Limited	4-bedroom detached bungalow at N 15 million (US$93,750); 3-bedroom semi-detached bungalow at N 12 million (US$75,000)	Water from borehole, electricity from the national grid with back-up generator, recreational park, shopping mall
4	Goshen and Jubilee Estates, Enugu (South East Nigeria)	COPEN Services Limited	2- and 3-bedroom detached and semi-detached bungalows at N 10 million (US$62500) to N 25 million (US$15,6250)	Tarred internal roads, water from public mains, electricity from the national grid, nursery/primary school
5	Cooperative City Gardens, Abuja, Federal Capital Territory (northern Nigeria)	El-Salam Limited	2- and 3-bedroom detached and semi-detached bungalows at N 50 million (US$31,2500) to N 75 million (US$46,8750)	High grade finishing, asphalted internal roads, paved parking lots, recreational space, landscaping

Source: Field survey by the author, 2011.

A second reason why the PPP strategy has failed to address the urban low-income housing challenge is what appears to be a limited understanding on the part of government of the workings of the housing market, leading to a lack of clarity on exactly what role government is to play. Take for instance the delegation of responsibility in the PPP guidelines for provision of on-site infrastructure in project sites to private developers – an area where they clearly do not have comparative advantage. The failure on the part of government to interpret and implement the PPP concept in housing delivery correctly is the main reason why the urban low-income housing delivery challenge has remained intractable. This is because current practices have succeeded in sidelining an important segment that is needed to address this challenge – the informal private sector.

Also, the inability of private housing developers in Nigeria to carry out massive housing projects (owing to their limited financial and technical resources) thereby creating the optimal size and reducing the cost of construction per square metre means that no quick progress can be made particularly on the issue of low-cost housing production.

Lack of sincerity of developers and government officials

There is often a lack of sincerity on the part of the developers resulting in outright fraud or attempts to cut corners in order to maximize profits. According to the PPP guidelines (FMHUD 2006: 7), private developers involved in PPP projects are expected to sign a Memorandum of Understanding with government. Government, by the terms of the agreement, is required to deliver to the prospective developers (through the Ministry of Lands and Housing) unencumbered land for housing development. There is evidence that in a good number of cases, prospective developers simply take advantage of the titles to land prepared in their names and do little or nothing after signing the Memorandum of Understanding. A Review Committee set up by the government in 2010 reported instances where prospective developers were found to have sublet portions of land allotted to them for PPP housing projects to other developers for uses not related to housing development. This development has created a problem for government of how to recover land from such non-performing and/or fraudulent contractors.

In states such as Imo, according to the Review Committee report, under the guise of providing land for prospective developers, government officials fraudulently sold off tracts of unutilized government land in choice locations in the state capital to wealthy individuals and speculators. This was made possible by the persistence of corrupt and secretive allocative procedures in government land delivery practices.

High level of inconsistency and policy somersaults

There is a high level of inconsistency as well as foot-dragging in policy development and implementation. Several recent developments point to a clear reluctance on the part of government to break with discredited practices characteristic of previous housing regimes, particularly public sector construction and sale of housing units. The main attraction of this strategy, it would appear, is that it creates opportunities for the elite in government to dispense favours to friends, kinsmen, tribesmen and associates through the award of contracts, often with resultant kickbacks.

The 500-unit Federal Housing Authority (FHA) Cooperative Housing Estate in Calabar (inaugurated in April 2011 by the Minister of Lands, Housing and Urban Development) is to be delivered partly through PPP and partly through direct construction by the FHA – a government agency. Also, at the foundation-stone laying ceremony for a Federal Civil Servants' Housing Estate in Abuja on the same day, the president gave the highlights of a proposed new national housing programme which includes the following:

(1) 600,000 housing units to be delivered by the Federal Ministry of Lands, Housing and Urban Development through direct construction;
(2) 250,000 housing units to be delivered by the FHA through direct construction; and
(3) 5,000 housing units to be delivered through the PPP strategy.

On the issue of foot-dragging in policy implementation, it is noteworthy that since the launch of the 2002 policy (which adopted the PPP strategy as the preferred housing delivery approach), it was not until July 2009 that a PPP Steering Committee was inaugurated by the Finance Minister with the mandate to ensure that global best practices are adopted in the implementation of PPP projects in Nigeria. Also, most of the proposals in the policy for reforming the mortgage institutions for optimal performance have not been implemented. In fact, it was only in November 2012 at a presidential retreat on housing that a resolution was made to set up a mortgage refinance company and to recapitalize the FMBN. Meanwhile, there is nothing to suggest that the implementation of this new resolution will fare any better than those before it.

It is difficult to speculate beyond the points outlined above on what the continuing implementation of the PPP strategy portends for the ongoing support approach (or enabling housing market) policy regime in Nigeria. Official corruption is, of course, a major issue and preliminary evidence already indicates that some government officials and private investors would cheat if the regulatory framework were not stringent enough. What is definitely beyond doubt, however, is that given the present distribution of income, the nature of the land market and the structure of the building industry, this strategy is unlikely to be able to meet sustainability and equity concerns in urban housing delivery in Nigeria any time soon.

The World Commission on the Environment and Development (1987), with the *Brundtland Commission Report*, defined sustainable development, or sustainability, as development that meets the needs of the people without compromising the ability of future generations to meet their own needs. Mitlin and Satterthwaite (1994) observe that sustainable development is not simply a new way to describe environmental protection, but a new concept of economic growth which provides for fairness and opportunity for all people in the world without destroying the world's natural resources and without further compromising the carrying capacity of the globe.

Sustainable housing development in this context therefore refers to housing development that has the capacity to replicate itself because of its affordability and the opportunity it offers all income groups without posing any significant threats to the environment or putting undue pressure on public resources.

In search of workable solutions

Three methods of categorizing housing production are:

- locus of decision-making (i.e. public or private);
- organization of production (i.e. capitalist or petty commodity); and
- degree of legality with respect to land and/or planning and building regulations (i.e. legal or unauthorized).

That public agencies in Nigeria often take this rigid categorization as sacrosanct is demonstrated by the numerous public-sponsored demolitions of 'illegal' housing in Nigeria's major towns and cities in the name of development control, particularly in Abuja and Lagos in the very recent past. A major incident in Lagos was the demolition of an entire low-income neighbourhood, Makoko, by the Lagos State government in 2011. And in Abuja, the federal capital, a low-income estate under construction by a private developer in the Kyami district of the city with about 500 units of housing at various stages of completion and valued at about 3 billion nairas (US$18.75 million) was pulled down by the Federal Capital Development Authority in 2012. Both incidents drew widespread public outrage and condemnation, and bring to the fore the dilemma of modern planning in poor and emerging economies. Watson (2009: 2259) captured this vividly when she observed that urban planning in many parts of the world reflects a growing gap between current approaches and growing problems of poverty, inequality, informality, rapid urbanization and spatial fragmentation.

But the limitations of a rigid categorization have been recognized (Ikejiofor 2009). Because an element may be, for example, given permission and funded by the public sector but installed by the private sector, analysts agree that there is usually no clear distinction between the two sectors. It is also possible that different elements in a residential package (land, shelter, infrastructure and services) may be produced in different modes of production with different legal statuses. Royston *et al.* (2005: 13), calling for a review of tenure terminology and concepts, observed that any dichotomy is problematic as it often indicates false polarization, when reality is more appropriately represented as a dynamic continuum in which the situation is moving towards more informality or formality.

At the moment, informality (in terms of forms of income generation, forms of settlement and housing, and forms of negotiating life in the city) has become the dominant mode of behaviour. In many urban centres, according to Roy (2005), this is now the norm and no longer the exception. This situation led Watson (2009: 2268) to conclude that finding a way in which planning can work with informality, supporting survival efforts of the urban poor rather than hindering them through regulation or displacing them with modernist megaprojects, is essential if it is to play a role at all in these new urban conditions.

It is against this backdrop that the appropriateness of incremental, self-built (or self-managed) and petty commodity housing production as a solution to the urban low-income housing delivery challenge is evaluated. It is the argument in this chapter that this strategy encompasses both formal and informal dynamic relationships that can combine the positive attributes of conventional and non-conventional as well as public and private strategies to satisfy both equity and sustainability concerns in low-income urban housing delivery in Nigeria. Also, it has the potential to address a major concern of the 2012 National Housing Policy, which is confronting the challenge of harnessing local resources and technological know-how for the mass production of housing.

For low-income earners in urban areas, the most economical housing option would be to rent a serviced plot from relevant government agencies and construct houses using their own labour. Where those in full-time wage employment are unable to afford the time needed to engage in self-building, the possibility of self-managed construction using small-scale producers presents a viable alternative. At present, this has not happened largely because low-income earners cannot afford the official and unofficial costs of plots in government land delivery programmes (Ikejiofor *et al.* 2004; Ikejiofor 2006). The difficulty in accessing land, among other factors, has contributed to the increasing population of prospective home seekers finding their housing solutions in slums and squatter settlements characterized by lack of secured tenure, basic services and generally poor housing conditions (Fadare and Mills-Tettey 1992; Coker *et al.* 2007).

As was illustrated earlier in this chapter, the proposed option fits perfectly into existing processes through which the bulk of housing in which the urban poor live are produced. Government's role will be to encourage and facilitate already existing processes by removing a major bottleneck: access to serviced land. Both local and international opinion recognizes the inherent positive attributes in this approach (Burns 1983; Fernandez 2003; Tibaijuka 2006; Ademiluyi and Raji 2008). These include:

- Owner-built housing construction allows the household to match its own priorities in terms of facilities and quality of housing with its ability to pay for them. It is, therefore, a viable option for producing housing appropriate to needs.
- Such an approach is cheaper than formal construction because it avoids the multiple overheads of the large contractor and utilizes the labour of the owner.
- Informal construction is more likely to use technologies that are appropriate to the scale, location, available finance, etc. of the site.
- Such small-scale construction will stimulate the appearance of small-scale manufacturers and suppliers of building materials, thereby adding to the building of the local economy.
- Incremental, informal housing construction provides housing for low-income families without relying on subsidy from government. Being a pro-poor and inclusive strategy, it satisfies both equity and sustainability criteria.
- Self-built housing allows owners to treat their dwelling as an investment. As a result, they can also invest in improvements or extensions in anticipation of future sale or rental income. It thus conforms to the call by the UN-Habitat Executive Director Anna Tibaijuka (2006) for planning practitioners to develop a different approach that places the creation of livelihoods at the centre of planning efforts.

The main disadvantage of self-built housing is the loss of control by the authorities over the visual and technical quality of the houses. However, this can be addressed if government effectively and efficiently discharges its enabling role by not only exercising control over plot layouts but also funding and implementing structural landscaping along the streets. Another measure government can take to improve visual quality is erecting a pilot scheme which will act as a guide for others to follow. This can take the form of the development of a group of houses illustrating the various methods of basic house construction and boundary treatments appropriate to this scale of building. The emphasis here should be on structural landscaping and boundary treatments, which are usually ignored in conventional sites-and-services programmes.

Conclusions

This chapter has demonstrated the limitations, in the critical areas of equity and sustainability, of a housing policy regime in a developing country that is anchored essentially on a formal interpretation of housing need. On the other hand, it has been argued that strategies that hold better prospects in addressing these concerns are more likely to be bottom-up approaches involving a return to first principles, to find out what the poor are able to do for themselves and how government intervention can make the greatest impact.

There is no doubt that, in line with global best practices, a market support approach in housing delivery is needed in Nigeria. Since small-scale informal producers account for the bulk of housing production that is affordable to the poor in both urban and rural areas in Nigeria, a strategy which draws on the proven capacity of this group within the overall framework of a market support approach is likely to make a greater impact on the low-income housing situation, particularly at a time of scarce public resources and enormous housing needs.

References

Ademiluyi, I. and Raji, B. (2008) 'Public and private developers as agents of urban housing in sub-Saharan Africa: the situation in Lagos State', *Humanity and Social Sciences*, 3(2): 143–150.

Arimah, B.C. and Adeagbo, D. (2000) 'Compliance with urban development and planning regulations in Ibadan, Nigeria', *Habitat International*, 24: 279–294.

Burns, L.S. (1983). 'Self-help housing: an evaluation of outcomes', *Urban Studies*, 20(3): 299–309.

Coker, A.O., Awokola, O.S., Olomolaiye, P.O. and Booth, C.A. (2007) 'Challenges of urban housing quality and association with neighbourhood environment: insights and experiences in Ibadan City, Nigeria', *Journal of Environment and Health*, 7(1): 27–35.

Duke-Lucio, J., Peck, L.R. and Segal, E.A. (2010) 'The latent and sequential costs of being poor: an exploration of housing', *Poverty & Public Policy*, 2(2): 254–268.

Drakakis-Smith, D.W. (1979) 'Low cost housing provision in the Third World: some theoretical and practical alternatives', in H. Murrison and J.P. Lea (eds) *Housing in Third World Countries: Perspectives on Theory and Practice*. London: Macmillan.

Fadare, W. and Mills-Tettey, R. (1992) 'Squatter settlements in Port Harcourt', *Habitat International*, 16(1): 71–81.

Fernandez, E. (2003) 'Illegal housing: law, property rights and urban space', in P. Harrison, M. Huchzermeyer and M. Mayekiso (eds) *Confronting Fragmentation: Housing and Urban Development in a Democratising Society*. Cape Town: University of Cape Town Press.

FMHUD (2006) *Public and Private Sector Partnership Guidelines for Investment in Housing Development*. Abuja: FMHUD.

Ikejiofor, U. (1997) 'The private sector and urban housing production process in Nigeria: a study of small-scale landlords in Abuja', *Habitat International*, 21(4): 409–425.

Ikejiofor, U. (1998a) 'Tyranny of inappropriate policies: sharing as housing strategy among middle/low income households in Abuja, Nigeria', *Cities*, 15(6): 429–436.

Ikejiofor, U. (1998b) 'Access to land, development control and low-income housing in Abuja, Nigeria: policy, politics and bureaucracy', *Planning Practice and Research*, 13(3): 299–309.

Ikejiofor, U. (1999) 'The god that failed: a critique of public housing in Nigeria, 1975–1995', *Habitat International*, 23(2): 177–188.

Ikejiofor, U. (2005) 'Land issues in the new National Housing Policy for Nigeria: lessons from research experience', *International Development Planning Review*, 27(1): 91–111.

Ikejiofor, U. (2006) 'Equity in informal land delivery: insights from Enugu, Nigeria', *Land Use Policy*, 23: 448–459.

Ikejiofor, U. (2009) 'Planning within a Context of Informality: Issues and Trends in Land Delivery in Enugu, Nigeria', Case Study prepared for United Nations Global Report on Human Settlements, 2009. Online. Available HTTM: www.unhabitat.org/grhs/2009 (accessed 12 December 2012).

Ikejiofor, U. (2012) 'Sustainability and the revised National Housing Policy: mistakes and misconceptions', paper presented at the 2012 Architects' Colloquium, Abuja, April.

Ikejiofor, U., Nwogu, K.C. and Nwanunobi, C.O. (2004) *Informal Land Delivery Processes and Access to Land for the Poor in Enugu, Nigeria*. Birmingham: University of Birmingham, School of Public Policy, International Development Department, Informal Land Delivery in African Cities Working Paper 2.

ILO (1975) *Urbanisation, Regional Development and Empowerment in Developing Countries*, Progress Report No. 4. Geneva: The ILO.

Mitlin, D. and Satterthwaite, D. (1994) *Cities and Sustainable Development: Background Paper for Global Forum 1994*. London: IIED.

NBS (2012) *Annual Abstract of Statistics*. Abuja: NBS.

NBRRI (2012) 'Compressed interlocking blocks: an alternative to Sandcrete blocks in achieving affordable housing in Nigeria'. Paper presented at the 2nd Meeting of the Officials of the National Council on Lands, Housing and Urban Development, Port Harcourt, 12–13 November.

NPC (2010) *2006 Population and Housing Census of the Federal Republic of Nigeria: Housing Characteristics and Amenities (Priority Tables), Volume II*. Abuja: NPC.

Ogu, V.I. and Ogbuozobe, J.E. (2001) 'Housing policy in Nigeria: towards enablement of private housing development', *Habitat International*, 25: 473–492.

Okpala, D.C.I. (1992) 'Housing production systems and technologies in developing countries: a review of experiences and possible future trends/prospects', *Habitat International*, 16(3): 9–32.

Onibokun, A.G., Famoriyo, S., Agbola, T. and Akanji, B. (1995) 'Urban land management, regularization policies and local development in Nigeria', paper presented at World Bank Seminar, Abidjan, 21–25 March.

Onyebueke, V. and Geyer, M. (2011) 'The informal sector in urban Nigeria: reflections from almost four decades of research', *Town and Regional Planning*, 59: 65–76.

Oruwari, Y. (2006) 'Lest we forget: the poor people need housing in the urban areas in Nigeria too – a reflection of low-income housing provision', in A.I. Okewole, A. Ajayi, A. Daramola, K. Odusanmi and O. Ogunba (eds) *The Built Environment: Innovation, Policy and Sustainable Development*. Ota: Covenant University.

Rakodi, C. (1992) 'Housing markets in third world cities: research and policy into the 1990s', *World Development*, 20(1): 39–55.

Roy, A. (2005) 'Urban informality: towards an epistemology of planning', *Journal of the American Planning Association*, 71: 147–158.

Royston, L., Cousins, T., Hornby, D., Kingwell, R. and Trench, T. (2005) 'Perspectives on land tenure security in rural and urban South Africa: an analysis of tenure context and a problem statement for LEAP', *Commissioned Paper*, LEAP.

Sa-Aadu, J. (1998) 'Conceptual framework for private-public partnership in housing delivery in Africa', *Housing Today; Journal of the Association of Housing Corporations of Nigeria*, 1(1): 40–51.

Tibaijuka, A. (2006) 'The importance of urban planning in urban poverty reduction and sustainable development', paper presented at World Planners Congress, Vancouver.

UNCHS (1996) *An Urbanizing World: Global Report on Human Settlements, 1996*. Oxford: Oxford University Press.

UN-Habitat (2003) *The Challenge of Slums: Global Report on Human Settlements, 2003*. London: Earthscan.

UN-Habitat (2006) *National Trends in Housing Production Practices, Volume 4: Nigeria*. Nairobi: UN-Habitat.

Watson, V. (2009) 'Seeing from the South: refocusing urban planning on the globe's central urban issues', *Urban Studies*, 46(11): 2259–2275.

World Bank (1987) 'Making housing markets more efficient', *Urban Edge*, 11(9): 1.

World Commission on Environment and Development (1987) *The Brundtland Commission Report*. New York: United Nations.

24

HOUSING AND THE URBAN POOR IN KENYA

Opportunities for increased partnerships and innovative practices

Bob Hendriks

Abbreviations

ABMT	Appropriate Building Materials and Technology
AMT	Akiba Mashinani Trust
ASO	Absentee structure owner
BHC	Bellevue Housing Cooperative
CAHF	Centre for Affordable Housing Finance in Africa
CCN	City Council of Nairobi
CLT	Community land trust
COHRE	Centre on Housing Rights and Evictions
CoK	Constitution of Kenya
CSUDP	Civil Society Urban Development Programme
DITs	Dweller-initiated transformations
ESC rights	Economic Social and Cultural rights
GoK	Government of Kenya
HCPI	Hass Consult Price Index
HDF	Housing Development Fund
ISSB	Interlocking Stabilized Soil Blocks
KENSUP	Kenya Slum Upgrading Programme
KISIP	Kenya Informal Settlements Improvement Project
KNT	Kaputiei New Town
KSUP	Korogocho Slum Upgrading Programme
MINA	Minimum intervention approach (to informal settlements upgrading)
MoH	Ministry of Housing
MoLG	Ministry of Local Government
MoU	Memorandum of Understanding
MUST	Muungano Support Trust
MUUNGANO	Muungano Wa Wanavijiji (Slum Dwellers Federation)

NACHU	National Cooperative Housing Union
NCAPD	National Coordinating Agency for Population and Development
NHC	National Housing Corporation
ODPM	Office of the Deputy Prime Minister
RSO	Resident structure owner
SACCOs	Savings and credit cooperative societies
SDI	Slum Dwellers International
SHH	Self-help housing

Introduction

Kenya has faced a considerable deficit in housing supply since independence. The authorities have been unable to ensure that the annual housing supply keeps pace with the estimated growing annual housing need, due to population growth and weak financial resources and management capacities of urban centres. Despite the introduction of new approaches, policies and programmes, meeting the high demand for housing has remained a major challenge since the 1990s.

Kenya is considered the third fastest urbanizing country and Nairobi the second fastest growing city in sub-Saharan Africa (UN-Habitat 2010a). The rising birth rates and natural growth of the urban population account for approximately 55 per cent of urban growth. Rural–urban migration – due to factors including drought, conflict and rural poverty – accounts for an estimated 25 per cent. In Central and Coast Provinces much of the migration was to urban areas, whereas in other provinces – except for Nairobi – migration was predominantly within the rural areas. The majority of the newly urbanized population are between 15 and 34 years, made up of primary and high school graduates looking for jobs in towns (GoK 2011).

The high demand for housing has further increased during the past decade with the growing middle class and reduced urban poverty, due to sustained economic growth at 4 to 7 per cent since 2003. In addition, national demand patterns have started altering, as for the first time more formal jobs were created in secondary towns than in Nairobi, with the latter especially catering for growth of informal jobs (GoK 2012).

Formal housing supply is currently estimated at 50,000 units annually, while housing demand is estimated at 156,000 units based on urban population growth and rapid urban migration. Therefore, the estimated annual housing requirement is 206,000 units, with 40 per cent being in urban areas. The current overall housing backlog is estimated at 2 million units (CAHF 2011). Overall, more than 80 per cent of new houses produced are for high-income and upper middle-income earners, yet the greatest demand is from low-income and lower middle-income earners who constitute 83 per cent of the demand (GoK 2007a). Table 24.1 presents relevant population, income and poverty statistics for housing supply and demand.

Recent planning, law and policies aim to improve housing provision, quality and rights for Kenyan citizens. Vision 2030 promises to work towards 'an adequately and decently housed nation in a sustainable environment'. The Constitution of Kenya (CoK 2010) guarantees to every person the right to accessible and adequate housing and reasonable standards of sanitation. The state will take legislative, policy and other measures, including the setting of standards, to accomplish its progressive realization. In alignment with the CoK 2010 and National

TABLE 24.1 Kenya country statistics

% population living in urban areas	8% (1970)
	19% (1979)
	32.3% (2009)
	44.5% (2015)
	54% (2030)
% urban growth	7.7% (1979)
	3.4% (1999)
	8.3% (2009)
Number of urban centres	17 (1948)
	91 (1979)
	230 (2009)
Concentration urban population (2009)	Nairobi 22%
	Mombasa 3.5%
% population earning (2008)	1.6% Upper-middle class (US$10–20 per day)
	15.2% Lower-middle class (US$4–10 per day)
	28.1% Floating class (US$2–4 per day)
	41.7% Poor (<US$2 per day)
	Kenya ranking third among sub-Saharan African countries
% population below poverty line	56% (2002)
	46%: urban 33.7%; rural 49.1% (2007)
% population below food poverty line	Urban 8.3% (2005/2006)
	Rural 21.9% (2005/2006)
% urban population able to afford mortgage	8% (2011)

Sources: GoK (2011); AfDB (2011).

Housing Policy 2004, the Eviction and Resettlement Guidelines Bill 2011 was drafted. The draft Housing Act 2011 and draft National Urban Development Policy 2012 were aligned with the CoK 2010, Intergovernmental Relations Acts 2011 and Urban Areas and Cities Act 2011 – including devolution of authority to counties and urban areas – and propose respectively the establishment of an enabling institutional regulatory framework for housing provision and the first comprehensive national urban policy framework for sustainable urban development.

This chapter discusses housing provision and the urban poor in Kenya. The following section analyses approaches, trends and impacts of housing provision through private, public and self-help housing streams. The section thereafter discusses institutional opportunities and constraints for housing provision to the urban poor related to the draft Housing Act 2011. The last section concludes on the contributions of the three streams of housing provision to accessible and adequate housing for the urban poor and how these can be improved.

Existing and emerging housing provision in Kenya

Figure 24.1 provides an overview of existing and emerging housing provision in Kenya. Regulated private sector housing provision has been dominant since independence. Regulated

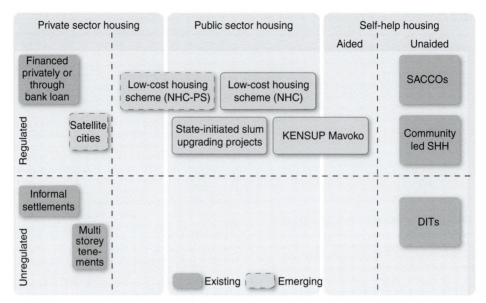

FIGURE 24.1 Existing and emerging housing provision in Kenya (numbers of units provided).

public sector housing through state-assisted sites-and-services projects was considerable during the 1970s and 1980s and only recently has reverted to a new round of state-provided affordable housing. Unaided self-help housing, often through hybrid initiatives of formal land access and informal subdivision and/or community land trust deeds, has a long tradition in Kenya and has been growing in the past two decades, especially in the absence of state-supported housing and adequate private market supply. The urban poor and low-income populations are largely dependent on unregulated private sector housing provision, and some unregulated self-help housing provision in Nairobi, and the over last decade considerably increased regulated self-help housing initiatives. The current regulated state-provided slum upgrading projects are not expected to reach the intended low-income target populations, although recent minimum approaches to informal settlement upgrading might provide improved opportunities. The following subsections discuss the various streams of housing provision, their impacts and future opportunities in detail.

Private sector housing

The formal private sector mainly provides housing for higher-income and upper middle-income housing market segments. Low-income, affordable housing units are estimated at less than 30 per cent of the private development portfolio (GoK 2007b). The relative share of private sector housing for ownership and rental is not fully clear, as available data are outdated. The Ministry of Lands, Housing and Urban Development carried out the Kenya National Housing Survey in 2012–2013, which has not been published yet. However, it is generally estimated that the private sector provides 50,000 units yearly. Rental tenure is estimated at 28.5 per cent countrywide, due to concentration in urban areas (Huchzermeyer 2007).

However, tenant populations for various cities are slightly above 80 per cent (Nairobi, Kisumu, Kericho, Embu, Kiambu, Nakuru, Kitale) and 90 per cent (Mavoko), and for towns 30–60 per cent (Kakamega, Garissa, Moyale, Kilifi, Wajir, Mandera) (Syagga 2006).

According to the Hass Consult Price Index (HCPI) 2001–2011, the past decade has shown a shift in the mix of property types provided through the formal private sector for both sales and rentals. Apartments gained the largest share in sales, going up from 23.5 to 30.4 per cent of the market, while town houses and stand-alone houses went slightly down from 24.5 to 23.9 per cent and 52 to 45.7 per cent, respectively. Apartments form the largest share in rentals, going up from 45.3 to 47.4 per cent, while townhouses went down from 20.5 to 17.4 per cent, and stand-alone houses slightly up from 34.1 to 35.3 per cent.

The secondary housing market of large-scale single- and multi-storey – largely unauthorized – dwellings owned by absentee private landlords dominates low-income and lower middle-income housing provision, respectively. This concerns both low-quality high-cost tenement slum dwellings and multi-storey rooming tenements which are often characterized by very high plot coverage, non-regulated maximization of unit numbers, higher number of storeys than the officially permitted four storeys without an elevator, and lack of inner estate infrastructure and facilities. Nairobi contains over 150 informal settlements (Pamoja Trust 2007) and over 10,000 multi-storey buildings, approximately housing 740,000 people, the latter accounting for 23 per cent of the city's population (Huchzermeyer 2011).

In response to the very rapid and largely unplanned growth of urban centres, private companies have recently developed plans for six satellite cities in Nairobi metropolitan area in alignment with Vision 2030 and largely financed through foreign direct investment. The cities will be attached to 'mother' cities, provide mixed-use residential and commercial urban environments for 60,000 to 100,000 residents, and offer public amenities for residents and businesses. The social housing aspects, however, are expected to remain minimal. Social division and exclusion, with the rich living in their own exclusive areas, might be accompanying phenomena.

Property prices rose steeply from 2001, by 100 per cent nationally and in Nairobi, and by 30–50 per cent in smaller urban areas. HCPI house price data indicate that the cheapest house on the formal market costs Ksh 1–2 million/US$13,000–26,000, requiring a monthly income of US$468–534 on a loan instalment of US$156–178 (CAHF 2011). This means only about 10 per cent are currently accommodated by formal, commercial private sector housing supply.

A recent mortgage market survey by the Central Bank of Kenya and World Bank showed that Kenya's mortgage market grew at an average rate of 30 to 40 per cent annually between 2006 and 2010, while the total number of mortgage loans grew from 7,275 to 15,049 (Walley 2011). The mortgage debt as a proportion of Kenya's gross domestic product (GDP) equals 2.5 per cent, which ranks third in sub-Saharan Africa behind South Africa and Namibia. However, the survey also found that only 8 per cent of the urban population can afford mortgages for a basic house. This means that most middle-income earners cannot afford an average fixed mortgage necessary to buy an entry-level house. Monthly instalments estimated at Ksh 42,615/US$527 are too high. The government is working on developing the mortgage market to partially fill the gap between housing supply and demand, through innovative mortgage products, tax incentives for real estate investors – including some related to low-income housing – and creation of a mortgage liquidity facility with competitively priced long-term bonds.

Public sector housing

Public sector housing provision mainly consists of recent government initiatives in slum upgrading and state-provided low-cost housing schemes. The government also aims to increase affordability through the Appropriate Building Materials and Technology Programme. These public sector initiatives are discussed in the following subsections.

Government initiatives in slum upgrading

Slum upgrading was incorporated into the National Housing Policy 2004 as one of the key components of the government's programme for Integrated Land and Urban Sector. In the international context of the focus on reduction of people living in the slums by 2015, the GoK in partnership with international donors, initiated the Kenya Slum Upgrading Programme (KENSUP) in 2003 – after initial agreement in 2000 – and the Kenya Informal Settlements Improvement Project (KISIP) in 2011. These programmes formally aim at improving the livelihoods of the people working and living in informal settlements in urban areas. This is increasingly done through an integrated housing and infrastructure development approach, including housing improvement, income generation, provision of tenure security, and physical and social infrastructure.

Kenya Slum Upgrading Programme

The KENSUP is based on an agreement between the government (GoK) and UN-Habitat. It is a first attempt to provide a nationwide framework on slum upgrading in Kenya. The KENSUP aims to adopt a mixed development approach, ranging from complete to partial redevelopment as well as provision of sites with secure tenure and infrastructural services for incremental improvement (IFRA 2011). In addition, it originally aimed at simultaneous slum upgrading and development of a slum upgrading policy contributing towards slum eradication by 2015. The National Slum Upgrading and Prevention Policy has recently been drafted since April 2012. The programme has started, in phase IA, within selected slums in Nairobi, Kisumu, Mavoko and Mombasa (see Table 24.2). All programmes are run by the Ministry of Housing (MoH), except the Korogocho Slum Upgrading Programme (KSUP) run by the Office of the Deputy Prime Minister (ODPM) and the Urban Development Department (UDD) of the Ministry of Local Government (MoLG). Phase IB intends to target Nakuru, Eldoret, Thika, Ongata, Rongai and Ruiru. Phase IIA will focus on secondary towns, phase IIB on small towns with less than 20,000 citizens.

The main provisional results of the KENSUP regarding housing concern the Kibera Soweto East pilot phase, particularly the temporary relocation of residents to the decanting site, with 632 apartments accommodating approximately 1,200 households. The pilot phase saw major challenges in reallocation, trade and subletting of relocation units to other than low-income groups, including the formation of a black market for residents selling their IDs – which allow for temporary occupation of units for a maximum period of 30 months – and future unit rights. Many structure occupants left and sublet their temporary units for socio-economic and physical reasons, such as loss of social networks and income sources, increased transport and unit costs (Ksh 1,000/US$11 – including service charges for shared facilities – versus Ksh 500/US$5,50 monthly for former room). Tenants who refused to pay higher rents than before

TABLE 24.2 KENSUP

Location	Year	Size in ha	Number of units	Types of housing provision	Service provision
Nairobi-Kibera Soweto East	2004	Current: Zone A: 6.9　Future: Zone B/C/D: 6.6/3.6/4.5　Total: 21.3	Current: Zone A: 876 structures　Future: Zone B/C/D: 522/410/588　Total: 2,396 structures/7,500 households	Slum redevelopment: *Pilot phase (zone A)*　Replacement old dwellings with 6-storey flats totalling 742 units	*Pilot phase (zone A)*　Spine road, including physical infrastructure
Nairobi-Korogocho Slum Upgrading Programme	2008	52.7	*Tentative figures:*　Proposed plots versus existing structures: 2,462/3,268　• Residential: 2,067/3,004　• Commercial: 317/269　• Public purpose: 70/60　• Waste disposal: 8/0　Negotiated principles: RSO: 1 plot/1 household　• ASO: 1 plot/2 households　• Tenant: 1 plot/5 households	• MINA　• Preparation physical development plan　• Provision tenure security: individual titles and share-certificates　• SHH construction with housing typologies to guide residents　• Possibility housing cooperatives	Sustainable integrated upgrading plan
Nairobi- Kahawa Soweto	2005			Tenure security through CLTs	
Mavoko- Sustainable Neighbourhood Programme	2004	78		• Resettlement　• SHH pilot project for slum residents in Mavoko linked to CB and IG　• ABMT	Improvement of basic services

TABLE 24.2 (*cont.*)

Location	Year	Size in ha	Number of units	Types of housing provision	Service provision
		22	• 40 (upper middle-income) • 120 (lower middle-income) • 252 (low-income)	• Mixed housing • Conventional construction methods through contracting • 2- and 3-bedroomed units • Framework for comparison two housing delivery options on affordability, delivery time, product quality, employment opportunities generated	Physical, employment/income generation, and social infrastructure
Kisumu–Urban Programme	2004				Construction of social amenities in slums: schools, clinics, water and sanitation facilities, social halls, markets
Mombasa–Slum Upgrading Programme	2007			*In situ* upgrading in various settlements	Prioritized implementation of physical and social infrastructures

Sources: UN-Habitat (2008); IFRA (2011); MoLG (2012).
CB: capacity building; IG: income generation.

were relocated to other zones of Soweto East. Currently, mainly middle-class citizens and university students are believed to occupy the relocation units (IFRA 2011). It is unclear whether the instrument of (partial) purchasing of final units through cooperative titles, with residents pooling resources, will suffice to overcome risks of selling out. Additional measures taken are differentiation of typologies (one-, two- and three-room apartments at respectively Ksh 400.000/US$4,400, Ksh 600,000/US$6,600 and Ksh 900,000/US$9,900, with the majority being two-room apartments) and allowing subletting of rooms.

KENSUP Kibera faces high risks for conflict due to non-compensation for absentee and resident structure owners, who constitute 10 per cent of the population. It adheres to the principle of one stakeholder (tenant/owner) one unit right. Structure owners who did not accept relocation often went to court, which ruled that tenants should move but that the government should not destroy the structures they occupied. Some structure owners still rented out these structures against lower rents than before (IFRA 2011).

Another major challenge, for slum upgrading projects in Kenya in general, concerns the transformation of governance from top-down programmes with some consultation over implementation to bottom-up programmes with community representation at all programme levels, including the meta-governance level. In addition, mechanisms for accountability, lodging, hearing of formal complaints and independent evaluations could be included (COHRE 2006). KENSUP Kibera has only limited consultation over implementation. KSUP Korogocho's steering committee, after heavy contestations which led to inclusion in the Kenya–Italy Debt for Development Programme, contains four resident representatives.

KSUP and Mavoko slum resettlement projects have opted for modalities of tenure security provision and facilitation of incremental self-help housing rather than redevelopment, i.e. the minimum intervention approach (MINA). Environmental sustainability is mostly limited to use of appropriate building technologies, primarily aimed at cost reduction.

Kenya Informal Settlements Improvement Project (KISIP)

KISIP is a project of the Ministry of Lands, Housing and Urban Development, supported by the World Bank, Agence Française de Développement (AFD) and the Swedish International Development Agency (SIDA). It is the second project in a series which supports the Kenyan government in the urban and local government sectors. The Kenya Municipal Program builds the institutional capacity and citywide infrastructure at municipal level, while the KISIP is explicitly oriented towards poverty reduction and improved living conditions in informal settlements of the same municipalities. The project comprises four components: institutional strengthening and programme management of the participating national and local authorities; enhancing tenure security; investing in infrastructure and service delivery; and planning for urban growth. It runs from 2011 until 2016 and targets 15 municipalities: Nairobi, Kisumu, Nakuru, Kakamega, Machakos, Garissa, Embu, Mombasa, Kericho, Naivasha, Malindi, Thika, Nyeri, Eldoret and Kitui. The focus is on areas where land tenure is already regularized. The KISIP hopes to be able to deal with the risks of non-affordability and relocation due to improved infrastructure and affected property values through coping mechanisms of scale (infrastructure improvement in multiple settlements), very basic infrastructure standards and new land for housing or densification, to influence and regulate the housing market. Adequate timing of infrastructure improvement and tenure security interventions is also important. If tenure security comes too late, infrastructure investments may largely benefit structure owners and target beneficiaries may be priced out. If tenure security arrives too early, it may complicate regularization processes since land tenure would have changed from public to either private or community tenure. Under the KISIP, the ministries have increasingly contracted civil society organizations (CSOs) for consultancy services, such as on land tenure regularization and socio-economic data collection. Contracting CSOs for short-term technical inputs seems quite feasible, though much less so for longer-term social interventions.

Low-cost housing schemes

Recently, the NHC has been reactivated for efficient development of decent and affordable housing, after having been largely dormant for a decade. The NHC's Strategic Plan 2009–2013 planned a direct development of 2,000 housing units annually; 22,000 more units are envisioned to be developed through facilitation and partnership arrangements (NHC 2010). It also planned housing projects in 90 other towns, totalling 6,000 units at a cost of Ksh 8 billion/US$70 million. These are mainly low-cost housing schemes. Low-cost prefabricated housing provision, with a low-cost prefabricated materials plant run by the NHC, through public–private partnerships offers opportunities to move to scale, with estimated 30 per cent savings in construction costs for decent housing and reduction of adverse environmental effects. However, these houses are considered unaffordable for the poor and do not yet substantially reduce the housing shortage. These developments constitute only a slight shift to low-cost affordable housing, especially on the outskirts of Nairobi, Thika and Kitengela. It does, however, contribute to some relaxation of market demand, relief of steeply rising prices, and stabilization of sales and rental prices in the long run. Impacts are also influenced by irregularities in house allocation processes, such as applications for 209 units by NHC staff, half of allocations going to people who never applied, 10 per cent of reservations for high-level personalities and non-allocation to applicants meeting required deposits (*Daily Nation* 2012).

Appropriate Building Materials and Technology (ABMT) programme

The MoH established the ABMT programme in 2006. ABMT refers to building processes, materials and tools that are cost-effective, safe, innovative, green/environmental friendly and acceptable to the climate, socio-economic conditions and natural resources of the area. Research and development regarding Interlocking Stabilized Soil Blocks (ISSB), micro-concrete roofing tiles and pozzolana/rice husks cement has been carried out. In addition, the revised Building Code was drafted, which allows for use of ABMT in designated areas. Practical implementation has so far concentrated on ISSB for walling. The regional ABMT centre at Mavoko is almost completed, while approximately 80 of 210 constituency ABMT centres are ready. By September 2012, about a hundred Hydraform machines for use by citizens had been procured through the centres. Training workshops are conducted to transfer skills and empower community groups to construct affordable houses, social facilities and other utilities.

Self-help housing

Social production of habitat through self-help housing has a long tradition in Kenya, especially since the redistribution of land in the resettlement period just after independence. Owing to

TABLE 24.3 Registered self-help housing initiatives in Kenya, 1990–2011

Type	Cumulative numbers
SACCOs and commercial land buying companies	3,305 (1998)
	4,678 (2005)
	5,444 (2010)
Housing cooperatives registered with MoCD	20+ (1990)
	424 (1999)
	512 (2005)
	625 (2009)
	708 (2010)
	867 (2011)
Housing cooperatives registered with NACHU	220 (2005)
	248 (2007)
	347 (2011)

Sources: Consultations MoCD (Ministry of Co-operative Development; NACHU; Merill *et al.* (2007); UN-Habitat (2010b).

the failure and absence of state provision of housing during the structural adjustment period, the mechanisms of middle-class savings and credit cooperative societies (SACCOs) and land buying companies as well as housing cooperatives of the poor were boosted (see Table 24.3). The latter mechanisms were further strengthened during the 1990s and 2000s, starting with savings to gain access to land and followed by acquiring affordable housing finance.

Self-help housing has been mainly unaided by the state until now, although regulatory frameworks for SACCOs and microfinance institutions have been established recently to improve performance and public confidence in these institutions. The main self-help housing models accessible for the urban poor are community-led incremental (in-situ) slum upgrading, with access to land and tenure through community land tenure with sectional titles for households; and (peri-)urban housing development through land buying cooperatives, trusts and societies, with formal collective land purchase and informal subdivision of individual plots, which may or may or not be followed by (gradual) formalization. Over the past two decades 16 self-help housing initiatives of the urban poor have planned for 6,988 housing units for members, of which 1,532 units have been completed so far. A special category of unregulated and unaided self-help housing are the Dweller-Initiated Transformations of formal housing. Former aided incremental sites-and-services projects of the 1970s and 1980s are not discussed here in detail. However, when analysing self-help housing provision it is important to remember their limited outcomes. Despite the large housing stock produced, two-thirds or more were not occupied by the target group of the urban poor.

Community-led (incremental) self-help housing

Community-led (peri-)urban land buying cooperatives, trust and societies

Research evidence shows that, however difficult it might be, it is possible for the poor and very poorest households to continue paying rent while saving or repaying a loan to purchase land, especially if there is a clear and unambiguous vision of the purpose of saving (Hendriks 2008). Eight community-led land buying initiatives, moving from informal settlements to peri-urban Nairobi, varying in size from 5 to 80, 300 and 600 acres, have planned for 2,593 housing units since the mid-1990s. To date 921 units have been completed by three initiatives (Bellevue Housing Cooperative, Kaputiei New Town and Shangilia Baba Na Mama), while three initiatives which gained access to land in the early 2000s have not started building yet (Toi Market Savings Scheme, Ghetto Saving Scheme and Original Wanpenda Afya Bidii Women's Group), and two initiatives were initiated recently (Eastern Greenfields and upcoming project). Generally, costs of building in advance of relocation – which mostly include provision of infrastructure and basic services, and advantages of economies of scale, volume and uniformity – are unaffordable for the poor.

One strategy to overcome these limitations is through incremental building and use of low-cost building materials, especially in combination with subletting rooms, such as in the case of the Bellevue Housing Cooperative (BHC) supported by the National Cooperative Housing Union (NACHU) (Hendriks 2008). The BHC was relatively successful, especially due to expansion of the industrial area ten years after settlement, which offered various income-generating opportunities. After 20 years, economic and social impacts were that 7 per cent of original owners had been able to change status from very poorest to poor based on criteria of food and absolute poverty line. Half of them can be considered non-poor on the basis of wealth ranking. Tenure security through record keeping and/or share certificates was considered sufficient for investment in plot development by half of the owners. Recently, however, residents have started aspiring to acquire formal titles due to steeply rising land prices in the area. Environmental and morphological impacts have been mixed. Process optimizations – such as strategic anticipation of longer-term socio-economic contextual prospects, and efficient and profitable utilization of idle land during delivery time – might improve impacts of similar projects.

A second strategy is cross-subsidizing of initiatives by adding middle-income units and/or by making a smaller margin on affordable units and a larger margin on middle-income units. Kaputiei New Town (KNT), supported by Jamii Bora, provides a recent example of the necessity of cross-subsidizing in cases of building in advance and insufficient economic opportunities. The project planned to house 2,000 low-income households from Nairobi's slums without additional cross-subsidizing units in 2000, but will end up selling two-thirds of the built units to non-members as first inhabitants. Prices have become too high for members: Ksh 1.2 million/US$13,200 and Ksh 1.6 million/US$17,600 for two- and four-bedroom houses, respectively. During the six-year land delivery time up to settlement, through dragging court cases up to the High Court over a politically instigated land conflict, building material costs had increased steeply. However, the originally planned monthly rents of Ksh 2,500/US$27.50 would also have been unaffordable for the poor. Moreover, the project insufficiently anticipated the medium- and long-term social-economic-political prospects for the settlement location, such as income-generating opportunities, access roads, transport costs (Ksh 500/US$5.50 for return trip Nairobi) and electricity provision, although KNT concluded a Memorandum of Understanding (MoU) with the local community, arranged temporary electricity provision and plans special transport arrangements after implementation of access roads. Environmental impacts in terms of building materials and wider sustainability are positive. KNT includes installation of solar panels to power houses and a water and sanitation system which recycles 70 per cent of waste water via man-made wetlands.

A third strategy is the combination of incremental building, low-cost building technologies and cross-subsidizing, which is the case in two upcoming projects supported by Muungano Slum Dwellers Federation (MUUNGANO) and Muungano Support Trust (MUST). In peri-urban Katani, 700 slum dwellers bought 8 acres of vacant land for Ksh 18 million, for mixed development. Five acres will be used for 400 incrementally built units by the poor and 200 ground-floor-plus-four units for sale. The remaining 3 acres are for sale or rental to support MUST's financial resources.

Community-led incremental (in-situ) slum upgrading

Community-led incremental slum upgrading programmes with access to land and tenure through special planning areas and sectional property titles, and/or temporary occupation licences in case of absence of further arrangements, have existed in Kenya since the early 2000s, initially mainly in Nairobi, but recently also in other cities such as Nakuru and Thika. Eight community-led initiatives planned for 3,137 upgraded housing units. To date 424 units have been completed by four initiatives, especially the Huruma Slum Upgrading and Habitat for Humanity projects, but also Nyamarutu and Shikamoo Projects in Nakuru and Kiandutu Project in Thika. Two major upcoming projects – Tushirikishe Jamii Project in the Mukuru slums in Nairobi and the Nakuru Greenfields Project – plan for mixed housing development with 2,000 and 200 ground-floor-plus-two low-income units respectively for incremental building, and 1,000 and 100 ground-floor-plus-three/-four units respectively for sale. The recently initiated court case by the MUUNGANO to claim land rights in the Mukuru slums due to failed usage of land for allocated purposes might provide additional space for community-led slum upgrading, although the High Court has awarded Ksh 11 billion compensation to Orbit Chemical Industries which acquired the land in 1987 and which submitted an application to dismiss the MUUNGANO's case.

The majority of projects are supported by the MUUNGANO, the MUST, the Akiba Mashinani Trust (AMT) and Slum Dwellers International (SDI), with additional incidental financial loans and grants from local and international banks. The main project so far has been the Huruma Slum Upgrading Project, which started formation of savings schemes in 2000 and commenced incremental *in situ* upgrading in 2003 – supported by Pamoja Trust and Cooperazione Internazionale (COOPI) for infrastructure since 2005. Its main aim was tenure regularization for residents to avoid evictions.

Social impacts are largely positive in terms of increased tenure security through sectional titles – which can be sold back to the community – and reduced need for relocation through construction of 20–30 units at a time. However, up to now the complicated ownership pattern has made it difficult to give titles to individual landowners, while the City Council of Nairobi (CCN) still holds the land title, and land transfer still has to be claimed by the community (IFRA 2011). Different guidelines and recommendations to secure land apply to different categories of informal settlements, i.e. those on government, private, indigenous freehold and private land owned by absentee landlords (Pamoja Trust 2011). Furthermore, impacts on perceived tenure security have been positive for savers, but have remained mixed for excluded non-savers in the area (Klopp 2005), including structure owners who felt uneasy about the rule to give up multiple structures for one regularized unit. Reduced membership fees to enter savings schemes and lowering the repayment burden might improve inclusion. Overall, limited availability of finances for low-income housing, limited scale of initiatives and relatively long delivery time remain challenges for large-scale housing delivery, although progress and achievements are consistent and reach the urban poor.

Economic impacts of affordability seem positive, but have not been researched thoroughly. Environmental impacts are positive although mainly related to the household itself for cost reduction, as the use of locally available lava stone blocks and application of the Laady building method of prefabricated mini-floor slabs reduce the need for expensive energy-intensive materials such as cement and steel. Recent initiatives increasingly make use of the affordable building techniques of ISSB and adobe block technology. Morphological impacts are generally positive.

Cooperation with the government has remained occasional, such as the one-time MoU with the CCN regarding the 'special planning area', the MoH technical support and provision of ISSB machines to the Shikamoo project and the expected infrastructure provision to Tushirikishe Jamii Project. Cooperation with private sector stakeholders such as banks and international funding organizations is mostly project related, while civic support in housing microfinance is generally structural. Cooperation between the NGOs Pamoja Trust and the MUST (started in 2010 by former Pamoja Trust staff) is tense and requires further clarification of roles and complementarity to sustain effectiveness.

Finally, in the context of the Revised Railway Relocation Action Plan, the MUUNGANO and Ngazi ya Chini – supported by the MUST and Hakijamii and in partnership with the World Bank – are working on relocation of 10,000 households residing or operating a business on railway reserves in Kibera and Mukuru slums for improved safety of passengers on faster commuter trains and of slum dwellers through land share in the Safety and Development Corridor from 2012.

Housing microfinance

The microfinance market in Kenya is well developed, including four large microfinance banks (Equity Bank, K-REP, Family Bank, Cooperative Bank), which mainly serve the upper-end market, and 50 microfinance organizations (Merill et al. 2007). Recently, the SACCO Societies Act 2008 and Regulations 2010 and MFI Act 2006 and Regulations 2007 have established enabling regulatory frameworks to improve performance and public confidence in these institutions. However, there is still a major gap in the provision of affordable housing microfinance for low-income groups. A few housing microfinance institutions, such as the NACHU, Jamii Bora Bank and the AMT, offer services accommodating the poor, including small loans, long-term loans, share certificates as collateral, flexible repayment terms and linked health insurance. In general, the sector has been unable to scale-up its operations and ensure long-term sustainability due to various factors, including limited funding, heavy donor dependency and relatively high repayment defaults. The SDI alliance formed by the AMT and the Urban Poor Fund shows repayment defaults as high as 50 per cent (SDI 2011), despite efforts towards improved savings through Muungano Development Fund shares. However, initiatives for further capacity building and scaling-up of housing microfinance and support services in partnership with international support organizations are ongoing. The NACHU strengthened its financial and technical capacities through increased revolving funds to reduce donor dependency and increase self-reliance, supported by Rooftops Canada and others. Jamii Bora Bank raised its core capital to acquire middle-tier status and plans to double its staff and run 12 branches countrywide, offering mortgage packages below Ksh 200,000/US$2,200 for low-income clients. AMT and K-Rep Bank jointly launched the low-cost housing finance company Makao Mashinani in 2010, which seeks to bridge the gap between development and market financing for slum upgrading. Finally, a regional support programme and national institutional structures are being developed, supported by FinMark Trust, Rooftops Canada and Habitat for Humanity.

Dweller-initiated transformations

Dweller-initiated transformations (DITs) of formal housing are common in middle-class housing estates in Nairobi (Makachia 2011). The large majority of homeowners in middle-class estates have extended their houses informally, especially in Eastlands. Initially DITs aimed at satisfying the family's qualitative and quantitative physical and/or socio-cultural spatial needs. Further expansion often aimed at the economic needs of additional income and/or pension through subletting of rooms or business premises.

DITs offer reasonably affordable rental housing for low-income households. However, informalization through incremental building often goes against the initial design and building standards of estates through deteriorated 'temporary' material and unplanned space uses. Due to congestion, the carrying capacity of physical infrastructure is frequently overburdened. Sometimes new informal codes are introduced around informal urbanism practices.

Recent research recommends a phased-design guided densification model through a socially inclusive process incorporating existing dwellership, in order to deal with the compromising of living environments. A precondition for effectiveness, however, is conferment of tenure security or legality within the CCN rental tenure system and within a legal physical framework.

Institutional context and housing the urban poor

Since 2006/2007 an encompassing Housing Act was drafted and realigned with the CoK 2010, which will replace the National Housing Policy 2004 and first Housing Act 1967. The draft Housing Act 2011 formulates an enabling regulatory framework, with new institutions such as the Housing Development Authority – run by the multi-stakeholder Kenya Housing Board – including the NHC, Housing Development Fund (HDF) and Housing Tribunal.

The two main conditions for the newly established institutional framework to work are access to land and availability of financial resources. Public land is very scarce in Kenya. Access to private land is difficult, mostly overpriced and, if available, often used for other purposes than housing. The Kenyan law, however, provides for the possibility to acquire land for public purposes. It remains to be seen whether claims for land on the Commissioner of Lands of the newly established National Land Commission will be effective. As for availability of finances, the draft Act proposes three major ways of financing through contributions of the government, employers and employees. Employers only contribute in the absence of a housing scheme. The central perspective is to consider housing investment not only as a social issue, but also as an economic issue contributing considerably to Kenya's GDP.

A major limitation to reaching the urban poor is that the Act does not require the private sector to set aside a certain portion for social housing. In addition, the need for demand-driven infrastructure development is not mentioned. Furthermore, only employees are supposed to contribute and thus gain access to housing, which excludes the majority of informally employed citizens. The question remains how the HDF will be distributed among groups.

A positive aspect is that different mechanisms of housing finance can be supported. While the emphasis might be on facilitating mortgages, current interest rates for mortgages are too high for most citizens. The Act, however, also includes the possibility of supporting housing cooperatives, including initiatives of the urban poor. Housing microfinance organizations currently explore opportunities for partnerships with the government in housing finance, either through the HDF or KENSUP. Finally, the Act enables supporting special housing programmes, including disabled friendly accommodation, women's shelters and student hostels.

The CoK 2010 mandates a minimum of 15 per cent of national revenue to be transferred unconditionally to counties. Allocation of revenue depends on the size of counties. Counties decide on the share of finances allocated for housing. In addition, counties can borrow against favourable interest rates from the HDF, which consists of 5 per cent of the government budget.

While the Act does not refer to the draft Eviction and Resettlement Guidelines Bill 2011, illegal occupants of land are legally better protected than before. Genuine consultations and adequate reasonable notice of occupants are legally required, which has already resulted in numerous disputes and court cases over (planned) evictions and resettlement. The Housing Tribunal provides an alternative mechanism for effective and efficient dispute resolution and might reduce the number of pending court cases.

Environmental sustainability was not integrated, but was said to be included in the final draft version. To guarantee improved results for the urban poor, current civil society engagement – which anticipates devolution to counties and urban areas – for proper urban planning, including housing provision to the urban poor, is a necessity, such as the CSUDP's campaigns and CSOs evaluating constitutional economic and socio-cultural rights.

Conclusion

This chapter discussed housing provision, institutions and the urban poor in Kenya. The private sector has been the dominant housing supplier, mainly providing for higher- and middle-income market segments. The government predominantly plays the role of facilitating an enabling environment for private sector housing provision, with recently increased incentives for investment in affordable housing. Until now it has scarcely been involved in enabling the self-help housing sector for the poor. Recently the government has also taken up a role as supplier of considerable numbers of affordable housing through low-income housing schemes by the NHC and state-initiated slum upgrading projects. The self-help housing sector plays the role of providing affordable housing to poor households, in the absence of accessible and adequate public and private sector supply. Community-based organizations cater for savings, local and international NGOs, and/or housing microfinance organizations for professional support to community-based organizations and housing microfinance. The numbers of housing units provided through this stream are relatively low compared to the other streams, but have grown rapidly and are expected to grow further.

The impacts of housing provision streams for the urban poor differ considerably. Overall, all streams mainly take into consideration impacts at the micro-level of the household and neighbourhood, rather than the meso- and macro-level of the city and nation. Social impacts in terms of tenure security are provided through formal titles in public and private sector housing, and through collective formal titles or sectional title deeds – either or not combined with individual titles and/or share certificates – in the self-help housing sector. Economic impacts in terms of affordability for the urban poor are mainly through the self-help housing sector – especially in the case of cross-subsidizing, incremental building and facilitation of income-generating opportunities, although affordability and selling out also remain issues of concern for this sector. The recently propagated minimum intervention approach by the government also offers opportunities for reaching the poor, although recent negotiations within the KSUP showed that the majority of slum residents opted for individual rather than collective titling, with high risks of selling out. Generally, there is a need for more transparency and longitudinal research on socio-economic impacts. Impacts on local and national economic growth are highest through private and public sector housing, partly related to the current scale of self-help housing. Environmental impacts considered in all streams mainly concern building materials and construction technologies, while only incidentally sustainable energy, predominantly because of costs. Climate responsive housing and settlement design is addressed through climate change and 'green design' agendas, though it is mostly not integrated in self-help housing initiatives. Cultural impacts in terms of physical and/or socio-cultural spatial needs of the urban poor are often taken more into account by the self-help housing sector, while aesthetic and morphological issues are less considered by DITs and some housing cooperatives.

The government has opted for the strategy of promoting affordable housing through private home ownership, from the perspective of contribution to economic growth. In order to meet its constitutional mandate to offer accessible and adequate housing to all Kenyans, including the urban poor, the government should consider additional housing provision strategies. First, it should consider increased and structural (financial) enablement of self-help housing for the urban poor. This could be through currently explored implementation of joint housing finance partnerships between government and housing microfinance organizations. Structural extension of current incidental support for infrastructure and land also provides opportunities. The self-help housing sector should also continue its capacity building and scaling-up of housing microfinance and support services – including the reduction of considerable repayment defaults. Furthermore, the self-help housing sector – and other sectors – should increasingly take into account social, economic, environmental and cultural impacts beyond household and neighbourhood, in order to become a more viable partner. Second, the current minimum intervention approach which provides tenure security and promotes opportunities for community-led (incremental) upgrading presents a good opportunity to further complement government and civil society roles. Third, the government could consider an additional strategy for subsidized (rental) housing, given the fact that only 10 per cent of the urban population can afford mortgages.

The recent institutional changes, aligned with the CoK 2010, potentially contribute to improved results, but remain subject to negotiations. Current civil society engagement – anticipating devolution to counties and urban areas from the general elections in 2013 – for proper urban planning and evaluation of constitutional ESC rights is necessary to guarantee improved results for the urban poor.

References

AfDB (2011) *The Middle of the Pyramid: Dynamics of the Middle-Class in Africa*. Tunis: AfDB.
CAHF (2011) *Yearbook. Housing Finance in Africa. A Review of Some of Africa's Housing Finance Market*. Parkview: CAHF.
COHRE (2006) *Listening to the Poor? Housing Rights in Nairobi, Kenya*. Geneva: COHRE.
Daily Nation (2012) 'Audit exposes NHC housing scam', 14 March.
GoK (2007a) *Vision 2030*. Nairobi: GoK.
GoK (2007b) *Economic Survey*. Nairobi: GoK.
GoK (2011) *State of Kenya Population 2011. Kenya's 41 Million People: Challenges and Opportunities*. Nairobi: NCAPD.
GoK (2012) *Economic Survey*. Nairobi: GoK.

Hendriks, B. (2008) 'The social and economic impacts of access to peri-urban land and secure tenure for the poor: the case of Nairobi, Kenya', *International Development Planning Review*, 30(1): 27–66.

Huchzermeyer, M. (2007) 'City: the emergence of multi-storey districts through large-scale private landlordism in Nairobi', *International Journal of Urban and Regional Research*, 31(4): 714–732.

Huchzermeyer, M. (2011) *Tenement Cities: From 19th Century Berlin to 21st Century Nairobi*. New Jersey: AWP.

IFRA (2011) 'Slum upgrading programmes in Nairobi: challenges in implementation', *Les Cahiers d'Afrique de l'Est*, 44. Nairobi: IFRA.

Klopp, J. (2005) *Enabling Community-Led Process: Pamoja Trust's Approach to Slum Upgrading in Nairobi, Kenya*. Columbia University: SIPA.

Makachia, P. A. (2011) 'Evolution of urban housing strategies and dweller-initiated transformations in Nairobi', *City, Culture and Society*, 2(4): 219–234.

Merrill, S., Wambugu, A. and Johnston, C. (2007) 'Housing for the poor in Kenya: NACHU's cooperative approach', *USAID, microNOTE 38*.

MOLG (2012) Project Documentation, Korogocho Slum Upgrading Project.

NHC (2010) 'Emerging opportunities in the housing industry in Kenya'. Presentation to Kenyan Diaspora in London.

Pamoja Trust (2007) *Nairobi Inventory*. Nairobi: Pamoja Trust.

Pamoja Trust (2011) *Securing Land Tenure for the Urban Poor in Kenya. A Policy Brief*. Nairobi: Pamoja Trust.

SDI (2011) *Country Indicators and Overview*. Nairobi: Pamoja Trust.

Syagga, P. (2006) 'Land ownership and use in Kenya: policy prescriptions from an inequality perspective', in SID (ed.) *Readings on Inequality in Kenya: Sectoral Dynamics and Perspectives*. Nairobi: SID.

UN-Habitat (2008) *UN-Habitat and the Kenya Slum Upgrading Programme*. Nairobi: UN-Habitat.

UN-Habitat (2010a) *The State of African Cities 2010*. Nairobi: UN-Habitat.

UN-Habitat (2010b) *The Organisation, Management and Finance of Housing Cooperatives in Kenya*. Nairobi: UN-Habitat.

Walley, S. (2011) *Developing Kenya's Mortgage Market*. Washington, DC: World Bank.

25

URBAN LOW-INCOME HOUSING IN GHANA

Paul W. K. Yankson and Katherine V. Gough

Abbreviations

FGBS	First Ghana Building Society
GLSS	Ghana Living Standards Survey
GREDA	Ghana Real Estate Developers Association
GSS	Ghana Statistical Service
SAP	Structural Adjustment Programme
SHC	State Housing Corporation
SSNIT	Social Security and National Insurance Trust
TDC	Tema Development Corporation

Introduction

Ghana has undergone rapid population growth and urbanisation since the mid-1950s offering potential as well as great challenges for national development. Today, with 51 per cent of the total population living in urban centres,[1] Ghana can be described as an 'urbanised society'. The housing supply, however, has not been able to keep up with this urban growth. One of the key challenges Ghana faces today is the inadequate provision of housing, both in quantity and quality, especially for low-income urban households. According to the draft National Housing Policy (Government of Ghana 2009), various data suggest that the housing deficit is in excess of 500,000 units whilst supply figures hover around 40,000 units per annum as against an annual requirement of 120,000 units.[2] The national annual housing supply to demand ratio (for new housing) is estimated at about 35 per cent. The inability of the housing delivery system to meet effective demand over the years has created strains on the existing housing stock and infrastructure, especially in urban areas. In addition to the surging deficit in housing delivery in the country, the decay of existing stock resulting from a poor maintenance culture is another constraint on the housing sector. Housing the urban poor has thus reached a crisis situation as housing provision from public sector agencies, as well as from formal private sector institutions, has not reached the poor (Songsore 2003).

The typical housing type in Ghana is the compound family house which is occupied by multiple households. This housing provides the type of low or no cost accommodation found in squatter areas of other countries. Relatives are allowed to live in family houses free of charge but, especially in urban areas, rooms are often rented out to non-family members. Where demand for accommodation is high, compound houses have been extended to enable the renting out of additional rooms. Consequently, the most common type of urban tenancy in Ghana is rental; in Accra, for example, almost two-thirds of households rent their accommodation (Grant and Yankson 2003). The vast majority of tenants rent one or more rooms from private individuals who in most cases reside in the same premises with their families (Konadu-Agyemang 2001a).

This chapter analyses the housing situation of urban low-income households in Ghana.[3] Following this introduction, Ghana's changing housing policies are outlined after which the nature of low-income housing provision is discussed. Housing tenure is then examined, focusing on rental housing, and finally the future policy directions for low-income housing provision are indicated.

Ghana's changing housing policies

Colonial period

The British colonial administration was interested in providing shelter on a subsidised rental basis in a congenial environment for the staff of the colonial bureaucracy (Tipple and Korboe 1998). Apart from isolated housing provision in response to emergency situations, the provision of low-income housing was left to the dictates of market forces (Songsore 2003). Consequently, Accra and the other major urban centres developed not as coherent physical units but rather assumed a segmented urban structure (Larbi 1996). On the one hand, there were 'European' townships, usually on higher or elevated ground (ridges), with well-constructed durable houses of the bungalow type. The 'natives', on the other hand, lived in their traditional compound houses in the 'African' or 'native' townships which developed in a haphazard manner (Songsore *et al.* 2004). This remained the situation essentially until Ghana attained political independence in 1957.

Post-independence housing policy

The development agenda of the first post-independence government was driven by a modernisation paradigm led by an urban-based, import-substitution industrialisation policy. A number of development plans were prepared which contained plan objectives and development strategies for various sectors of the economy including housing. The main urban centres of Ghana, such as Accra (and the industrial city of Tema), Kumasi and Sekondi-Takoradi, were the centres of investment. These cities experienced rapid growth due largely to rural–urban migration (Addo 1972), which was the key factor of urban growth in Ghana in the 1960s. As the rising urban population, particularly in Accra, exceeded the increase in housing provision, housing became very expensive and unaffordable for many.

The housing policy of the post-independence government was one of direct production of houses by state institutions such as the Tema Development Corporation (TDC), which produced houses in Tema New Town, and the State Housing Corporation (SHC), which produced housing in the other main cities. These two institutions constructed 24,000 single household dwellings between 1957 and 1990 (Tipple and Korboe 1998). Government housing policy also involved a number of measures to influence demand including subsidies for renting and the subsequent purchase of government-built dwellings; subsidised interest rates for borrowers from a few institutions concerned with housing finance; and a rent-control regime (Tipple et al. 1999). State financial institutions such as the State Insurance Corporation (SIC), the Social Security and National Insurance Trust (SSNIT) and the First Ghana Building Society (FGBS) were also encouraged to invest in low-cost housing. These state institutions, however, performed poorly in housing production during the 1970s into the early 1980s and the recipients were relatively well-off formal sector employees (Tipple and Korboe 1998). In light of the incapacity of state agencies to provide adequate housing, the private sector accounted for about 80 per cent of the official housing output. The rent and price controls introduced in the early 1980s to make housing affordable to the poor had the unintended effect of discouraging private developers from building rental units (Tipple and Willis 1989).

A shift in policy direction commenced in 1987 with the state abandoning direct intervention in housing to act as facilitator for private sector-led housing production. Consequently, the Home Finance Company (HFC) and the Ghana Real Estates Developers Association (GREDA) emerged dealing with home finance and housing delivery, respectively. Together with the SSNIT these organisations provided housing mainly in residential estates for the middle and upper segments of the housing market. By the year 2000, approximately 2,000 housing units out of the anticipated 4,100 units had been built (Ministry of Works and Housing 2001).

Era of structural adjustment, economic liberalisation and globalisation

The late 1980s to the present is described as the era of economic recovery, structural adjustment and economic liberalisation. The liberalisation programme indirectly contributed to the physical expansion of Accra (Grant and Yankson 2003) and to a lesser degree in the other major urban centres of the country. There have been two salient consequences of liberalisation for the urban housing market. First, in response to the more liberal conditions of the Structural Adjustment Programme (SAP), the expatriate community has increased in size, which along with an expanding middle class has intensified pressure on housing. Second, the liberalisation of the financial sector has enabled foreign currency transactions resulting in many Ghanaians working abroad investing in real estate (Arku 2006; Briggs and Yeboah 2001). House building also attracts investment from middle-income Ghanaians seeking to insulate their savings from inflation. Consequently, individuals build in areas that are not serviced in anticipation of future service provision and speculate on the lower land cost in these areas (Briggs and Yeboah 2001). Estimates suggest that up to 50 per cent of all buildings erected since the introduction of the SAP have not had building permits (Yeboah 2001).

Despite the rapid expansion of housing units in Accra, about 85 per cent of the housing stock is provided by numerous small builders and individual owners (Ministry of Works and Housing 2001). Only 15 per cent is provided by quasi-public corporations that operate like commercial developers, guided by the policy and programmes of the government, and the private real estate developers who operate under the umbrella of the GREDA. Almost all the houses constructed by members of the GREDA are found in the major cities, particularly in the Accra-Tema area. The housing units produced by the private sector are targeted at the middle- and upper-income earners while those of the state corporations are targeted largely at the middle-income category. The question then is, how do poor households access housing in the light of increasing demand and the inability of the housing supply to keep pace with it?

Low-income housing provision

The 2010 Population and Housing Census recorded a total of 3,392,745 dwelling units for a total population of 24,658,823. According to UN-Habitat (2011: 49) the amount of space available to households in urban Ghana is only 1.7 rooms, giving a mean occupancy rate in urban Ghana of 2.3 persons per room. About one-third of urban households manage to obtain two rooms (31 per cent in Accra) but very few enjoy three or more rooms (UN-Habitat 2011: 52). Furthermore, over 75 per cent of households are said to share a dwelling.

Access to land

It is essential to outline the land allocation system in Ghana in order to understand housing provision. In Ghana, there are four main categories of land holdings: state lands, which are acquired by government and are held in trust for the people of Ghana; vested lands, which are lands vested in the state in trust for the original owners under the Administration of Lands Act, 1962 (Act 123); stool/family lands, which are group-owned lands governed by customary tenure systems and held by stools/family heads in trust for all members of the group; and private lands held by individuals, corporate bodies, institutions, etc. Stools have retained their customary rights to use and administer land and to allocate according to prevailing social customs. Consequently, the land market in Ghana is in effect two markets, one traditional and one modern, operating side by side (Gough and Yankson 2000).

With increasing urbanisation, customary lands in and around cities have become the focal point of settlement and housing development. As a result, access to land in both the modern and customary sectors has become increasingly difficult (Agyapong 1995). With increasing urbanisation, much of the customary land has entered the market, though informally, and formal documentation is not an essential part of the process (Antwi and Adams 2003). Access to land by the indigenous people in peri-urban Accra, both for farming and for housing, has been severely restricted owing to shortage of land within reach of the villages. Much of the land has been sold to new land acquirers on leasehold and mainly for residential development. Furthermore, some have acquired residential plots for speculative purposes (Gough and Yankson 2000). A similar process has occurred in and around Kumasi metropolitan area and to a lesser extent in the regional capitals and other urban centres in the country.

Access to land for housing by low-income groups in urban and peri-urban areas, especially in the metropolitan areas, is a real challenge, even for indigenes who belong to the various land-owning groups. Tables 25.1 and 25.2 illustrate the changes in the cost of building plots to both indigenes and migrants in urban and peri-urban areas of Ghana. The tables show that the proportion of respondents who had free land for housing declined dramatically between 1995 and 2005. The tables also show that while a significant proportion of both indigenes (39.5 per cent) and migrants (37.4 per cent) paid between 50,000 cedis (US$40) and 500,000 cedis (US$400) for housing plots in 1995, this proportion had reduced to 3.5 and 2.1 per cent of indigenes and migrants, respectively, by 2005 partly due to the inflationary situation that characterised the economy of Ghana during that period and partly to the commodification

TABLE 25.1 Changes in price of housing land for indigenes in urban/peri-urban areas in Ghana, 1995–2005 (percentage; number of respondents in brackets)★

Price in Cedis	1995	2000	2005
Free	10.2	3.8	0.8
<50,000	5.4	0.7	–
50,000–500,000	39.5	14.6	3.5
500,001–5,000,000	37.9	56.8	42.9
5,000,001–20,000,000	6.5	20.4	36.2
20,000,001–40,000,000	0.4	2.8	9.6
>40,000,000	0.1	0.9	7.0
Total	100.0 (798)	100.0 (841)	(880)

Source: ISSER Land Tenure and Land Policy Research Project: National Survey reported in Yankson and Kala (2008).
★ Figures in cedis: 10,000 cedis = 1 Ghana cedi (average exchange rate of cedis to US$1: 1,250 (1995); 5,120 (2000); 9,200 (2005)).

TABLE 25.2 Changes in price of housing land for migrants in urban/peri-urban areas in Ghana, 1995–2005 (percentage; number of respondents in brackets)★

Price in cedis	1995	2000	2005
Free	7.6	3.1	0.6
<50,000	3.8	0.6	–
50,000–500,000	37.4	10	2.1
500,001–5,000,000	40.4	51.6	37.5
5,000,001–20,000,000	10	24.8	32.5
20,000,001–40,000,000	0.6	3.9	16.3
>40,000,000	0.2	1.4	11
Total	100 (658)	100 (683)	100 (715)

Source: ISSER Land Tenure and Land Policy Research Project: National Survey reported in Yankson and Kala (2008).
★ Figures in cedis: 10,000 cedis = 1 Ghana cedi (average exchange rate of cedis to US$1: 1,250 (1995); 5,120 (2000); 9,200 (2005)).

of urban and peri-urban land in Ghana. The proportion of migrants who paid between half a million and five million cedis (US$400–4,000) for land increased appreciably between 1995 and 2000, and the proportion who paid more than five million cedis (more than US$4,000) increased between the years 2000 and 2005. The same is generally applicable to indigenes who acquired building plots.

Land prices in the metropolitan areas and other major urban areas have risen rapidly as the situation of specific areas in Accra and Kumasi shows[4] (see Table 25.3). This constrains access to land for housing by low-income groups and households in the metropolitan and other major urban centres. A related land issue is that of land disputes. Other claimants, boundary disputes and encroachments were the most pressing issues militating against smooth delivery of land for housing in urban areas. There are thousands of land cases in the courts in the country, which causes delays in securing documents on land and building permits (Gough and Yankson 2000). Consequently, many landlords have built without first securing the necessary permits.

TABLE 25.3 Trends in price (in new Ghana cedis) of indigene and migrant housing land per acre (0.4 hectare) in selected areas of Accra and Kumasi, 1995–2005

	Accra							Kumasi				
	Ofankor/Amansaman		Nungua		Nii Boi Town			Ayeduase		Fankyenebra	
	Mean price (¢)	% change	Mean price (¢)	% change	Mean price (¢)	% change		Mean price (¢)	% change	Mean price (¢)	% change
Indigene housing land price											
1995	2,950	–	2,210	–	2,780	–		5,000	–	3,120	–
2000	6,210	110.5	5,690	157.5	8,270	197.5		14,500	190	8,340	167.3
2005	20,000	254.3	16,500	190.0	21,700	162.4		35,400	144	17,200	106.2
1995–2005	–	578	–	646.6	–	680.6		–	608	–	454.5
Migrant housing land price											
1995	2,840	–	1,560	–	2,500	–		1,740	–	3,300	–
2000	6,610	132.7	4,390	181.4	9,040	261.9		9,250	431.6	8,380	153.9
2005	24,300	267.6	11,700	166.5	20,600	127.0		24,700	167	18,600	122
1995–2005	–	755.6	–	650	–	724		–	1377	–	463.6

Source: ISSER Household Land Survey, 2005 (Owusu 2008) as presented in Government of Ghana (2010, Table 2.9).
*Figures in cedis: 10,000 cedis = 1 Ghana cedi (average exchange rate of cedis to US$1: 1,250 (1995); 5,120 (2000); 9,200 (2005)).

TABLE 25.4 Sources of housing finance in some selected low-income urban communities in Ghana (%)

Source	Ashiaman	Nima	James Town	Saltpond	Tamale
Own savings	80	72	66	42.5	32.5
Relatives/friends	18	24	20	52.5	62.5
Susu and money lender	2	4	2	7.5	–
Credit union	–	–	–	–	2.5
Bank credit	–	–	–	–	–
Others	–	2	–	–	–

Source: UN-Habitat (2011: 100).

Housing finance

Formal sector housing finance is poorly developed in Ghana, particularly for small-scale private individuals. Several attempts made over the years to establish institutions to provide housing finance ostensibly targeted at ordinary Ghanaians have not worked but rather the institutions have turned to the higher-income market for a safe lending environment (UN-Habitat 2011). The development of a housing finance system capable of financing shelter for the majority of the population requires a three-pronged approach: the mobilisation of resources at the national as well as the beneficiary levels; the creation of appropriate financial assistance; and the development of loan and savings schemes adapted to the needs and financial capacities of low-income residents (Government of Ghana 2009). The existing financial systems are short term in character with high commercial lending rates depending on short-term borrowing to finance long-term assets. Virtually all existing finance institutions do not have access to adequate long-term funds, hence the tendency to depend on short-term funds to finance long-term mortgages (Government of Ghana 2009). This situation raises the cost of borrowing significantly, making the existing housing financing schemes unaffordable to low- and medium-income groups. Consequently, homeowners finance their housing through private savings, leading to incremental development and delays in completing buildings, resulting in many engaging 'caretakers' to live in their incomplete houses as a form of security (Gough and Yankson 2011).

A survey of five low-income urban communities showed how savings and assistance from relatives provide over 90 per cent of the money for housing construction as well as the insignificant role played by formal financial mechanisms as a source of loans for house building in several communities in Ghana (see Table 25.4).[5] Similar findings were obtained from a study of peri-urban Accra (Gough and Yankson 2000), where only 4 per cent of homeowners had borrowed money from a bank and 88 per cent used their own savings. 'Own savings' entails a multitude of strategies including remittances from abroad and the assembly of materials ahead of construction as seen from the piles of sand, stones and *sandcrete* blocks on building sites or on a convenient location in the street. Some relied on windfall gains such as retirement lump-sums, whilst others had worked overseas or had sources of cash from relatives overseas. Friends, family members and occasionally an employer are the usual sources of additional finance (UN-Habitat 2011: 102).

Building materials

One of the challenges confronting the production of houses for low-income groups in urban areas is the high cost of building materials, which can account for 60 per cent of construction cost (Government of Ghana 2009). This is partly due to the high import-content of building materials used for constructing houses in urban areas. The results of the 2010 Population and Housing Census (GSS 2012) show that the majority of low-income builders use cement blocks or concrete for wall construction (57.5 per cent), followed by mud, brick or earth (34.2 per cent). Corrugated metal sheets (71.4 per cent), slate/asbestos (13 per cent), thatch or palm leaves or raffia (8.6 per cent) are the main materials used for roofing collectively, accounting for 93 per cent of all materials used. Doors are mainly panelled or flush doors that are mass produced locally and sold on the open timber market. Floors are mainly cement screed, and ceiling materials, when used, are mostly plywood (UN-Habitat 2011). Local materials such as compacted laterite used for buildings in rural areas and the older parts of towns and cities are not being used for new buildings. Although it is cheap, durable and highly thermally efficient, it is not approved by building regulations in urban areas. The Draft National Housing Policy 2009 has noted that improvements in the local building materials industry constitute the foundation of any strategies to improve housing delivery in the country (Government of Ghana 2009).

Infrastructure

Inadequate infrastructure is a key feature of housing environments in Ghana, especially low-income housing areas in cities and urban areas. There are two distinctly different urban infrastructure levels within Ghanaian cities: relatively well-serviced areas in which most of the occupants are rich, and poorly serviced areas occupied by all income groups. According to the 2010 Population and Housing Census, 46.5 per cent of households have access to pipe-borne water while 29.1 per cent use a well or borehole. The rest depend on natural water sources such as rain water, rivers and ponds. The proportion of the population with access to safe water in urban areas was estimated at 58 per cent in 2010 (GSS 2012). Despite this being an improvement, there are still real problems. In the major cities, in particular, the water systems experience operational problems such as disrepair of the distribution systems leading to serious leakages and water loss. In many areas of cities in Ghana, water flows once or twice a week for a few hours. Currently, low-income areas in urban Ghana face a shortfall in the water supply. The urban poor in the informal, low-income settlements are the hardest hit by the shortage in water supply, relying on public standpipes, neighbours' taps or water vendors for their daily supply and consequently paying 10 to 20 times more than those connected to the network (UN-Habitat 2011).

Sanitation provision is also inadequate. The results of the 2010 Population and Housing Census show that public toilets are the main facility used by 34.6 per cent of the population in the country, up from 31.4 per cent in 2000, while the proportion without a toilet facility reduced slightly from 20 per cent to 19 per cent (GSS 2012). On the other hand, the proportion using a water closet toilet facility increased notably from 8.5 per cent in 2000 to 15.4 per cent in 2010. The situation in urban low-income areas is worse than these statistics suggest. A study by Owusu and Afutu-Kotey (2010) in low-income areas of Accra and Sekondi-Takoradi metropolitan areas shows that just over a fifth (20.2 per cent) had no access to a specific toilet facility.

With respect to solid waste disposal, a large proportion of households (61.5 per cent) use public dumpsites (37.7 per cent in open space and 23.8 per cent in containers) with only 14 per cent having access to a collection service (GSS 2012). Solid waste often remains uncollected for long periods and the dumping of solid waste is done haphazardly. In low-income areas in cities such as Kumasi and Accra, despite improvements in waste collection generally this has not translated into improved environmental conditions. Communal containers are constantly overflowing and every possible open space and drainage channels are targets for indiscriminate dumping (UN-Habitat 2011: 127).

Lack of drainage is also a critical issue. Drains in urban Ghana are generally inadequate and local floods and flash-floods are common. Waste water tends to be disposed of through open drains, a predominant feature of low-income and other informal neighbourhoods, and only a few households have a sewer or septic tank for their sullage. In 2010, about 35 per cent of all households in Ghana threw their liquid waste onto the compound of their homes; 28.1 per cent onto streets or outside their homes; 18.7 per cent into gutters; and only 10.9 per cent disposed of their liquid waste through plumbing systems into gutters (GSS 2012).

Housing tenure

In Ghana, the 2010 Population and Housing Census shows that 47.2 per cent of dwelling units are occupied by their owners; 31.1 per cent are rented out; and 20.8 per cent are occupied rent-free. The latter are usually homes for extended families whose original owners may have died. About 53 per cent of the dwelling units are owned by household members, 26.3 per cent are owned by other private individuals, another 15.6 per cent are owned by relatives who are not household members and only 3.7 per cent are owned by employers (public and private) (GSS 2012). Rental units are provided by landlords who may be a private individual, a non-profit organisation such as a housing association or a government body as in public housing (Government of Ghana 2009). Having dealt with factors that affect the provision of low-income housing above, we now turn to focus on the most common form of urban tenancy: rental housing.

Provision of rental housing

Rental housing can be divided into formal and informal segments. The formal public rental sector has been diminishing since liberalisation of the housing sector started in the 1990s, which resulted in the selling off of public agencies' rental homes to the occupants (Arku *et al.* 2012). Most rental units are provided by informal landlords, making it difficult to obtain adequate data on the extent of and trends in the sector. The chief motivation for informal landlords to produce rental housing is to serve as a safety net (60 per cent), for income generation (23 per cent) and for consumption expenditure (10 per cent) (Yankson 2012a). Tipple *et al.* (1999) have suggested that the chief reason for owning a house in Ghana is for future security. This was found to be the case not only for the landlords themselves but also for the security of their children. The same authors found that rental income was not a great motivating factor in the decision to move from renting to owning. The results of the Accra study (Yankson 2012a) showed that rental income had become an important motivator in rental housing production (23 per cent of respondents), with rental income being an important supplement to the earnings of landlords. For the female landlords covered in the study, their rental housing was first and foremost a form of safety net and secondly, to support their consumption expenditure. Male landlords had similar motivations but predominantly considered renting as a form of business.

In Yankson's 2012a study, 67 per cent of the landlords had built by themselves the houses they let, acquiring the materials and hiring artisans to build the houses under their own supervision. Consequently, most rental units are produced informally and are built or altered without official planning permission (Arku et al. 2012). Fifteen per cent of landlords bought their houses outright from medium- and large-scale real estate companies or from other individuals, and a further 18 per cent had inherited the houses they were renting. About 50 per cent of the rental units had been built since the early 1990s, while another 30 per cent were built between 1981 and 1990. This indicates the relatively recent origin of most of the rental housing units in the areas covered in the survey (Yankson 2012a). Landlords encounter many challenges in building their rental units. As indicated above, land and finance are the major challenges confronting house producers generally and especially low-income house owners.

Rent levels

There has long been a general perception in Ghana that rents are high, especially compared with monthly earnings, but studies have refuted that landlords are a group of rich people exploiting poorer tenants. Many landlords charged lower rents than the controlled levels in the 1980s (Willis *et al.* 1990), and many landlords' households had lower per capita incomes than their tenant households and only slightly higher household incomes (Tipple *et al.* 1997). The Ghana Living Standards Survey Round 5 (GLSS 5) data shows that owner households have only slightly higher annual expenditure than renters in urban areas (GSS 2008). A housing sector profile survey also showed that between 2.5 per cent and 11.5 per cent of expenditure was being spent on rent (UN-Habitat 2011: 165). Rental values in Accra, however, are higher than other cities in Ghana and are reported to have surged in recent years (Arku *et al.* 2012).

An important feature of rental housing in Ghana that has developed since the early 1990s has been landlords demanding rent in advance, usually the value of at least one year and often up to several years of rent. This sum of money, which may add up to several months' income for prospective tenants, makes it extremely difficult for low-income households to enter the rental market (Tipple *et al.* 1999). In addition to the problem of rising rents, it can be extremely difficult to find rental accommodation, a problem that is accentuated by lack of information on vacant premises to let. Most people find accommodation through personal inquiries or through friends and relatives (Konadu-Agyemang 2001b), although at times informal 'estate agents' are used who charge both the owner and the tenant for their services. 'Estate agents' link prospective tenants to the landlords and assist both landlords and tenants to prepare and sign contract agreements, and usually serve as witnesses or as arbiters in lease contracts.

Landlord–tenant relationships

The landlord–tenant relationship is a highly important issue with regard to security and stability within the rental housing market, though earlier writers on this issue had differing views. For instance, Konadu-Agyemang (2001a) argued that in Accra landlords exploited the relationship at the expense of tenants, whereas Tipple and Willis (1990) postulated that rents in Kumasi were low relative to construction costs, hence renters had gained at the expense of landlords. The results of a study in Accra (Yankson 2012b) suggest a more complex picture and highlight the financial, legal and social dimensions of landlord–tenant relationships. The financial dimension includes: firstly, a change in the mode of rent payment from monthly to advance payments; secondly, rents not being negotiated but mainly fixed by landlords, with arbitrary and frequent rent increases; and thirdly, the bitter experiences and conditions meted out to tenants who were unable to pay the rent or rent advance promptly. With respect to the legal dimension, respondents mentioned the introduction of written contract agreements as a major positive step which, they claimed, had brought some regularity and security into the relationship. However, if the huge daily attendance at the proceedings of the Rent Control Department is used as a yardstick, this suggests that both parties, especially the landlords, do not adequately recognise the written documents. With respect to the social dimension, prospective tenants in the past rented accommodation only from people with whom they had prior relations, while landlords also let rooms along similar lines. In the early 2000s, this situation changed to one where people rented rooms in areas they could afford. Some landlords indicated that they select prospective tenants on the basis of ethnic or religious origin to avoid tenants they consider might be noisy, difficult or have large families (Yankson 2012b). Landlords have also been reported to restrict the types of home-based enterprises that they allow their tenants to operate, which are often an important source of income especially for low-income households (Gough 2010).

The landlord–tenant relationships for low-income households in Accra could be described neither as wholly exploitative nor as wholly cordial. They vary from one relationship to another and from one residential area to another, depending largely on the conduct of tenants and their households as well as the level of interaction with the landlord and the socio-economic circumstances of the latter. These relationships, however, have been found to be more cordial in situations where tenants partly or fully financed the construction or completion of the units they occupy or carry out maintenance (Yankson 2012b). However, as Arku *et al.* (2012: 9) claim, many tenants described the rental market as 'wearisome and stressful' and tenants expressed many concerns including 'long-term advance rents, breaches of rental agreements, threats of eviction, tense relations with property owners, rising rent costs and long searches for units' (Arku *et al.* 2012: 14).

Future policy directions for urban low-income housing

The goal of Ghana's housing policy (Government of Ghana 2009) is to provide adequate, decent and affordable housing that is accessible and sustainable with infrastructural facilities to satisfy the needs of Ghanaians. Broad policy initiatives for the various sectors or components of housing have been outlined in the Draft National Housing Policy (Government of Ghana 2009) but no specific policy objectives and initiatives for low-income housing have been outlined. UN-Habitat (2011) proposes shifting the current focus of providing housing and fully serviced plots for middle- and higher-income households to creating conditions that will refocus the housing supply towards low-cost accommodation. Correspondingly, policymakers need to widen their focus from single household villas for ownership to encourage multi-occupancy types for renting and provision of family houses.

In light of the high cost of inputs into house production, particularly land and building materials, most low-income households are not likely to own their own dwellings but will remain tenants (Arku *et al.* 2012). Individual landlords on their own cannot respond fully to the urgent need of low-income households for housing delivery unless there is a significant advancement of private sector investment infused into the sector. Tax holidays, rebates and other incentives should be provided to the private sector to encourage investment in affordable housing and supporting infrastructure. Collaboration with public sector institutions and agencies as well as with land owning groups, traditional authority and civil society organisations generally will also be required. Despite the challenges of trying to regulate an informal rental market, there is a need to enforce legislation against excessive rent advances and to 'revamp' the Rent Control Department (Arku *et al.* 2012).

Local government also needs to play a lead role in assembling lands, providing services and ensuring that land development is guided by structure plans for urban areas. Planning standards, including those regarding building densities and building heights, will have to be reviewed in the light of the current realities of urbanisation in Ghana. Incentives to encourage the private sector to invest in housing and related infrastructure need to be supported with the establishment of financing schemes to facilitate access to housing finance, and banks should be encouraged to support micro-lenders. These loans would be suitable for incremental building or housing improvements such as roofing, wall protection, sanitary latrines or an extra room (UN-Habitat 2011). In relation to building materials, the Draft National Housing Policy (Government of Ghana 2009) proposes the sustainable exploitation of local raw materials for the building industry, promotion of local building materials, and strengthening the capacity of the local building and construction materials industry.

To conclude, there is no doubt about the enormity of the urban housing problem in Ghana, particularly for low-income groups. As highlighted above, this calls for innovative ideas and adequate investment in order to address all the key issues militating against achieving the adequate delivery of housing units. Housing provision both for owner-occupancy and renting needs to be focused upon, as well as reviewing legislation governing construction and tenancy agreements. This is essential if there is to be any hope of meeting the current shortfall in housing provision and the ever increasing urban housing demand, especially from low-income groups.

Notes

1. Settlements with a population of 5,000 or more are officially defined as urban centres in Ghana.
2. It is important to recognise that there is a lack of reliable statistics on housing in Ghana and that most studies on urban housing focus on the two major cities of Accra and Kumasi. The final version of the draft national housing policy is yet to be produced.
3. We are using the term 'low income' generically here rather than following the standard definition of low income as household daily income of US$1 a day or less.
4. This may be less so in the case of medium-sized and smaller towns where pressure on building plots may not be that high.
5. These low-income communities differ in size of population and in character. Some are essentially indigenous communities while others are migrant dominated. Tamale metropolis is the largest urban centre in the three northern regions of Ghana. It is an indigenous settlement with a population of 375,000 in 2010. Ashiaman (population 191,000 in 2010) is a large migrant-dominated dormitory town of Tema metropolis, while Nima is a well-known migrant-dominated community (population 81,274 in 2010) close to the central business district of Accra metropolitan area. James Town (population 16,221 in 2010) is an indigenous-dominated community at the heart of the city of Accra. Saltpond is an indigenous town (population 20,114 in 2010) in the Central Region of Ghana.

References

Addo, N.O. (1972) 'Population, migration and employment in Ghana', in S.H. Ominde and C.N. Ejiogu (eds) *Population Growth and Economic Development in Africa*. London: Heinemann.

Agyapong, T. (1995) 'Increasing Access to Land and Shelter', National Preparatory Process for Habitat II, Draft Report.

Antwi, A.Y. and Adams, J. (2003) 'Rent-seeking behaviour and its economic costs in urban land transactions in Accra, Ghana', *Urban Studies*, 40(10): 2083–2098.

Arku, A. (2006) 'Housing and development strategies in Ghana, 1945–2000', *International Development Planning Review*, 28(3): 333–358.

Arku, G., Luginaah, I. and Mkandawire, P. (2012) '"You either pay more advance rent or you move out": landlords/ladies' and tenants' dilemmas in the low-income housing market in Accra, Ghana', *Urban Studies*, 49(14): 3177–3193.

Briggs, J. and Yeboah, I. (2001) 'Structural adjustment and the contemporary sub-Saharan African city', *Area*, 33: 18–26.

Gough, K.V. (2010) 'Continuity and adaptability of home-based enterprises: a longitudinal study from Accra, Ghana', *International Development Planning Review*, 32(1): 45–70.

Gough, K.V. and Yankson, P.W.K. (2000) 'Land markets in African cities: the case of peri-urban Accra, Ghana', *Urban Studies*, 37(13): 2485–2500.

Gough, K.V. and Yankson, P.W.K. (2011) 'A neglected aspect of the housing market: the caretakers of peri-urban Accra, Ghana', *Urban Studies*, 48(4): 793–810.

Government of Ghana (2009) *Draft National Housing Policy*. Accra: Ministry of Water Resources, Works and Housing.

Government of Ghana (2010) *Draft National Urban Policy*. Accra: Ministry of Local Government and Rural Development.

Grant, R. and Yankson, P. (2003) 'City Profile, Accra', *Cities*, 20(1): 65–74.

GSS (2008) *Ghana Living Standards Survey Report on the Fifth Round (GLSS5)*. Accra: GSS, Government of Ghana.

GSS (2012) *2010 Population and Housing Census: Summary Report of Final Results*. Accra: GSS, Government of Ghana.

Konadu-Agyemang, K. (2001a) *The Political Economy of Housing and Urban Development in Africa: Ghana's Experience from Colonial Times to 1998*. Westport, CT: Praeger.

Konadu-Agyemang, K. (2001b) 'Structural adjustment programmes and housing affordability in Accra, Ghana', *The Canadian Geographer*, 45(4): 528–544.

Larbi, W. (1996) 'Spatial planning and urban fragmentation in Accra', *Third World Planning Review*, 18: 193–214.

Ministry of Works and Housing (2001) *National Shelter Strategy*. Accra.

Owusu, G. (2008) 'Indigenes' and migrants' access to land in peri-urban areas of Ghana's largest city of Accra', *International Development Planning Review*, 30(2): 1–22.

Owusu, G. and Afutu-Kotey, R.L. (2010) 'Poor urban communities and municipal interface in Ghana: a case study of Accra and Sekondi-Takoradi Metropolis', *African Studies Quarterly*, 12(1): 1–16.

Songsore, J. (2003) 'The urban housing crisis in Ghana: capital, the state versus the people', *Ghana Social Science Journal* (New Series), 2: 1–31.

Songsore, J., McGranahan, G. and Kjellen, M. (2004) 'Tenure, housing and environmental management among families in the Greater Accra Metropolitan Area (GAMA) of Ghana', *Research Review* Supplement, 15: 69–83.

Tipple, A.G. and Korboe, D. (1998) 'Housing policy in Ghana: towards a supply-oriented future', *Habitat International*, 22(3): 245–257.

Tipple, A.G. and Willis, K.G. (1989) 'The effects on household and housing of strict public intervention in a private rental market: a case study of Kumasi, Ghana', *Geoforum*, 20(1): 15–26.

Tipple, A.G. and Willis, K.G. (1990) 'Cost-benefit of rent control: a case study in Kumasi, Ghana' *World Bank Discussion Paper* 74, Washington, DC: World Bank.

Tipple, A. G., Korboe, D. and Garrod, G. (1997) 'Income and wealth in house ownership studies in urban Ghana', *Housing Studies*, 12(1): 111–126.

Tipple, G., Korboe, D., Garrod, G. and Willis, K. (1999) 'Housing supply in Ghana: a study of Accra, Kumasi and Berekum', *Progress in Planning*, 51(4): 253–323.

UN-Habitat (2011) *Ghana-Housing Profile*. Nairobi: UN-Habitat.

Willis, K.G., Malpezzi, S. and Tipple, A.G. (1990) 'An econometric and cultural analysis of rent control in Kumasi, Ghana', *Urban Studies*, 27(2): 241–258.

Yankson, P.W.K. (2012a) 'Landlordism and housing production in Greater Accra Metropolitan Area', in E. Ardayfio-Schandorf, P.W.K. Yankson and M. Bertrand (eds) *The Mobile City of Accra (Accra, Capitale en Mouvement)*. Dakar: CODESRIA.

Yankson, P.W.K. (2012b) 'Rental housing and tenancy dynamics with particular focus on low-income households in Greater Accra Metropolitan Area', in E. Ardayfio-Schandorf, P.W.K. Yankson and M. Bertrand (eds) *The Mobile City of Accra (Accra, Capitale en Mouvement)*. Dakar: CODESRIA.

Yankson, P.W.K. and Kala, M. (2008) *Access to Land, Tenure Security and Growth Within the Informal Economy in the Urban and Peri-Urban Areas of Ghana*, Technical Publication No. 82. Institute of Statistical, Social and Economic Research (ISSER), University of Ghana, Legon (USAID-Ghana and ISSER Publication).

Yeboah, I. (2001) 'Structural adjustment and emerging urban form in Accra, Ghana', *Africa Today*, 7: 61–89.

Conclusion

26
PRO-POOR HOUSING POLICIES REVISITED
Where do we go from here?

Paul van Lindert, Peer Smets and Jan Bredenoord

This book contains a collection of thematic state of the art reviews on affordable housing and well-informed accounts of housing policies and practices in Asia, Latin America and Africa. Even though the 17 country case chapters scrutinize housing policies and practices in their specific national and local contexts, overall, three broad thematic fields stand out throughout this book. The first field relates, by definition, to the affordability of housing options for the urban poor. A second common topic is the issue of the sustainability of low-income urban housing. The governance aspects of housing provision, including the role of the various stakeholders involved in the production of low-income housing, represent the third general theme that connects the chapters.

This final chapter discusses the main common findings from the chapters in this book. In doing so, it also aims to draw lessons which may be of use for policymakers and housing professionals whose ambition is to arrive at affordable and sustainable solutions for the urban housing question in the Global South.

The first section below provides background information on the different trajectories of urbanization in the Latin American, Asian and African macro-regions. Next follows a discussion based upon the key messages that emerge from the chapters in this book. The final section of this chapter concludes by presenting suggestions for the housing research and policy agendas.

Different regions, different backgrounds

This book focuses on low-income urban housing policies and practices in Asia, Africa and Latin America. After the thematic perspectives presented in Part I, the following three parts focus on the housing experiences in each of the three macro-regions. The rationale for such organization of the book is that various relevant and distinct characteristics make such geographical clustering of chapters meaningful. Most importantly, the majority of the countries in each of the macro-regions are in relatively similar stages of their urban transition. Together with remarkable differences in their economic development trajectories, the distinct urbanization processes occurring in the countries also have a varied imprint on related issues of urban housing, sustainability and local governance. Starting with a concise account of relevant urban practices in the most urbanized region (Latin America), this section then draws a comparison with current experiences in Asia and Africa.

Latin America is by far the most urbanized region of the Global South. Current urbanization levels in Africa and Asia still compare relatively poorly with those of Latin America, although currently the respective *rates* of urbanization in Africa and Asia are much higher than in Latin America. An important consequence of the long-standing urbanization track record of Latin America is the early expansion of informally built settlements in all major cities across the region. Another distinguishing reality is the tradition of urban social movements in Latin American cities. Urban grassroots organizations boast a long-standing history of demand-making, advocacy and lobbying, by actively pressuring state institutions for security of housing tenure and improved public services in informal settlements, and thus of claiming their 'right to the city'. In the 1950s and 1960s, the state's classic answer to the massive and illegal land invasions across the region was still eviction, often combined with relocation to places outside the city. However, since the 1970s the various city administrations in Latin American countries have gradually come to realize that self-build construction in informal settlements is a solution to the massive housing demand of the urban poor – something the state cannot possibly offer. This is not to say that the eviction of settlers from illegal settlements has been totally abandoned – for example, as witnessed by the *favela* demolitions in Rio de Janeiro in anticipation of the mega-events of the 2014 FIFA World Cup and the Olympic Games in 2016. But such evictions are now the exception rather than the rule in Latin America.

A pioneering role played by the city governments throughout the region relates to their often sophisticated urban planning mechanisms. This holds true in particular to the megacities and the metropolitan areas of the region. However, in secondary and rural towns there is still a blatant lack of management capacity. Nonetheless, in many cities – including the smaller ones – some form of participatory budgeting has already become an institutionalized phenomenon. Starting from Brazil and Bolivia with some interesting experiences in participatory planning and budgeting in the 1990s, today in most of the Latin American countries such participatory mechanisms have been put in place, either in a formal or an informal way. Thus, many urban neighbourhood residents – including those living in informal settlements – have the opportunity to voice their demands for decent housing and serviced neighbourhoods. The traditionally high levels of organization and mobilization of citizens across the Latin American region, often also resulting in a considerable capacity of neighbourhood-based associations to exert pressure on their local authorities, may offer an important explanation for relatively speedy and effective processes of self-help dwelling consolidation and neighbourhood improvement.

In Asia and Africa, the process of massive urbanization mostly started once the decolonization process was completed. Various Asian countries – especially the so-called newly industrializing countries – maintained consistently high levels of economic growth paired with high urbanization rates. China is the most prominent example in this respect, with a housing delivery system that is not available – nor immediately replicable – in other countries of the region. However, in many other Asian countries, industrial and urban development lagged behind. In Africa, and more particularly in the countries of sub-Saharan Africa, urbanization levels are still relatively low but urbanization rates projected for the next decades are among the world's highest. However, today's urban growth in sub-Saharan Africa occurs in an environment which, by and large, is characterized by an absence of substantial industrial development in these rapidly expanding cities.

Although the Latin American urbanization experience includes pioneering approaches with respect to urban planning and urban governance, including participatory practices and the overall attitude of considering the existence of informal settlements as *faits accomplis*, these and other positive experiences are not necessarily being replicated in Asia or Africa. Most alarmingly, slum eradication by the state is quite common across both continents. Instead of evictions being an undesired remnant from the past, it seems that for some local governments (e.g. in South Africa and India) slum removal has become a renewed target which neatly fits within their concept of 'slum-free cities'.

Against this background of regional varieties of urbanization and economic development, we will now discuss some of the key messages that emerge from the chapters in this book.

Discussion

First of all, it has become clear from most chapters that informal settlements have mushroomed in most countries and that this phenomenon will undoubtedly continue to exist for some time to come. Actually, self-managed housing by incremental construction seems to be the most universal process that is practised worldwide by urban low-income citizens. Affordability is the keyword to explain this phenomenon. In most cases, self-build housing is the only way to secure a home that is affordable for the lower income groups, the so-called 'incremental affordability' (see Chapter 1). Even when the residual income approach is used,[1] which is far better than the housing expenditure-to-income ratio, in general, public housing programmes are mainly delivering dwellings that are too expensive for the urban poor.

A key factor for self-help housing is access to land and security of tenure, no matter whether that means *de jure* or *de facto* security. Considerable experience has already been gained in practice with housing programmes and projects that aim to foster the self-build activities of the urban poor. Preconditions for assisted self-help housing projects include the availability of sufficient financial resources and a competent municipal apparatus in charge of urban planning, land use and land allocation. However, for the success of assisted self-help projects, the involvement of the civil sector is no less important than the role of (local) governments. Many successful cases of assisted self-help schemes are based on the principle of community participation. We will get back to such cases below once we arrive at the governance aspects of housing provision.

In comparison to our first statement, our second observation perhaps appears to be somewhat paradoxical: notwithstanding the huge housing deficits for the urban poor, some countries which throughout the years have boasted massive public housing provision programmes (e.g. Mexico and Egypt) also present considerable housing vacancies. Is it possible that there is an overproduction of housing in these countries? It is tempting indeed to speculate about the reasons for high vacancy rates in countries with housing deficits. As mentioned above, conventional public housing often is unaffordable for the poorest citizens. Housing vacancies thus mainly refer to turn-key homes, constructed by private construction firms but in the framework of state-regulated housing programmes. More often than not, such housing projects are realized at considerable distances from the built-up cities, which makes it difficult and expensive for prospective residents to get to their jobs, to do their shopping or to pay social visits to their family and friends in town. Sometimes a severe lack of infrastructure and connection with the urban areas are additional factors that make such housing an unsatisfactory solution, even for middle-income groups. On top of being unaffordable to the majority of the urban population, such housing programmes are also particularly unsustainable, since they may become drivers of urban sprawl and add to the carbon footprint by occupying rural land that is more suitable for agricultural production.

Our third observation regards housing finance for lower income groups. In the Latin American case studies, during the past decade an interesting new model of housing finance was highlighted. The so-called *Ahorro-Bono-Crédito* (ABC) model originated in Chile and then was adjusted to local realities and adopted in the housing policies of many other Latin American countries. The constituent parts of the ABC model are the households' savings (ahorro) which are necessary to make a down payment; a subsidy (bono) provided by the housing agency; and a credit (crédito) from a bank or other private financial institution that can be used to finance outstanding debts for housing. The interesting fact is that, in theory, such a model of 'mixed' finance packages can be applied flexibly both to acquire ready-made homes provided by private or public parties and to finance *in situ* expansion or improvement of owner-occupied houses in existing neighbourhoods. However, the Latin American case studies also show that while middle-income groups do indeed tend to benefit from the combined subsidy–credit schemes, many ABC schemes are still beyond the reach of the lowest income groups.

A fourth message follows from our preceding observations. Many housing policy packages – including the ABC schemes – have a dual intention of creating a country of home-owners while at the same time stimulating national economic production. The focus then is on fostering private sector activities, particularly in the construction and financial sectors. Through house construction programmes, the state can indeed give a boost to the economy. But the impact this has on lower-income households is questionable. A somewhat gloomy conclusion then is that cities will continue to grow through the expansion of new informal settlements, based on the self-help and self-finance performance of the poor. On the other hand, many urban residents live in rental housing. So far, such rental housing opportunities are mainly provided by private actors, such as real estate agents and petty landlords. The possibilities for the involvement of institutional rental housing actors, in order to produce rental dwellings for special social target groups in cities, are evident. Thus, when rethinking state housing policies, the inclusion of rental housing as an affordable solution to accommodate the poor should be seriously considered.

Fifth, the Asian country chapters especially presented some quite promising examples of innovative approaches to tackle the urban housing question. That Asian evidence is encouraging indeed, as it shows a variety of ways for new forms of governance which are based on direct stakeholder involvement. The motto for these new approaches is 'community-driven development', which implies (though not exclusively) community organization and improvement of dwellings and services in existing informal neighbourhoods. This community participation in Asia did not originate from grassroots initiatives exactly, which rather contrasts with the Latin American experience. Actually, many community contracting partnership arrangements were strongly guided by national governments and other (international) agencies. In the past decade, the Asian Development Bank has become one of the most prominent champions of community contracting. There is a remarkable parallel in this respect with other current stakeholder approaches. The housing cooperatives that have gained importance in Asia since the 1990s also originated as mainly state-driven entities; in comparison, African cooperatives were mainly stimulated by non-governmental organizations (NGOs) while those in Latin America originated from urban social movements. Other promising and effective examples of stakeholder approaches include the experiences of collective negotiation by local communities with the state and with private sector parties (e.g. contractors). The organization, mobilization and empowerment of these communities are often supported by NGOs – most prominently Slum/Shack Dwellers International – which also adds to their capacity to negotiate with local authorities. Together with other stakeholder approach experiences – such as those based on public–private partnerships – new forms of governance have definitely contributed to the implementation of pro-poor housing policies.

The sixth key message from the preceding chapters is that blueprint solutions or blanket approaches to solve the urban housing crisis are unsustainable. If something has become clear throughout the book, it is that uniform solutions do not exist for such a complicated challenge as providing adequate shelter to everyone. National and municipal housing policies should allow for maximum degrees of flexibility and diversity. Projects should be tailored to the needs and possibilities of diverse categories of urban poor. They should differentiate according to, among others, earning capacity and solvency, and tenure status. In addition, such projects should take into account relevant socio-cultural characteristics such as gender. Tenure security, affordability and location are key ingredients of pro-poor housing policies. Broadening the scope of self-build support programmes which target a diversity of low-income residents can make all the difference to the urban poor. However, such a diversified approach presupposes, among other things, that adequate tools for urban planning and land management are in place. In this respect, the role of local governments is of vital importance for the design and implementation of a range of self-build housing 'packages'. The recent processes of public reform and administrative decentralization in most countries of the Global South have resulted in many new responsibilities and challenges for local governments. Especially at the level of the small towns and intermediate cities – where most of the current and projected urban growth takes place – governments' most immediate challenges are related to their lacking competences. Local government capacity development – including the development of skills to implement targeted housing projects – should therefore be prioritized by national governments.

Our final point concerns the issue of the sustainability of future urbanization and housing strategies. Worldwide, the phenomenon of urban sprawl is rapidly reaching its limits and it should be reversed for the sake of sustainable urban futures in which the themes of ecology, energy, technology, economy, social issues and relevant policies are taken into account. Most typically, the occupation of new land on the peripheries of cities by the poor is the standard procedure to start up incremental, self-build housing. Without proper assistance, it will remain very unlikely that the self-builder will be able to use techniques and building materials which permit sustainable housing. In addition, the incremental housing experience demonstrates that it takes a long time to reach higher construction densities, with considerable vertical expansion of the buildings. Thus the intensification of urban land use will hardly be possible without the development of high-rise housing solutions. Even though such solutions would be affordable to the middle and higher income groups, most land developers and construction companies which cater for these groups also develop such private housing projects in essentially peri-urban areas; their product is mainly (semi-)detached housing and row-housing. Many state-promoted housing projects have similar characteristics, although we have also seen cases where stacked homes and high-rise housing projects are becoming more common. From the viewpoint of the low-income housing market, we see that diverse solutions have been presented in many of the chapters. This diversity might lead to a better equilibrium between efficiency and resilience of the housing market and, as a consequence, its sustainability.

Research directions

What do the various key messages from the book imply for the research agenda? In this final section, we present the following recommendations for further research.

First of all, it should be recognized that the frequently used concepts of affordability and sustainability should be linked in such a way as to lead to synergy. Therefore attention should be paid to how synergetic relations between different sustainability areas are created and maintained. In this way, urban housing production and provision could be improved tremendously. There is an urgent need to unpack both concepts and even to distinguish between different kinds of affordability and sustainability. While we have started this exercise in the first chapter of the book, it is beyond doubt that a much more profound elaboration is needed.

A second field for future research relates to the governance of housing supply for the urban poor. This is a sizable research theme indeed. On one hand, such research should focus on the role of national and local governments. As a result of recent decentralization laws, local governments in many countries have become the principal actors with respect to housing provision. Good local governance and effective urban management are vital ingredients for sustainable urban planning, including the provision of (land for) housing and public services. City administrations need effective information and monitoring systems, population and land registry systems, and tax collection systems, to name but a few. These are distinct themes for future empirical studies. What can be learned from good practices? And what are the possibilities for replication?

On the other hand, more in-depth empirical research is desirable with respect to innovative practices of stakeholder arrangements. It is important to analyse and document the successes and weaknesses of both civil sector and private sector initiatives in the fields of housing provision and settlement upgrading in order to assess whether and how such initiatives can be replicated and upscaled nationally and internationally. How effective are such stakeholder arrangements for solving the housing deficit? How successful are they in terms of settlement upgrading? Do they effectively contribute to the empowerment of the urban poor? How do these initiatives cope with the danger of (political) patronage and encapsulation? These are some of the questions that are of particular relevance for empirical research on neighbourhood based initiatives. Similar research is due for innovative models of low-income housing (micro) finance. For example, how can finance models for housing be tailored better to the needs of the very poor? Can such models be replicated elsewhere? What adaptations are necessary for such replication? In sum, and in more general terms, our suggestion is to investigate successful approaches to low-income housing provision and settlement upgrading in order to assess whether and how such experiences can be introduced or adjusted in other contexts to also serve the poorest segments of society.

Another issue concerns incremental building, which should be redefined. Turnerian incremental building (e.g. Turner 1976) requires relatively large plots which enable mainly horizontal extensions, but this entails a diverse number of consequences concerning *inter alia* energy, food prices and urban land scarcity. While rising energy and food prices, and urban land scarcity conflict with the Turnerian incremental building approach, new solutions can be developed by studying the daily practices in an informal vertical community such as in Torre David (Tower David) in Caracas, Venezuela (Brillembourg and Klumpner 2013). Or perhaps we should consider empty offices, storehouses and industrial enclaves that could house communities where an incremental approach could occur inside of a larger complex. This may offer possibilities for a roofed settlement instead of separate roofed shelter.

A final recommendation for research is meant to provide a better understanding of the functioning of urban housing markets. One aspect that merits further attention is the issue of housing vacancy. While there is only circumstantial evidence for why massive housing vacancies exist, it is very relevant that more specific research is done, if only because it is needed to devise well-informed housing policies. Another distinct theme for housing market research relates to the issue of rental housing. So far, the majority of rental housing is provided by (petty) landlords who often live in their own, self-built houses. Most studies on informal housing focus on those owner-occupiers, whereas the tenants often remain beyond the scope of housing research. Related to this research suggestion, there is an additional important theme for policy-related research. In this sense, it is pertinent to assess the possibilities and potential of institutional rental housing provision. If affordable rental housing is made available to the urban poor through public housing programmes, it may be assumed that many will opt for that possibility – if only because they have no access to land. Yet, rental housing provision, as a policy tool to accommodate the urban poor that is complementary to other housing instruments, is only rarely part of public housing policy. In line with our earlier claims to devise diversified and targeted housing policies, such research is particularly relevant.

Notes

1 The residual income approach looks at the amount of finance that can be allocated for housing once non-housing needs are paid for. Policies based on this approach help the poor to meet their basic non-housing needs first.

References

Brillembourg, A. and Klumpner, H. (2013) *Torre David: Informal Vertical Communities*. Zurich: Lars Müller.
Turner, J. (1976) *Housing by People: Towards Autonomy in Building Environment*. London: Marion.

INDEX

ABC model 5, 219, 260–1, 265, 267, 275–6, 288, 400
accessibility xxii–xxiv, 355
Accra 382–92
adequate housing xxi–xxiv, 44, 196, 274, 305, 365, 379, 383
adequate shelter xxiii, 1, 56, 200, 401
administration 19, 23–4, 58, 63, 119, 126, 171, 247, 249, 261–5, 272, 278–80, 282, 283, 288, 306, 329, 334, 351, 398, 402; *see also* land administration
advocacy 26, 112, 398
affordability 1, 9, 10, 46, 75, 117, 140, 207
affordable housing 22, 40–52, 58, 121, 125, 137, 139, 141, 145, 149, 205, 207–8, 210–14
Africa xxii, 2, 12, 16, 17, 20, 33, 43, 46, 55, 63, 88, 89, 91, 93, 103, 107, 110, 111, 112, 133, 184, 198, 317–20, 397, 398, 399
agglomeration xxii, 322, 325
Ahmedabad 141, 182, 183
Alexandria 325–6
apartments 68, 82, 84, 90, 93, 135, 145, 149, 155–6, 160–3, 172, 193–4, 199, 200–1, 213, 230, 232, 234, 236–8, 257, 267, 283, 288, 294–5, 314, 334, 367–8, 371
Apex cooperative 105, 107, 108, 112
Argentina 43, 106, 110
Asia xxii, 2, 12, 16, 17, 20, 22, 41, 55, 63, 66, 89, 91, 93, 103, 105, 106, 110–13, 133–6, 170, 184, 198, 317, 397–9, 400
Asian Coalition for Housing Rights (ACHR) 198–9
Asian Development Bank (ADB) 135, 182–9, 400
assistance xxii, 16, 59, 63–7, 69, 70, 77–9, 82, 104, 106, 108, 113, 129, 134, 139, 178, 182, 185, 187, 199, 225, 235, 244, 278, 283, 291, 309–10, 318, 337–8, 387, 401; financial 194, 195, 200, 324, 387; technical 47, 49, 56, 64, 66–7, 70, 112, 156, 188–9, 195, 200, 234–5, 243, 246–7, 273, 291, 302, 304, 309, 314–15

Baan Mankong 106, 110, 133
backyard 90–1, 93, 124, 340–1
bamboo 16, 51, 74, 82–3, 85, 292
Bangkok 89, 90, 110
Bangladesh 28, 36, 47, 49, 154, 183, 188
banks 5, 15, 28, 45, 57, 76, 84, 121, 123, 147, 161–3, 170–1, 188, 220–1, 225, 227–9, 231–2, 259, 261, 263–4, 276, 287–8, 307–11, 315, 375–6, 387, 392, 400; commercial 45, 50, 53, 142, 150, 195, 228, 275, 307; development 34, 73–4, 97, 181, 199, 328; housing 3, 5, 155, 161, 194, 241–5, 260, 287
Banmat 274–6, 280–3
barriadas 58, 272–4, 283
base of the income pyramid (BOP) 41–2, 44, 46–50
basic service(s) 3, 16, 51, 56, 59, 82, 117–19, 127, 129, 194, 272–3, 323–4, 328, 338, 340, 344, 359, 369, 374
Beijing 207, 212
Bogotá 25, 36, 80, 88, 92, 99, 257–8, 261, 266–8
Bolivia 27, 36, 43, 49, 58, 60–1, 89, 106, 271, 289, 398
Brazil 23, 27, 32, 42–3, 45–6, 52, 53, 67–8, 89, 106, 110, 219–54, 265, 275, 289, 398
Brundtland report 6, 358
bureaucratic machinery 337
Buen Vivir 221, 289, 297

Buenos Aires 93
building code(s) xxi, 74, 77, 83–4, 139, 145, 229, 231, 322, 352, 372
building companies 15, 70, 230, 249, 252, 318
building control 68–9, 160
building industry 42, 81, 84, 87, 149, 155, 358, 392
building materials 3, 7, 10, 11, 15–16, 45, 48–9, 64, 67–9, 73–4, 76, 80–5, 108, 111, 125–6, 141, 149, 169, 195–6, 224, 233–5, 237, 258, 274, 281, 284, 307–8, 328, 353, 360, 368, 372, 374, 379, 388, 391–2, 401
building materials bank 67, 304, 312
building permit 64, 83, 385
building skills 2–3, 76
building technology(ies) 16, 51, 67, 76, 82, 84, 187, 371, 374
bureaucracy 219, 249, 342–3, 345, 382
bustee 58, 90

Cairo 95, 325–6, 334
Calcutta *see* Kolkata
Cambodia 21, 25, 30, 35
Cameroon 35
capacity 17, 47, 55, 57, 63, 75, 77, 81, 84, 108, 112, 119–21, 134, 155, 166, 168–9, 171–4, 176–8, 189, 245, 307, 311, 315, 343, 349–50, 358, 360, 371, 377, 392, 398, 401
capacity building 4, 80–1, 107, 123, 133, 188, 197, 200, 309, 343, 376, 379
capacity development 309, 401
Cape Town 118, 341, 343
Capital: financial 177; human 173–4, 176–7, 339; physical 173–4, 176–7; natural 173, 175–7; social 109, 117, 173, 176–7, 200, 353
capital subsidy(ies) 89, 129, 257, 318, 336–8, 343, 345–6
Caracas 403
carbon: emissions 7, 47, 81; footprint 7, 74, 83–4, 400
Caribbean 46, 90, 219
central city 91–2, 352
Chad 36
Chile 5, 43, 51, 77, 88, 90, 97, 106, 110, 219, 234, 260, 268, 275, 283, 287, 289, 310, 336, 400
China 23, 29–31, 35, 42–3, 52, 59, 68, 89, 97–9, 106, 134–5, 204–16
Chongqing 135, 207, 209, 212–13, 215
Cities without Slums 58, 73, 76, 343
city administration(s) 58, 63, 398, 402
City Summit 4, 56, 349
civil society xxiii, 3–4, 6, 26, 30–1, 34, 57, 120, 196, 198–9, 346, 372, 378–9, 392
climate change 6, 16, 36, 47, 73–84, 86, 379
climate friendly building materials 74, 76, 83–4

Colombia 5, 25, 43, 80, 83, 92, 97, 219–20, 256–68, 275, 289, 336
Colombo 135, 193–4, 196–9
collaboration 5, 7, 26, 47–9, 52, 63, 107, 134, 167, 173, 176, 178, 246, 292, 297, 392
collective organisation(s) 103, 108, 112, 128
community action 17, 80, 103, 109, 196–7, 199
community-based organisation (CBO) 4, 57, 62–3, 66, 69, 103, 139, 221, 308, 311, 315, 352, 378
community: building 30, 301; development 7, 105, 134, 199
community: cohesion 79, 184; engagement 81, 169, 195; involvement 79, 198, 200; mobilisation 198–9
community contracting 6–7, 135, 181–9, 198, 400
Community Development Councils 135, 194, 196
community-driven development 121, 135, 183, 185, 188, 400; *see also* community-led development
community facilities 84, 148
community groups 59, 62, 118, 122, 185, 187–8, 195, 372; *see also* community-based organisation
community land trust 22, 103, 109, 366
community-led development 6, 117–30; *see also* community-driven development
community savings 106, 117
compound 319, 382, 389
condominium(s) 51, 68, 104, 194, 231, 237, 314
consolidation: of dwelling/housing 58, 68, 75, 82, 177, 247, 398; of settlements 59, 353
construction 2, 5, 6, 11, 15, 16, 44–7, 49–51, 56, 64–5, 68–70, 74, 76–7, 80–4, 88, 103–4, 108–9, 111–12, 121–2, 125–6, 128, 135, 144, 151, 156–7, 160, 162, 170, 172, 183, 185, 187–9, 194–6, 211, 215, 220–1, 224, 226, 229, 231, 234, 241–52, 254, 259–60, 262, 264–5, 272–3, 276–80, 283, 288, 291, 301, 303–7, 309–12, 314, 321–4, 326–7, 329, 333–4, 339–40, 346, 350–1, 353–5, 357–8, 360, 369–70, 375, 379, 387, 391, 400–1; formal 5, 56–7, 324, 360; incremental 17, 55, 62–5, 119, 128, 160, 332–3, 399; informal 57, 324, 360; self-help 3, 56, 62, 74, 83–4, 92, 124, 126, 187, 220, 225, 241–4, 253, 272, 301, 303–4, 309, 315, 359, 398
construction companies 5, 57, 120, 123, 221, 229, 235, 245, 275, 278, 280, 283, 399, 401
construction costs 9, 10, 65, 123, 171, 194, 237, 274, 293, 302, 311–13, 324, 329, 333, 357, 372, 388, 390
construction industry 81, 83, 188, 198, 250, 258, 275
construction materials 2, 3, 16, 56, 66, 83, 189, 195, 235, 243–4, 247, 293, 295, 304, 307, 392
construction standards 85, 253

contractor 78, 82, 121, 184, 186, 189, 324, 342, 360
cooperative 22, 89, 102–13, 139, 193, 228, 235, 245–7, 351, 371, 373; housing xxii, 5–6, 17, 57, 59, 62, 64, 67, 69–70, 89, 104–13, 118, 122, 125, 128–9, 139, 174, 220–1, 234–5, 244–6, 248–9, 274, 291, 305, 307–9, 315, 319, 328, 351–2, 354, 356–7, 369, 373, 377–9, 400; laws 107–11; principles 104, 109–10
core: house/housing 16, 56, 64, 82, 121, 172, 182, 313, 325–6, 329, 355; unit 59, 75, 353
corruption 28, 32, 52, 105, 163, 281, 337, 339–40, 344, 351, 358
cortiços 241–3, 247
Costa Rica 106, 219, 275, 336
craftsmen 5, 56, 83, 303
credit xxiii, 9–11, 34, 43–5, 47–9, 51, 74, 76, 81, 84, 98, 104, 108–9, 113, 161–2, 167, 170–4, 186, 189, 195, 199, 228–9, 231–2, 234, 245, 248–9, 259–60, 262–4, 266–7, 275–6, 280, 282–3, 293, 306, 314, 324–5, 334, 336, 340, 353, 387, 400
credit: associations 45, 57; cooperatives 103, 105, 248, 373
credit facilities 3, 149, 327
crime 33, 41, 47, 51–2, 186, 344
cross-subsidising 123, 148, 374, 378
Cuba 66, 106
customary: land 319, 384; practices 25; rights/rule 61, 384; tenure 384

decentralisation 4, 163, 167, 170–1, 178, 212, 244, 289, 401–2
decision making xxiii, 4–6, 23, 104, 110, 196, 200, 245, 343, 358
Delhi 25, 31, 105, 119, 139–41
demolition 56, 58, 97, 127, 157, 318, 358, 398
densification 7, 68, 75, 126, 134, 156, 159–60, 168, 232, 302, 314, 371, 377
density 22, 26, 29, 51, 68, 73, 80–2, 121–2, 124, 126, 134, 145, 149–50, 156, 168–9, 210, 213, 233, 242, 314, 343
desert 157, 318, 321, 328, 331–2, 334
diversification 329, 345, 346
down payment 10–11, 48, 173, 259, 275, 324, 328–9, 331, 400
drainage 66, 122, 169, 182, 185–6, 199, 356, 389
Dubai 27, 29
duplex 231, 234, 238, 356
durable: housing 20, 51, 69, 79, 237, 305, 382; materials 73, 78, 83–4, 224, 288, 388
Durban 340, 343

earthquake: resilience 68, 83, 155; resistance 65, 187–8; vulnerability 6, 47, 73, 76–7, 84, 182, 186, 257, 262
East Asia 33, 43, 46–7, 97, 211

economic activities 4, 7, 174, 352
economic crisis 124, 126, 170, 244, 250, 262, 275, 287
Ecuador 5, 73–6, 80, 83, 85, 88, 106, 219, 221, 286–97
education 27, 104, 111, 187, 196, 220, 286, 317, 353; basic 170, 344; services/facilities 95, 134; technical 68, 70, 158
Egypt 22, 43, 89, 95, 107, 317–18, 321–34, 399
electricity 25, 36, 51, 64–6, 95, 122, 125, 159, 273, 279, 302, 328, 332, 356, 374
elites 15, 19, 24, 27–33, 36, 91, 160, 322, 334, 357
El Salvador 47, 67, 106, 219
empowerment 4, 5, 25, 76, 103, 109, 133, 170, 177–8, 184, 194, 249, 372, 401–2
enabling: approach 3, 16, 36, 102, 133, 138; environment 353, 378; housing markets 40–2, 44, 52, 358; policy(ies) xxiii, 107, 112; regulatory framework 365, 376–7
entitlement 186, 197–8, 342
entrepreneurship: housing 41, 49, 52; social 50, 189
enumeration 17, 63, 120, 123, 128, 197
environmental: disasters 193, 200; hazards 169; impact 374–5, 379; integrity 6; management 4, 80; protection 82, 177, 358; sustainability 7, 109, 284, 371, 378; vulnerability 36, 47, 266
ethnic: conflict/tension 163–4; groups 96, 160, 163–4; minorities 97
ethnicity 96, 162
Ethiopia 68, 108
eviction xxi, 23, 30, 56, 58, 94–5, 120, 123–4, 127–30, 157, 375, 378, 391, 398, 399; *see also* relocation and resettlement

facilitation 3, 65, 184, 187, 307, 351, 371–2, 378
favela 23, 58, 242–3, 246–7, 253–4, 398
financial crisis 7, 9, 41, 140, 171, 206–7, 210, 228, 262
financial institutions 15, 42, 45, 49, 52–3, 93, 123, 163, 185, 189, 227, 229, 232, 275, 283, 383, 400
financial management 82, 121, 200
flood/flooding 6, 42, 47, 66, 68, 80, 82, 155, 182, 186, 199, 257, 265, 310, 389
floor area 141, 173, 354
floor area ratio (FAR) 36, 141
floor space 59, 204, 207–8, 210, 214, 230, 312–13
floor space index (FSI) 26, 121, 141
foundation(s) 18, 59, 65, 75, 121
fraud 262, 264, 281, 339, 357
fund 27, 228, 231, 233–4, 247, 250; housing fund 249, 273, 304, 351; provident fund 205–6; revolving fund 190, 196, 274

garbage 65; collection 66, 309; disposal 169; dumping 175; *see also* waste

gated communities 28, 257, 322, 334
Ghana 95, 317, 319, 381–92
gini coefficient/index 29, 36, 288
Global Shelter Strategy 102, 140
goth 58, 154, 158–9
governance 107, 399–402; good 184; local 4, 6, 163, 210, 288, 398, 402; system 162–3, 371; urban 7, 34, 164, 328, 399
government: central 3, 27, 32, 35, 52–3, 136, 151, 167, 170–1, 177, 205, 210–12, 215–16, 264, 278; local 4, 15, 20, 24–5, 27, 35, 50–2, 55–7, 62–4, 66–7, 70, 74–6, 81, 84, 113, 126, 129, 136, 163, 167, 170–1, 176–8, 184–6, 199, 204–6, 208, 210, 212, 215–16, 221, 231, 248, 262, 277–8, 289, 301–2, 307–9, 315, 324, 343–4, 354, 371, 392, 399, 401–2
grant(s) 125, 185, 187, 231, 249, 280, 288, 296, 306, 325, 337–9, 344, 375
grassroots organisation(s) 6, 17, 57, 117, 200, 322, 398
group credit 108, 189
Guatemala 36, 49, 106
Guayaquil 83, 85, 88, 287–9, 291–4

habitat xxiii, 3, 6, 16–17, 47, 51, 70, 186, 188–9, 221, 235, 238, 288, 290–1, 294–5, 297, 309, 349, 372
habitat agenda xxi, xxiii, 1, 4, 56, 188
habitat awards 27, 106
Habitat for Humanity 51, 77–8, 235, 308–10, 375–6
Haiti 36, 76–8, 80–1, 84–5, 106, 221, 301
Harare 17, 117, 119, 124–9
hazards 7, 16, 52, 73–5, 169
health 41, 66, 82, 120, 134, 147–8, 156, 158–9, 169–70, 172, 186–7, 196, 210, 220, 268, 302, 317, 343, 353, 376
high-rise buildings: 68, 121–3, 127, 135, 145, 148, 156, 196, 201, 213, 401
home improvement 47–9, 76, 84, 127, 175, 183, 186, 189, 206, 220, 231, 238, 273, 276, 280, 296, 309, 314
home renovation 220, 224, 231, 234, 304–7, 309, 315
Honduras 36, 47, 106
Hong Kong 182
household income xxii, 9–11, 41, 44, 46, 48, 99, 141–2, 144, 150, 207, 284, 329, 390
house improvement 161–2; *see also* home improvement
housing: adequate xxi–xxiv, 44, 196, 257, 274, 293, 305, 365, 379, 383; basic 20, 59, 229, 231, 312; decent 1, 5, 55–6, 63, 238, 257, 261, 267, 303, 315, 355, 372, 391, 398; formal 57, 70, 84, 118–19, 155, 178, 211, 257, 259–60, 292, 294, 322–4, 337, 345, 364, 373, 377; hybrid 62, 234, 322–3; informal xxii, 57–8, 70, 92, 123, 274, 291, 318, 322–4, 326, 360, 403; semi-informal 322–3
housing association 5, 98, 108, 128, 305, 345, 389
housing backlog 161, 232, 337, 339, 364; *see also* housing shortage
housing cooperatives *see* cooperatives
housing corporations 170, 173–4, 220, 228, 308, 372, 382
housing credit, 10, 45, 48, 51, 171, 173, 189, 283; debt 16, 52, 262; *see also* housing loan
housing crisis 139, 321, 323, 401
housing delivery 1, 70, 166, 171, 224, 318–19, 323, 336–7, 339–42, 345–6, 349–56, 358–60, 370, 375, 381, 383, 388, 392, 398
housing demand xxi, 49, 63, 89, 134, 155, 164, 166–8, 171–2, 188, 192, 204, 207, 211, 224, 235, 252, 277, 283, 304–5, 307, 332–3, 338–40, 364, 392, 398
housing developer(s) 5, 16, 49, 178, 230, 235, 310, 312, 357
housing-expenditure-to-income ratio 9, 399
housing finance 40–52, 231, 245
housing loan 9–11, 150, 152, 164, 195, 228, 244, 248; *see also* housing credit
housing micro finance (HMF) 48–51
housing movement 112, 244, 246–9
housing need(s) xxi, 10, 17, 46, 69, 138, 155, 232, 234–5, 275, 350, 360–1, 364, 403
housing provision 7, 56, 58–9, 62, 65, 145, 151, 167–8, 173, 178, 189, 196, 205–6, 220, 241, 247, 248, 253–4, 288, 303–5, 318–19, 351–3, 364–70, 372–3, 378–9, 381–2, 384, 392, 397, 399, 402–3; affordable 5, 58, 134, 137, 139; formal 57, 62, 70; hybrid 62; informal 57, 62, 70; sustainable 16, 55
housing price 46, 96, 140, 149, 206–7, 210–11, 229, 283, 326
housing quality 68–9, 141, 144–5, 234–5, 238, 302
housing reconstruction 77, 182, 186–8
housing reform 97, 106, 135, 204–5, 215, 220, 272, 283
housing shortage 47, 139, 143, 166, 205, 242, 249, 253, 287–8, 290, 297, 315, 321, 326, 372; *see also* housing backlog
housing stock 2, 47, 55, 58, 68, 89, 91, 94, 96, 105–6, 121, 171, 193, 196, 213, 221, 224, 233, 237, 257, 268, 287–8, 291, 295, 297, 304–5, 314–15, 373, 381, 383
housing subsidy 41, 44, 228, 260, 264–5, 280, 290, 329, 338–40
housing supply 3, 16, 56, 58, 133–4, 140–1, 150, 271, 275–6, 278–9, 283, 319, 350, 364, 367, 381, 384, 391, 402; *see also* housing provision
housing typology 221, 229, 237, 288, 302, 311–12, 315, 369

illegal occupation 61, 322, 325
incremental building 11, 52, 56–7, 149–50, 189, 237, 374–5, 377–8, 392, 402
incremental construction 5, 17, 62–5, 333, 399
incremental housing 40–1, 44–5, 48, 50, 63, 65, 69–70, 75, 79, 81, 118–19, 128–9, 156, 182, 198, 219–22, 253, 271–3, 282–4, 287–9, 312, 317–19, 401
India 5, 11, 17, 22, 24–5, 27, 29, 31–3, 42–3, 45, 49, 52, 58, 61, 66–8, 89, 96–7, 105, 109–13, 119–25, 134, 137–52, 156, 182–3, 188, 399
Indonesia 21, 43, 81, 133–5, 166–78, 181–3, 185–6, 188
industrial area 157, 168, 374
informal development 74, 159, 271
informal sector 2, 45, 70, 92, 129, 133, 157–8, 162, 189, 219, 261, 319, 351–2
informal settlement(s) 1, 5, 17, 23, 25, 34, 40, 47, 56, 59, 62–3, 65–6, 74–5, 80, 84, 94, 99, 109, 117, 119–20, 122–4, 127–30, 133–5, 156–8, 161, 164, 168–9, 173–4, 182, 188, 198, 200–1, 219, 245, 257, 264, 271, 273–4, 288, 292, 294, 318, 326, 340–6, 353, 366–8, 371, 373, 375, 398–400
informality xxii, 242, 291–2, 321–5, 333–4, 359
infrastructure xxi, xxiii–xxxiv, 10, 22, 28, 35, 41, 50, 51, 57, 59, 62, 64, 66, 68, 70, 74–6, 82, 85, 99, 112, 118, 120–4, 128, 130, 143, 147–8, 156–7, 159, 176–7, 182–3, 185, 187, 193, 196, 199, 200, 225–6, 243, 251, 259, 265, 268, 333, 345, 355, 356, 359, 367–8, 369–71, 372, 374–7, 379, 381, 388, 392, 399; basic 168–9, 173–5, 199, 291, 371; physical 59, 369, 377; social 147, 156, 344, 368, 370
inner city 89, 134, 142, 160, 164, 168, 232, 340, 342
innovation 25, 31, 51, 121, 130, 174, 183, 187, 189, 215, 265, 321–2, 346
innovative approaches 22–3, 187, 400
institutional support 108, 112, 169, 171
institutions xxi, xiv, 3–6, 15, 17, 55, 63–4, 70, 103, 110, 120, 128, 162, 171, 174, 183, 185, 197, 204, 206, 208, 220, 227–9, 235, 238, 259, 263, 275, 291, 319, 322–5, 328, 334, 351, 373, 376–8, 381–4, 387, 392, 398; housing 76, 220, 224–6, 229, 231, 235, 237, 323–4; mortgage 195, 220, 227, 319, 328, 353, 358; *see also* financial institutions
Inter-American Development Bank (IDB) 300, 306–7, 309, 314
interest rate 10–1, 42–3, 45, 49, 53, 109, 126, 161–4, 173, 206, 220, 249, 257, 263–5, 274–6, 306–7, 310–11, 327–9, 377–8, 383

Jaipur 141
Johannesburg 93, 95, 333, 340–3

kampung 21, 133, 167–9, 170, 173, 175–8
Kampung Improvement Programme (KIP) 134, 167, 169–70, 175, 182
Karachi 3, 66–7, 134, 154–64
katchi abadi(s) 134, 154–5, 157, 160, 164
Kathmandu 89
Kenya 26, 32, 96–7, 103, 107, 109–10, 112, 317, 319, 363–79
Kibera 96, 368–9, 371, 376
Kingston 97
Kolkata 90, 134, 138, 140, 145, 147, 152
Kumasi 382, 384–6, 389–90, 392

La Paz 58, 60–1
Lagos 89, 318, 356, 358
Lahore 26, 35, 36, 38
land: acquisition 126, 155, 157, 194, 249; administration 19, 24–5, 31, 33–5, 189; agricultural 168, 318, 321–4, 326, 328, 333–4; allocation 25, 319, 327, 332, 384, 399; bank 64, 109, 266, 307; developer 5, 25, 57, 61, 64, 168, 318, 334, 401; development xxii, 1, 22, 26–7, 41, 64–5, 104, 182, 188, 224, 233, 243–4, 310, 324, 392; dispute 162, 385; invasion 88, 90, 92, 157, 244, 257, 292, 339, 398; management xxiii, 22, 24–5, 28, 31, 33–5, 289, 291, 401; market 15, 24, 31, 34, 319, 352, 358, 384; market management 19–37; rural 61, 210, 216, 293, 400; ownership 66, 105–6, 155, 167, 194, 216, 238, 247, 290, 327; policy(ies) xxii, 23, 26–7, 32, 46, 67–8; price 35, 133, 233, 244, 266, 294, 333, 374, 385–6; provision 150, 167, 170, 182; regularisation 189, 242, 247, 250; revenue 215–16; speculation 109, 113, 159, 163, 207, 271, 291, 293, 323; subdivision 51, 61–2, 88, 93, 126, 157, 220, 241, 366, 373; supply 31, 61, 182; tenure 23, 34, 59, 88, 109–10, 133, 186, 197, 199, 216, 243, 245, 250, 317, 319, 326, 371–3; title(s) 26, 64, 157–8, 163–4, 196, 199, 274, 294, 375; titling 2–3, 219, 354; use xxi, 24, 26, 46, 64, 68, 193–4, 210, 214, 283–4, 297, 302, 311, 314, 353, 399, 401; use management 15, 19; *see also* land market management; use regulations 139, 224; use rights 35, 214, 216; value 121, 127, 163, 171, 248, 259, 284
landlord 16, 87, 89–99, 193, 367, 375, 385, 389–91, 400, 403
landlord–tenant: conflict 95–7; relationship 319, 390–1
Latin America xxii, 5, 12, 16–7, 20, 41–7, 55, 61, 63, 88, 89, 91, 95, 98, 103, 106, 109–13, 133, 219, 256–8, 260, 271–3, 276–8, 283–4, 289, 291, 306–7, 317, 397–400
leadership 6, 19, 24, 35, 74, 157–8, 176–7, 309
leasehold title/right 197, 198, 384

letting 96, 98, 238; subletting 238, 368, 371, 374, 377
Lima 67–8, 90, 220, 273–4, 276–80, 282–4
livelihood 11, 30, 79, 118, 170, 173, 177, 187, 199, 201, 343
living conditions xxii–xxiii, 6, 20, 28, 30, 35, 58, 65, 87, 94, 174–6, 185, 204, 210–11, 258–9, 371
local development 171, 212, 215, 221, 283, 309
Los Angelos 47, 88, 99
low-cost housing 3, 10, 51, 63, 83–4, 141–2, 220, 224–5, 233, 260, 295, 314, 326, 329, 332, 351, 357, 366, 368, 372, 376, 388
low-income housing 1–3, 5, 7, 9, 12, 15, 49, 56, 75, 108, 141, 155, 167, 169, 172, 178, 194, 221, 228, 243, 259, 303, 319, 323–4, 340, 349–50, 354–6, 359, 368, 375, 378, 381–2, 384, 389, 391, 397, 401–2

Managua 221, 300–4, 306, 308–10, 312–15
Manilla 32, 97, 185
mapping 17, 63–4, 72, 120, 128
Master Plan 26, 36, 146, 157
Medellin 257, 268
Mexico 3, 5, 42, 43, 90, 93, 95–6, 219–20, 223–38, 265, 275, 399
Mexico city 88, 90–1, 225–6
microfinance institutions (MFI) 45, 48–51, 57, 64, 142, 150, 186, 189, 265, 373, 376
Middle East 33, 43
middle-income housing 5, 138, 144, 367
migrant housing 92, 386
migrant workers 208, 210–11, 213, 215
Millennium Development Goals (MDG) xxii–xxiii, 58, 73, 103, 343–4
Mongolia 36, 183, 188
mortgage 5, 9, 16, 35, 40–5, 47–8, 51–3, 55, 57, 87, 129, 140, 155–6, 161, 171, 181–2, 189, 193, 195, 206, 227–9, 232, 237, 257, 259–60, 263, 282–3, 291, 310, 319, 329, 351, 354, 365, 367–8, 376–7, 379, 387
mortgage institutions *see* institutions
multi-family housing 231, 238, 283
multi-story housing 51, 75, 230, 232, 234, 238, 367
Mumbai 17, 22, 26, 31–2, 35–6, 66, 88–9, 109–10, 117, 119–23, 127–30, 140–1, 143–5, 149–50
municipal housing policy 68, 247, 401

Nairobi 89, 93–4, 109, 319, 364–9, 371–2, 374–5, 377
Nakuru 367–8, 371, 375
Namibia 367
national housing programme 167, 193–4, 198, 200, 231, 244, 273, 291, 357
neoliberalism 2, 15, 144
neoliberal policy 102, 161
New Delhi *see* Delhi

new town(s) 28, 80, 145, 147–8, 152, 168, 214, 318, 321–2, 326–9, 332–4, 382
Nicaragua 67, 106, 219, 221, 271, 300–15
Niger 36
Nigeria 5, 43, 95, 317–19, 349–61
North Africa 317

Orissa 96
overcrowding 210, 297, 353
overproduction of housing 235, 238, 252, 399
owner-occupied housing 2, 15, 198, 219, 237, 400
owner-occupier(s) 17, 56–7, 62, 88, 224, 327, 403
ownership: document(s) 161; home 16, 40, 52, 68, 70, 87, 88, 92, 96–9, 141, 151, 167, 182, 206, 216, 219, 224, 229, 233, 257, 263, 266, 295, 329, 379; house 17, 90, 155, 161, 193–4, 198, 253, 318, 330, 337; land 17, 25, 66, 105–6, 155, 162, 164, 167, 194, 216, 238, 247, 290, 327

Pakistan 22, 35, 47, 66, 105, 134–5, 154–64, 182–3, 185, 187–8
Panama 43, 76, 80
Paraguay 106
participation: of community 23, 81–2, 109, 169–70, 183–4, 187, 193–4, 196–8, 200–1, 232, 243, 245, 399–400; of residents 4, 15, 76–7, 117, 135, 185, 246, 249, 252–3, 276; of stakeholders xxi–iv, 4, 31, 79, 138, 140, 196
participatory budgeting 27, 219, 398
participatory planning 4, 289, 398
participatory upgrading 135, 196
partnerships 4, 26, 31, 35, 41, 62, 66, 81, 125, 139, 184, 189, 198, 200, 235, 244–5, 247, 249, 363, 368, 372, 376, 378–9, 400; *see also* public–private partnerships
Patna 141
patronage 5, 25, 110, 402
pavement dwellers 120, 123, 129–30
peripheral area 30, 214, 216, 220, 244, 251–2, 271, 278, 337
peripheral settlement 160, 272–3
peri-urban area 61, 168, 188, 373–4, 384–5, 387, 401
Peru 5, 36, 43, 61, 68, 89, 107, 219–20, 271–84
Philippines 32, 183
pilot projects 2, 50, 249
political economy 15–16, 19, 27, 30, 33, 40, 52
political will 163, 170, 194
Port au Prince 76–7, 84
Porto Alegre 248–9
price-to-income ratio 207
progressive housing 40, 44–6, 50–2, 262, 273, 284, 346
property market 211, 215, 340
property prices 32, 51, 140, 279, 367

property title 34, 246, 273–4, 375
pro-poor housing 69–70, 135, 139, 148–9, 174, 220–1, 283, 360, 397, 401
provident fund 155, 205–6
public facilities 169, 173–4, 177
public–private partnerships 5, 25, 63, 141, 145, 319, 349–50, 354, 372, 400
pueblos jóvenes 58

Quito 75, 84, 88, 92, 97, 287–9, 291–2, 294

real estate: businesses/companies 94, 210, 284, 390; developers 50, 57, 205, 214, 252, 293, 295, 318, 353, 367, 383, 400; development 90, 162, 291; investment 277, 279; markets 111, 140, 149, 206–7, 211, 245, 271, 294, 334, 383; prices 193; subsidy 252
real property 16, 42–3, 46, 51–3
regulatory framework 3–4, 133, 358, 365, 373, 376, 377
regulatory reform 118, 140, 151
relocation 23, 77, 82, 120–1, 123, 129–30, 135, 195–6, 199, 201, 292, 339, 343–4, 368, 371, 374–6, 398; *see also* resettlement
rental accommodation 16, 61, 87, 89, 91–2, 94, 98, 319, 390
rental housing xxii, 2, 5, 15–17, 62, 70, 87, 89–99, 135–6, 182, 192, 205–6, 208–16, 220, 224, 233, 250, 257, 266, 268, 295, 311–12, 319, 345, 377, 379, 382, 389, 390, 400, 403
rent control 17, 91, 94–5, 97–8, 109, 257, 383, 391–2
resettlement 62, 84, 135, 182, 193, 196, 198–200, 292, 296, 325, 365, 369, 371–2, 378; *see also* relocation
residual income approach 9–10, 399, 403
resilience 2, 7–9, 16, 30, 35, 66, 73–4, 83, 345, 402
retrofitting 40, 57, 76, 81, 84
revolving fund 190, 196, 274, 376
right to the city 15, 27, 30, 291, 398
row houses/housing 51, 236–7, 355, 401
Rwanda 23

SACCO (Savings and credit cooperative societies) 366, 373, 376
safety xxi, 69–70, 78, 93, 210, 238, 301, 344, 353, 376, 389, 390
sanitation 20, 51, 58, 64, 82, 122–4, 126, 169, 185–6, 297, 353, 365, 370, 374, 388
São Paulo 220, 242–3, 245–9, 251, 253–4
satellite city 142, 168, 292, 366–7
savings 9–11, 24, 42, 44, 49, 57, 106, 117–18, 120, 123, 127–8, 133, 140, 157–8, 206, 234, 258–60, 262–6, 274–5, 288, 307, 323, 336, 342, 349, 353, 372–3, 376, 378, 383, 387, 400
savings and credit associations 45, 57, 155

savings groups 106, 121, 199
savings programme/schemes 17, 117–19, 125–6, 128, 189, 206, 265, 342, 375, 387
second-tier liquidity facilities 42, 50, 53, 287
security of tenure xxi, 1, 3, 224, 399; *see also* tenure security
segregation xxii, 29, 216, 242, 253, 284, 322, 337, 343
Sekondi-Takoradi 382, 388
self-builder 55–7, 62, 65–70, 83, 234, 302, 401
self-building 44, 55, 66, 70, 237, 310, 353, 359
self-financed/financing 36, 45–6, 65, 121, 139, 194, 245, 400
self-help construction 3, 16–17, 62, 74, 83–4, 92, 124, 126, 187, 220, 241
self-help housing: aided 182, 188, 193–7, 353, 366, 373; assisted 1, 6, 16, 55–6, 63–5, 70, 135, 175, 193, 232, 234, 276, 291, 303, 324, 399; mutual 16, 67
self-help housing solutions 66, 221, 233, 260, 288, 291, 293–4
self-managed housing 1, 5, 56, 67, 183, 198, 219–20, 224, 231, 234, 237, 280, 300, 352–3, 359, 399
sewage/sewerage 36, 40, 65–6, 122, 125–6, 130, 156, 159, 177, 182, 257, 266, 273, 302, 309, 313, 328, 332
Shack/Slum Dwellers International (SDI) 17, 34, 63, 117–30, 133, 199, 375–6, 401
Shanghai 29, 99, 207, 212
shanty area/town 97, 194, 196, 211–12, 241
Singapore 23, 29, 355
sites and services 2, 9, 16, 40, 56, 59, 61–2, 75–6, 80–2, 124, 139, 156, 161, 174, 182, 193–5, 220–1, 243, 253, 258, 261–2, 301, 303, 323, 325–6, 333, 340, 351, 360, 366, 373
slum dwellers xxiii, 20, 41, 58, 108–9, 113, 120–1, 133, 141, 317, 343, 374, 376
slum dwellers federation 63, 120, 374
slum/settlement eradication 243, 318, 343, 345, 368, 399
slum-free cities 58, 193, 399
social housing 61–2, 70, 89, 91, 98, 103, 106–9, 139, 150, 220, 221, 225, 228–31, 233–4, 237, 257–8, 260, 262–7, 272, 277–9, 283–4, 300, 302–3, 307, 310, 312–15, 340, 354, 367, 377
social housing delivery system 1, 224
social housing policy 224, 233, 275, 282, 297
social housing programme 243, 253, 272, 275–6, 278, 280, 282, 290, 297, 303–4, 306, 311, 333, 345
social housing production 68, 224–6, 232, 235, 238, 241, 244, 250
social movements 17, 106, 108, 110, 112, 219, 235, 398, 401
solid waste 3, 182, 186, 389

Solomon Islands 24
South Africa 29, 36, 58, 65, 89–91, 95, 98, 103, 107, 109–10, 112, 125, 317–18, 336–46, 367, 399
South Asia 46, 61, 63, 66, 105, 107, 112, 133, 192
South Korea 99, 182
Southeast Asia 105
spatial planning 70, 232, 288, 291, 343
squatter settlement 55–6, 75, 173, 241, 247, 359
Sri Lanka 66, 133–5, 183–4, 192–201
structural adjustment 107, 158, 373, 383
subdivision of land 51, 61–2, 88, 93, 126, 157, 220, 241, 366, 373
sub-Saharan Africa 20, 45, 317, 364–5, 367, 398
subsidy(ies) 5, 10–11, 16–17, 34, 37, 40–2, 44, 47, 49, 51–2, 57, 65, 70, 89, 94, 98, 104, 110, 118, 121, 123, 127, 129, 135, 139, 141, 143, 148, 150–1, 158, 163, 171–5, 181, 195, 199, 206, 211, 220, 226–9, 231–3, 249–52, 254, 257, 259–68, 275, 277–8, 280–3, 288, 290, 294, 301, 304–12, 314–15, 318, 329, 333, 336–40, 342–3, 345–6, 351, 360, 383, 400
Surat 96, 141
sustainability xxi, 1–3, 6–9, 69–70, 74, 83, 149, 156, 162, 176–7, 183, 232–3, 283, 337, 345, 352, 358–60, 371, 374, 376, 397–9, 401–2
sustainable building 68, 83
sustainable building materials 69, 82, 85, 233, 237
sustainable housing 1, 16, 42, 55, 68–9, 74, 84, 225–6, 232–3, 235, 237, 319, 358, 401
sustainable urban development xxiii, 4, 142, 220, 226, 365
Syria 23

technical assistance *see* assistance
technical education *see* education
technical quality of housing 16, 68, 352, 360
technical training 3, 68
Tema 382–3, 392
tenant(s) 63, 87–99, 109, 194, 266, 371, 382, 390–1, 403
tenure security xxi, 1, 3, 17, 59, 64, 109–10, 126, 186, 224, 273, 317, 340, 352, 368–9, 371–2, 374–5, 377–9, 399, 401
Thika 368, 371–2, 375
toilet(s): community 122; household 123; public 123, 175, 185, 388; *see also* sanitation
townships 27, 105, 140, 163, 196, 327, 382
transferable development rights (TDR) 5, 22, 36, 121, 123, 128

tsunami 6, 47, 81, 135, 182, 186, 198–201
Turkey 36, 89
Tunisia 23

UN-Habitat xxii, xxi, 31, 34, 44, 55, 58, 183–4, 187–8, 198–9, 207, 228, 360
uninhabited housing 225, 235, 237
upgrading of slums/settlements 1–3, 34, 40–1, 44, 57–9, 62, 66, 70, 76, 81, 84, 97–8, 106, 109, 118–19, 123, 128, 133, 135, 139, 167, 169–70, 175, 182, 185, 188, 193–6, 198–200, 220–1, 238, 242–3, 247, 253–4, 261–2, 273–4, 276, 278, 280, 291–2, 295, 318–19, 323, 325–6, 342–6, 366, 368–70, 371, 373, 375, 378–9, 402
urban expansion 65, 73, 88, 214, 233, 238, 301, 303, 312
urban fringe 22, 40, 46, 321
urban outskirts 152, 242–3, 251, 253–4, 301, 309, 314, 372
urban planning 30–1, 33, 37, 68–9, 182, 193, 214, 221, 225–6, 233, 235, 259, 265, 278, 287, 291, 302, 359, 378–9, 398–9, 401–2
urban poverty 4, 20, 37, 94, 189, 231, 364
urban renewal 141, 182, 189, 207, 214, 220, 238
urban renovation 215–16, 314
urban sprawl 47, 80, 99, 201, 232, 291, 326, 400–1
Uruguay 43, 67, 106, 109–13, 219, 246, 309

Venezuela 89, 107, 403
violence 41, 47, 51–2, 124, 186, 235, 264–5, 274

water 6, 20, 25, 32, 36, 40, 51, 58, 64–6, 69, 78, 82, 95, 119, 122, 124–6, 128, 130, 149, 156, 159, 169, 175–7, 185–6, 198, 233, 257, 266, 273, 279, 289, 297, 302, 307, 310, 328, 356, 370, 374, 388
West Africa 61
World Bank 8, 15, 27, 34, 41–2, 44, 55, 58, 76, 80–1, 102, 139, 181–2, 184, 275, 279, 351, 371, 376
World Urban Forum 27, 127

Xiamen 207

Yinchuan 207

Zimbabwe 17, 97, 103, 108, 119, 124–9